perspectives

Abnormal Psychology

Academic Editor
Kathleen J. Sexton-Radek
Elmhurst College

coursewise
publishing
inc.

Bellevue • Boulder • Dubuque • Madison • St. Paul

Our mission at **Coursewise** is to help students make connections—linking theory to practice and the classroom to the outside world. Learners are motivated to synthesize ideas when course materials are placed in a context they recognize. By providing gateways to contemporary and enduring issues, **Coursewise** publications will expand students' awareness of and context for the course subject.

For more information on **Coursewise,** visit us at our web site: http://www.coursewise.com

To order an examination copy:
Houghton Mifflin Sixth Floor Media 800-565-6247 (voice) / 800-565-6236 (fax)

Coursewise Publishing Editorial Staff

Thomas Doran, ceo/publisher: Environmental Science/Geography/Journalism/Marketing/Speech
Edgar Laube, publisher: Political Science/Psychology/Sociology
Linda Meehan Avenarius, publisher: **Courselinks**™
Sue Pulvermacher-Alt, publisher: Education/Health/Gender Studies
Victoria Putman, publisher: Anthropology/Philosophy/Religion
Tom Romaniak, publisher: Business/Criminal Justice/Economics
Kathleen Schmitt, publishing assistant
Gail Hodge, executive producer

Coursewise Publishing Production Staff

Lori A. Blosch, permissions coordinator
Mary Monner, production coordinator
Victoria Putman, production manager

Printed in the United States of America by Coursewise Publishing, Inc.
7 North Pinckney Street, Suite 346, Madison, WI 53703

10 9 8 7 6 5 4 3 2 1

from the
Publisher

Edgar Laube

Coursewise Publishing

I admit to being completely clueless about abnormal psychology and issues pertaining to mental health. About the only time I think about such things is when there's a big news story about someone doing something bizarre or pleading insanity as a defense tactic in a courtroom. Such situations don't provide much context for understanding, though, because the story is really about something else—the act or crime—and not the mental condition of the person in question.

The other problem in understanding mental health issues is that they can be quite subtle. Sure, some people who are mentally unstable make the news. But many other people suffer silently, out of view, their afflictions taking a daily toll that is never measured and often unnoticed. This is so because many abnormalities are understood to be a matter of degree. It's okay to be a little bit compulsive or to be preoccupied with body fat or to drink alcohol some of the time. But it's not okay to be ruled by compulsive obsessions or to throw up after a big meal or to drink excessively. Understanding where the gray zone is, where normal starts to become something else, must be very difficult.

So I'm guessing that most people are as clueless as I am. And that's why I'd like to commend you students who are taking a course in abnormal psychology. Whether you intend to become some sort of health professional, whether you're a psych major and want (or need) to understand the science of psychopathology, or whether you're in the course out of curiosity about your own thoughts and feelings—or those of others— abnormal psychology is a worthy subject because it's so poorly understood. Whatever you can do to lift the shade and let some light shine on these various phenomena will probably benefit us all.

I'd like to extend a special note of thanks to Kathy Sexton-Radek for her hard work and persistence in pulling this project together. I wanted her to take on this project as soon as I realized that her primary focus was you students—what you learn, how you learn, and how to get more out of you than you thought you had. You'll feel her warmth and focus as you read through her introductions and summaries of the articles here.

Good luck with your studies! And remember, there's a great web site that supports this reader at www.courselinks.com. While you're there, please let Kathy or me know what you think of these selections and the electronic resources.

from the
Academic Editor

Kathleen J. Sexton-Radek
Elmhurst College

Abnormal psychology courses challenge you with their technical information, theory, and principles of behavior. In addition, textbooks present, to varying degrees, the practice of clinical work where abnormal psychology theory is applied. Given this complexity, you sometimes leave the course with only a partial understanding of this important area. I invite you to consider these readings as a means of strengthening your understanding. Experience tells me that your interest and desire to apply your knowledge of abnormal psychology is strong. I hope you will find these readings helpful in learning abnormal psychology.

With the profound relevance of the topic of abnormal psychology, student interest has not been lacking in the enrollments in this course. In fact, health professional areas (that is, pre-medicine, nursing, pre-physical therapy) are classically represented in these classrooms. I think that the translation of material into its real-world applications is essential in the abnormal psychology course. I believe that you will learn "how to think" and "how to think about" psychology when such translations are done.

In selecting materials for *Perspectives: Abnormal Psychology*, I specifically searched for readings written by and for practitioners. First, I looked for materials that addressed major areas, such as diagnosis, assessment, and disorders. Then, I searched for articles exemplifying applied research—that is, the testing of a concept or measurement of a treatment effect. And finally, I selected articles that addressed themes that may not be addressed in your textbook and/or that represent contemporary issues necessitating study.

Because I am an experienced mentor and educator, my selection of section topics and readings always keeps students in mind's eye. This guides all of my work. Quite literally, I represented this notion with article summaries that are constructed to relate to the student of abnormal psychology. I sincerely hope that these readings add context to your understanding of abnormal psychology and provide you with a comfortable format for the application of abnormal psychology knowledge. I also hope that they motivate you in your learning and help you to focus on how to think about the issues in your textbook and classroom lectures/discussions from a prospective practitioner's perspective.

Kathleen J. Sexton-Radek received her Ph.D. in clinical psychology from Illinois Institute of Technology in 1988. She is a professor and chairperson of the Psychology Department at Elmhurst College. She teaches courses in undergraduate, industrial organizational graduate, and human services administration programs. In addition to teaching, Dr. Sexton-Radek is an allied medical staff member at a local hospital and a consultant to the sleep clinic, and also maintains a small private practice. She is the co-coordinator (with Peter Petrosian, Education Directorate, APA) of the Undergraduate Consulting Service. She is a member of the American Psychological Association, the Association for the Advancement of Behavior Therapy, and the Society for Behavioral Medicine. She is the author of approximately thirty-five professional publications, including three book chapters. She has approximately thirty projects/presentations that include the mentorship of student work. She and her husband reside in North Riverside, Illinois, with their three sons—Brett, Neal, and Ted. She enjoys watching her sons' baseball and theater participation.

Editorial Board

WiseGuide Introduction

Critical Thinking and Bumper Stickers

Question Authority

The bumper sticker said: Question Authority. This is a simple directive that goes straight to the heart of critical thinking. The issue is not whether the authority is right or wrong; it's the questioning process that's important. Questioning helps you develop awareness and a clearer sense of what you think. That's critical thinking.

Critical thinking is a new label for an old approach to learning—that of challenging all ideas, hypotheses, and assumptions. In the physical and life sciences, systematic questioning and testing methods (known as the scientific method) help verify information, and objectivity is the benchmark on which all knowledge is pursued. In the social sciences, however, where the goal is to study people and their behavior, things get fuzzy. It's one thing for the chemistry experiment to work out as predicted, or for the petri dish to yield a certain result. It's quite another matter, however, in the social sciences, where the subject is ourselves. Objectivity is harder to achieve.

Although you'll hear critical thinking defined in many different ways, it really boils down to analyzing the ideas and messages that you receive. What are you being asked to think or believe? Does it make sense, objectively? Using the same facts and considerations, could you reasonably come up with a different conclusion? And, why does this matter in the first place? As the bumper sticker urged, question authority. Authority can be a textbook, a politician, a boss, a big sister, or an ad on television. Whatever the message, learning to question it appropriately is a habit that will serve you well for a lifetime. And in the meantime, thinking critically will certainly help you be course wise.

Getting Connected

This reader is a tool for connected learning. This means that the readings and other learning aids explained here will help you to link classroom theory to real-world issues. They will help you to think critically and to make long-lasting learning connections. Feedback from both instructors and students has helped us to develop some suggestions on how you can wisely use this connected learning tool.

WiseGuide Pedagogy

A wise reader is better able to be a critical reader. Therefore, we want to help you get wise about the articles in this reader. Each section of *Perspectives* has three tools to help you: the WiseGuide Intro, the WiseGuide Wrap-Up, and the Putting It in *Perspectives* review form.

WiseGuide Intro

In the WiseGuide Intro, the Academic Editor introduces the section, gives you an overview of the topics covered, and explains why particular articles were selected and what's important about them.

Also in the WiseGuide Intro, you'll find several key points or learning objectives that highlight the most important things to remember from this section. These will help you to focus your study of section topics.

At the end of the WiseGuide Intro, you'll find questions designed to stimulate critical thinking. Wise students will keep these questions in mind as they read an article (we repeat the questions at the start of the articles as a reminder). When you finish each article, check your understanding. Can you answer the questions? If not, go back and reread the article. The Academic Editor has written sample responses for many of the questions, and you'll find these online at the **Courselinks**™ site for this course. More about **Courselinks** in a minute. . . .

WiseGuide Wrap-Up

Be course wise and develop a thorough understanding of the topics covered in this course. The WiseGuide Wrap-Up at the end of each section will help you do just that with concluding comments or summary points that repeat what's most important to understand from the section you just read.

In addition, we try to get you wired up by providing a list of select Internet resources—what we call R.E.A.L. web sites because they're **R**elevant, **E**nhanced, **A**pproved, and **L**inked. The information at these web sites will enhance your understanding of a topic. (Remember to use your Passport and start at http://www.courselinks.com so that if any of these sites have changed, you'll have the latest link.)

Putting It in *Perspectives* Review Form

At the end of the book is the Putting It in *Perspectives* review form. Your instructor may ask you to complete this form as an assignment or for extra credit. If nothing else, consider doing it on your own to help you critically think about the reading.

Prompts at the end of each article encourage you to complete this review form. Feel free to copy the form and use it as needed.

The Courselinks™ Site

The **Courselinks** Passport is your ticket to a wonderful world of integrated web resources designed to help you with your course work. These resources are found at the **Courselinks** site for your course area. This is where the readings in this book and the key topics of your course are linked to an exciting array of online learning tools. Here you will find carefully selected readings, web links, quizzes, worksheets, and more, tailored to your course and approved as connected learning tools. The ever-changing, always interesting **Courselinks** site features a number of carefully integrated resources designed to help you be course wise. These include:

- **R.E.A.L. Sites** At the core of a **Courselinks** site is the list of R.E.A.L. sites. This is a select group of web sites for studying, not surfing. Like the readings in this book, these sites have been selected, reviewed, and approved by the Academic Editor and the Editorial Board. The R.E.A.L. sites are arranged by topic and are annotated with short descriptions and key words to make them easier for you to use for reference or research. With R.E.A.L. sites, you're studying approved resources within seconds—and not wasting precious time surfing unproven sites.

- **Editor's Choice** Here you'll find updates on news related to your course, with links to the actual online sources. This is also where we'll tell you about changes to the site and about online events.

WiseGuide Wrap-Up

http://www.courselinks.com

- **Course Overview** This is a general description of the typical course in this area of study. While your instructor will provide specific course objectives, this overview helps you place the course in a generic context and offers you an additional reference point.

- **www.orksheet** Focus your trip to a R.E.A.L. site with the www.orksheet. Each of the 10 to 15 questions will prompt you to take in the best that site has to offer. Use this tool for self-study, or if required, email it to your instructor.

- **Course Quiz** The questions on this self-scoring quiz are related to articles in the reader, information at R.E.A.L. sites, and other course topics, and will help you pinpoint areas you need to study. Only you will know your score—it's an easy, risk-free way to keep pace!

- **Topic Key** The online Topic Key is a listing of the main topics in your course, and it correlates with the Topic Key that appears in this reader. This handy reference tool also links directly to those R.E.A.L. sites that are especially appropriate to each topic, bringing you integrated online resources within seconds!

- **Web Savvy Student Site** If you're new to the Internet or want to brush up, stop by the Web Savvy Student site. This unique supplement is a complete **Courselinks** site unto itself. Here, you'll find basic information on using the Internet, creating a web page, communicating on the web, and more. Quizzes and Web Savvy Worksheets test your web knowledge, and the R.E.A.L. sites listed here will further enhance your understanding of the web.

- **Student Lounge** Drop by the Student Lounge to chat with other students taking the same course or to learn more about careers in your major. You'll find links to resources for scholarships, financial aid, internships, professional associations, and jobs. Take a look around the Student Lounge and give us your feedback. We're open to remodeling the Lounge per your suggestions.

Building Better Perspectives!

Please tell us what you think of this *Perspectives* volume so we can improve the next one. Here's how you can help:

1. Visit our **Coursewise** site at: http://www.coursewise.com

2. Click on *Perspectives*. Then select the Building Better *Perspectives* Form for your book.

3. Forms and instructions for submission are available online.

Tell us what you think—did the readings and online materials help you make some learning connections? Were some materials more helpful than others? Thanks in advance for helping us build better *Perspectives*.

Student Internships

If you enjoy evaluating these articles or would like to help us evaluate the **Courselinks** site for this course, check out the **Coursewise** Student Internship Program. For more information, visit:

http://www.coursewise.com/intern.html

Contents

At **Coursewise,** we're publishing connected learning tools. That means that the book you are holding is only a part of this publication. You'll also want to harness the integrated resources that **Coursewise** has developed at the fun and highly useful **Courselinks**™ web site for *Perspectives: Abnormal Psychology.* If you purchased this book new, use the Passport that was shrink-wrapped to this volume to obtain site access. If you purchased a used copy of this book, then you need to buy a stand-alone Passport. If your bookstore doesn't stock Passports to **Courselinks** sites, visit http://www.courselinks.com for ordering information.

section

1

Assessment and Diagnosis

section 2

Self-Control and Regulation

section 3

Anxiety and Stress

section 4

Biological Factors Related to Schizophrenia

section 5

Depression

section

6

Child and Adolescent Pathology

section

7

Treatment

Topic Key

This Topic Key is an important tool for learning. It will help you integrate this reader into your course studies. Listed below, in alphabetical order, are important topics covered in this volume. Below each topic, you'll find the reading numbers and titles, and R.E.A.L. web site addresses, relating to that topic. Note that the Topic Key might not include every topic your instructor chooses to emphasize. If you don't find the topic you're looking for in the Topic Key, check the index or the online topic key at the **Courselinks**™ site.

Biological Factors
11 Schizophrenia and Bipolar Disorder: Origins and Influences
14 Genetic and Environmental Contributions to Depression Symptomatology: Evidence from Danish Twins 75 Years of Age and Older

Behavioral and Brain Sciences
http://www.princeton.edu/~harnad/bbs.html

Cultural Perspective
1 Cultural Diversity and the Cultural Epistemological Structure of Psychoanalysis: Implications for Psychotherapy with Latinos and Other Minorities
4 Common Mental Disorders and Disability Across Cultures: Results from the WHO Collaborative Study on Psychological Problems in General Health Care
17 Clinical Characteristics of Attention Deficit Hyperactivity Disorder in African American Children

The Atlantic Monthly
http://www.theatlantic.com

APA's PsycNet
http://www.apa.org/

Impact of Disorders
11 Schizophrenia and Bipolar Disorder: Origins and Influences
12 Seasonal Influence on Platelet 5-HT Levels in Patients with Recurrent Major Depression and Schizophrenia
20 A 10-Year Longitudinal Study of Body Weight, Dieting, and Eating Disorder Symptoms

Psychology Self-Help Resources
http://www.psychwww.com/resource/
   selfhelp.htm

Behavior OnLine
http://www.behavior.net/

Measurement
2 Integrating Psychobiological Approach to Psychiatric Assessment and Treatment

Department of Health and Human Services
http://www.os.dhhs.gov/

Helplessness-L
Send email to: Listserv@netcom.com

Research/Models
3 Lifetime and 12-Month Prevalence of DSM-III-R Psychiatric Disorders in the United States: Results from the National Comorbidity Survey
10 The Structure of Work-Related Stress and Coping among Oncology Nurses in High-Stress Medical Settings: A Transactional Analysis

Helplessness-L
Send email to: Listserv@netcom.com

Symptom Expression
19 Adolescent Depressed Mood, Reports of Suicide Attempts, and Asking for Help

Psychology Self-Help Resources
http://www.psychwww.com/resource/
   selfhelp.htm

Yanx-Dep
Send email to: Listserv@sjuvm.st.johns.edu

Theory Application
9 The Relation between Personality and Anxiety: Findings from a Three-Year Prospective Study
13 Manual and Saccadic Reaction Time with Constant and Variable Preparatory Intervals in Schizophrenia
15 Cognitive Theory and the Generality of Pessimism among Depressed Persons

16 Structural Relationships among Dimensions of the DSM-IV Anxiety and Mood Disorders and Dimensions of Negative Affect, Positive Affect, and Autonomic Arousal

APA's PsycNet
http://www.apa.org/

Department of Health and Human Services
http://www.os.dhhs.gov/

Treatment
7 Prevalence and Risk Factors of Problem Gambling Among College Students
18 Group Treatment for Prepubescent Boys with Sexually Aggressive Behavior: Clinical Considerations and Proposed Treatment Techniques
21 Computer-Assisted Psychological Intervention: A Review and Commentary
22 Mental Health: Does Therapy Help?

APA's PsycNet/
http://www.apa.org/

Treatment Outcome
5 Resolution of Alcohol Problems without Treatment: Methodological Issues and Future Directions of Natural Recovery Research
6 Retrospective Review of Treatment Outcome for 63 Patients with Trichotillomania
8 Does Concurrent Drug Intake Affect the Long-Term Outcome of Group Cognitive Behaviour Therapy in Panic Disorder with or without Agoraphobia?

APA's PsycNet
http://www.apa.org/

Department of Health and Human Services
http://www.os.dhhs.gov/

section

1

Learning Objectives

- The student will become aware of cultural factors that influence the expression of symptoms.

- The student will develop knowledge about the correspondence between assessment and treatment.

- The identification of symptoms, their severity, and their duration will provide the student with a fuller explanation of diagnosis in applied settings.

Questions

Reading 1. Briefly describe what Lacanian psychoanalysis is and identify one implication relevant to the Latino culture.

Reading 2. Explain how "temperament" is addressed with respect to the integrative psychobiological approach.

Reading 3. What is comorbidity and why is it important to study?

Reading 4. What is the most prevalent disorder in the United States? Include the demographic correlates in your response.

Assessment and Diagnosis

The theoretical groundwork to the study of abnormal behavior is laid out in this first section. Various means to assess symptomology and thereby determine a diagnosis are addressed in this section. Of particular note is the attention paid to cultural diversity issues.

As you will read in the Moncayo article, the focus on culture and diagnosis represents a strong challenge. To complicate the circumstance, a psychoanalytic approach that is in itself very abstract presents unique conceptual challenges. At the heart here is the issue of how generalizable psychoanalytic conceptualizations are to cultures other than the white affluent class they were designed from. Moncayo reconciles this issue with a clear presentation of clinical practice issues, using a Lacanian (type of psychoanalytic application) approach.

The second article in this section introduces you to the biological approach to assessment and treatment. Drs. Cloninger and Svrakic present their views, using patterns of development (temperament) as an important clinical feature to include in assessment. The psychiatrists write how this approach will provide the necessary sensitivity to connecting the correct diagnosis to treatment that will work. The third article in this section provides a scope to the types and amounts of diagnosable conditions in the United States. Although it is dated from *DSM III-R* diagnoses, the thorough review has not been done with the *DSM IV* to date. In reading this work, you will be able to get an idea of the number of individuals presenting with a diagnosed disorder. Your study of the textbook material about the specificity of the symptom being presented, the severity of the symptom, and the length of time the person has been experiencing it will come into application with the reading of this article. As you read, glance back at the tables to obtain a quick conclusion of what disorders are diagnosed in the United States.

To build the idea in a broader sense, the final article in this section was chosen. The World Health Organization administers the General Health Questionnaire on a regular basis to determine the scope of diagnosed problems in the world. Ormel and associates carefully point out the cultural differences in symptom presentation as it is then reflected in prevalence figures. This issue is advanced by the concept of higher-order human capacities, in which factors such as expression of emotion and motivation are considered as determinants of a disorder.

Briefly describe what Lacanian psychoanalysis is and identify one implication relevant to the Latino culture.

Cultural Diversity and the Cultural and Epistemological Structure of Psychoanalysis:

Implications for Psychotherapy with Latinos and Other Minorities

Raul Moncayo, Ph.D.

Mission Mental Health and California School of Professional Psychology

This article offers a critique of assumptions made by both the majority psychoanalytic culture and minority groups regarding the suitability of psychoanalysis for Latinos and other underserved ethnic groups. Both sides of the aforementioned controversy are rooted in the larger conflict between modern and traditional paradigms as well as in the epistemological and political contradictions of the "master's discourse" prevailing within educational institutions. The proposed theory articulates intrapsychic and extrapsychic dimensions into a single theoretical framework. The proposed reconceptualization includes a redefinition of the psychoanalytic concept of insight more in keeping both with the concept of the unconscious and with the conception of knowledge found in traditional cultures.

It is important to periodically examine the assumptions that, consciously or unconsciously, determine the course and results of psychoanalytic work; unexamined and unrecognized assumptions establish the parameters of what may be possible or impossible within the scope of our professional practice and activity as psychotherapists and analysts. Minorities have shown high underuse of services as well as high dropout rates. Thus, the question regarding the role of culture in psychotherapy and in the field of mental health has arisen around the practical problem of providing effective mental health services to ethnic minority populations. Within the majority, dominant culture, the stated or unstated assumption is often made that many ethnic minority groups, as a result of economic, cultural, and educational deficits, are simply not "good candidates" for the mental health services available within Western culture (i.e., "insight" forms of psychotherapy or psychoanalysis). Within psychoanalysis, such an assumption has followed from the criteria of "analyzability," whereas, outside psychoanalysis, it has found confirmation in psychotherapy outcome research data that support the view that intelligent, verbal, attractive, and successful upper-class individuals tend to benefit the most from psychotherapy. It goes without saying that White majority subjects are overrepresented within those defined as ideal candidates for psychotherapy. In addition, until recently the psychoanalytic literature in the United States has not been known for addressing the concerns of the minority mental health literature or those of minorities in general.

In contradistinction to this perspective, literature on minority mental health produced by minorities for minorities comes to the different conclusion that mental health services have to be provided by bilingual and bicultural professionals to more effectively deliver services to underserved groups. Here the assumption is made that most therapists are not familiar with the cultural backgrounds and lifestyles of diverse ethnic groups because they have received training primarily developed for treating Anglo Americans (Bernal & Padilla, 1982; Sue & Zane, 1987). Western insight-oriented forms of psychotherapy and psychoanalysis, as a whole, are often summarily dismissed by minority researchers and clinicians as being appropriate and effective only with majority or mainstream individuals. For example, it is said that Latinos cannot benefit from psychodynamic treatment because they like to focus on the present, want the direct guidance of authority figures, can conceive only of medical–physical symptoms, or cannot self-disclose regarding their experience (Cortese, 1979; Meadow, 1982; Ruiz & Padilla, 1987; Sue & Zane, 1987; Szapocznik, Santisteban, Kurtines, Hervis, & Spencer, 1982).

From the ideological underpinnings of both dominant and minority groups, many inaccurate clinical observations and generalizations have been derived regarding the kinds of interventions that may benefit the various cultural groups. I argue that both sides need to be held responsible for a portion of the responsibility for what has led to the historical misunderstanding between minorities and psychoanalysis in the United States. The risk one always takes, in attempting to link and place two sets of independent discourses into a relationship with one another, is that neither side will accept modifications of their basic assumptions. However, the dominant European culture can no longer afford not to listen to the concerns of cultural minorities, and it may have to reconsider and develop some of its own assumptions. Minority groups, on the other hand, may be neglecting and underusing many points of convergence between psychoanalytic theory and practice and their own emancipatory interests.

Carefully designed research studies would not necessarily be helpful in debunking faulty assumptions of this kind, as the empirical research literature recommends; from my perspective, what is also needed is a congruent and coherent theoretical and epistemological critique and not merely more empirical research. Empirical evidence and clinical practices are at least codetermined by the conceptual assumptions made in the research and therapeutic process. After many years of working with Latinos within a Latin American psychoanalytic frame of reference, I want to argue that inaccurate assumptions about Latinos or psychoanalysis stem not from Latino culture or Latino populations but from the dualisms and conceptual–political contradictions of the "master's discourse" that rules clinicians as well as institutions of higher education. In this article, I address critical issues regarding the definition of social science; the relationship between social science and traditional culture, interrelationships among culture, class, and psychotherapy; and the practice of psychodynamic interpretation and its cultural significance.

Although the literature on minority mental health has explained the difficulties encountered in providing effective mental health services to minorities in terms of differences between Western culture and various other cultural traditions, I want to argue that the problem is rooted not solely in relative cultural differences but also in the larger conflict between modern and traditional paradigms as well as in the epistemological underpinnings of empiricist social science culture. In this article, I elucidate why I place social science in the category of a relative cultural phenomenon. I begin with a discussion of traditional and modern approaches to knowledge. I then describe an alternative postmodern epistemological framework that could prove more effective in the understanding and treatment of ethnic minorities. The final section focuses on the application of this framework to the clinical process, using Lacanian principles, and includes a redefinition of the psychoanalytic concept of insight more in keeping both with the concept of the unconscious and with the conception of knowledge found in traditional cultures. The fact that Lacanian theory is very influential in Latin America (because of its historical focus on social and political theory) makes it specially relevant for the task at hand. This is not to say that other schools of psychoanalysis do not exist in Latin America or that the same task could not be undertaken from other vantage points within psychoanalysis. Unfortunately, as would also be the case with other possible formulations, every process of knowledge throws some light but also some darkness on other modes of understanding.

The terms *traditional, modern,* and *postmodern* are used here not merely as words but to designate specific conceptual structures. The common use of these terms merely designates a temporal reference: *Modern* is synonymous with contemporary, new, or current, whereas *traditional* refers to the old and the past (i.e., the often-mentioned reference to "traditional" psychotherapy). Within the present postmodern paradigm, *modern* refers to modernity as the secular scientific paradigm with all of its accompanying aesthetic and ethical values, whereas *tradition* or *traditional* refers to cultural traditions existing before and outside the Western scientific paradigm. *Postmodern* points in the direction of a new cross-cultural paradigm that permutates and combines traditional and modern conceptual structures.

Modern and Traditional Epistemologies

The so-called Western scientific paradigm developed in Europe, beginning with the Renaissance and culminating in the 18th and 19th centuries with the social, cultural, and political movement known as the Enlightenment. Out of this period came most of the values and ideas we associate with the modern world. However, the European scientific tradition, which rules most learning institutions in developed as well as developing countries, is not a single and unitary phenomenon. Basically, within the social or human sciences there are two European traditions or discourses: empiricism and various forms of rationalism, some of which include the transrational (what is beyond the a priori categories of reason) in their perspectives.

Empiricism is the tradition associated with Anglo-Saxon or English culture, whereas what, for the moment, I am calling rationalism is associated with continental Europe, including romance language cultures and certain aspects of German culture. Marxism and critical social thinking developed out of this latter tradition and led to the critique of oppression of minority or disempowered groups, whether through political or cultural forms of colonialism.

The Frankfurt school (Adorno, 1978; Habermas, 1968; Horkheimer, 1978) proposed that political domination is ingrained within the epistemological structure of empiricism. According to empiricism, science, as the presupposed superior form of knowledge, is the sole arbiter of truth, and anything that cannot be empirically and atheoretically demonstrated is false or an error. From this kind of misleading assumption developed the modern and current dualistic distinction between modern scientific facts and traditional mythological beliefs.

Out of this dualistic conceptual structure that regards the mythological thinking of traditional cultures as a prescientific form of knowledge develops the condescending attitude of regarding other different cultures as primitive, inferior, or incapable of benefiting from the light of scientific culture. Because empiricist culture resists knowledge and cognition to narrow formal logical structures, members of other cultures that are based on broader, more intuitive, more right-brain forms of cognition will continue to fail "normative" expectations. Concurrently, the empiricist paradigm also discredits and invalidates the ways of knowledge of traditional cultures. This has become a political reality in contemporary society.

Nevertheless, despite the strength and momentum of the empiricist world view, trends can be found in modern culture that contradict the view of rational thought as superior to mythical or intuitive thought. This is seen not only within spiritual quarters and the works of Jung (1964) and Campbell (1967, 1968) but also within the discourse of the social sciences. The writings of anthropologist Claude Levi-Strauss (1949/1969) would be an example. Although a social scientist

and the founder of structuralism in anthropology, he rejected the notion that mythical thought is somehow less rigorous and demanding than scientific thought. The difference between the two is not based on the quality of intellectual operations but found in the nature of the object or the dimension of reality being studied. Mythical thought is not without a conceptual language but is used to describe a reality that cannot be fully captured by language. Myth simultaneously organizes a historical and timeful perspective, on the one hand, and a timeless–eternalist and ahistorical perspective, on the other. The perception of the mythical mentality as a primitive, false, pathological, or infantile consciousness is a dogmatic and ethnocentric bias of empiricist science. In taking this stance, science becomes the very shadow of the dogmatic theological paradigm it rose to supplant.

Despite any actual claim to ethical and political neutrality, epistemology has definite political consequences in terms of the socioeconomic power and authority that comes from establishing criteria regarding credible or legitimate knowledge. In addition to the political issue involved in the relationship between power and knowledge across cultures, however, the question still remains as to whether empiricism is the only adequate and valid paradigm for the social sciences. Can the structural complexities of culture and of the human subject be adequately approached, interpreted, and explained with purely behavioral, descriptive, and "objectivistic" references? Are there entire levels of social, psychical, and subjective reality that remain unaccounted for within the structure of logical empiricism? Conversely, could it be that, despite their inferior political and economic status, traditional epistemological forms are more adequate than empiricist social science in this regard?

Toward a Postmodern Epistemology

In contrast to traditional, intuitive forms of knowledge that are based on becoming intimate with what one knows, empiricist scientific knowl-

edge remains separate from the object. In the guise of being objective and nonsubjective, the scientist misses something essential to himself or herself and the object. Knowledge in science is intrinsically associated with the split between subject and object. This split may result in dualistic views regarding the nature of reality because the scientist and the technocrat think they are manipulating an object that is separate from themselves.

It is true that the fallibility of a scientific hypothesis (to use Popper's concept) serves as an antidote against human beings projecting their own wishes and expectations onto the world of nature. Such is the usual empiricist critique of mythical thought as distinguished from the world of facts. However, traditional cultures also contain vehicles for the reality testing of perceptions or for bridging the symbolic and the real, theory and reality. It could be argued that the process of differentiating between true and false knowledge seems to be similar for both traditional culture and social science. It is misleading to think that intuitive knowledge is subjective and scientific knowledge is objective. The scientific approach seeks an objective knowledge that describes phenomena independently from personal and subjective beliefs (i.e., values, attitudes, opinions, sensations, impressions, and feelings). It strives to describe things in themselves "just as they are," free from subjective distortion. However, although empiricists believe that true knowledge comes from the senses, they fail to realize that the senses, as something different from subjective "sensual" desire, derive their "sense" from a rational–symbolic function. Following Lacan (1975), any symbolic–cultural system can be understood as providing an objective mediation between social cultural reality and subjective desire.

It is a mistake to think that reality is translucently reflected in human analytical consciousness, as a naive empirical realism would have it. Empiricism fails to notice how a theory and the logic of the experiment or the technical procedures involved determine or at least interact with the nature of the data produced. Facts and theory belong together because facts do not exist on their own without theoretical elucidation or interpretation. If no theory can be declared true, neither can any fact for that matter. Moreover, knowledge (as rational theory or empirical fact) and truth can never completely coincide because, as Lacan (1975) has argued, truth can be only half-stated or half-said. In other words, whatever is said beyond the medium point fails to hit the mark, because the other half is beyond theory and measurement.

From a postmodern perspective, "what things are" does not signify an external object for a separate subject. The practice of observation, experimentation, and concentration produces mutations in people's subjectivity that allow a phenomenon to be simultaneously revealed as it is outside and inside the mind. In addition, what things are does not mean either a singular, univocal signification such as they are only this and not that, as would follow from the identity principle of formal logic prevalent in logical empiricism. Within the arena of the social sciences, what things are unfolds within a dialectical, polyvocal, and symbolic system in which things being what they are can also be something else or more.

Lacan (1959) pointed out that all things of the human world are structured by language. In the subjectivization of the external world symbols, as representations, memories, and images, color and screen the perceptions and impressions coming from the external world. In this view, the world is not perceived naturally, spontaneously, but is interpreted according to one's desires, languages, and culturally guided theories. The symbolic structure is interposed between perception and consciousness. The something out there as a phenomenon in the external world, which has objective existence in reality, is found there by human endeavor and purposive action only to be used for some utility that exists within a world of subjective expectations and goals.

Finally, that so-called objective discoveries are corrective subjective experiences or a rectification of one's subjectivity (Bachelard, 1975) does not mean that, ultimately, one is left with pure objectivity and no subjectivity. This is still a dualistic view

representing a partial perspective. If an objective discovery changes one subjectively, this means that both the object and the subject are changed. Thus, one arrives not at a position of no subjectivity but at a position of true, rectified–corrected subjectivity. Thus, the difference between false beliefs and authentic knowledge, whether in science or traditional culture, is not that between objective and subjective knowledge but that between true and false subjectivity.

Culture, Lacanian Psychoanalysis, and Clinical Practice

In addition to cultivating a cultural critique of social oppression based on both Judeo-Christian and Marxist sources, the continental European tradition also developed a psychoanalytic and hermeneutic tradition. These latter two have in common an incorporation of myth, interpretation, and the "beyond reason" into the structure of a social or human science. It is only here that it becomes possible to conceive of a continuity and compatibility between what Lyotard (1989) called the narrative knowledge of traditional ethnic cultures and the culture of Western science. The hermeneutic tradition is associated with the philosophy of science of Dilthey and, more currently, with that of Ricoeur (1970) and Habermas (1968). Both Habermas and Ricoeur define psychoanalysis as hermeneutic science operating through the medium of language and interpretation of meaning.

Freud's twin concepts of the unconscious and of a symbolic order were meant to account for what is beyond rational measurement and what was traditionally associated with intuition and nonlinear, paralogical metaphoric thinking. However, there are also positivistic elements running through Freud's thought in that he accepted the modernistic assumptions of his time regarding the advancement of culture from animism to religion to science. Thus, only the work of Lacan provides a postmodern interpretation of Freud that allows for a more sympathetic understanding of traditional culture.

Although many of Freud's views on ethnology, as outlined in

"Totem and Taboo" (1913/1953) and "Moses and Monotheism" (1939/1964), have been criticized as inaccurate, they are so only insofar as they are presented to be positivistic, objective, and scientific historical facts. I follow Lacan in his conception of these Freudian works as modern mythological structures. The two works aforementioned contain truths not as facts but as myths and metaphors. In this area of his work, Freud's texts ironically become akin to narrative biblical or traditional stories describing events that need to be interpreted symbolically and hermeneutically, as opposed to literally or objectively. Nevertheless, it should also be recognized that Freud's myths reflect certain key concerns and characteristics of modern Western culture (e.g., the importance and meaning attributed to sexuality and to parent–child relationships).

Following Freud, who, in *The Psychopathology of Everyday Life* (1901/1965), called psychoanalysis his psychomythology, Lacan taught that psychoanalysis is half-science and half-metaphor or myth. This field is neither completely one or the other nor a symmetrical complement of the two. Moreover, this state of affairs is consistent with the aforementioned Lacanian aphorism that truth can be only half-stated or half-said (whatever is said beyond the medium point fails to hit the mark, because the other half is beyond knowledge and measurement). In this sense, metaphor or myth may be the preferable symbolic medium needed for accessing a dimension of reality and of human experience that cannot be grasped by reason or scientific method. In addition, metaphor leaves one with the echo and evocation of something that is beyond words and logic. Lacan's work differs from the school of hermeneutics in that his theory also includes a register of experience that is beyond words and the symbolic order. This has important consequences for the practice of interpretation in psychotherapy. I return to this later.

It is important to note that the United States also developed a particular psychoanalytic tradition and a psychoanalytically influenced psychiatric culture that, in my opinion, increases the gap between modern psychiatry and traditional minority groups. This is a pivotal point, because it again underscores the fact that one cannot speak of a single and monolithic Western culture. Moreover, certain aspects of Western culture blend better with traditional non-Western cultures than others.

The North American psychoanalytic school has produced a culturally guided reformulation of psychoanalysis. In the land of empiricism and pragmatism, psychoanalysis partially moved away from the unconscious and from those symbolic intangibles that cannot be measured. More important for the purposes of this article, however, psychoanalysis was adapted to the popular North American ideology of individualism and the self-made entrepreneur. North American psychoanalysis developed the school of ego psychology out of this cultural juncture. In lieu of the unconscious, the emphasis shifted to the problem of adaptation to society. The latter can lead to a dichotomy between adaptive and normal–normative behavior and maladaptive and abnormal behavior. The problem with the concept of adaptation is that one has to ask "Adaptation to what society?" One possible answer is the society of dominant Anglo-Saxon ego-based individualism. Thus, it is no accident that those from different cultural groups could fail to function within certain cultural imperatives. Entire groups may fall out of the "norm" and the "normal" and into pathology and deviance. In contrast to this, the concept of the unconscious is nondual because it is found in both normality and pathology. For example, the Oedipus myth is involved in the production of both functional states. Moreover, primitive symbolic logic constitutes the logic of the unconscious and, as such, establishes a continuity between abnormal and normal and between primitive and developed mental phenomena.

In some respects, this critique could also apply to more current schools of psychoanalysis. Although the object relations and self psychology schools cannot be identified with ego psychology, they share an interest in ego development and use a developmental model to differentiate normal from abnormal behavior. It can be argued that linear developmental models that establish tempo-

ral norms to differentiate normal from abnormal behavior—and that therefore reify culture-bound norms into so-called objective criteria—run the risk of either pathologizing individuals from other cultures or imposing on them behavioral standards of the dominant culture. Finally, wittingly or unwittingly, the three schools mentioned earlier (with the exception of the Kleinian school of object relations) lose sight of the unconscious and its symbolic and cultural interpretation. In doing so, they inevitably disregard atemporal dimensions of experience. Mythical, metaphoric, and linguistic mediums have the advantage of simultaneously organizing both time-bound and timeless dimensions. In contrast to this, developmental models are always bound to culturally relative conceptions of time.

Under the influence of Lacanian thought, socially informed psychoanalysis in Latin America has continued to center psychoanalysis around the therapeutic task not of ego adaptation but of interpreting unconscious desire and undoing repression. This latter treatment task establishes a different therapeutic relationship with oppressed minority groups. The undoing of psychological repression resonates in unison with the emancipatory social interests of minority groups, whereas adaptation to culture-bound norms is analogous to a process of assimilation in which a core of desired values is lost or repressed. This point can be elaborated further by using the contrast that Levi-Strauss (1955/1965) made between two basic mechanisms of cultural organization: anthropophagy and anthropemy. The former refers to the tendency of a culture or society to expel or exclude differences from the social or public body, and the latter refers to the tendency to include and welcome differences and foreign influences into the social body. Thus, the social movement toward including differences can be compared with the psychical task of undoing repression and incorporating the "other" into the core of one's being. In contrast, the movement toward expelling differences can be seen as analogous to the task of adaptation to a normative environment by conforming and excluding differences to the norm. Finally, the

focus on ego adaptation is consistent with an assimilationist or melting pot model of acculturation.

Lacan often pointed out the danger that ego psychology constructs can reinforce an implicit master's mentality or attitude in which the ego is the master or rider and the id is the servant or the tamed animal. This equestrian metaphor shares formal similarities with the political relationship whereby a dominant majority group governs over a dominated minority. This relationship, in turn, can be replicated within the psychotherapeutic relationship with ethnic minority individuals. Lacan's critique of an ego-mastery ideal does, in fact, coincide with how North American values and cultural standards are scrutinized within the minority mental health literature. However, most minorities in the United States are not aware of this possible and plausible way of combining psychoanalysis and social theory. Making these points explicit, I think, can help bridge the gap and misunderstanding between these two sets of human discourses.

Lacan argued that Freud invented a new relationship and situation that subverts the normative discourses of both government and education. By using language nonconventionally and occupying a different psychical position than that emanating from the master's discourse of the ruling or governing classes, the discourse of psychopathology may be understood and healed in the psychotherapeutic process.

Thus, this framework purports to address concerns raised within the minority mental health literature regarding how the psychotherapy process can be impeded when individuals and their psychotherapists are members of different socioeconomic classes or possess different sets of cultural values. This has been considered an important issue in work with working-class Latinos because the majority of Latinos have lower incomes, fewer years of education, and overrepresentation in menial occupations that nevertheless sustain and support the upper structures of the North American economy. Many Latinos are literally working as servants, maids, janitors, gardeners, and in-home child-care workers.

However, although the literature on psychotherapy with Latinos has emphasized the importance of extrapsychic factors of class and culture, it has not articulated extrapsychic and intrapsychic factors into a coherent theoretical model (Ruiz & Padilla, 1977). The proposed theory combines these dimensions into a nondual framework: What is intrapsychic can become extrapsychic, and vice versa. Thus, in the metaphor used earlier, the extrapsychic social relationship between master and servant—the ruling majority and the ruled minority—finds its correlate and equivalent process at the intrapsychic level in the relationship between the ego and the unconscious. From the perspective of this parallel process, it then becomes possible to understand how extrapsychic and intrapsychic, social and psychical elements may impede or facilitate the psychotherapy situation.

When a psychotherapist is a member of a racial or cultural minority group, he or she will, at minimum, belong to a higher socioeconomic stratum than the lower-class minority patient, and class differences will arise secondary to educational differences. Altman (1995) pointed out that the social location of psychologists and psychoanalysts is in the professional–managerial class and that "they have nothing more tangible by way of capital to hold on to than their knowledge and expertise" (p. 81). On the other hand, when psychotherapist and patient belong to different racial, cultural, and linguistic groups, class differences will be subsumed or expressed through these categories. In the latter case, cultural and language barriers will prevent the therapist from understanding and communicating with the minority patient. In the former case, although a therapist may be knowledgeable about language and culture, a class barrier may lead the therapist to impose his or her own class-bound values, therapeutic or otherwise, on the lower-class individual. Thus, from my perspective, beyond a mere recognition of the existence of a class difference, what is required is the neutralization of the class-bound "master" position and discourse of the psychotherapist; this needs to be distinguished from the psychotherapist's professional credibility.

Sue and Zane (1987) identified credibility and giving as two basic processes that are important to consider in doing psychotherapy with members of ethnic minority groups. Credibility refers to a patient's perception of the psychotherapist as an effective and trustworthy helper, whereas giving is the perception that something was received from the therapeutic encounter. According to Sue and Zane, because of skepticism toward Western forms of treatment, the minority individual needs to perceive, almost immediately, a direct benefit from the treatment.

From my vantage point, the credibility of the psychotherapist is based on two elements: (a) the fact that the psychical symptom is something unknown and uncontrolled by the subject and (b) the fact that the patient attributes a certain knowledge to the doctor regarding the symptom. In the Lacanian school, these elements are understood as the basis for a positive transference relationship. The latter is what functions as a structural basis for the perceived credibility of the psychotherapist. As such, it provides the initial immediate gratification (benefit) needed to engage an individual in a treatment relationship. In fact, a reduction in symptomatology is often reported in the very early phase of psychotherapy. Within the psychoanalytic field, this phenomenon is known as a "transference cure."

Thus, I want to argue that, on the one hand, the analyst–therapist needs to establish his or her credibility on the basis of knowledge regarding psychopathology, psychical structures, and psychotherapeutic processes; on the other hand, to satisfy the aforementioned considerations of class as well as the ingredients of effective psychotherapeutic use of the transference relationship, the therapist–analyst needs to renounce the power and privilege given to him or her by educational class differences as well as the transference of the subject. Here the curative factor comes not from the class-bound knowledge of the analyst (the master's discourse) but from an unconscious knowing not based on formal education that the suffering subject (the client or analysand) does not know that he or she knows. When the analyst renounces the ego

knowledge or expertise of the master's discourse and functions out of an attitude of not knowing (in the non-dual sense of a not knowing that includes knowing by the subject and not the ego), he or she becomes a vehicle for the nonrepressed "unknown knowing" and understanding contained within the symbolic, or what Lacan calls the treasure chest of the signifier. "Unknown knowing" here includes both the repressed signifying chain of the analysand and the participation of the analyst in the larger unknown (unconscious in a descriptive sense) structure of language and the symbolic. On this side of the dialectic, credibility is achieved by a symbolic horizontal leveling of the ego-based authority of the analyst–psychotherapist in favor of the transformative power of the unconscious.

Thus, two different forms of credibility can be postulated: vertical and horizontal. Vertical credibility would refer to credibility based on the professional knowledge of the clinician, whereas horizontal credibility would refer to credibility flowing from a subjective position of not knowing or "unknown knowing" on the part of the analyst. This is the meaning that should be assigned to the aforementioned symbolic renunciation on the part of the analyst–psychotherapist. This latter form of credibility would be associated with unconscious and subjective dimensions of experience (the subject) and would be a direct function of the degree of conflict and resolution within the clinician's own psychical structure.

Consistent with Hegel's philosophy, within this model the true subject is found in the position of service and servitude. True mastery is attained not by the ego but in relationship to the unconscious and through a process of benevolent ego deconstruction. Mastery, thus defined, allows the psychotherapist to renounce his or her own desire to obtain ego gratification through the patient's idealization of him or her in transference. This kind of subjective maturity on the part of the psychotherapist would constitute a central characteristic of the horizontal type of credibility. It can be argued that this secular symbolic type of subjective position is very much consistent and congruent with key properties of traditional and symbolic cultural systems (e.g., Chinese Confucianism and Taoism, Chinese or Japanese Buddhism, Native American shamanistic traditions, or Western Judaic and Christian traditions).

In line with this, Lacan reformulated and redeployed Freudian principles regarding the process of the cure. In "The Direction of the Treatment and the Principles of Its Power," Lacan (1966/1979) outlined how the two elements of direction and power are correlated and how, if there is to be a direction to the cure, the analyst has to renounce the power granted to him or her by the analysand's transference. Lacan in France, along with his followers in Latin America, has emphasized the need to call the analysand *analizante* instead of *analizado* (analyzed). The English word *analysand* implies a position of empowerment, analytical activity, and responsibility. The unconscious of the analysand knows the textual truth (the signifying chain of symbolic language resembles a latent text) manifesting through the symptom; as a result of repression and concomitant disguises, however, the subject appears to ignore it. From this place of ignorance, the analysand searches for a master in the analyst.

It is the unconscious of the analysand, and not the ego of either analyst or analysand, that directs the process of the cure. Thus, the autonomy granted to the subject of analysis is not so that he or she may become a repressive master of another colonized part of the self or of yet another more vulnerable subject or social group. Emancipation is achieved by bracketing and renouncing the traps and allures of the master's discourse. Especially when working with individuals of a different culture or a lower socioeconomic class, the analyst has to renounce being a representative of the ego ideals of the ruling classes, instead operating out of a position of not knowing or "unknowing knowing" and letting the culturally and linguistically ciphered unconscious of the analysand speak in its own true voice. Conversely, the analysand has to surrender not to the class and status-bound ego of the analyst or to his or her own imaginary ego demands but to the voice of his or her

own symbolic language and culture. From a social cultural perspective, the idealizing transference to the analyst as an ego ideal can be regarded as a movement toward searching for assimilation: to want to be and speak with the words of the White upper-class master (of the rulers) rather than with one's own.

The therapeutic task of undoing repression and the concept of cure direction (as defined earlier), constitute key elements of psychotherapy in general but also have a special importance and meaning essential to doing psychotherapy with minority groups. Both point in the direction of empowerment of the subject and reconciliation with and inclusion of otherness. Lacan used the term *the Other* to designate the Freudian unconscious. This term has the advantage of simultaneously conveying both the symbolic and social meanings of the unconscious. Given that otherness encompasses the subject of the unconscious and the presence of a different social other (i.e., an ethnic minority individual or group), acceptance and reconciliation with the Other of the unconscious will lead to a qualitative change in the nature of the social link and nexus with other subjects.

The relational or intersubjective school of psychoanalysis (Altman, 1995) argues that psychoanalysis has neglected social or class issues because the "one-person" conceptual framework, with its emphasis on intrapsychic drive processes, does not lend itself to an analysis of intersubjective social phenomena. However, from a Lacanian perspective, the problem is not drive theory per se but how the drive is defined. In the United States, the mainstream ego-psychological psychoanalytic view of the drive has been that of the model of a biological instinct. Lacan, following Freud, postulates that the drive, as opposed to a biological instinct, can be known only through psychical representations that are organized within a cultural symbolic order. The symbolic order immediately places the drive not only within a dyadic dual or "two-person psychology" but within a triadic "three-person psychology." The symbolic is analogous to the category of the social, linguistic, and cultural dimensions of experience.

The unconscious as the Other encompasses the place of a repressed symbolic drive and the psychosocial space of the socially different. The social other of a same race or class represents the general social other–will of society, the nurture side of the nurture–nature relationship. For the master class (the class in power), the place of minorities, of the socially different by virtue of race and class, symbolically represents the place of forbidden satisfaction (*jouissance*), the natural *jouissance*, the place of the lack of discipline that the law demands. Thus, minorities, the masses, people of color, and the lower classes have been classically perceived and defined as representing the other of the primitive mentality found in nature, passion, and drive. Finally, the exceptions to and failures of the law produce a reinforcement and a heightened awareness of the law. What the servant is seen as wanting or doing is what the master cannot have or do. This also explains, in my view, how the other of social difference is metaphorically held responsible not only for representing the drive but also for reminding members of the master class of what they cannot do or have.

The ego psychology school also differentiates between defensive and nondefensive forms of ego functioning. For Lacan, the category of nondefensive ego functioning is associated with the subject of the unconscious, from which stems the capacity to experientially and not necessarily rationally know the unconscious. The objection could be raised that the distinctions between the ego and the unconscious, master and servant, and the repressive and the repressed are not absolute given that, for Freud, the ego also had an unconscious dimension. Nevertheless, I do not think that Freud's ideas regarding an unconscious part of the ego refer to a distinction between defensive and nondefensive ego functioning. For Freud, the nondefensive ego was the rational conscious ego. Freud's unconscious part of the ego refers to the source of unconscious repression and therefore is bound up with a defensive function of the ego. Freud (1923/1953) believed that the unconscious part of the ego, as the unconscious source of repression, had to be of a different nature than the repressed unconscious.

Freud never clarified very well or added much content to his assertion that the repressive ego is unconscious but not repressed. Freud did not provide a systematic definition of the unconscious part of the ego or of how this concept is similar to or different from the repressed unconscious. In "The Ego and the Id" (1923/1953), instead of defining the unconscious part of the ego, he moved on to introduce the id. Freud conceived of a connection between repression, the unconscious part of the ego, and the faculty of self-criticism and conscience. In addition, Freud associated the faculty of criticism with the superego. However, he never established a systematic relationship between the superego and the unconscious part of the ego, although all of his thinking pointed in this direction. To explain the unconscious part of the ego, Freud pointed out that the ego extends into the id. Moreover, because Freud established a close connection between the superego and the energetic cathexis of the id, it is my contention that he advanced the concept of the superego precisely to explain the relationship between an unconscious self-critical faculty, the unconscious part of the ego, and the id. Moreover, later he contradicted himself by arguing that the ego can also repress the superego (the unconscious part of the ego on whose behest the ego carries out the repressions). Thus, this would seem to indicate that the unconscious repressive force may also be repressed.

The unconscious ego can precisely refer to suppressed or repressed values and class prejudices of a particular culture as they are embodied in a particular individual. The superego, as an aspect or differentiation within the ego, is the unconscious taskmaster, the master class overlord capable of thinking and making derogatory comments of deprived people of color who rarely have access to mental health treatments available to the White upper classes. As opposed to the rational ego and the unconscious superego, the subject of the unconscious is in the position of not knowing and, therefore, in a symbolic position similar to that of the other, the socially different and humble. I believe that this subjective position, which is in fact non-defensive, should be differentiated from the concepts of the ego and the superego as a differentiation within the ego.

The emphasis given to undoing repression over adaptation to normative society should not be misunderstood as giving priority to cognitive insight over affect or social behavioral change. The emphasis on social engineering and behavioral change and management through positive reinforcement of socially adaptive behavior needs to be understood not as value neutral but as a direct way of reinforcing the norms and values of a particular society. On the other hand, insight should not be understood either as a purely intellectual or as a verbal exercise without any actual emotional or practical consequence. Up until now, the psychoanalytic concept of insight has been primarily regarded as cognitive in nature (Stricker, 1992). The question regarding the function of insight in psychotherapy has important characteristics for the purposes of this article. For example, it is often critiqued as ineffective both as a therapeutic tool leading to interminable and exceedingly long treatments and as a treatment for minority groups because of the assumption that insight is based on formal education, intelligence, and cognitive processes primarily characteristic of Western culture.

Lacan redefined the classical psychoanalytic concept of transference around the question of "knowing" (*savior* in French or *saber* in Spanish). Knowing is not based on formal rational ego knowledge (*conocimiento* in Spanish and *conaissance* in French), because Lacan makes a distinction between the referential knowledge of science and a textual knowing in the psychoanalytic situation regarding the text of the unconscious. This form of knowing would not be characterized by cognitive or secondary ego processes. The unconscious has to do with an associative chain of representations that convey an emotional knowing regarding experiences apparently ignored by the ego. In other words, the analysand does not know that he or she knows. Thus, Lacan can be understood in his contention that analysis is about a search for a knowing that is not based on book knowledge: In every session, the analysand is looking for an "unknown knowing." When the analysand says, "I do not *know* what is wrong with me," the analysand knows that the symptom means something (although this something is unknown).

It is well known (within Lacanian circles) that Lacan's aphorism—the unconscious is structured like a language—should not be interpreted as meaning that the structure of the unconscious is identical to the structure of social language. Rather, the unconscious has the structure of a different kind of language: the language of the unconscious. Lacan even gave a different name to the symbolic language of the unconscious: *lalangue*. *Lalangue* thrives on the symbolic rather than grammatical or syntactic elements of language. From this perspective, it becomes imperative to differentiate between a preconscious (unconscious in a descriptive sense), rational language and the language of the unconscious. Thus, the importance given in minority mental health to the necessity that the analyst be familiar with the language of the analysand refers to the preconscious, cognitive knowledge of a language. However, the function of language in psychoanalysis specifically refers to the intimate knowing (*saber*) of the language of the unconscious, to the ability of the subject to listen for those places in which the signifier intersects the "real" of unconscious experience. It goes without saying that the knowledge of the former is obviously a requirement for the experiential knowing of the latter.

Lacan's concept of cure direction should also be contrasted with the classical notion of an analytical contract. The latter implies a series of quasi-legislative standard norms that define a "proper" analytical frame (Harari & Moncayo, 1997). Such attempts at strict uniformity and conformity regarding the length and frequency of sessions, among other things, constitute what Octave Mannoni called a Procrustean couch (if someone does not fit into the frame, cut an arm, then a leg, etc.). Lacan insisted that the question of the frame be considered on a case-by-case basis and not in standard fashion. This is especially important when working with different cultural groups; instead of attempting to "adapt" the minority client to the frame, the frame should be adapted to match the cultural and linguistic styles within which the unconscious of the subject is ciphered.

I would like to conclude this exposition by returning to the question of the practice of interpretation and its cultural significance. I stated earlier that metaphor leaves one with the echo or evocation of something that is beyond words or logic. In a well-known paper on symbolic efficacy, Levi-Strauss (1949/1963) investigated the parallels between psychoanalytic treatment and the shamanic practices of healers or *curanderos*. He concluded that both work with symbols and with the relationship between a signifier or symbol and that which is signified or symbolized. The shaman provides an ill subject with a particular symbolic language to symbolize unconscious psychical and physiological states that may otherwise remain beyond formulation or symbolization. The symptoms–symbols are resolved or transformed not because of a professional knowledge or insight that the patient acquires but because the symbolic process produces a specific experience on the side of the patient and on the half-side of truth that remains outside and yet also intrinsically connected with culture-bound symbolization. Lacanian analysis and psychotherapy engages the subject in a parallel healing process.

A Case Example

An example case provides a concrete illustration of how the unconscious is ciphered in the language and culture of the subject. Velia, a Mexican woman in her mid-40s, presented to the clinic complaining of major depression with insomnia, crying spells, and panic attacks. She came from a peasant family from Mexico's rural countryside, had finished third grade only (at age 13), and was working part time cleaning houses. During her first session, she described her suffering in terms of feeling inside as though she were *"pesada, pisada and como nada"* (heavy and disliked by others, stepped on and a nothing). This example makes

painfully clear the need to know the linguistic and cultural context so as to understand how the unconscious producing the symptom is ciphered. The Spanish language makes possible the formation of a series or a signifying chain of unconscious meaning. *"Pesada, pisada and como nada"* shares a homophonic rhyme that is not the case in the English translation. From a Lacanian perspective, homophony between words is one of the ways in which the unconscious organizes meaning within language. Knowing this, I repeated these signifiers back to her, including the repetition of the phoneme *ada* in the three words, and asked her to say more about them. No cognitive explanation was given at this point. In turn, she produced the following additional material.

Ada she associated with *"Ada Madrina"* (fairy godmother). In addition, *ada* connoted the "beautiful fantasy" of being someone instead of nothing. Velia spoke of the fairy tale of Cinderella, who was made to suffer in the position of servitude by a cruel stepmother but who nevertheless later became a princess. In her own experience, both her stepmother and godmother had been cruel to her. Velia's sister once told her that their stepmother had asked her to tell Velia that she was a nothing or "like a fly landing everywhere." Her stepmother once refused to shake her hand because of the fear of "contracting prostitution" from her. Both of these metaphors were allusions to Velia having led a sexually active life outside marriage and having been a prostitute in a bordello for a short period of time. Velia's mother had also been too strict and severe with her, and, before she died, Velia refused to kneel to receive her final blessing. This was a source of much guilt.

Velia loved her father very much. She saw him as a very gentle man who was not respected by others because he was a peasant with a humble character. People often referred to him as a *"palo viejo"* (old stick). She regarded her sexual experiences as having brought further disrespect and humiliation to her father. When discussing this subject in one of our sessions, she referred to herself as *"palo caido de camino real"* (fallen stick on a royal road). This is a saying (*dicho*) or aphorism in

Spanish that, in her case, became a signifier expressing unconscious meaning. Thus, beyond solely incorporating cultural sayings into the work, as is often recommended in the minority mental health literature, these aphorisms need to be understood as cultural and linguistic vehicles of the unconscious. I ended the session after she produced the aphorism and its signifying context was preliminarily explored. At least on the surface, it was clear that she identified herself with the image of a fallen stick as a metaphor for failure, impotence, and lack of social advancement, but this interpretation was not yet given to her.

In the following session, she brought up a dream that further deepened our understanding of the aphorism. She was flying in an airplane made of *"palos"* (sticks). This time she associated *palo* with *chile* and went on to explain that both *palo* and *chile* are vulgar metaphors used in Mexico to represent the penis. I interpreted the dream as her wish for the stick to "rise" as opposed to remaining in a "fallen" position. This time, because she had introduced the phallic metaphor, I interpreted "fallen stick" as a metaphor or signifier for male impotence and for her father, with whom she was identified. She agreed and said that in her family the women were the "men" and her father was the "humble" or the "woman" (like her). She also added that once, when she was 14 years old, a boyfriend of hers had tried to force her to have sex, but she was so strong in fighting him back that he lost his erection. After this incident, her boyfriend became ill for 4 months and was thin like a *"palo."*

The next session she began by correcting something she had said during the previous session. She had said that her father had wanted a son when she was born because the first-born had been a boy who "fell" (*cayo*) or died on his 40th day. This time she said that it was her sister's only son who fell on the 40th day. At this point, I began to notice the repeated appearance of the number 4 in the context of a signifying chain linking *fallen stick* with *male* and *female*. From my training and reading of psychoanalytic literature, I knew that numbers can also function as symbolic signifiers. I simply stated that the number 4 had appeared more than once. She said that 4 is her favorite number. Why? Because it is "*pares*" (an even number). The grammatically correct way of saying even in Spanish would have been "*par*." Thus, *pares* also means "you give birth." With regard to giving birth, she brought up with sadness her inability to have children. She added that recently she had been craving to hold a newborn in her arms and to smell the fresh smell of the infant's head and mouth, as she had done with her younger siblings. She also felt envy and anger when seeing pregnant women, although she enjoys seeing a baby nursing at the breast. I interpreted that, in this maternal scene, there is no *palo caido* (fallen stick); there is both a baby and a breast. She agreed and was happy that we had discussed many topics. I agreed and ended the session. There was marked improvement in Velia's symptoms in the course of these sessions.

The process material presented in these sessions illustrates the capacity of any working-class Latino or Latina without formal education to benefit from psychodynamic psychotherapy or psychoanalysis, provided that the aforementioned theoretical and practical conditions are met (by the psychotherapist). The example also shows how the unconscious is ciphered within cultural–linguistic forms and, therefore, how both knowledge of the culture and language and knowing the language of the unconscious are needed for its correct interpretation. Thus, psychoanalysis centered on the analysis of a mythical and linguistic unconscious (with myth and language being key ingredients of traditional culture) could be much more likely to be socially and culturally congruent with the subjective experience of ethnic minorities in a postmodern world.

Conclusion

This work has offered a critique of assumptions made by both the majority psychoanalytic culture and minority groups regarding the suitability of psychoanalytically based psychotherapy for Latinos and other underserved ethnic groups. I have argued that what is needed to

rectify such mistaken assumptions is not only more empirical research but an epistemological critique and a theoretical reformulation of the problem.

Difficulties encountered in providing effective mental health services to minorities are rooted in the larger conflict between modern and traditional paradigms as well as in the epistemological underpinnings of empiricist social science culture. Both sides of the controversy are reflections of the conceptual and political contradictions inherent to what, following Lacan, I call the master's discourse that rules clinicians as well as institutions of higher education.

Empiricist social science is not the best conceptual framework for understanding the experience of ethnic minorities, because its epistemological foundation invalidates the ways of knowledge of traditional cultures. Contrary to empiricism, a postmodern epistemological framework combining modern and traditional elements does not pair false beliefs with subjectivity and valid knowledge with objectivity. Truth will always remain rooted within a subjective ground, and objectivity will always remain limited and relative to the cognitive interests and desiring structure of the human subject.

As a science of interpretation of meaning, psychoanalysis includes the traditional cultural mediums of myth and metaphor and therefore is in a better position to understand the culture-bound experiences of minority groups. However, an effective psychoanalytic approach to psychotherapy with minorities also requires an internal critique of ego-psychological constructs. I have argued that the ego-psychology school and its influence on North American psychiatry widen the gap between Western and traditional cultures mainly for two reasons. First, the ego as a concept is the psychological equivalent of the social concept of a master class, and, second, insight as a therapeutic tool has been primarily construed as a cognitive process heavily loaded with educational characteristics of Western culture and cognitive styles that are dissimilar to those prevalent in traditional cultures. A psychoanalysis centered on the analysis of a mythical and linguistic unconscious is more likely to be socially and culturally congruent

with the subjective experience of ethnic minorities.

Despite a lack of formal education, the working-class ethnic minority individual lives within a rich cultural symbolic universe that does not require cognitive sophistication to encode or decode social–psychical experiences. However, for the symbolic phenomena previously described to manifest in the psychotherapeutic situation, a certain subjective–objective method is required on the part of the psychotherapist. The analyst–psychotherapist has to hold a certain subjective position (or psychical state) if the subjectivity of the individual is to be permutated and transformed under the direction of the unconscious. I have described the social and cultural meanings and dynamics of such a position in terms of the master–servant dialectic. If the psychotherapist can maintain a creative tension between the vertical need for credibility and the horizontal need for leveling and renouncing the ego-based authority that contains his or her master-class values, then psychodynamic psychotherapy can be effective with the minority individual and perhaps with any individual for that matter. I propose that the subjective position of the analyst, as a symbolic renunciation and a position of not knowing or unknown knowing, not only facilitates the psychotherapeutic process and the exploration of the unconscious, as modern people understand it, but also profoundly resonates and is consistent with key properties of traditional symbolic systems.

In addition, the example provided earlier shows that cognitive insight based on formal education is not necessary for analytically based treatment and that metaphor (fallen stick on a royal road) or myth (*ada*–fairy) may be a preferable medium needed for accessing a dimension of human experience that cannot be grasped by reason or scientific method. Moreover, from a Lacanian perspective, psychotherapy mostly requires an unconventional use of language rather than one based on learned, grammatically correct formal language. I postulate that this is an especially important principle to observe with members of ethnic and immigrant minorities who are already struggling with problems associated with bilingualism and difficulties in the use of their original or newly acquired language.

Members of ethnic minorities are perfectly capable of self-disclosure and, given a different understanding of the frame for psychotherapy, can produce material usually associated with traditional psychoanalysis. A great portion of the individual's difficulty with self-disclosure can be attributed to the psychotherapist's lack of intimacy with the social dimensions of his or her own unconscious subjectivity. The self-disclosure of a minority patient with a majority therapist or analyst may be impeded by the latter's own unexamined unconscious issues with class and racial differences. In other words, the self-disclosure of the ethnic individual is obstructed by the psychotherapist's own resistance. For the majority-class psychotherapist, ethnic, cultural, or class differences come to symbolically represent the otherness and ego-alien nature of unconscious experience.

Finally, one could argue that the aforementioned falls under the general classical category of the countertransference that should be handled in the analyst's own personal analysis. However, this would be true only if the personal analysis focused on such topics and the analyst's analyst had an interest in understanding—and a theoretical framework in which to understand—phenomena arising at the intersection of social and unconscious experience.

References

Adorno, T. (1978). Subject and object. In A. Arato & E. Gebhardt (Eds.), *The essential Frankfurt school reader* (pp. 497–527). New York: Urizen Books.

Altman, N. (1995). *The analyst in the inner city*. Hillsdale, NJ: Analytic Press.

Bachelard, G. (1975). *La formacion del espiritu cientifico*. [The formation of the scientific spirit]. Buenos Aires: Siglo Ventiuno Editores.

Bernal, M. E., & Padilla, A. M. (1982). Status of minority curricula and training in clinical psychology. *American Psychologist, 37*, 780–787.

Campbell, J. (1967). *The hero with a thousand faces*. Cleveland, OH: Meridian.

Campbell, J. (1968). *The masks of God* (4 vols.). New York: Viking.

Cortese, M. (1979). Intervention research with Hispanic Americans: A review. *Hispanic Journal of Behavioral Sciences, 1,* 4–20.

Freud, S. (1953). The ego and the id. In J. Strachey (Ed. and Trans.), *The standard edition of the complete psychological works of Sigmund Freud* (Vol. 19, pp. 1–60). (Original work published 1923)

Freud, S. (1953). Totem and taboo. In J. Strachey (Ed. and Trans.), *The standard edition of the complete psychological works of Sigmund Freud* (Vol. 13, pp. 1–161). London: Hogarth Press. (Original work published 1913)

Freud, S. (1964). Moses and monotheism. In J. Strachey (Ed. and Trans.), *The standard edition of the complete psychological works of Sigmund Freud* (Vol. 23, pp. 1–138). (Original work published 1939).

Freud, S. (1965). *The psychopathology of everyday life*. New York: Norton. (Original work published 1901)

Habermas, J. (1968). *Knowledge and human interests*. Boston: Beacon Press.

Harari, R., & Moncayo, R. (1997). Principles of Lacanian clinical practice. *Journal of the Lacanian School of Psychoanalysis, 1*, 13–28.

Horkheimer, M. (1978). On the problem of truth. In A. Arato & E. Gebhardt (Eds.), *The essential Frankfurt school reader* (pp. 407–443). New York: Urizen Books.

Jung, C. (1964). *Man and his symbols*. New York: Basic Books.

Lacan, J. (1959). *La etica del psicoanalisis* [The ethics of psychoanalysis]. Buenos Aires: Paidos.

Lacan, J. (1975). *El reverso del psicoanalisis* [The underside of psychoanalysis]. Buenos Aires: Paidos.

Lacan, J. (1979). The direction of the treatment and the principles of its power. In *Ecrits* (pp. 226–280). New York: Norton. (Original work published 1966)

Levi-Strauss, C. (1963). The effectiveness of symbols. In *Structural anthropology* (pp. 186–205). New York: Basic Books. (Original work published 1949)

Levi-Strauss, C. (1965). *Tristes tropiques*. New York: Atheneum. (Original work published 1955)

Levi-Strauss, C. (1969). *The elementary structures of kinship*. Boston: Beacon Press. (Original work published 1949)

Lyotard, J. F. (1989). *The postmodern condition*. Minneapolis: University of Minnesota Press.

Meadow, A. (1982). Psychopathology, psychotherapy, and the Mexican-American patient. In E. E. Jones & S. J. Korchin (Eds.), *Minority mental health* (pp. 331–361). New York: Praeger.

Ricoeur, P. (1970). *Freud and philosophy: An essay on interpretation*. New Haven, CT: Yale University Press.

Ruiz, A. R., & Padilla, A. M. (1977). Counseling Latinos. *Personnel and Guidance Journal, 55*, 401–408.

Stricker, G. (1992). The relationship of research to clinical practice. *American Psychologist, 47*, 543–549.

Sue, S., & Zane, N. (1987). The role of culture and cultural techniques in psychotherapy. *American Psychologist, 42*, 37–45.

Szapocznik, J., Santisteban, D., Kurtines, W. M., Hervis, O. E., & Spencer, F. (1982). Life enhancement counseling: A psychosocial model of services for Cuban elders. In E. E. Jones & S. J. Korchin (Eds.), *Minority mental health* (pp. 296–330). New York: Praeger.

Article Review Form at end of book.

Explain how "temperament" is addressed with respect to the integrative psychobiological approach.

Integrative Psychobiological Approach to Psychiatric Assessment and Treatment

C. Robert Cloninger and Dragan M. Svrakic

Center for Psychobiology of Personality and the Departments of Psychiatry and Genetics, Washington University School of Medicine

A developmental approach to integrative psychobiology provides a flexible framework for both clinical assessment and treatment planning. Assessment of seven dimensions of personality using the Temperament and Character Inventory (TCI) allows for comprehensive description of individual differences in feelings, thoughts, and actions. Four temperament factors that are stable throughout life can be decomposed in terms of their underlying genetic structure. Character factors that mature in response to social learning can be decomposed in terms of the components that unfold in a stepwise fashion from infancy through adulthood. Pharmacotherapy and psychotherapy can be systematically matched to the personality structure and stage of character development of each individual. This provides comprehensive paradigm that integrates psychodynamic, cognitive-behavioral, interpersonal, and neurobiological insights into case formulation. Use of the TCI in clinical assessment and treatment planning

was illustrated by a case independently assessed by Mardi Horowitz using another approach.

Psychiatric formulation and treatment can be substantially improved by recent improvements in methods for personality assessment that are highly efficient, reliable, and clinically valid. The Temperament and Character Inventory (TCI) distinguishes components of personality that differ in terms of their etiology, pattern of development, and responses to psychotherapy and pharmacotherapy. This provides a foundation for integrating diagnosis and treatment planning, including both psychotherapy and pharmacotherapy, in a manner that is generalizable, but sensitive to differences among individual patients. In addition, the TCI allows the clinician to detect discrepancies between a patient's self-report and their actual performance style, so that the therapist can immediately know when there is misrepresentation due to cognitive distortion or purposeful deception. In this way, it is possible for the clinician to know the basic structure of personality at the time of the first visit with the patient. This can improve both the efficiency and effectiveness of treatment, by facilitating establishment of a therapeutic al-

liance, a valid case formulation, and planning for an optimal sequence of interventions.

The TCI was originally developed to permit quantitative ratings of the seven dimensions of personality needed to describe individual differences in normal personality development, and for the differential diagnosis of personality disorders (Cloninger 1987a; Cloninger, Svrakic, and Przybeck 1993). This original description has been extended to specify a general quantitative model of personality development (Svrakic, Svrakic, and Cloninger 1996). Using this model, personality development can be described in terms of a sequence of 15 steps, in which transformations of attitudes, values, and emotions occur as a result of complex interactions among heritable predispositions, social learning, and individual experiences. The rate and direction of these transitions in quantitative ratings of personality can be predicted in terms of the dynamic interactions among multiple components of the model.

This psychobiological model of personality development has many implications for the assessment and treatment of all forms of mental disorder. For example, the presence and severity of personality disorders can be reliably assessed using interview or questionnaire versions of the Temperament and Character Inventory (TCI), which rates the seven basic dimensions of personality and each of the 15 steps in character development (Cloninger, Przybeck, Svrakic, and Wetzel 1994). Also, individual differences in personality structure and development have a strong influence on the risk of all forms of psychopathology, including psychoses, mood disorders, antisocial behavior, and substance abuse (Bayon, Hill, Svrakic, Przybeck, and Cloninger 1996; Cloninger, Svrakic, and Svrakic in press). Likewise, responses to pharmacotherapy and psychotherapy depend on personality structure and development (Joyce et al. 1994; Cloninger et al. 1994, 1996).

In this article, we will describe the general psychobiological model of personality, and then illustrate its use in practical assessment and treatment in terms of a particular case. The same case is evaluated by Mardi Horowitz (1997, this issue) using his method of configurational analysis, so that these two approaches can be compared. Our integrative psychobiological approach does not advocate a particular form of therapy, such as supportive, cognitive-behavioral, psychodynamic, or pharmacological techniques. Instead, our developmental approach may use any or all of these techniques, specifying a systematic sequence of different techniques for use as the personality organization of the patient changes in response to treatment and other experiences.

General Psychobiological Model of Personality

The way that people learn from experience, and then adapt their feelings, thoughts, and actions, is what characterizes their personality. Specifically, personality can be broadly defined as the dynamic organization within an individual of the psychobiological systems that modulate adaptation to a changing environment (Cloninger et al. 1993). This includes systems regulating cognition, emotion and mood, personal impulse control, and social relations. Hence, personality traits are enduring patterns of per-

Table 1 Differences in Learning between Temperament and Character

Learning Variable	Temperament	Character
Awareness level	Automatic	Intentional
Memory form	Percepts	Concepts
	Procedures	Propositions
Activity type	Habits, skills	Goals, values
Emotion type	Reactive (basic)	Evaluative (complex)
Learning principle	Associative	Conceptual
	Conditioning	Insight
Acquisition rate	Gradual (quantitative)	Abrupt (qualitative)
Key brain system	Limbic system	Temporal cortex
	Striatum	Hippocampus

ceiving, relating to, and thinking about oneself, other people, and the world as a whole.

Personality is comprised of both temperament and character traits. Temperament refers to differences between individuals in their automatic responses to emotional stimuli, which follow the rules of associative conditioning or procedural learning of habits and skills. Temperament traits include basic emotional response patterns, such as fear versus calm, thrill versus anger, disgust versus attachment, and tenacity versus discouragement. Temperament has been defined as those components of personality that are heritable, fully manifest in infancy, and stable throughout life (Goldsmith et al. 1987). Fortunately, each approach defines essentially the same traits, which are all present from infancy onwards, and are moderately heritable and stable throughout life. In contrast, character refers to individual differences in our voluntary goals and values, which are based on insight learning of intuitions and concepts about ourselves, other people, and other objects. Character traits describe individual differences in our self-object relationships, which begin with parental attachments in infancy, then self-object differentiation in toddlers, and then continue to mature in a step-wise manner throughout life. Whereas temperament refers to the way we are born (our emotional predispositions), character is what we make of

ourselves intentionally. Some of the major differences between temperament and character in this psychobiological processes and rules of operation are summarized in Table 1.

Both propositional and procedural learning processes can be dissociated experimentally, but they usually interact to change the salience and significance of all that we experience. Likewise, the limbic and cortical structures underlying procedural and propositional learning are dissociable but interactive components in brain and personality development. For example, amnestic patients with lesions in the medial temporal lobe exhibit deficits in propositional (declarative) learning, but normal procedural learning of skills and habits, whereas patients with Parkinson's disease, with lesions in the neostriatum, have deficits in procedural learning but not in propositional learning (Robbins 1996; Knowlton, Mangels, and Squire 1996). Models of personality and learning that do not specify the dimensions of procedural learning, the dimensions of propositional learning, and their interactions during development, give a misleading and oversimplified account of personality structure and development.

Factor analytic studies confirm that temperament and character are each multidimensional. For example, four dimensions of temperament and three dimensions of character have been distinguished in the TCI. Each dimension is roughly normally distributed. Descriptors for individuals who score high and who score low are summarized in Table 2 for temperament and Table 3 for character.

The four TCI temperament dimensions are called harm avoidance, novelty seeking, reward dependence, and persistence. For example, individuals low in harm avoidance have little anticipatory anxiety or fear about danger; consequently, they are optimistic risk-takers and, if they are not mature in character, frequently use hypochondriasis and isolation as defense mechanisms (Mulder, Joyce, Sellman, and Cloninger 1996). Individuals who are high in novelty seeking are impulsive, quick-tempered whenever frustrated, and prone to break rules and regulations in order to pursue what they think will give them pleasure or thrills; those low in novelty seeking are reflective and law abiding. Immature novelty seekers often use dissociation, splitting, and devaluation as defenses under stress (Mulder et al. 1996). Individuals who are low in reward dependence are aloof and insensitive to social cues; when immature and under stress, such individuals frequently use projection and fantasy as defenses. Individuals who are high in reward dependence are more likely to form warm social attachments readily and to respond to sentimental appeals. Individuals low in persistence are underachievers with labile moods, who give up easily when frustrated. Individuals high in persistence are overachievers, who frequently use suppression and anticipation as defense mechanisms.

Each of these is inherited independently of one another, so all possible combinations of scores on these dimensions occur. Such different configurations predispose individuals to qualitatively distinct patterns of emotional response because of functional interactions among the dimensions. Traditional subtypes of temperament and personality disorder correspond to the possible configurations of the three temperaments harm avoidance, novelty seeking, and reward dependence, as depicted in Figure 1.

Different temperament configurations are associated with different risks of particular behaviors and emotions, such as violence or compassion. However, the accuracy of predictions about behavior in indi-

Table 2 Descriptors of Individuals Who Score High and Low on the Four Temperament Dimensions

Temperament Dimension	Descriptors of Extreme Variants	
	High	Low
Harm avoidance	pessimistic	optimistic
	fearful	daring
	shy	outgoing
	fatigable	energetic
Novelty seeking	exploratory	reserved
	impulsive	rigid
	extravagant	frugal
	irritable	stoical
Reward dependence	sentimental	critical
	open	aloof
	warm	detached
	sympathetic	independent
Persistence	industrious	lazy
	determined	spoiled
	ambitious	underachiever
	perfectionist	pragmatist

Table 3 Descriptors of Individuals Who Score High and Low on the Three Character Dimensions

Character Dimension	Descriptors of Extreme Variants	
	High	Low
Self-directedness	responsible	blaming
	purposeful	aimless
	resourceful	inept
	self-accepting	vain
	disciplined	undisciplined
Cooperative	tender-hearted	intolerant
	empathic	insensitive
	helpful	hostile
	compassionate	revengeful
	principled	opportunistic
Self-transcendent	self-forgetful	unimaginative
	transpersonal	controlling
	spiritual	materialistic
	enlightened	possessive
	idealistic	practical

vidual cases is low unless the character configuration is also specified. For example, the adventurous temperament (i.e., low harm avoidance, high novelty seeking, and low reward dependence) may lead to either antiso-cial personality disorder and type-2 alcoholism (when character is immature), or imaginative exploration and objective independence in scientific research (when character is mature) (Cloninger 1987b). Persistence acts as

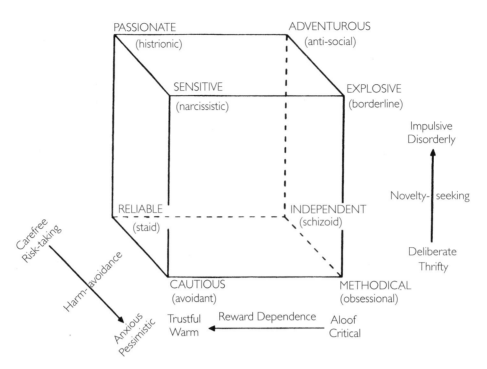

Figure 1. The Temperament Cube: Descriptors of the possible combination of Harm Avoidance, Novelty Seeking, and Reward Dependence (subtype in parenthesis if personality disorder is present). (Used by permission of the Center for Psychobiology of Personality.)

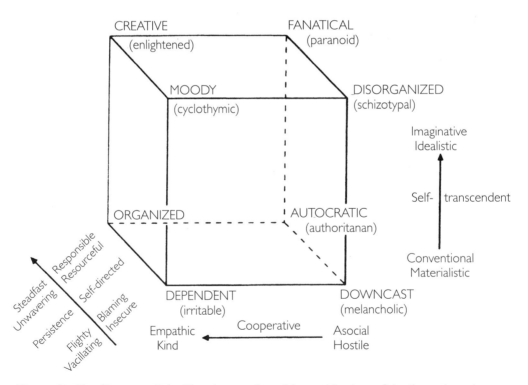

Figure 2. The Character Cube: Descriptors of possible combinations of the three character dimensions and Persistence. (Used by permission of the Center for Psychobiology of Personality.)

a general moderator of self control and influences character development, so it also has an important role in emotional regulation and personality development.

All possible combinations of the three character dimensions also occur, as depicted in Figure 2. Low self directedness is associated with irresponsible, aimless, and undisciplined behavior characteristic of poor impulse control and personality disorder in general. Low cooperativeness is associated with deficits in empathy, so that uncooperative individuals are described as hostile, aggressive, hateful, and revengeful opportunists. Low self transcendence is associated with deficits in transpersonal identification or conscience; those low in self transcendence show conventional and materialistic behavior, with little or no concern for absolute ideals, such as goodness and universal harmony. Consequently, low character development, as in melancholic and disorganized character configurations in Figure 2, are associated with deficits in impulse control, empathy, and conscience that are often associated with substance abuse and antisocial behavior.

Furthermore, temperament and character configurations are related to one another in complex but systematic ways. Temperament constrains character development, but does not fully determine it, because of the systematic efforts of sociocultural learning and the stochastic effects of experience. For example, the explosive temperament configuration, which is also called borderline temperament (i.e., high novelty seeking and harm avoidance plus low reward dependence) according to DSM-IIIR criteria (Svrakic et al. 1993), predisposes to the underdevelopment of self directedness and cooperativeness. Antisocial and obsessional temperament are also likely to have the same predisposition, as shown in Table 4. However, temperament structure is not an inevitable or necessary determinant of character structure, which also depends substantially on social learning and luck (i.e., random environmental events that can be measured but not predicted in advance).

Fortunately, the complex patterns of relationship among temperament structure, character structure, and histories of behavioral conditioning and insight (social) learning, can be quantified in a rigorous manner as a non-linear dynamic network of variables (Kauffman 1993).

Correspondence of Emotionality and Personality

Each dimension of personality is associated with different moods and emotional states, depending on current stimulus conditions. This correspondence allows a clinician to predict emotional responses to particular situations, or to infer personality structure from patterns of emotional reactivity. These correspondences between personality and emotions are summarized in Table 5. Another way of thinking about character development is that basic negative emotions associated with temperament, such as fear, anger, disgust, and discouragement, are transformed by steps to more complex secondary and positive emotions, such as hope, love, and joy, with progressive maturation.

Table 4 Relative Risk of Immaturity (i.e., Mild and Severe Personality Disorder) as a Function of Temperament Type in a Sample from the General Community (Cloninger et al. 1994)

Temperament Type	Configuration	N	% Immature
High risk			
Borderline	NHr	39	72
Obsessional	nHr	44	59
Antisocial	Nhr	25	48
Passive-Aggressive	NHR	30	40
Average	—	15	33
Low risk			
Avoidant	nHR	30	17
Schizoid	nhr	31	16
Histrionic	NhR	50	12
Reliable	nhR	36	6
Total		300	33

Table 5 Effects of Reward (+) and Punishment (–) on Emotional States Depending on the Seven Personality Dimensions

Personality Dimension	High Scorers		Low Scorers	
	+	–	+	–
Harm avoidance	Anxious	Depressed	Cheerful	Fearless
Novelty seeking	Euphoric	Angry	Placid	Stoic
Reward dependence	Sympathetic	Disgusted	Aloof	Indifferent
Persistence	Enthusiastic	Steadfast	Unstable	Discouraged
Self-directed	Hopeful	Resourceful	Vain	Shameful
Cooperative	Loving	Forgiving	Scornful	Revengeful
Transcendent	Joyful	Peaceful	Greedy	Miserable

Table 6

Table 6 15 Steps in Full Personality Development, as Measured by the Temperament and Character Inventory: The Canonical or Usual Sequence of Healthy Development

Steps	Self-Directed	Cooperative	Self-Transcendent
TCI Tier 1			
[1] co1		Tolerant-v-Suspicious (Trustful-v-Mistrustful)	
[2] sd1	Responsible-v-Blaming (Confident-v-Shameful)		
[3] st1			Obedient-v-Intractable (Respectful-v-Judgmental)
TCI Tier 2			
[4] sd2	Purposeful-v-Aimless (Moderate-v-Indulgent)		
[5] co2		Empathic-v-Cruel (Prudent-v-Scornful)	
[6] st2			Conscientious-v-Unjust (Worshipful-v-Defiant)
TCI Tier 3			
[7] sd3	Resourceful-v-Inept (Hopeful-v-Helpless)		
[8] co3		Generous-v-Disagreeable (Kind-v-Hostile)	
[9] st3			Spiritual-v-Materialistic (Contemplative-v-Greedy)
TCI Tier 4			
[10] sd4	Self-accepting-v-Vain (Humble-v-Impatient)		
[11] co4		Forgiving-v-Revengeful (Compassionate-v-Callous)	
[12] st4			Enlightened-v-Possessive (Joyfully free-v-Controlling)
TCI Tier 5			
[13] sd5	Integrity-v-Conflict (Peaceful-v-Undisciplined)		
[14] co5		Wise-v-Unprincipled (Loving-v-Harsh)	
[15] st5			Creative-v-Dualistic (Idealistic-v-Practical)

Note. co = cooperativeness; sd = self directedness; st = self transcendence.

A 15-Step Model of Personality Development

It is highly informative to consider problems in emotional regulation and interpersonal adjustment from a developmental perspective. Fortunately, the subscale structure of the TCI was formulated to specify character in terms of the component steps of its development, as shown in Table 6. Each of the five subscales of each character dimension (self-directedness, cooperativeness, and self-transcendence) are numbered in the usual order of their development. These 15 steps most often occur in the interlocking sequence shown in Table 6, which is called the "canonical sequence," because it is the usual rule and natural order despite occasional pathological exceptions (Cloninger et al. 1997).

Table 7	Comparison of Different Descriptions of Personality Development			
TCI Developmental Step	**Piaget**	**Freud**	**Erikson**
[1] co1-Trust	Sensorimotor (reflexive)	Oral (passive)	Trust
[2] sd1-Confidence	Sensorimotor (enactive)	Anal (negativistic)	Autonomy
[3] st1-Obedience	Self-object differentiation	Early phallic	
[4] sd2-Purposefulness	Intuitive	Late phallic (exploratory)	Initiative
[5] co2-Empathy	Operational (concrete)	Latency (conforming)	
[6] st2-Conscientiousness	Operational (abstract)	Early genital (conscientious work)	Identity
[7] sd3-Resourcefulness			
[8] co3-Generosity		Later genital (social maturity)	Intimacy
[9] st3-Spirituality			
[10] sd4-Humility			
[11] co4-Compassion			Generativity
[12] st4-Enlightenment/joy			
[13] sd5-Integrity/peace			Integrity
[14] co5-Wisdom/pure love			
[15] st5-Creativity/goodness			

Note. co = cooperativeness; sd = self directedness; st = self transcendence.

This canonical sequence of 15 steps provides a more detailed and quantitative account of development than prior qualitative descriptions, but is fully compatible with the prior accounts. The TCI character subscales have high internal consistency. Each is moderately correlated with other components in the same dimension, but weakly correlated with components in other dimensions. The TCI sequence shown in Table 6 corresponds to descriptions derived from observations of cognitive development, psychosexual development, and ego maturation. As shown in Table 7, the TCI sequence corresponds to the stages of development distinguished by Piaget (1975), Freud (1949), and Erikson (1963). For example, the oral, anal, and phallic phases of Freud correspond to the first subscales of cooperativeness (co1 = oral or trustful vs suspicious), self directedness (sd1 = anal or responsible vs shame prone), and self transcendence (st1 = phallic or obedient vs defiant). Descriptions from different perspectives help in understanding the de-

velopmental significance of each TCI subscale.

More generally, developmental sequences are expected to differ in individuals with different temperaments and life experiences, but the sequence described in Tables 6 and 7 correspond to the modal pathway that leads to full character development, that is, high scores on all three character dimensions. Accordingly, the TCI provides a quantitative way of measuring the interrelations among each step in the developmental sequence, with antecedent temperament traits as well as prior character development. The correlations of each step in character development with the temperament dimensions and the prior step is shown in Table 8. These steps can be organized into five tiers by grouping the corresponding steps from each of the three character dimensions as in Table 5. Alternatively, the steps can be organized into seven levels in a progressive hierarchy, as shown in Table 8, making divisions at the seven points where arrests in development are most frequent. Such arrests occur when a step is moderately correlated with the prior step, but not with the subsequent step. In other words, such points of division correspond to frequent fixation points in development. Self directedness and cooperativeness are positively correlated, so that development of one facilitates the development of the other. However, the subscales of self transcendence progress from a negative correlation between st1 to increasingly positive correlations with self-directedness and cooperativeness, particularly for st4 and st5. As a result, the transitions from one level of self transcendence to the next, which reflect increasingly more inclusive concepts of self, are the most difficult steps in personality development.

A hierarchical model of the different types of problems occurring in each step in personality development is shown in Table 9. Problems in the first group, involving problems in basic trust (step 1) and confidence (step 2), are characteristic of individuals who have sexual or physical abuse beginning in early infancy, and is associated with highly disorganized disorders. Such patients have been characterized as having severe borderline and narcissistic disorders, with "dyadic deficits" if they are arrested at step 1 (which leads to impairments in the sense of self along with impaired mother-child relations), or "dyadic conflicts" if they are arrested at step 2 (which leads to severely impaired object relations, such as difficulty of the child separating from the mother) (Karasu 1994). Such fundamental impairments predispose to vulnerability to psychosis.

Problems at the second level involve severe personality disorders with negativism, disobedience, and lack of purposefulness and empathy. They are described as having mild borderline and narcissistic disorders, characterized by problematic three-person (i.e., mother-child-father) relationships. This group includes patients with "triadic deficits" if they are arrested at step 3 (which leads to poor impulse control and severe Oedipal problems, such as a lack of capacity for intimacy and social commitment), or "triadic conflicts" (arrested at steps 4 or 5, leading to milder Oedipal conflicts, such as

Table 8 Correlations of Each Step in Character Development (Designated as Step N) with Temperament Dimensions, the Prior Step in Character Development (Designated as Step N–1), and Spiritual Acceptance (st3)

Developmental Step N [N] Subscale - Label	Correlation (X100) with TCI Scales					
	NS	**HA**	**RD**	**PS**	**N-1**	**ST3**
Level I = Walking together						
[1] co1 trust	–2	–25	**35**	13	–	14
[2] sd1 confidence	1	**–45**	15	18	**30**	2
Level II = Working together						
[3] st1 obedience	17	–7	11	18	–13	**43**
[4] sd2 purposefulness	–2	**–47**	22	**40**	7	15
[5] co2 empathy	–6	–22	**55**	20	**36**	22
Level III = Hearts beating as one						
[6] st2 conscientiousness	–5	–19	25	**30**	11	**43**
[7] sd3 resourcefulness	7	**–58**	12	**55**	10	9
[8] co3 generosity	–9	–19	**41**	19	**32**	15
Level IV = Spirits feeling as one						
[9] st3 spirituality	2	–8	**33**	15	14	100
[10] sd4 humility	–24	–12	12	–7	7	7
[11] co4 compassion	–21	–12	**40**	9	**35**	20
Level V = Minds thinking as one						
[12] st4 enlightenment/joy	–11	–1	**33**	8	**31**	**75**
[13] sd5 integrity/peace	–19	**–43**	23	**43**	16	13
Level VI = Listening in silence						
[14] co5 wisdom/pure love	–16	-4	**30**	1	21	23
Level VII = Experiencing in unity						
[15] st5 creativity/goodness	–16	5	**34**	8	25	**58**

Note. co = cooperativeness; sd = self directedness; st = self transcendence.

Data based on 593 individuals representative of general population of metropolitan St. Louis (Cloninger et al., in press)

Correlations of .30 or higher in bold.

inhibited sexuality or impaired internalization of group values) (Karasu 1994). Such individuals have severe problems in working, socialization, and impulse-control.

Problems in the third level, involving low conscientiousness, low self confidence and resourcefulness, and little generosity, are typical of individuals with mild personality disorders, type-1 alcoholism, and many cases of anxiety disorder or major depression associated with mild problems in self-esteem, social intimacy, or group identification. Progress through level three reflects "ego strength," which can be measured as the sum of TCI scores on self-directedness and cooperativeness. This is consistent with Freud's notions of mature personality organization.

The fourth and higher levels involve progressive steps in cognitive and spiritual development among socially mature individuals seeking fulfillment with health and happiness. Such overall personality integration can be measured by the sum of scores on all three character dimensions, consistent with Jung's notion of the self-transcendent leader (Jung 1939). These higher levels of personality integration may be associated with psychopathology at times of existential crisis.

Identifying an Optimal Pathway through the 15-Step Sequence

Each step in character development is differentially influenced by temperament and prior development, as was shown in Table 8. Initially, infants are fully dependent on their caretakers, so the initial step involves the development of trust or mistrust, depending on temperament and quality of care. The development of trust is facilitated in children who are high in reward dependence and low in harm avoidance (see Table 8). In turn, high trust facilitates

Table 9

Table 9 A Hierarchical Model of Mental Order and Disorder Based on Level of Personality Developments

Character Deficits	Associated Mental Health Features
Level I = Walking together	(Disorganized disorders)
[1] co1 mistrust	Self-injurious behavior
[2] sd1 doubt & shame	Sado-masochistic sexuality
Level II = Working together	(Severe personality disorders)
[3] st1 poor impulse control	Bipolar affective lability
[4] sd2 aimlessness	Unemployment, criminality
[5] co2 lack of empathy	Polysubstance abuse
Level III = Hearts beating as one	
[6] st2 no conscience	Mild personality disorder
[7] sd3 low self-esteem	Social dysfunction
[8] co3 selfishness	Frequent negative emotions
Level IV = Spirits feeling as one	
[9] st3 materialism	Personal dissatisfaction
[10] sd4 arrogance	Lack of generativity
[11] co4 revengefulness	Occasional negative emotions
Level V = Minds thinking as one	
[12] st4 possessiveness	Mature but lack of joy and lack of serenity
[13] sd5 unintegrated	
Level VI = Listening in silence	Mature but lack of intuitive wisdom
[14] co5 unloving at times	
Level VII = Experiencing in unity	Mature but judgmental and not fully harmonious
[15] st5 dualistic	

Note. co = cooperativeness; sd = self directedness; st = self transcendence.

the development of self confidence and a sense of personal responsibility (step 2); there is a positive correlation of .30 between these two steps. However, the development of confidence depends even more strongly on the individual being low in harm avoidance.

When self-object differentiation occurs, the development of obedience instead of negativism (step 3) depends mostly on temperament and experiences unique to the individual, rather than on prior character development. The capacity for self-object absorption and obedience is facilitated by high persistence ($r = .18$) and high novelty seeking ($r = .17$). Feeling self confident is actually negatively associated with being obedient; there is little association of step 3 with step 2 ($r = -.13$) or step 1 ($r = -.03$).

Such relationships come into play at each transition point. Accordingly, each step in development emerges as a consequence of a

complex set of facilitating and inhibitory influences. The dynamics of such a complex adaptive system is nonlinear. In other words, the effect of each variable depends on the other variables with which it is combined. The particular sequence described by the 15-step model is the one which optimizes character development for most people. However, it is likely that other paths may be optimal for particular temperament types, but this remains under investigation.

The observation that character development depends on both the temperament configuration and prior development has many implications for assessment and treatment. In order to take such information into account, reliable and systematic assessments are needed. Once the information is in hand, pharmacotherapy may be useful, since individual differences in temperament are heritable and predict responses to psychotropic med-

ication like antidepressants, which may be useful in regulating temperament. Further, different psychotherapy techniques may be indicated to facilitate particular steps in development, so a multi-step approach is indicated, rather than trying to accomplish all tasks with the same technique.

A Developmental Program of Personality Treatment

These developmental observations indicate that the techniques most beneficial to patients depend on their stage of personality integration. A brief outline of this integrative psychobiological approach to treatment is given in Table 10, suggesting the techniques for each step in development. When there is more than one gap in development, we recommend that the clinician focus on the earliest problem in order to build a foundation for later work, although the patient may want at least some stabilization of the most salient presenting problem.

Steps in treatment are organized into seven levels, corresponding to the seven levels of development described earlier. The first level involves supportive and reality-based techniques, including basic trust building, encouragement, and the teaching of basic living skills. The clinician's most basic responsibility is to help assure the safety of patients, despite their disorganization and destructive impulses. Trust building and encouragement within safe limits are basic components of all therapy, and are essential at this level, because patients are filled with all of the negative emotions, such as patients whose temperaments are explosive (borderline) or whose characters are severely immature (melancholic or schizotypal). However, if the patient is psychotic or prepsychotic, therapy may be limited to supportive functions. Such supportive function may require somatic therapies, like electroconvulsive therapy or high doses of antipsychotic medication. The "holding" aspects of the psychotherapeutic environment are crucial at this level, and include

Table 10 A 15-Step Program for Integrative Psychobiological Treatment of Personality and Psychopathology

Level	Developmental Steps	Effective Methods of Treatment
I. Supportive-realistic therapy		
	[1] Trust	Acceptance, trust-building
		Establish supportive environment
		Anti-psychotic medication if needed
		Detoxification if needed
	[2] Stop denial and vain self-sufficiency	Maintain safety and support
		Teach basic living skills and social interdependence
II. Directive rational-expressive behavioral therapy		
	[3] Obedience	Instruction about temperament
	Stop defiance	Set limits and respect for boundaries
	[4] Purposefulness	Explore goals and role models and make a searching personal inventory
		Model problem-solving skills for analysis and imitation
	[5] Empathy	Encourage sharing of personal feelings
		Empathy training and teamwork
		+ Objectively monitor treatment compliance
		+ Pharmacotherapy of impulsivity, violence, craving (e.g. lithium, Tegretol, valproate)
		+ Treatment of comorbid depression
		+ Conditioning of impulse control by repetitive drills & homework
III. Non-directive dynamic-humanistic-interpersonal therapy		
	[6] Conscientiousness	Discursive reflection on goals and values as motivation to adapt
		Identification with role models
	[7] Resourcefulness	Non-directive discussion of options for coping with problems, then self-willed action
		Persistence/resourcefulness training
	[8] Generosity	Making amends, helping others
		Sharing, accepting help from others
		+ Monitor treatment compliance by self-report
		+ Education about character steps
		+ Cognitive analysis of basic emotions, defenses, and virtues
		+ Antidepressant medication if needed

the therapist being dependable, patient, non-retaliatory, and compassionate despite frequent crises, and being able to provide a more hopeful and constructive understanding of patient needs and opportunities than the patients can provide themselves (Pine 1990). Such relations with the therapist allow the patient to build trust and self confidence.

The second level of treatment involves directive cognitive-behavioral techniques that emphasize rational behavioral analysis and repetitive drills to improve obedience, discipline, and impulse control. This level involves initial treatment of individuals with moderately severe personality and mood disorders, characterized by poor impulse control and emotional lability, such as seen in most patients with antisocial personality disorder, severe ob-

sessional, or mild borderline personalities. Pharmacotheapy for labile affect and impulsivity, such as carbamazepine or other mood stabilizers, and for hostility, such as low-dose neuroleptics like thioridazine, may be beneficial. Discussion of personality structure and emotional needs in such patients is focused on their understanding of their temperament structure and basic emotional needs, along with education about mature ways of satisfying those needs. For example, hatha yoga or martial arts training are appealing methods for teaching self control at this level, leading to enhancement of self esteem and impulse control. Such structured approaches minimize conflict about setting limits, but there must be much patient repetition of practical problem solving skills, and encour-

agement by discussion of attractive role models. This makes constructive use of such patient's craving for pleasure and power.

The third level of treatment involves non-directive dynamic, humanistic, and interpersonal techniques, to foster increases in conscientiousness, resourcefulness, and generosity. At this stage, direction is counterproductive, because the patient needs to internalize group values and to develop confidence in their self-willed action. Depression and anxiety are common at this level, and may be treated with antidepressants as needed, in combination with the non-directive therapy. The standard six exercises of autogenic training (Schulz and Luthe 1959) are useful at this level, providing relaxation and preparation for meditative exercises at more advanced levels.

Table 10 *Continued*

Level Developmental Steps	Effective Methods of Treatment
IV. Experiential-existential therapy	
[9] Spirituality	Charitable action
	Mindful meditation with undistracted body scanning and automatic breathing
	Disidentification with mind-body
	Identification as mind-body-spirit
	Spiritual empowerment/communion
[10] Humility, patience	Self-knowledge, disclosure, acceptance
[11] Compassion	Recognize social interdependence
	Identification in spirit with others
	Consider work with support groups
	+ Cognitive analysis of mature character development
V. Transcendence therapy	
[12] Detachment, freedom (unconditional joy and trust)	Whole-hearted compassionate activity
	Contemplation with automatic devout vocalization
	All-inclusive identification
[13] Integrity, power, peace, courage	Spirit-guided contemplation (Ego-less channelling)
	Integration of personal goals and values, eliminating distractors
	Empowerment of Mind (integrating of mind and spirit)
	Mind-body healing practices
	+ Cognitive analysis of conditions for joy and peace
VI. Advanced spiritual guidance	
[14] Unity of wisdom and love	Social integration for love with enhanced intuitive awareness
	Superconscious contemplation with automatic visualization and revelation (Spirit = all-inclusive Self)
	Supernatural (spiritual) healing
	+ Cognitive analysis of unity and obstacles to integration
VII. Full integration	
[15] Creativity	Maintain contemplative awareness in all daily activities
Bliss	Object-less contemplation (non-dual consciousness)
	+ Integrated creative development

Note. + = Common to all steps in this level.

The patient is educated about their character structure and the first nine steps in character development.

The fourth level of treatment involves experiential and existential therapy techniques, such as mindful meditations and spiritual identification exercises. This involves a conscious expansion of the self concept to include a transpersonal (i.e., spiritual) component, in addition to that of the mind and body. Disidentification with the mind and body can be elicited by exercises in intuitive awareness in scanning body functions (i.e., spontaneous flow of breath, changes in temperature of various body parts, or vibrations throughout the nervous system) or awareness of the stream of mental consciousness (Assagioli 1965). The meditative exercises of autogenic training (Schulz and Luthe 1959),

mindfulness meditation exercises based on yoga traditions (Goldstein and Kornfield 1987; Goleman 1988; Low 1989), or contemplative prayer (Burke 1992; St. John of the Cross 1906), are all helpful to promote direct awareness of an intuitive consciousness more basic than categorization or the logical analysis of experience. Antidepressant or anti-anxiety medication may be useful at times of existential crisis, but are used sparingly and transiently, because strong motivation is needed to promote the leaps of faith needed to transform consciousness and self concepts.

Levels five through seven involve advanced guidance in meditation and other techniques needed to transcend ordinary self concepts. Many patients with such mature personality development are seldom

very impaired by ordinary standards, but seek superior character integration, emotional fulfillment, and healthy longevity. Along with cognitive analysis and guidance by the therapist, advanced techniques of meditative practice are helpful (Assagioli 1991; Norbu 1986; Benson 1975). These stages of character development correspond closely to the stages of practice leading to enlightenment or atonement in Buddhist traditions (Cleary 1983; Goldstein and Kornfield 1987), Judeo-Christian traditions (St. John of the Cross 1906), and the twelve-step program of Alcoholics Anonymous (Cloninger 1997). Medication is contraindicated, since the goal here is enhancement of natural neuroendocrine regulation and the integration of emotional needs with conscious goals and values (Rossi 1993).

Transcendence therapy at level five involves expansion of self concept to participation in a transpersonal consciousness shared with other sentient beings (Jung 1939; Assagioli 1991). Contemplation with automatic vocalizations and gestures is used to achieve egoless detachment from selfish desires, leading to a feeling of joyful freedom. This enlightenment (or joyful detachment) motivates further integration of personal activities to become congruent with idealistic values, eliminating whatever was distracting and unessential. Such individuals are often highly effective and influential because of their integration, perseverance, and strength of conviction. There are controversial reports that some, but not all, people at this level of character development acquire extraordinary abilities for telepathy and healing. More consistently, such individuals live balanced and well-integrated lives, so, not surprisingly, they are unusually happy and healthy, and promote similar positive adjustments in others around them.

Level six and seven involve further stepwise increases in intuitive awareness, compassion, and creative inspiration. Information processing in the right occipital cortex, involving preconceptual visuo-spatial information, becomes more prominent coincident with the increases in cooperativeness and self-transcendence (Vedeniapin, A., Rohrbaugh, J., and Cloninger, C. R., unpublished results in preparation, 1997). Essentially, this holistic mode of information processing minimizes the subject-object differentiation that is artificially imposed on experience by conceptual processing. The identification of self becomes all-inclusive at level six, but there is still subject-object differentiation, and therefore some tendency for materialistic or personal attachments. At level seven, consciousness becomes non-dualistic (i.e., absolute or object-less), so that all is unique and seemingly perfect, because there is no other to judge. These holistic paradigms of intuitive experience are stimulated by direct experience during contemplation of spontaneous visualizations, involving little or no categorical (e.g., this versus that) or judgmental (e.g., good versus bad) processing. Such creative visualiza-

tion techniques have been described in the advanced meditative exercises of autogenic training (Schulz & Luthe 1959; Luthe 1983) and meditation of complex geometric figures (Norbu 1986; Cleary 1983). Advanced visualization work should be limited to mature patients, in order to reduce the risk of perceptual aberrations. It should also be supervised by a guide experienced in such meditation, in order to avoid errors of practice or attitude. For example, vanity in one's achievements, and unrealistic extremes of pessimistic nihilism and grandiose externalism, are attitudes that frequently block the progress of solitary meditators. Such counterproductive attitudes can be avoided by guides with experience in facilitating unpretentious creativity and the positive emotions of hope, love, and joy.

A Case Example: Personality Analysis of Sue Smith

To illustrate the application of the TCI in clinical assessment and treatment planning, the test was administered to someone who will be called Sue Smith in this report and related papers in this issue (Zinner 1997; Horowitz 1997). Mrs. Smith is a 35 year old widow, a college student, and the mother of two children. Her TCI was scored and interpreted according to explicit algorithms implemented by the computerized TCI analysis program. Interpretation has not been modified based on additional information, so that the use of the TCI in case formulation, blind to additional data, can be evaluated.

Mrs. Smith's self-report about her personality is summarized in Table 11. In character, she depicted herself as mature and well organized; she scored moderately high in self-directedness (85th percentile) and cooperativeness (85th percentile), and moderately low in self-transcendence (20th percentile). She also described herself as self-reliant (i.e., highly self-directed) but helpful to others, and pragmatic (i.e., not idealistic or self-transcendent), which is a common ideal for social maturity in Western society. In temperament, she depicted herself as mildly adventurous; she scored mildly high in novelty seeking

(70th percentile) and low in harm avoidance (10th percentile) and reward dependence (35th percentile). She described herself as exploratory and uninhibited by fear (i.e., low harm avoidance) or social sentiment (i.e., low reward dependence), but low in persistence. In short, she depicted herself as courageous and mature in a conventional manner.

We suspected the validity of this self-report profile because such mature character structures seldom arise in individuals with an adventurous temperament. Invalid self-reports can arise in clinical practice because of careless test taking, cognitive distortion, or deliberate misrepresentation. In order to evaluate such problems, several validity scales that measure the actual performance style of the subject are embedded within the TCI. These performance-based scales allow objective estimates of each of the personality dimensions, independent of variation in any of the self-reported content scale. The relationships between the performance scales and self-reported content scales in the general population are summarized in Table 12. Basically, performance style was objectively assessed by constructing scales that measured careful responding, acquiescence, conventionality, and social deviance. Careful responding is directly assessed by measuring internal consistency in sets of items that are highly positively correlated (i.e., scale of like items) or highly negatively correlated (i.e., scale of unlike items). Docility or acquiescence is directly assessed by measuring the number of true answers in sets of 16 items with close to a 50/50 ratio of true to false responses. Conventionality or intermediacy is assessed by measuring the number of answers in the modal direction for a set of 20 items, half of which have response frequencies of 2/3 true, and half of which have response frequencies of 2/3 false. Social deviance or rarity was measured by counting the number of answers in the unusual direction from a scale of 25 items, composed of each of the least frequently endorsed item from each of the TCI subscales. Accordingly, each of the performance scales are independent of content. Further information about emotionality is obtained by examin-

Table 11	Self-Reported TCI Profile of Susan Smith		
	Raw Score	**T Score**	**Percentile**
Novelty seeking	23	56	70
Exploratory excitability	7	53	60
Impulsiveness	5	56	70
Extravagance	8	63	90
Disorderliness	3	44	25
Harm avoidance	5	39	10
Anticipatory worry	0	37	9
Fear of uncertainty	1	37	9
Shyness	1	40	15
Fatigability	3	52	55
Reward dependence	14	47	35
Sentimentality	8	53	60
Attachment	3	43	20
Dependence	3	47	35
Persistence	4	42	20
Self-directedness	39	61	85
Responsibility	8	61	85
Purposefulness	7	58	75
Resourcefulness	5	58	75
Self-acceptance	8	56	70
Congruent second nature	11	58	75
Cooperativeness	41	62	85
Social acceptance	8	59	80
Empathy	6	55	65
Helpfulness	8	61	85
Compassion	10	59	80
Pure-heartedness	9	62	85
Self-transcendence	15	43	20
Self-forgetfulness	2	36	8
Transpersonal identification	3	43	20
Spiritual acceptance	10	54	65

ing sequence contingencies among the items in these scales with the antecedent and subsequent items. Overall, in a volunteer sample from the general population in which there is no systematic advantage for misrepresentation, the multiple regression between performance style and each personality dimension varies from 0.52 to 0.74. For example, cooperativeness is estimated primarily on the basis of high consistency on the scale of like items and infrequent endorsement of rare items (see Table 12). High harm avoidance is indicated by endorsing few items with intermediate response frequencies.

Mrs. Smith's self-report and performance-based profiles are compared in Table 13. Overall, the authenticity of her self-report, measured as the sum of the squared differences between the self-report and performance scores for each of the seven dimensions, was very low (5th percentile). There was much distortion of both her temperament profile (30th percentile in agreement) and her character profile (2nd percentile in agreement). In particular, her ob-

jective performance style indicated much lower cooperativeness than she reported (9th percentile versus 85th percentile, $p < .05$).

When such discrepancies are found, clinical experiences and spouse reports suggest that the performance profile is more valid. The performance profile indicates that Mrs. Smith has a mildly autocratic or authoritarian character (that is, she is higher in self-directedness and low in cooperativeness), which is characterized by preoccupation with personal goals, need to control others, and hostile irritability when these wishes are frustrated. According to Table 10, however, she operates at Level III, with frequent negative emotions, but slightly above the traditional boundary for personality disorder in DSM-IV; her performance-based score for self-directedness plus cooperativeness is 60, which places her at about the 35th percentile in character development in a general population sample. In addition, she is independent or schizoid in temperament, with below average scores on each of the temperament dimensions except persistence. She is particularly low in her sensitivity to social cues from others (i.e., 10th percentile in reward dependence), which often leads to low cooperativeness.

Further analysis showed that the performance-based character profile agreed well with that expected for the performance-based temperament profile. Given her performance-based temperament, she was expected to mature well in a neutral environment through step six (i.e., conscientious) or step seven (i.e., resourceful) of character development, but then to arrest at step eight (i.e., helpfulness) (Cloninger et al. 1997). About 35 percent of the general population mature positively through step seven, without progressing further. In other words, with her low reward dependence, it will be difficult for her to be genuinely charitable and generous to others (step eight) without therapy to enhance her empathy and capacity for compassion and selfless love. Her depiction of herself as more cooperative than her current performance style indicates a readiness for therapy, with a positive motivation to enhance her ability to give love.

Table 12 Estimation of TCI Personality Dimensions by Regression in Normative General Population (N = 300) on TCI Performance Style Scales Independent of Self-Report Content

Objective Measures of Performance Style	Standardized Partial Regressions of TCI Self-Report on Performance Scales						
	NS	HA	RD	PS	SD	CO	ST
Careful discernment							
Scale of like items	-10			11	9	23	
Scale of unlike items		-9	9	20	17	15	6
Number of true answers	-12	-6	-10	34	4	-16	13
Docility							
Acquiescence	6	10			-49		37
Acquiescence-prior			5		-8		
Acquiescence-rare prior	22			-9		14	27
Conventionality							
Intermediacy	18	-47	17	28	41		31
Intermediacy-prior					-5		-10
Intermediacy-next		15		-13	-7		
Social deviance							
Scale of rare items	15		-47	-9	-13	-58	-13
Rarity-prior					-10	-17	
Rarity-next	37	-6	5	-17	-26	-7	8
Multiple regression	52	52	53	56	74	70	60

Note. Partial regressions over .20 in **bold** ($p < .0001$).

Table 13 Comparison of Self-Report and Performance-Based TCI Profiles of Susan Smith

Personality Dimension	Self-Report Score/Percentile		Performance Based Score/Percentile		Score Difference
Novelty seeking	23	70	19	30	4
Harm avoidance	5	10	15	45	10
Reward independence	14	35	15	10	1
Persistence	4	20	6	70	2
Self-directedness	39	85	31	60	8
Cooperativeness	41	85	29	9	12*
Self-transcendence	15	20	13	20	2

* A difference this large occurs in less than 5% of cases, and may indicate significant response bias.

Comparison of TCI Analysis with Clinical Presentation

Mrs. Smith's 11 year old son Adam was in treatment following sexual and physical abuse by a day care worker. His father had abandoned the family when Adam was young. Adam often fails to show Mrs. Smith the respect and obedience she wants, which provokes her anger. She complains that he does not listen to her, so she must get his attention with angry demands. He feels ambivalent toward his mother, combining defiance with rejection sensitivity, leading to somatization with suicidal gestures. This suggests that both Adam and Mrs. Smith have arrests at step eight in character development, that is, they have limited ability to be helpful and generous toward others.

Consequently, Mrs. Smith's autocratic expectations of Adam are unfulfilled, and Adam has failed to receive the nurturance from his mother that is needed for him to develop greater cooperativeness.

In contrast, Mrs. Smith's four-year-old son John, the half-brother of Adam, is not defiant, and consistently tries to please his autocratic mother. Consequently, he receives her approval. John appears to have become conscientious at an early age, internalizing his mother's values and frequently defending her from criticism. In other words, he has already matured through step six in character development (i.e., conscientiousness) by age four.

The two sons reveal the alternative ways of responding to an authoritarian parent—with defiance, as in Adam's case, or with compliance, as in John's case. Mrs. Smith's frustration when she is not in control is indicated by her complaint about feeling excluded from Adam's care, as well as by her criticism and anger about his defiance. She feels unable to respond to the children's needs for attention and affection. Her low reward dependence is indicated by her lack of sympathy toward Adam's needs, and her indifference toward the man who abused him. As a single parent, she faces a dilemma about priorities for her own career advancement and the nurturance of her children. This conflict elicits negative emotions of discouragement, shame, scorn, and anger. Hostility and lack of compassion for her children are her most prominent and frequent emotional responses, as expected from her autocratic character structure (see Table 5).

Recommendations for Treatment

The most important area for character development in Mrs. Smith and her son Adam is to improve their capacity for empathy and mutual identification, so that they can enjoy helping and making sacrifices for one another. According to our model of integrative psychobiology, such lack of charity and generosity (step eight) is most effectively addressed by nondirective psychodynamic or interpersonal approaches (see Table 10).

First, in view of the mother's autocratic character structure, it would be prudent to meet with her individually as soon as possible, to review her TCI report as a starting point to understanding her needs and goals. Her self-report can be presented as "the way you would like to be," whereas the performance-based profile is likely to be closer to "the way you are functioning in the current situation." The discrepancy between the two profiles can be seen as a favorable sign, indicating her awareness, at some level, of the crucial ways she must change in order to enhance the quality of her life and those of her children. Specifically, she is experiencing much hostility and guilt because of her difficulty satisfying her children's needs for attention and affection, which is exacerbated by Adam's low cooperativeness. In order to avoid becoming overly directive, or initiating a confrontation, this should be discussed hopefully and compassionately in tentative terms, allowing her to clarify her understanding of what is meant by the test results. She is recognized as the one person who knows the true facts, and she can help understand what she is feeling, so that the therapist can serve her and her family effectively as an informed and experienced consultant. In our experience, this allows much sensitive material to be put on the table for open discussion in a constructive, problem-solving spirit. The earlier it is discussed in non-pejorative terms, the less defensive is the patient, and the more quickly therapy can proceed to the heart of the issue.

Once Mrs. Smith and the therapist are in agreement that increases in mutual understanding and helpfulness within the family would be beneficial, Mrs. Smith can be invited to suggest ways that she can take the initiative in making amends to reduce hostility and encourage mutual sharing and generosity. This is likely to require much work to get her to empathize with the children's needs, in order that she can anticipate their feelings and behavior in problematic situations. However, she responded with tears to the therapist's empathy in the videotaped therapy session, indicating that she may quickly learn the benefits of empathy and generosity. Once she has made progress in

individual therapy for a few sessions, sessions with the two sons might proceed. Discussion of particular arguments and conflicts should focus on clarifying the feelings and wishes of each participant, and then promote generalization to the overriding issues of empathy, generosity, and cooperation. The feelings and needs of each family member can be discussed in terms of their individual personalities, so that members of the family become more skilled at anticipating conflict and promoting harmony. Adam's anger and low self-esteem might benefit if he became involved in a martial arts course of physical and mental discipline, like Tae Kwon Do, which positively channels anger and fear into calm confidence.

From a psychodynamic perspective, personality can also be thought of as another way of accounting for individual differences in ego defense mechanisms (Mulder et al. 1996). For example, her low reward dependence is likely to be associated with use of projection under stress, but her moderately high performance-based persistence and self-directedness scores indicate she is able to use more mature defenses, such as suppression and sublimation, in most situations. Greater identification with other people will help reduce her experience of the negative emotions of hostility or scorn.

From a cognitive-behavioral perspective, the therapist can reinforce any effort to be generous or giving and compassionate or forgiving, while responding to signs of hostility and anger by questions about what the other person may be feeling. Complaints about limited time can be cognitively reframed in terms of questions about priorities and opportunities for kindness and loving sacrifice.

From an interpersonal systems perspective, cooperative behavior has the advantage of being self-fulfilling prophecy that elicits positive emotions in oneself as well as in others, and promotes social support, which confirms its original assumption that most people are trustworthy and helpful. In contrast, uncooperative behavior has the disadvantage that it is self-fulfilling prophecy that elicits negative emotions in oneself as well as in others, and provokes anger and revenge, which confirms its original assumption that most people are untrustworthy and vicious (Svrakic et al. 1996). Everyone is free to adopt their own style of either cooperation or of distrust, but then must be prepared to accept the emotional consequences of that choice. Great care must be taken to avoid prescriptive statements about particular situations. Only when the therapist remains non-directive can the patients learn from whatever choice they make; both cooperative and uncooperative choices have consequences that are equally instructive if accurately predicted. According to integrative psychobiology at this level of character development, the role of the therapist is merely to help patients learn to accurately anticipate the emotional consequences of their unrestricted personal choices among alternative intentions. Particularly in treating an autocratic character, such nondirectiveness is crucial in promoting the development of mutual trust and respect.

References

Assagioli, R. *Psychosynthesis: A Manual of Principles and Techniques.* Crucible, 1965.

Assagioli, R. *Transpersonal Development: The Dimension Beyond Psychosynthesis.* Crucible, 1991.

Bayon, C., Hill, K., Svrakic, D. M., Przybeck, T. R., and Cloninger, C. R. Dimensional assessment of personality in an outpatient sample: Relations of the systems of Millon and Cloninger. *Journal of Psychiatric Research* (1996) 30:341–352.

Benson, H. *The Relaxation Response.* Avon, 1975.

Burke, G. *Lighting the Lamp: Practical Instruction in Interior Prayer According to the Hesychastic Tradition of the Christian East.* St. George Press, 1992.

Cleary, T. *Entry into the Inconceivable: An Introduction to Hua-Yen Buddhism.* University of Hawaii Press, 1983.

Cloninger, C. R. A systematic method for clinical description and classification of personality variants. *Archives of General Psychiatry* (1987a) 44:573–588.

Cloninger, C. R. Neurogenetic adaptive mechanisms in alcoholism. *Science* (1987b) 236:410–416.

Cloninger, C. R. A 15-step model of personality development: Assessment and treatment implications for alcoholism. In J. D. Sellman, ed., *Progress in Management of Alcoholism and Substance Abuse.* New Zealand Department of Health, 1997.

Cloninger, C. R., Przybeck, T. R., Svrakic, D. M., and Wetzel, R. D. *The Temperament and Character Inventory (TCI): A Guide to Its Development and Use.* Washington University, Center for Psychobiology of Personality, 1994.

Cloninger, C. R., Svrakic, D. M., Bayon, C., and Przybeck, T. R. Personality Disorders. In S. B. Guze, Ed., *Washington University Adult Psychiatry.* Mosby, pp. 301–317, 1996.

Cloninger, C. R., Svrakic, D. M., and Przybeck, T. R. A psychobiological model of temperament and character. *Archives of General Psychiatry* (1993) 50:975–990.

Cloninger, C. R., Svrakic, N. M., and Svrakic, D. M. The role of personality self-organization in the development of mental order and disorder. *Psychopathology and Development* (1997) in press.

Erikson, E. *Childhood and Society.* (Second Edition.) Norton Publishing, 1963.

Freud, S. *An Outline of Psychoanalysis.* W. W. Norton, 1949.

Goldsmith, H. H., Buss, A. H., Plomin, R., Rothbart, M. K., Thomas, A., Chess, S., Hinde, R. A., and McCall, R. B. What is temperament? Four approaches. *Child Development* (1987) 58:505–527.

Goldstein, J., and Kornfield, J. *Seeking the Heart of Wisdom: The Path of Insight Meditation.* Shambala, 1987.

Goleman, D. *The Meditative Mind: The Varieties of Meditative Experience.* Crucible, 1989.

Horowitz, M. J. Configurational analysis for case formation. *Psychiatry Interpersonal and Biological Processes* (1997) 60:111–1119.

Joyce, P. R., Mulder, R. T., and Cloninger, C. R. Temperament predicts clamipramine and desipramine response in major depression. *Journal of Affective Disorders* (1994) 30:35–46.

Jung, C. G. *The Integration of the Personality.* (Translated by Stanley M. Dell) Farrar & Rinehart, 1939.

Karasu, T. B. A developmental metatheory of psychopathology. *American Journal of Psychotherapy* (1994) 48:581–599.

Kauffman, S. A. *The origins of order: Self-organization and selection in evolution.* Oxford University Press, 1993.

Knowlton, B. J., Mangels, J. A., Squire, L. R. A neostriatal habit learning system in humans. *Science* (1996) 273:1399–1402.

Low, A. *An Invitation to Practice Zen.* C. E. Tuttle Co., 1989.

Luthe, W. *Creativity Mobilization Technique.* Grune & Stratton, 1983.

Mulder, R. T., Joyce, P. R., Sellman, J. F., Cloninger, C. R. Towards an understanding of defense style in terms of temperament and character. *Acta Psychiatrica Scandinavica* (1996) 93:99–104.

Norbu, N. *The Crystal and the Way of Light: Sutra, Tantra, and Dzogchen.* (Compiled and Edited by John Shane) Routledge and Kegal Paul, 1986.

Piaget, J. *The Development of Thought: Equilibration of Cognitive Structures.* Viking, 1975.

Pine, F. *Drive, Ego, Object, & Self.* Basic Books, 1990.

Robbins, T. W. Refining the taxonomy of memory. *Science* (1996) 273:1353–1354.

Rossi, E. L. *The Psychobiology of Mind-Body Healing: New Concepts of Therapeutic Hypnosis.* (Revised Edition) W. W. Norton & Co, 1993.

Schultz, J. H., and Luthe, W. *Autogenic Training: A Psychophysiologic Approach to Psychotherapy.* Grune & Stratton, 1959.

St. John of the Cross *The Ascent of Mount Carmel* (Translated by David Lewis) Thomas Baker, 1906.

Svrakic, N. M., Svrakic, D. M., and Cloninger, C. R. A general quantitative theory of personality development: Fundamentals of a self-organizing psychobiological complex. *Development and Psychopathology* (1996) 8:247–272.

Zinner, J. A journey from blame to empathy in a family assessment of a mother and her sons. *Psychiatry Interpersonal and Biological Processes* (1997) 60:104–110.

 Article Review Form at end of book.

What is comorbidity and why is it important to study?

Lifetime and 12-Month Prevalence of *DSM-III-R* Psychiatric Disorders in the United States:

Results from the National Comorbidity Survey

Ronald C. Kessler, Ph.D.;
Katherine A. McGonagle, Ph.D.;
Shanyang Zhao, Ph.D.;
Christopher B. Nelson, M.P.H.;
Michael Hughes, Ph.D.;
Suzann Eshleman, M.A.;
Hans-Ulrich Wittchen, Ph.D.;
and Kenneth S. Kendler, M.D.

Background: This study presents estimates of lifetime and 12-month prevalence of 14 *DSM-III-R* psychiatric disorders from the National Comorbidity Survey, the first survey to administer a structured psychiatric interview to a national probability sample in the United States.

Methods: The *DSM-III-R* psychiatric disorders among persons aged 15 to 54 years in the noninstitutionalized civilian population of the United States were assessed with data collected by lay interviewers using a revised version of the Composite International Diagnostic Interview.

Results: Nearly 50% of respondents reported at least one lifetime disorder, and close to 30% reported at least one 12-month disorder. The most common disorders were major depressive episode, alcohol dependence, social phobia, and simple phobia. More than half of all lifetime disorders occurred in the 14% of the population who had a history of three or more comorbid disorders. These highly comorbid people also included the vast majority of people with severe disorders. Less than 40% of those with a lifetime disorder had ever received professional treatment, and less than 20% of those with a recent disorder had been in treatment during the past 12 months. Consistent with previous risk factor research, it was found that women had elevated rates of affective disorders and anxiety disorders, that men had elevated rates of substance use disorders and antisocial personality disorder, and that most disorders declined with age and with higher socioeconomic status.

Conclusions: The prevalence of psychiatric disorders is greater than previously thought to be the case. Furthermore, this morbidity is more highly concentrated than previously recognized in roughly one sixth of the population who have a history of three or more comorbid disorders. This suggests that the causes and consequences of high comorbidity should be the focus of research attention. The majority of people with psychiatric disorders fail to obtain professional treatment. Even among people with a lifetime history of three or more comorbid disorders, the proportion who ever obtain specialty sector mental health treatment is less than 50%. These results argue for the

importance of more outreach and more research on barriers to professional help-seeking.
(*Arch Gen Psych.* 1994;51:8-19)

This report presents data on the lifetime and 12-month prevalence of 14 *DSM-III-R* psychiatric disorders assessed in the National Comorbidity Survey (NCS). The NCS is a congressionally mandated survey designed to study the comorbidity of substance use disorders and nonsubstance psychiatric disorders in the United States. The NCS is the first survey to administer a structured psychiatric interview to a representative national sample in the United States. The need for such a survey was noted 15 years ago in the report of the President's Commission on Mental Health and Illness.[1] It was impossible to undertake such a survey at that time, though, due to the absence of a structured research diagnostic interview capable of generating reliable psychiatric diagnoses in general population samples. Recognizing this need, the National Institute of Mental Health, Bethesda, Md, funded the development of the Diagnostic Interview Schedule (DIS),[2] a research diagnostic interview that can be administered by trained interviewers who are not clinicians. The DIS was first used in the Epidemiologic Catchment Area (ECA) Study, a landmark study that interviewed more than 20 000 respondents in a series of five community epidemiologic surveys. The ECA Study has been the main source of data in the United States on the prevalence of psychiatric disorders and utilization of services for these disorders for the past decade.[3-5]

The NCS was designed to take the next step beyond the ECA Study. Three main advances are noteworthy. First, the NCS diagnoses are based on *DSM-III-R*[6] rather than *DSM-III*[7] criteria. Questions are also included in the interview that allow some comparisons with *DSM-IV*[8] and with the *International Classification of Diseases (ICD-10)* Diagnostic Criteria for Research.[9] Second, while the ECA Study was designed primarily as a prevalence and incidence study, the NCS was designed to be a risk factor

Table 1 Characteristics of NCS Respondents Compared with Those of the Total U.S. Population*

	%		
	U.S. Population[†]	NCS Weighted	NCS Unweighted
Sex			
M	49.1	49.5	47.5
F	50.9	50.5	52.5
Race			
W	75.0	75.3	75.1
B	11.9	11.5	12.5
Hispanic	8.6	9.7	9.1
Other	4.5	3.5	3.3
Education, y			
0–11	22.5	22.3	18.2
12	36.8	37.4	33.1
13–15	21.2	21.7	26.3
≥ 16	19.5	18.6	22.4
Marital status			
Married/cohabitation	59.8	62.9	54.4
Separated/widowed/ divorced	10.1	10.0	15.5
Never married	30.1	27.1	30.1
Region			
Northeast	20.0	20.2	19.2
Midwest	24.6	23.8	25.6
South	33.7	36.4	35.6
West	21.7	19.6	19.6
Age, y			
15–24	25.5	24.7	21.8
25–34	30.8	30.1	32.4
35–44	25.9	27.1	27.7
45–54	17.8	18.1	18.1
Urbanicity			
Large MSAs	71.2	67.8	68.9
Small MSAs	8.1	7.5	6.5
Not MSAs	20.7	24.7	24.6
Total N	65,244[‡]	8098	8098

* NCS indicates National Comorbidity Survey; large MSAs, counties in the U.S. Bureau of the Census—defined metropolitan statistical areas with 250 000 or more residents; small MSAs, counties in MSAs containing less than 250 000 residents; and not MSAs, counties that are not in MSAs.

† The U.S. population characteristics are based on results from the 1989 U.S. National Health Interview Survey.

‡ There were 65,244 household members in the sample households interviewed as part of the 1989 U.S. National Health Interview Survey.

Methods

Sample

The NCS is based on a stratified, multistage area probability sample of persons aged 15 to 54 years in the noninstitutionalized civilian population in the 48 coterminous states. The inclusion of respondents aged as young as 15 years, compared with the 18-year-old lower age limit found in most general population surveys, was based on an interest in minimizing recall bias of early-onset disorders. The exclusion of respondents aged older than 54 years was based on evidence from the ECA Study that active comorbidity between substance use disorders and nonsubstance psychiatric disorders is much lower among persons aged older than 54 years than among those aged 54 years and younger. The NCS also includes a supplemental sample of students living in campus group housing. The survey was administered by the staff of the Survey Research Center at the University of Michigan (UM), Ann Arbor, between September 14, 1990, and February 6, 1992. The response rate was 82.6%. Cooperation in listed households did not differ markedly by age or sex, the only two listing variables available for all selected respondents. A total of 8098 respondents participated in the survey. Based on previous evidence that survey nonrespondents have higher rates of psychiatric disorder than respondents,[11,12] a supplemental nonresponse survey was carried out in parallel with the main survey. In this supplemental survey, a random sample of initial nonrespondents was offered a financial incentive to complete a short form of the diagnostic interview. Elevated rates of both lifetime and current psychiatric disorders were found among these initial nonrespondents. A nonresponse adjustment weight was constructed for the main survey data to compensate for this systematic nonresponse. A second weight was used to adjust for variation in probabilities of selection both within and between households. A third weight was used to adjust the data to approximate the national population distributions of the cross-classification of age, sex, race/ethnicity, marital status, education, living arrangements, region, and urbanicity as defined by the 1989 US National Health Interview Survey.[13] A comparison of weighted and unweighted NCS data with national distributions on a range of demographic variables is presented in Table 1.

Diagnostic Assessment

The psychiatric diagnoses reported below are based on the *DSM-III-R*.[6] The diagnostic interview used to generate these diagnoses is a modified version of the Composite International Diagnostic Interview (CIDI),[14] a state-of-the-art structured diagnostic interview based on the DIS and designed to be used by trained interviewers who are not clinicians.[15] We deleted diagnoses known to have low prevalence in population-based surveys, such as somatization disorder. We also deleted the Folstein-McHugh Mini-Mental State Examination, which is included in the full CIDI, based on pilot test results showing that respondents in the 15- to 54-year-old age range only rarely have high error scores and that those with high error scores in this age range disproportionately come from the foreign-born and the poorly educated population groups. Our modifications of the remaining sections of the CIDI included adding commitment and motivation probes for recall of lifetime episodes, and including clarifying probes for CIDI questions found in pilot work to be unclear or confusing to respondents.

The *DSM-III-R* diagnoses included in the core NCS include major depression, mania, dysthymia, panic disorder, agoraphobia, social phobia, simple phobia, generalized anxiety disorder, alcohol abuse, alcohol dependence, drug abuse, drug dependence, antisocial personality disorder (ASPD), and nonaffective psychosis (NAP). Twelve-month diagnoses of substance use disorders were made in the subsample of respondents who qualified for the lifetime diagnosis and who reported at least one *DSM-III-R* symptom in the 12 months prior to the interview. Nonaffective psychosis is a summary category made up of schizophrenia, schizophreniform disorder, schizoaffective disorder, delusional disorder, and atypical psychosis. We also constructed a summary category for 12-month "severe" disorder, defined as (1) 12-month mania or NAP, (2) lifetime mania or NAP with 12-month treatment or role impairment, or (3) 12-month depression or panic disorder with severe impairment (hospitalization or use of antipsychotic medication).

World Health Organization field trials of the CIDI have documented good interrater reliability,[16,17] test-retest reliability,[18,19] and validity of almost all diagnoses.[20-26] The exception is acute psychotic disorder, which has been shown to be diagnosed with low reliability and validity in structured interviews like the CIDI.[27,28] Based on this evidence, the NCS included clinical reinterviews with respondents who reported any evidence of psychotic symptoms. These reinterviews were administered by experienced clinicians using an adapted version of the Structured Clinical Interview for *DSM-III-R*,[29] an instrument with demonstrated reliability in the diagnosis of schizophrenia.[30] The NCS diagnoses of schizophrenia and other nonaffective psychotic disorders (NAPs) are based on these clinical reinterviews rather than on the UM-CIDI interviews.

Interviewers and Interviewer Training

As noted above, the NCS was carried out by the field staff of the Survey Research Center at the UM. The 158 interviewers who participated in the NCS had an average of 5 years of prior interviewing experience with the Survey Research Center. In addition, the NCS interviewers went through a 7-day study-specific training program in the use of the UM-CIDI. Fieldwork was closely monitored throughout the entire data collection period. Three field quality control procedures are worth noting. First, completed interviews were by one of 18 regional supervisors before they were returned to the national field office. This allowed rapid detection of missing data and unclear responses. Incomplete interviews were returned to the interviewer, who recontacted the respondent to obtain the missing information. Second, a random sample of respondents was recontacted by the field supervisors to verify the accuracy of interviewer performance. Third, the field edits were checked at the national field office as soon as interviews were received. This provided a second check on interviewer performance as well as a check on the accuracy of the supervisor's editing. Supervisors were contacted whenever errors were found, and the interview was sent back to the field for resolution.

Analysis Procedures

As a result of the complex sample design and weighting, special software was required to estimate SEs. Standard errors of proportions were estimated by using the Taylor series linearization method.[31] The PSRATIO program in the OSIRIS software package[32] was used to make these calculations. Standard errors of odds ratios (ORs) were estimated by using the method of Balanced Repeated Replication in 44 design-based balanced subsamples.[33,34] The LOGISTIC program in the SAS software package[35] was used to make these calculations.

Table 2 Lifetime and 12-Month Prevalence of UM-CIDI/*DSM-III-R* Disorders*

| | Male | | | | Female | | | | Total | | | |
| | Lifetime | | 12 mo | | Lifetime | | 12 mo | | Lifetime | | 12 mo | |
Disorders	%	SE	%	SE	%	SE	%	SE	%	SE	%	SE
Affective disorders												
Major depressive episode	12.7	0.9	7.7	0.8	21.3	0.9	12.9	0.8	17.1	0.7	10.3	0.6
Manic episode	1.6	0.3	1.4	0.3	1.7	0.3	1.3	0.3	1.6	0.3	1.3	0.2
Dysthymia	4.8	0.4	2.1	0.3	8.0	0.6	3.0	0.4	6.4	0.4	2.5	0.2
Any affective disorder	14.7	0.8	8.5	0.8	23.9	0.9	14.1	0.9	19.3	0.7	11.3	0.7
Anxiety disorders												
Panic disorder	2.0	0.3	1.3	0.3	5.0	1.4	3.2	0.4	3.5	0.3	2.3	0.3
Agoraphobia without panic disorder	3.5	0.4	1.7	0.3	7.0	0.6	3.8	0.4	5.3	0.4	2.8	0.3
Social phobia	11.1	0.8	6.6	0.4	15.5	1.0	9.1	0.7	13.3	0.7	7.9	0.4
Simple phobia	6.7	0.5	4.4	0.5	15.7	1.1	13.2	0.9	11.3	0.6	8.8	0.5
Generalized anxiety disorder	3.6	0.5	2.0	0.3	6.6	0.5	4.3	0.4	5.1	0.3	3.1	0.3
Any anxiety disorder	19.2	0.9	11.8	0.6	30.5	1.2	22.6	0.1	24.9	0.8	17.2	0.7
Substance use disorders												
Alcohol abuse without dependence	12.5	0.8	3.4	0.4	6.4	0.6	1.6	0.2	9.4	0.5	2.5	0.2
Alcohol dependence	20.1	1.0	10.7	0.9	8.2	0.7	3.7	0.4	14.1	0.7	7.2	0.5
Drug abuse without dependence	5.4	0.5	1.3	0.2	3.5	0.4	0.3	0.1	4.4	0.3	0.8	0.1
Drug dependence	9.2	0.7	3.8	0.4	5.9	0.5	1.9	0.3	7.5	0.4	2.8	0.3
Any substance abuse/dependence	35.4	1.2	16.1	0.7	17.9	1.1	6.6	0.4	26.6	1.0	11.3	0.5
Other disorders												
Antisocial personality	5.8	0.6	. . .	. . .	1.2	0.3	. . .	. . .	3.5	0.3	. . .	. . .
Nonaffective psychosis†	0.6	0.1	0.5	0.1	0.8	0.2	0.6	0.2	0.7	0.1	0.5	0.1
Any NCS disorder	48.7	0.2	27.7	0.9	47.3	1.5	31.2	1.3	48.0	1.1	29.5	1.0

* UM-CIDI indicates University of Michigan Composite International Diagnostic Interview; NCS, National Comorbidity Survey.

† Nonaffective psychosis includes schizophrenia, schizophreniform disorder, schizoaffective disorder, delusional disorder, and atypical psychosis.

study as well. As a result, the NCS interview contains a much more comprehensive risk factor battery than the ECA Study, including family history Research Diagnostic Criteria[10] assessments of parental psychopathology, questions about childhood family adversity, measures of social networks and support, and information about stressful life events and difficulties. Third, while the goals of the ECA Study to include institutional respondents and clinical reappraisals made it necessary to carry out the ECA Study in a small number of local samples, our different goals made it possible to carry out the NCS in a national sample. As a result, we are able to study regional variations in specific psychiatric disorders and urban-rural differences in

unmet need for services as well as to provide the first nationally representative data that can be used in the current debate about health care policy in the United States.

Results
The Prevalence of Psychiatric Disorders

The results in Table 2 show UM-CIDI/*DSM-III-R* prevalence estimates of the 14 lifetime and 12-month disorders assessed in the core NCS interview. Lifetime prevalence is the proportion of the sample who *ever* experienced a disorder, while 12-month prevalence is the proportion who experienced the dis-

order at some time in the 12 months before the interview. The prevalence estimates in Table 2 are presented without exclusions for *DSM-III-R* hierarchy rules. Standard errors are reported in parentheses.

The most common psychiatric disorders were major depression and alcohol dependence. More than 17% of respondents had a history of major depressive episode (MDE) in their lifetime, and more than 10% had an episode in the past 12 months. More than 14% of respondents had a lifetime history of alcohol dependence, and more than 7% continued to be dependent in the past 12 months. The next most common disorders were social and simple phobias, with lifetime prevalences of 13% and 11%, respectively, and 12-month prevalences

No. of Lifetime Disorders	Proportion of Sample		Proportion of Lifetime Disorders		Proportion of 12-mo Disorders		Proportion of Respondents with Severe 12-mo Disorders*	
	%	SE	%	SE	%	SE	%	SE
0	52.0	1.1	. . .	. . .	. . .	. . .	. . .	. . .
1	21.0	0.6	20.6	0.6	17.4	0.8	2.6	1.7
2	13.0	0.5	25.5	1.0	23.1	1.0	7.9	2.1
≥3	14.0	0.7	53.9	2.7	58.9	1.8	89.5	2.8

*Severe 12-month disorders include active mania, nonaffective psychosis, or active disorders of other types that either required hospitalization or created severe role impairment.

close to 8% and 9%, respectively. As a group, substance use disorders and anxiety disorders were somewhat more prevalent than affective disorders. Approximately one in every four respondents reported a lifetime history of at least one substance use disorder, and a similar number reported a lifetime history of at least one anxiety disorder. Approximately one in every five respondents reported a lifetime history of at least one affective disorder. Anxiety disorders, as a group, are considerably more likely to occur in the 12 months before the interview (17%) than either substance use disorders (11%) or affective disorders (11%), suggesting that anxiety disorders are more chronic than either substance use disorders or affective disorders. The prevalence of other NCS disorders was quite low. Antisocial personality disorder, which was only assessed on a lifetime basis, was reported by more than 3% of respondents, while schizophrenia and other NAPs were found among only 0.7% of respondents. It is important to remember that the diagnosis of NAP was based on clinical reinterviews using the Structured Clinical Interview for *DSM-III-R* diagnosis rather than on the lay CIDI interviews. The prevalence estimates for NAP based on the UM-CIDI were considerably higher but were found to have low validity when judged in comparison with the clinical reappraisals (K.S.K., William Eaton, PhD, Janie Abelson, MSW, R.C.K., oral communication, September 1992).

As shown in the last row of Table 2, 48% of the sample reported a lifetime history of at least one UM-CIDI/*DSM-III-R* disorder, and 29% had one or more disorders in the 12 months before the interview. While there is no meaningful sex difference in these overall prevalences, there are sex differences in the prevalences of specific disorders. Consistent with previous research, [36-40] men are much more likely to have substance use disorders and ASPD than women, while women are much more likely to have affective disorders (with the exception of mania, for which there is no sex difference) and anxiety disorders than men. The data also show, consistent with a trend found in the ECA Study, [41] that women in the household population are somewhat more likely to have NAP than men, although this sex difference is not statistically significant ($P > .05$).

A final observation about the results in Table 2 is that the sum of the individual prevalence estimates across the 14 disorders consistently exceeds the prevalence of having any disorder. This means that there is considerable comorbidity among these disorders. For example, while the 48% lifetime prevalence in the total sample means that 48 of every 100 respondents in the sample reported a lifetime history of at least one disorder, a summation of lifetime prevalence estimates for the separate disorders shows that these 48 individuals reported a total of 102 lifetime disorders (2.1 per person). As demonstrated in the next section of the article, this comorbidity is quite important for understanding the distribution of psychiatric disorders in the United States.

The Importance of Comorbidity

It is beyond the scope of this article to delve into the many different types of comorbidity that exist in the NCS. Nevertheless, the aggregate results in Table 3 document that these patterns are very important in understanding the distribution of psychiatric disorders among persons aged 15 to 54 years in the United States and provide an empirical rationale for more detailed examination of particular types of comorbidity in future analyses. The four rows of Table 3 represent the number of lifetime disorders reported by respondents. As shown in the first column, 52% of respondents never had any UM-CIDI/*DSM-III-R* disorder, 21% had one, 13% had two, and 14% had three or more disorders. Only 21% of all the lifetime disorders occurred in respondents with a lifetime history of just one disorder. This means that the *vast majority* of lifetime disorders in this sample (79%) were comorbid disorders. Furthermore, an even greater proportion of 12-month disorders occurred in respondents with a lifetime history of comorbidity. It is particularly striking that close to six (59%) of every 10 12-month disorders and nearly nine (89%) of 10 severe 12-month disorders occurred in the 14% of the sample with a lifetime history of three or more disorders. These results show that while a history of some psychiatric disorder is quite common among persons aged 15 to 54 years in the United States, the major burden of psychiatric disorder in this sector of our society is concentrated in a group

Table 4	Lifetime and 12-Month Utilization of Professional Services*		
	No Disorder	**Any Disorder**	**≥3 Disorders**
Lifetime			
Any professional†			
%	15.3	42.0	58.8
SE	1.3	1.1	1.8
Mental health specialty‡			
%	8.1	26.2	41.0
SE	1.2	1.1	2.1
Substance abuse facility§			
%	0.3	8.4	14.8
SE	0.2	0.7	1.5
12 mo			
Any professional			
%	7.0	20.9	34.2
SE	0.7	1.1	3.0
Mental health specialty			
%	2.7	11.5	22.5
SE	0.6	0.8	2.6
Substance abuse facility			
%	0.1	4.0	8.6
SE	0.04	0.7	2.5

* Top part of Table 4 relates to lifetime disorders/utilization; bottom part, 12-month disorders/utilization.

† Any professional indicates hospitalization or outpatient treatment by a mental health specialist, physician, social worker, counselor, nurse, or other health professional, including treatment in a substance abuse facility.

‡ Mental health specialty indicates hospitalization or outpatient treatment by a psychiatrist or psychologist or treatment in a substance abuse facility.

§ Substance abuse facility indicates hospitalization for drug or alcohol problems or treatment in a drug or alcohol outpatient clinic or drop-in center or program for people with emotional problems with alcohol or drug abuse.

of highly comorbid people who constitute about one sixth of the population. The more detailed disaggregation and investigation of these people is a major focus of the NCS.

Utilization of Services

Although previous national surveys have asked about utilization of professional services for emotional problems,[42,43] no national survey until now has included a diagnostic assessment that could be used to define unmet need. This was done in the NCS by assessing both lifetime and recent utilization of services from a wide variety of professionals in a number of different treatment settings. Summary results (Table 4) show that only four of every 10 respondents with a lifetime history of at least one UM-CIDI/*DSM-III-R* disorder ever obtained professional help for their disorders, only one in four obtained treatment in the mental health specialty sector, and about one in 12 were treated in substance abuse facilities. While nearly six in 10 persons who have a lifetime history of three or more disorders ever received professional treatment, only four in 10 of these highly comorbid people were treated in the mental health specialty sector, and about one in seven received treatment in substance abuse facilities. Among respondents with a 12-month disorder, only one in five obtained any professional help in the past year, one in nine obtained treatment in the mental health specialty sector, and one in 25 were treated in substance abuse facilities. Only about one third of persons with three or more disorders in the past year received any professional treatment in the past year, slightly more than one in five were treated in the mental health service sector, and about one in 12 received treatment in substance abuse facilities. These national patterns are broadly consistent with those from the five-site ECA sample,[5,44] in showing that the vast majority of people with recent disorders have not had recent treatment.

Demographic Correlates of Disorder

Bivariate risk factor associations are reported for groupings of disorders in Table 5 (lifetime) and Table 6 (12 months). Based on findings in Table 3 that the majority of both lifetime and 12-month disorders, and the vast majority of severe disorders, occurred in people with a history of three or more disorders, we also included three or more disorders as an outcome variable in Tables 5 and 6. Associations are shown in the form of ORs with 95% confidence intervals (CIs) As noted above, these CIs are based on complex variance estimation techniques that adjust for the weighting and clustering of the sample data.

Sex

As mentioned previously in the discussion of Table 2, the NCS data are consistent with those of previous epidemiologic studies, in finding that women have higher prevalences than men of affective disorders (with the exception of mania, for which there is no sex difference), anxiety disorders, and NAP, and that men have higher rates than women of substance use disorders and ASPD. Furthermore, we find that women have higher prevalences than men of both lifetime and 12-month comorbidity of three or more disorders.

Age

In the absence of an extremely young age at onset, cohort effects, differen-

Table 5 Demographic Correlates of Lifetime Psychiatric Disorders*

	Any Affective Disorder		Any Anxiety Disorder		Any Substance Use Disorder		ASPD†		Any Disorder		≥3 Disorders	
	OR	95% CI	OR	95% CI	OR	95% CI	OR	95% CI	OR	95% CI	OR	95% CI
Sex												
M	1.00	...	1.00	...	1.00	...	5.16‡	2.90–9.20	1.00	...	1.00	...
F	1.82‡	1.56.–2.12	1.85‡	1.58–2.16	0.40‡	0.34–0.46	1.00	...	0.95	0.83–1.08	1.24‡	1.02–1.50
Age, y												
15–24	0.85	0.65–1.11	1.13	0.90–1.43	1.36‡	1.01–1.83	2.56‡	1.52–4.30	1.15	0.92–1.43	1.18	0.88–1.58
25–34	0.97	0.77–1.22	1.13	0.90–1.42	1.99‡	1.53–2.57	1.83‡	1.08–3.12	1.36‡	1.12–1.65	1.47‡	1.07–2.02
35–44	1.06	0.81–1.38	1.05	0.83–1.34	1.58‡	1.25–1.99	1.01	0.50–2.03	1.20	0.99–1.46	1.19	0.87–1.62
45–54	1.00	...	1.00	...	1.00	...	1.00	...	1.00	...	1.00	...
Race												
W	1.00	...	1.00	...	1.00	...	1.00	...	1.00	...	1.00	...
B	0.63‡	0.46–0.87	0.77	.058–1.01	0.35‡	0.27–0.46	0.89	0.56–1.41	0.50‡	0.41–0.60	0.67‡	0.45–0.98
Hispanic	0.96	0.72–1.27	0.90	0.71–1.15	0.80	0.62–1.03	1.43	0.92–2.23	0.86	0.69–1.06	0.99	0.73–1.35
Income, $												
0–19 000	1.56‡	1.23–1.98	2.00‡	1.66–2.41	1.27‡	1.05–1.54	2.98‡	1.71–5.20	1.49‡	1.25–1.78	2.46‡	1.87–3.24
20 000–34 000	1.19	0.89–1.60	1.52‡	1.21–1.90	1.06	0.80–1.41	2.16‡	1.15–4.06	1.21	0.95–1.53	1.71‡	1.20–2.43
35 000–69 000	1.16	0.88–1.51	1.48‡	1.16–1.90	1.06	0.83–1.36	1.59	0.82–3.10	1.21	0.97–1.49	1.55‡	1.12–2.15
≥70 000	1.00	...	1.00	...	1.00	...	1.00	...	1.00	...	1.00	...
Education, y												
0–11	0.98	0.80–1.20	1.86‡	1.53–2.26	0.99	0.77–1.27	14.13‡	6.05–32.99	1.17	0.96–1.42	2.15‡	1.60–2.90
12	1.00	0.82–1.24	1.76‡	1.42–2.20	1.25‡	1.05–1.48	4.29‡	2.07–8.90	1.25‡	1.07–1.46	2.09‡	1.52–2.86
13–15	1.05	0.89–1.25	1.44‡	1.15–1.79	1.20‡	1.01–1.43	3.32‡	1.43–7.72	1.21‡	1.04–1.40	1.73‡	1.25–2.39
≥16	1.00	...	1.00	...	1.00	...	1.00	...	1.00	...	1.00	...
Urbanicity												
Major metropolitan	1.26	0.91–1.76	0.98	0.76–1.26	1.09	0.82–1.45	1.27	0.80–1.99	1.10	0.83–1.47	1.20	0.86–1.68
Other urban	1.20	0.85–1.71	1.00	0.74–1.35	1.10	0.80–1.51	0.98	0.61–1.58	1.09	0.78–1.53	1.18	0.80–1.73
Rural	1.00	...	1.00	...	1.00	...	1.00	...	1.00	...	1.00	...
Region												
Midwest	1.06	0.85–1.33	1.17	0.93–1.46	1.21	0.96–1.54	1.34	0.89–2.00	1.19	0.94–1.49	1.00	0.76–1.33
Northeast	1.00	0.76–1.30	1.29‡	1.07–1.56	1.33‡	1.04–1.69	1.49	0.83–2.69	1.25‡	1.03–1.52	1.35	0.98–1.85
West	1.32	1.00–1.74	1.15	0.87–1.52	1.57‡	1.15–2.14	2.40‡	1.49–3.85	1.38‡	1.05–1.81	1.43‡	1.03–1.98
South	1.00	...	1.00	...	1.00	...	1.00	...	1.00	...	1.00	...

* ASPD indicates antisocial personality disorder; OR, odds ratio; and CI, confidence interval.

† Results concerning ASPD exclude respondents aged 15 to 17 years because the diagnosis requires that the rspondent be at least 18 years of age.

‡ P < .05 (two tailed).

tial mortality, selection bias associated with age, and age-related differences in willingness to report symptoms, one would expect to find increasing lifetime prevalence of all disorders with age. However, the results in Table 5 show quite a different pattern, with the highest prevalences generally in the group aged 25 to 34 years and declining prevalences at later ages. This pattern is broadly consistent with the results of recent epidemiologic surveys,[36,45] in documenting increasing psychopathology in more recent cohorts. The pattern is even more pronounced in Table 6, where it is shown that 12-month disorders are consistently most prevalent in the youngest cohort (age range, 15 to 24 years) and generally decline monotonically with age.

Table 6 Demographic Correlates of 12-Month Psychiatric Disorders*

	Any Affective Disorder		Any Anxiety Disorder		Any Substance Use Disorder		Any Disorder		≥3 Disorders	
	OR	95% CI	OR	95% CI	OR	95% CI	OR	95% CI	OR	95% CI
Sex										
M	1.00	. . .	1.00	. . .	1.00	. . .	1.00	. . .	1.00	. . .
F	1.76†	1.43–2.18	2.19†	1.88–2.55	0.37†	0.31–0.43	1.18†	1.07–1.31	1.55†	1.15–2.10
Age, y										
15–24	1.67†	1.14–2.44	1.40†	1.09–1.80	3.65†	2.29–5.84	2.06†	1.66–2.56	2.08†	1.17–3.70
25–34	1.32	0.89–1.96	1.13	0.85–1.51	2.65†	1.72–4.06	1.51†	1.20–1.88	1.66	0.88–3.16
35–44	1.35	0.93–1.96	0.98	0.76–1.26	2.00†	1.31–3.05	1.24	0.98–1.56	1.36	0.75–2.49
45–54	1.00	. . .	1.00	. . .	1.00	. . .	1.00	. . .	1.00	. . .
Race										
W	1.00	. . .	1.00	. . .	1.00	. . .	1.00	. . .	1.00	. . .
B	0.78	0.54–1.14	0.90	0.65–1.26	0.47†	0.35–0.64	0.70†	0.55–0.90	1.04	0.53–2.06
Hispanic	1.38†	1.02–1.86	1.17	0.93–1.49	1.04	0.74–1.46	1.11	0.91–1.35	1.86†	1.23–2.82
Income, $										
0–19 000	1.73†	1.29–2.32	2.12†	1.63–2.77	1.92†	1.36–2.71	1.92†	1.54–2.39	3.36†	1.95–5.79
20 000–34 000	1.13	0.80–1.59	1.56†	1.18–2.06	1.12	0.79–1.60	1.24	0.97–1.57	2.10†	1.16–3.83
35 000–69 000	1.01	0.75–1.37	1.50†	1.15–1.97	1.11	0.75–1.64	1.20	0.93–1.55	1.66†	1.02–2.73
≥70 000	1.00	. . .	1.00	. . .	1.00	. . .	1.00	. . .	1.00	. . .
Education, y										
0–11	1.79†	1.31–2.43	2.82†	2.26–3.51	2.10†	1.56–2.84	2.33†	1.91–2.84	3.76†	2.45–5.76
12	1.38†	1.00–1.89	2.10†	1.66–2.67	1.80†	1.40–2.32	1.79†	1.46–2.21	2.54†	1.70–3.78
13–15	1.37†	1.02–1.84	1.60†	1.19–2.15	1.70†	1.20–2.42	1.58†	1.28–1.96	2.06†	1.18–3.59
≥16	1.00	. . .	1.00	. . .	1.00	. . .	1.00	. . .	1.00	. . .
Urbanicity										
Major metropolitan	1.21	0.76–1.92	1.04	0.77–1.41	1.09	0.79–1.50	1.05	0.75–1.47	1.44†	1.00–2.08
Other urban	1.11	0.69–1.79	1.18	0.85–1.63	1.12	0.77–1.64	1.11	0.78–1.60	1.41	0.97–2.04
rural	1.00	. . .	1.00	. . .	1.00	. . .	1.00	. . .	1.00	. . .
Region										
Midwest	0.84	0.63–1.13	1.07	0.81–1.41	1.22	0.97–1.53	1.04	0.80–1.34	0.79	0.56–1.11
Northeast	0.87	0.62–1.21	1.24	0.99–1.57	1.30	0.98–1.72	1.09	0.85–1.39	1.08	0.74–1.59
West	0.98	0.59–1.64	1.12	0.86–1.47	1.13	0.86–1.48	1.02	0.77–1.33	1.07	0.61–1.88
South	1.00	. . .	1.00	. . .	1.00	. . .	1.00	. . .	1.00	. . .

* OR indicates odds ratio; CI, confidence interval.

† P < .05 (two tailed).

Race

While the NCS results concerning sex and age are consistent with those of previous epidemiologic studies, this is less true for the results concerning race. Blacks in the NCS have significantly lower prevalences of affective disorders, substance use disorders, and lifetime comorbidity than whites. There are no disorders where either lifetime or active prevalence is significantly higher among blacks than whites. More detailed analyses (results available from the first author [R.C.K.]) show that these effects cannot be explained by controlling for income and education. The lower prevalence of affective disorders is consistent with, but more pronounced than, the ECA finding of a slightly lower rate in the 30- to 64-year-old age range among blacks than whites.[46] The lower prevalence of substance use disorders among blacks is consistent with the ECA finding of higher prevalence of drug and alcohol abuse and dependence among young whites compared with that among young blacks.[47,48] Our failure to find black-white differences in anxiety disorders (or, in more detailed analyses not reported here, in panic disorder, simple phobia, or agoraphobia) is consistent with the ECA finding that blacks and whites have similar prevalences of panic disorder[49] but inconsistent with the ECA finding that blacks have nearly twice the lifetime prevalence of simple phobia and agoraphobia.[50]

Hispanics in the NCS have significantly higher prevalences of current affective disorders and active comorbidity than non-Hispanic whites. There are no disorders where either lifetime or active prevalence is significantly lower among Hispanics than among non-Hispanic whites. The higher rate of affective disorders is inconsistent with that of the ECA Study, which found higher lifetime rates among whites and no race difference in active prevalence.[46] The failure to find a white vs Hispanic difference in anxiety disorders is inconsistent with the ECA finding that Hispanics have significantly lower lifetime rates of panic.[50] Furthermore, the NCS does not replicate the ECA finding that Hispanics have elevated rates of alcohol use disorders compared with whites.[47]

Socioeconomic Status

Consistent with previous research,[3,37,51-54] rates of almost all disorders decline monotonically with income and education. The ORs in Tables 5 and 6 comparing the lowest with highest income groups are significant in all equations. The coefficients comparing the middle vs highest income groups are significant in predicting anxiety disorders, ASPD, and comorbidity. The ORs for education are somewhat more variable, but the general pattern is still one of decline in the ORs from the lowest to highest education groups. One noteworthy exception is that lifetime substance use disorder is significantly higher in the *middle* education subsamples than among those with either the lowest or highest education. The significant ORs for both income and education are consistently larger in predicting 12-month than lifetime prevalence, which means that socioeconomic status is associated not only with onset but also with course of disorder. It is unclear from these data, though, whether this is due to causal influence or to drift. Finally, there is a consistent tendency for socioeconomic status to be more powerfully related to anxiety disorders than to affective disorders, suggesting indirectly that the resources associated with socioeconomic status are more protective against the onset and/or exacerbation of worries and fears than of sadness. We are unaware of any previous research on this issue, although this consistent pattern in our data suggests that this might be a fruitful area for future investigation.

Urbanicity

Urbanicity is examined here at the county level by distinguishing major metropolitan counties (major metropolitan areas), urbanized counties that are not in major metropolitan areas (other urban areas), and rural counties (rural). It is important to note that significant within-county differences in the prevalence of some disorders has been found in previous research.[55] Within-county comparisons will be made in later analyses of the NCS, but these comparisons cannot yet be carried out because of current incompleteness in the NCS geocoding, pending release of final matching information from the 1990 census.

As seen in Tables 5 and 6, the effects of urbanicity at the county level are generally not significant. The single exception is that residents of major metropolitan counties are more likely than residents of rural counties to have comorbidity in the 12 months before the interview (OR=1.44). The coefficient that compares residents of other urbanized counties with residents of rural counties on the same outcome is very similar in magnitude (OR=1.41) and significant at the .06 level, which means that it is the low rate of comorbidity in rural America rather than a high rate in major metropolitan counties that underlies this pattern. This one significant coefficient could have occurred by chance in 22 different comparisons (two urbanicity coefficients for each of 11 outcomes), although there is a general trend in the data for rural residents to have the lowest levels of disorder (in 10 of the 11 outcomes in Tables 5 and 6).

Region

There are a number of significant regional differences in lifetime prevalence. Substance use disorders, ASPD, and comorbidity are all highest in the West. Anxiety disorders are highest in the Northeast. Virtually all disorders are lowest in the South. None of these patterns, however, is replicated in parallel analyses of 12-month disorders, implying that region is associated in different ways with onset and course.

Comment

Limitations

Two data collection limitations need to be noted. First, the NCS is a cross-sectional survey that relies entirely on retrospective reports to assess the prevalence of lifetime disorders. Commitment and memory probes were used to minimize recall problems, but we recognize that whatever success we had in this regard was only partial. Long-term longitudinal data collection is needed to evaluate the magnitude of recall failure and to adjust for its effects on prevalence estimates. Second, even in cases where respondents describe recent disorders, our diagnostic assessment is based on only a single structured interview administered by nonclinicians. This is a practical necessity in a survey as large and geographically dispersed as the NCS. Yet, it is important to recognize that we pay a price for this ease of implementation in reduced diagnostic precision, which could have been improved if it had been possible to use clinical interviewers, to carry out multiple interviews, and to use ancillary information from informants and institutional records. The fact that these things were not done means that the prevalences reported here should be interpreted as estimates rather than as definite diagnoses.

Prevalence

The NCS results show that psychiatric disorders are more prevalent than previous research would lead us to believe. Close to half of all respondents report a lifetime history of at least one UM-CIDI/*DSM-III-R* disorder. One fifth of respondents have a lifetime history of an affective disorder, one fourth have a history of an anxiety disorder, and one fourth have a history of a substance use disorder. A 12-month prevalence of at least one disorder is nearly 30% in the sample as a whole, with more respondents reporting a 12-month anxiety disorder (17.2%) than either affective disorders (11.3%) or a substance use disorder (11.3%). The high ratio of a 12-month to lifetime anxiety disorder prevalence suggests indirectly that they are more chronic than either affective disorders or substance use disorders.

The fact that the NCS prevalence estimates are higher than in previous epidemiologic surveys could be due, at least in part, to secular trends. A number of methodologic factors could also be involved, including the fact that the NCS is based on a national sample, concentrates on a younger age range than previous surveys, uses a correction weight to adjust for nonresponse bias, and reports *DSM-III-R* diagnoses while earlier epidemiologic surveys used the *DSM-III* diagnostic system. Any attempt to compare prevalence estimates in the NCS with those in earlier surveys needs to grapple with the implications of all these issues.

It is also important to recognize that while the diagnostic instrument used in the NCS is very similar to the diagnostic instrument used in the ECA Study and other recent epidemiologic studies (the DIS), there are differences in wording and depth of probing that could have important effects on prevalence estimates. For example, the UM-CIDI assesses phobias by presenting the respondent with three separate lists containing a total of 20 prototypic feared objects and situations (six for social phobia, nine for simple phobia, and five for agoraphobia), while the version of the DIS used in the ECA Study combined all these objects and situations into a single list containing a total of only 15 items. The assessment of social phobia, in particular, is more thorough in the UM-CIDI than in the DIS, and this may explain why the NCS estimate of the prevalence of social phobia is much higher than the ECA estimate.

A final methodologic factor of importance in accounting for the comparatively higher NCS prevalence estimates is that the NCS included more sensitive probes for lifetime recall than did earlier epidemiologic surveys. Two aspects of this probing are noteworthy. First, based on the results of pilot tests that showed that respondents underreport stem questions once they recognize that positive responses will lead to more detailed questions, we included diagnostic stem questions for a number of disorders in a life review section that was administered before probing any positive stem responses. Second, this life review section used probes to stimulate motivation for lifetime recall in an effort to aid memory search. Based on these refinements, NCS respondents reported more positive responses to virtually all stem questions than ECA respondents. This, in turn, led to higher prevalence estimates.

The higher prevalence in the NCS compared with that in the ECA Study is particularly pronounced for MDE (lifetime prevalence of 17.1% in the NCS compared with 6.3% in the ECA Study). We suspect that this is due, at least in part, to the fact that failure to recall lifetime episodes of MDE is greater than for other disorders and that our refinements to aid recall had a more powerful effect on estimates of MDE than other disorders. This cannot explain the fact, though, that 12-month prevalence of MDE is much higher in the NCS than in the ECA Study. A factor relevant to this difference is that the NCS used three separate stem questions for MDE concerning periods of feeling "sad, blue, or depressed," feeling "down in the dumps or gloomy," and "losing interest in most things like work, hobbies, or things you usually like to do for fun." The ECA Study, in comparison, used only one stem question that combined the content of our first and third questions. It is noteworthy that the estimated prevalence of MDE in the NCS is quite similar to the estimates in previous epidemiologic studies that used clinical interviews like the Schedule for Affective Disorders and Schizophrenia and the Structured Clinical Interview for *DSM-III-R* [56-58] The fact that our refinements did not lead to overreporting is indicated by the fact that blind clinical reappraisals of the UM-CIDI diagnosis of MDE in a random subsample of NCS respondents using the Structured Clinical Interview for *DSM-III-R* [29] as the validation standard yielded a positive predictive value of 0.70 (±0.10), a rate that compares favorably with that of similar investigations of the ECA diagnostic classification of MDE. [2,27,28]

Comorbidity

One important accomplishment of the ECA Study was that it documented that comorbidity among psychiatric disorders is quite high in the general population. More than 60% of the ECA respondents with at least one lifetime disorder had two or more disorders. [3] The ECA respondents with comorbidity were also found to have higher utilization of services. [59] It was also found that mental disorders are associated with substance abuse prevalence and specialty sector treatment. [60] The NCS was designed to build on these results and to provide more fine-grained data about the prevalence, causes, and consequences of psychiatric comorbidity. We have taken a first step in that direction in the present report. We find that 56% of NCS respondents with a history of at least one disorder had two or more disorders. We also find that the majority of lifetime disorders and an even greater percentage of 12-month disorders occur in the roughly one sixth of the population with a lifetime history of three or more disorders. The fact that this segment of the population accounts for a higher percentage of 12-month disorders than lifetime disorders means that comorbidity is, in general, associated with a more serious course of illness, a result consistent with the findings of clinical investigations. [61-65] Future analyses of the NCS data will disaggregate this overall pattern to investigate the possibility that the effect of comorbidity on course can be further specified as due to particular primary disorders, secondary disorders, or primary-secondary combinations and whether these effects are specified by age at onset, family history, and other individual differences.

Utilization of Services

Our findings regarding utilization of services are broadly consistent with those of previous research, [5,43,44] in showing that the majority of people with psychiatric disorders receive no professional treatment and that fewer yet receive treatment in the mental health specialty sector. Although more likely than others to obtain treatment, we also found that fewer than half of people with three or more lifetime comorbid disorders ever obtained mental health specialty sector treatment.

It is noteworthy that the ECA estimate of the percentage of people with a disorder who received any professional treatment during the past 12 months is roughly 25% higher than the NCS estimate.[5] This finding, coupled with the fact that the NCS finds a considerably higher 12-month prevalence of disorder than the ECA Study, means that the NCS finds considerably more unmet need for mental health services than the ECA Study. More detailed analyses are planned to investigate this difference and to determine how much of it is due to time trends, to the fact that the ECA Study was based on a largely urbanized population where access to professional services is greater than in the rest of the population, or to other reasons.

Risk Factors

For the most part, the risk factor results reported above are consistent with previous investigations in finding more affective disorders and anxiety disorders among women, more substance use disorders and ASPD among men, and declining rates of most disorders with age and higher socioeconomic status. The other risk factor results are more provisional, though, due to the fact that they either fail to replicate previous research (in the case of the results regarding race) or are new results (in the cases of urbanicity and region). It is important to remember, in this regard, that we examined close to 200 separate coefficients in the risk factor analysis. It is quite likely that some of the significant results in this large set are due to chance. Future analyses of the NCS need to examine these risk factor results in more detail to determine whether they are stable. Perhaps the most interesting of these results concerns the fact that respondents living in rural areas have a 40% lower odds of 12-month comorbidity of three or more disorders than their urban counterparts. This association is much more powerful than the associations of urbanicity with the prevalence of individual disorders, which means that while rural Americans are no more likely to suffer from a psychiatric disorder, their disorders are more likely to be "pure" than comorbid. If this result is stable, it has important implications for the provision of services to the rural mentally ill, where medical care is more likely to come from the general medical sector than from the specialty mental health sector. Comorbidity is recognized as a major complication that impedes the ability of the general medical sector to provide effective care.[63] The fact that 1-year comorbidity of three or more disorders is lowest in rural areas means that the magnitude of this complication is considerably less than expected from our total population estimate.

Another intriguing aspect of the results regarding low prevalence of disorder in rural counties is that this is true despite the fact that rural Americans are exposed to much greater financial adversity than their urban counterparts.[66] The same can be said for the low prevalence of affective and substance use disorders among blacks compared with that among whites, patterns that exist despite the fact that blacks have much lower aggregate levels of both income and education than whites.[66] Future analyses of the NCS data will explore these patterns in more depth with the expectation that some as yet unknown resources protect rural people and blacks from the adverse psychiatric effects that we would otherwise expect to be associated with their stressful lives.

References

1. The President's Commission on Mental Health and Illness, eds. *Report to the President From the President's Commission on Mental Health, Volume 1.* Washington, DC: US Government Printing Office; 1978. Stock No. 040–000–00390–8.
2. Robins LN, Helzer JE, Croughan JL, Ratcliff KS. National Institute of Mental Health Diagnostic Interview Schedule: its history, characteristics and validity. *Arch Gen Psychiatry.* 1981;38:381–389.
3. Robins LN, Locke BZ, Regier DA. An overview of psychiatric disorders in America. In: Robins LN, Regier DA, eds. *Psychiatric Disorders in America: The Epidemiologic Catchment Area Study.* New York, NY: Free Press; 1991:328–366.
4. Bourdon KH, Rae DA, Locke BZ, Narrow WE, Regier DA. Estimating the prevalence of mental disorders in U.S. adults from the Epidemiologic Catchment Area Study. *Public Health Rep.* 1992;107:663–668.
5. Regier DA, Narrow WE, Rae DS, Manderscheid RW, Locke BZ, Goodwin FK. The de Facto US Mental and Addictive Disorders Service System: Epidemiologic Catchment Area prospective 1-year prevalence rates of disorders and services. *Arch Gen Psychiatry.* 1993;50:85–94
6. American Psychiatric Association. *Diagnostic and Statistical Manual of Mental Disorders, Revised Third Edition.* Washington, DC: American Psychiatric Association; 1987.
7. American Psychiatric Association. *Diagnostic and Statistical Manual of Mental Disorders, Third Edition.* Washington, DC: American Psychiatric Association; 1980.
8. Task Force on *DSM-IV:* American Psychiatric Association. *Diagnostic and Statistical Manual of Mental Disorders, Fourth Edition Draft Criteria.* Washington, DC: American Psychiatric Association; March 1993.
9. World Health Organization. Mental health and behavioral disorders (including disorders of psychological development). In: *International Classification of Diseases—10th Revision.* Geneva, Switzerland: World Health Organization; 1991:chap 5. Diagnostic Criteria for Research, Draft for Field Trials.
10. Endicott J, Andreasen N, Spitzer RL. *Family History Research Diagnostic Criteria.* New York, NY: Biometrics Research, New York State Psychiatric Institute; 1978.
11. Allgulander C. Psychoactive drug use in a general population sample, Sweden: correlates with perceived health, psychiatric diagnoses, and mortality in an automated record-linkage study. *Am J Public Health.* 1989;79:1006–1010.
12. Eaton WW, Anthony JC, Tepper S, Dryman A. Psychopathology and attrition in the Epidemiologic Catchment Area Study. *Am J Epidemiol.* 1992;135:1051–1059.
13. US Department of Health and Human Services. *National Health Interview Survey: 1989 (Computer File).* Hyattsville, Md: National Center for Health Statistics; 1992.
14. World Health Organization. *Composite International Diagnostic Interview (CIDI), Version 1.0.* Geneva, Switzerland: World Health Organization; 1990.
15. Robins LN, Wing J, Wittchen H-U, Helzer JE. The Composite International Diagnostic Interview: an epidemiologic instrument suitable for use in conjunction with different diagnostic systems and in different cultures. *Arch Gen Psychiatry.* 1988;45:1069–1077.
16. Wittchen H-U, Robins LN, Cottler LB, Sartorius N, Burke JD, Regier DA, and

Participants in the Multicentre WHO/ADAMHA Field Trials. Cross-cultural feasibility, reliability and sources of variance in the Composite International Diagnostic Interview (CIDI). *Br J Psychiatry.* 1991;159:645–653.

17. Cottler LB, Robins LN, Grant BF, Blaine J, Towle LH, Wittchen H-U, Sartorius N, and Participants in the WHO/ADAMHA Field Trials. The CIDI-core substance abuse and dependence questions: cross-cultural and nosological issues: *Br J Psychiatry.* 1991;159:653–658.

18. Semler G, von Cranach M, Wittchen H-U, eds. Comparison between the Composite International Diagnostic Interview and the Present State Examination. Report to the WHO/ADAMHA Task Force on Instrument Development; February 1987; Geneva, Switzerland.

19. Wacker HR, Battegay R, Mullejans R, Schlosser C. Using the CIDI-C in the general population. In: Stefanis CN, Rabavilas AD, Soldatos CR, eds. *Psychiatry: A World Perspective.* Amsterdam, the Netherlands: Elsevier Science Publishers; 1990:138–143.

20. Semler G, ed. *Reliabilitat und Validitat des Composite International Diagnostic Interview: Inaugural-Dissertation zur Erlangung des akademischen Grades eines Doktors der Philosophie.* Mannheim, Germany: Universitat Mannheim; 1989.

21. Spengler P, Wittchen H-U. Procedural validity of standardized symptom questions for the assessment of psychotic symptoms: a comparison of the CIDI with two clinical methods. *Compr Psychiatry.* 1989;29:309–322.

22. Janca A, Robins LN, Cottler LB, Early TS. Clinical observation of CIDI assessments: an analysis of the CIDI field trials—wave II at the St. Louis site. *Br J Psychiatry.* 1992;160:815–818.

23. Leitmeyer P, ed. *Zur Symptomerfassung mit dem standarisierten Interview CICI-C in der Allgemeinpraxis: Inaugural Dissertation zur Erlangung des medizinischen Doktorgrades fur klinische Medizin.* Mannheim, Germany: Universitat Mannheim; 1990.

24. Farmer AE, Katz R, McGuffin P, Bebbington P. A comparison between the Present State Examination and the Composite International Diagnostic Interview. *Arch Gen Psychiatry.* 1987;44:1064–1068.

25. Farmer AE, Jenkins PL, Katz R, Ryder L. Comparison of CATEGO-derived *ICD-8* and *DSM-III* classifications using the Composite International Diagnostic Interview in severely ill subjects. *Br J Psychiatry.* 1991;158:177–182.

26. Wittchen H-U, Burke JD, Semler G, Pfister H. Recall and dating of psychiatric symptoms: test-retest reliability of time-related symptom questions in a standardized psychiatric interview. *Arch Gen Psychiatry.* 1989;46:437–443.

27. Anthony JC, Folstein M, Romanoski AJ, von Korff MR, Nestadt GR, Chahal R, Merchant A, Brown CH, Shapiro S, Kramer M, Gruenberg EM. Comparison of the lay Diagnostic Interview Schedule and a standardized psychiatric diagnosis: experience in eastern Baltimore. *Arch Gen Psychiatry.* 1985;42:667–675.

28. Helzer JE, Robins LN, McEvoy LT, Spitznagel E. A comparison of clinical and Diagnostic Interview Schedule diagnoses. *Arch Gen Psychiatry.* 1985;42:657–666.

29. Spitzer RL, Williams JBW, Gibbon M, First MB. The structured clinical interview for *DSM-III-R* (SCID), I: history, rationale, and description. *Arch Gen Psychiatry.* 1992;49:624–629.

30. Williams JBW, Gibbon M, First MB, Spitzer RL, Davies M, Borus J, Howes MJ, Kane J, Harrison GP Jr, Rounsaville B, Wittchen H-U. The structured clinical interview for *DSM-III-R* (SCID), II: multisite test-retest reliability. *Arch Gen Psychiatry.* 1992;49:630–636.

31. Woodruff RS, Causey BD. Computerized method for approximating the variance of a complicated estimate. *J Am Stat Assoc.* 1976;71:315–321.

32. University of Michigan. *OSIRIS VII.* Ann Arbor, Mich: Institute for Social Research, The University of Michigan; 1981.

33. Kish L, Frankel MR. Balanced repeated replications for standard errors. *J Am Stat Assoc.* 1970;65:1071–1094.

34. Koch GG, Leneshow S. An application of multivariate analysis to complex sample survey data. *J Am Stat Assoc.* 1972;67:780–782.

35. SAS Institute. *SAS 6.03.* Cary, NC: SAS Institute; 1988.

36. Robins LN, Regier DA, eds. *Psychiatric Disorders in America: The Epidemiologic Catchment Area Study.* New York, NY: Free Press; 1991.

37. Canino GJ, Bird HR, Shrout PE, Rubio-Stipec M, Bravo M, Martinez R, Sesman M, Guevara L. The prevalence of specific psychiatric disorders in Puerto Rico. *Arch Gen Psychiatry.* 1987;44:727–735.

38. Hwu, H-G, Yeh EK, Chang LY. Prevalence of psychiatric disorders in Taiwan defined by the Chinese Diagnostic Interview Schedule. *Acta Psychiatr Scand.* 1989;79:136–147.

39. Wells JE, Bushnell JA, Hornblow AR, Joyce PR, Oakley-Browne MA. Christchurch Psychiatric Epidemiology Study, I: methodology and lifetime prevalence for specific psychiatric disorders. *Aust N Z J Psychiatry.* 1989;23:315–326.

40. Wittchen H-U, Essau CA, von Zerssen D, Krieg JC, Zaudig M. Lifetime and six-month prevalence of mental disorders in the Munich follow-up study. *Eur Arch Psychiatry Clin Neurosci.* 1992;241:247–258.

41. Keith SJ, Regier DA, Rae DS. Schizophrenic disorders. In: Regier DA, Robins LN, eds. *Psychiatric Disorders in America: The Epidemiologic Catchment Area Study.* New York, NY: Free Press; 1991:33–52.

42. Gurin G, Veroff J, Feld SC. *Americans View Their Mental Health.* New York, NY: Basic Books Inc Publishers; 1960.

43. Veroff J, Kulka RA, Douvan E. *Mental Health in America: Patterns of Help-Seeking From 1957 to 1976.* New York, NY: Basic Books Inc Publishers; 1981.

44. Shapiro S, Skinner EA, Kessler LG, von Korff M, German PS, Tischler GL, Leaf PJ, Benham L, Cottler L, Regier DA. Utilization of health and mental health services: three Epidemiological Catchment Area sites. *Arch Gen Psychiatry.* 1984;41:971–978.

45. Cross-National Collaborative Group. The changing rate of major depression. *JAMA,* 1992;268:3098–3105.

46. Weissman MM, Bruce ML, Leaf PJ, Florio LP, Holzer C III. Affective disorders. In: Robins LN, Regier DA, eds. *Psychiatric Disorders in America: The Epidemiologic Catchment Area Study.* New York, NY: Free Press: 1991:53–80.

47. Helzer JE, Burnam A, McEvoy LT. Alcohol abuse and dependence. In: Robins LN, Regier DA, eds. *Psychiatric Disorders in America: The Epidemiologic Catchment Area Study.* New York, NY: Free Press; 1991:81–115.

48. Anthony JC, Helzer JE. Syndromes of drug abuse and dependence. In: Robins LN, Regier DA, eds. *Psychiatric Disorders in America: The Epidemiologic Catchment Area Study.* New York, NY: Free Press; 1991:116–154.

49. Horwath E, Johnson J, Hornig CD. Epidemiology of panic disorder in African-Americans. *Am J Psychiatry.* 1993;150:465–469.

50. Eaton WW, Dryman A, Weissman MM. Panic and phobia. In: Robins LN, Regier DA, eds. *Psychiatric Disorders in America: The Epidemiologic Catchment Area Study.* New York, NY: Free Press; 1991:155–179.

51. Bruce ML, Takeuchi DT, Leaf PJ. Poverty and psychiatric status: longitudinal evidence from the New Haven Epidemiologic Catchment Area Study. *Arch Gen Psychiatry.* 1991;48:470–474.

52. Holzer CE, Shea B, Swanson JW, Leaf PJ, Myers JK, George L, Weissman MM, Bednarski P. The increased risk for specific psychiatric disorders among persons of low socioeconomic status. *Am J Psychiatry.* 1986;6:259–271.

53. Stansfeld SA, Marmot MG. Social class and minor psychiatric disorder in British civil servants: a validated screening survey using the General Health Questionnaire. *Psychol Med.* 1992;22:739–749.

54. Myers JK. Social factors related to psychiatric disorders. *Soc Psychiatry Psychiatr Epidemiol.* 1984;19:53–61.

55. Robins LN, Helzer JE, Weissman MM, Orvaschel H, Gruenberg E, Burke JD Jr, Regier DA. Lifetime prevalence of specific psychiatric disorders in three sites. *Arch Gen Psychiatry*. 1984;41:949–958.

56. Boyd JH, Weissman MM. Epidemiology of affective disorders: a reexamination and future directions. *Arch Gen Psychiatry* 1981;38:1039–1046.

57. Kendler KS, Neale MC, Kessler RC, Heath AC, Eaves LJ. A population-based twin study of major depression in women. *Arch Gen Psychiatry*. 1992;49:257–266.

58. Weissman MM, Myers JK, Harding PS. Psychiatric disorders in a U.S. urban community: 1975–1976. *Am J Psychiatry* 1978;135:459–462.

59. Helzer JE, Pryzbeck TR. The co-occurrence of alcoholism with other psychiatric disorders in the general population and its impact on treatment. *J Stud Alcohol*. 1988;49:219–224.

60. Regier DA, Farmer ME, Rae DS, Locke BZ, Keith SJ, Judd LL, Goodwin FK. Comorbidity of mental disorders with alcohol and other drug abuse: results from the Epidemiologic Catchment Area (ECA) Study. *JAMA*. 1990;264:2511–2518.

61. Bukstein OG, Brent DA, Kaminer Y. Comorbidity of substance abuse and other psychiatric disorders in adolescents. *Am J Psychiatry*. 1989;146:1131–1141.

62. Hesselbrock MN, Meyer RE, Keener JJ. Psychopathology in hospitalized alcoholics. *Arch Gen Psychiatry*. 1985;42:1050–1055.

63. Kessler RC, McGonagle KA, Carnelley KB, Nelson CB, Farmer MA, Regier DA. Comorbidity of mental disorders and substance use disorders: a review and agenda for future research. In: Leaf P, ed. *Research in Community and Mental Health*. Greenwich, Conn: JAI Press Inc. In press.

64. Marlatt GA, Gordon JR. Determinants of relapse: implications for the maintenance of behavioral change. In: Davidson P, Davidson S, eds. *Behavioral Medicine: Changing Health and Lifestyles*. New York, NY: Brunner/Mazel Inc; 1980.

65. Vaillant GE. Natural history of male psychological health VIII: antecedents of alcoholism and 'orality'. *Am J Psychiatry*. 1980;137:181–186.

66. Rosenblatt PC. *Farming Is in Our Blood: Farm Families in Economic Crisis*. Ames: Iowa State University Press; 1990.

Article Review Form at end of book.

What is the most prevalent disorder in the United States? Include the demographic correlates in your response.

Common Mental Disorders and Disability Across Cultures:

Results from the WHO Collaborative Study on Psychological Problems in General Health Care

Johan Ormel, Ph.D.;
Michael VonKorff, Sc.D.;
T. Bedirhan Ustun, M.D., Ph.D.;
Stefano Pini, M.D.;
Ailsa Korten, B.Sc.;
and Tineke Oldehinkel, M.Sc.

Objective.—To examine the impact of common mental illness on functional disability and the cross-cultural consistency of this relationship while controlling for physical illness. A secondary objective was to determine the level of disability associated with specific psychiatric disorders.

Design.—A cross-sectional sample selected by two-stage sampling.

Setting.—Primary health care facilities in 14 countries covering most major cultures and languages.

Patients.—A total of 25,916 consecutive attenders of these facilities were screened for psychopathology using the General Health Questionnaire (96% response).

Screened patients were sampled from the General Health Questionnaire score strata for the second-stage Composite International Diagnostic Interview administered to 5447 patients (62% response).

Main Outcome Measures.—Patient-reported physical disability, number of disability days, and interviewer-rated occupational role functioning.

Results.—After controlling for physical disease severity, psychopathology was consistently associated with increased disability. Physical disease severity was an independent, although weaker, contributor to disability. A dose-response relationship was found between severity of mental illness and disability. Disability was most prominent among patients with major depression, panic disorder, generalized anxiety, and neurasthenia; disorder-specific differences were modest after controlling for psychiatric comorbidity. Results were consistent across disability measures and across centers.

Conclusions.—The consistent relationship of psychopathology and disability indicates the compelling personal and socioeconomic impact of common mental illnesses across cultures. This suggests the importance of impairments of higher-order human capacities (eg, emotion, motivation, and cognition) as determinants of functional disability.
(*JAMA*. 1994;272:1741–1748)

Recent epidemiologic studies in community, primary care, and outpatient settings have reported an association of depression and anxiety with functional disability.[1–15] Depressed and anxious patients show higher levels of disability relative to patients without significant psychiatric symptoms. The level of disability among patients with depression appears similar or elevated compared with the disability found among patients with chronic medical illnesses.[1] This cross-sectional association between psychopathology and disability holds longitudinally. Two studies in primary care settings, by VonKorff et al.[3]

"Common Mental Disorders and Disability Across Cultures: Results from the WHO Collaborative Study on Psychological Problems in General Health Care," by Johan Ormel, Michael VonKorff, T. Bedirhan Ustun, Stefano Pini, Ailsa Korten, and Tineke Oldehinkel, *JAMA*, 272 (22), December 14, 1994, pp. 1741–1748.

and Ormel et al.[15] reported that improvement in psychiatric symptoms was associated with corresponding changes in disability, while patients whose symptoms ran a chronic course experienced chronic disability. Disability associated with affective illness may have a considerable impact on personal well-being, social relationships, and work productivity,[16] owing to its high prevalence[17-23] and the recurrent or chronic course of depressive and anxiety disorders.[18,24-30]

Because all studies to date have been carried out in western European and North American communities and health care centers, it is unknown whether the psychopathology-disability association is culture specific. Cross-cultural invariance of the disabling effects of depression and anxiety is not self-evident. For example, the World Health Organization (WHO) International Pilot Study on Schizophrenia found that schizophrenia ran a more favorable and less disabling course in developing countries.[31-33]

Disability is typically defined in the context of the triad of impairment, personal disability, and role handicap as "any restriction or lack of capacity to perform an activity in a manner or within a range considered normal for a human being."[34] In the current study, we focused on disability as indicated by (1) limitations in physical activities that ranged from vigorous to basic self-care, (2) occupational role limitations (a restriction or lack of capacity to perform activities and/or manifest behaviors as expected in a person's occupational role), and (3) the number of days the patient was unable to carry out his or her usual daily activities. We did not seek a comprehensive assessment of all aspects of functioning[35] but focused on aspects that are well defined and relevant from a health-economic and a quality-of-life perspective.

The objective was to examine among primary care patients (1) the relationship of psychiatric status with disability in a wide variety of cultural settings; (2) the contribution of specific psychiatric disorders as defined by the *International Statistical Classification of Diseases, 10th Revision (ICD-10)* and the *Diagnostic and Statistical Manual of Mental Disorders, Revised Third Edition (DSM-III-R)* to

disability; and (3) whether the association of psychopathology and disability was explained by global severity of physical disease. We will also discuss to what extent the disability associated with psychiatric disorder may be confounded by impairment criteria embedded in the diagnostic interview and in the diagnostic algorithms.

The data were collected within the framework of the WHO Collaborative Study on Psychological Problems in General Health Care.[36] The purpose of this study was to investigate the form, frequency, course, and outcome of psychological problems commonly seen in primary care settings in 15 different sites around the world. Participating centers include Ankara, Turkey; Athens, Greece; Bangalore, India; Berlin, Germany; Groningen, the Netherlands; Ibadan, Nigeria; Mainz, Germany; Manchester, England; Nagasaki, Japan; Paris, France; Rio de Janeiro, Brazil; Santiago, Chile; Seattle, Wash; Shanghai, China; and Verona, Italy.

Methods

The design and methods are described elsewhere.[36,37] Therefore, only essential information is presented herein.

Design and Patient Selection

The 15 centers selected represent a broad variation in socioeconomic development, ecology, and culture, although most are based in large cities. Main requirements for selection were (1) available capacity (manpower and infrastructure) to ensure full adherence to sampling protocol, training of personnel, administration of instruments, and monitoring quality of data collection; (2) experience in collaboration with the WHO in one of the many areas WHO is active; (3) experience with research in primary care settings; (3) access to a primary care patient population; (4) access to medical records of the primary care patients; and (5) ethical approval to implement the study from relevant bodies. Secondary selection criteria and a full description of the centers and sites are provided elsewhere.[36]

At each of the 15 participating centers, 1300 to 2800 consecutive at-

tenders, aged 15 to 65 years, of primary health care facilities were screened using the 12-item General Health Questionnaire (GHQ-12)[38] and rated by the physician seeing the patient using an encounter form. A total of 25 916 screens were completed (response rate, 96%; range, 91% to 99%). The GHQ-12 was chosen as the screening mechanism because (1) it is brief, (2) it has been shown to be associated with mental disorders in primary health care settings, (3) it has acceptable levels of sensitivity and specificity for case detection, and (4) it has been successfully used in diverse cultural settings. The population screened was stratified into low GHQ (60%), medium GHQ (20%), and high GHQ (20%) scorers. Eligible patients for second-stage assessments included all high GHQ scorers, a one of three random sample from the medium GHQ scorers, and a one of 10 random sample from the low GHQ scorers. A total of 5447 patients of the eligible 8729 completed the structured interview and self-report instruments in the second stage (response rate, 62%). Second-stage nonresponse rates differed significantly across centers and were associated with GHQ score. Information regarding the sampling plan and center-specific response rates are provided elsewhere.[36,37]

Instruments

The physician seeing the patient at index consult (stage 1) was asked to complete an encounter form for each patient stating the reason for contact; level of overall health (excellent, very good, good, fair, or poor); physical health status (completely healthy, some symptoms but subclinical, mildly ill, moderately ill, or severely ill); psychological health status (completely normal, subclinical, mild case, moderate case, or severe case); and treatment prescribed (if given). The physical and mental health ratings were done on the basis of all information available to the physician. The ratings on these two dimensions were also global, ie, the severity of individual disorders was not assessed but the global physical (or mental) health status was assessed, taking into account all physical (or mental) disorders present. The physicians completing the form were all MDs and considered primary care physicians in their respective countries, although medical qualifications differed between centers. Some held a specialization in family medicine (eg, Seattle and Groningen), others in internal medicine (eg, Athens, Rio de Janeiro, and Nagasaki, but most had only completed their regular basic MD training. In general, they had not received additional training in psychiatry beyond their regular medical training. The purpose of the encounter form was explained carefully to them and discussed and practiced in a joint session with the investigators. The reliability of the physician ratings was not established.

During the second-stage interview, a series of questions were asked to establish the presence of seven chronic medical conditions, including high blood pressure (17%), diabetes (5%), arthritis (13%), heart disease (10%), bronchitis/emphysema (10%), stomach disorder (15%), and common parasitic diseases (2%). In addition, a stem question was asked regarding whether other serious physical diseases were present. If so, they were recorded by the interviewer. Diseases frequently mentioned were stroke, asthma, thyroid disorder, human immunodeficiency virus, kidney disease, bladder disease, tuberculosis, colitis, vasculitis, cancer, epilepsy, anemia, and malnutrition. Prevalence of these ranged from 0.2% to 2.5%. There were significant differences across centers in the number of chronic medical diseases (Poisson regression, $P<.001$).

Psychopathology was assessed with the WHO primary care version of the Composite International Diagnostic Interview (CIDI).[39] In this version, the sections on anxiety, depression, somatization, and neurasthenia were modified to also provide assessment of the clinical state of the respondent in the month preceding the interview. Both *ICD-10* and *DSM-III-R* psychiatric diagnoses were assigned using the CIDI algorithms.

Disability was measured with the Brief Disability Questionnaire (BDQ), the Occupational Role section of the Social Disability Schedule (SDS),[40] and a question on the number of days in the past month the subject had not been able to carry out his or her usual activities. The BDQ is an eight-item self-report scale of

largely physical disability[41] adapted from items in the Medical Outcomes Study Short-Form General Health Survey.[42] The BDQ asked subjects whether they were limited because of health problems during the last month in (1) the kinds or amount of vigorous activities they could do, like lifting heavy objects, running, or sports; (2) the kinds or amount of moderate activities they could do, like moving a table or carrying groceries or goods; (3) climbing stairs or walking uphill; (4) bending, lifting, or stooping; (5) walking long distances (>1 mile); (6) eating, dressing, bathing, or using the toilet; (7) whether they had cut down or stopped any activity they used to do, such as hobbies; and (8) whether they had been unable to do things that the family expected as part of daily routine. Each item was rated as no, not at all; yes, sometimes or a little; and yes, moderately or definitely. The BDQ items constitute a nonparametric, hierarchical, one-dimensional scale with similar measurement properties across the centers. The reliability of this scale as indicated by the internal consistency statistic, Cronbach's α, ranged from 0.84 to 0.95 across centers, with a pooled estimate of 0.88.[41]

The SDS is a semistructured interview on role functioning. It allows culture-specific expectations to be taken into account. The criteria against which performance was evaluated by the interviewer were the expectations prevailing in the local community.[40] Within the framework of the SDS, disability is conceptualized as a restriction or lack of capacity to perform activities as expected in well-defined social roles. The restriction or lack of capacity is inferred from behavioral deviations from norms and expectations as these prevail within the context of the relevant reference group, typically the local community. The occupational role concerns daily activities at work (gainful employment, volunteer work, and housekeeping), activities directed at securing a job (study and job searching), and structuring of daily activities in case of retirement. Interviewer ratings range from 0 (no disability) through 1 (mild disability) and 2 (moderate disability) to 3 (severe disability). For each role, these severity categories have been defined

in behavioral terms. For instance, in the occupational role for people in gainful employment, three dimensions are distinguished: daily routine, performance, and contacts with others at work. Mild, moderate, and severe disability in the first two dimensions are defined as follows: Daily routine, mild disability: some difficulties in adjusting to daily routine; absence for up to 25% of the time. Daily routine, moderate disability: major difficulties in adjusting to daily routine; absence for 25% to 75% of the time. Daily routine, severe disability: there is hardly any adjustment to daily routine; absence for more than 75% of the expected time. Performance, mild disability: performance falls short of expectations; complaints have been expressed; superiors may have discussed the reduced performance with the person but no consequences are imminent. Performance, moderate disability: performance is considered poor; regardless of the individual's efforts, adequacy and/or efficiency is lacking; dismissal or removal from the job may be imminent. Performance, severe disability: performance is very poor; regardless of the individual's efforts, adequacy and/or efficiency is almost completely or totally absent; dismissal has already occurred or is nearly unavoidable. Interviewer-observer reliability of the SDS occupational role has been shown to be good in a variety of populations (Cohen's κ ranged from 0.63 to 0.93).[40]

Considerations of cross-cultural applicability were important in the selection of instruments. Most instruments had been used extensively in prior cross-national research. All instruments were translated by a group of bilingual experts, checked by local professional staff, and back-translated into English. These translations were checked by WHO staff on linguistic equivalence with the original texts. All procedures were pretested at each site, and necessary modifications were made. Reliability studies were carried out at each center.

The interviews were administered by well-trained local personnel who typically had experience with psychiatric patients. The interviewers included social workers, clinical psychologists, senior medical students, and, in some centers, psychiatrists (in training). Interviewer mix varied across centers. It should be stressed that the CIDI and BDQ are fully standardized instruments and therefore (largely) insensitive to who administers the instrument provided he or she is well trained in its use. This does not apply to the SDS, which is less structured to allow local norms and expectations to be taken into account.

Measures

Psychiatric Status.—The CIDI data were used to assign *ICD-10* and *DSM-III-R* psychiatric diagnoses according to well-defined computerized diagnostic algorithms. In this article we only present *ICD* diagnoses for reasons of economy, the similarity in results for comparable *DSM-III-R* diagnoses (data available on request), and because the study was an international study organized by the WHO. The following *ICD-10* disorders were included in the current analyses: current depression (F32/33), agoraphobia (F40; with and without panic), panic disorder (F41.0), generalized anxiety disorder (F41.1), hypochondriasis (F45.2), neurasthenia (F48.0), somatization disorder (F45.0), and alcohol dependence (F10.1/2). Neurasthenia refers to persistent, unusual, and distressing mental or physical fatigue (or both) after performing or attempting to perform everyday tasks that do not require much effort. Patients with at least one of these disorders were defined as a definite psychiatric case. Subthreshold versions of these disorders were defined as having all but one or two of the symptoms needed for the full diagnosis.[36] Symptomatic patients were defined as patients without a (subthreshold) disorder but with some symptoms in at least two of the following areas: depression, anxiety, somatization, and alcohol abuse.[36] Patients were considered psychiatrically well if they were not symptomatic or if they did not have a (subthreshold) disorder. Since the categories of subthreshold and symptomatic do not represent a clear-cut severity difference, the two were usually combined. For all psychiatric disorders, prevalence rates differed significantly across centers (logistic regression, *P*<.001).

Disability.—Three indicators were used: (1) interviewer-rated SDS disability in the occupational role

(none, 56%; mild, 27%; moderate, 14%; and severe, 4%); (2) the total score of the BDQ self-report physical disability (mean, 3.0) and a recoded version (0 to 2=none, 59%; 3 to 4=mild, 14%; 5 to 9=moderate, 19%; and 10 to 16=severe, 7%); and (3) the number of disability days in the past month (mean, 3.2 days). The three indicators correlated approximately .50 (Pearson correlation coefficient).

Nonpsychiatric Medical Illness.—Two measures were used: (1) the physician rating on the severity of physical health status (healthy, 18%; symptoms but not ill, 30%; mild, 36%; moderate, 14%; and severe, 2%); and (2) the reported number of chronic diseases (none, 49%; one, 30%; two, 14%; and three or more, 7%). Rates differed significantly across centers (Poisson regression, *P*<.001).

Analysis

All prevalence and proportions presented have been weighted back to represent the population screened with the GHQ, ie, the population of consecutive attenders.[36] This was done for various reasons: the nonproportionally stratified sampling scheme for the second stage; and the response rate among those sampled for the second-stage interview varied from one GHQ stratum to another, between the sexes, and between centers. For each of the six GHQ-by-sex strata within each center (S_i; $_i$=stratum 1, 2, 3, 4, 5, or 6), the weight was estimated by the inverse of the response rate in S_i times the inverse of the probability of selection for the second-stage interview in S_i times the proportion interviewed in the center, yielding 90 weights (six GHQ-sex strata times 15 centers).

Two series of logistic regression analyses were performed using the SPSS logistic regression module. The first series controlled for sociodemographic and stratification variables (ie, sex, age, years of schooling, GHQ stratum, and sex by GHQ stratum) by entering those variables as covariates. The second series controlled for the sociodemographic variables only. This series was done because controlling for GHQ stratum in the first series results in underestimation of the impact of psychiatric illness on disability since GHQ stratum is strongly

associated with psychiatric status. We only present the conservative results of the first series unless indicated otherwise.

Results

Prevalence and Psychiatric Comorbidity

Pooled across centers, 21% of the consecutive attenders had one or more of the eight selected current definite *ICD* psychiatric disorders listed in Table 1 (any disorder). The highest prevalence rates for any disorder were found in Santiago (53%) and Rio de Janeiro (34%), and the lowest rates were in Shanghai (8%). Rates in the other centers ranged from 9% to 28%. Table 1 presents the pooled prevalence of eight specific current psychiatric disorders and the proportion of patients with psychiatric comorbidity for each diagnosis. In most centers, the disorders with relatively high prevalences were depressive episode, generalized anxiety disorder, and neurasthenia. For all psychiatric disorders, rates varied substantially across centers, even when the Santiago center was not taken into account. For instance, the prevalence of current depressive episode ranged from 3.6% in the three centers with the lowest prevalences (Nagasaki, 2.6%; Shanghai, 4.0%; and Ibadan, 4.2%) to 15.2% for the three centers with the highest prevalences (Groningen, 15.9%; Paris, 13.8%; and Rio de Janeiro, 15.9%). For current panic disorder, these upper and lower rates were 0.2% and 2.3%, and for alcohol dependence, they were 0.6% and 5.6%.

Psychiatric comorbidity, defined as the copresence of another current *ICD-10* psychiatric disorder, was common: 13.0% had one, 5.4% had two, and 2.7% had three or more. All specific psychiatric disorders had comorbidity rates higher than 50% except alcohol dependence (Table 1).

Disability by Psychiatric Status

At each center, disability levels were markedly increased among persons with definite psychiatric disorder (Table 2). In each center and for each disability measure, the percentages indicate a strongly increased level of disability among psychiatric cases and a moderately increased level among subthreshold-symptomatic cases. Across the participating centers, moderate to severe disability was typically found in four to five times as many patients with a definite psychiatric disorder compared with psychiatrically well patients.

Disability by Diagnosis

The upper portion of Table 3 presents data pooled across centers on the association of eight psychiatric disorders with disability. For all diagnostic categories, the proportion of patients with moderate or severe disability was approximately three to five times higher than the proportion among psychiatrically well patients. This pattern was consistent across all three measures of disability. For each

 Table 1 Prevalence of Current *ICD-10* Diagnoses and Proportion with Psychiatric Comorbidity, Pooled across Centers (All Patients, Weighted Estimates)*

Current Definite ICD-10 Diagnosis	Prevalence, %	Psychiatric Comorbidity, %	No. of Cases, Unweighted
Any *ICD* diagnosis†	21.1	39	1955
ICD depressive episode	10.5	62	1174
ICD panic disorder	1.1	71	116
ICD agoraphobia	1.5	67	159
ICD neurasthenia	5.5	71	591
ICD hypochondriasis	0.8	58	66
ICD generalized anxiety	7.9	54	705
ICD alcohol dependence	2.7	43	206
ICD somatization disorder	2.8	61	232

*ICD-10 indicates *International Statistical Classification of Diseases, 10th Revision.*

†"Any" refers to the diagnoses listed below.

Table 2 Disability by Current Psychiatric *ICD-10* Status per Center (Weighted Estimates)*

Center	Moderate or Severe Occupational Role Dysfunction, % Psychiatric Status*			Moderate or Severe Self-reported Physical Disability, % Psychiatric Status*			Mean No. of Disability Days Psychiatric Status*			Observed, n
	Well	Sub	Definite	Well	Sub	Definite	Well	Sub	Definite	
Ankara, Turkey	0	2	27	1	16	43	0.5	2.1	6.2	400
Athens, Greece	0	11	31	5	24	44	0.9	2.4	6.4	196
Bangalore, India	2	18	45	7	41	75	1.4	7.4	11.9	398
Berlin, Germany	8	15	34	14	21	36	2.3	3.0	3.9	400
Groningen, the Netherlands	4	28	59	7	33	52	2.8	3.5	9.5	340
Ibadan, Nigeria	18	37	50	4	22	53	2.5	7.5	11.9	269
Mainz, Germany	18	20	33	17	23	35	2.9	5.3	5.2	400
Manchester, England	10	29	55	20	41	64	3.0	4.1	7.2	428
Nagasaki, Japan	6	20	25	12	33	36	1.6	3.5	6.7	336
Paris, France	4	9	33	8	19	38	1.7	1.6	4.0	405
Rio de Janeiro, Brazil	1	8	26	7	26	59	0.4	2.8	7.4	393
Santiago, Chile	0	15	25	0	17	35	0.3	1.5	1.0	274
Seattle, Wash	1	15	13	24	27	45	1.6	3.6	4.2	373
Shanghai, China	8	22	55	11	32	60	0.9	1.6	4.4	576
Verona, Italy	10	5	15	25	29	46	1.2	2.1	2.5	259
All centers	7	16	35	12	26	48	1.7	3.0	5.9	5447

*Three categories of psychiatric status are distinguished: "Well" includes psychiatrically well patients; "Sub," subthreshold and symptomatic patents; and "Definite," patients with at least one of the following *International Statistical Classification of Diseases, 10th Revision (ICD-10)* disorders: current depression (F32/33), dysthymia (F34), agoraphobia (F40; with and without panic), panic disorder (F41.0), generalized anxiety disorder (F41.1), hypochondriasis (F45.2), neurasthenia (F48.0), somatization disorder (F45.0), or alcohol dependence (F10.1/2).

Table 3 Prevalence, Psychiatric Comorbidity, and Disability by Current *ICD-10* Diagnosis, Pooled across Centers (Weighted Estimates)*

	Moderate or Severe, %		Mean No. of Disability Days in Past Month	No. of Cases, Unweighted
	Occupational Role Dysfunction	Self-reported Physical Disability		
Current ICD-10 diagnosis, all patients				
Psychiatrically well patients†	7	12	1.7	1114
ICD depressive episode	48	58	7.7	1174
ICD panic disorder	58	55	10.0	116
ICD agoraphobia	41	60	7.3	159
ICD neurasthenia	53	61	8.5	591
ICD hypochondriasis	39	44	4.7	66
ICD generalized anxiety	38	59	6.3	705
ICD alcohol dependence	32	31	5.1	206
ICD somatization disorder	38	58	6.3	232
Current ICD-10 diagnosis, patients with ≥ 2 psychiatric disorders are excluded				
Psychiatrically well patients†	7	12	1.7	1114
ICD depressive episode	39	46	6.1	438
ICD panic disorder	53	34	6.7	22
ICD agoraphobia	14	47	2.3	38
ICD neurasthenia	37	48	6.7	130
ICD hypochondriasis	42	45	6.3	25
ICD generalized anxiety	26	53	4.4	272
ICD alcohol dependence	20	18	4.2	83
ICD somatization disorder	21	42	2.6	53

*ICD-10 indicates *International Statistical Classification of Diseases, 10th Revision.*

†Well patients do not include patients with a definite or a subthreshold disorder or symptomatic patients.

of the most prevalent disorders (depression, generalized anxiety, and neurasthenia), we examined the disorder-specific robustness across centers of the psychiatric disorder-disability relationship. Although the strength of the association varied across centers, disability was consistently increased in patients with the specific psychiatric disorder relative to psychiatrically well patients (data not shown, available on request).

Controlling for Psychiatric Comorbidity

Because of the high level of psychiatric comorbidity, the disorder-specific disability estimates in the upper portion of Table 3 may not represent the disability associated with the pure form of a specific disorder. For example, depressed patients could show higher disability levels because psychiatric comorbidity was more prevalent or consisted of a different mix among depressed patients than among patients with an anxiety disorder. Therefore, we also examined disability levels among patients with only one psychiatric disorder, thus excluding those with psychiatric comorbidity. The disability levels associated with the pure form of each disorder are shown in the lower portion of Table 3. Compared with the upper portion of Table 3, they suggest that part of the disability is due to psychiatric comorbidity. For all disability measures, disability levels dropped after excluding patients with psychiatric comorbidity, although they still are substantially increased compared with the level of disability in psychiatrically well patients. In particular, the association of agoraphobia and somatization with disability appeared to be due to other co-occurring psychiatric disorders.

Considering all three indicators of disability, the psychiatric disorders with the strongest association with disability appeared to be depression, panic disorder, generalized anxiety, and neurasthenia. Except for panic disorder, these were also the most prevalent disorders among primary care patients.

Table 4

Results for Logistic Regression of Disability on Psychiatric Status, Controlling for Physical Health Status (All Patients)*

Psychiatric Status	No. of Cases, Unweighted	Odds Ratio (95% Confidence Interval)		
		Occupational Role Dysfunction	Self-reported Physical Disability	No. of Disability Days
Disorder absent, reference category	1046	. . .	. . .	. . .
Symptomatic or subthreshold psychiatric disorder	2051	2.1 (1.7–2.8)	1.7 (1.4–2.1)	1.5 (1.3–1.8)
One definite psychiatric disorder	986	4.3 (3.3–5.6)	3.1 (2.5–3.9)	2.6 (2.1–3.2)
≥2 definite psychiatric disorders	845	8.2 (6.2–10.7)	5.6 (4.5–7.1)	3.5 (2.8–4.4)

*We controlled for sex, age, years of education, General Health Questionnaire (GHQ) stratum, sex by GHQ stratum, number of chronic medical diseases, and physical-rated physical health status. Occupational role and physical disability were dichotomized as none and mild vs moderate and severe; and number of disability days, as none vs 1 or more. Psychiatric status consisted of four categories; well, subthreshold or symptomatic disorder, one definite *International Statistical Classification of Diseases, 10th Revision (ICD-10)* psychiatric disorder, and two or more definite ICD-10 psychiatric disorders.

Controlling for Nonpsychiatric Medical Disease

The increased disability among patients with a psychiatric disorder may be due to an increased level of co-occurrence of nonpsychiatric medical disease. Two measures of physical disease status, physician-rated physical health status and subject-reported number of chronic medical conditions, were each weakly correlated (pooled Pearson r) with occupational role dysfunction (.13 and .11), self-reported physical disability (.19 and .23), and number of disability days (.11 and .05). In comparison, the correlations of psychiatric status with these three disability indicators were .39, .36, and .26, respectively. Kendall's tau-β coefficients were similar.

The relationship between psychiatric status and disability level was maintained when severity of physical disease and the number of chronic conditions were controlled for by entering those as covariates in the multivariate logistic regression of disability on psychiatric status (Table 4). For these analyses, patients with a psychiatric disorder were further subdivided into those with one disorder vs those with two or more disorders. The impact of psychiatric illness on disability remained substantial even with physical health status controlled. For instance, patients with two or more psychiatric disorders had an 8.2-fold

higher risk of moderate or severe occupational role dysfunction than psychiatrically well patients. The consistent increase in the odds ratio with increasing severity of psychiatric illness further suggests a strong dose-response relationship between severity of psychiatric illness and disability. The dose-response relationship became even more pronounced when we did not control for the stratification variable GHQ stratum (but continued controlling for physical health status indicators; data not shown; odds ratios typically increased by 30%).

Table 5 presents the results of stratified multivariate logistic regression, ie, at each level of physician-rated physical health status and the number of chronic medical conditions. The odds ratios clearly show the robustness of the dose-response relationship between severity of psychiatric illness and disability.

Comment

The results of this multicenter, cross-national study support five important conclusions. First, in major cultures around the world, psychiatric disorder in primary care is common and associated with substantial levels of disability. Irrespective of the specific psychiatric disorder and controlling for socio-demographic characteristics and severity of co-occurring medical illness, disability levels were increased among patients with psychiatric illnesses. Second,

the differences in associated disability between diagnostic categories were modest, but disability was most strongly related to major depression, panic disorder, generalized anxiety, and neurasthenia, all prevalent illnesses except panic disorder. Third, part of the disability was due to psychiatric comorbidity, a common phenomenon among psychiatrically ill primary care attenders. Fourth, physical health status did not explain the relationship between psychopathology and disability. Nonpsychiatric medical morbidity was an independent, although weaker, contributor. Fifth, results were consistent across the disability measures used. The interviewer-rated culturally adaptive rating of disability in the occupational role showed results similar to those obtained with self-report measures of limitations in physical activities and disability days.

The consistency of the findings on the relationship of psychopathology and disability across centers was striking, considering the substantial differences in prevalence rates, characteristics of the primary health care settings, and cultural and socioeconomic environment.[36,43] This cross-cultural consistency, of course, does not imply that center-specific factors were unimportant. Part of the disability observed was associated with nonmeasured center-associated factors (data not shown).

Current psychopathology among consecutive attenders of primary care facilities was common in

Table 5 Results for Logistic Regression of Disability on Psychiatric Status*

Psychiatric Status	No. of Cases, Unweighted	Odds Ratio (95% Confidence Interval)		
		Occupational Role Dysfunction	Self-reported Physical Disability	No. of Disability Days
No physical illness†				
Disorder absent, reference category	248	...	...	...
Symptomatic or subthreshold psychiatric disorder	350	2.5 (1.2-5.0)	1.3 (0.9-2.1)	1.5 (1.0-2.3)
One definite psychiatric disorder	137	8.9 (4.2-18.8)	2.3 (1.4-4.1)	2.6 (1.6-4.4)
≥2 definite psychiatric disorders	120	16.5 (7.7-35.3)	4.1 (2.3-7.2)	6.1 (3.5-10.6)
Mild physical illness†				
Disorder absent, reference category	703	...	...	...
Symptomatic or subthreshold psychiatric disorder	1440	2.1 (1.6-3.1)	1.9 (1.5-2.5)	1.5 (1.2-1.9)
One definite psychiatric disorder	690	4.2 (3.1-6.0)	3.7 (2.9-4.9)	2.7 (2.1-3.5)
≥2 definite psychiatric disorders	556	8.6 (6.0-12.2)	7.2 (5.4-9.7)	3.1 (2.4-4.2)
Severe physical illness†				
Disorder absent, reference category	141	...	...	
Symptomatic or subthreshold psychiatric disorder	356	1.9 (1.1-3.1)	2.0 (1.3-3.2)	1.6 (1.0-2.4)
One definite psychiatric disorder	208	3.1 (1.8-5.5)	3.6 (2.2-6.1)	2.5 (1.6-4.1)
≥2 definite psychiatric disorders	194	4.9 (2.8-8.7)	5.2 (3.0-8.8)	3.9 (2.3-6.6)
No chronic disease‡				
Disorder absent, reference category	614	...	...	
Symptomatic or subthreshold psychiatric disorder	1026	1.8 (1.3-2.6)	2.0 (1.5-2.8)	1.6 (1.2-2.0)
One definite psychiatric disorder	435	4.7 (3.2-6.9)	3.8 (2.7-5.4)	2.7 (2.0-3.6)
≥2 definite psychiatric disorders	336	9.5 (6.3-14.3)	8.4 (5.8-12.2)	3.7 (2.7-5.2)
One chronic disease‡				
Disorder absent, reference category	340	...	...	...
Symptomatic or subthreshold psychiatric disorder	702	3.2 (2.0-5.0)	1.3 (1.0-1.9)	1.7 (1.2-2.2)
One definite psychiatric disorder	305	4.8 (2.9-7.9)	2.2 (1.5-3.2)	2.9 (2.0-4.1)
≥2 definite psychiatric disorders	283	9.4 (5.8-15.3)	4.1 (2.8-6.1)	4.2 (2.9-6.0)
Two or more chronic diseases‡				
Disorder absent, reference category	160	...	...	...
Symptomatic or subthreshold psychiatric disorder	470	2.0 (1.2-3.5)	2.2 (1.5-3.4)	1.5 (1.0-2.4)
One definite psychiatric disorder	321	3.9 (2.2-6.7)	4.7 (3.0-7.3)	2.7 (1.7-4.3)
≥2 definite psychiatric disorders	275	6.4 (3.6-11.3)	5.4 (3.3-8.9)	3.4 (2.1-5.4)

*We controlled for sex, age, years of education, General Health Questionnaire (GHQ) stratum, and sex by GHQ stratum. Occupational role and physical disability were dichotomized as none and mild vs moderate and severe; and number of disability days, as none vs 1 or more. Psychiatric status consisted of four categories: well, subthreshold or symptomatic disorder, one definite *International Statistical Classification of Diseases, 10th Revision (ICD-10)* psychiatric disorder, and two or more definite ICD-10 psychiatric disorders.

†Stratified by physician-rated physical health status.

‡Stratified by chronic disease status.

all centers, with a pooled estimate of 21% for the eight disorders included. The prevalence rates for any current psychiatric disorder as well as for specific current psychiatric disorders varied considerably across centers. The causes of the between-center differences in prevalence rates are many and include cultural factors, sociodemographic differences in patient mix, factors associated with the catchment area, and characteristics of the primary care clinics. As differences in prevalence rates were not the focus of this article, they have been discussed elsewhere.[43]

Common psychiatric illnesses are conditions that are only defined on the basis of the presence of symptom patterns. There are neither objective, biological markers, nor asymptomatic psychiatric illnesses. This raises the issue of operational confounding between the measures of psychiatric disorder (the symptoms) and the measures of disability. Some of the disorder-disability association may be due to the use of impairment criteria in diagnostic interviews and diagnostic algorithms. The WHO primary care version of the CIDI included two types of impairment criteria. At the individual item level, some symptom questions allowed a response of 2, implying that the symptom was present but not sufficiently severe to satisfy diagnostic criteria. An individual symptom may pass this severity screen in three ways: a medical professional was consulted, the respondent used medication for the symptom, or the symptom interfered with life or activities significantly. The interference criterion is the third in the hierarchy of severity criteria and is only asked if one of the first two is not satisfied. Recording of a 2 code does not specify which severity criterion was passed. At the disorder level, some diagnostic criteria include overall impairment criteria. In these cases, respondents would have to report some level of impairment to satisfy diagnostic criteria. Herein, we present a disorder-specific overview of impairment criteria used at either level in the WHO primary care version of the CIDI. For the *ICD* depressive episode and *ICD* generalized anxiety, no 2 codes or impairment criteria apply. This implies that opera-

tional confounding was not possible. For *ICD* panic disorder and *ICD* hypochondriasis, a single screening item allowed a 2 code. Consequently, some respondents may have been asked about interference and included on that basis. For *ICD* agoraphobia, the diagnostic algorithm included a disorder-level impairment criterion. Respondents must endorse one of the three severity criteria. So, again some respondents may have been included on the basis of interference. For *ICD* alcohol dependence, one of the items addressed interference. For *ICD* neurasthenia and *ICD* somatization disorder, the majority of the symptom questions allowed 2 codes; consequently, confounding was most likely here. Given this use of impairment criteria in the diagnostic algorithms, we believe that the observed association between psychiatric illness and disability was largely genuine and only minimally due to operational confounding for two reasons. First, the role of disability-related criteria in diagnostic algorithms was absent or minor for most disorders. Second, the level of associated disability was relatively low for disorders that were most vulnerable to confounding (somatization and alcohol dependence) and relatively high for disorders that were not confounded (depression and generalized anxiety).

Results could also be confounded by the possibility that patients with psychiatric illness may give overly pessimistic appraisals of their functioning and disabilities. This confounding may operate most among those with current depression and affect the measure of disability days in particular because of its subjective nature. Although the possibility of confounding by pessimistic appraisals cannot be ruled out, it is unlikely that it has seriously biased our results. The rating of occupational disability by the interviewer (SDS) was based as much as possible on factual information about daily routine, performance, and contacts with others at work, thereby rendering this measure relatively insensitive to confounding by pessimistic appraisals. Nevertheless, it was occupational disability, and not the measure of disability days, that was the strongest factor associated with psychopathology.

Our cross-sectional data on psychiatric illness and disability show association but not how and why this association occurs. There is some evidence that this cross-sectional association holds longitudinally. Patients whose psychiatric symptoms substantially improve show corresponding changes in disability level, while patients with unimproved or only slightly improved symptoms show, on average, no improvement in disability level.[3,15] But this does not imply a specific causal ordering. For instance, it cannot be excluded that unemployment is a cause rather than a consequence of psychiatric illness. To avoid this risk, the scoring rules of the occupational disability instrument instruct the interviewer to not rate unemployment as disability when it is clearly owing to extraneous factors, such as a high level of local unemployment. In that case, the interviewer assessed how subjects spent their days, including the efforts to find work. The most plausible hypothesis is that in general psychiatric illness and disability are mutually reinforcing, with initial psychiatric distress leading to impairment in role function, which in turn reduces social reinforcement and self-esteem, further propelling psychiatric illness.

Severity of physical illness was also associated with disability but less strongly than psychiatric illness. Similar results were reported by Ormel and colleagues[15] for a Dutch primary care sample. The finding from the Medical Outcomes Study[1] that the functioning of depressed patients is comparable or worse compared with patients with a major chronic medical disease point in the same direction. The surprisingly weak association of physical illness with disability may be due to the spectrum of severity of physical illness observed among primary care patients. Although chronic medical illness was prevalent among our second-stage sample—49% had at least one chronic medical condition and 21% had two or more—only 14% were rated as moderately physically ill and 2% were rated as severely ill by their physician. The modest impairments in physical capacities typically observed among primary care patients may be substantially less disabling than moderate dysregulation in cognitive, motivational, and emotional function. It is highly plausible that the effects of physical disease on disability only become pronounced at severe levels of physical impairment.

It seems counterintuitive that mental illness would show a stronger association with disability than severity of physical disease. While physical and psychiatric illness both cause disability, the underlying mechanisms likely differ. Physical illness may produce disability because of limitations in physical capacities, such as mobility, vision, aerobic capacity, lower and upper body strength, manual dexterity, and incontinence, whereas psychiatric illness may produce disability through limitations in cognitive and motivational capacities, affect regulation, social perception, and a tendency to amplify physical symptoms (eg, fatigue and pain).[44,45] Impairments in cognitive, motivational, and emotional function associated with psychiatric illness affect the highest order capacities of the human organism. The impairments caused by psychiatric illness may directly affect social disability (eg, occupational role functioning, social contacts, parenting, and partner role), whereas physical illness may produce social disability indirectly through physical impairments and the resulting limitations in physical functioning.

Although compliance with the first stage of data collection, the screening with the GHQ-12, was excellent (96%), only 62% of those eligible completed all aspects of the data collection in the second stage. At a few centers, nonresponse was moderately associated with the first-stage GHQ score. We do not know whether disability was associated with nonresponse as no measure of disability was obtained in the first stage. However, it is unlikely that, among nonresponders, severity of psychiatric illness and level of disability were correlated inversely to such an extent that inclusion of the nonresponders would radically have changed the patterns observed among the responders.

The consistent relationship of psychological illness with disability across a wide range of countries and cultures underscores the worldwide public health significance of the common forms of psychological illness experienced by primary care patients. Our results confirm the poor level of functioning of depressed patients that Wells and colleagues[1] observed in the Medical Outcomes Study and extend their results across cultures and to other common mental disorders. Effective prevention and treatment of these illnesses may ameliorate physical disability and restore social role functioning among psychiatrically ill primary care patients. The results suggest the importance of impairments of higher-order human capacities (emotion, motivation, and cognition) as determinants of functional disability across a wide range of cultural settings.

References

1. Wells KB, Steward A, Hays RD, et al. The functioning and well-being of depressed patients: results from the Medical Outcomes Study. *JAMA.* 1989;262:914–919.
2. Broadhead WE, Blazer DG, George LK, Kit Tse C. Depression, disability days, and days lost from work in a prospective epidemiologic survey. *JAMA.* 1990;264:2524–2528.
3. VonKorff M, Ormel J, Katon W, Lin EHB. Disability and depression among high utilizers of health care: a longitudinal analysis. *Arch Gen Psychiatry.* 1992;49:91–100.
4. Wohlfarth TD, vanden Brink W, Ormel J, Koeter MWJ, Oldehinkel AJ. The relationship between social dysfunctioning and psychopathology. *Br J Psychiatry.* 1993;163:37–44.
5. Berkman LF, Berkman C, Kasl S, et al. Depressive symptoms in relation to physical health and functioning in the elderly. *Am J Epidemiol.* 1986; 124:372–389.
6. Turner R, Beiser M. Major depression and depressive symptomatology among the physically disabled: assessing the role of chronic stress. *J Nerv Ment Dis.* 1990;178:343–350.
7. Hurry J, Sturt E. Social performance in a population sample: relations to psychiatric symptoms. In: Wing JK, Bebbington P, Robins LN, eds. *What Is a Case?* London, England: Grant McIntyre; 1981.
8. Dohrenwend BS, Dohrenwend BP, Link B, Levav I. Social functioning of psychiatric patients in contrast with community cases in the general population. *Arch Gen Psychiatry.* 1983;40:1174–1182.
9. Casey PR, Tyrer PJ, Platt S. The relationship between social functioning and psychiatric symptomatology in primary care. *Soc Psychiatry.* 1985;20:5–9.
10. Hecht H, Zerssen D, Wittchen HU. Anxiety and depression in a community sample: the influence of comorbidity on social functioning. *J Affect Disord.* 1990;18:137–144.
11. Rodin G, Voshart K. Depression in the medically ill: an overview. *Am J Psychiatry.* 1986;143:696–705.
12. Craig TJ, Van Natta PA. Disability and depressive symptoms in two communities. *Am J Psychiatry.* 1983;140:598–601.
13. Blumenthal MD, Dielman TE. Depressive symptomatology and role function in a general population. *Arch Gen Psychiatry.* 1975;32:985–991.
14. Paykel ES, Weissmann MM. Social adjustment and depression. *Arch Gen Psychiatry.* 1973;28:659–663.
15. Ormel J, VonKorff M, vanden Brink W, Katon W, Brilman E, Oldehinkel T. Depression, anxiety, and disability show synchrony of change. *Am J Public Health.* 1993;83:385–390.
16. Stoudemire A, Frank R, Hedemark N, Kamlet M, Blazer D. The economic burden of depression. *Gen Hosp Psychiatry.* 1986;8:387–394.
17. Shepherd M, Cooper B, Brown AC, Kalton GW. *Psychiatric Illness in General Practice.* New York, NY: Oxford University Press Inc; 1966.
18. Ormel J, vanden Brink W, Koeter MWJ, et al. Recognition, management, and outcome of psychological disorders in primary care: a naturalistic follow-up study. *Psychol Med.* 1990;20:909–923.
19. VonKorff M, Shapiro S, Burke JD, Anxiety and depression in a primary care clinic: comparison of DIS, GHQ, and practitioner assessments. *Arch Gen Psychiatry.* 1987;44:152–156.
20. Bartlett JE, Barrett JA, Oxman TE, Gerber PD. The prevalence of psychiatric disorders in a primary care practice. *Arch Gen Psychiatry.* 1988; 45:1100–1106.
21. Hoeper EW, Nycz GR, Cleary PD, Regier DA, Goldberg ID. Estimated prevalence of RDC mental disorder in primary medical care. *Int J Ment Health.* 1979;8:6–15.
22. Murphy JM, Olivier DC, Sobol M, Monson RR, Leighton AH. Diagnosis and outcome: depression and anxiety in a general population. *Psychol Med.* 1986;16:117–126.
23. Hankin JR, Oktay JS. *Mental Disorder and Primary Medical Care: An Analytic Review of the Literature.* Washington, DC: US Dept of Health and Human Services; 1979. Publication ADM 78–661, National Institute of Mental Health series D5.
24. Blacker CVR, Clare AW. Depressive disorder in primary care. *Br J Psychiatry.* 1987;150:737–751.
25. Mann AH, Jenkins R, Belsey E. The twelve-month outcome of patients with neurotic illness in general practice. *Psychol Med.* 1981;11:535–550.
26. Schulberg HC, McClelland M, Gooding W. Six-month outcomes for

medical patients with major depressive disorders. *J Gen Intern Med.* 1987;2: 312–317.

27. Regier DA, Burke JD, Manderscheid RW, Burns BJ. The chronically mentally ill in primary care. *Psychol Med.* 1985;15:265–273.

28. Cooper B, Fry J, Kalton GW. A longitudinal study of psychiatric morbidity in a general practice population. *Br J Preventive Soc Med.* 1969;23:210–217.

29. Hankin JR, Locke BZ. The persistence of depressive symptomatology among prepaid group practice enrollees: an exploratory study. *Am J Public Health.* 1982;29:2–10.

30. Kessler LG, Cleary PD, Burke JD. Psychiatric disorders in primary care: results of a follow-up study. *Arch Gen Psychiatry.* 1985;42:583–587.

31. Leff J, Sartorius N, Jablensky A, Korten A, Ernberg G. The International Pilot Study of Schizophrenia: five-year follow-up findings. *Psychol Med.* 1992;22:131–145.

32. Jablensky A, Sartorius N, Ernberg G, et al. Schizophrenia: manifestations, incidence, and course in different cultures. *Psychol Med.* 1992:monograph suppl 20.

33. Lefley HP. Culture and chronic mental illness. *Hosp Community Psychiatry.* 1990;41:177–286.

34. World Health Organization. *International Classification of Impairments, Disabilities, and Handicaps.* Geneva, Switzerland: World Health Organization; 1980.

35. Susser M. Disease, illness, sickness: impairment, disability, and handicap. *Psychol Med,* 1990;20:471–473.

36. VonKorff M, Ustun TB. Methods of the WHO Collaborative Study of psychological problems in primary care settings. In: Sartorius N, Ustun BT, eds. *Mental Illness in Primary Care: An International Study.* New York, NY: John Wiley & Sons Inc; In press.

37. Sartorius N, Ustun TB, Costa e Silva JA, et al. An international study of psychological problems in primary care: preliminary report from the WHO Collaborative Project on Psychological Problems in General Health Care. *Arch Gen Psychiatry.* 1993;50:819–824.

38. Goldberg D, Williams P. *A User's Guide to the General Health Questionnaire.* Windsor, England: NFER/Nelson; 1988.

39. World Health Organization. *Composite International Diagnostic Interview.*

Geneva, Switzerland: World Health Organization, Division of Mental Health; 1989. Publication MNH/NAT/89.

40. Wiersma D, DeJong A, Ormel J. The Groningen Social Disability Schedule: development, relationship with ICIDH, and psychometric properties. *Int J Rehab Res.* 1988;11:213–224.

41. VonKorff M, Ustun TB, Ormel J, et al. Self-report of disability: the reliability and validity in an international primary care study. *J Clin Epidemiol.* In press.

42. Stewart AL, Hays RD, Ware JE. The MOS Short-Form General Health Survey: reliability and validity in a patient population. *Med Care.* 1988; 26:724–732.

43. Ustun TB, Sartorius N, eds. *Mental Illness in Primary Care: An International Study.* New York, NY: John Wiley & Sons Inc; In press.

44. Barsky AJ, Goodson JD, Lane RS, Cleary PD. The amplification of somatic symptoms. *Psychosom Med.* 1988;50:510–519.

45. Katon W, Sullivan M. Depression and chronic medical illness. *J Clin Psychiatry.* 1990;51:3–11.

Article Review Form at end of book.

WiseGuide Wrap-Up

Cultural diversity, temperament, and applied research are just a few of the issues related to assessment and diagnosis. Further reading on training to diagnose and on various tools, such as structured interviews, will prove to be quite useful to you as a "practitioner to be."

R.E.A.L. Sites

This list provides a print preview of typical **Coursewise** R.E.A.L. sites. (There are over 100 such sites at the **Courselinks**™ site.) The danger in printing URLs is that web sites can change overnight. As we went to press, these sites were functional using the URLs provided. If you come across one that isn't, please let us know via email to: webmaster@coursewise.com. Use your Passport to access the most current list of R.E.A.L. sites at the **Courselinks** site.

Site name: APA's PsycNet
URL: http://www.apa.org
Why is it R.E.A.L.? This is a good resource for material about the professional practice of psychology. Articles from the *Monitor* (American Psychological Association publication), information on careers in psychology, and documents of interest to the general public are included.
Key topics: cultural diversity, temperament

Site name: The Atlantic Monthly
URL: http://www.theatlantic.com
Why is it R.E.A.L.? The *Atlantic* magazine periodically publishes articles related to psychologial issues.
Key topic: cultural diversity

Site name: Psychology Self-Help Resources
URL: http://www.psychwww.com/resource/selfhelp.htm
Why is it R.E.A.L.? Information on impulse disorders as well as other disorders are offered on this site.
Key topics: epidemiological research, temperament

section 2

Self-Control and Regulation

Traffic accidents, altercations with the law, and employment incidents are related to individuals' inability to regulate themselves. The most common culprits are substance use and a growing concern in our country—expressed aggression. The articles in this section focus on these topics and highlight the problems they have on both individuals and society.

Watson and Sher present a unique treatment approach called natural recovery. While this rather official sounding title does refer to the obvious recovery from substance abuse without treatment, the wonderful literature review on substance use treatment is less obvious from the title and very scholarly. In addition, the clinical researcher addresses the valuable issue of the lack of specificity of current research methods to measure and track substance use. As prospective practitioners, you should find the section on definition of treatment quite useful.

The second article in this section, by Keuthen and associates, provides an excellent example of applied clinical research. The treatment outcome method is thoroughly described. This useful tool provides practitioners with valuable information on whether their interventions are effective and in what way.

The final article in this section, by Winters and associates, provides an example of how demographic studies are conducted and how results are generated. The findings in terms of prevalence figures for college students are surprising; the dollar estimates given in the articles are compelling.

As you read the articles in this section, you should develop an understanding of self-control and regulation issues—particularly when they become problematic for individuals.

Learning Objective

- The student will learn control and impulse themes as they apply to pathological levels.

Questions

Reading 5. What is natural recovery research and how does it compare with other treatments of alcohol problems?

Reading 6. Summarize the treatments used for trichotillomania.

Reading 7. What treatment(s) would be effective for compulsive gambling in college students?

What is natural recovery research and how does it compare with other treatments of alcohol problems?

Resolution of Alcohol Problems without Treatment:

Methodological Issues and Future Directions of Natural Recovery Research

**Amy L. Watson
and Kenneth J. Sher**

University of Missouri Columbia

Natural recovery appears to be the major path to recovery from alcohol use disorders (AUDs). Studies of this phenomenon have implications for designing formal treatments, self-change strategies, and preventive interventions, and for contributing to current knowledge of the course of AUDs. The research conducted to date is limited by a number of important methodological issues associated with sampling, diagnostic criteria, and research design. Furthermore, previous research has failed to consider a number of sociocultural, developmental, and individual difference variables that clinical and epidemiological literature have established as influential to the course of AUDs. This article critically reviews the existing natural recovery literature and elaborates on areas of interest that have been neglected by previous natural recovery researchers.

In recent years there has been an increased interest in the resolution of alcohol problems without treatment.

The study of this phenomenon has important implications for designing self-change strategies, improving formal treatment, developing effective preventive interventions, and contributing to our knowledge of the natural history of alcohol use disorders (AUDs).[1] Much of this research has been subsumed under the rubric of "natural recovery" (also known as "spontaneous remission" or "self-change"). Although it is a commonly held assumption that significant resolutions in alcohol consumption follow active attempts to change, many individuals resolve alcohol problems without actively attempting self-change and are not included in the focus of many "natural recovery" studies. The current review adopts a more comprehensive scope and considers clinical and epidemiological literature, not only the "natural recovery" literature, in order to characterize the processes involved in the moderation or cessation of problem drinking more broadly.

The phenomenon of natural recovery is important for a number of reasons. Primarily, it appears that recovery without treatment is the most common path to recovery. As many as three quarters of the individuals who recover from an AUD apparently do so without treatment (Knupfer, 1972; Sobell, Cunningham, & Sobell, 1996; Sobell, Sobell, & Toneatto, 1992; Vaillant, 1995). The effectiveness of formal treatment might be enhanced by including successful self-change strategies. Additionally, many individuals do not initially seek treatment because they believe it would be stigmatizing and would prefer to handle their problem on their own (Cunningham, Sobell, Sobell, Agrawal, & Toneatto, 1993; Sobell, Cunningham, Sobell, & Toneatto, 1993; Tucker, 1995). Alternative treatment programs for AUDs could be designed to appeal to individuals who would otherwise not seek treatment (Sobell, Sobell, Toneatto, & Leo, 1993). Indeed, interventions based on self-change strategies are currently being tested (Sobell, Cunningham, Sobell, Agrawal et al., 1996).

In addition to the clinical relevance of studying natural recovery, a greater understanding of the factors associated with recovery across the

Amy L. Watson and Kenneth J. Sher, "Resolution of Alcohol Problems without Treatment: Methodological Issues and Future Directions of Natural Recovery Research," *Clinical Psychology: Science and Practice,* 5 (1), Spring 1998, pp. 1–18. Reprinted by permission of Oxford University Press.

life span would contribute to our understanding of the progression of AUDs. Clinical and epidemiological literature, on both adolescents and adults, examines a range of sociocultural, developmental, and individual difference variables to explain the cessation of drinking problems. However, researchers focused on "natural recovery" have failed to examine many of these variables. The purpose of the present article is to clarify the methodological issues associated with the research strategies employed to date and to critically review the existing literature on natural recovery. Furthermore, by integrating the natural recovery literature with current knowledge about AUDs across the life span, we will expand on those sociocultural, developmental, and individual factors that might influence recovery and have been overlooked by previous research focused on "natural recovery" processes.

Methodological Issues

Definitional Issues

Perhaps the greatest limitation to generalizing about the findings from the numerous natural recovery studies is the diversity of research criteria employed. To derive a sample of natural recoverers, researchers must verify the existence of a prior AUD, define what constitutes a current recovery status (including drinking status and duration of that status), and determine what constitutes treatment (which definitionally precludes "natural recovery"). A great variety of definitions have been utilized, making it difficult to generalize about participants across studies. According to Roizen, Cahalan, and Shanks (1978), much of the variation in rates of remission can be attributed to variation in these criteria.

Prerecovery Drinking Status

To identify individuals who previously had an AUD, researchers have focused on a range of problematic drinking statuses from less severe indices, such as alcohol-related problems alone (Knupfer, 1972; Roizen et al., 1978) or alcohol problems with above average consumption (Armor & Meshkoff, 1983), to more severe in-

dices such as, alcohol-related problems with dependence symptoms (Guze, Goodwin, & Crane, 1969; Klingemann, 1991; Ojesjo, 1981; Saunders & Kershaw, 1979; Sobell et al., 1992; Tuchfeld, 1981) or diagnoses of an AUD (Imber, Schultz, Funderburk, Allen, & Flamer, 1976; Kendell, 1966; Kissin, Rosenblatt, & Machover, 1968). Other studies have employed prerecovery drinking statuses with ambiguous severity by including individuals who had gone through detoxification or sought referrals for help (Humphreys, Moos, & Finney, 1995) or individuals who had exhibited "specific signs of problem drinking" (Stall, 1983, p. 193). Clearly, previous research has studied individuals with a range of problem severity, which is likely to affect outcomes.

Postrecovery Drinking Statuses

Researchers have defined recovery in a number of ways, including subjective ratings of improvement (Edwards et al., 1977), decreased consumption (Klingemann, 1991), problem-free drinking (Guze et al., 1969; Saunders & Kershaw, 1979), or abstinence (Ludwig, 1985; Tucker, Vuchinich, & Gladsjo, 1994; Tucker, Vuchinich, & Pukish, 1995; Vaillant, 1995). Some authors have acknowledged the potential for different recovery types and have included multiple outcomes such as abstinence and problem-free drinking (Humphreys et al., 1995; Kissin et al., 1968; Sobell, Cunningham, & Sobell, 1996; Sobell et al., 1992; Sobell, Sobell, & Kozlowski, 1995) or abstinence and decreased consumption (Ojesjo, 1981; Tuchfeld, 1981).

Variation in this criterion has important implications for interpreting recovery research, as there is evidence that differences exist between individuals who have different drinking outcomes. For example, individuals who select abstinence tend to have more severe drinking problems, have lower socioeconomic status, are more likely to have received treatment or participated in Alcoholics Anonymous, and feel less in control over their drinking problem than individuals who select moderation (Armor & Meshkoff, 1983; Humphreys et al., 1995; Saunders & Kershaw, 1979; Sobell et

al., 1992; Vaillant, 1995). These differences suggest that variation in the definition of a recovery drinking status may result in somewhat different recovery experiences.

Duration of Recovery Status

Studies also vary in the duration required for an achieved recovery, which ranges from 6 months (Armor & Meshkoff, 1983) to 3 years (Sobell et al., 1992), with the mode being 1 year (Klingemann, 1991; Ludwig, 1985; Stall, 1983; Tuchfeld, 1981). Most studies have employed relatively short recovery periods, despite evidence that risk of relapse is greatest during the first several years after recovery (De Soto, O'Donnell, & De Soto, 1989; Sobell et al., 1992). Therefore, a number of studies with shorter recovery periods may assess individuals who eventually relapse and do not represent stable recoveries.

Definition of Treatment

Finally, what is considered treatment and criteria for exclusion from studies of natural recovery varies as well. Some studies include individuals who participated in self-help groups such as Alcoholics Anonymous (Edwards et al., 1977; Humphreys et al., 1995; Imber et al., 1976), completed detoxification (Humphreys et al., 1995), or reported ineffectual treatment experiences (Klingemann, 1991; Stall, 1983). Therefore, a number of studies may actually assess individuals who have benefitted from contact with both lay and professional helpers and do not represent "natural" recoveries. All of the above definitional differences may account for inconsistencies between studies as well as raise questions about their generalizability.

Sample Heterogeneity

Another issue that affects evaluation of the current literature is the lack of sample heterogeneity. Most studies have assessed primarily (or entirely) White, middle-aged males, although there is evidence that the development and cessation of AUDs are related to a number of sociocultural, developmental, and individual variables, especially ethnicity, age, and gender. Therefore, the findings of many natural recovery studies may not generalize to individuals in minority ethnic groups, younger and older age groups, or women.

Ethnicity

Very little is known about the recovery process for members of minority ethnic groups. Three important issues need to be addressed when considering ethnic differences in the recovery process. First, minority status is related to increased stress due to lower socioeconomic status (SES) and discrimination. Second, members of some ethnic groups appear to have an increased likelihood of experiencing certain alcohol-related consequences. Third, being a member of a minority ethnic group appears to be related to increased barriers to treatment.

Minority Status. For many individuals, being a member of a minority group also means having a lower SES and facing discrimination. The effect of ethnicity on drinking patterns appears to interact with SES. Lower SES is related to increased rates of drinking problems for African-American men and women while higher SES is related to increased rates of AUDs among White men and women (Darrow, Russell, Cooper, Mudar, & Frone, 1992; Jones-Webb, Hsiao, & Hannan, 1995). A number of explanations have been offered regarding this difference. Among lower SES African Americans, alcohol use may be seen as an acceptable form of coping with discrimination and poverty (Lex, 1987). Also, lower SES African-American men may have fewer social and financial resources available to them, which may exacerbate their drinking problems and make recovery more difficult (Jones-Webb et al., 1995).

One natural recovery study found that African-American men were less likely to recover from an AUD than White men (Goodwin, Crane, & Guze, 1971). This study, however, used an unrepresentative sample of felons after release from prison and may reflect the different effects of low SES on African-American and White men. In particular, there is evidence that African-American men have greater difficulty adjusting after release from

prison, especially in finding employment (Menon, Blakely, Carmichael, & Snow, 1995; Myers, 1983).

Alcohol-Related Consequences. Studies attempting to understand ethnic differences in drinking behavior often define problem drinking in terms of alcohol-related consequences such as health problems or citations for driving while intoxicated (driving under the influence, DUI). However, some ethnic groups appear to be at higher risk of experiencing certain alcohol-related consequences (Hollinger, 1984; Jones-Webb et al., 1995; Zylman, 1972). For example, there is evidence that African-American and Native-American individuals may be more susceptible to health-related consequences of drinking, such as cirrhosis of the liver (Lex, 1987). Additionally, non-Whites are more likely to receive DUIs than Whites (Hollinger, 1984; Zylman, 1972). Interestingly, this difference does not appear to result from biased enforcement by individual police officers but is related to living in more heavily patrolled areas with congested traffic (Hollinger, 1984; Jones-Webb et al., 1995; Zylman, 1972). The increased likelihood of experiencing alcohol-related problems affects the study of natural recovery in two ways. First, it may artificially produce apparent group differences in recovery. Second, due to the increased likelihood of experiencing legal and medical alcohol-related problems, minorities may come into contact more often with interventions for AUDs, excluding them from study.

Barriers to Treatment. Finally, members of minority ethnic groups are less likely to seek and successfully complete formal treatment for mental health problems (Chen, 1991; Neighbors, 1985; Raynes & Warren, 1971; Smear & Smithy-Willis, 1982). When minorities seek help, they are more likely to seek advice from general physicians or clergy than from mental health professionals (Leaf, Bruce, Tischler, & Holzer, 1987; Neighbors, 1985). These differences may be related to beliefs about drinking problems. For example, in one study, Hispanic and African-American adults were more likely than White adults to believe that alcoholism was a sign of moral weakness and less likely to believe in the disease concept of alcoholism

(Caetano, 1989). Additionally, related to lower SES and lower educational attainment, minorities are more likely to face barriers to treatment (e.g., time and money constraints; Chen, 1991; Grant, 1996; Leaf et al., 1987). Beliefs that confer greater control to the individual over a drinking problem combined with less access to treatment may lead a large number of minority individuals to attempt to recover from an alcohol problem without formal treatment. Unfortunately, because minority ethnic groups are underrepresented in studies of natural recovery, the recovery process and the rate of natural recovery among ethnic minorities are unclear.

Age

It is likely that a number of age-related processes influence the likelihood of recovery and types of processes involved in recovery. There are data suggesting that a large number of natural recoverers can be found in younger and older age groups (Chen & Kandel, 1995; Fillmore, 1988; Helzer, Burnam, & McEvoy, 1991). Here we consider these two age groups that have been overlooked in studies of natural recovery.

Young Adult Recoveries. The initiation and cessation of drug use generally occur by the late twenties (Chen & Kandel, 1995; Fillmore, 1988; Helzer et al., 1991). Recovery from an AUD early in life could represent a particular "developmentally limited" subtype of AUD (Zucker, 1987). This particular subtype may reflect a large number of natural recoveries as it is characterized by resolution in early adulthood and the infrequent seeking of treatment. There is evidence that young adults are particularly more likely to feel that treatment is stigmatizing and prefer to handle their problem on their own (Cunningham et al., 1993; Sobell, Cunningham et al., 1993). Also, it is important to note that age-related patterns of alcohol consumption need to be considered within the context of ethnicity and that this pattern may primarily apply to White individuals. Among Whites, alcohol use peaks during the twenties and decreases in the thirties (Fillmore, 1988; Helzer et al., 1991). However, among African Americans and Hispanics, alcohol use peaks during "middle age" and decreases thereafter (Caetano & Herd, 1984; Caetano & Katsukas, 1995).

Late-Life Recoveries. It has been observed that the prevalence of AUDs decreases over the life span, with significant decreases after middle age (Helzer et al., 1991). Although this decrease is partially related to increased mortality, it is also related to a large number of recoveries that occur in older age groups (Fillmore, 1988; Helzer et al., 1991). Older drinkers differ from younger drinkers in a number of ways. For example, age-related physiological processes that reduce tolerance for alcohol may play a significant role in late-life recoveries (Nordstrom & Berglund, 1987). Additionally, drinking problems in late life appear to be associated with life stress, isolation, depression, and anxiety, suggesting that symptomatic improvement in these domains would be associated with recovery for older adults (Atkinson, 1994; Blow, Cook, Booth, Falcon, & Friedman, 1992; Dufour & Fuller, 1995; Schonfeld & Dupree, 1991; Schuckit & Gunderson, 1977; Seymour & Wattis, 1992).

Of particular interest are older adults with late-onset AUDs. Compared to older drinkers with earlier onset, they appear to be more stable psychologically, more likely to complete treatment programs, have greater motivation for treatment, and are more likely to recover without treatment as well (Atkinson, 1994; Atkinson, Tolson, & Turner, 1990; Schonfeld & Dupree, 1991; Seymour & Wattis, 1992).

It is possible that many studies of natural recovery have excluded individuals with early or late recoveries and that the process of change varies according to age of onset and age of recovery. Age-related variation in the recovery process wold have important implications for designing developmentally appropriate interventions. To the extent that alcoholism can be viewed as a disorder of development (Zucker, 1987), it seems very likely that recovery processes are tied to developmental changes and transitions in adulthood. By examining only a restricted range of age, many studies of natural recovery are unable to examine these processes.

Gender

An important individual difference variable that has been overlooked in studies of natural recovery is gender. Many women recover from AUDs without treatment. In a comparison of the rates of alcohol problems and remission in men and women, women in all age groups had higher rates of remission (Fillmore, 1987). Additionally, it has been observed that women receive less social support for and greater opposition to entering treatment than men (Beckman & Amaro, 1986). As a result, women may be more likely to attempt to recover without treatment. Perhaps due to the greater prevalence of AUDs among men (Helzer et al., 1991), most studies of natural recovery have assessed only men or have had too few women in their samples to make meaningful comparisons.

It would be of interest to compare the rates of natural recovery, and determine if the self-change process varies, for men and women. For example, natural recovery researchers might attempt to clarify the effect of pregnancy on drinking. It is unclear how many women permanently decrease alcohol consumption as a result of pregnancy. Some reports indicate that women decrease alcohol consumption during pregnancy and then return to previous levels after giving birth (Ihlen, Amundsen, & Daae, 1990; Serdula, Williamson, Kendrick, Anda, & Byers, 1991). One study, however, found that becoming pregnant was related to permanent decreases in alcohol consumption among women who were "heavy social drinkers" (Fried, Barnes, & Drake, 1985). The picture is further complicated by evidence that women tend to underreport the amount they drink during pregnancy (Ernhart, Morrow-Tlucak, Sokol, & Martier, 1988). The effect of pregnancy on women's alcohol consumption is one gender-specific question that might be examined in studies of natural recovery.

Clearly, cultural, developmental, and individual difference variables must be considered in studies that examine the initiation and cessation of AUDs. This, however, is not possible in studies that assess samples that are homogeneous in terms of ethnicity, age, and gender.

Strategies Employed for Studying Natural Recovery

In addition to problems due to variation in research criteria and the lack of sample heterogeneity, a number of limitations arise from the differing strategies that have been employed for studying natural recovery. These strategies include (a) retrospective assessments of samples ascertained either systematically via random community samples (Saunders & Kershaw, 1979; Sobell, Cunningham, & Sobell, 1996) or unsystematically by obtaining volunteers or anecdotal reports (Klingemann, 1991, 1992; Lemere, 1953; Ludwig, 1985; Sobell et al., 1992; Sobell, Sobell et al., 1993; Stall, 1983; Tuchfeld, 1981; Tucker & Gladsjo, 1993; Tucker et al., 1994; Tucker et al., 1995) and (b) prospective studies assessing samples of treatment seekers (Edwards et al., 1977; Humphreys et al., 1995; Imber et al., 1976; Kendell, 1966; Kissin et al., 1968) or nonclinical samples drawn from the general population (Armor & Meshkoff, 1983; Goodwin et al., 1971; Knupfer, 1972; Ojesjo, 1981; Roizen et al., 1978; Sobell et al., 1995; Vaillant, 1995). Here, we address the strengths and weaknesses of each of these approaches.

Retrospective Studies

In a number of cross-sectional studies, samples of recovered individuals have been selected from the general population or recruited through advertisements and asked to recall events prior to, concurrent with, and following their recoveries. Using retrospective methods, researchers can target individuals with the desired characteristics allowing for larger sample sizes and eliminating the lengthy intervals and high costs associated with longitudinal research.

Due to the nature of retrospective reports, it is unclear to what degree these reports suffer from recall bias. Many studies attempt to describe the change process by identifying events that led to recovery or were concurrent with recovery. In some cases, participants were asked to recall details about events that had occurred 6–8 years previously (Saunders & Kershaw, 1979; Tuchfeld, 1981). Due to possible inaccuracies in participants' recall concerning the ordering of events, conclusions about the direction of effect can not confidently be drawn in many cases.

Many of these studies are additionally limited by a lack of appropriate control groups. A control group of unrecovered alcohol abusers who have never sought treatment is necessary to distinguish those experiences specific to natural recovery versus those experiences that are a function of an AUD. For example, many natural recoverers have reported events such as legal problems, health problems, and interventions by family and friends as critical to their recoveries. Two natural recovery studies including control groups have attempted to determine if natural recoverers actually experience these events more frequently than unrecovered alcohol abuses. In one study, self-changers experienced more health and legal concerns in the year preceding recovery than a control group of current alcohol abusers (Tucker et al., 1994). Another study, however, found that the frequency of life events was related to age rather than recovery (Sobell, Cunningham et al., 1993). Another informative control that has been studied infrequently consists of individuals treated for AUDs that can illustrate how the change process differs for those in treatment versus those who recover without treatment. For example, it appears that seeking treatment is related to greater psychosocial problems (Tucker & Gladsjo, 1993).

Two types of control groups have not been utilized by natural recovery researchers. First, relapse may be an important experience in the recovery process (Brownell, Marlatt, Lichtenstein, & Wilson, 1986). Natural recovery researchers are in an ideal position to identify and study unstable recoveries. By including control groups of individuals who experience one or more relapses, researchers could help clarify the role of relapse in recovery. Second, role transitions and changes in peer interactions appear to influence recovery (Klingemann, 1992; Ludwig, 1985; Saunders & Kershaw, 1979; Stall, 1983; Stall & Biernacki, 1986; Tuchfeld, 1981; Vaillant, 1995), and age-matched controls of non-problem drinkers can help illustrate the degree to which these events are related to problematic drinking and

recovery or are a function of chronological age.

Unsystematically Ascertained Samples. A number of limitations arise due to the sampling methods of many retrospective studies. One of the earliest studies of "natural recovery" used anecdotal reports about deceased relatives of the author's clients (Lemere, 1953). Although second-hand accounts spanning a lifetime of information are severely limited by potential inaccuracies of reporting, it is important to note that this remains a landmark study as it was one of the first to establish natural recovery as a possible outcome for "alcoholics."

More recently, a majority of natural recovery studies have used another unsystematic sampling method by advertising for participants who had recovered from an alcohol problem without treatment (Klingemann, 1991, 1992; Ludwig, 1985; Sobell et al., 1992; Sobell, Sobell et al., 1993; Stall, 1983; Tuchfeld, 1981; Tucker & Gladsjo, 1993; Tucker et al., 1994; Tucker et al., 1995). Although this method increases researchers' ability to reach a large number of individuals outside of a treatment setting, it tends to be haphazard as it involves a self-selected sample of unknown representatives. Furthermore, this sampling method may rely largely on individuals who have self-identified as having a previous drinking problem. Although many 12-step programs assert that identifying oneself as an alcoholic is critical to recovery (Anonymous, 1972), it is possible that a number of natural recoverers decrease their drinking to problem-free levels without ever believing they had a problem. In fact, labeling oneself as an alcoholic may not be necessary for successful outcomes (Miller, 1985). Additionally, coerced treatment appears to have equal success rates to voluntary treatment (Miller, 1985).

Systematically Ascertained Samples. Two retrospective studies have systematically ascertained subjects by recruiting through random community samples (Saunders & Kershaw, 1979; Sobell, Cunningham, & Sobell, 1996). This method improves on unsystematically ascertained samples by eliminating self-selection and some degree of self-identification, but still suffers

from potential recall bias. One of these studies is additionally limited by the lack of informative control groups (Saunders & Kershaw, 1979).

Prospective Studies

Prospective studies improve on retrospective studies by enabling researchers to more accurately characterize the change process over time, reduce the amount of retrospection about events, and provide multiple comparison groups (e.g., age-matched individuals with similar drinking problems who do not recover). Although improving on retrospective studies, a number of limitations are associated with prospective studies. In particular, prospective studies are less efficient than retrospective studies. In prospective studies, stable recoveries are identified in cohorts of individuals followed over time, requiring larger sample sizes and lengthy follow-ups. Although providing more representative samples than possible in many retrospective studies, sample composition in prospective studies may be biased due to the higher likelihood of individuals with an AUD being lost at follow-up as a result of alcohol-related mortality, alcohol-related problems which prevent participation (e.g., incarceration, illness), and less willingness to participate. Note, however, that retrospective sampling methods may also underrepresent many individuals due to the same reasons.

Prospective Studies of Treatment Seekers. A number of prospective studies have employed treatment seekers, either by assessing individuals on a wait-list control group in treatment outcome studies (Edwards et al., 1977; Kissin et al., 1968) or individuals who sought treatment but subsequently declined it (Humphreys et al., 1995; Imber et al., 1976; Kendell, 1966). The advantage of using a clinical sample is the assurance that individuals have reached or exceeded a common threshold of "clinical significance." Furthermore, individuals who exhibit problem drinking can be easily identified among clinical populations, allowing for an efficient design. Although these studies determine the outcome of those individuals who refused treatment and provide estimates of the prevalence of their natural recovery, they have substantial limitations.

This method of sampling limits the generalizability of the findings because a number of differences that affect the likelihood of recovery exists between individuals who seek treatment and those who do not. For example, clinical samples tend to overrepresent problem severity and comorbidity (Cohen & Cohen, 1984; NIAAA, 1993). Evidence also suggests that these individuals are more likely to have experienced alcohol-related psychosocial problems (Hingson, Scotch, Day, & Culbert, 1980; Sobell, Cunningham, & Sobell, 1996; Tucker & Gladsjo, 1993; Tucker et al., 1995). Furthermore, as in the case of recruitment through advertisements, the role of self-recognition in these recoveries is unclear. For example, information regarding coerced versus voluntary treatment is not provided.

Nonclinical Prospective Studies. Prospective studies employing nonclinical samples improve on studies assessing treatment seekers by providing a more representative sample of recovered alcohol abusers and allowing for an examination of natural recovery that occurs independent of problem recognition (Armor & Meshkoff, 1983; Knupfer, 1972; Ojesjo, 1981; Roizen et al., 1978; Sobell et al., 1995; Vaillant, 1995). In addition, these studies can provide a critical type of control group: alcoholic individuals drawn from the same cohort whose problems do not remit. However, in practice, these studies are often limited in their ability to accurately describe changes in drinking behavior prior to and following recovery, as most do not have more than two assessments. Only one nonclinical prospective study has included more than two assessments (Vaillant, 1995). This study, however, relied on a large degree of retrospection about one's drinking history as a lengthy period of time elapsed between some follow-ups, requiring individuals to retrospect about periods of 15–20 years. Finally, although in a better position to study the role of self-recognition, this variable has been overlooked by prospective researchers.

Furthermore, some prospective studies have been conducted that rely on potentially unrepresentative samples. For example, Goodwin et al. (1971) assessed a sample of convicted felons, which is likely to be unrepresentative in a number of ways, especially regarding variables related to antisocial personality and psychosocial adjustment. In another study, a sample of self-identified individuals who already recovered from an alcohol problem were recruited, thereby relying on self-recognition and retrospection of the events preceding recovery (Sobell et al., 1995).

Summary of Strategies Employed

Although numerous cross-sectional and prospective studies of natural recovery have been conducted, there are a number of limitations inherent in the design of these studies. Primarily, there is great variation in the definitions used for prerecovery and postrecovery during statuses and for what kinds of experiences are considered treatment. Additionally, most studies have assessed primarily White, middle-aged males, and may represent recovery processes that are not generalizable to women, minorities, and other age groups.

Many retrospective studies are limited by the use of volunteer samples who are self-selected and have self-identified as having an AUD. It is unknown how many individuals recover subsequent to self-recognition of an AUD. Other patterns of recovery might exist that occur independent of self-recognition. Furthermore, retrospective studies are limited by potential recall bias and many lack appropriate control groups.

Prospective studies can improve on many of the limitations of retrospective studies; however, in practice, those conducted still suffer from a number of limitations. Ideally, individuals in a prospective study would be drawn from the general population. However, several prospective studies have potentially unrepresentative samples including treatment seekers, felons, and self-selected volunteers. Finally, in practice, existing studies have relied on a large degree of retrospection and may suffer from recall bias, as the majority only have two assessment points and some have lengthy follow-up intervals. As interest in natural recovery has increased, many researchers have made advances in the research strategies employed and despite the limitations we have discussed, the studies conducted to date have yielded a number of important findings.

Current Findings

In attempting to review and integrate findings from various studies conducted by researchers of diverse interests, it is helpful to categorize the literature using several different frames of reference. First, researchers have attempted to identify processes involved in a recovery. Second, researchers have identified immediate circumstances that appear to surround a change in drinking behavior. Third, a range of individual difference variables have been associated with natural recovery. Although these categories are conceptually distinct, they are highly overlapping. Nevertheless, by focusing on these conceptually distinct areas, we are in a better position to generalize about the findings of the studies.

Processes of Self-Directed Change

Many studies have focused on strategies self-changers use and key events they experience while overcoming an addiction. No discussion of behavior change would be complete without addressing the change model proposed by Prochaska and colleagues that is commonly cited in the addiction literature (Prochaska, DiClemente, & Norcross, 1992). In their research, they have derived 10 distinct processes individuals experience while recovering from an addiction. The 10 processes are associated with five stages: *precontemplation* (i.e., no intention to change), *contemplation* (i.e., awareness of problem with consideration of change), *preparation* (i.e., intention to change with small behavioral changes), *action* (i.e., modification of behavior), and *maintenance* (i.e., prevention of relapse and continuation of change). According to the authors, each process may be seen during several stages, but is particularly significant to one or two stages.

Of these 10 processes, eight appear frequently in the literature of natural recovery from AUDs. *Consciousness raising,* acquiring information about the problem, occurs very early in recovery. In the natural recovery literature, it is most likely to come in the form of an intervention by friends, family, or a physician (Saunders & Kershaw, 1979; Tuchfeld, 1981). *Self-reevaluation* and *environmental evaluation* occur when individuals evaluate themselves, their problem, and the effect of their problem on their environment. Examples of these processes that appear frequently in the recovery literature are "hitting rock bottom" or "a personal bottom," in which the individual is dissatisfied with several aspects of his or her life, and "weighing the pros and cons" of problematic drinking, in which the person decides that the negative consequences of drinking outweigh the benefits (Klingemann, 1992; Ludwig, 1985; Sobell, Sobell et al., 1993). Examples of when the individual commits to making a change, *self-liberation,* include frequent references to turning points, rites of quitting, and the individual's use of willpower and motivation to overcome the addiction (Klingemann, 1992; Ludwig, 1985; Stall & Biernacki, 1986). Behavioral strategies appear to be successfully employed by many self-changers. These strategies include *counterconditioning* (substituting nonaddictive substances or activities), *stimulus control* (avoiding situations where the substance itself, or cues for the substance, are present), and *reinforcement management* (giving oneself a reward for quitting; Sobell & Sobell, 1994; Stall & Biernacki, 1986). Finally, *helping relationships,* relying on support from significant others, appear to be central to many recoveries (Sobell, Sobell et al., 1993; Stall & Biernacki, 1986; Tuchfeld, 1981). Interestingly, however, in one study recoverers reported withdrawing from social support networks at the time of their recovery (Klingemann, 1992). Many of these events will be discussed in greater detail in the following sections. Examples of the two remaining processes, *dramatic relief* ("experiencing and expressing feelings about one's problems and solutions"; Prochaska et al., 1992, p. 1108) and *social liberation* ("increasing alternatives for non-problem behaviors available in society" through social action; Prochaska et al., 1992, p. 1108) do not appear frequently in the natural recovery literature.

An important criticism of this model is that behavior modifications can also occur because the "functional significance" (Davidson, 1992, p. 821) of a behavior changes and that many individuals modify a behavior without awareness of the change process. In response to this criticism, Prochaska, DiClemente, Velicer, and Rossi (1992) acknowledge that their research is based only on intentional change and point to the need for research that compares other forms of behavior change with their model of change. By assessing volunteers who evidence recognition of their AUD, most of the natural recovery literature does not contribute to understanding the process of "unintentional" change. We propose that one way the "functional significance" of alcohol use can change is through role transitions and discuss the importance of role transitions in a following section.

Bandura (in press) also discusses several criticisms of the change model. First, he argues that it is not a true stage model because stages are formed on the basis of quantitative changes in behavior instead of qualitatively different behaviors. For example, some stages are distinguished on the basis of whether or not a behavior has been performed for more or less than 6 months. Second, he argues that the model does not provide explanations for behavior at different stages and suggests that researchers consider a number of "determinants of inaction" (Bandura, in press, p. 7), including risk perception, outcome expectations, and efficacy belief.

Circumstances Surrounding Change

Many studies have used open-ended interviews of life-event checklists in an attempt to identify specific circumstances surrounding a change in drinking behavior. A variety of events have been identified as reasons for change, and this discussion includes those reasons that appear most frequently in the natural recovery literature. Although researchers have conceptualized these data in a number of ways, the most commonly cited reasons for change can be assigned to three superordinate categories: (a) events that promote

self-recognition of a drinking problem, (b) health-related concerns, and (c) role transitions.

Events That Promote Self-Recognition

Events that promote self-recognition of a problem are frequently identified as having been an impetus for change. These processes can be understood in terms of accumulative processes or, alternatively, singular key events. For example, many individuals attribute their change to having "hit rock bottom" or having reached their "personal bottom" (Klingemann, 1992; Ludwig, 1985). This describes a self-evaluative process in which one recognizes having experienced a number of disappointing or humiliating alcohol-related consequences leading to a relative low point in his or her life (Klingemann, 1991; Ludwig, 1985). For others, a change appears to follow singular key events that had great meaning for them, such as spiritual experiences or religious conversions (Klingemann, 1991; Ludwig, 1985; Tuchfeld, 1981). According to Tucker et al. (1994), accumulative processes are more likely to precede recovery than singular key events.

It would appear as though events promoting self-recognition are key to many recoveries. However, it is unknown if all recovered alcohol abusers experience these events and processes since the vast majority of research on recovery has employed treated samples or self-selected volunteers, who are likely to have experienced self-recognition of their drinking problems.

Health-Related Concerns

Health-related concerns represent an important type of event that promotes self-recognition of an alcohol problem. However, they should be considered separately from events that promote self-recognition because health-related concerns may also promote change as part of a general health regime without self-recognition of an actual problem. Many individuals report making positive changes in health habits concurrent with recovery (Tucker et al., 1995). A number of health-related concerns are often attributed as the cause for change, including medical conditions that preclude drinking, concerns with general health and fitness, or advice from a physician (Klingemann, 1991; Ludwig, 1985; Ojesjo, 1981; Saunders & Kershaw, 1979; Smart, 1975; Tuchfeld, 1981; Tucker et al., 1994; Vaillant, 1995). These reports are corroborated by the finding that physician advice appears to be an effective form of intervention for "heavy drinkers" (Anderson & Scott, 1992). Similarly, some alcoholics have reported that having a friend who becomes seriously ill or dies as a consequence of drinking prompted the change in their drinking behavior (Tuchfeld, 1981). Heightened health concerns appear to play a major role in many recoveries and, thus, deserve further inquiry by natural recovery researchers.

A number of factors affect the likelihood of a change in drinking behavior in response to health concerns. Applying the Health Belief Model (Rosenstock, 1974), two factors appear to influence the likelihood of seeking treatment for AUDs: perceived control over one's health and perceived severity of health problems (Beckman, 1988; Dean & Edwards, 1990). It is likely that recovery without treatment in response to heightened health concerns would also reflect increases in these domains. As previously noted, Bandura (in press) suggests that researchers examine the influence of a number of health-related beliefs on unhealthy practices.

Additionally, it is possible that other variables influence the likelihood of responding to health-related concerns. For example, older adults may be more responsive to health problems than younger adults. One study found that health concerns were attributed more often as a cause of recovery by participants over 30 than those under 30 (Knupfer, 1972). Identifying who is most likely to respond to health concerns has important implications for understanding the recovery process and designing interventions.

Role Transitions

The initiation and continuation of substance use are known to be related to a number of social factors (Bachman, O'Malley, & Johnston, 1984). It is also evident that social factors play a significant role in natural recovery. Pressure from family and friends, use of social support, a change in lifestyle to a new nondrinking peer group and nondrinking leisure activities, and role transitions such as marriage and new occupations are all frequently cited causes of change (Klingemann, 1992; Ludwig, 1985; Saunders & Kershaw, 1979; Stall, 1983; Stall & Biernacki, 1986; Tuchfeld, 1981; Vaillant, 1995). There is evidence that the adoption of adult roles (e.g., pregnancy, parenthood, marriage, full-time employment) is associated with a general reduction in alcohol use (Chassin, Presson, Sherman, & Edwards, 1992; Esbensen & Elliot, 1994; Fried et al., 1985; Ihlen et al., 1990; Miller-Tutzauer, Leonard, & Windle, 1991; Schulenberg, O'Malley, Bachman, Wadsworth, & Johnston, 1996; Yamaguchi & Kandel, 1985). To gain a clearer understanding of the process of change, several questions should be addressed in future research.

The relation between roles and substance use is generally understood in terms of role selection and role socialization. Role selection occurs when substance use influences the roles one adopts, and role socialization occurs when characteristics of a role influence one's substance use (Yamaguchi & Kandel, 1985). In natural recovery studies, the reduction in substance use is generally attributed to the role transition, suggesting that role socialization has taken place. However, as these studies usually rely on retrospection the direction of effect is not always clear. As noted by Yamaguchi and Kandel (1985), individuals self-select into the roles they occupy and the degree to which role selection has taken place must always be considered in studies of role socialization. It is possible that role transitions reflect improvement that has already occurred. For example, it appears that, in some cases, "anticipatory socialization" occurs: An individual decreases use before assuming a role they believe will be incompatible with substance use (Yamaguchi & Kandel, 1985). To understand the effects of role transitions on natural recovery, studies that prospectively examine both processes are necessary.

The mechanisms through which role socialization promotes self-change are unknown. We propose several mechanisms. The first mechanism involves *deterrence*, which includes direct social sanctions to desist drinking and subsequent rewards for quitting (Klingemann, 1992). It has been observed that a reduction in drug use is related to the perception of disapproval by peers (Bachman, Johnston, O'Malley, & Humphrey, 1988). Second, a reduction in drinking behavior may reflect *prior role socialization*. This may occur if an individual was previously in a role that promoted drinking. For young adults, initiation and continued use of drugs are related to association with drug-using peers (Bachman et al., 1984; Brennan, Walfish, & AuBuchon, 1986). It is unclear how persistent the effect of this association is after one leaves a drug-abusing peer group. Third, *role incompatibility* may occur when an increase or change in responsibilities is incompatible with a drinking lifestyle, when a newly adopted role has less tolerance for impairment, or when access to alcohol becomes limited (Wilsnack & Cheloha, 1987; Yamaguchi & Kandel, 1985). Studies that examine role properties, such as peer support for drinking, opportunities for drinking, and tolerance for impairment in the roles occupied prior to and following recovery, would contribute to our knowledge of how role socialization occurs.

Finally, it appears that there is a complex relation between roles and substance use, which varies by types and combinations of roles, ethnicity, age, and gender. Characteristics of the role may influence likelihood of alcohol use. For example, Mandell, Eaton, Anthony, and Garrison (1992) found that some jobs (e.g., restaurant waitstaff) were related to a higher risk of alcohol abuse and others (e.g., management-related occupations) were related to lower risk. The study authors theorize that less supervision or greater availability of alcohol may increase the risk of alcohol abuse among employees. Additionally, combinations of roles may have diverse effects. For example, one study found that being a mother was related to lower alcohol consumption, but being a mother who worked full-time was related to an increase in alcohol consumption (Wilsnack & Cheloha, 1987).

A number of social influences on drinking may have different effects for members of various ethnic groups. For example, one study found that African-American women were more likely than Puerto Rican women to endorse social reasons for drinking, especially spousal drinking (Fernandez-Pol, Bluestone, Missouri, Morales, & Mizruchi, 1986). Thus, changes in drinking environments would be especially influential on African-American women's drinking. Also, African-American youth appear to be more influenced by parental disapproval for drinking, whereas White youth appear to be more influenced by peer disapproval (Ringwalt & Palmer, 1990). Changes in drinking behavior may be related to pressure to quit from different social spheres depending on one's ethnic group.

The effects of role transitions also appear to vary by age. Wilsnack and Cheloha (1987) found that alcohol use was predicted by a lack of stable marital and work roles for younger women and by divorce or children leaving home for middle-aged women. For older women, two different patterns were observed: Alcohol use was predicted by being unemployed and married to a problem drinker or by being unmarried and working away from the home.

Finally, the effect of role transitions on alcohol use may vary by gender. For example, men decrease substance use before marriage and after becoming a parent, while women decrease substance use before and after marriage and before becoming a parent (Yamaguchi & Kandel, 1985). Additionally, spousal relationships have different effects for men and women. There is evidence that a husband's drinking before marriage affects the wife's drinking during the first year of marriage, but the wife's premarital drinking does not significantly affect the husband's subsequent drinking (Leonard & Eiden, 1996). Women attempting to change their drinking behavior might be encouraged to evaluate the effects of their spouse's drinking on their own drinking.

Clearly, there is evidence that role transitions affect alcohol use via role selection and role socialization. Natural recovery researchers have identified some of these transitions as important to recovery. Future research should attempt to differentiate between role selection and role socialization and examine the mechanisms through which these transitions affect alcohol use while considering the potential interactions of type and combinations of roles, age, gender and ethnicity.

Individual Difference Variables

A question that has been less frequently examined is what individual difference variables distinguish natural recoverers from other alcohol abusers. Natural recovery may be associated with a number of individual difference variables, including severity of the drinking problem, family history of AUDs, comorbid psychopathology, and personality traits. As of yet, few researchers have examined the relationship of these variables to natural recovery, and existing findings are often contradictory.

Problem Severity

One way in which natural recoverers appear to differ from other alcohol abusers is the severity of their drinking problem. The results from several studies indicate that naturally recovered alcohol abusers had less severe drinking histories and fewer dependence symptoms (Armor & Meshkoff, 1983; Knupfer, 1972; Ojesjo, 1981; Saunders & Kershaw, 1979; Vaillant, 1995). Other studies, however, found no difference in drinking severity between naturally recovered alcoholics and other alcoholics (Goodwin et al., 1971; Tucker & Gladsjo, 1993).

Family History of Alcoholism

Related to problem severity, natural recoverers may be less likely to have a family history of alcoholism, which is a known risk factor for alcoholism (Sher, 1991). Although Vaillant (1995) reported finding no differences in family history among recovered and current alcohol abusers, three other studies have found that natural re-

coverers were less likely to have a family history of alcoholism (Goodwin et al., 1971; Knupfer, 1972; Sobell & Sobell, 1994). Unfortunately, these studies lack comprehensive criteria for determining family history.

Comorbid Psychopathology

A number of disorders are highly comorbid with, and possibly etiologically significant to, AUDs including depression, antisocial personality, and other substance use disorders (Helzer et al., 1991; NIAAA, 1993; Sher & Trull, 1994). Comorbid psychopathology might be expected to negatively impact one's ability to recover without treatment; however, the findings to date regarding the relation between comorbid psychopathology and natural recovery are conflictual.

Depression. Two studies have reported that recovered alcohol abusers were less depressed than current alcohol abusers (Goodwin et al., 1971; Knupfer, 1972). However, these observations were noted following recovery and could reflect a consequence of decreased consumption. Interestingly, in a study of late-life remission from alcohol problems, depression was a significant predictor of recovery, suggesting that distress provided motivation for overcoming an AUD (Schutte, Brennan, & Moos, 1994). Although this study did not distinguish between individuals who recovered with or without treatment, this finding may be applicable for natural recoverers as many describe reaching a low point in their lives prior to recovering (Ludwig, 1985).

Antisocial Personality. Two studies of natural recovery have included measures of antisocial personality. One prospective study found no difference between naturally recovered alcoholics and other alcoholics in terms of "sociopathy," but this study systematically excluded individuals exhibiting delinquent behavior (Vaillant, 1995). Additionally, Goodwin et al. (1971) reported no difference in criminality between those who recovered and those who did not. However, this sample consisted of prison inmates and is likely to have been homogeneous in terms of criminality. Interestingly, existing research examining antisocial personality are limited by restricted variance, both at the low and high ends of this dimension.

Other Substance Use Disorders. It is likely that comorbid substance use disorder is related to a poorer prognosis for AUDs. Most research on comorbid alcohol and tobacco use disorders has focused on the influence of alcohol use on smoking (Sobell et al., 1995). For example, one study found that smokers were less likely to quit if they had a history of alcohol abuse (Breslau, Peterson, Schultz, Andreski, & Chilcoat, 1996). In terms of the influence of smoking on alcohol use, one prospective study of dual recoveries from AUDs and tobacco dependence found that relapse to alcohol abuse was more likely for individuals who continued smoking or had relapsed to smoking (Sobell et al., 1995). However, another study found that comorbid tobacco dependence did not significantly impact the likelihood of recovery from an AUD in young adults (Sher, Gotham, Erickson, & Wood, 1996).

Additionally, some data suggest that multiple drug users have greater difficulty successfully recovering from addictions. Cocaine use appears to predict relapse to alcohol use (Brown, Seraganian, & Tremblay, 1993). Also, continued alcohol abuse appears to predict relapse in recovering cocaine abusers (Moos, Mertens, & Brennan, 1994). Researchers should compare rates of natural recovery among individuals with and without comorbid substance use disorders. If the path to recovery is more difficult for individuals with comorbid substance use disorders, they may also be less likely to recover without treatment. In that case, more intensive self-change strategies and treatment plans may need to be designed for individuals with comorbid substance use disorders.

Personality

A number of personality traits (e.g., behavioral undercontrol and negative affectivity) are related to AUDs and potentially affect one's ability to recover (Sher & Trull, 1994). For example, negative affectivity, a risk factor for AUDs, is of interest as it has been implicated as a predictor of relapse (Brownell et al., 1986). One

study examined a number of personality variables with a sample of natural recoverers and found that recovered alcoholics were lower in "guilt," "need for approval," and introversion (Knupfer, 1972). To date, no comprehensive evaluation of personality and comorbid psychopathology using prospective data has been conducted with a sample of natural recoverers.

By identifying factors that differentiate individuals who are more likely to recover without formal treatment, less intensive interventions based on successful self-change strategies could be targeted to those individuals. These alternative treatments would be consistent with the Institute of Medicine (1990) recommendations that future treatment programs be developed that incorporate graduated levels of treatment and match individuals with the level of treatment they require.

Conclusions and Directions for Future Research

The need for better designed studies of natural recovery is indicated by a number of significant methodological issues associated with the research strategies that have been employed to date. There is a particular need for prospective studies with multiple assessments. Prospectively examining the phenomenon would enable researchers to measure variables of interest contemporaneously with drinking behaviors and help resolve questions of causality. Furthermore, frequent multiple assessments are necessary to establish chronicity of AUDs, the stability of recoveries, and reduce the risk of recall bias about previous events.

A number of improvements in sample selection are needed in both retrospective and prospective research. First, future studies should include relevant control groups. Several researchers have made significant contributions to the study of natural recovery by including individuals with AUDs that recovered with treatment and individuals with current alcohol problems (Sobell et al., 1992; Tucker et al., 1994). These control groups are useful in clarify-

ing how natural recovery is different from treated recovery and how those who recover are different from those who do not recover. However, there are several potentially informative control groups that have yet to be assessed. Unstable recoveries might be identified and included in order to increase our understanding of the role of relapse in the change process. Additionally, individuals who do not have AUDs are important for distinguishing which traits and experiences are products of developmental or cultural processes and which are specific to alcohol use.

Second, studies are needed that examine the change process independent of self-recognition of an alcohol problem. It is likely that a number of individuals experience processes unlike those described by Prochaska, DiClemente, & Norcross (1992) that require or lead to self-recognition of a problem. Several researchers using self-selected volunteers have examined cognitive processes involved in recovery and report that many individuals go through in-depth evaluations of their problems (Ludwig, 1985; Sobell, Sobell et al., 1993). However, individuals who change "unintentionally" would not necessarily go through a similar process. By assessing only individuals who changed after recognizing their alcohol problem, many studies have overlooked the impact of developmental and environmental influences, such as role transitions and social interactions, which might affect alcohol use independent of self-recognition. Finally, due to the use of relatively homogeneous samples, the findings of many studies may not generalize to individuals of all ethnic backgrounds, various ages, and women.

Although findings from previous research must be taken somewhat tentatively in light of the substantial limitations present in the research conducted to date, there are a number of important findings of interest to researchers, clinicians, and individuals making self-change attempts. First, it appears that many individuals experience similar processes when overcoming an AUD, many of which correlate well with 8 of 10 processes identified by Prochaska, DiClemente, & Norcross (1992). Additionally, a number of events (those that encourage recognition of a problem, health-related concerns, and role transitions) appear particularly influential to the change process. Finally, although less research has been conducted on this issue, there is evidence to suggest that natural recovery may be associated with certain individual difference variables such as problem severity, family history of alcoholism, comorbid psychopathology, and personality traits.

Future research should expand on previous findings regarding processes, events, and individual difference variables related to recovery in order to clarify their role in recovery. Additionally, variables that have been examined in clinical and epidemiological research, but overlooked by natural recovery researchers, such as ethnicity, gender, age, and age-related role transitions, should be considered.

A greater understanding of how a number of variables affect the change process has important implications for designing formal treatment programs. First, by identifying factors that differentiate those individuals more likely to recover without treatment, less intensive treatment programs that encourage the use of self-change strategies can be targeted to those individuals. For example, it is unclear whether individuals with comorbid psychopathology have greater difficulty recovering. If natural recovery studies indicate that they do have greater difficulty, more intensive self-change strategies or formal treatment plans may be appropriate for those individuals. Additionally, natural recovery research should make attempts to study individuals who appear to face more barriers to completing formal treatment, such as women and minorities. If self-change appears to be a viable option for these individuals, they could be provided early in treatment with information about self-change strategies that they can attempt should they decide not to complete treatment.

Second, formal treatment can benefit from understanding factors that influence individuals to change independent of self-recognition. For example, natural recovery researchers can attempt to clarify the mechanisms through which role tran-

sitions influence recovery. Therapists could utilize that information to help clients evaluate their lifestyles in terms of processes that appear to be the most influential to recovery (i.e., deterrence, prior role socialization, role incompatibility). For example, if role incompatibility is supported as a major vehicle toward recovery, clients may be asked in what ways their lifestyle (including their drinking behaviors) is incompatible with roles they occupy currently or intend to occupy in the future. If prior role socialization appears to affect recovery, clients who currently occupy roles that encourage drinking might be asked to consider the benefits of alternate roles they would like to occupy and be encouraged to make lifestyle changes. Finally, if deterrence appears to be an important process for some individuals, those individuals whose drinking might be beneficially influenced by their spouses and children should be encouraged to attend premarital, marital, and family counseling.

When viewed in a larger context, it becomes apparent that research in natural recovery can contribute not only to designing self-change strategies and improving formal treatment, but also to designing more effective universal preventive interventions. We offer several examples of how natural recovery studies might expand on previous natural recovery, epidemiological, and clinical research with implications for designing more effective interventions. First, studying the influence of role occupancy on natural recovery has implications for designing educational and workplace policies. Certain role characteristics that appear to influence rates of alcohol consumption such as supervision and alcohol availability should be studied by natural recovery researchers (Mandell et al., 1992). Role characteristics that appear to beneficially influence natural recovery might be incorporated into workplace and institutional policies in order to discourage unhealthy drinking behaviors among students and employees. Second, by studying how the recovery process is different for various demographic groups, interventions can target segments of the population by identifying concerns most salient to different groups of in-

dividuals. For example, the process may vary for members of different age groups. Based on the finding that drinking in older adults is often related to depression and anxiety (Schonfeld & Dupree, 1991), natural recovery studies could determine if symptomatic improvement in those domains leads to reduced alcohol consumption. If so, interventions attempting to reach older drinkers might encourage members of this age group to focus on combating their depression and/or anxiety in order to recover from an alcohol problem. Also, natural recovery studies might attempt to determine what ethnic differences exist in the effects of social factors on drinking in order to make their message more salient to members of different ethnic groups. For example, in light of the finding that drinking by African-American and White youth is differentially affected by peer and parental disapproval (Ringwalt & Palmer, 1990), campaigns targeting youth drinking should stress parental disapproval for African-American youth and peer disapproval for White youth.

In sum, a number of contributions to the study of the development and cessation of AUDs, the development of more effective self-change strategies and formal treatments, and the creation of preventive interventions can arise from the study of natural recovery. However, in order to realize the full potential of studying natural recovery, a number of improvements need to be made in the research strategies employed by natural recovery researchers.

Note

1. In the present article, "alcohol use disorders" is used to refer to a range of problematic drinking statuses that have been studied by researchers of natural recovery.

References

Anderson, P., & Scott, E. (1992). The effect of general practitioners' advice on heavy drinking men. *British Journal of Addiction, 87*, 891–900.

Anonymous (1972). *Alcoholics Anonymous.* New York: Alcoholics Anonymous World Services.

Armor, D. J., & Meshkoff, J. E. (1983). Remission among treated and untreated alcoholics. *Advances in Substance Abuse, 3,* 239–269.

Atkinson, R. M. (1994). Late onset drinking in older adults. *International Journal of Geriatric Psychiatry, 9*, 321–326.

Atkinson, R. M., Tolson, R. L., & Turner, J. A. (1990). Late versus early onset problem drinking in older men. *Alcoholism: Clinical and Experimental Research, 14*, 574–579.

Bachman, J. G., Johnston, L. D., O'Malley, P. M., & Humphrey, R. H. (1988). Explaining the recent decline in marijuana use: Differentiating the effects of perceived risks, disapproval and general lifestyle factors. *Journal of Health and Social Behavior, 29*, 92–112.

Bachman, J. G., O'Malley, P. M., & Johnston, L. D. (1984). Drug use among young adults: The impacts of role status and social environment. *Journal of Personality and Social Psychology, 47*, 629–645.

Bandura, A. (in press). Health promotion from the perspective of social cognitive theory. *Psychology and Health: An International Journal.*

Beckman, L. J. (1988). The health belief model and entry into alcoholism treatment. *International Journal of the Addictions, 23*, 19–28.

Beckman, L. J., & Amaro, H. (1986). Personal and social difficulties faced by women and men entering alcoholism treatment. *Journal of Studies on Alcohol, 47*, 135–145.

Blow, F. C., Cook, C. A., Booth, B. M., Falcon, S. P., & Friedman, M. J. (1992). Age-related psychiatric comorbidities and level of functioning in alcoholic veterans seeking outpatient treatment. *Hospital and Community Psychiatry, 10*, 990–995.

Brennan, A. F., Walfish, S., & AuBuchon, P. (1986). Alcohol use and abuse in college students. II. Social/environmental correlates, methodological issues, and implications for intervention. *The International Journal of the Addictions, 21*, 475–493.

Breslau, N., Peterson, E., Schultz, L., Andreski, P., & Chilcoat, H. (1996). Are smokers with alcohol disorders likely to quit? *American Journal of Public Health, 86*, 985–990.

Brown, T. G., Seraganian, P., & Tremblay, J. (1993). Alcohol and cocaine abusers 6 months after traditional treatment: Do they fare as well as problem drinkers? *Journal of Substance Abuse Treatment, 10*, 545–552.

Brownell, K. D., Marlatt, G. A., Lichtenstein, E., & Wilson, G. T. (1986, July). Understanding and preventing relapse. *American Psychologist, 41*, 765–782.

Caetano, R. (1989). Concepts of alcoholism among Whites, Blacks, and Hispanics in the United States. *Journal of Studies on Alcohol, 50*, 580–582.

Caetano, R., & Herd, D. (1984). Black drinking practices in northern California. *American Journal of Drug and Alcohol Abuse, 10*, 571–587.

Caetano, R., & Katsukas, L. A. (1995). Changes in drinking patterns among Whites, Blacks, and Hispanics. *Journal of Studies on Alcohol, 56*, 558–565.

Chassin, L., Presson, C., Sherman, S. J., & Edwards, D. A. (1992). The natural history of cigarette smoking and young adult social roles. *Journal of Health and Social Behavior, 33*, 328–347.

Chen, A. (1991). Noncompliance in community psychiatry: A review of clinical interventions. *Hospital and Community Psychiatry, 42*, 282–286.

Chen, K., & Kandel, D. B. (1995). The natural history of drug use from adolescence to the mid-thirties in a general population study. *American Journal of Public Health, 85*, 41–47.

Cohen, P., & Cohen, J. (1984). The clinician's illusion. *Archives of General Psychiatry, 41*, 1178–1182.

Cunningham, J. A., Sobell, L. C., Sobell, M. B., Agrawal, S., & Toneatto, T. (1993). Barriers to treatment: Why alcohol and drug abusers delay or never seek treatment. *Addictive Behaviors, 18*, 347–353.

Darrow, S. L., Russell, M., Cooper, M. L., Mudar, P., & Frone, M. R. (1992). Sociodemographic correlates of alcohol consumption among African-American and White women. *Women & Health, 18*, 35–51.

Davidson, R. (1992). Prochaska and DiClemente's model of change: A case study? *British Journal of Addiction, 87*, 821–822.

Dean, P. R., & Edwards, T. A. (1990). Health locus of control beliefs and alcohol-related factors that may influence treatment outcomes. *Journal of Substance Abuse Treatment, 7*, 167–172.

De Soto, C. B., O'Donnell, W. E., & De Soto, J. L. (1989). Long-term recovery in alcoholics. *Alcoholism: Clinical and Experimental Research, 13*, 693–697.

Dufour, M., & Fuller, R. K. (1995). Alcohol in the elderly. *Annual Reviews in Medicine, 46*, 123–132.

Edwards, G., Orford, J., Egert, S., Guthrie, S., Hawker, A., Hensman, C., Mitcheson, M., Oppenheimer, E., & Taylor, C. (1977). Alcoholism: A controlled trial of "treatment" and "advice." *Journal of Studies on Alcohol, 38*, 1004–1031.

Ernhart, C. B., Morrow-Tlucak, M., Sokol, R. J., & Martier, S. (1988). Underreporting of alcohol use in pregnancy. *Alcoholism: Clinical and Experimental Research, 12*, 506–511.

Esbensen, F., & Elliot, D. B. (1994). Continuity and discontinuity in illicit drug use: Patterns and antecedents. *The Journal of Drug Issues, 24*, 75–97.

Fernandez-Pol, B., Bluestone, H., Missouri, C., Morales, G., & Mizruchi, M. S. (1986). Drinking patterns of inner-city Black Americans and Puerto Ricans. *Journal of Studies on Alcohol, 47*, 156–160.

Fillmore, K. M. (1987). Women's drinking across the adult life course as compared to men's. *British Journal of Addiction, 82*, 801–811.

Fillmore, K. M. (1988). *Spontaneous remission from alcohol problems: A critical review.* Unpublished manuscript.

Fried, P. A., Barnes, M. V., & Drake, E. R. (1985). Soft drug use after pregnancy compared to use before and during pregnancy. *American Journal of Obstetrics and Gynecology, 151*, 787–792.

Goodwin, D. W., Crane, J. B., & Guze, S. B. (1971). Felons who drink. *Quarterly Journal of Studies on Alcohol, 32*, 136–147.

Grant, B. F. (1996). Toward an alcohol treatment model: A comparison of treated and untreated respondents with DSM-VI alcohol use disorders in the general population. *Alcoholism: Clinical and Experimental Research, 20*, 583–591.

Guze, S. B., Goodwin, D. W., & Crane, B. J. (1969). Criminality and psychiatric disorders. *Archives of General Psychiatry, 20*, 583–591.

Helzer, J. E., Burnam, A., & McEvoy, L. T. (1991). Alcohol abuse and dependence. In L. N. Robins & D. A. Regier (Eds.), *Psychiatric disorders in America* (pp. 81–115). New York: Free Press.

Hingson, R., Scotch, N., Day, N., & Culbert, A. (1980). Recognizing and seeking help for drinking problems. *Journal of Studies on Alcohol, 41*, 1102–1117.

Hollinger, R. C. (1984). Race, occupational status, and proactive police arrest for drinking and driving. *Journal of Criminal Justice, 12*, 173–183.

Humphreys, K., Moos, R. F., & Finney, J. W. (1995). Two pathways out of drinking problems without professional treatment. *Addictive Behaviors, 20*, 427–441.

Ihlen, B. M., Amundsen, A., & Daae, S. L. (1990). Changes in the use of intoxicants after onset of pregnancy. *British Journal of Addiction, 85*, 1627–1631.

Imber, S., Schultz, E., Funderburk, F., Allen, R., & Flamer, R. (1976). The fate of the untreated alcoholic. *The Journal of Nervous and Mental Disease, 162*, 238–247.

Institute of Medicine. (1990). *Broadening the base of treatment for alcohol problems: Report of a study by a committee of the Institute of Medicine, Division of Mental Health and Behavioral Medicine.* Washington, DC: National Academy Press.

Jones-Webb, R. J., Hsiao, C., & Hannan, P. (1995). Relationships between socioeconomic status and drinking problems among Black and White men. *Alcoholism: Clinical and Experimental Research, 19*, 623–627.

Kendell, R. E. (1966). The fate of untreated alcoholics. *Quarterly Journal of Studies on Alcohol, 27*, 30–41.

Kissin, B., Rosenblatt, S. M., & Machover, S. (1968). Prognostic factors in alcoholism. In J. O. Cole (Ed.), *Clinical research in alcoholism* (pp. 22–43). Washington, DC: American Psychiatric Association.

Klingemann, H. K. (1991). The motivation for change from problem alcohol and heroin use. *British Journal of Addiction, 86*, 727–744.

Klingemann, H. K. (1992). Coping and maintenance strategies of spontaneous remitters from problem use of alcohol and heroin in Switzerland. *The International Journal of the Addictions, 27*, 1359–1388.

Knupfer, G. (1972). Ex-problem drinkers. In M. Roff, L. N. Robins, & M. Pollack (Eds.), *Life history research in psychopathology* (Vol. 2, pp. 256–280). Minneapolis: University of Minnesota Press.

Leaf, P. J., Bruce, M. L., Tischler, G. L., & Holzer, C. E. (1987). The relationship between demographic factors and attitudes toward mental health services. *Journal of Community Psychology, 15,* 275–284.

Lemere, F. (1953). What happens to alcoholics? *American Journal of Psychiatry, 109,* 674–676.

Leonard, K. E., & Eiden, R. (1996, June). *Husbands and wives drinking: Unilateral or bilateral influences.* Paper presented at the annual meeting of the Research Society on Alcoholism, Washington, DC.

Lex, B. W. (1987). Review of alcohol problems in ethnic minority groups. *Journal of Consulting and Clinical Psychology, 55,* 293–300.

Ludwig, A. M. (1985). Cognitive processes associated with "spontaneous" recovery from alcoholism. *Journal of Studies on Alcohol, 46,* 53–58.

Mandell, W., Eaton, W. W., Anthony, J. C., & Garrison, R. (1992). Alcoholism and occupations: A review and analysis of 104 occupations. *Alcoholism: Clinical and Experimental Research, 16,* 734–746.

Menon, R., Blakely, C., Carmichael, D., & Snow, D. (1995). Making a dent in recidivism rates: Impact of employment on minority ex-offenders. In G. Thomas (Ed.), *Race and ethnicity in America: Meeting the challenge in the 21st century* (pp. 279–294). Washington, DC: Taylor and Francis.

Miller, W. R. (1985). Motivation for treatment: A review with special emphasis on alcoholism. *Psychological Bulletin, 98,* 84–107.

Miller-Tutzauer, C., Leonard, K. E., & Windle, M. (1991). Marriage and alcohol use: A longitudinal study of "maturing out." *Journal of Studies on Alcohol, 52,* 434–440.

Moos, R. H., Mertens, J. R., & Brennan, P. L. (1994). Rates and predictors of four-year readmission among late-middle-aged and older substance abuse patients. *Journal of Studies on Alcohol, 55,* 561–570.

Myers, S. L. (1983). Racial differences in post prison employment. *Social Science Quarterly, 64,* 655–669.

Neighbors, H. W. (1985). Seeking professional help for personal problems: Black Americans' use of health and mental health services. *Community Mental Health Journal, 21,* 156–166.

NIAA (1993). Psychiatric comorbidity with alcohol use disorders. In *The eighth special report to the U.S. Congress on alcohol and health* (pp. 37–59). Alexandria, VA: National Institute on Alcohol Abuse and Alcoholism.

Nordstrom, G., Berglund, M. (1987). Ageing and recovery from alcoholism. *British Journal of Psychiatry, 151,* 382–388.

Ojesjo, L. (1981). Long-term outcome in alcohol abuse and alcoholism among males in the Lundby general population, Sweden. *British Journal of Addiction, 76,* 391–400.

Prochaska, J. O., DiClemente, C. C., & Norcross, J. C. (1992). In search of how people change. *American Psychologist, 47,* 1102–1114.

Prochaska, J. O., DiClemente, C. C., Velicer, W. F., & Rossi, J. S. (1992)., Comments on Davidson's 'Prochaska and DiClemente's model of change: A case study?' *British Journal of Addiction, 87,* 1102–1114.

Raynes, A. E., & Warren, G. (1971). Some distinguishing features of patients failing to attend a psychiatric clinic after referral. *American Journal of Orthopsychiatry, 41,* 581–588.

Ringwalt, C. L., & Palmer, J. H. (1990). Differences between White and Black youth who drink heavily. *Addictive Behavior, 15,* 455–460.

Roizen, R., Cahalan, D., & Shanks, P. (1978). "Spontaneous remission" among untreated problem drinkers. In D. B. Kandel (Ed.), *Longitudinal research on drug use* (pp. 197–221). Washington, DC: Hemisphere.

Rosenstock, I. M. (1974). Historical origins of the health relief model. *Health Education Monographs, 2,* 328–335.

Saunders, W. M., & Kershaw, P. W. (1979). Spontaneous remission from alcoholism—a community study. *British Journal of Addiction, 74,* 251–265.

Schonfeld, L., & Dupree, L. W. (1991). Antecedents of drinking for early- and late-onset elderly alcohol abusers. *Journal of Studies on Alcohol, 52,* 587–592.

Schuckit, M. A., & Gunderson, E. K. (1977). Alcoholism in young men. *American Journal of Drug and Alcohol Abuse, 4,* 581–592.

Schulenberg, J., O'Malley, P. M., Bachman, J. G., Wadsworth, K. N., & Johnston, L. D. (1996). Getting drunk and growing up: Trajectories of frequent binge drinking during the transition to young adulthood. *Journal of Studies on Alcohol, 57,* 289–304.

Schutte, K. K., Brennan, P. L., & Moos, R. H. (1994). Remission of late-life drinking problems: A 4-year follow-up. *Alcoholism: Clinical and Experimental Research, 18,* 835–844.

Serdula, M., Williamson, D. F., Kendrick, J. S., Anda, R. F., & Byers, T. (1991). Trends in alcohol consumption by pregnant women: 1985 through 1988. *Journal of the American Medical Association, 265,* 876–879.

Seymour, J., & Wattis, J. P. (1992). Alcohol abuse in the elderly. *Reviews in Clinical Gerontology, 2,* 141–150.

Sher, K. J. (1991). *Children of alcoholics: A critical appraisal of theory and research.* Chicago: University of Chicago Press.

Sher, K. J., Gotham, H. J., Erickson, D. J., & Wood, P. K. (1996). A prospective high-risk study of the relationship between tobacco dependence and alcohol use disorders. *Alcoholism: Clinical and Experimental Research, 20,* 485–491.

Sher, K. J., & Trull, T. J. (1994). Personality and disinhibitory psychopathology: Alcoholism and antisocial personality disorder. *Journal of Abnormal Psychology, 103,* 92–102.

Smart, R. G. (1975). Spontaneous recovery in alcoholics: A review and analysis of the available research. *Drug and Alcohol Dependence, 1,* 277–285.

Smear, V. S., & Smithy-Willis, D. (1982). Utility of sex, marital status, race, and age in targeting populations for mental health services. *Psychological Reports, 50,* 843–855.

Sobell, L. C., Cunningham, J. A., & Sobell, M. B. (1996). Recovery from alcohol problems with and without treatment: Prevalence in two population surveys. *Journal of Public Health, 86,* 966–972.

Sobell, L. C., Cunningham, J. A., Sobell, M. B., Agrawal, S., Gavin, D. R., Leo, G. I., & Singh, K. N. (1996). Fostering change among problem drinkers: A proactive community intervention. *Addictive Behaviors, 21,* 817–833.

Sobell, L. C., Cunningham, J. A., Sobell, M. B., & Toneatto, T. (1993). Life-span perspective on natural recovery (self-change) from alcohol problems. In J. S. Baer, G. A. Marlatt, & R. J. McMahan (Eds.), *Addictive behaviors across the life span* (pp. 34–66). London: Sage.

Sobell, L. C., & Sobell, M. B. (1994, June). *Naturally recovered alcohol abusers: What maintains their resolutions?* Paper presented at the annual meeting of the Research Society on Alcoholism, Maui, Hawaii.

Sobell, L. C., Sobell, M. B., & Toneatto, T. (1992). Recovery from alcohol problems without treatment. In N. Heather, W. R. Miller, & J. Greeley (Eds.), *Self-control and the addictive behaviors* (pp. 198–242). New York: Maxwell Macmillan.

Sobell, L. C., Sobell, M. B., Toneatto, T., & Leo, G. I. (1993). What triggers the resolution of alcohol problems without treatment? *Alcoholism: Clinical and Experimental Research, 17,* 217–224.

Sobell, M. B., Sobell, L. C., & Kozlowski, L. T. (1995). Dual recoveries from alcohol and smoking problems. In J. B. Fertig & J. P. Allen (Eds.), *Alcohol and Tobacco: From basic science to clinical practice* (research monograph No. 3; pp. 207–224) Alexandria, VA: National Institute on Alcohol Abuse and Alcoholism.

Stall, R. (1983). An examination of spontaneous remission from problem drinking in the bluegrass region of Kentucky. *Journal of Drug Issues, 13,* 191–206.

Stall, R., & Biernacki, P. (1986). Spontaneous remission from the problematic use of substances: An inductive model derived from a comparative analysis of the alcohol, opiate, tobacco, and food/obesity literatures. *The International Journal of the Addictions, 21,* 1–23.

Tuchfeld, B. S. (1981). Spontaneous remission in alcoholics: Empirical observations and theoretical implications. *Journal of Studies on Alcohol, 42,* 626–641.

Tucker, J. A. (1995). Predictors of help-seeking and the temporal relationship of help to recovery among treated and untreated recovered problem drinkers. *Addiction, 90,* 805–809.

Tucker, J. A., & Gladsjo, J. A. (1993). Help-seeking and recovery by problem drinkers: Characteristics of drinkers who attended alcoholics anonymous or formal treatment or who recovered without assistance. *Addictive Behaviors, 18,* 529–542.

Tucker, J. A., Vuchinich, R. E., & Gladsjo, J. A. (1994). Environmental events surrounding natural recovery from alcohol-related problems. *Journal of Studies on Alcohol, 55,* 401–411.

Tucker, J. A., Vuchinich, R. E., & Pukish, M. M. (1995). Molar environmental contexts surrounding recovery from alcohol problems by treated and untreated problem drinkers. *Experimental and Clinical Psychopharmacology, 3,* 195–204.

Vaillant, G. E. (1995). *The natural history of alcoholism revisited.* Cambridge, MA: Harvard University Press.

Wilsnack, R. W., & Cheloha, R. (1987). Women's roles and problem drinking across the lifespan. *Social Problems, 34,* 231–248.

Yamaguchi, K., & Kandel, D. B. (1985). On the resolution of role incompatibility: A life event history analysis of family roles and marijuana use. *American Journal of Sociology, 90,* 1284–1325.

Zucker, R. A. (1987). The four alcoholisms: A developmental account of the etiologic process. In P. C. Rivers (Ed.), *Nebraska symposium on motivation, 1986: Alcohol & addictive behavior* (pp. 27–83). Lincoln: University of Nebraska Press.

Zylman, R. (1972). Race and social status discrimination and police action in alcohol affected collisions. *Journal of Safety Research, 4,* 75–84.

 Article Review Form at end of book.

Summarize the treatments used for trichotillomania.

Retrospective Review of Treatment Outcome for 63 Patients with Trichotillomania

Nancy J. Keuthen, Ph.D.,

Richard L. O'Sullivan, M.D.,

Paige Goodchild, B.A.,

Dayami Rodriguez, B.A.,

Michael A. Jenike, M.D.,

and Lee Baer, Ph.D.

Objective

The authors' goal was to assess naturalistic treatment outcome in trichotillomania. Method: Sixty-three patients who had been treated in a specialty clinic for trichotillomania over a period of 6 years were contacted. The patients were given paper-and-pencil instruments that assessed current severity of hairpulling, depression, anxiety, self-esteem, and psychosocial functioning. Results: Significant mean improvement was found on measures of hairpulling, depression, anxiety, self-esteem, and psychosocial functioning. Improvement in hairpulling was associated with greater depression at the time of their index clinic evaluation as well as more improvement in depression after treatment. Conclusions: State-of-the-art behavioral and pharmacological treatments offer substantial clinical benefit to patients with trichotillomania, both in hairpulling symptoms and ancillary measures of functioning.
(Am J Psychiatry 1998; 155:560–561)

Trichotillomania is widely viewed as a chronic disorder that can be refractory to treatment efforts. The existing treatment literature is sparse; there are few controlled trials and meager long-term follow-up data.[1] To our knowledge, there is only one clinical report that documents naturalistic treatment outcome;[2] this study reported minimal benefit.

To examine treatment outcome in trichotillomania, we conducted a retrospective survey using multiple measures of functioning in a large group of patients with the disorder. We hypothesized that these patients would experience improvement in measures of hairpulling, self-esteem, and psychosocial functioning but not in measures of anxiety or depression. We also examined whether comorbid depression and anxiety, severity and impact of hairpulling at the time of their index clinic evaluation, or demographic variables were related to treatment response.

Method

All patients with trichotillomania treated in the Massachusetts General Hospital Trichotillomania Clinic and Research Unit between August 1990 and November 1996 were contacted by phone or letter. Surveys were completed by 63 (79%) of the 80 patients successfully reached. All subjects satisfied DSM-IV criteria for trichotillomania and provided written informed consent.

The subjects' mean age was 33.5 years (SD=9.3, range=15–60), and their mean age at onset of trichotillomania was 12.4 years (SD=6.5, range=1–48). Fifty-eight respondents (92%) were female and five (8%) were male. Thirty subjects (48%) were married, 32 (51%) were single, and one (2%) was divorced.

Fifty-seven patients (90%) received behavioral treatment, and 46 patients (73%) received medication treatment. Forty-one patients (65%) received both medication treatment and behavioral treatment. Of those who received medication treatment, 27 (59%) were given clomipramine, 27 (59%) fluoxetine, 23 (50%) paroxetine, 11 (24%) venlafaxine, 10 (22%) sertraline, 10 (22%) fluvoxamine, and seven (15%) lithium carbonate. Other medications were used infrequently (in five or fewer patients). Seven patients (15%) participated in an open trial of paroxetine; of these, six (86%) pursued subsequent treatment. In addition, 23 (37%) of the 63 patients were treated with hypnosis, 31 (49%) were treated with psychotherapy, and 21 (33%) participated in a support group.

At questionnaire completion, 32 subjects (51%) were still in active treatment; of these, 20 subjects (62%)

each were still receiving behavioral treatment or medication treatment; eight subjects (25%) were still receiving both behavioral and medication treatment. Twenty-seven subjects (43%) were no longer in active treatment. Current treatment status was unknown for four subjects (6%).

Paper-and-pencil measures of functioning included the Massachusetts General Hospital Hairpulling Scale, Beck Depression Inventory, Beck Anxiety Inventory, Trichotillomania Impact Scale, Sickness Impact Profile, and Rosenberg Self-Esteem Scale. For the Sickness Impact Profile and the Rosenberg Self-Esteem Scale, subjects were asked to assess themselves before treatment initiation retrospectively, as was done in an earlier follow-up study of obsessive-compulsive disorder.[3] The Hairpulling Scale, Beck Depression Inventory, Beck Anxiety Inventory, and Trichotillomania Impact Scale scores at clinic evaluation were extracted from the medical charts. (Data on these scales were available for 43 patients, although scores were not available on each scale for every patient.) Global self-ratings of improvement in hairpulling were based on a 7-point scale on which 1=very much improved and 7=very much worse. Subjects were rated as responders if their self-ratings of improvement were 1 or 2; they were rated as nonresponders if their self-ratings of improvement were higher than 2.

The Hairpulling Scale is a seven-item self-report instrument that measures the number of hairpulling urges, the intensity of the urges, the ability of the patients to distract themselves from the urge to pull their hair, the number of hairpulling incidents, attempts to resist hairpulling, the ability to resist hairpulling, and feeling uncomfortable about hairpulling. Individual items are rated for severity from 0 (no symptoms) to 4 (extreme symptoms).

At the time of their index clinic evaluation (baseline), the patients self-reports of hairpulling symptoms on the Hairpulling Scale indicated that they experienced hairpulling urges often (mean=2.31, SD=1.05), urges were moderate in intensity (mean=2.38, SD=0.94), and the patients were able to distract themselves from urges some of the time

(mean=2.31, SD=0.84). They reported pulling their hair often (mean=2.10, SD=1.12), attempted to resist pulling their hair some of the time (mean=2.14, SD=0.78), and were able to resist hairpulling some of the time (mean=3.05, SD=0.94). Patients reported feeling noticeably uncomfortable about their hairpulling at baseline (mean=2.12, SD=1.13). Mean Beck Depression Inventory and Beck Anxiety Inventory scores at baseline were in the range of a mild mood disturbance (mean score=12.18, SD=8.44) and mild anxiety (mean score=10.59, SD=8.71), respectively.

Paired t tests were used for within-subject comparisons, and independent t tests were used for between-group comparisons. The significance level was set at p=0.05 for both one-tailed directional hypotheses and two-tailed nondirectional hypotheses.

To protect against type I error caused by multiple tests, multivariate analysis of variance (MANOVA) was used to compare treatment response groups (responder versus nonresponder) and a composite of eight dependent variables (age; age at onset of trichotillomania; baseline Beck Depression Inventory, Beck Anxiety Inventory, Hairpulling Scale, and Trichotillomania Impact Scale scores; and difference between Beck Depression Inventory and Beck Anxiety Inventory scores from baseline to questionnaire completion).

Results

Significant improvement occurred from baseline to questionnaire completion in total Hairpulling Scale scores (t=5.11, df=41, p<0.001). Thirty-three subjects (52%) rated themselves as treatment responders, and 30 (48%) rated themselves as nonresponders.

Comparisons between current and retrospective ratings of functioning revealed significant improvement in Rosenberg Self-Esteem Scale scores (t=6.95, df=51, p<0.001) and Sickness Impact Profile total scale scores (t=2.21, df=38, p=0.02). Significant improvement in psychosocial functioning was also found, reflected in Trichotillomania Impact Scale total scores (t=4.33, df=42, p<0.001).

Contrary to our hypotheses, we found significant reductions in both

depression and anxiety symptoms (Beck Depression Inventory: t=3.20, df=36, p=0.003; Beck Anxiety Inventory: t=3.90, df=30, p=0.001).

We computed a MANOVA for eight dependent variables comparing treatment response groups (Wilks's lambda=0.49, F=2.22, df=8, 17, p=0.08). Baseline Beck Depression Inventory scores differed significantly between groups (t=2.21, df=36, p=0.03): responders had higher baseline depression scores than nonresponders. Improvement in depression scores from baseline to questionnaire completion also differed significantly between responders and nonresponders (t=2.81, df=35, p=0.008). On average, Beck Depression Inventory scores for responders decreased by 8.68 points, but scores for nonresponders stayed the same (mean difference=0.13). No significant group differences were found for age, age at onset of trichotillomania, baseline or difference in Beck Anxiety Inventory scores, or baseline Hairpulling Scale and Trichotillomania Impact Scale scores.

Discussion

The existing treatment literature raises serious concerns as to whether health care professionals have effective treatments for trichotillomania. Treatment studies are plagued with conflicting results, a lack of large-scale controlled treatment trials, and limited long-term follow-up of patients.

Our investigation offers treatment outcome data for a large group of well-characterized subjects with trichotillomania as well as assessment with multiple measures. Our satisfactory study return rate of 79% enables us to provide a representative picture of treatment outcomes. Given that all subjects received part or all of their treatment in our specialty clinic, we can be confident that adequate trials of each treatment modality were attempted in most cases.

Our outcome data reveal clinically meaningful and significant improvement with treatment according to all of our assessment measures. These findings are paralleled by subjective ratings of hairpulling improvement. Although many of the medications prescribed for treatment of hairpulling are effective anxiolytics and antidepressants, 16 (25%) of the patients in our study had received behavioral treatment alone and 27 (43%) were not in treatment at the time of questionnaire completion. Thus, improvements in anxiety, depression, self-esteem, and psychosocial functioning may be indirect benefits of treatment for hairpulling.

Higher baseline levels of depression as well as greater reductions in depression with treatment were associated with higher patient global ratings of hairpulling improvement. Our results, however, do not allow us to comment on whether alleviation of depression precedes reductions in hairpulling or vice versa. Future longitudinal studies should prospectively follow patients with trichotillomania to identify whether reductions in depression precede or follow improvement in hairpulling.

In summary, our findings are optimistic for treatment outcome in trichotillomania and are in direct contrast to earlier reports indicating limited treatment efficacy. While clinical and research investigations into better treatments for trichotillomania continue, our results suggest that current state-of-the-art treatment methods benefit a substantial proportion of patients with trichotillomania who seek care.

References

1. Keuthen NJ, O'Sullivan RL, Jefferys D: Trichotillomania: clinical concepts and treatment approaches, in *Obsessive-Compulsive Disorders*, 3rd ed. Edited by Jenike MA, Baer L, Minichiello WE. Littleton, Mass, PSG (in press)
2. Cohen LJ, Stein DJ, Simeon D, Spadaccini E, Rosen J, Aronowitz B, Hollander E: Clinical profile, comorbidity, and treatment history in 123 hair pullers: a survey study. *J Clin Psychiatry* 1995; 56:319–326
3. Baer L, Rauch SL, Ballantine T, Martuza R, Cosgrove R, Cassem E, Giriunas I, Manzo PA, Dimino C, Jenike M: Cingulotomy for intractable obsessive-compulsive disorder. *Arch Gen Psychiatry* 1995; 52:384–392

 Article Review Form at end of book.

What treatment(s) would be effective for compulsive gambling in college students?

Prevalence and Risk Factors of Problem Gambling among College Students

Ken C. Winters and Phyllis Bengston
University of Minnesota, Twin Cities

Derek Dorr
University of Minnesota, Duluth

Randy Stinchfield
University of Minnesota, Twin Cities

College students from 2 Minnesota universities were surveyed about their gambling involvement. Gambling was reported to be a common experience, with 87% having participated at least once in the previous year. Most students reported gambling at fairly infrequent levels, and few identified financial, social, or personal consequences as a result of gambling. The odds of being identified as a probable pathological gambler was high for men, those indicating a positive parental history for gambling problems, regular (weekly plus) users of illicit drugs, and those with poor grades.

The recent expansion of legalized gambling in the United States has raised the health concern that this trend will contribute to an increased rate of pathological gambling (Volberg, 1996). As defined in the fourth edition of the *Diagnostic and Statistical Manual of Mental Disorders* (*DSM-IV*; American Psychiatric Association, 1994), pathological gambling is characterized by 10 criteria that are conceptually similar to substance use disorder criteria, such as a persistent pattern of loss of control, negative consequences, and diminished functioning in expected roles. Pathological gambling criteria also include symptoms suggesting psychological tolerance (i.e., a need to gamble with increasing amounts of money to achieve the desired excitement) and withdrawal-like phenomena (i.e., restlessness or irritability when attempting to cut down or stop gambling).

Within the past decade, several prevalence studies have been conducted in an effort to estimate the extent of this so-called "addiction of the 1990s." As summarized in Volume 12 of the *Journal of Gambling Studies* (1996) devoted to this topic, prevalence rates of adult problem gambling (often referred to as "probable pathological gambling") are estimated to be 1%–3% (Volberg, 1996), and prevalence rates among adolescents are estimated at 2%–6% (Shaffer & Hall, 1996). Admittedly, this body of research has not benefited from the vast resources and rigorous research designs that characterize such prominent epidemiological studies as the National Institute on Drug Abuse Household Survey (National Institute on Drug Abuse, 1990). However, numerous large-scale gambling surveys have been conducted, representing diverse national and international communities. Many of them have recruited large, representative samples and used sound sampling strategies. Furthermore, nearly all of them based their findings on the same gambling measure: the South Oaks Gambling Screen (SOGS; Lesieur & Blume, 1987). This nearly-universal use of the 20-item self-report SOGS in gambling surveys allows for cross-study comparisons.

Somewhat surprisingly, one high-risk group that has not received much research attention is college students. One factor relevant to risk status is that the college years are generally associated with a wide range of at-risk behaviors, including heavy use of psychoactive substances (Windle, 1991). It appears that substance abusers are more likely than nonsubstance abusers to develop a gambling problem, an association that has been empirically demonstrated in adults (Lesieur & Heineman, 1988; Stinchfield & Winters, 1996) and adolescents (Jacobs, 1989; Shaffer & Hall, 1996; Stinchfield, Cassuto, Winters, & Latimer, 1997; Winters, Stinchfield & Fulkerson, 1993). For example, Winters et al. (1993) found in their adolescent sample that regular (weekly or daily) substance users were many times more likely to be defined as problem gamblers. Thus, to the extent that gambling and substance abuse empirically go hand in hand, the college years may be an unusually risky period for the development of gambling problems (Landouceur, Dube, & Bujold, 1994; Lesieur et al., 1991).

Another factor that may affect this heightened risk is the fact that in many states the legal age for gambling, including high-stakes games, is 18 years. Because the vulnerability associated with problem gambling seems to increase during the early adulthood years (Lesieur & Heineman, 1988), the relaxed legal age for gambling further accentuates its potential health risk to college students. These converging factors of concern have led one national expert to recommend that all college students should be screened for potential problems with gambling (Lesieur et al., 1991).

To date, the research literature on college gambling is sparse. Browne and Brown (1993) reported that among 288 marketing students at an Oregon state university, attitudes, game preferences, and reasons for play pertaining to the State of Oregon lottery were similar to results from the general population. The researchers did not report the extent of lottery playing. Casino use was the focus of a survey of 238 Connecticut college students (Devlin & Peppard, 1996). About 15% of respondents indicated having visited a local casino, and few reported problems related to gambling involvement.

Perhaps the most comprehensive estimate of gambling involvement among college students was provided by a study of 1,771 college students from New York, New Jersey, Nevada, Oklahoma, and Texas (Lesieur et al., 1991). Eighty-five percent of the students reported gambling at any level, and 23% gambled weekly. The most frequent forms of gambling were slot machines, video poker, card games, casino games, and lotteries. Similar to the literature on adolescents, men tended to gamble more than women, and most bettors risked small amounts of money (although 12% of the college students reported gambling with $100 or more). On the basis of SOGS results, 9.3% of the men and 2.4% of the women scored in the range indicating probable pathological gambling.

However, the past few years have been characterized by the combination of several trends that suggest a need for additional monitoring of college-aged gambling: A national law increasing the legal age for drinking to 21 years of age; a rapid expansion of casino gambling and state lotteries; and the spread of gambling venues and options for 18-year-olds. Many campuses in the United States today are faced with the situation in which the majority of their students cannot legally drink but they can legally participate in high-stakes gambling. In addition, given that most Americans now live within a 4-hr drive of a casino, it is likely that most American university students have easy access to gambling venues. Given these trends, there is reason to expect that college gambling may be more prevalent today than in previous years.

The aims of this study were threefold. First, we wanted to characterize the risk of problem gambling among college students in close proximity to high-stakes gambling venues compared with known rates for adults and college students from previous studies. The participants' status as college students was viewed as an individual risk factor for involvement in risky behaviors (Lesieur & Heineman, 1988), and their close proximity to high-stakes casinos was hypothesized to be an environmental risk factor for gambling (Jacobs, 1989). The second aim of the study was to further explore whether specific psychosocial factors would be related to college problem gambling. Of particular interest were drug use and parent gambling, two variables that have been consistently linked to adolescent problem gambling (e.g., Winters et al., 1993). Examining psychosocial correlates may further inform pathogenic models of gambling and assist in developing prevention efforts aimed at college students. A final aim of the study was to examine the association between gambling habits and credit card debt. Because the independence of college life and the transition into young adulthood often includes access to lines of credit (e.g., credit cards), the college student is often faced with newfound spending freedoms. We were interested in whether students who overindulged in gambling also would be more likely to show a more general problem of money management as evidenced by high levels of credit card debt.

The study focused on the findings from a 1993 gambling survey conducted at two universities in Minnesota. Minnesota was an appropriate state to address the study aims because gambling is legal at age 18, both universities are located within a 30-min drive of at least one high-stakes casino, and the rapid and widespread expansion of gambling in the state has created a progambling culture of which the majority of its residents approve (Emerson, Laundergan, & Schaefer, 1994).

Method

Survey

A college gambling survey was designed for this study. It consisted of (a) demographic, school performance, and drug use frequency items routinely included in the University of Minnesota yearly student survey; (b) the 20-item SOGS (Lesieur & Blume, 1987); and (c) questions about amount lost while gambling, perceptions of peer gambling, and personal finances and spending (income during the previous year, average monthly disposable income, and total credit card debt as of the previous month). The SOGS, which represents the core variables of the survey, was developed from criteria from the third edition of the *DSM* for screening populations for gambling problems. It has been widely used in epidemiological surveys and for clinical and forensic screening, and its psychometric properties are excellent (Lesieur & Blume, 1987). The SOGS measures the frequency of gambling for money across several activities, the amount gambled, familial history of gambling, and signs of problem gambling (e.g., signs of guilt, loss of control, interference with responsibilities, and the consequences of gambling). Most items require a yes or no response. It has established reliability and validity in a wide range of settings and across clinical and community groups as a screening tool (Lesieur & Blume, 1993). On the basis of validation studies with clinical and nonclinical samples, a cutoff score of 5+ has been identified as the most ac-

Table 1 Characteristics of the College Sample (*N* = 1,361)

Variable	n	%
Classification		
Freshman	370	27.2
Sophomore	350	25.8
Junior	324	23.8
Senior	315	23.2
Age		
18 and under	117	8.7
19–22	1,008	75.1
23 and older	217	16.2
Gender		
Male	652	48.7
Female	687	51.3
Ethnicity		
White	1,266	94.6
Non-White	72	5.4
Employed		
Not employed	548	42.7
Part time[a]	628	48.9
Full time[b]	107	8.3
Grade point average		
A	219	16.6
B	764	57.8
C	326	24.7
D–F	12	0.9
Income previous 12 months[c]		
Less than $5,000	548	40.6
$5,000–$10,000	524	38.8
$10,000 and over	277	20.5
Disposable income per month		
Less than $50	405	29.9
$50–$100	512	37.8
$100–$200	268	19.8
$200 and over	168	12.4
Licit drug use frequency[d]		
Never use	138	10.1
Twice per month or less	523	38.4
Weekly or more	700	51.4
Illicit drug use frequency		
Never use	925	68.0
Twice per month or less	323	23.7
Weekly or more	113	8.3

Note. Frequencies for some characteristics vary slightly because of missing data.

[a]Less than 30 hr per week; [b]Thirty hours or more per week; [c]Includes earned wage, loans, money sent by relatives, and grant or scholarship funds not dedicated to tuition; [d]Tobacco and alcohol.

curate designation of clinical-level gambling, referred to by the developers as "probable pathological gambler" (Lesieur & Blume, 1987; Stinchfield, 1997).

Participants

Students were recruited from two university campuses in Minnesota, each located in cities with populations of less than 100,000. The two campus samples of undergraduate students (*ns* = 846 and 515) were combined (*N* = 1,361) because (a) each group was recruited with the same procedures (classroom testing), had equivalent participation rates (more than 95% of eligible participants completed the survey), and represented about 10% of their respective student bodies, and (b) no statistical differences were found in terms of demographic characteristics, drug and alcohol frequency, gambling frequency, and SOGS scores between the two groups.

The sampling procedure targeted classrooms that attracted the general student body. With the help of school officials, a group of representative classrooms was identified by a computerized random selection procedure. For the one instance that the instructor refused participation, another classroom within the same subject area was chosen as a replacement.

As summarized in Table 1, participants were predominantly White (95%) and 19–22 years old (73%). A slight majority were women (52%). The sample was equally distributed in terms of college year. Nearly 60% were employed full or part time, and 21% had an income of $10,000 or higher during the past 12 months.

Procedure

Students in the target classrooms were approached by a research assistant about participation during class time. The purpose of the study and the voluntary nature of participation were explained. Students not wishing to take the survey were instructed to work quietly until the others had finished. The combined percentage of refusals and absent students was small (<5%).

Results

Gambling Involvement in the Past Year

Ninety-one percent and 84% of the men and women, respectively, reported gambling at least once during the previous 12 months (see Table 2). Except for bingo, men reported a higher rate of gambling than did women across all activities. The rates for men were the same or more than double those of women for several activities (e.g., playing cards with friends, cards at casino, betting on horse or dog races, betting on sports, and playing dice games for money). In terms of the total sample, the most popular games were gambling machines (67%) and lotteries (63%).

Twelve percent of the participants reported gambling at least weekly or daily for at least one activity, and proportionally more men (19%) than women (5%) did so at this level. Betting on games of skill was the category most often played weekly or daily by men (7%); for women, lottery playing (2%) was the activity with the highest percentage of weekly or daily involvement. Reported estimates of the amount of money lost due to gambling during the previous year were generally at the low end. Among gamblers, 30% reported no gambling losses (included those indicating net gain), whereas 10% reported total loss of $100 or more. (Gambling loss data should be viewed with caution because of unknown validity. It is not clear whether individuals are accurate in monitoring net losses for games that involve the reuse of the same money throughout the course of a gambling episode, such as playing casino cards.)

SOGS scores revealed a highly skewed frequency distribution (see Table 3). Nearly 3% (2.9%) of the participants ($n = 41$) scored in the probable pathological range (5+), and nearly 80% of them were men ($n = 32$). An additional 4.4% reported a SOGS score in the potential pathological range (3–4). Again, men dominated this group (78%). None of the elevated SOGS scorers exceeded a score of 11, which is the average SOGS score found among treatment-seeking problem gamblers

(Stinchfield & Winters, 1996). At the other end of the distribution, 68.3% had a zero SOGS score (which included nongamblers).

Variables Associated with Gambling Involvement

Given that subject variables were categorical, we chose an odds ratio (OR) analysis to examine the relationship between subject characteristics and probable pathological gambling status. To facilitate the interpretation of OR results, we dichotomized the categorical variables on the basis of (a) their natural division into two categories (e.g., gender); (b) a cut score that adequately divided a bimodal distribution (e.g., monthly disposable income); or (c) a cut score that identified an "outlier" group for a variable believed to a high risk factor (e.g., use of illicit drugs). On the basis of these guidelines, the following subject variables were identified: gender, college class (lower division or upper division), student status (part time or full time), employment status (employed <10 hr or >10 hr per week), approximate cumulative grade point average (As and Bs or Cs, Ds, and Fs), yearly income (<$10,000 or >$10,000), monthly disposable income (<$200 or >$200), use of licit substances (less than weekly use or more than weekly use of alcohol or tobacco), use of illicit drugs (less than weekly use or more than weekly use), positive or negative parental history (positive indicated that one or both parents were rated by the participant as having a gambling problem), and previous month total credit card debt (<$2,000 or >$2,000).

As summarized in Table 4, the OR results indicate that several variables were significantly associated with probable pathological gambling: a positive parental history (OR = 8.2), more than weekly illicit drug use (OR = 4.5), being male (OR = 4.4), having a high disposable income ($200+ per month) (OR = 2.9), and more than weekly licit drug use (OR = 2.3). None of the other variables, including credit card debt, produced significant findings.

Because the identified risk variables could significantly covary, we conducted a stepwise logistic regression to evaluate their nonredundant

association with probable pathological gambling status (see Table 5). These variables were identified as nonredundant significant risk factors: positive parental history, being male, more than weekly illicit drug user, and $200+ disposable monthly income. The largest OR was associated with the parent history variable (8.1). The stepwise logistic model confirmed the significance of the association between problem gambling status and a core group of subject variables, and it emphasized the role of parental gambling history as a prominent risk factor.

Discussion

In many ways, the study findings are consistent with the results of previous gambling surveys. Similar to recent adult and adolescent prevalence studies, we found gambling to be a common experience (about 87% had gambled in the previous year), and few students reported financial consequences or met criteria for probable pathological gambling. Thus, gambling appeared to be a relatively benign activity for the majority of college students we surveyed. In this context, the study findings were reassuring to university health officials who had expressed concern to us that the close proximity and legal access of high-stakes gambling would produce high rates of problem gambling.

It is interesting to note, however, that our obtained rate of probable pathological gambling (2.9%) was slightly higher than the rate of 1.1% reported in a recent survey of Minnesota adults (Emerson et al., 1994). This finding could be taken to support the notion that university students, particularly those who have easy access to high-stakes gambling, are at elevated risk to experience problem gambling. Yet, the data need to be viewed within the context of two major considerations. The first is statistical in nature. The standard error of estimates for both our college study and adult study used for reference exceeded the respective estimates of the low-base-rate phenomenon of probable pathological gambling. Thus, we should be cautious about overinterpreting the difference between a 2.9% rate and a 1.1% rate.

Table 2 Gambling Involvement During the Previous 12 Months

Group	Any Game n	Any Game %	Cards with Friends[a] n	Cards with Friends[a] %	Cards at a Casino n	Cards at a Casino %	Bet on Animals n	Bet on Animals %	Bet on Sports[b] n	Bet on Sports[b] %	Dice for Money n	Dice for Money %
Total	1,197	88.0	555	40.8	546	40.1	139	10.2	497	36.5	209	15.4
Men	598**	91.7	361**	55.4	365**	56.0	102**	15.6	366**	56.1	131**	20.1
Women	583	84.9	185	26.9	176	25.6	37	5.4	124	18.0	75	10.9
Freshmen	336	90.8	178**	48.1	143	38.6	39	10.5	137	37.0	68	18.4
Sophomores	306	87.4	149	42.6	162	46.3	33	9.4	140	40.0	57	16.3
Juniors	285	88.0	138	42.6	125	38.6	31	9.6	113	34.9	45	13.9
Seniors	269	85.4	89	28.3	116	36.8	26	11.4	106	33.7	39	12.4

[a]Played cards for money with friends; [b]Bet on the outcome of a sporting event; [c]Played the numbers (including scratch tabs, lottery, daily numbers); [d]Played slot machines, poker machines, or other gambling machines; [e]Bowled, shot pool, played golf, or played some other game of skill for money; [f]Wagered or gambled on high-risk stock, commodities, markets, or real estate.

*$p \leq .05$.

**$p \leq .01$; chi-squares between men and women within each type of gambling and among freshmen, sophomores, juniors, and seniors within each type of gambling.

Table 3 South Oaks Gambling Screen (SOGS) Scores by Group ($N = 1,361$)

Group	0 n	0 %	1–2 n	1–2 %	3–4 n	3–4 %	5+ n	5+ %
Total	924	67.9	336	24.7	61	4.5	40	2.9
Men	385**	59.0	187**	28.7	48**	7.4	32**	4.9
Women	524	76.3	143	20.8	13	1.9	7	1.0
Freshmen	230*	62.2	107	28.9	19	5.1	14	3.8
Sophomores	241	68.9	87	24.9	14	4.0	8	2.3
Juniors	229	70.7	73	22.5	13	4.0	9	2.8
Seniors	223	70.8	68	21.6	15	4.8	9	2.9

Note. Total frequencies for some groups vary slightly because of missing data.

*$p \leq .05$.

**$p \leq .01$; chi-square between men and women within each SOGS group or among freshmen, sophomores, juniors, and seniors within each SOGS group.

The second consideration pertains to developmental interpretations of the findings. Experience from adolescent studies suggests that precocious addictive-like behaviors, such as smoking or alcohol abuse, are predictive of adult addictive disorders (U.S. Department of Health and Human Services, 1994). Furthermore, there is evidence that the course of early gambling involvement is characterized by a shift in preference as the adolescent ages into young adulthood. It was found in an adolescent prospective study that participants who recently became of legal age (18 years old) had shifted their gambling preference from informal games (e.g., playing cards with friends) toward the legal and more high-stake games, such as lottery playing and video gaming (Winters, Stinchfield, & Kim, 1995). There is even some evidence that involvement in high-stakes and easy-access games has a clinical link. Reports from pathological gamblers indicate that they play the lottery and casino-type games, such as gambling machines and casino cards, more frequently than other gambling activities (Stinchfield & Winters, 1996). Thus, our finding that college students commonly play high-stakes games is consistent with the view that early gambling patterns may lay the foundation for future problems for some individuals.

A counter health position could be advanced by arguing that problem gambling at the college level may fall by the wayside during the maturation process. This phenomenon has been observed for other adolescent problem behaviors, such as alcohol and drug use (e.g., Blum, 1987; Donovan, Jessor, & Jessor, 1983). There is some retrospective data that gambling interest peaks in the 18- to 24-year-old range, after which there is a steady decline (Kallick, Suits, Dielman, & Hybels, 1976; Mok & Hraba, 1991). Also, our results did not yield a large percentage of afflicted individuals, even with a definition of probable pathological gambling that has been criticized as yielding too many false positives (e.g., Walker & Dickerson, 1996). Finally, one could make a cogent argument that college students

Table 2 *Continued*

Lottery[c]		Bingo for Money		Machines[d]		Game of Skill[e]		Pulltabs		High-Risk Stocks[f]	
n	%	n	%	n	%	n	%	n	%	n	%
866	63.6	262	19.3	927	68.1	390	28.7	414	30.4	64	4.7
442**	67.8	118	18.1	461	70.7	289**	44.3	224**	34.4	50**	7.7
413	60.1	140	20.4	455	66.2	95	13.8	184	26.8	13	1.9
238	64.3	80	21.6	270**	73.0	116*	31.4	103	27.8	16	4.3
226	64.6	72	20.6	263	75.1	112	32.0	103	29.4	16	4.6
204	63.0	61	18.8	213	65.7	92	28.4	103	31.8	19	5.9
197	62.5	49	15.6	180	57.1	70	22.2	105	33.3	12	3.8

Table 4 Significant Odds Ratios of Client Variables Associated with Assignment to the Gambling Involvement Groups

Client Variable	Probable Pathological Gambler (SOGS 5+)
Parents have a gambling problem	8.2**
Being male	4.4**
Weekly or greater illicit drug use	4.5**
Disposable income of $200+ per month	2.9**
Weekly or greater licit drug use	2.3*
Taking less than 12 credits	0.4*

Note. SOGS = South Oaks Gambling Screen.

*$p \leq .05$.

**$p \leq .01$.

Table 5 Logistic Stepwise Regression Model of Variables Associated with Assignment to the Gambling Involvement Groups

Client Variable	Probable Pathological Gambler (SOGS 5+)
Parents have a gambling problem	8.1**
Being male	5.9**
Weekly or greater illicit drug use	2.8*
Disposable income of $200+ per month	2.5*

Note. SOGS = South Oaks Gambling Screen.

*$p \leq .05$.

**$p \leq .01$.

are unlikely to experience truly severe gambling problems because most of them lack easy access to large sums of money and thus are essentially insulated from suffering devastating financial consequences over gambling losses.

These two polar positions are similar to the debate regarding the health implications of adolescent gambling (Shaffer & Hall, 1996). Admittedly, the true seriousness of problem gambling by young people is not yet clear. It is not known the extent to which young adult problem gamblers will develop a full-blown clinical condition. More prospective investigations are needed on the possible consequences brought on by early gambling and what effect these consequences have on young adult development.

Also, more research is needed to identify the mediational factors and processes of problem and pathological gambling. At the very least, prevalence surveys should include measures of possible predispositional and precipitating psychosocial variables so that hypotheses about the underlying determinants can be explored. Our finding that problem gambling is strongly linked to certain characteristics, such as gender, illicit drug use, and student performance, is consistent with the literature on adolescent gambling (Jacobs, 1989). Furthermore, these risk variables are conceptually similar to the cluster of problem behaviors that have been linked to youth alcohol abuse (Jessor & Jessor, 1977). Thus, it may be meaningful to include problem gambling as part of the problem behavior pattern of adolescence and young adulthood. In this light, problem gambling among young people may be mediated by factors common to a larger problem behavior syndrome rather than by unique risk factors.

The association between parental gambling and college problem gambling further supports the familial nature of gambling (Gambino, Fitzgerald, Shaffer, Renner, & Courtnage, 1993). The adult literature indicates that the relative risk of problem gambling is about three to five times greater when the family history is positive, and similar findings have been reported in adolescent studies (Jacobs, 1989). Family studies may clarify how parents and the home environment contribute to youthful gambling. Broader environmental factors should be examined as well. Peer influences, which often have been identified as a determinant of youth substance use (e.g., Newcomb, 1988), are relevant considerations in this context.

There are weaknesses and limitations associated with our study that merit discussion. First, the findings are limited to self-report. The SOGS has been validated against alternate measures of gambling severity, but few researchers have included independent criterion measures not based on self-report. Also, our use of the SOGS did not permit a detailed inquiry about the association of excessive gambling and heavy betting and the development of problems related to gambling. This topic is an important line of research for future longitudinal study given that heavy involvement in gambling does not always correspond with clinical problems. Furthermore, the study's focus on college students who had easy access to high-stakes casinos means that the obtained prevalence data should not be considered representative of young adults or college students in general. A final generalizability issue concerns the possible confusion resulting from comparisons between lifetime SOGS and current SOGS data. We used the current SOGS (previous year), whereas the majority of the literature is based on lifetime data, including the Lesieur et al. (1991) benchmark college survey. As reported by Volberg (1996), rates of probable pathological gambling based on the lifetime SOGS are routinely two to three times higher than current SOGS rates.

References

American Psychiatric Association. (1994). *Diagnostic and statistical manual of mental disorders* (4th ed.). Washington, DC: Author.

Blum, R. W. (1987). Adolescent substance abuse: Diagnostic and treatment issues. *Pediatric Clinics of North America, 34,* 523–537.

Browne, B. A., & Brown, D. J. (1993). Using students as subjects in research on state lottery gambling. *Psychological Reports, 72,* 1295–1298.

Devlin, A. S., & Peppard, D. M. (1996). Casino use by college students. *Psychological Reports, 78,* 899–906.

Donovan, J., Jessor, R., & Jessor, L. (1983). Problem drinking in adolescence and young adulthood: A follow-up study. *Journal of Studies on Alcohol, 44,* 109–137.

Emerson, M. O., Laundergan, J. C., & Schaefer, J. M. (1994). *Adult survey of Minnesota problem gambling behavior: A needs assessment of changes from 1990 to 1994.* Unpublished manuscript, University of Minnesota, Duluth.

Gambino, B., Fitzgerald, R., Shaffer, H., Renner, J., & Courtnage, P. (1993). Perceived family history of problem gambling and scores on SOGS. *Journal of Gambling Studies, 9,* 169–184.

Jacobs, D. F. (1989). Illegal and undocumented: A review of teenage gambling and the plight of children of problem gamblers in America. In H. J. Shaffer, S. A. Stein, B. Gambino, & T. N. Cummings (Eds.), *Compulsive gambling: Theory, research and practice* (pp. 249–292). Lexington, MA: Lexington Books.

Jessor, R., & Jessor, S. I. (1977). *Problem behavior and psychosocial development: A longitudinal study of youth.* New York: Academic Press.

Kallick, M., Suits, D., Dielman, T., & Hybels, J. (1976). *Survey of American gambling attitudes and behavior* (Appendix 2). Washington, DC: U.S. Government Printing Office.

Landouceur, R., Dube, D., & Bujold, A. (1994). Prevalence of pathological gambling and related problems among college students in the Quebec metropolitan area. *Canadian Journal of Psychiatry, 39,* 289–293.

Lesieur, H. R., & Blume, S. B. (1987). The South Oaks Gambling Screen (SOGS): A new instrument for the identification of pathological gamblers. *American Journal of Psychiatry, 144,* 1184–1188.

Lesieur, H. R., & Blume, S. B. (1993). Revising the South Oaks Gambling Screen in different settings. *Journal of Gambling Studies, 9,* 213–223.

Lesieur, H. R., Cross, J., Frank, M., Welch, M., White, C. M., Rubenstein, G., Mosely, K., & Mark, M. (1991). Gambling and pathological gambling among university students. *Addictive Behaviors, 16,* 517–527.

Lesieur, H. R., & Heineman, M. (1988). Pathological gambling among youthful multiple substance abusers in a therapeutic community. *British Journal of Addiction, 83,* 765–77).

Mok, W. P., & Hraba, J. (1991). Age and gambling behavior: A declining and shifting pattern of participation. *Journal of Gambling Studies, 7,* 313–336.

National Institute on Drug Abuse. (1990). *National household survey on drug abuse.* Rockville, MD: Author.

Newcomb, M. D. (1988). *Drug use in the workplace: Risk factors for disruptive substance use among young adults.* Dover, MA: Auburn House.

Shaffer, H. J., & Hall, M. N. (1996). Estimating the prevalence of adolescent gambling disorders: A quantitative synthesis and guide toward standard gambling nomenclature. *Journal of Gambling Studies, 12,* 193–214.

Stinchfield, R. (1997, June). *Reliability, validity, and classification accuracy of the South Oaks Gambling Screen (SOGS).* Paper presented at the 10th International Conference on Gambling and Risk-Taking, Montreal, Quebec, Canada.

Stinchfield, R., Cassuto, N., Winters, K. C., & Latimer, W. W. (1997). Prevalence of gambling by Minnesota public school students in 1992 and 1995. *Journal of Gambling Studies, 13,* 25–48.

Stinchfield, R., & Winters, K. C. (1996). *Effectiveness of six state-supported compulsive gambling treatment programs in Minnesota.* St. Paul: Minnesota Department of Human Services.

U.S. Department of Health and Human Services. (1994). *Preventing tobacco use among young people: A report of the surgeon general.* Washington, DC: Author.

Volberg, R. A. (1996). Prevalence studies of problem gambling in the United States. *Journal of Gambling Studies, 12,* 111–128.

Walker, M. B., & Dickerson, M. G. (1996). The prevalence of problem and pathological gambling: A critical analysis. *Journal of Gambling Studies, 12,* 233–249.

Windle, M. (1991). Alcohol use and abuse: Some research findings from the National Adolescent Student Health Survey. *Alcohol Health and Research World, 15,* 5–10.

Winters, K. C., Stinchfield, R., & Kim, L. (1995). Monitoring gambling among Minnesota adolescents. *Journal of Gambling Studies, 11,* 165–183.

Winters, K. C., Stinchfield, R., & Fulkerson, J. (1993). Patterns and characteristics of adolescent gambling. *Journal of Gambling Studies, 9,* 371–387.

Article Review Form at end of book.

WiseGuide Wrap-Up

This new section of the *DSM IV* reflects careful thinking by the American Psychiatric Association on the potential problems for society from individuals with these disorders. Interesting behavior management and pharmacological treatments are being developed; try a web search to find further information on treatments.

R.E.A.L. Sites

This list provides a print preview of typical **Coursewise** R.E.A.L. sites. (There are over 100 such sites at the **Courselinks**™ site.) The danger in printing URLs is that web sites can change overnight. As we went to press, these sites were functional using the URLs provided. If you come across one that isn't, please let us know via email to: webmaster@coursewise.com. Use your Passport to access the most current list of R.E.A.L. sites at the **Courselinks** site.

Site name: APA's PsycNet

URL: http://www.apa.org

Why is it R.E.A.L.? The career information and division materials provided by this web site will provide students with valuable information about their vocational decision-making and referral resources.

Key topics: alcohol problems, trichotillomania, compulsive gambling

Site name: Addict-L

URL: Send e-mail to: Listserv@kentum.kent.edu

Why is it R.E.A.L.? By subscribing to this list, you will be able to communicate with researchers who study addictions.

Key topics: alcohol problems, compulsive gambling

Site name: Behavior OnLine

URL: http://www.behavior.net/

Why is it R.E.A.L.? Discussion on contemporary relevant issues, such as impulse control disorders may be addressed here. The discussions are sometimes technical and thus will give you a chance to apply your knowledge of psychological terminology.

Key topics: trichotillomania, alcohol problems, compulsive gambling

section

3

Learning Objectives

- The student's understanding of conditions exacerbated by stress will be fostered.

- The presentation of empirically valid and contemporary treatments of anxiety will increase the student's understanding of professional psychological practice.

- The student will develop a knowledge of personality factors, such as attribution and style, that influence the experience of stress.

? Questions ?

Reading 8. Comment on the theme of predisposing factors to anxiety and the commonplace expression of anxiety that a practitioner would encounter.

Reading 9. In what way(s) does self-esteem influence the experience of anxiety and stress?

Reading 10. What is transactional analysis? Does it explain medical-setting stress?

Anxiety and Stress

The series of articles in this section discusses issues around the commonly presented problem of anxiety. The section begins with an epidemiological study and ends with an article presenting results from a study conducted in a stressful environment—the hospital.

Oei and associates present the picture of anxiety disorders specific to panic disorder symptomology. One of the many values in this article is the realistic aspect of the experience of panic disorder that is presented. It is very common for patients to be on medication while involved in behavioral therapy. The difficult question then becomes: Is the demonstrated effect, the relief the patient expresses, attributed to the medicine or the intervention? The aspects of the cognitive behavioral approach are highlighted in this article and thus provide a brief primer of sorts on this common treatment technique.

In the second reading, Gershuny and Sher hypothesize about the connection between personality style and anxiety. While the modeling terms *intraversion* and *extraversion* are dated, the conclusions point to their heartiness in explaining how some people become anxious.

Florio and associates provide a unique conceptualization of anxiety. Transactional analysis provides a step-by-step approach to the ways in which an individual becomes aware of symptoms/discomfort, the steps he or she takes to resist and cope with the circumstance, and the rationale for the intervention.

This section is designed to provide the reader with a view of what anxiety is and how it is commonly manifested. The articles in this section also give a good understanding of conceptual models for understanding anxiety.

Comment on the theme of predisposing factors to anxiety and the commonplace expression of anxiety that a practitioner would encounter.

Does Concurrent Drug Intake Affect the Long-Term Outcome of Group Cognitive Behaviour Therapy in Panic Disorder with or without Agoraphobia?

Tian P. S. Oei,[1] Michael Llamas[2] and Larry Evans[3]

[1]Department of Psychology, The University of Queensland, Brisbane, Australia,
[2]Consultation—Liaison Psychiatry Service, Princess Alexandra Hospital, Brisbane, Australia
[3]Department of Psychiatry, The University of Queensland, Brisbane, Australia

Introduction

Panic disorder and agoraphobia are chronic conditions which have serious social consequences and impact significantly on quality of life (Weissman, 1990, 1991; Weissman & Merikangas, 1986). The literature to date suggests that cognitive-behavioural therapy (CBT) is an effective treatment for these conditions at least in the short term (Llamas & Oei, 1993). Based on several recent reviews (Llamas, Oei & Devilly, 1997; Mattick, Andrews, Hadzi-Pavlovic & Christensen, 1990;

Michaelson & Marchione, 1991; Steketee & Shapiro, 1995), CBT appears to be therapeutically effective in the short-term alleviation of a wide range of symptoms, including: panic attacks, anticipatory anxiety, phobic avoidance, generalised anxiety, depression, and personality factors associated with vulnerability to neurosis. Two studies (Barlow, 1990; Evans, Holt & Oei, 1991) have investigated the long-term efficacy of CBT in the treatment of panic disorder and agoraphobia. In the first of these studies, Barlow (1990) demonstrated long-term benefits for up to two years following CBT of panic disorder and agoraphobia. In the second study, Evans et al. (1991) found that, compared to waiting-list controls, patients treated with a brief intensive (2-day) group cognitive-behavioural therapy (BIGCBT) program for agoraphobics with panic attacks were significantly improved at 3 yr long-term follow-up on self-report measures of panic disorder and agoraphobia. Furthermore, 85%

of the treated patients were either symptom free or their symptoms had reduced to a manageable level and these effects of treatment had been maintained at long-term follow-up.

Taken together, the studies by Barlow (1990) and Evans et al. (1991) suggest that CBT and BIGCBT may be effective interventions for up to 3 yr in the treatment of panic disorder with or without agoraphobia. It should be noted, however, that in the Evans et al. (1991) study a significant proportion (60%) of patients studied were taking medications concurrent with their psychological treatment and the effects of this medication on long-term outcome of the BIGCBT program was not analysed by the authors. Recently, there have been several systematic evaluation programs comparing CBT in combination with pharmacological treatments with either CBT or pharmacological treatments alone in the treatment of panic disorder with or without agoraphobia (e.g., Sharp et al., 1996; Beurs, van Balkom, Lange, Koele & van Dyke,

Reprinted from *Behavioral Research and Therapy*, 35 (9), Tian P.S. Oei, M. Llamas, and L. Evans, "Does Concurrent Drug Intake Affect the Long-Term Outcome of Group Cognitive Behaviour Therapy in Panic Disorder with or without Agoraphobia?" 1997, with permission from Elsevier Science.

1995; Marks *et al.*, 1993). The findings suggest that both CBT and drug treatment are effective; however, the combined CBT and drug treatment seems to be more effective than CBT or drug alone. Similarly, various studies have reported similar results of the relative effectiveness of behavioural therapy alone (in particular, exposure) to behavioural therapy combined with medication (for review see Clum, 1989). It seems reasonably clear that CBT and drug treatment is a useful combined treatment for panic disorder and panic disordered and agoraphobic patients.

While the research findings from the laboratory suggest the usefulness of combined treatment, it is still unclear whether the laboratory findings can be replicated in the community clinics. Patients attending for psychotherapy treatment in community clinics usually take prescribed medications for panic disorder and panic disordered agoraphobic patients. Furthermore, the literature does show that medical practitioners commonly use drugs in the treatment of these conditions (e.g., Evans, Oei & Hoey, 1988). Consequently, in clinical practice, patients referred for CBT are often already taking prescribed psychotropic medications of one form or another (e.g., Evans *et al.*, 1991). The impact of the medication on the efficacy of CBT is unclear. It is important to ascertain whether such medications in any way enhance or detract from the short- and long-term outcome of CBT in a clinical setting.

The present study primarily sought to determine whether the concurrent use of different classes of pharmacotherapy would enhance or detract from a BIGCBT program when used in the treatment of panic disordered and agoraphobic patients in a community clinic.

Method
Subjects
Patients were selected from a group of 206 treated at the Anxiety Disorders Clinic, Brisbane, between 1980 and 1987, and for whom long-term follow-up data was available. Patients were included in the study if they met the following criteria:

1. a diagnosis of panic disorder with or without agoraphobia following a semi-structured clinical interview based on DSM-III (American Psychological Association, 1980) criteria;

2. aged between 17 and 65 yr;

3. attended and completed the BIGCBT program at the clinic;

4. medication information at assessment was available; and

5. informed consent had been given to use data collected for research purposes and publication.

Patients were excluded from the study according to the following criteria:

1. presence of concurrent Axis I diagnosis;

2. receiving anti-psychotic medication;

3. receiving beta-blocking agents; and

4. medication information at assessment was unknown.

The final sample comprised 106 patients (74 females). Of these, 93 had a diagnosis of agoraphobia with panic attacks (code: 300.21), and 13 were diagnosed as having panic disorder (code: 300.01) (American Psychological Association, 1980). Their ages ranged from 17 to 64 yr (X = 37.2 yr; SD = 10.4 yr). The mean age of onset of the panic disorder and agoraphobia conditions was 28.9 yr (SD = 9.8 yr; range = 8.0–55.0 yr). The mean reported duration of the current episode was 3.4 yr (SD = 3.5 yr; range = 0.1–14.0 yr.

Patients were retrospectively allocated to one of four treatment groups on the basis of their self-reported pre-existing medication status:

1. *BIGCBT without medication group (40 patients):* patients who were not taking any anti-anxiety or anti-depressant medication.

2. *BIGCBT plus anti-anxiety medication group (40 patients):* patients who were taking anti-anxiety medication (e.g., alprazolam, diazepam, oxazepam).

3. *BIGCBT plus anti-depressant medication group (10 patients):* patients who were taking anti-depressant medication (e.g., doxepin, imipramine, phenelzine).

4. *BIGCBT plus combined medications group (16 patients):* patients who were taking combinations of anti-anxiety and anti-depressant medication.

The mean drug doses reported by the patients in the BIGCBT with pharmacotherapy groups were comparable with the therapeutic dosage levels that have been recommended in the literature (e.g., Ballenger, 1990) and recognised standards such as the *MIMS Annual* (Craig, Underwood, Ashley, Ashley & Piper, 1991).

The demographic characteristics of the patients allocated to each of the above four treatment groups are shown in Table 1.

Chi-squared analyses showed that there were no significant differences across the treatment conditions ($P > 0.05$) with regard to the categorical variables of sex [$\chi^2(3, N = 106) = 3.98$] and marital status [$\chi^2(6, N = 106) = 6.08$]. One-way analyses of variance also showed that there were no significant differences across the treatment conditions ($P > 0.05$) on the following continuous variables: mean age [$F(3,102) = 0.38$]; mean age of onset [$F(3,95) = 2.11$]; number of previous episodes [$F(3,63) = 1.59$]; mean duration of present episode [$F(3,72) = 0.48$] and the mean period to long-term follow-up [$F(3,102) = 0.99$]. Hence, it can be concluded that the four treatment groups did not differ significantly with respect to demographic characteristics.

Assessment Measures
The assessment measures administered at pre-treatment and at long-term follow-up included:

1. Hamilton Anxiety Rating Scale (HAM-A: Hamilton, 1959);

2. Hamilton Depression Rating Scale (HAM-D: Hamilton, 1960);

3. State–Trait Anxiety Inventory (STAI: Spielberger, Gorsuch & Lushene, 1970);

4. Fear Questionnaire (FQ: Marks & Matthews, 1979);

Table 1 Demographic Characteristics of the Four Treatment Groups

Characteristics	No Medication	Anti-Anxiety	Anti-Depressant	Combined Medication
Patients (n)	40	40	10	16
Sex (female/male)	28/12	30/10	8/2	8/8
Mean age (yr)	36.2	38.5	36.1	36.9
Marital status				
Single	11	5	2	4
Married or de facto	28	33	8	10
Separated, divorced or widowed	1	2	0	2
Mean age of onset (yr)	26.3	29.9	28.1	33.3
No. previous episodes (mean)	1.0	1.5	1.0	1.3
Mean duration of present episode (months)	34.1	45.2	30.5	44.9
Mean long-term follow-up (months)	37.3	35.1	43.5	38.5

5. Modified Fear Survey Schedule (FSS-M: Oei, Cavallo & Evans, 1987); and

6. Life History Questionnaire (Oei, Wanstall & Evans, 1990). The Life History Questionnaire is a comprehensive instrument compiled by staff at the Anxiety Disorders Clinic to obtain pre-treatment information from the patient on a wide range of areas, including

1. demographics and details relating to condition;

2. frequency of panic attacks (rated 1–4; 1 = 'no panic attacks' and 4 = 'three or more panic attacks per week');

3. physical symptoms experienced during panic attacks (rated 1–5; 1 = 'not present at all' and 5 = 'present very much');

4. catastrophic cognitions during panic attacks (rated 1–5; 1 = 'not present at all' and 5 = 'present very much');

5. behavioural avoidance of situations (rated 1–5; 1 = 'not at all' and 5 = 'very much'); and

6. current medication status (categorized as: "taking no medication," "taking anti-anxiety medication,"

"taking anti-depressant medication" or "taking a combination of anti-anxiety agents and anti-depressants").

A Follow-up Questionnaire (Evans *et al.*, 1991) developed by staff at the Anxiety Disorders Clinic was included at long-term follow-up for the purpose of collecting long-term follow-up information from patients who had previously attended the BIGCBT program at the clinic. Long-term follow-up information collected included:

(a) frequency of panic attacks;

(b) physical symptoms during a panic attack;

(c) catastrophic cognitions during a panic attack;

(d) avoidance of particular situations; and

(e) current medication status.

Each of these areas was measured and rated in a fashion similar to that already described for the Life History Questionnaire (Oei *et al.*, 1990).

Assessment Procedures

Data gathered for the purposes of the present study were collected during pre-treatment and long-term follow-up phases of the BIGCBT program

offered at the Anxiety Disorders Clinic, Brisbane. Pre-treatment assessment procedures were similar to those previously outlined by Oei *et al.* (1987, 1990). The long-term assessment procedures were similar to those previously outlined by Evans *et al.* (1991) and occurred during 1987 for all 106 patients who participated in the present study. These patients completed a battery of questionnaires similar to the one completed at initial assessment. The patients were then assessed further at a clinical interview arranged for the purpose of administering the HAM-A and HAM-D. The mean long-term follow-up period for the group of patients studied was 3.1 yr (SD = 1.2 yr) and ranged from 1.1 to 6.2 yr.

Description of Brief Intensive Group Cognitive-Behavioural Therapy Program

The BIGCBT program is presented in an intensive 3-day workshop format developed by staff at the Anxiety Disorders Clinic, Brisbane (Evans *et al.*, 1988, 1991).

Statistical Analyses

All statistical analyses were conducted using the Statistical Package for the Social Sciences (SPSS, 1990) adjusting for unequal sample sizes. The statistical procedures used to analyse the demographic data were chi-square tests for categorical variables and one-way analyses of variance (ANOVAs) for continuous variables. As part of the preliminary data analyses, a series of one-way ANOVAs were conducted on each of the variables, including catastrophic cognitions, physical symptoms, avoidance behaviour, frequency of panic attacks and psychological questionnaire measures, to determine whether there were any pre-treatment differences across the four treatment groups on any of these measures. The probability level of significance for the main effects derived from each of these separate ANOVAs was set at $P < 0.05$. For the main data analyses—to examine and contrast differences across treatment conditions and assessment phases—a series of 4 (treatment conditions) × 2 (assessment phases) repeated-measures ANOVAs were conducted on catastrophic cognitions, physical symptoms, avoidance behaviour, frequency of panic attacks and psychological questionnaire variables. To control for the "familywise" cumulative Type I error rate resulting from a large series of separate ANOVAs, a "Bonferroni" adjustment was employed as described by Keppel (1991). Based on this adjustment, the probability level of significance for main effects derived from each of the separate ANOVAs in the main analyses was set at $P < 0.001$. Evaluations of assumptions of normality, linearity, homogeneity of variance, homogeneity of regression and reliability of covariates prior to conducting the above statistical analyses were satisfactory. Further, it was decided not to substitute means for any missing data values because of the likely distortion of results and bias this would introduce into any interpretations.

Results
Preliminary Analyses of Pre-Treatment Group Differences

Preliminary analyses using one-way ANOVAs were conducted on all of the dependent variables to determine whether any significant pre-

treatment differences existed between the four treatment groups. It was found that the pre-treatment means of the shopping avoidance behaviour, FSS-M and STAI-T were significantly different for the four groups. ANCOVAs were then used to further examine the data for these variables across treatment conditions and assessment phases. The pattern of results obtained from these ANCOVAs was also similar to that obtained when repeated-measures ANOVAs were performed. Consequently, for these variables, the results obtained from the repeated-measures ANOVAs are presented in the main analyses, rather than the results of the ANCOVAs, in order to be consistent with the analyses reported for other variables.

Main Analyses of Dependent Measures

Data pertaining to the main statistical analyses conducted on dependent measures for which results were not statistically significant have not been reported, for purposes of conciseness.

Group differences at pre-treatment and long-term follow-up. Statistical analyses revealed no significant treatment group effects ($p > 0.001$) or significant interaction effects between treatment groups and time ($P > 0.001$) on any of the dependent measures of interest. Specifically, this indicates that the four treatment groups did not differ significantly from one another at any point in time with respect to pre- and long-term follow-up measures of catastrophic cognitions, physical symptoms, avoidance behaviours, frequency of panic attacks and clinician-rated and self-report questionnaires that were employed during the present study. Hence, it can be said that the concurrent use of pre-existing anti-anxiety, anti-depressant or combined (anti-anxiety and anti-depressant) medication regimes with BIGCBT did not significantly enhance or detract from its long-term outcome on these dependent measures.

Long-term outcome of BIGCBT (with or without pharmacotherapy). Table 2 shows the means, standard deviations and results of the ANOVAs conducted on those dependent measures for which results were statistically significant.

Statistically significant time main effects were noted across all four treatment groups on most dependent measures employed. Specifically, all four BIGCBT treatment groups significantly ($P < 0.001$) improved from pre-treatment to long-term follow-up on their reported frequency of panic attacks, most self-ratings of avoidance behaviour and also clinician-rated and self-report questionnaire measures of anxiety, depression and agoraphobia. Hence, it can be concluded that BIGCBT (with or without pharmacotherapy) was associated with significant long-term improvements on these dependent measures. Statistical analyses with respect to self-ratings of catastrophic cognitions and physical symptom revealed, however, no statistically significant changes ($P > 0.001$) from pre-treatment to follow-up for any of the four treatment groups concerned.

Medication status. As a long-term outcome measure, change in the medication status of patients was assessed across time for each of the four treatment groups. Table 3 shows the percentage of patients in each of the four treatment groups who reported taking anti-anxiety, anti-depressant or combined (anti-anxiety and anti-depressant) medications at pre-treatment and long-term follow-up.

It can be seen that of all the patients who underwent BIGCBT without any pre-existing medication regimes for their condition, the large majority (80%) remained medication-free at long-term follow-up. The percentages of patients from the remaining three treatment groups who reported not taking any anti-anxiety, anti-depressant or combinations of these medications at long-term follow-up were as follows: BIGCBT plus anti-anxiety medication, 47.5%; BIGCBT plus antidepressant medication, 60.0%; and BIGCBT plus combined medications, 25.0%. Overall, it can be said that a large percentage (44%) of patients who underwent BIGCBT whilst on pre-existing medication regimes for their conditions became medication-free at long-term follow-up.

Discussion

The present study primarily demonstrates that, on the dependent mea-

Table 2 Means, Standard Deviations and Results of Repeated-Measures ANOVAs

Dependent Measure		BIGCBT X (SD)		BIGCBT + AA X (SD)		BIGCBT + AD X (SD)		BIGCBT + COMB X (SD)		F-ratio** (time)	F-ratio*** (Treatment Effect)
Panic freq.	Pre	3.1	(0.9)	3.2	(0.8)	2.8	(0.9)	3.1	(0.9)	108.68	< 1
	F/u	1.5	(0.6)	1.6	(0.8)	2.1	(1.0)	1.8	(0.8)		
Crowds	Pre	3.4	(1.2)	3.9	(1.2)	4.1	(0.9)	3.8	(1.3)	29.68	2.03
	F/u	2.4	(1.1)	2.8	(1.2)	2.3	(1.3)	3.3	(1.3)		
Lifts	Pre	3.1	(1.2)	3.1	(1.3)	3.3	(1.4)	4.1	(1.4)	36.44	< 1
	F/u	2.1	(1.0)	2.1	(1.0)	2.0	(1.7)	2.1	(1.4)		
Shopping	Pre	3.2	(1.1)	3.7	(1.1)	4.0	(1.3)	4.3	(0.9)	45.67	3.96
	F/u	2.0	(1.2)	2.4	(1.2)	2.4	(1.5)	3.2	(1.5)		
Boat	Pre	3.5	(1.5)	3.6	(1.3)	4.0	(1.3)	3.5	(1.4)	20.09	< 1
	F/u	2.3	(1.5)	2.7	(1.5)	3.3	(2.1)	2.3	(1.5)		
Bus	Pre	3.7	(1.2)	3.5	(1.2)	3.9	(1.1)	3.8	(1.1)	19.34	< 1
	F/u	2.6	(1.6)	2.6	(1.6)	3.0	(1.9)	2.8	(1.8)		
Plane	Pre	3.7	(1.4)	4.6	(0.8)	3.7	(1.3)	3.6	(1.5)	20.39	1.98
	F/u	2.9	(1.7)	3.4	(1.6)	3.0	(1.9)	2.9	(1.6)		
Train	Pre	3.9	(1.2)	3.7	(1.3)	4.0	(1.3)	4.0	(1.3)	15.2	< 1
	F/u	2.7	(1.6)	2.7	(1.6)	3.9	(1.6)	2.8	(1.9)		
HAM-A	Pre	16.8	(8.6)	18.5	(5.7)	18.7	(6.2)	18.9	(6.5)	32.54	1.87
	F/u	7.1	(5.9)	11.6	(7.5)	12.2	(7.0)	11.4	(11.5)		
HAM-D	Pre	9.3	(6.6)	12.9	(5.0)	9.8	(5.6)	13.8	(5.5)	18.74	4.04
	F/u	3.7	(4.3)	7.2	(5.8)	8.7	(6.3)	7.1	(8.7)		
FSS-M	Pre	90.0	(31.7)	121.1	(41.6)	113.2	(45.7)	100.1	(42.7)	56.57	2.83
	F/u	58.8	(36.1)	70.8	(43.8)	72.8	(34.5)	72.5	(44.2)		
FQ-Ag	Pre	16.4	(11.7)	22.6	(9.8)	19.2	(6.1)	16.5	(10.9)	22.58	1.41
	F/u	9.9	(11.6)	11.8	(9.4)	13.0	(6.7)	12.4	(12.1)		
STAI-S	Pre	42.1	(11.3)	50.2	(12.0)	44.2	(12.0)	52.1	(14.1)	17.62	2.86
	F/u	36.2	(11.2)	39.5	(12.0)	33.2	(10.5)	44.8	(17.9)		
STAI-T	Pre	44.2	(11.1)	53.8	(8.2)	54.2	(12.0)	58.5	(13.3)	19.95	6.26
	F/u	38.8	(10.6)	47.3	(10.9)	44.6	(14.2)	54.5	(13.1)		

AA, anti-anxiety medication; AD, anti-depressant medication; BIGCBT, brief intensive group cognitive behavioural therapy program; COMB, combined (anti-anxiety and anti-depressant) medication; FQ-Ag, Fear Questionnaire Agoraphobia Subscale; FSS-M, Modified Fear Survey Schedule; HAM-A, Hamilton Anxiety Scale; HAM-D, Hamilton Depression Scale; STAI-S, State–Trait Anxiety Inventory: State Subscale; STAI-S, State–Trait Anxiety Inventory: Trait Subscale; Pre, pre-treatment; F/u, long-term follow-up.

**P < 0.001; ***P > 0.001.

sures employed, patients with panic disorder with or without agoraphobia who received BIGCBT concurrent with their pre-existing regimes of anti-anxiety, anti-depressant or combined (anti-anxiety and anti-depressant) medications did not differ significantly (P > 0.001) from one another or from patients who underwent the program without medication, either at pre-treatment assessment or at mean long-term follow-up

of 3.2 yr. Hence, the concurrent use of these pre-existing medication regimes did not significantly enhance or detract from the long-term outcome of the BIGCBT program used in the treatment of panic disorder with or without agoraphobia.

From a clinical point of view, the above finding has important implications. First, we know from the literature that patients with panic disorder and agoraphobia are commonly

prescribed medications (e.g., Evans et al., 1988). Consequently, in clinical practice, a large proportion of patients with these conditions who are referred for CBT are on pre-existing medication regimes (e.g., Evans et al., 1991). Psychologists and other clinicians have therefore had to contend with the possibility that such medication regimes may have a positive or a negative impact on the outcome of their CBT interventions. These

Table 3 Medication Status at Pre-Treatment and Long-Term Follow-Up (Four Treatment Groups)

Treatment Group/ Assessment Phase	No Medication (%)	Anti-Anxiety Medication Only (%)	Anti-Depressant Medication Only (%)	Combined Medication (%)
BIGCBT without medication				
Pre-treatment	100.0	0.0	0.0	0.0
Long-term F/u	80.0	12.5	5.0	2.5
BIGCBT + AA				
Pre-treatment	0.0	100.0	0.0	0.0
Long-term F/u	47.5	40.0	5.0	7.5
BIGCBT + AD				
Pre-treatment	0.0	0.0	100.0	0.0
Long-term F/u	60.0	0.0	20.0	20.0
BIGCBT + COMB				
Pre-treatment	0.0	0.0	0.0	100.0
Long-term F/u	25.0	31.3	0.0	43.7

AA, anti-anxiety medication; AD, anti-depressant medication; BIGCBT, brief intensive group cognitive behavioural therapy program; COMB, combined (anti-anxiety and anti-depressant) medication; F/U, follow-up.

clinicians should receive some comfort from the results of the present study, since it appears that the concurrent use of pre-existing, anti-anxiety, anti-depressant or combined (anti-anxiety and anti-depressant) medication regimes with BIGCBT neither contribute to nor detracted significantly from its long term outcome.

Second, our results would imply that the role of pharmacotherapy in the treatment of panic disorder and agoraphobia possibly requires re-evaluation. While the short-term efficacy of both anti-anxiety and anti-depressant drugs is well established (Ballenger, 1990; Mattick *et al.*, 1990; Michelson & Marchione, 1991; Tesar, 1990), the literature to date suggests that the beneficial effects of these medications does not extend beyond their period of administration (Michelson & Marchione, 1991; Pollack, 1990). The resultant high relapse rates on cessation of therapy, combined with toxicity and dependency problems, call into question the role of medications in the treatment of panic disorder with or without agoraphobia. The demonstration in the present study of the lack of any significant enhancing effects of pre-existing medication regimes on the long-term outcome of BIGCBT in the treatment of panic disordered and

agoraphobic patients further questions the impact of medications commonly used in the long-term management of these conditions.

The results of the present study additionally showed that BIGCBT (with or without pharmacotherapy) was associated with significant improvements ($P < 0.001$) between pre-treatment assessment and long-term follow-up in self-reported frequency of panic attacks, in most self-ratings of avoidance behaviour (crowds, lifts, shopping, boat, bus, plane and train travel) and in most clinician-rated and self-report questionnaire measures employed (HAM-A, HAM-D, FSS-M, FQ-Ag and STAI). In contrast, BIGCBT (with or without pharmacotherapy) was not associated with any significant improvements or deterioration ($P > 0.001$) between pre-treatment and long-term follow-up in any self-ratings of catastrophic cognitions or physical symptoms experienced during a panic attack. This latter finding, coupled with the significant improvement over time in the frequency of reported panic attacks, would indicate that the panic attacks had improved quantitatively rather than qualitatively at long-term follow-up for those patients investigated. With respect to medication status at long-term follow-up, most (80%) patients

who underwent BIGCBT without medications for their conditions were reporting that they still remained medication-free at long-term follow-up. Furthermore, a large percentage (44%) of patients who underwent BIGCBT concurrent with pre-existing pharmacotherapy (either anti-anxiety, anti-depressant or combinations of these) for their conditions reported no longer taking any such medications at long-term follow-up.

Limitations of the Present Study

The present study is unique in its attempts to investigate the relative long-term impact of different classes of pharmacotherapy when combined with BIGCBT treatment of panic disorder with or without agoraphobia. The study does, however, have some methodological and empirical limitations. Firstly, any conclusions that can be drawn from its findings with respect to the long-term efficacy of BIGCBT in the treatment of panic disorder with or without agoraphobia are limited by the fact that the present study did not include a "no treatment" control group. Nevertheless, the improvements noted corroborate the earlier findings of Evans *et al.* (1991), who evaluated the long-term efficacy of the same BIGCBT program employed in the present study in comparison with such a control group. These authors reported long-term efficacy of BIGCBT in the treatment of agoraphobics for up to 3 yr. Additionally, the findings of the present study are consistent with the long-term benefits of CBT demonstrated by Barlow (1990) in similar patients. Hence, the results of the present study, taken in the light of previous literature, suggest that BIGCBT has long-term treatment benefits for panic disordered and agoraphobic patients.

A second limitation of the present study concerns the fact that patients were not randomly allocated to treatment groups. Nevertheless, it was previously stated in this paper that, in clinical practice, patients with panic disorder with or without agoraphobia who undergo CBT treatments are frequently already on pre-existing medication regimes. Often, these regimes are out of the control of the clinician administering the CBT treatment. Consequently, the present study chose to allocate patients to treatment groups on the basis of their self-reported pre-existing medication regimes. The disadvantages of this research approach include the inability to control for the specific types of medications that patients have been prescribed, the dosage levels of these medications, the duration of drug therapy, as well as possible inaccuracies of patient self-reports with respect to data pertaining to these factors. Nevertheless, it was considered to be a more clinically relevant and practical approach to attempt to discern the effects of pre-existing medication regimes on the long-term outcome of a BIGCBT program in the treatment of panic disorder with or without agoraphobia.

Finally, a further limitation of the present study concerns the sample sizes of the various treatment groups evaluated. While most of these treatment groups (BIGCBT without medication, BIGCBT plus anti-anxiety medication, BIGCBT plus combined anti-anxiety and anti-depressant medications) comprised reasonably large numbers of patients (ranging from 16 to 40), the BIGCBT plus anti-depressant group contained only 10 patients. Consequently, comparisons with this sub-group remain somewhat suspect until otherwise confirmed by future research.

References

American Psychological Association (1980). *Diagnostic and statistical manual of mental disorders* (3rd ed.). Washington, DC: American Psychological Association.

Ballenger, J. C. (1990). Efficacy of benzodiazepines in panic disorder and agoraphobia. *Journal of Psychiatric Research, 24* (2), 15–25.

Barlow, D. H. (1990). Long-term outcome for patients with panic disorder treated with cognitive behavioural therapy. *Journal of Clinical Psychiatry, 51* (12), 17–23 (Suppl. A).

Beurs, E., van Balkom, A., Lange, A., Koele, P., & van Dyke, R. (1995). Treatment of panic disorder with agoraphobia: Comparison of fluvoxamine, placebo, and psychological panic management combined with exposure and of exposure *in vivo* alone. *American Journal of Psychiatry, 15,* 683–691.

Clum, G. A. (1989). Psychological interventions versus drugs in the treatment of panic. *Behaviour Therapy, 20,* 429–457.

Craig, S., Underwood, B. R., Ashley, J. J., Ashley, M. H., & Piper, D. W. (1991). *MIMS Annual 1991.* Crows Nest, NSW: Intercontinental Medical Statistics.

Evans, L., Holt, C., & Oei, T. P. S. (1991). Long-term follow-up of agoraphobics treated by brief intensive group cognitive behavioural therapy. *Australian and New Zealand Journal of Psychiatry, 25,* 343–349.

Evans, L., Oei, T. P. S., & Hoey, H. (1988). Prescribing patterns in agoraphobia with panic attacks. *Medical Journal of Australia, 148,* 74–77.

Hamilton, M. (1959). The assessment of anxiety states by rating. *British Journal of Medical Psychology, 32,* 50–55.

Hamilton, M. (1960). A rating scale for depression. *Journal of Neurology, Neurosurgery and Psychiatry, 23,* 56–62.

Keppel, G. (1991). *Design and analysis: A researcher's handbook* (3rd ed.). Englewood Cliffs, NJ: Prentice-Hall.

Llamas, M., & Oei, T. P. S. (1993). The efficacy and cognitive processes of cognitive behaviour therapy in the treatment of panic disorder with agoraphobia. In S. Wang (Ed.), *Proceedings of the Second Afro-Asian Psychological Congress* (August 1993, pp. 710–714). Beijing: Beijing University.

Llamas, M., Oei, T. P. S., & Devilly, G. (1997). Cognitive change in cognitive behaviour therapy for panic disorder with agoraphobia. *Journal of Cognitive and Behavioural Psychotherapy* (in press).

Marks, I. M., & Matthews, A. M. (1979). Brief standard self-rating scale for phobic patients. *Behaviour Research and Therapy, 17,* 263–267.

Marks, I., Swinson, R., Basoglu, M., Kuch, K., Noshirvani, H., O'Sullivan, G., Lelliott, P., Kirby, M., McNamee, G., Sengun, S., & Wickwire, K. (1993). Alprazolam and exposure alone and combined in panic disorder with agoraphobia: A controlled study in London and Toronto. *British Journal of Psychiatry, 162,* 776–787.

Mattick, R. P., Andrews, G., Hadzi-Pavlovic, D., & Christensen, H. (1990). Treatment of panic and agoraphobia: An integrative review. *Journal of Nervous and Mental Disease, 178* (9), 567–576.

Michelson, L. K., & Marchione, K. (1991). Behavioural, cognitive, and pharmacological treatments of panic disorder with agoraphobia: Critique and synthesis. *Journal of Consulting and Clinical Psychology, 59* (1), 100–114.

Oei, T. P. S., Cavallo, G., & Evans, L. (1987). Utility of fear survey schedule with Australian samples of anxiety disorder patients. *Journal of Behaviour Therapy and Experimental Psychiatry, 18* (4), 329–336.

Oei, T. P. S., Wanstall, K., & Evans, L. (1990). Sex differences in panic disorder with agoraphobia. *Journal of Anxiety Disorders, 4,* 317–324.

Pollack, M. H. (1990). Long-term management of panic disorder. *Journal of Clinical Psychiatry, 51* (5), 11–13.

Sharp, D., Power, K., Simpson, R., Swanson, V., Moodie, E., Anstee, J., & Ashford, J. (1996). Fluvoxamine, placebo, and cognitive behavior therapy used alone and in combination in the treatment of panic disorder and agoraphobia. *Journal of Anxiety Disorders, 10,* 219–242.

Spielberger, C. D., Gorsush, R. L., & Lushene, R. E. (1970). *Manual of the state–trait anxiety inventory.* Palo Alto, CA: Consulting Psychologists.

SPSS (1990). *Statistical package for the social sciences* (Release 4) [computer software]. Chicago: SPSS.

Steketee, G., & Shapiro, L. (1995). Exposure vs cognitive restructuring in the treatment of panic disorder with agoraphobia. *Clinical Psychology Review, 15,* 317–346.

Tesar, G. E. (1990). High-potency benzodiazepines for short-term management of panic disorder: The U.S. experience. *Journal of Clinical Psychiatry, 51* (5), 4–10.

Weissman, M. M. (1990). The hidden patient: Unrecognized panic disorder. *Journal of Clinical Psychiatry, 51* (11), 5–8.

Weissman, M. M. (1991). Panic disorder: Impact on quality of life. *Journal of Clinical Psychiatry, 52* (2), 6–8.

Weissman, M. M., & Merikangas, K. R. (1986). The epidemiology of anxiety and panic disorders: An update. *Journal of Clinical Psychiatry, 47* (6), 11–17.

 Article Review Form at end of book.

In what way(s) does self-esteem influence the experience of anxiety and stress?

The Relation between Personality and Anxiety:

Findings from a Three-Year Prospective Study

**Beth S. Gershuny
and Kenneth J. Sher**

University of Missouri—Columbia

The authors tested the extent to which the personality dimensions of neuroticism, extraversion, and psychoticism (H. J. Eysenck & S. B. G. Eysenck, 1975) prospectively predicted global anxiety (assessed by items from the Brief Symptom Inventory; L. R. Derogatis & M. S. Spencer, 1982). The authors also examined prospective relations among these personality dimensions and depression to evaluate the specificity of findings. Participants were 466 young adults, primarily undergraduate students, assessed twice over a 3-year interval. An interaction between neuroticism and extraversion predicted both global anxiety and depression 3 years later. Findings indicated that personality, in particular the combination of high neuroticism and low extraversion, may play an important predisposing, etiological role in anxiety. Interpretations and implications of the predictive importance of the Neuroticism × Extraversion interaction in anxiety are discussed, and further speculations about the relation between anxiety and depression are put forth.

Theories and empirical interest in the relation between personality and psychopathology have been long-standing (see Maher & Maher, 1994, for a review), but interest in relations between personality and anxiety specifically began to wane as behavioral theories dominated the field. Recently, however, there has been a resurgence of interest in the relation between personality and anxiety (e.g., Reich, Noyes, Coryell, & O'Gorman, 1986; Trull & Sher, 1994), with particular interest paid to the possible etiological relevance of personality to anxiety. However, to date, few studies have examined the *prospective* relation between these constructs, and no reported studies have examined the longitudinal relevance of personality dimension *interactions* to the prediction of anxiety, both of which are necessary to help further our current understanding of personality–anxiety relations. To narrow these gaps in empirical knowledge, we examined the prospective relation between personality dimensions (and their interactions) and anxiety.

Theories of the Relation between Personality and Anxiety

Researchers and clinicians hypothesized that personality predisposes in-dividuals to specific psychological disorders such as depression and anxiety (e.g., Boyce, Parker, Barnett, Cooney, & Smith, 1991; M. Eysenck, 1987; Gray, 1981; Levenson, Aldwin, Bosse, & Spiro, 1988; Widiger & Trull, 1992). For example, Eysenck, Gray, and others (e.g., H. J. Eysenck, 1957; H. J. Eysenck & Eysenck, 1985; M. Eysenck, 1987; Gray, 1981, 1987; Zinbarg & Revelle, 1989) have posited that introverted and neurotic individuals may be more prone to anxiety than extraverted and non-neurotic individuals. These researchers speculated that people who are introverts experience greater susceptibility to punishment cues and less susceptibility to reward cues, and are prone to greater arousal; introverted individuals are, therefore, more conditionable to anxiety than extraverts. In addition, neurotic individuals are hypothesized as more sensitive to signals of punishment than nonneurotic individuals. Thus, both introversion and neuroticism may predispose an individual to anxiety because these personality traits may influence one's condition-ability to a variety of anxiety-provoking cues. Although these theories address the potential roles of intro-version and neuroticism in the development of anxiety, they are relatively silent about the potential role of psychoticism; therefore, the nature of the relation between psychoticism and anxiety is uncertain.

It remains unclear if extraversion and neuroticism work additively or interactively. Existing theories suggest that an *interaction* between neuroticism and introversion would lead to greater anxiety. That is, if one is introverted and thus more conditionable to punishment cues, anxiety would likely arise in more extreme forms if one is also more neurotic and thus more susceptible to negative affect and higher arousal in response to punishment cues. Thus, neuroticism and extraversion *should* interact synergistically in predicting anxiety.

Research on the Relation between Personality and Anxiety

To date, most studies of the relation between personality and anxiety have been cross-sectional, and few longitudinal studies have been conducted (L. A. Clark, Watson, & Mineka, 1994). Of the longitudinal studies reported in the literature (Faravelli & Albanesi, 1987; Levenson et al., 1988; Noyes, Clancy, Hoenk, & Slymen, 1980), none controlled for baseline anxiety, and thus they did not address the predictive importance of personality to anxiety above and beyond preexisting anxiety levels. However, with this caveat in mind, the identified longitudinal studies, of both nonclinical and clinical samples, reported a positive relation between neuroticism and anxiety (Levenson et al., 1988; Noyes et al., 1980),[1] and suggested a negative relation between extraversion and anxiety (Faravelli & Albanesi, 1987; Levenson et al., 1988). No identified studies examined the longitudinal relation between psychoticism and anxiety.

Of the cross-sectional studies identified in the literature, results consistently indicated that neuroticism (or negative affectivity) was positively related to both dimensional anxiety and anxiety disorders (e.g., Arrindell & Emmelkamp, 1987; Chambless, 1985; D. A. Clark &

Hemsley, 1985; Darvill, Johnson, & Danko, 1992; Kenardy, Oei, & Evans, 1990; Lolas, 1991; Trull & Sher, 1994; van Oppen, 1992; Zinbarg & Barlow, 1996). However, unlike neuroticism, cross-sectional relations between extraversion and anxiety were less clear: Some studies found a negative relation, albeit one that was less strong than a neuroticism–anxiety relation (e.g., Arrindell & Emmelkamp, 1987; Chambless, 1985; Darvill et al., 1992; Lolas, 1991; Trull & Sher, 1994), and other studies found no relation (e.g., D. A. Clark & Hemsley, 1985; Kenardy et al., 1990; van Oppen, 1992). Similarly, equivocal findings were shown for psychoticism–anxiety relations: Some studies found a positive relation (e.g., Lolas, 1991), but others found no relation (e.g., Chambless, 1985; D. A. Clark & Hemsley, 1985; Darvill et al., 1992; van Oppen, 1992). Still another study (Trull & Sher, 1994) found a negative relation between agreeableness–conscientiousness (traits related to psychoticism such that low agreeableness and low conscientiousness correspond to high psychoticism; e.g., Watson, Clark, & Harkness, 1994) and certain anxiety types (e.g., a composite anxiety score, posttraumatic stress disorder), but no relation between agreeableness–conscientiousness and other anxiety types (e.g., agoraphobia, social phobia, or simple phobia).

As noted earlier, both neuroticism and extraversion have been linked theoretically to anxiety, but it is unclear if these variables act additively or interactively to predict anxiety empirically. At least two studies have addressed a related issue by examining the cross-sectional relation between personality dimension interactions and general mood or subjective well-being. Hotard, McFatter, McWhirter, and Stegall (1989) and McFatter (1994) found a significant relation between a Neuroticism × Extraversion interaction and subjective well-being: Extraversion was related to subjective well-being only in high-neuroticism participants and was virtually unrelated for low-neuroticism participants. In addition, McFatter found that Neuroticism × Extraversion was significantly related to positive affect,

negative affect, and depression; low extraversion and high neuroticism were related to low levels of positive affect and high levels of negative affect and depression. Thus, a Neuroticism × Extraversion interaction may be an important cross-sectional correlate of subjective well-being, positive and negative affect, and depression. However, it remains unclear if this interaction would predict anxiety (and other types of negative affect) prospectively.

Summary

Reported findings suggest a positive relation between neuroticism and anxiety, a generally negative but inconsistent relation between extraversion and anxiety, and an unclear relation between psychoticism and anxiety. Related findings also suggest the importance of a Neuroticism × Extraversion interaction in predicting subjective well-being and mood or affect; however, no research specifically examined the potential interactive effects of personality on anxiety, despite the theoretical importance of such interactions. In addition, there is a paucity of prospective data, and those that do exist do not control for baseline anxiety. This is an important issue for understanding the personality–anxiety relation and establishing a direction of effect because (a) it is important to show that a relevant predictor (i.e., personality dimension) antedates the criterion (i.e., anxiety), and (b) if no unique effect is afforded by personality over an autocorrelation of anxiety with itself over time, then the need for introducing personality as a predictor variable is suspect. Recent articles in this area of research have noted a lack of longitudinal, prospective studies of personality–anxiety relations and have emphasized the importance of such longitudinal designs; indeed, most called for more studies of this kind (e.g., L. A. Clark et al., 1994; Zimbarg & Barlow, 1996). To address these issues and the global question of whether personality plays a *predisposing* role in anxiety, we examined the prospective relation between anxiety and personality dimensions (and personality dimension interactions).

To this end, we hypothesized that neuroticism would positively relate to anxiety, and extraversion would negatively relate to anxiety; however, the neuroticism–anxiety relation should appear stronger than the extraversion–anxiety relation. Because of the paucity of past research on the relation between psychoticism and anxiety, we made no specific predictions about this relation. However, we did expect an interaction effect between neuroticism and extraversion to emerge such that individuals low on extraversion and high on neuroticism would be at especially high risk for experiencing anxiety 3 years later, beyond the additive effects of neuroticism and (low) extraversion.

Method

Basic Design

As part of a longitudinal study of young adults at high and low risk for alcoholism, four waves of data were collected at yearly intervals with each participant tracked for approximately 3 years after being initially assessed as first-time college freshmen. The current study focused on two waves of data: those collected at Years 1 and 4. We focused on these two waves because (a) a relatively long interval with the largest number of participants was provided, (b) the statistical analyses were simplified by conserving the number of parameters that needed to be estimated, and (c) the stability (autoregressivity) of statelike aspects of anxiety was theoretically reduced and thus provided more efficiency in detecting prospective effects.

Participants

In the current study, 466 young adults, with a mean age of 18.2 (SD = 0.96) years at Year 1 and 21.2 (SD = 0.92) years at Year 4, served as participants. This sample size represents approximately 95% of participants targeted for follow-up at Year 1 (N = 489). Each participant received $25 for participation at each wave of data collection, with an additional travel stipend given to those who had relocated out of town. On the basis of participants' self-reports, approximately 93% were White, 5% were Black, 1% were Hispanic, and 1%

were Asian American.[2] All participants were first-time freshmen at baseline. By the completion of the fourth wave of data, approximately 75% were full-time college or university students, 5% were part-time college or university students, 5% were attending community colleges or trade schools, and 15% were no longer students.

Although a detailed description of participant ascertainment procedures was provided by Sher, Walitzer, Wood, and Brent (1991), a summary is provided here. Briefly, 3,156 freshmen (80% of the class) at a large midwestern university were first screened with a form of the Short Michigan Alcoholism Screening Test (SMAST; Selzer, Vinokur, & van Rooijen, 1975) adapted to assess biological fathers' (F-SMAST) and mothers' (M-SMAST) drinking problems (Crews & Sher, 1992). After this initial screening, participants were tentatively classified as high risk (HR) or low risk (LR), depending on whether they reported a history of alcoholism in their biological fathers. These participants were rescreened with selected sections of the Family History Research Diagnostic Criteria interview (FH-RDC; Endicott, Andreasen, & Spitzer, 1978) for the presence of alcoholism, drug abuse, antisocial personality disorder, and depression in all first-degree relatives and for alcoholism and drug abuse in all second-degree relatives. Participants included in the HR group (men, n = 110; women, n = 127) were those whose biological fathers met criteria for alcoholism on the basis of the F-SMAST and FH-RDC. Participants included in the LR group (men, n = 111; women, n = 118) were those whose biological parents did not meet SMAST criteria for alcoholism, whose first-degree relatives did not meet FH-RDC criteria for alcohol abuse, drug abuse, or antisocial personality disorder, and whose second-degree relatives did not meet FH-RDC criteria for alcoholism or drug abuse. Participants with an alcoholic biological mother were included in the HR group only if their biological fathers were also alcoholic (n = 24).

The current sample provided an opportunity to examine an age group that had not yet been examined in a longitudinal study of the re-

lation between personality and anxiety. Also, prior research has shown heightened levels of anxiety in individuals with a family history of alcoholism (Kushner, Sher, & Beitman, 1990), which potentially increases the base rates of anxiety, thus increasing the likelihood for detecting personality–anxiety relations. However, oversampling individuals at high risk for alcoholism introduced potential sample biases, and statistical analyses were conducted to determine the generalizability of findings across risk status. Family history was statistically controlled in all analyses, and interactions between family history and all other predictor variables were estimated to determine if comparable relations between personality and anxiety were obtained in high- and low-risk samples.

Measures

The *Eysenck Personality Questionnaire* (EPQ; H. J. Eysenck & Eysenck, 1975) contains questions that probed participants about characteristics they believed were pertinent to themselves *in general over the past several years*. This instrument assessed three dimensions of personality (regarded as traitlike in nature): neuroticism (23 items, α = .85), extraversion (21 items, α = .83), and psychoticism (25 items, α = .65). Alphas roughly corresponded to the alphas included in the EPQ manual. The factor structures of these personality dimensions were generally and consistently supported (e.g., McKenzie, 1988).

The *Brief Symptom Inventory* (BSI; Derogatis & Spencer, 1982) contains questions that probed participants about types of distress and various mood states that they experienced *during the past week*. This instrument assessed global anxiety and depression (both regarded as statelike in nature). Depression was assessed with the Depression subscale of the BSI (6 items; α = .79 at Year 1, α = .76 at Year 4; alphas were slightly lower than those reported in the BSI manual), and global anxiety was assessed with a combination of items from the anxiety subscales of the BSI. This composite global anxiety factor was derived by computing the mean for the 17 items (α = .85 at Year 1, α = .83 at Year 4) from the anxiety subscales of General Anxiety (6 items),

Phobic Anxiety (5 items), and Obsessive–Compulsive Anxiety (6 items). To examine the BSI's factor structure with the current data, we subjected items obtained from the three face-valid anxiety scales (Phobic, General, and Obsessive–Compulsive) to an exploratory factor analysis. When the entire sample was included in the analysis, there was not compelling evidence for more than one factor (determined by eigenvalues ≥ 1). In addition, the alpha for the composite Global Anxiety factor was higher than the alphas for the individual subscale factors, and Global Anxiety provided the broadest conceptualization of anxiety. Thus, the composite factor of Global Anxiety was included in our analyses.

Procedure

Participants were initially assessed during the 1987–1988 academic year and were reassessed on three subsequent annual assessments (1988–1991), totaling to four waves of data collection. We obtained informed consent regarding study participation from each participant at each wave. In addition, participants completed a battery of questionnaires that included the EPQ and the BSI (the EPQ was administered only at the first assessment wave; the BSI was administered at all four waves). Questionnaires were self-report paper-and-pencil tests administered in person at baseline to all participants. However, some participants were unable to be present for assessments at later waves of data collection and thus completed questionnaires by mail (13% at Wave 4). In addition to completing the EPQ and BSI, participants completed additional interviews and questionnaires at all four waves and a neuropsychological battery at Wave 1. However, these do not receive focus in the current study and thus are not discussed further.

Results

For all regression analyses, interaction terms between personality dimensions and family history and between personality dimensions and gender were computed and entered into regression equations (after all main effects were modeled) to test for generalizability of findings. No significant interactions were found; thus, analyses were not conducted separately for HR and LR participants or for male and female participants. However, family history and gender were entered into early steps in the regression models to control for possible main effects of family history and gender.

Prior to computing cross-product and quadratic terms (quadratic terms of individual personality dimensions were computed and included in our regression model to control for spurious moderator effects; see Lubinski & Humphreys, 1990), all variables were centered to eliminate nonessential collinearity. In addition, regression analyses were rerun on normalized data (data were normalized by rank transforming all data and then referencing each score percentile to a standard normal distribution; SAS Institute, 1985, Proc Rank procedure, Blom option) to assess whether findings were an artifact of distribution anomalies. Findings from the normalized data replicated findings from the nonnormalized data and thus are not discussed further.

Pearson product–moment correlations were computed among all predictor and criterion variables. Table 1 presents these correlations. Individuals with a family history of alcoholism reported slightly more neuroticism and psychoticism than individuals without this family history. In addition, men reported somewhat higher levels of psychoticism than women. As anticipated, correlations between primary personality dimensions (neuroticism, extraversion, psychoticism) tended to be small with correlation coefficients ranging from −.13 to .19. Also as expected, baseline global anxiety was highly correlated with Year 4 global anxiety, baseline depression was highly correlated with Year 4 depression, and global anxiety was consistently strongly correlated with depression contemporaneously. Neuroticism demonstrated a strong relation to baseline anxiety and depression, and a lesser but still strong relation to Year 4 anxiety and depression. Extraversion did not reveal an association with anxiety or depression at either wave, and psychoticism showed a moderate relation

to baseline anxiety and depression, with a very weak relation to Year 4 anxiety.

Cross-Sectional Regression Analyses

Prior to examining our data prospectively, we conducted a hierarchical ordinary least square regression analysis on data obtained at Year 1 to examine relations between main and interactive effects of personality on global anxiety and the replicability of McFatter's (1994) findings. Variables were entered in five steps: (a) family history and gender, (b) personality dimensions of neuroticism, extraversion, and psychoticism, (c) quadratic terms of individual personality dimensions, (d) two-way interactions among personality dimensions, and (e) a three-way interaction among personality dimensions. All betas presented in Table 2 are drawn from the final step. As shown in Table 2, adding the step of personality main effects resulted in a significant increment in the variance of anxiety, ΔAdj $R^2 = .30$, $F (3,456) = 68.45$, $p < .001$; both neuroticism ($\beta = .43$, $p < .001$) and psychoticism ($\beta = .28$, $p < .001$) related positively to anxiety (neuroticism appeared more strongly related to anxiety than did psychoticism). The psychoticism quadratic ($\beta = −.12$, $p < .05$) related negatively to anxiety, but adding the quadratic step did not account for a significant amount of the variance in anxiety. However, adding the step of two-way interaction terms did result in a significant increment in variance, ΔAdj $R^2 = .02$, $F(3, 450) = 4.36$, $p < .01$; the Neuroticism × Psychoticism interaction ($\beta = .14$, $p < .01$) related positively to anxiety. This Neuroticism × Psychoticism interaction was probed in two ways. First, we plotted the interaction using a technique described by Aiken and West (1991); the plot revealed that individuals with high neuroticism scores showed a strong positive relation between psychoticism and anxiety. Although this method of plotting interactions has the virtue of using all information from regression analyses, it potentially portrays data points that may not exist in reality. Thus, as a secondary check on the fidelity of these interaction plots, we conducted regression analyses separately for par-

Table 1

Table 1 Pearson Product—Moment Correlations Among Primary Study Variables

Variable	GA1	GA4	D1	D4	N	E	P	FH	Gender
GA1	—								
GA4	.44***	—							
D1	.67***	.32***	—						
D4	.30***	.67***	.37***	—					
N	.51***	.30***	.51***	.26***	—				
E	−.04		−.03	−.08	−.08	−.13**	—		
P	.27***	.11*	.22***	.07	.19***	−.02	—		
FH	.10*	.12*	.14**	.10*	.17***	−.03	.16***	—	
Gender	.13**	.09	.10*	.04	.07	.07	−.31***	.02	—

Note. Means and standard deviations for the main predictors and criteria are as follows: for GA1, $M = 0.45$, $SD = 0.40$; for GA4, $M = 0.24$, $SD = 0.32$; for D1, $M = 0.54$, $SD = 0.60$; for D4, $M = 0.29$, $SD = 0.46$; for N, $M = 9.34$, $SD = 4.93$; for E, $M = 15.78$, $SD = 4.06$; for P, $M = 2.77$, $SD = 2.43$. Coding for FH was 1 = *high risk*, 0 = *low risk*. Coding for gender was 0 = *male*, 1 = *female*. GA1 = global anxiety measured at Year 1; GA4 = global anxiety measured at Year 4; D1 = depression measured at Year 1; D4 = depression measured at Year 4; N = neuroticism; E = extraversion; P = psychoticism; FH = family history.

*$p < .05$. **$p < .01$. ***$p < .001$.

Table 2 Cross-Sectional Linear Multiple Regression Analysis of Personality Dimensions Predicting Global Anxiety

Predictor	ΔAdj R^2	β	B	SE
Intercept			.362***	.033
Step 1	.02**			
FH		−.030	−.024	.032
Gender		.183***	.148***	.033
Step 2	.30***			
N		.429***	.035***	.003
E		.058	.006	.005
P		.280***	.047***	.009
Step 3	.00			
N^2		.067	.001	.001
E^2		.068	.001	.001
P^2		−.119*	−.004*	.002
Step 4	.02**			
N × E		.040	.001	.001
N × P		.138**	.004**	.001
E × P		−.038	−.001	.001
Step 5	.00			
N × E × P		−.025	−.000	.000

Note. Regression coefficients were taken from the last step of the model. β = standardized regression coefficients; B = unstandardized regression coefficients; FH = family history; N = neuroticism; E = extraversion; P = psychoticism; N^2 = neuroticism quadratic; E^2 = extraversion quadratic; P^2 = psychoticism quadratic. Coding for FH was 0 = *high risk*, 1 = *low risk*. Coding for gender was 0 = *male*, 1 = *female*.

*$p < .05$. **$p < .01$. ***$p < .001$.

ticipants at varying levels of psychoticism and neuroticism. In so doing, it appeared that, indeed, high neuroticism potentiates the psychoticism–anxiety relation, and high psychoticism potentiates the neuroticism–anxiety relation.

Previous literature (e.g., Gotlib, 1984) suggests high degrees of covariation among self-report measures of anxiety and depression, and some researchers posit that extraversion is differentially related to anxiety and depression (e.g., Watson, Clark, & Carey, 1988). Although we are specifically interested in personality–anxiety relations, we believed it necessary to determine if the effects we found were specific to anxiety or similar to those found for depression. Thus, we conducted parallel statistical analyses using depression as the criterion. As shown in Table 3, results similarly revealed that adding the steps of personality main effects accounted for a significant increment in the variance of depression, ΔAdj $R^2 = .25$, $F(3, 456) = 56.88$, $p < .001$; neuroticism (β = .42, $p < .001$) and psychoticism (β = .17, $p < .01$) related positively to depression (again, neuroticism appeared to reveal a stronger association). No other steps showed a significant increment in the variance of depression. However, the neuroticism quadratic (β = .08, $p < .05$) showed a weak positive association with depression, as did the Neuroticism × Psychoticism interaction (β = .09, $p < .05$). Probing the Neuroticism × Psychoticism interaction revealed that, again, neuroticism potentiates the psychoticism–anxiety relation, and psychoticism potentiates the neuroticism–anxiety relation.

Prospective Regression Analyses

Before conducting prospective analyses controlling for baseline anxiety, we explored simple regression models (of Year 1 personality predicting Year 4 anxiety) to examine basic types of effects and to determine if the relative youth of our sample at baseline might have contributed to the difference between our cross-sectional findings and McFatter's (1994). To this end, five steps analogous to those previously described

<table>
<tr><th colspan="2">Table 3</th><th colspan="4">Cross-Sectional Linear Multiple Regression Analysis of Personality Dimensions Predicting Depression</th></tr>
<tr><th>Predictor</th><th>ΔAdj R^2</th><th>ß</th><th>B</th><th>SE</th></tr>
</table>

Predictor	ΔAdj R^2	ß	B	SE
Intercept		.000***	.388***	.051
Step 1	.03***			
FH		.030	.036	.048
Gender		.123**	.146**	.050
Step 2	.25***			
N		.422***	.051***	.005
E		−.001	−.000	.007
P		.169**	.041**	.014
Step 3	.01			
N^2		.084*	.002*	.001
E^2		.067	.002	.001
P^2		−.037	−.002	.003
Step 4	.00			
N × E		.032	.001	.001
N × P		.089*	.004*	.002
E × P		.006	.000	.002
Step 5	.00			
N × E × P		.059	.000	.000

Note. Regression coefficients were taken from the last step of the model. β = standardized regression coefficients; B = unstandardized regression coefficients; FH = family history; N = neuroticism; E = extraversion; P = psychoticism; N^2 = neuroticism quadratic; E^2 = extraversion quadratic; P^2 = psychoticism quadratic. Coding for FH was 0 = high risk, 1 = low risk. Coding for gender was 0 = male, 1 = female.

*p < .05. **p < .01. ***p < .001.

for the cross-sectional analyses were entered into the regression model. Results indicated that adding the steps of personality main effects, ΔAdj R^2 = .08, F(3, 458) = 14.44, p < .001, and quadratics, ΔAdj R^2 = .02, F(3, 455) = 3.89, p < .01, accounted for a significant increment in the variance of global anxiety 3 years later. In addition, the regression coefficients of neuroticism (β = .22, p < .001) and psychoticism (β = .18, p < .01) and of the quadratic of psychoticism (β = −.16, p < .05) were significant. Perhaps most important, however, the Neuroticism × Extraversion interaction revealed a significant regression coefficient (β = −.12, p < .01), indicating that Neuroticism × Extraversion accounted for a significant amount of variance in global anxiety 3 years later. Parallel analyses using depression as the criterion revealed similar findings. Adding the steps of personality main effects, ΔAdj R^2 = .06, F(3, 458) = 10.60, p <

.001, and two-way interactions, ΔAdj R^2 = .01, F(3, 452) = 2.85, p < .05, accounted for a significant increment in the variance of depression 3 years later. The main effect of neuroticism revealed a significant regression coefficient (β = .22, p < .001), as did the Neuroticism × Extraversion interaction (β = −.14, p < .01). Thus, these prospective regression analyses not controlling for baseline measures of mood yielded the hypothesized Neuroticism × Extraversion interaction, and the form of this interaction was highly similar to that controlling for baseline anxiety (and depression) as described below.[3]

Because some might argue that anxiety is merely a facet of neuroticism and thus would be expected to correlate with neuroticism both cross-sectionally and prospectively, controlling for baseline anxiety is important for theorizing etiological relations. To this end, hierarchical (ordinary least square) multiple regression analyses

predicting Year 4 anxiety from Year 1 personality dimensions, while controlling for baseline anxiety, were performed to test potential prospective main and interactive (configural) effects of personality dimensions on global anxiety measured 3 years later. Variables were entered in six steps: (a) baseline anxiety, (b) family history and gender, (c) personality dimensions of neuroticism, extraversion, and psychoticism, (d) quadratic terms of individual personality dimensions, (e) two-way interactions among personality dimensions, and (f) a three-way interaction among personality dimensions. All betas presented in Table 4 are drawn from the final step.

As illustrated in Table 4, baseline anxiety accounted for a significant amount of the variance in global anxiety assessed 3 years later. The step adding the main effects of personality did not account for a significant increment in variance, and none of the individual regression coefficients for personality main effects were significant. Adding the quadratic step, however, did account for a significant increment in variance, ΔAdj R^2 = .01, F(3, 452) = 2.86, p < .05. (Note, however, that in the final model, none of the individual regression coefficients for quadratic effects reached a conventional level of statistical significance.) Adding the two-way interactions also accounted for a significant increment in variance in later global anxiety, ΔAdj R^2 = .01, F(3, 449) = 2.76, p < .05, above and beyond baseline anxiety, family history, gender, main effects of personality dimensions, and quadratic effects of personality dimensions. The Neuroticism × Extraversion interaction revealed a significant regression coefficient (β = −.14, p < .01). None of the other regression coefficients (except for baseline anxiety) were significant.

The Neuroticism × Extraversion interaction was probed in exactly the same way as described earlier. Figure 1 shows the interaction plots of the regression slope between neuroticism and anxiety for participants at three levels of extraversion. As indicated within Figure 1, individuals with high extraversion did not differ on anxiety levels at Year 4 regardless of their neuroticism levels. However, for those individuals with

	Table 4	Longitudinal Linear Multiple Regression Analysis of Personality Dimensions Predicting Global Anxiety after Controlling for Baseline Anxiety			

Predictor	ΔAdj R^2	β	B	SE
Intercept			.075*	.031
Step 1	.19			
BAI		.369***	.284***	.039
Step 2	.00			
FH		.047	.029	.027
Gender		.054	.034	.028
Step 3	.00			
N		.067	.004	.003
E		−.012	−.001	.004
P		.078	.010	.008
Step 4	.01*			
N^2		.072	.001	.000
E^2		.002	.000	.001
P^2		−.106	−.003	.002
Step 5	.01*			
N × E		−.138**	−.002**	.001
N × P		−.003	−.000	.001
E × P		.003	.000	.001
Step 6	.00			
N × E × P		.067	.000	.000

Note. Regression coefficients were taken from the last step of the model. β = standardized regression coefficients; B = unstandardized regression coefficients; BAI = baseline anxiety for Year 1; FH = family history; N = neuroticism; E = extraversion; P = psychoticism; N^2 = neuroticism quadratic; E^2 = extraversion quadratic; P^2 = psychoticism quadratic. Coding for FH was 0 = *high risk*, 1 = *low risk*. Coding for gender was 0 = *male*, 1 = *female*.

*$p < .05$. **$p < .01$. ***$p < .001$.

low extraversion, there was a very strong positive relation between anxiety and neuroticism. Separate regression analyses supported these conclusions: High neuroticism potentiated the extraversion–anxiety relation, and low extraversion potentiated the neuroticism–anxiety relation.

As was done previously, parallel analyses were conducted using depression as the criterion. Results indicated that after controlling for baseline depression, adding the step of two-way interaction terms accounted for a significant increment in the variance of depression, ΔAdj $R^2 = .01$, $F(3, 449) = 3.72$, $p < .05$ (see Table 5). Indeed, a negative interaction between neuroticism and extraversion significantly predicted higher levels of depression 3 years

later ($\beta = -.15$). This interaction is explicated in Figure 1 and supported in subsequent analyses. For individuals with low extraversion, there was a strong positive relation between neuroticism and depression. High neuroticism potentiated the extraversion–depression relation, and low extraversion potentiated the neuroticism–depression relation. It is quite clear that in this study, the prospective (and cross-sectional) statistical patterns obtained for global anxiety were indeed similar to those found for depression.[4]

Discussion

Our findings extend previously reported cross-sectional data by demonstrating bivariate relations be-

tween neuroticism and global anxiety and between psychoticism and global anxiety. However, in a prospective context controlling for baseline anxiety, these main effects of personality were not statistically significant, perhaps partially because of the statistically conservative nature of such a design. Also note that extraversion did not relate to anxiety in any of our experimental contexts.

Of greatest interest, however, is the finding that the *interaction* between neuroticism and extraversion appeared most etiologically relevant; it predicted global anxiety over a 3-year interval above and beyond baseline anxiety and the main effects of personality.[5] Indeed, this interaction effect was significant even without controlling for baseline anxiety. Individuals scoring low on extraversion *and* high on neuroticism were especially likely to experience higher levels of global anxiety 3 years later. Similarly, findings from Hotard et al. (1989) and McFatter (1994) demonstrated a significant cross-sectional relation between a Neuroticism × Extraversion interaction and subjective well-being (and according to McFatter, 1994, positive and negative affect and depression were also significantly related to this interaction).

It is interesting that our cross-sectional data revealed a different pattern: Neuroticism × Extraversion did not predict anxiety; rather, neuroticism, psychoticism, and Neuroticism × Psychoticism predicted anxiety. Why might these findings differ from McFatter's (1994) findings and our own longitudinal examination? First, it is difficult for us to explain why these findings differed from McFatter's because it is nearly impossible to directly compare our methods, samples, and so forth. However, we speculate that perhaps there is something different about our cross-sectional (Year 1) sample and McFatter's sample in that we were testing only first-time freshmen with a mean age of about 18 years during the first wave of our study. McFatter (personal communication, June 1997), on the other hand, stated that the mean age of his sample was about 19 to 20 years and that it was comprised mostly of freshmen and sophomores, with some juniors and seniors as well. On further scrutiny of our data, we found that by the age of 19 to 20, our

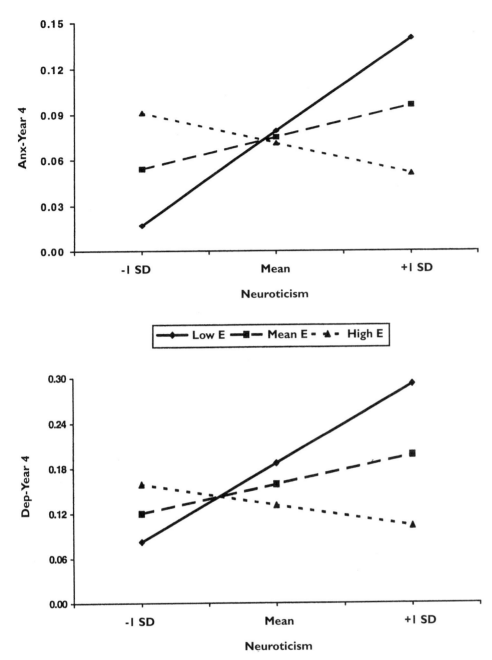

Figure 1. Regression plots of the linear relation between Year 1 neuroticism and Year 4 anxiety and depression conditional on Year 1 extraversion (low = 1 *SD* below the sample mean, medium = sample mean, and high = 1 *SD* above the sample mean). These regression plots control for all terms included in the regression models. Anx-Year 4 = global anxiety measured at Year 4; Dep-Year 4 = depression measured at Year 4; −1 *SD* = 1 *SD* below the mean; +1 *SD* = 1 *SD* above the mean; Low E = low levels of extraversion; Mean E = mean levels of extraversion; High E = high levels of extraversion.

participants began to reveal patterns similar to those demonstrated in our prospective analyses and in McFatter's (1994) analyses. We also found that the Neuroticism × Extraversion interaction was still a significant predictor of Year 4 anxiety when we did *not* control for baseline anxiety; thus, the findings from our pseudo-cross-sectional analysis of Year 4 data were consistent with our prospective reports and, again, with McFatter's (1994) data.

We are still, however, left with the task of further explaining why our Year 1 cross-sectional analyses did not yield the same findings as our prospective analyses. One possible explanation suggested by other findings from this sample is that the first 2 years of college are marked by higher levels of distress than the last 2 years (Sher, Wood, & Gotham, 1996). Much of the variance in the adjustment of freshmen and sophomores could be attributable to situational factors. For example, it is possible that a great deal of anxiety felt and reported during Year 1 of college is situational; students are in a new environment, are faced with new academic and social experiences, are virtual strangers with those around them, and so forth. Perhaps, over time, these students mature developmentally, grow accustomed to their surroundings, and develop social support through the making of friendships. For some (e.g., extraverted students who seek out others), this social support may help ameliorate and manage anxiety over time. However, for others who may be more introverted and solitary, this social support may not be available, and thus these individuals may be more prone to experiencing anxiety over time. In other words, an interaction between neuroticism and extraversion may become more salient and apparent in the prediction of anxiety over the course of a few years because individuals with high neuroticism but low extraversion may have fewer coping resources (e.g., social support) available to them; thus, their anxiety goes unabated.

Another possible explanation is that during a period of acute stress (e.g., beginning college), anxiety levels may be raised which, in turn, increases perceived levels of aversiveness to any potentially negative events that occur during that time. As a consequence, previously unconditioned stimuli may become conditioned and associated with feelings of anxiousness (Davey & Matchett, 1994), and higher and more frequent levels of anxiety may result. Thus, what we may be finding in our own study is that a Neuroticism × Extraversion interaction is actually predicting a more chronic form of anxiety, one that perhaps waxes and

Table 5

Longitudinal Linear Multiple Regression Analysis of Personality Dimensions Predicting Depression after Controlling for Baseline Depression

Predictor	ΔAdj R^2	ß	B	SE
Intercept			.159***	.045
Step 1	.13			
BDI		.320***	.246***	.040
Step 2	.00			
FH		.034	.031	.041
Gender		.011	.010	.043
Step 3	.01			
N		.084	.001	.005
E		−.061	−.007	.006
P		.035	.007	.012
Step 4	.00			
N^2		.012	.000	.001
E^2		−.055	−.001	.001
P^2		−.089	−.003	.002
Step 5	.01*			
N × E		−.153**	−.003**	.001
N × P		.004	.000	.002
E × P		−.006	−.000	.002
Step 6	.00			
N × E × P		.014	.000	.000

Note. Regression coefficients were taken from the last step of the model. β = standardized regression coefficients; B = unstandardized regression coefficients; BDI = baseline depression for Year 1; FH = family history; N = neuroticism; E = extraversion; P = psychoticism; N^2 = neuroticism quadratic; E^2 = extraversion quadratic; P^2 = psychoticism quadratic. Coding for FH was 0 = *high risk*, 1 = *low risk*. Coding for gender was 0 = *male*, 1 = *female*.

**p < .01. ***p < .001.

wanes over time but is still present and felt (such as is found in the anxiety disorders), rather than a transient state of anxiety derived from a temporary situational stressor (e.g., beginning college).

Whatever the possible reasons for the lack of a Neuroticism × Extraversion effect in our Year 1 cross-sectional analyses, the potency and replicability of our Neuroticism × Extraversion effect remain prospectively (with and without controlling for baseline anxiety). In addition, this interaction is theoretically supported; thus, it receives primary focus throughout the remainder of this article. To this end, we introduce possible explanations of why an interaction between neuroticism and extraversion may predict anxiety over time.

Relation between Neuroticism × Extraversion and Anxiety—Possible Explanations

Extraversion's and neuroticism's potential *etiological* roles in anxiety were potent when considered jointly in our study. Why is the interaction between neuroticism and extraversion integral to the *prediction* of anxiety? Eysenck (e.g., H. J. Eysenck, 1957; H. J. Eysenck & Eysenck, 1985; H. J. Eysenck & Levey, 1972) and Gray (1981, 1987), as well as other prominent researchers (e.g., Zinbarg & Revelle, 1989), speculated that neuroticism and extraversion predispose one's conditionability, sensitivity to signals of reward and punishment, and vulnerability to arousal and the

development of anxiety. Low extraversion and high neuroticism relate to greater susceptibility to negative affect, less susceptibility to signals of reward, greater susceptibility to signals of punishment, and higher vulnerability to arousal and anxiety. Even if an individual is highly neurotic, this same individual with high extraversion would more likely also be sensitive to signals of reward, which may offset or mask feelings of extreme anxiety. Similarly, even if an individual is highly introverted, this same individual with low neuroticism and low emotional reactivity would be less likely to react to signals of punishment with negative affect such as anxiety. Thus, there are multiple plausible reasons to hypothesize that the effects of neuroticism are contingent on extraversion (and vice versa).

Most theories on the relations among neuroticism, extraversion, and anxiety have focused on the role of conditioning and sensitivity to particular cues. Alternative perspectives are also possible. For example, perhaps an introverted neurotic person is prone to experiencing greater anxiety because of a lack of social support (e.g., Amirkhan, Risinger, & Swickert, 1995; Parkes, 1986) to aid in the amelioration of such anxiety (an introverted person may not seek much interaction with others). Thus, an introverted person may not have the coping strategy of seeking social support as an option, which then maintains and potentially exacerbates anxiety, an explanation that was alluded to earlier in this article. It is also possible that an introverted neurotic person places greater focus on internal processes (i.e., feelings, thoughts), which potentially magnifies the experience of subjective anxiety and leads to reports of greater anxiousness.

Are Anxiety and Depression Two Sides of the Same Coin? Further Speculations

On the basis of the writings of Clark, Watson, and their colleagues (e.g., L. A. Clark & Watson, 1991; L. A. Clark et al., 1994), we conducted analyses on depression to examine the specificity of our findings. The same pattern of findings was obtained for depression as for global anxiety, suggesting a lack of specificity. Indeed, it seems that there exists a synergistic effect of neuroticism and extraversion on Year 4 anxiety and Year 4 depression in which individuals scoring high on neuroticism are more likely to experience each of these forms of distress if also scoring low on extraversion.

Let us consider here the relative importance of the behavior activation system (BAS) and the behavior inhibition system (BIS). "There is little reason that higher BIS sensitivity (introversion) should be connected with [negative affect] to any great degree more than high BAS sensitivity (extraversion), except under conditions in which the tendency to inhibit responding is accompanied by high NAS (nonspecific arousal system) activation (neuroticism) with its high readiness to respond" (McFatter, 1994, p. 576). Drawing primarily from the theories of Gray (1981) and Fowles (1987), introverts are speculated to have a dominant BIS and thus to be more sensitive to punishment cues than reward cues. Thus, perhaps it is possible that both anxious and depressed individuals have dominant BIS systems and are sensitive to punishment, which leaves them more vulnerable to anxiety and depression.

Indeed, speculation of a common diathesis for anxiety and depression echoes the findings and interpretations of a study on genetic and environmental influences on anxiety and depression. Kendler, Heath, Martin, and Eaves (1987) found that genes influence the level of psychiatric symptoms but not the specific development of these symptoms into anxiety, depression, or both. However, they also found that one's environment influenced whether these symptoms would specifically take the form of depression or anxiety. Kendler et al. (1987) suggested that a distinction between anxiety and depression symptoms is largely the result of environmental influences, and that genes, although perhaps an influence on overall levels of distress, do not distinguish the form in which that distress will manifest itself. Thus, if we speculate that personality is substantially genetic, it would logically follow that personality traits may not adequately distinguish one's symptomatic expression of distress.

Study Limitations

Despite the strengths of this study, there exist limitations that warrant attention. The sample we examined was not representative of the general university population. Because this study was part of an ongoing longitudinal study of risk factors for alcohol-related problems, participants comprised an oversampling of individuals with a family history of alcoholism. However, the effects of personality on anxiety were not conditional on family history, so it seems unlikely that our findings could be an artifact of our sampling strategy. Also, we controlled for family history and gender in early steps of the statistical models to ascertain effects of personality on anxiety beyond any potential confounding of family history and gender. Thus, we feel reasonably confident that our findings are generalizable to similar populations. However, it is unclear if our findings would replicate in different populations (e.g., community samples) of varying ages; thus, generalizations to a variety of populations warrant caution.

As noted earlier, our findings were not specific to anxiety but indeed generalized to depression. The BSI's ability to distinguish between anxiety states and depression is difficult to determine; the BSI assesses both with relatively few items, and these indexes show high degrees of covariation. However, most scales of anxiety and depression are highly correlated (Gotlib, 1984), and even those (e.g., Beck Depression Inventory, and Beck Anxiety Inventory) posited to demonstrate better discrimination ability than other self-report measures "are nevertheless moderately correlated (.49–.61)" (D. A. Clark, Steer, & Beck, 1994, p. 646). It is presently unclear whether alternative self-report measures of dimensional depression and anxiety would yield a pattern of findings similar to that obtained in the current study.

Another limitation to our study involves the inclusion of EPQ assessment at only Wave 1. Because of this, we were unable to examine whether Year 1 anxiety predicts Year 4 personality dimensions; evaluating possible changes in personality over time was not possible. Although this is an important issue that should be addressed in later studies, the question of differential changes in personality was not integral to our current empirical investigation.

Conclusions

In summary, findings from our current study revealed that an interaction between neuroticism and extraversion predicted anxiety and depression 3 years later; individuals reporting high neuroticism and low extraversion were the most anxious and depressed. However, this interaction was not relevant to understanding the concurrent experience of these moods during a period of life marked by high situational stress (Sher et al., 1996). Thus, it seems that understanding and being aware of the synergistic effect between neuroticism and extraversion is most useful to us in predicting more chronic forms of anxiety and depression that are not necessarily expected reactions to a situational stressor and may, indeed, correspond to forms of anxiety found in an anxiety disorder (e.g., generalized anxiety disorder) or forms of depression found in a mood disorder (e.g., major depression). In the future, researchers may wish to replicate the current study with anxiety disordered individuals (and individuals diagnosed with major depression) and may wish to include other measures of anxiety (e.g., categorical diagnoses) and personality (e.g., five-factor model), as well as measures of other types of distress. In addition, it would be useful for future researchers to include additional variables (e.g., life events) speculated to interact with personality in the prospective prediction of anxiety.

Notes

1. Findings from a study conducted by Faravelli and Albanesi (1987) did not show a relation between neuroticism and level of agoraphobic symptoms in agoraphobic patients. However, it is important to note that a nonanxious control group was not included in Faravelli and Albanesi's (1987) study; thus, we cannot determine whether neuroticism does indeed relate to level of agoraphobic symptoms because they examined only a sample of individuals high in such symptoms, and the level of variance between these individuals is likely to have been low.

2. Ethnic breakdown differs from prior reports (e.g., Sher et al., 1991) because follow-up examinations of the data revealed that a number of participants who reported themselves to be Native American at baseline then reported themselves to be White in other data collection contexts. We suspect that some participants did not understand what was meant by Native American when they were first asked to report their ethnic identification.

3. We also conducted analogous analyses on data from Years 2 and 3 to examine potential patterns in our data. Findings yielded from Year 2 analyses (i.e., predicting Year 2 anxiety from Year 1 EPQ personality dimensions both with and without controlling for baseline anxiety) were remarkably similar to those garnered from Year 1 cross-sectional analyses; findings yielded from Year 3 analyses were extremely similar to those obtained from Year 4 analyses. It appeared that the strength of the Neuroticism × Extraversion interaction as a predictor of anxiety and depression increased over the course of 4 years of college.

4. To conserve space, betas and p values from the interaction-probing analyses (for all longitudinal and cross-sectional analyses using anxiety and depression as criteria) are not provided here. These data are available from Kenneth J. Sher.

5. Some may argue that the 1% of the variance accounted for by the Neuroticism × Extraversion interaction in our study is not substantial. However, empirical studies, particularly longitudinal studies, typically find interaction and moderator effects extremely difficult to detect in a dimensional context using multiple regression analyses. McClelland and Judd (1993) noted that the "efficiency of the moderator parameter estimate and statistical power is much lower" (p. 386) for such studies and that "moderator effects are so difficult to detect that even those explaining as little as 1% of the total variance should be considered important" (p. 377). In addition, our findings revealed a strong relation between neuroticism and anxiety for individuals reporting low extraversion, but virtually no relation for individuals reporting high levels of extraversion. Thus, the effects of neuroticism appear strongly conditional on one's level of extraversion (and vice versa), further emphasizing the strength of our findings.

References

Aiken, L. S., & West, S. G. (1991). *Multiple regression: Testing and interpreting interactions*. Newbury Park, CA: Sage.

Amirkhan, J. H., Risinger, R. T., & Swickert, R. J. (1995). Extraversion: A "hidden" personality factor in coping? *Journal of Personality, 63,* 189–212.

Arrindell, W. A., & Emmelkamp, P. M. G. (1987). Psychological states and traits in female agoraphobics: A controlled study. *Journal of Psychopathology and Behavioral Assessment, 9,* 237–253.

Boyce, P., Parker, G., Barnett, B., Cooney, M., & Smith, F. (1991). Personality as a vulnerability factor to depression. *British Journal of Psychiatry, 159,* 106–114.

Chambless, D. L. (1985). The relationship of severity of agoraphobia to associated psychopathology. *Behaviour Research and Therapy, 23,* 305–310.

Clark, D. A., & Hemsley, D. R. (1985). Individual differences in the experience of depressive and anxious, intrusive thoughts. *Behaviour Research and Therapy, 23,* 625–633.

Clark, D. A., Steer, R. A., & Beck, A. T. (1994). Common and specific dimensions of self-reported anxiety and depression: Implications for the cognitive and tripartite models. *Journal of Abnormal Psychology, 103,* 645–654.

Clark, L. A., & Watson, D. (1991). Tripartite model of anxiety and depression: Psychometric evidence and taxonomic implications. *Journal of Abnormal Psychology, 100,* 316–336.

Clark, L. A., Watson, D., & Mineka, S. (1994). Temperament, personality, and the mood and anxiety disorders. *Journal of Abnormal Psychology, 103,* 103–116.

Crews, T., & Sher, K. J. (1992). Using adapted Short MASTs for assessing parental alcoholism: Reliability and validity. *Alcoholism: Clinical and Experimental Research, 16,* 576–584.

Darvill, T. J., Johnson, R. C., & Danko, G. P. (1992). Personality correlates of public and private self consciousness. *Personality and Individual Differences, 13,* 383–384.

Davey, G. C. L., & Matchett, G. (1994). Unconditioned stimulus rehearsal and the retention and enhancement of differential "fear" conditioning: Effects of trait and state anxiety. *Journal of Abnormal Psychology, 103,* 708–718.

Derogatis, L. R., & Spencer, M. S. (1982). *The Brief Symptom Inventory (BSI): Administration, scoring, and procedures manual—1*. Baltimore: Johns Hopkins University School of Medicine, Clinical Psychometrics Unit.

Endicott, J., Andreasen, N., & Spitzer, R. L. (1978). *Family History Research Diagnostic Criteria (FH-RDC)*. New York: New York State Psychiatric Institute.

Eysenck, H. J. (1957). *The dynamics of anxiety and hysteria*. New York: Praeger.

Eysenck, H. J., & Eysenck, M. (1985). *Personality and individual differences: A natural science approach*. New York: Plenum Press.

Eysenck, H. J., & Eysenck, S. B. G. (1975). *Eysenck Personality Questionnaire manual*. San Diego, CA: Educational and Industrial Testing Service.

Eysenck, H. J., & Levey, A. (1972). Conditioning, introversion–extraversion and the strength of the nervous system. In V. Nebylitsyn & J. Gray (Eds.), *Biological bases of individual behavior* (pp. 96–106). New York: Academic Press.

Eysenck, M. (1987). Trait theories of anxiety. In J. Strelau & H. J. Eysenck (Eds.), *Personality dimensions and arousal* (pp. 79–94). New York: Plenum Press.

Faravelli, C., & Albanesi, G. (1987). Agoraphobia with panic attacks: 1-year prospective follow-up. *Comprehensive Psychiatry, 28,* 481–487.

Fowles, D. (1987). Application of a behavioral theory of motivation to the concepts of anxiety and impulsivity. *Journal of Research in Personality, 21,* 417–435.

Gotlib, I. H. (1984). Depression and general psychopathology in university students. *Journal of Abnormal Psychology, 93,* 19–30.

Gray, J. A. (1981). A critique of Eysenck's theory of personality. In H. J. Eysenck (Ed.), *A model for personality* (pp. 91–98). New York: Springer.

Gray, J. A. (1987). Perspectives on anxiety and impulsivity: A commentary. *Journal of Research in Personality, 21,* 493–509.

Hotard, S. R., McFatter, R. M., McWhirter, R. M., & Stegall, M. E. (1989). Interactive effects of extraversion, neuroticism, and social relationships on subjective well-being. *Journal of Personality and Social Psychology, 57,* 321–331.

Kenardy, J., Oei, T. P. S., & Evans, L. (1990). Neuroticism and age of onset for agoraphobia with panic attacks. *Behavior Therapy and Experimental Psychiatry, 21,* 193–197.

Kendler, K. S., Heath, A. C., Martin, N. G., & Eaves, L. J. (1987). Symptoms of anxiety and symptoms of depression: Same genes, different environment? *Archives of General Psychiatry, 44,* 451–457.

Kushner, M. G., Sher, K. J., & Beitman, B. D. (1990). The relation between alcohol problems and the anxiety disorders. *American Journal of Psychiatry, 147,* 685–695.

Levenson, M. R., Aldwin, C. M., Bosse, R., & Spiro, A. (1988). Emotionality and mental health: Longitudinal findings from the normative aging study. *Journal of Abnormal Psychology, 97,* 94–96.

Lolas, F. (1991). Personality effects on verbally expressed anxiety and hostility. *Personality and Individual Differences, 12,* 581–584.

Lubinski, D., & Humphreys, L. G. (1990). Assessing spurious "moderator effects": Illustrated substantively with the hypothesized ("synergistic") relation between spatial and mathematical ability. *Psychological Bulletin, 107,* 305–393.

Maher, B. A., & Maher, W. B. (1994). Personality and psychopathology: A historical perspective. *Journal of Abnormal Psychology, 103,* 72–77.

McClelland, G. H., & Judd, C. M. (1993). Statistical difficulties of detecting interactions and moderator effects. *Psychological Bulletin, 114,* 376–390.

McFatter, R. M. (1994). Interactions in predicting mood from extraversion and neuroticism. *Journal of Personality and Social Psychology, 66,* 570–578.

McKenzie, J. (1988). An item-factor analysis of the Eysenck Personality Questionnaire (E.P.Q.): Will the real personality factors stand up? *Personality and Individual Differences, 9,* 801–810.

Noyes, R., Clancy, J., Hoenk, P. R., & Slymen, D. J. (1980). The prognosis of anxiety neurosis. *Archives of General Psychiatry, 37,* 173–178.

Parkes, K. R. (1986). Coping in stressful episodes: The role of individual differences, environmental factors, and situational characteristics. *Journal of Personality and Social Psychology, 51,* 1277–1292.

Reich, J., Noyes, R., Coryell, W., & O'Gorman, T. W. (1986). The effect of state anxiety on personality measurement. *American Journal of Psychiatry, 143,* 760–763.

SAS Institute, Inc. (1985). *SAS user's guide: Statistics* (Version 5 ed.). Cary, NC: Author.

Selzer, M., Vinokur, A., & van Rooijen, L. (1975). A self-administered Short Michigan Alcoholism Screening Test (SMAST). *Journal of Studies on Alcohol, 36,* 117–126.

Sher, K. J., Walitzer, K., Wood, P., & Brent, E. (1991). Characteristics of children of alcoholics: Putative risk factors, substance use and abuse, and psychopathology. *Journal of Abnormal Psychology, 100,* 427–448.

Sher, K. J., Wood, P. K., & Gotham, H. J. (1996). The course of psychological distress in college: A prospective high-risk study. *Journal of College Student Development, 37,* 42–50.

Trull, T. J., & Sher, K. J. (1994). Relationship between the five-factor model of personality and Axis I disorders in a nonclinical sample. *Journal of Abnormal Psychology, 103,* 350–360.

van Oppen, P. (1992). Obsessions and compulsions: Dimensional structure, reliability, convergent and divergent validity of the Padua Inventory. *Behaviour Research and Therapy, 30,* 631–637.

Watson, D., Clark, L. A., & Carey, G. (1988). Positive and negative affectivity and their relation to anxiety and depressive disorders. *Journal of Abnormal Psychology, 97,* 346–353.

Watson, D., Clark, L. A., & Harkness, A. R. (1994). Structures of personality and their relevance to psychopathology. *Journal of Abnormal Psychology, 103,* 18–31.

Widiger, T. A., & Trull, T. J. (1992). Personality and psychopathology: An application of the five-factor model. *Journal of Personality, 60,* 363–393.

Zinbarg, R., & Revelle, W. (1989). Personality and conditioning: A test of four models. *Journal of Personality and Social Psychology, 57,* 301–314.

Zinbarg, R. E., & Barlow, D. H. (1996). Structure of anxiety and the anxiety disorders: A hierarchical model. *Journal of Abnormal Psychology, 105,* 181–193.

 Article Review Form at end of book.

What is transactional analysis? Does it explain medical-setting stress?

The Structure of Work-Related Stress and Coping among Oncology Nurses in High-Stress Medical Settings:

A Transactional Analysis

Gerard A. Florio,
James P. Donnelly,
and Michael A. Zevon

Roswell Park Cancer Institute

A transactional approach was used to examine stress and coping among 59 oncology nurses. Nine work stress clusters were identified: Physician-Related Stress, Organizational Factors, Observing Suffering, Ethical Concerns, Death and Dying, Carryover Stress, Negative Self-Thoughts, Inadequate Resources, and Coworker Stress, with the first 3 rated as most frequent and most intense. Ten coping clusters were also identified: Coworker Support, Positive Reappraisal, Developing a Growth Perspective, Positive Involvement in Treatment, Affective Regulation, Balancing Work Stress, Negative Coping, Apathy, Withdrawal, and Catharsis, with the first 3 rated as most frequently used and most effective. The relationships among the clusters, as well as the theoretical and clinical implications of these results, were discussed.

Although all professions are susceptible to work-related stress, the nursing profession has been identified as particularly stressful (Ivancevich & Matteson, 1980; Numerof & Abrams, 1988). Oncology nursing, in particular, is often described as among the most stressful specialty areas (Lederberg, 1989), with oncology nurses reported to be vulnerable to a host of related effects, such as burnout and job dissatisfaction (Jenkins & Ostchega, 1986), increased health complaints (Ullrich & FitzGerald, 1990), disturbances in sleep patterns (Herschbach, 1992), clinical depression and anxiety (Molassiotis & van den Akker, 1995), and increased interpersonal problems (Herschbach, 1992; Papadatou, Anagnostopoulis, & Monos, 1994).

These significant negative effects have been related in prior studies to a number of stressors endemic to oncology nursing, such as administering intense cancer treatments (Molassiotis & van den Akker, 1995), dealing with the death of patients (Jenkins & Ostchega, 1986; Ullrich & FitzGerald, 1990), poor relationships with medical staff (Molassiotis & van den Akker, 1995), ethical and moral issues related to patient care and research (Peteet et al., 1989), interpersonal staff conflicts (Molassiotis & van den Akker, 1995), highly demanding patients and families (Molassiotis & van den Akker, 1995), developing close relationships with patients during long-term hospitalizations (Herschbach, 1992; Molassiotis & van den Akker, 1995; Ullrich & FitzGerald, 1990), and finding a balance between one's personal and professional life (Herschbach, 1992; Papadatou et al., 1994).

The majority of the empirical literature examining work-related stress among oncology nurses is based on a stimulus–response model of stress. This model focuses on identifying the working conditions that are predictive of various forms of distress, as well as the organizational, demographic, and personality factors that moderate these associations. Dewe (1991), however, argued that the stimulus–response model is conceptually sterile and fails to incorporate essential elements of the theoretically richer but less empirically tested transactional model of stress (Lazarus & Folkman, 1984). The transactional model views stress as a transaction between a person and the environment that is mediated by two processes: cognitive appraisal and coping. Because the stimulus–response model fails to assess these important mediating processes, Dewe argued that a significant gap exists between our theoretical and empirical understanding of work-related stress among oncology nurses. He and others have argued for the development of new methodologies that operationalize and render testable the essential components of the transactional approach to stress (Bhagat & Beehr, 1985; Dewe, 1992; Lazarus, 1995).

The overall purpose of this study was to capture the essential elements of the transactional model of stress and subject them to a rigorous empirical evaluation in the context of a particularly high-stress medical environment, that is, medical oncology. The specific goal was to develop a conceptually rich, yet empirically derived, description of work-related stress and coping among medical oncology nurses. This was accomplished by using concept mapping (Trochim, 1989; Trochim & Linton, 1986), a relatively new methodology previously unused in the study of stress and coping. Specifically, the cognitive structure underlying the constructs of work-related stress and coping was identified in a sample of oncology nurses and graphically portrayed as concept maps. Four elements of the transactional stress model formed the basis for these maps: (a) identification of the specific encounters that oncology nurses perceived as stressful; (b) evaluations of the seriousness of the encounters (primary appraisals); (c) identification of the specific coping responses that they used to manage the stressful encounters; and (d) evaluations of the coping responses (secondary appraisals).

Method
Sample
The sample consisted entirely of registered nurses caring for inpatients at Roswell Park Cancer Institute

(RPCI), a National Cancer Institute-designated comprehensive cancer research and treatment center located in Buffalo, New York. Participants were drawn from two hematologic oncology services providing care to patients receiving high-dose chemotherapy, bone marrow transplantation, or both. This group of nurses was chosen because of the challenging nature of their responsibilities. Specifically, they were required to provide highly technical treatments to seriously ill patients who were hospitalized for extended periods of time.

All full-time oncology nurses from the two units were invited to participate in the study ($N = 79$). The nurses were informed that participation was voluntary and that their refusal to participate would not affect them in any fashion. Eighty percent ($N = 59$) of the nurses from these units participated in the study. Of this total, 33 nurses worked on the transplant unit (56%) and 26 nurses worked on the high-dose chemotherapy unit (44%). Demographic information collected from the nurses included age, race, nursing degree status, length of employment at RPCI, length of employment on the present unit, and prior nursing experience (oncology and nononcology).

Data Collection
A free-response methodology was used to identify the work-related stressors and coping responses most relevant to these oncology nurses. The specific methodology used in this study was based on a series of concrete, operationally defined steps described in detail by Trochim (1989) and Trochim and Linton (1986).

Step 1: Defining the conceptual domain. Twenty-four randomly selected nurses participated in one of four free-response item-generating sessions. One session with each of the following groups was held: (a) 6 nurses randomly selected from the day shift on the transplant unit; (b) 6 nurses randomly selected from the night shift on the transplant unit; (c) 6 nurses randomly selected from the day shift on the chemotherapy unit; and (d) 6 nurses randomly selected from the night shift on the chemotherapy unit. Within these

groups, the nurses were asked to generate responses to the following focus statements:

1. Generate statements that describe specific stresses that you encounter in your job as a hematologic oncology nurse.

2. Generate statements that describe specific things that you think or do to cope with the stress that you encounter on your job as a hematologic oncology nurse.

The nurses were encouraged to generate as many statements as possible. No criticism or discussion about the statements took place as the statements were being generated. The facilitator recorded the statements as they were generated so that the nurses could see the entire set of statements as they evolved.

A total of 220 work-related stress items were generated by the nurses at the four sessions. After the four lists were edited for redundancies, 164 work-related stress items remained. Because of the nature of the sorting and rating tasks to be performed on these items, we decided that the item pool should not exceed 100 items for the stress and coping domains. A panel of experts was used to further refine the item pool and to reduce the number to a maximum of 100 items, a number large enough to ensure coverage of the domain and manageable in terms of the required sorting and rating. The panel included the two head nurses from the units participating in the study and two psychologists with expertise in the areas of medical oncology and stress and coping. Each panel member used the following rating system to rank the 164 items in terms of their relative priority: 3 = *high priority items*; 2 = *medium priority items*; and 1 = *low priority items*. Ninety-seven items with a mean priority rating of greater than or equal to 2 were included in the next phase of the study.

A total of 147 work-related coping items were generated by the nurses in the four sessions. Editing the four lists for redundancies resulted in a final list of 79 work-related coping behaviors. Because editing alone reduced the coping items to less than 100, all of these items were included in the next phase of the study.

Step 2: Structuring the statements. The second phase of data collection involved the total sample of 59 inpatient hematologic oncology nurses. Structuring the statements involved first sorting and then rating the stress and coping items. For the sorting task, each nurse received two sets of 3 × 5 cards: one set containing the 97 work-related stress items and one set containing the 79 work-related coping items. The nurses performed individual unstructured sorts for both the stress and coping cards. Specifically, they were told to "separate the cards into piles of similar items in any way that makes sense to you." The only restrictions were the following: (a) An item cannot be placed simultaneously into two separate piles; (b) all items cannot be placed into a single pile; (c) all items cannot be placed into their own piles; and (d) items that do not appear to be related to any others should be in their own pile rather than a miscellaneous pile.

For the rating task, the stress and coping items were listed in a questionnaire form. The nurses were asked to rate the 97 work-related stress items on three appraisal dimensions: frequency of occurrence (1 = *rarely* and 7 = *very frequently*); intensity of the associated distress (1 = *very minor distress*; 7 = *unbearable distress*); and perceived controllability (0 = *no control*; 7 = *completely controllable*). The work-related coping items were rated on two appraisal dimensions: frequency of use (1 = *rarely* and 7 = *very frequently*) and effectiveness in reducing distress (1 = *very little effect*; 7 = *dramatic effect*).

Data Analysis

On the basis of the sorting of the items, we used multidimensional scaling (MDS) and hierarchical cluster analyses to analyze and graphically represent the underlying structure of the work-related stress and coping responses of the oncology nurses. These analyses were performed by using *The Concept System* (Trochim, 1995), a software package designed specifically for this methodology.

Two-dimensional nonmetric MDS analyses were performed for the work-related stress and coping items. This was accomplished in several steps. First, individual binary square similarity matrices were created from each nurse's stress and coping sorting results. These matrices had as many rows and columns as there were statements in the particular domain (i.e., 97 × 97 for stress and 79 × 79 for coping items). The values in the binary matrices were 1 (if the statements in that row and column were placed in the same pile) or 0 (if they were not). Next, a group similarity matrix for the stress and coping domains was created by aggregating the individual similarity matrices across participants. These group similarity matrices also had as many rows and columns as there were items in the particular domain. The values in these matrices corresponded to the total number of nurses who included the items represented by the particular rows and columns in the same sort.

The group similarity matrices for the work-related stress and coping items were used as the input for the two-dimensional nonmetric MDS analyses. These analyses resulted in two dimensional (x-y) point maps that represent each item as a point on a spatial map. A separate spatial map was created for the work-related stress and work-related coping data. Placement of the points on these maps is mathematically determined so that the distance between the points has the strongest possible relation to the perceived similarities and dissimilarities among the sorted work-related stress and coping items. Specifically, statements that were closer together on the map were, in general, sorted together more frequently; more distant statements on the map were sorted together less frequently.

Hierarchical agglomerative cluster analysis was performed for the work-related stress and coping domains to group the individual items on the MDS point map into clusters of similar statements. Specifically, the x-y coordinate values from MDS solutions were used as the input for the hierarchical cluster analyses. Ward's (1963) algorithm was used to partition the MDS configuration into nonoverlapping clusters in two-dimensional space. Ward's algorithm is designed to minimize the variance within clusters and optimize the distinctiveness across clusters. The end-product of this analysis is referred to as a *concept map*, which shows how the sorted items on the MDS point maps were grouped together into broader conceptual units.

A problem common to cluster analysis pertains to deciding the number of clusters that are present in the data set. Although several procedures have been developed (see Aldenderfer & Blashfield, 1984), there is no simple or widely accepted method. Trochim provided a heuristic approach that can be used with the results generated by *The Concept System* (Trochim, 1989; Trochim & Linton, 1986). He advised that a range of cluster solutions be examined when deciding the number of clusters for the final map, using both an item content and quantitative goodness-of-fit criterion.

For item content, Trochim (1989) advised that the range of cluster solutions should be examined in reverse order. At each reverse step, two clusters are merged. The clusters that are merged at each step are examined, and a subjective determination is made as to whether the two merged clusters obscure an important distinction preserved by retaining the separate clusters. When the entire range of solutions is examined in this way, a judgment can be made about the cluster solution that yields the fewest number of clusters but still preserves the maximum amount of substantive detail.

A goodness-of-fit measure known as a bridging value is used to analyze the range of cluster solutions quantitatively. A bridging value can be computed for each item, and an average bridging value can be computed for each cluster. The bridging value for an individual item indicates whether the item was sorted more frequently with other items that are close to it on the map. The cluster-average bridging value is the mean of the individual item values and indicates how clearly a cluster reflects the content in its specific portion of the map. Bridging values range from 0 to 1, and decisions about the final cluster solution should try to minimize the cluster-average bridging values while still providing sufficient substantive detail.

The mean appraisal ratings for the stress and coping items were also calculated. As previously stated, nurses rated the work-related stress items in terms of the three appraisal dimensions of frequency, intensity, and controllability. The work-related coping items were rated on the two appraisal dimensions of frequency and effectiveness. For the final stress and coping clusters, means and standard deviations were calculated for each appraisal dimension. In addition, analyses of the internal consistency of the appraisal ratings were performed for the final stress and coping clusters.

Results

Table 1 describes the sample in terms of demographic and work variables. The sample was predominantly female (90%) and White (71%). On average, the sample had less than 4 years experience in oncology nursing and less than 4 years of employment at RPCI.

Work-Related Stress

Multidimensional scaling analysis. The 97 work-related stress items identified by the nurses were analyzed in a two-dimensional nonmetric MDS. Eighteen iterations resulted in a solution with a final Kruskal stress value of 0.13. This represents a stable solution for an analysis of 97 complex items. The MDS solution for the 97 work-related stresses is included in Figure 1. In the figure, each work-related stress item is indicated by a small box with a statement-identifying number beside it. Items that are close together were sorted together more frequently and show a high degree of similarity.

The reliability or consistency of the work-related stress MDS solution was assessed by computing a coefficient analogous to a split-half reliability. This was done by randomly dividing the 59 nurses into two groups (30 in one and 29 in the other). Similarity matrices were constructed separately for each random group, and separate MDS configurations were computed from these matrices. To estimate reliability, we computed the correlation between the similarity matrices and applied the Spearman–Brown correction. The reliability estimate for the similarity

Table 1 Descriptive Data for the Hematologic Oncology Nurse Sample

Variable	Range	M	SD	n
Age (years)	24–48	32.6	6.84	
Employment at Roswell Park Cancer Institute (years)	0.5–14	3.4	2.29	
Experience on present unit (years)	0.8–7.1	2.9	1.59	
Total nursing experience (years)	0.8–12.75	4.2	2.79	
Oncology nursing experience (years)	0.4–12	3.6	2.17	
Highest nursing degree earned				
Registered nurse				33
Bachelor of Science in Nursing				17
Master's of Nursing				3
Not specified				8
Race				
White				42
African American				6
Native American				1
Not specified				10

matrices was .96 ($df = 4753$, $p < .001$), indicating a very reliable solution.

Hierarchical cluster analysis. A hierarchical cluster analysis of the MDS configuration was used to group the work-related stress items into internally consistent stress clusters. All potential cluster solutions from 4 through 15 clusters were examined in terms of statistical fit (i.e., the bridging indexes) and item content. The 9-cluster solution minimized the average-cluster bridging value while providing the most substantively interpretable units. The 9-cluster work-related stress concept map for oncology nurses is also presented in Figure 1. In the figure, the clusters are identified by bounded groups of points. Examples of the item content and bridging indexes of the 9-cluster stress solution are presented in Table 2. Labels were assigned to the 9 clusters on the basis of an examination of the items. In labeling the clusters, we emphasized items with lower bridging values because they are more central to the meaning of the cluster.

Understanding the work-related stress concept map for oncology nurses involves examining the spatial relationships among the nine stress clusters. Physician-Related Stress and Ethical Concerns are in close proximity to each other on the

map and can be viewed as composing the larger dimension of role conflict. Death and Dying and Observing Patient and Family Suffering are close in proximity and represent the emotional stress associated with oncology nursing. The personal impact of oncology nursing is represented by the clusters Carryover Stress and Negative Self-Thoughts, which are very close together. Finally, Organizational Factors, Coworker Stress, and Inadequate Resources are close in proximity and relate to stress from the work environment.

Appraisal of the work-related stress clusters. Figure 2 graphically presents the mean appraisal ratings (i.e., frequency, intensity, and controllability) of the nine work-related stress clusters. The large number of significance tests required to examine the mean differences between all combinations of the nine stress clusters for all three appraisal dimensions (i.e., 36 tests–appraisal dimension) would obviously inflate the Type I error rate. Therefore, we used paired t tests to examine the mean differences between the highest and lowest ratings for each of the appraisal dimensions to evaluate the most extreme contrasts for each appraisal dimension.

Organizational Factors, Death and Dying, Observing Patient and

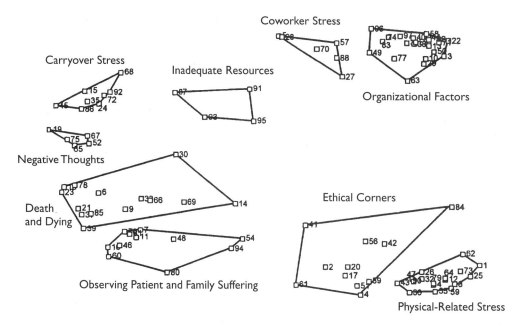

Figure 1. Nine-cluster work-related stress concept map for hematologic oncology nurses. Each box with a statement-identifying number beside it indicates a work-related stress item.

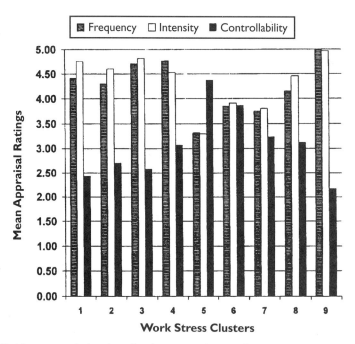

Figure 2. Mean appraisal ratings for the stress clusters. Cluster codes: 1 = Physician Stress, 2 = Ethical Concerns, 3 = Observing Suffering, 4 = Death and Dying, 5 = Carryover Stress, 6 = Negative Self-Thoughts, 7 = Inadequate Resources, 8 = Coworker Stress, 9 = Organizational Factors.

Family Suffering, Physician-Related Stress, and Ethical Concerns were rated as the most frequently occurring stress clusters. The clusters Carryover Stress, Inadequate Resources, and Negative Self-Thoughts were rated as least frequently occurring. The mean difference between the frequency ratings of Organizational Factors and Carryover Stress was statistically significant, $t(58) = 5.87$, $p < .001$.

Organizational Factors, Observing Patient and Family Suffering, and Physician-Related Stress were rated as the most intense stress clusters. The clusters Carryover Stress, Inadequate Resources, and Negative Self-Thoughts were rated as the least intense. The mean difference between the intensity ratings of Organizational Factors and Carryover Stress was statistically significant, $t(58) = 5.71$, $p < .001$.

The stress clusters that were perceived to be the least controllable were Organizational Factors, Physician-Related Stress, and Ethical Concerns. The clusters rated as the most controllable were Carryover Stress and Negative Self-Thoughts. The mean difference between the controllability ratings of Organizational Factors and Carryover Stress was statistically significant, $t(58) = -8.45$, $p < .001$.

There was a strong positive correlation between the cluster frequency and intensity ratings ($r = .94$), indicating that stress clusters that were perceived as more frequent were also rated as more intense. There was also a strong inverse relationship between the frequency and controllability ratings of the stress clusters ($r = -.89$). In general, stress clusters that were rated as more frequent were also rated as less controllable. Finally, a strong inverse

Table 2 Sample Items and Cluster Bridging Values for the Nine Oncology Nurse Work Stress Clusters

Work-Related Stress Cluster/Item	Bridging Value	Work-Related Stress Cluster/Item	Bridging Value
Physician-Related Stress		**Negative Self-Thoughts**	
Physicians avoiding communication with patients and their families	0.16	Feeling guilt about my lower personal commitment to the job and my patients	0.62
Physicians ordering aggressive treatments that seem unnecessary	0.12	Fears about my ability to perform my job	0.65
Physicians' reluctance to discuss resuscitation procedure with patients and families	0.16	Seeing myself change in negative ways, like joking about grim topics	0.68
Physicians who appear to abandon patients who are not doing well	0.17	Cluster bridging average	0.67
Cluster bridging average	0.27	**Carryover Stress**	
Ethical Concerns		Difficulties separating work and home conflicts	0.83
Observing unnecessary suffering by patients because of inadequate pain control	0.53	Work anxiety (e.g., difficulty sleeping before a shift)	0.80
Lack of information and/or failure to give realistic information about treatment and prognosis for patients and families	0.40	Overreacting at home due to stress at work	0.86
Newly diagnosed patients not being told about their disease and treatment by the physician	0.35	Conflict between work and family responsibilities (e.g., when your child is sick)	0.76
Cluster bridging average	0.62	Cluster bridging average	0.81
Death and Dying		**Coworker Stress**	
No chance to grieve after the death of a patient	0.45	Interpersonal conflicts among the nursing staff	0.96
Not being able to forget patients who have died	0.48	Getting flack from health care aides when you confront them about their lack of performance	0.68
Death of patients whom we get close to during long hospital stays	0.45	Cluster bridging average	0.71
Watching people in the final days of their lives	0.44	**Organizational Factors**	
Cluster bridging average	0.54	Difficulty getting personal leave time	0.11
Observing Patient and Family Suffering		Nursing administration out of touch with the day-to-day life of nurses	0.08
Dealing with angry and aggressive family members	0.49	Lack of vacation time or having to take short vacations	0.26
Seeing what people go through from the treatments that we give them	0.44	No incentives or rewards for career development and advancement	0.10
Watching patients' family members deal with the treatment of their loved ones	0.48	Inadequate pay	0.26
Cluster bridging average	0.60	Cluster bridging average	0.18
		Inadequate Resources	
		Fear about my ability to perform my job because of inadequate training	0.91
		Having to perform multiple roles (i.e., supervisory, critical care, etc.)	0.89
		No response to grief by anyone in the hospital	0.83
		Not enough charting or personal contact with other services	0.87
		Cluster bridging average	0.88

relationship was also found between the intensity and controllability ratings of the stress clusters ($r = -.97$). In general, stress clusters that were more intense were also rated as less controllable.

Table 3 presents the stress cluster appraisal ratings for the day- and night-shift nurses. Multivariate analysis of variance (MANOVA) was used to determine whether there were significant differences in the appraisal ratings of the stress clusters between day- and night-shift nurses.

Work shift was the independent variable. Each set of appraisal ratings (frequency, intensity, and controllability) were the dependent variables in a separate MANOVA. Day and night nurses did not differ significantly in their appraisals of the frequency, intensity, or controllability of the work stress clusters.

The internal consistency estimates of the three appraisal dimensions are summarized in Table 4. The internal consistency of the frequency ratings ranged from .46 (Coworker

Stress) to .92 (Physician-Related Stress). Most clusters revealed good to excellent internal consistency. The cluster intensity ratings also showed good to excellent internal consistency, with values ranging from .66 (Coworker Stress) to .91 (Organizational Factors). Finally, the internal consistency of the controllability ratings ranged from .46 (Inadequate Resources) to .94 (Organizational Factors), with most clusters revealing good to excellent internal consistency.

Table 3 Stress Cluster Appraisal Ratings for Day- and Night-Shift Nurses

Cluster	Frequency		Intensity		Controllability	
	Day Shift	Night Shift	Day Shift	Night Shift	Day Shift	Night Shift
Physician-Related Stress	4.30	4.52	4.53	4.98	2.44	2.42
Ethical Concerns	4.16	4.48	4.48	4.72	2.67	2.72
Observing Suffering	4.71	4.70	4.76	4.87	2.53	2.61
Death and Dying	4.83	4.69	4.56	4.50	3.03	3.09
Carryover Stress	4.15	3.53	4.10	3.72	3.79	3.94
Negative Self-Thoughts	3.45	3.19	3.18	3.40	4.45	4.29
Inadequate Resources	3.49	4.01	3.37	4.23	3.32	3.13
Coworker Stress	4.17	4.13	4.37	4.54	3.09	3.14
Organizational Factors	4.98	5.03	4.82	5.11	2.22	2.10

Table 4 Alpha Reliability Coefficients of the Appraisal Ratings for the Nine Work-Related Stress Clusters

Work-Related Stress	Frequency	Intensity	Controllability
Physician-Related Stress	.92	.90	.90
Ethical Concerns	.88	.84	.79
Death and Dying	.82	.89	.80
Observing Patient and Family Suffering	.83	.84	.79
Carryover Stress	.72	.75	.67
Negative Self-Thoughts	.62	.66	.63
Organizational Factors	.89	.91	.94
Coworker Stress	.46	.67	.49
Inadequate Resources	.63	.77	.46

Work-Related Coping

Multidimensional scaling analysis. The 79 coping items were analyzed in a two-dimensional nonmetric MDS. After 10 iterations, a final Kruskal stress value of 0.23 was obtained for the MDS solution. Though not optimal, this represents a reasonably stable solution for a set of 79 complex items. The MDS solution for the 79 work-related coping behaviors is presented in Figure 3. Again each work-related coping item is indicated by a small box with a statement-identifying number beside it in the figure. Analysis of this figure reveals that, in general, items that are close together are conceptually similar to each other.

The same procedure that was used to calculate the reliability of the work–related stress MDS concept map was used to estimate the reliability of the work-related coping MDS concept map. After applying the Spearman-Brown correction to the correlation between the split similarity matrices, we obtained a final reliability estimate of .91 ($df = 3160$, $p < .000$), indicating a very reliable solution.

Hierarchical cluster analysis. The work-related coping items were also grouped into internally consistent clusters through a hierarchical cluster analysis of the MDS configuration. Ward's (1963) minimum variance method was used to optimize the distinctiveness across clusters. All potential cluster solutions from 2 through 15 clusters were examined in terms of the bridging indexes and item content. The 10-cluster solution was chosen as the solution that minimized the average bridging value while providing

the most substantively understandable and interpretable units. The 10-cluster work-related coping concept map for oncology nurses is also presented in Figure 3. Examples of the item content and bridging indexes for the 10-cluster coping solution are presented in Table 5. Labels were assigned to the 10 clusters on the basis of an examination of the items that compose them. In labeling the clusters, we emphasized items with lower bridging values because they were more central to the meaning of the cluster.

Interpreting the coping concept map for oncology nurses involved examining the spatial relationships among the 10 coping clusters and the two coping meta-dimensions. The clusters Coworker Support and Positive Involvement in Treatment are close to each other in the lower left portion of the map. These clusters relate to vocational characteristics that are used to manage stress. Affective Regulation, Balancing Work Stress, and Positive Reappraisal are in close proximity on the right side of the map and represent positive ways of managing the emotional impact of oncology nursing. Bridging these left and right portions of the map is the cluster titled Developing a Growth Perspective. This cluster represents an existential coping dimension. The location seems appropriate because the cluster relates to both a positive orientation toward nursing and managing the impact of the job. The clusters Apathy, Negative Coping, Withdrawal, and Catharsis/Break Room are all located in the upper

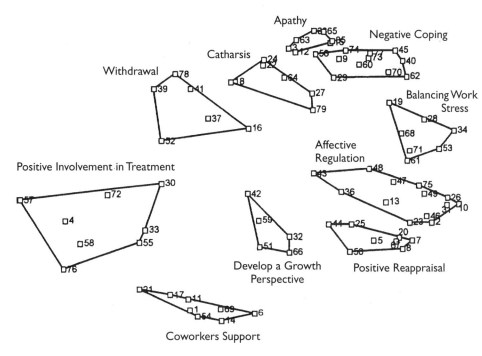

Figure 3. Ten-cluster coping concept map for the hematologic oncology nurses. Each box with a statement-identifying number beside it indicates a work-related stress item.

portion of the map. They are close in proximity and form a less adaptive coping meta-dimension.

Appraisal of coping clusters. Figure 4 graphically presents the mean appraisal ratings (i.e., frequency and effectiveness) of the 10 work-related coping clusters. Once again, the large number of significance tests required to examine the mean differences between all combinations of the 10 coping clusters for both appraisal dimensions (i.e., 45 tests–appraisal dimension) would result in an inflated Type I error rate. Therefore, paired t tests were used to examine the mean differences between the highest and lowest ratings for both appraisal dimensions.

Positive Reappraisal, Coworker Support, and Developing a Growth Perspective were rated as the most frequently used coping clusters. The least frequently used clusters were Apathy, Negative Coping, and Withdrawal. The mean difference between the frequency ratings of Positive Reappraisal and Apathy was statistically significant, $t(58) = 20.38, p < .001$.

Coworker Support, Positive Reappraisal, and Developing a Growth Perspective were rated as the most effective coping clusters.

The least effective clusters were Apathy, Negative Coping, and Withdrawal. The mean difference between the effectiveness ratings of Positive Reappraisal and Apathy was also statistically significant, $t(58) = 16.59, p < .001$.

Significant differences were observed across both coping appraisal dimensions when the most extreme contrasts were tested. As with the stress clusters, there was consistency in the appraisal of coping clusters. Specifically, Positive Reappraisal was used frequently and perceived as most effective, and Apathy was used least frequently and perceived as least effective.

The internal consistency estimates of the coping appraisals are summarized in Table 6. The internal consistency of the coping frequency ratings ranged from .01 (Withdrawal) to .72 (Negative Coping). For the effectiveness ratings, the internal consistency ratings ranged from .30 (Balancing Work Stress) to .78 (Negative Coping). The coping clusters generally had lower reliability ratings than the stress clusters. This is not surprising given the vast individual differences in coping behavior. Finally, there was a strong positive correlation ($r = .97$) between the fre-

quency and effectiveness ratings of the coping clusters. In general, clusters that were rated as more frequently used were also rated as more effective.

Discussion

The present study used an innovative methodology to provide an in-depth analysis of the structure of work-related stress and coping among a sample of oncology nurses from a single cancer center. Furthermore, the study was designed to integrate the essential conceptual elements of the transactional stress model into a viable empirical strategy.

Structure of Work-Related Stress among Oncology Nurses

The present study suggests that nurses who work on hematologic oncology units experience high levels of occupational stress. The free-response methodology yielded 97 specific work-related stress items. Because this method does not limit the scope of potential responses, this set of items represents a relatively unbiased assessment of the work stresses that challenge these oncology nurses. Consequently, this study provides significantly more detail about the nature of work-related stress for oncology nurses than prior investigations.

In addition, the results of the MDS and hierarchical cluster analyses graphically represented the nurses' perceived relationships among these detailed items. The work-related stress concept map is a two-dimensional representation of the perceptions of these nurses. In interpreting the map, one must identify the implicit dimensional axes around which the points and clusters appear to be configured. Inspection of the work stress concept map suggests that the items and clusters are organized along two dimensions: patient contact (high vs. low) and source of stress (externally vs. internally generated). Clusters in the lower portion of the map are related to direct patient contact responsibilities, whereas clusters in the upper portion of the map are not. Clusters in the right region of

Coping Cluster/Item	Bridging Value	Coping Cluster/Item	Bridging Value
Coworker Support		Become more passive rather than assertive in my dealings with physicians and administration	0.44
Friendships among the nurses whom I work with	0.36	Cluster bridging average	0.36
Helping each other out when we get difficult assignments	0.37	**Catharsis/Break Room**	
Rotate assignments so that we don't have to work with one patient too long	0.37	Gripe and complain	0.13
		Drink coffee	0.05
Flexibility with my coworkers about assignments and scheduling	0.40	Joke about serious situations	0.05
Cluster bridging average	0.42	Cluster bridging average	0.10
Positive Involvement in Treatment		**Balancing Work Stress**	
Reading and learning about people with disease	0.40	Have fun on my time off	0.15
Use my personal experiences with cancer to better understand what patients experience	0.47	Spend more time with my family	0.24
		Exercise	0.07
Taking part in the grieving process with families	0.71	Remind myself about the positive things that I have in my life outside of work	0.10
Cluster bridging average	0.65	Cluster bridging average	0.12
Affective Regulation		**Positive Reappraisal**	
Indulge myself	0.18	Remind myself about the value of life	0.13
Shopping	0.08	Appreciate my health	0.12
Eating	0.12	Talking about things to get them out of my system	0.09
Crying	0.11	Sense of increased appreciation for life because of my job	0.14
Cluster bridging average	0.15	Cluster bridging average	0.14
Negative Coping		**Develop a Growth Perspective**	
Hold things in until I explode	0.00	Participation in continuing education	0.17
Overreacting to situations at home	0.10	Finding spiritual meaning in my work	0.17
Repressing strong emotions related to work and then inadvertently releasing them in nonwork situations	0.00	Develop a personal perspective about death and dying	0.17
		Cluster bridging average	0.17
Drink alcohol	0.01	**Apathy**	
Lower my expectations	0.00	Lower my personal commitment to the job and to my patients	0.06
Sleep excessively	0.05	Adopt a "who cares" attitude	0.02
Cluster bridging average	0.05	Give up talking to people who I don't work with because they don't understand	0.08
Withdrawal		Cluster bridging average	0.05
Think about getting another job that has absolutely nothing to do with nursing	0.51		
Think about different career paths and options in nursing	0.44		

the map pertain to externally generated stress, whereas clusters in the left region pertain to internally generated stress.

On the basis of these implicit axes, four distinct work-related stress quadrants can be identified. These quadrants are presented in Figure 5. These four quadrants reflect four larger meta-dimensions of stress for oncology nurses. Quadrant I (internally generated–low patient care) reflects the personal impact of oncology nursing. This meta-dimension included two clusters: Negative Self-Thoughts and Carryover Stress.

Quadrant II (externally generated–low patient care) represents an overriding stressful work environment meta-dimension. This quadrant includes Organizational Factors and Coworker Stress. Role conflict, precipitated by the nurses' position as an intermediary between the patient and physician, is represented by Quadrant III (externally generated–high patient care). This meta-dimension encompasses Physician-Related Stress and Ethical Concerns. Quadrant IV (internally generated–high patient care) represents the emotional stress encountered by

oncology nurses. This meta-dimension included two clusters, Death and Dying and Observing Patient and Family Suffering.

The cluster Inadequate Resources is a small cluster that contains two items that fall within Quadrant I and two items that fall within Quadrant II. If the assumption of the analyses are correct, the items that make up this cluster will be conceptually appropriate to their respective dimensional quadrants. Item 87 ("Fear about my ability to perform my job because of inadequate training") and Item 93 ("No response to

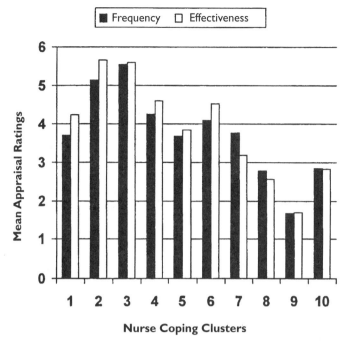

Figure 4. Mean appraisal ratings for the coping clusters. Cluster codes: 1 = Positive Involvement in Treatment, 2 = Coworker Support, 3 = Growth Perspective, 4 = Positive Reappraisal, 5 = Balancing Stress, 6 = Affective Regulation, 7 = Catharsis/Break Room, 8 = Negative Coping, 9 = Apathy, 10 = Withdrawal.

| Table 6 | Alpha Reliability Coefficients of the Appraisal Ratings for the 10 Work-Related Coping Clusters | |

Work-Related Coping Clusters	Frequency Rating	Effectiveness Rating
Coworker Stress	.68	.74
Positive Involvement in Treatment	.50	.47
Balancing Work Stress	.53	.68
Affective Regulation	.43	.30
Positive Reappraisal	.70	.72
Develop a Growth Perspective	.62	.50
Apathy	.51	.78
Negative Coping	.72	.78
Withdrawal	.01	.40
Catharsis/Break Room	.66	.67

grief by anyone in the hospital") relate to Quadrant II (internally generated–low patient contact) in that they reflect internal discomfort resulting from inadequate hospital resources. Conversely, Item 91 ("Having to perform multiple roles, i.e., supervisory, critical care, etc.") and Item 95 ("Not enough contact with other services") relate to stress from a lack of coworker resources and are appropriate for Quadrant II.

It is also important to compare the nine work-related stress clusters identified in this study with prior investigations of oncology nursing stress. The present study identified one stress dimension that was not identified in previous research. This dimension was labeled Negative Thoughts About Self and relates to doubts and guilt feelings about one's performance. Eight of the stress di-

mensions identified in this study support previous findings about the sources of stress for oncology nurses: stress related to death and dying, physician-related stress, stress from ethical conflicts, stress from observing patient/family suffering, carryover effects of work stress, organizational factors, coworker stress, and stress from inadequate resources (Herschbach, 1992; Jenkins & Ostchega, 1986; Molassiotis & van den Akker, 1995; Papadatou et al., 1994; Ullrich & FitzGerald, 1990). It should be noted, however, that the present study extends knowledge about these stress dimensions in two important ways. First, it provides detailed data about the specific concerns that constitute these dimensions (i.e., the 97 stress items). In addition, the present study provides valuable information about how oncology nurses appraise these dimensions in relation to each other.

Appraisal of Work-Related Stress among Oncology Nurses

Previous studies of work-related stress among oncology nurses have generally failed to examine the way that stress is cognitively appraised by the individuals who encounter it. This study assessed three specific cognitive appraisals (frequency, intensity, and controllability) of the 97 work-related stress items. Organizational Factors was rated as the most frequent and most intense stress cluster. The stress clusters pertaining to high patient contact (Physician Related Stress, Death and Dying, Observing Patient and Family Suffering, and Ethical Concerns) were also highly rated for frequency and intensity. The clusters relating to the personal impact of oncology nursing (Negative Self-Thoughts and Carryover Stress) were among the least frequent and least intense stress cluster. The nurses also felt that they had the most control over the occurrence of these personal impact clusters. In contrast, they believed that they had the least control over the stress clusters that related to dealings with others, that is, Organizational Factors, Physician Related Stress, and Observing Patient and Family Suffering.

Quadrant I	Quadrant II
Low Pt. Contact/ Internal Stress	**Low Pt. Contact/ External Stress**
1) Carryover Stress 2) Negative Self-Thoughts	1) Organizational Factors 2) Coworker Stress
Quadrant IV	Quadrant III
High Pt. Contact/ Internal Stress	**High Pt. Contact/ External Stress**
1) Death & Dying 2) Observing Pt. & Family Suffering	1) Physician-Related Stress 2) Ethical Concerns

Figure 5. A two-dimensional model of oncology nursing stress. (pt. = patient)

Quadrant I	Quadrant II
Emotion-Focused/ Negative	**Low Pt. Contact/ External Stress**
1) Withdrawal 2) Apathy 3) Negative Coping 4) Catharsis/Break Room	1) Develop A Growth Perspective 2) Positive Reappraisal 3) Affective Regulation 4) Balancing Work Stress
Quadrant IV	Quadrant III
Problem-Focused/ Negative	**Problem-Focused/ Positive**
	1) Positive Involvement in Treatment 2) Coworkers Support

Figure 6. A two-dimensional model of coping in oncology nursing.

It is also interesting to examine the relationships between the different appraisal ratings. As one would expect, there was a strong positive association between the frequency and intensity of the stress clusters. The strong negative relationship between the controllability and frequency ratings suggests that the rate at which a stress occurs is an important determinant of perceived control. In terms of the strong negative association between the controllability and intensity ratings, this relationship is more difficult to interpret. This study does not provide information about the causal directionality of this association. Consequently, it cannot be determined whether less controllability makes a stress seem more intense or

whether more intensity makes a stress appear less controllable.

There were no significant differences in the frequency, intensity, and controllability appraisals of the stress clusters by the day- and night-shift nurses. This finding may partially reflect the nature of the hematologic oncology services surveyed in this study. Specifically, several important aspects of the day- and night-shift work environments are quite similar. Both services provide 24-hr critical care to acutely ill patients. Both services have around-the-clock visiting hours. Consequently, both the day- and night-shift nurses experience high levels of physician contact, both perform a large number of interventions and procedures, and both have extended interactions with family members.

Structure of Work-Related Coping among Oncology Nurses

In the present study, oncology nurses on high-stress units report using a wide range of coping strategies to manage their work environment. The free-response methodology yielded 79 specific coping behaviors. The MDS and hierarchical cluster analyses resulted in a coping concept map with 10 coping clusters. The two implicit dimensions that appear to organize the placement of these clusters are coping focus (problem focused vs. emotion focused) and outcomes (positive vs. negative). Based on these implicit axes, four distinct work-related coping quadrants can be identified. These quadrants, which are presented in Figure 6, represent four larger coping meta-dimensions.

Quadrant I contains the clusters Apathy, Withdrawal, Negative Coping, and Catharsis/Break Room and represents emotion-focused coping with negative outcomes. Quadrant II represents emotion-focused coping with positive outcomes and contains the clusters Positive Reappraisal, Developing a Growth Perspective, Affective Regulation, and Balancing Work Stress. In Quadrant III, Positive Involvement in Treatment and Coworker Support represent problem-focused coping with positive outcomes. Finally, Quadrant IV represents a meta-dimension of problem-focused coping with negative outcomes. This quadrant is empty.

Only two previous studies examined coping among oncology nurses. Zevon, Donnelly, and Starkey (1990) reported that oncology nurses used more emotion-focused than problem-focused coping behaviors. The present study confirmed that finding. In Molassiotis and van den Akker (1995), nurses identified 13 behaviors that they use to cope with work stress, including gathering in informal meetings, participating in workshops and inservice training, seeking social support, crying, emphasizing the positive aspects of work, empathy, tension reduction through hobbies, and self-blame. Several of these coping responses were also identified in this study;

however, the present study identified many additional coping behaviors that oncology nurses use to manage work stress.

Appraisal of Work-Related Coping among Oncology Nurses

In addition to identifying specific coping responses used by oncology nurses, this study provided data about how these responses were appraised in terms of frequency and effectiveness. The clusters in the positive outcomes quadrants (Quadrants II and IV) were rated as the most frequently used coping behaviors. These clusters were also rated as the most effective for managing work stress. The clusters in the emotion-focused–negative outcomes quadrant were rated as the least effective and the least frequently used. These results suggest that oncology nurses appear to be selecting coping responses on the basis of their expectations about the effectiveness of a particular response.

The reliability coefficients of the coping ratings were weaker than those of the stress ratings. This is not unexpected. The coping appraisals focused on individual evaluations of behavior. It is generally well accepted that there are large differences in an individual's preferences for or predisposition toward certain coping responses. It is not surprising, therefore, that the reliability coefficients would reflect these individual differences. The stress appraisals, on the other hand, focused on individual evaluations of environmental events. It is not surprising that there was more consistency in the ratings of these more commonly experienced stimuli that are less dependent on individual personality differences.

Clinical Significance

The concept maps that were generated in this study provide an effective guide for planning stress reduction interventions. On the basis of the work-related stress concept map, specific interventions can be designed and implemented to target specific stress dimensions. This is

important because different stress reduction interventions are differentially suited for particular types of stress. For example, skills training in conflict resolution and assertiveness may be more helpful with stressful physician contacts and less helpful when dealing with patient and family suffering. The work-related stress concept map increases the likelihood that stress reduction intervention will provide the specific skills necessary for reducing job stress. For this group of oncology nurses, these interventions could include skills training, relaxation training, job redesign, support groups, and policy changes.

The stress appraisal data can be used to prioritize the order in which the stress clusters are addressed. It seems reasonable to give the most frequent and most intense clusters highest priority. The appraisal data can also be used to evaluate the intervention. Specifically, the nurses can appraise the stress items for a second time after the intervention is developed and implemented. By comparing this to the preintervention appraisal data, the nurses can determine areas of success and failure in the intervention program.

The coping concept map provides a guide to the behaviors that the nurses are presently using to manage the stress that they encounter at work. Furthermore, the appraisal data provide a basis for evaluating the nurses' perceptions about the effectiveness of each of these responses. These data can be used in two ways. First, interventions can be developed that capitalize on the coping strengths that the nurses already possess. For example, interventions can be developed that match the most effective coping clusters to the sources of stress for which they would appear to be most helpful. Second, the map can be used to evaluate potentially helpful coping responses that the nurses currently lack. For example, the use of relaxation exercises was not identified by the nurses. This is a basic stress management technique that could be provided to the nurses as part of an intervention.

Although the methodology used in this study was designed to assess the specific work stressors and

coping behaviors of a particular group of oncology nurses, the data can also be used with other groups of oncology nurses. Specifically, oncology nurses from other services could rate the stress and coping items on the dimensions specified in this study. Different groups of oncology nurses could then be compared on specific stress and coping items, clusters, or broad dimensions. On the basis of these ratings and comparisons, determinations can be made about which items, clusters, and broad dimensions generalize to other groups of oncology nurses.

The data from this study can also be used to develop measures of stress and coping for oncology nurses that would be applicable to oncology nurses in different work settings. Items for the measures would be chosen on the basis of high appraisal ratings by many different groups of oncology nurses. The measures can be constructed so that they would reflect the clusters and broader dimensions that were appraised as highly relevant by oncology nurses from diverse work settings.

Future Research

Future research should focus on determining the impact of work stress on the overall health of oncology nurses. Several studies have established links between the presence of stress and the occurrence of specific diseases (for reviews of this literature, see Kiecolt-Glaser et al., 1986; Rosch, 1996). The results from this study could be used to explore whether different levels of work stress significantly influence mental and physical health outcome variables among oncology nurses. The mediating effect of coping on this relationship should also be examined.

An additional focus of future research should be on developing models for understanding how oncology nurses select coping strategies for managing work stress. The coping with cancer literature provides a suggestion for developing such a model. Blanchard and Harper (1996) proposed a dynamic model of coping with the stress of cancer. They stated that the selection of coping strategies by cancer patients is influenced by the appraisal of a specific threat, individual factors (age, gender, personality style, and past coping experience), situational factors (site and stage of disease, symptoms, and effects of treatment), and sociocultural factors (attitudes about disease, disability, and death). The authors of this study are presently applying a similar model to the study of coping with work stress by oncology nurses. Specifically, they are exploring whether the presence of specific work stress clusters is significantly associated with specific coping responses. They are also exploring whether individual and work environment variables significantly influence the appraisal of stress by oncology nurses.

Conclusion

The present study extensively analyzed the unique structure of work-related stress and coping in a group of hematology oncology nurses who work in high-stress units at a National Cancer Institute comprehensive cancer treatment center. Overall, our results represent the first application of the concept mapping strategy to the study of stress and coping in a medical environment. The integration of this rigorous empirical methodology and the theoretically advanced transactional model of stress yielded a rich description of the structure underlying this complex environment. In turn, the results of this integration provided for a relatively seamless transition from theory to research to intervention, a sequence that has historically posed a significant challenge for both the scientist and the practitioner.

References

Aldenderfer, M. S., & Blashfield, R. K. (1984). *Cluster analysis.* In J. L. Sullivan (Ed), *Quantitative applications in the social sciences* (Series No. 44, pp. 7–61). Beverly Hills, CA: Sage.

Bhagat, R. S., & Beehr, T. A. (1985). An evaluation summary and recommendations for future research. In T. A. Beehr & R. S. Bhagat (Eds.), *Human stress and cognition in organizations: An integrated perspective* (pp. 401–415). New York: Wiley.

Blanchard, C. G., & Harper, G. R. (1996). Coping with the stress of cancer. In C. L. Cooper (Ed.), *Handbook of stress, medicine and health* (pp. 357–374). Boca Raton, FL: CRC Press.

Dewe, P. J. (1991). Primary appraisal, secondary appraisal and coping: Their role in stressful work encounters. *Journal of Occupational Psychology, 64,* 331–351.

Dewe, P. J. (1992). Applying the concept of appraisal to work stressors: Some exploratory analysis. *Human Relations, 45,* 993–1013.

Herschbach, P. (1992). Work-related stress specific to physicians and nurses working with cancer patients. *Journal of Psychosocial Oncology, 10,* 79–89.

Ivancevich, J. M., & Matteson, M. T. (1980). Nurses and stress: Time to examine the potential problem. *Journal of Nurse Leader Management, 11,* 17–22.

Jenkins, J. F., & Ostchega, Y. (1986). Evaluation of burnout in oncology nurses. *Cancer Nursing, 9,* 108–116.

Kiecolt-Glaser, J. K., Glaser, R., Strain, E. C., Stout, J. C., Torr, K. L., Holliday, T. E., et al. (1986). Modulation of cellular immunity in medical students. *Journal of Behavioral Medicine, 9,* 5–21.

Lazarus, R. S. (1995). Psychological stress in the workplace. In R. Crandall & P. Perrewe (Eds.), *Occupational stress: A handbook* (pp. 3–15). Washington, DC: Taylor & Francis.

Lazarus, R. S., & Folkman, S. (1984). *Stress, appraisal, and coping.* New York: Springer.

Lederberg, M. (1989). Psychological problems of staff and their management. In J. C. Holland & J. Rowland (Eds.), *Handbook of psychooncology* (pp. 631–646). New York: Oxford University Press.

Molassiotis, A., & van den Akker, O. (1995). Psychological stress in nursing and medical staff on bone marrow transplant units. *Bone Marrow Transplantation, 15,* 449–454.

Numerof, R. E., & Abrams, M. N. (1988). Sources of stress among nurses: An empirical investigation. *Journal of Human Stress, 10,* 88–100.

Papadatou, P., Anagnostopoulis, F., & Monos, D. (1994). Factors contributing to burnout in oncology nursing. *British Journal of Medical Psychology, 67,* 187–199.

Peteet, J., Murray-Ross, D., Medeiros, C., Walsh-Burke, K., Rieker, P., & Finkelstein, D. (1989). Job stress and satisfaction among staff members at a cancer center. *Cancer, 64,* 975–982.

Rosch, P. J. (1996). Stress and cancer: Disorders of communication, control, and civilization. In C. L. Cooper (Ed.), *Handbook of stress, medicine and health* (pp. 27–60). Boca Raton, FL: CRC Press.

Trochim, W. M. (1989). An introduction to concept mapping for planning and evaluation. *Evaluation and Program Planning, 12,* 1–16.

Trochim, W. K. (1995). *The concept system.* Ithaca, NY: Concept System.

Trochim, W. M., & Linton, R. (1986). Conceptualization for planning and evaluation. *Evaluation and Program Planning, 9,* 289–308.

Ullrich, A., & FitzGerald, P. (1990). Stress experienced by physicians and nurses in the cancer ward. *Social Science and Medicine, 31,* 1013–1022.

Ward, J. H. (1963). Hierarchical grouping to optimize an objective function. *Journal of the American Statistical Association, 58,* 236–244.

Zevon, M. A., Donnelly, J. P., & Starkey, E. A. (1990). Stress and coping relationships in the medical environment: A natural experiment. *Journal of Psychosocial Oncology, 8,* 65–77.

Article Review Form at end of book.

WiseGuide Wrap-Up

Conduct a literature search using the author David Barlow to find the definitive resource on anxiety disorders. The concept also forwarded by Dr. Barlow on a treatment center and short-term behavior therapy approach reflects progressive thinking about treatment in today's marketplace for health care.

R.E.A.L. Sites

This list provides a print preview of typical **Coursewise** R.E.A.L. sites. (There are over 100 such sites at the **Courselinks™** site.) The danger in printing URLs is that web sites can change overnight. As we went to press, these sites were functional using the URLs provided. If you come across one that isn't, please let us know via email to: webmaster@coursewise.com. Use your Passport to access the most current list of R.E.A.L. sites at the **Courselinks** site.

Site name: Yanx-Dep
URL: Send email to: Listserv@sjuvm.st.johns.edu
Why is it R.E.A.L.? This is a discussion group of researchers and practitioners working with anxiety disorders in children and adolescents.
Key topics: personality style, panic disorder, anxiety

Site name: Psychology Self-Help Resources
URL: http://www.psychwww.com/resource/selfhelp.htm
Why is it R.E.A.L.? This page contains links to noncommercial sites providing information about and help for anxiety, fears, stress, panic, trauma, dissociation, and other disorders.
Key topics: panic disorder, transactional model, anxiety

Learning Objectives

- The student will understand the science of psychology through the readings on schizophrenia.

- The student's awareness of the severity of schizophrenia pathology will be enriched by the description of the biological and psychophysiological factors of schizophrenia.

Questions

Reading 11. What is expressed emotion and how does it relate to schizophrenia?

Reading 12. How does the experience of major depression and schizophrenia provide evidence for seasonal influences on platelet 5-HT levels?

Reading 13. Summarize the psychophysiological findings (particularly, saccadic reaction time) associated with schizophrenia.

Given the complexity and chronicity of schizophrenia, advancements in knowledge in this area are always needed. The articles in this section provide information about distinct clinical features related to schizophrenia.

Suinn writes about the biological approaches to studying schizophrenia. The complexity of schizophrenia is addressed here with explanations about gene studies, receptor sites, and medications. The reader will obtain a solid understanding of the biological model as it is applied to practice. Expressed emotion has been examined with schizophrenia because it represents a means of examining the varying emotionality in individuals with this disorder. This concept also represents a convenient way to obtain measurement of emotionality. Behaviorists have made strides in this direction.

The second article in this section is written by psychiatrists and presents aspects of the biological model of schizophrenia. The question of seasonal influences on the incidence of schizophrenia is an old one but is still unanswered. A curious phenomenon of more births resulting in the schizophrenia diagnosis occurs during specific times of the year. In addition, at certain latitudes, the amount of environmental light is reduced, which may cause some individuals who are vulnerable to depression to have seasonal affective disorder. This article is an example of a careful study conducted to track serotonin, which is related to the etiology of schizophrenia and seasonal affective disorder.

Zahn and associates report remarkable findings in their article on psychophysiological assessment. Information-processing models are tested by indirect measurement of eye movements. As you learn about the clinical features of schizophrenia, the manner in which schizophrenics regulate their attention is different from that of those without the disorder. The eye movement measure represents an indirect means of determining the deployment of attention in schizophrenics.

The articles in this section were selected to provide you with information that will expand your understanding of schizophrenia. In practice, several approaches are used to conceptualize how this disordered behavior occurs; the articles in this section provide a means of approaching a greater understanding of schizophrenics.

What is expressed emotion and how does it relate to schizophrenia?

Schizophrenia and Bipolar Disorder:

Origins and Influences

Richard M. Suinn

Colorado State University

This 1993 AABT presidential address offers a brief survey of some factors associated with schizophrenia and bipolar disorder. Highlighted are findings regarding the influence of biological, psychological and cultural factors. The magnitude of the influence of biological factors is illustrated in research on morbidity risk, twin concordance, chromosome localization, brain glucose metabolism, ventricle size, smooth eye movement impairment, and dopamine function. The psychological evidence that is presented emphasizes the data on Expressed Emotion (EE) and includes discussion of cross-cultural research findings. The article concludes with the position that research on origins and influences must examine multiple factors, and offers an attempt to integrate the various findings.

Studies on the origins and major influences that affect the development or recurrence of schizophrenia or bipolar disorder have focused on a variety of variables. It is the purpose of this paper to highlight some of the major findings on biological, psychological, and sociocultural factors and to demonstrate the interdependence of data from these three domains for understanding severe psychopathology. This is something of a departure from presidential addresses that mainly aim to review behavioral literature. However, I sought to summarize the broad scientific literature, thereby drawing attention to the vastly different kinds of influence affecting these forms of serious psychopathology. I especially wish to emphasize the role of cross-cultural findings. Further, although some of the information will be familiar to readers, data will be reviewed that will demonstrate the magnitude of influence of these variables.

The format consists of a review of studies on biological factors, followed by a summary of findings regarding a major psychological/behavioral variable. Finally, some reports suggesting the role that culture might have on psychopathology in general will be examined.

I will begin with the varied research evidence that documents the strength of biological influences in schizophrenia, namely evidence from research on genetics, brain glucose metabolism, ventricle size, eye movement impairment, and dopamine dysfunction. Where comparable evidence has been reported for bipolar disorder, such research will also be cited.

This will be followed by a summary of the major role that expressed emotion (EE) behaviors by family members play in relapse of schizophrenia patients (even those on medication). Information that suggests the mediating influence of culture on EE and on psychopathol-

ogy will be reviewed. Finally, a perspective integrating the diverse data will be offered.

Biological Evidence

Genetic Evidence

Data on genetics come from three areas: morbidity risk, concordance, and chromosome localization studies. Each of these methodologies has contributed data to strengthen the hypothesis of the influence of genetics in schizophrenic and bipolar disorder.

Morbidity Risk Data

For morbidity risk, the logic is that if genetics influences psychopathology, then the closer the relationship of a person to a patient, the greater the morbidity risk should be. These data have appeared before in the literature and are summarized for schizophrenia in Table 1 (Gottesman, 1991; McGue, 1992) and in Table 2 for bipolar disorder (Bertelsen, Harvald, & Hauge, 1977; Gottesman & Shields, 1982; McGuffin & Sargeant, 1991). These findings provide clear evidence for a genetic component, confirming that morbidity risks increase with the immediacy of closeness of family relationship. Thus, although the risk of schizophrenia for someone in the general population is about 1 in 100, this risk increases to about 1 in 10 for a sibling

Table 1 Morbidity Risk for Schizophrenia

General Population	0.9
Half-Siblings	4.2
Full Siblings	9.6
Dizygotic Twins	11.4
Monozygotic Twins	45.4

Based on: Gottesman & Shields, 1982; McGue, 1992.

Table 2 Morbidity Risk for Bipolar Disorder

General Population	0.4
Half-Siblings	16.7
Full Siblings	23.0
Dizygotic Twins	26.3
Monozygotic Twins	95.7

Based on: Bertelsen, Harvald & Hauge, 1977; Gottesman & Shields, 1982; McGuffin & Sargeant, 1991.

of a person with a schizophrenic disorder. For bipolar disorder, the risks are even higher, from less than 1 in 200 to better than 1 in 5.

Concordance Data

In research on concordance with twins, the same type of logic is used. If genetics is a causative influence, then the closer the twin relationship, the greater should be the concordance in psychopathology. Again, across many studies on schizophrenia, this relationship has been amply demonstrated. Gottesman (1991) summarized the findings of recent studies, which show a 48% concurrence for monozygotic twins versus a 17% rate for dizygotic twins. For bipolar disorder, the evidence is stronger; Rushton, Russell, and Wells (1985) summarized the data indicating a 73% concordance rate for monozygotic twins versus a 12% rate for dizygotic twins. These data are consistent with the hypothesis of a genetic influence, given that monozygotic twins are identical in genetic make-up but dizygotic twins may potentially share only half their genes.

In summary, both the data on morbidity risk and on concordance rates suggest that heredity must be viewed as a strong contributing factor in schizophrenia and bipolar disorder (Rushton et al., 1985; see also

Allen, Cohen, Pollin, & Greenspan, 1974; Gottesman & Shields, 1982; McGue, 1992; McGue & Gottesman, 1989; Torrey, 1992; Walker, Downey & Caspi 1991).

Chromosome Localization Data

Finally, in genetic research, modern technology now permits chromosome localization studies. A reference point is the logs of the odds ratio, or (LOD), score, a quantitative method for indicating the likely linkage of a trait to a locale on a chromosome (Morton, 1955). Such a score is another method for estimating the magnitude of genetic influence on a human characteristic. A LOD value of 1.0 means that a genetic linkage is 10 times more likely to exist than no linkage. A score of 3.0 is considered the critical value needed to suggest a significant linkage exists (Risch, 1992). In studies across two countries, Great Britain and Iceland, chromosome localization research has identified chromosome 5 from a sample of over 100 patients as the probable culprit for schizophrenia (Sherrington et al., 1988). The corresponding LOD score has been calculated to be 4.33 for this disorder, clearly above the minimum level for significance (Holzman & Matthysee, 1990). Caution is still essential in concluding that the specific locus for schizophrenia has been found be-

cause others, such as McGuffin et al. (1990), have failed to replicate the finding of Sherrington et al. Yet even McGuffin et al. comment: "We think that an important genetic contribution to schizophrenia certainly does exist, but the evidence for this comes not from linkage studies but from classical family, twin, and adoption investigations. Nor do the negative linkage data discussed (in our report) invalidate the pursuit of genetic marker strategies in studying the genetic basis of schizophrenia" (p. 534).

For bipolar disorder, a preliminary study reported a LOD score of 7.52 (Baron et al., 1987) and Egeland, Gerhard, Pauls, Sussex, and Kidd (1987) reported a linkage to chromosome 11. However, these findings also have not been replicated (Wesner & Winokur, 1990).

In closing, the conclusion of Nigg and Goldsmith (1994) is worth repeating. Following their own extensive review and evaluation of genetic methodologies and findings, they concurred that "a growing body of research over the past two decades has revealed an important genetic influence on liability for schizophrenia" (p. 351).

Evidence from Biological Characteristics

In addition to genetic studies, other research has looked for physiological, anatomical, or sensory-motor characteristics that might reflect biological influences on schizophrenic or bipolar disorders. Such evidence associating various biological characteristics with schizophrenia may prove useful for understanding the physical basis for the disorder. For example, four such characteristics have been suggested as conceptually relevant for schizophrenia: low brain glucose metabolism, enlarged ventricles, eye movement impairment, and dopamine dysfunction. For bipolar disorder, eye movement dysfunction has also been studied.

Glucose Metabolism

Glucose metabolism of the frontal lobes is one such biological characteristic. Such evidence has been made possible by modern technology for measuring brain functions. Scientists have long had suspicions about the possible involvement of the frontal lobes in schizophrenic symptoms (Pearlson, 1991). After all, this is what explains the historical reliance on prefrontal lobotomies as a medical treatment for schizophrenia. Even today, the involvement of the frontal area remains a prime suspect. For instance, data on the dorsolateral prefrontal cortex confirm that trauma to this area of the brain leads to symptoms similar to those of schizophrenia; these symptoms tend to occur during adolescence (similar to the developmental course for schizophrenic symptoms); and such damage leads to dopamine dysfunction, which is implicated in schizophrenia (Breslin & Weinberger, 1990; Freedman & Oscar-Berman, 1986; Gold, Goldberg, & Weinberger, 1992; Goldman-Rakic & Brown, 1982; Levin, 1984; Luria, 1980; Morice, 1986).

Even more convincing direct sources of evidence exist involving glucose metabolism. With the technology of positron emission tomography (PET) scans, it is possible to compare the functioning of a "normal" person with a patient. There is strong evidence showing that patients with schizophrenic disorders show reduced brain glucose metabolism in the frontal area when compared with the metabolism of a healthy person (Buchsbaum, 1990; Buchsbaum et al., 1990; Clark et al., 1989; Gur & Pearlson, 1992; Waddington, 1993). Further, Volkow et al. (1987) discovered a correlation between low metabolism and negative symptoms, e.g., blunted affect, emotional withdrawal, anhedonia, and attentional dysfunction, $r = .32$. Finally, it is fascinating that at least one group demonstrated the presence of reduced metabolic activity localized in the dorsolateral prefrontal cortex, previously isolated as a possible major site in schizophrenic dysfunction (Weinberger, Berman, & Illowsy, 1988).

Ventricles

Another biological characteristic associated with schizophrenia, ventricle size, has been identified during examinations of brain anatomy. Computerized tomography (CT) scans and Magnetic Resonance Imagery (MRI) supported the conclu-

sion that enlarged ventricles may be such a marker for schizophrenia (Andreasen et al. 1990; Giordano, Fasullo, Rubino, & Cordovana, 1989; Straube & Oades, 1992). For instance, Degreef et al. (1992) found first-episode schizophrenic patients to show a 26% greater ventricular volume than a control sample.

Studies have also reported that patients with larger ventricles tended to exhibit more severe negative symptoms as well as poorer premorbid childhood adjustment (Klausner, Sweeney, Deck, Haas, & Kelly, 1992). Correlations between ventricular size and blunted affect were .33, and .36 with anhedonia. Of added interest is the finding of enlarged ventricles among high-risk children of schizophrenic mothers (Schulsinger et al., 1984). In fact, it is speculated that there are genetic origins for enlargement of ventricles (Cannon et al., 1993; Crow et al., 1989; Silverton, Mednick, Schulsinger, Parnas, & Harrington, 1988).

Smooth Pursuit Movements

A third biological characteristic involves impaired smooth pursuit eye movement (SPEM). SPEM characterizes the eye movements of normal persons as they track a moving object. In contrast, impaired movements characteristic of schizophrenia are seen in erratic rather than smooth tracking motions, called saccadic movements (Cegalis & Sweeney, 1979).

Interest in observational measurement of eye movements of psychiatric patients was reported as early as 1908 (Diefendorf & Dodge, 1908). Later rediscovery of such observations was initiated by Holzman, Proctor, and Hughes (1973), leading to the hypothesis that the same genetic transmitter of schizophrenia may also be responsible for eye movement dysfunction (Matthyesse & Holzman, 1987).

The consistency of current research findings has led some Harvard researchers (Abel, Levin, & Holzman, 1992; Holzman, 1987; Holzman, Solomon, Levin, & Waternaux, 1984) to believe eye movement dysfunction is not only another biological characteristic of schizophrenic patients, but one that may be helpful for differential diag-

nosis of schizophrenia. Similarly, a Japanese report suggests the use of SPEM evaluation as an especially valuable tool in differential diagnosis with older patients (Berger, Nezu, Iga, Hosaka, & Nakamura, 1990).

Saccadic movements are more frequently found in schizophrenic patients (86%) than in normal persons (8%) (Holzman et al., 1988; Holzman et al., 1974; Levy, Holzman, Matthysse, & Mendell, 1993; Sweeney, Haas, & Li, 1992). Further, greater severity of SPEM dysfunction corresponds with greater severity of psychotic symptoms (Clementz, Grove, Iacono, & Sweeney, 1992; Iacono & Lykken, 1979). In addition, substantial correlation between saccadic movements and negative symptoms has been reported (Mackert & Flechtner, 1989; see also Thaker, Nguyen, & Tamminga, 1989). In particular, Katsanis and Iacono (1991) reported a correlation of .54 between deviant eye tracking and negative symptoms.

Other data confirm the association between saccadic movements among relatives of patients and the appearance of schizophrenic symptoms among these relatives (Clementz, Sweeney, Hirt, & Haas, 1990; Iacono, Moreau, Beiser, Fleming, & Lin, 1992). Further, although saccadic movements might also appear in other psychiatric patients, their presence is still substantially higher in schizophrenic patients than in persons with other disorders (Holzman et al., 1984).

These SPEM results have implications for data previously cited regarding schizophrenia and glucose metabolism, the frontal lobes, and the dorsolateral prefrontal cortex. First, SPEM impairment has been found to be associated with low brain glucose metabolism (Thaker et al., 1989). In addition, SPEM dysfunction appears to be associated with neuropsychological test results related to frontal lobe dysfunction (Clementz & Sweeney, 1990; Clementz et al., 1992; Katsanis & Iacono, 1991). Finally, schizophrenic patients showed more eye-tracking errors of the anti-saccadic type than nonpatients and other psychiatric patients (Clementz, McDowell, & Zisook, 1994). This same type of error is common among patients with dorsolateral prefrontal lesions (Pierrot-Deseilligny, Rivaud,

Gaymard, & Agid, 1991). The documentation on SPEM and schizophrenia has been consistent enough as to lead Sweeney et al. (1994) to conclude: "Eye tracking dysfunction is one of the most promising psychobiological markers for schizophrenia . . . and is one of the most robust findings in schizophrenia research" (p. 222).

While not as powerful as the SPEM data relating to schizophrenia, similar data on SPEM and bipolar disorder is also suggestive. The prevalence of SPEM among bipolar patients has been reported as 41% (Holzman et al., 1984), which is higher than that for normal persons although lower than the rate for schizophrenic patients. However, unlike results for schizophrenic patients, the rates for relatives of bipolar patients is similar to the level for normal persons (Abel et al., 1992; Iacono et al., 1992).

Dopamine Dysfunction

The fourth major biological characteristic relevant to schizophrenia is dopamine function. The findings involving dopamine are readily summarized: drugs known to increase dopamine lead to an increase in schizophrenic symptoms; medication that displaces dopamine leads to decreases in schizophrenic symptoms; schizophrenic patients have been found to possess a greater number of dopamine receptors (Davis, 1978; Davis, Kahn, Ko, & Davidson, 1991; Farde, Wiesel, Halldin, & Sedvall, 1988; Gur & Pearlson, 1992; Healy, 1991; Heritch, 1990; Sedvall, 1990; Seeman & Niznik, 1990; Wei, Ramchand, & Hemmings, 1992). All these findings strongly support that dopamine dysfunction is a variable associated with schizophrenia. In fact, a standard medical treatment for schizophrenia has been reliance on medication that blocks dopaminergic neurotransmission in the patient.

Psychological Evidence
Expressed Emotion

Research on schizophrenia has been characterized by major interest in the behavioral variable EE. George Brown of the Institute of Psychiatry at Maudsley in England noted that schizophrenic patients tended to relapse when returning home (Brown, Carstairs, & Topping, 1958). Observation was a key component in the formulation of the concept of EE. EE involves the following behaviors among the relatives of the patient: high criticism, hostility, and emotional overinvolvement (Brown, Monck, Carstairs, & Wing, 1962; Vaughn & Leff, 1976). A series of research reports have confirmed the important association between EE and relapse.

Two hypotheses were tested in confirming the influence of EE: (a) greater relapse rates should be found for families high in EE than for families low in EE; (b) among families high in EE, greater relapse should be found for patients who had high contacts with their EE families than for patients who had low contacts with their EE families (Vaughn & Leff, 1976).

Vaughn and Leff (1976) collected data on relapse rates to test these hypotheses. If EE significantly influences relapse, then the relapse rates would show a gradually increasing level with the following hierarchy of categories: low EE family, high EE with low family contact, and high EE with high family contact. The respective percentage of relapse rates over 9 months, 13%, 28%, and 69%, aligned with this predicted pattern.

Even with medication, EE appears to have a mediating influence, leading to higher relapse rates. Specifically, the rates of relapse were: 12% for low EE family with the patient on medication, 15% for high EE family of low contact with the patient on medication, and 53% for high EE family of high contact with the patient on medication. Put in another way, patients with high EE families were four times more likely to relapse than patients with low EE families (the percentage relapse for all high EE families together was 51%).

Further supporting data have shown that relapse decreases after families are trained to reduce their EE behaviors; patients from untrained families showed 78% relapse compared to 20% for patients from families trained to lower their EE behaviors (Leff, Kuipers, & Berkowitz, 1983; see also Leff et al., 1989).

Similar research on EE has also surfaced regarding bipolar disorder patients (Kavanagh, 1992; Miklowitz, 1994). Persons suffering from bipolar disorder with high EE parents show 5.5 times greater relapse rate than patients with low EE parents (Miklowitz, Goldstein, Nuechterlein, Snyder, & Mentz, 1988). The presence of EE among parents of bipolar patients was equivalent to that of schizophrenic patients; however, the parents of schizophrenic patients exhibited more criticism and intrusiveness in behavioral problem-solving tasks (Miklowitz, Goldstein, Nuechterlein, Snyder, & Doane, 1987).

Cultural Influences on EE

Cross-cultural factors influencing EE are being identified through continuing research. A report from UCLA cross-validated the British EE findings using an American sample; but the percentage of U.S. families exhibiting the EE characteristic was different than that of the British. Other reports confirm that the EE levels differ across cultures: U.S. 67%, Great Britain 48%, Mexico 41%, India 23%, and Scotland 13% (Jenkins & Karno, 1992; Kuipers et al., 1987; Wig et al., 1987). However, such differences might not be relevant provided that EE continues to be predictive of relapse among patients in those cultures. Several international studies, such as in Australia (Vaughan et al., 1992), Czechoslovakia (Mozny & Votypkova, 1992), France (Berrelet, Ferrero, Szigethy, Giddy, & Pellizer, 1990), and Italy (Bertrando et al., 1992), offer cross-validation for the EE hypothesis.

Other research is less supportive. Leff et al. (1990) found that EE did not predict relapse in a follow-up study done in India 2 years later, although initial ratings of hostility continued to show a significant association. Stirling et al. (1991) also failed to confirm the relationship between EE and relapse in a British sample. Other failures to replicate appear in reports from Australia (Parker, Johnston, & Hayward, 1988) and Spain (Montero, Gomez-Bereyto, Ruis, Puche, & Adam, 1992). In addition, the study by Moline, Singh, Morris, and Meltzer (1985), which examined the validity of EE to predictive relapse among lower socioeconomic level patients, found that

EE could be predictive with a change in cutoff point. However, EE was not associated with relapse for African Americans, even with revision of the cutoff score.

Variable success in replicating the results on EE across cultures raises a caution. Are EE behaviors, as originally conceived, consistently predictive of relapse in all cultures? The failures to replicate may be due to chance (Kavanaugh, 1992), differences in research design, problems in defining EE behaviors due to language translation difficulties, a real absence of influence of EE in a specific culture, or the mediating influence of different cultural environments.

Closing Comments

This review provides evidence of the powerful contributions of biological variables to schizophrenia and perhaps to some forms of bipolar disorder. As behavioral psychologists, we might sometimes forget the magnitude of such influence. On the other hand, the role of biological factors is not the only part of the picture. The EE behaviors of family members appear to also exert profound influence, at least in influencing relapse rates among schizophrenic patients. In turn, cultural factors might mediate the nature of the EE effect.

Therefore, two conclusions may be drawn from this review. First, research reports have uncovered some of the major variables that represent either the origins or later influences on schizophrenia and, possibly, bipolar disorder. However, such research reports, crucial as they are, are often presented in isolation from studies that report on the contributions of other variables, as if the variables are nonoverlapping. This leads to the second conclusion that caution about strict acceptance of deterministic interpretations is essential, especially when the direction of causality could well be reciprocal among multiple factors.

In addition to offering these two conclusions, it is possible to offer at least a brief attempt at integration. Certainly, a leading conceptualization is the diathesis-stress model (Fowles, 1992; Rosenthal, 1970). In this model, biological factors (diathesis) contribute the vulnerability, and

the environment acts as precipitant or protector. Gottesman and Shields (1982) offer the specific theory that schizophrenia develops from a liability deriving from both genetic and environmental sources, that there is a threshold before the disorder is expressed, and that three sources of liability, specific genetic, general genetic, and general environmental, interact to reach this threshold. The specific genetic liability refers to the genetic characteristic that conveys a specific risk for schizophrenia. The general genetic and environmental liabilities represent modifiers or potentiators of the specific liability. On the basis of my review, it might make sense to add emphasis to a specific environmental liability.

Such a diathesis-stress model would suggest that among the specific genetic liabilities are perhaps glucose metabolism and dopamine function. SPEM characteristics might represent an associated symptom that reflects the genetic vulnerability of the individual, or at least confirms the genetic-familial source of the vulnerability. Of course, different subtypes of schizophrenia would be associated with different specific genetic liabilities.

Heightened psychophysiological reactivity might be considered one such general genetic liability. For instance, cardiovascular hyperreactivity has been associated with risk of heart disease for Type A persons (Krantz & Manuck, 1984). Reiss, Peterson, Gursky, and McNally (1986) have described anxiety sensitivity as involving a tendency for some persons to be reactive to arousal sensations; such reactivity is said to promote susceptibility to panic disorder or agoraphobia. In a similar way, the diathesis-stress model would hypothesize that schizophrenia is associated with a general disposition, although what this might be is yet unknown.

General genetic characteristics can also be protective. Rutter (1979) has identified temperament as a protective factor in preventing psychiatric disorder among high risk children. Similarly, Garmezy (1985) identified temperament or disposition as characterizing risk-resistant children. Therefore, schizophrenia

might be understood as involving deficiency in protective general genetic characteristics, rather than only the presence of general genetic liabilities.

Among general environmental liabilities might be those external events known to be associated with stress. Brown and Birley (1968) found increased numbers of stressful life events in the weeks prior to symptom onset of schizophrenic patients, and Ventura, Nuechterlein, Lukoff, and Hardesty (1989) identified high numbers of stressful life events preceding relapse.

In integrating the data, we might highlight the category of specific environmental liabilities. This is the category that parallels the category of specific genetic liabilities and refers to environmental triggers specific to schizophrenic symptoms. Expressed emotion behaviors might be understood in this way. Tarrier et al. (1979) measured skin conductivity of schizophrenic patients when interacting with their parents. They discovered schizophrenic patients with high EE parents do not habituate during interactions with their parents, although patients with low EE parents do. Therefore, we might interpret EE parental communication style as a specific stressor for schizophrenia-vulnerable persons.

In keeping with this hypothesis, Miklowitz et al. (1987) found that there were the same number of high EE parents among bipolar patients as among schizophrenic patients in their sample. However, the parents of schizophrenic patients were characterized as exhibiting more critical, intrusive behaviors during problem-solving discussions. This finding is consistent with the premise that a specific stressor, such as critical and intrusive family behaviors, might be the trigger for schizophrenia while differing behaviors trigger bipolar disorder.

Finally, the concept of specific environmental liabilities offers perspective on the inconsistent cross-cultural findings on EE. Jenkins and Karno (1992) suggest that the association between EE and relapse is a valid one, although the component variables (criticism, hostility, overinvolvement) that are most relevant for predicting relapse might differ among cultures. Their view is consistent with my premise that it is reasonable to speak of specific environmental liabilities associated with schizophrenia, but adds the view that these specific environmental events might vary cross-culturally. According to Jenkins and Karno, there are two ways in which cultural differences can modify the influence of EE. First, EE is defined as including emotional overinvolvement, but Jenkins and Karno observe that some cultures tend not to engage in such behaviors within families. Hence this facet of EE would be absent as an environmental stressor. Second, the linguistic term to refer to the illness can determine the parents' response. For instance, Jenkins (1988) found that the term *nervios*, used to describe schizophrenia, destigmatizes the disorder and prompts supportiveness rather than criticism of the patient.

The accumulation of evidence supporting roles for both biological and environmental factors, with the latter mediated by culture, underscores the importance of understanding the etiology and course of this illness from a multidimensional perspective.

References

Abel, L., Levin, S., & Holzman, P. (1992). Abnormalities of smooth pursuit and saccadic control in schizophrenia and affective disorders. *Vision Research, 32,* 1009–1014.

Allen, M., Cohen, S., Pollin, W., & Greenspan, S. (1974). Affective illness in veteran twins. *American Journal of Psychiatry, 131,* 1234–1239.

Andreasen, N., Swayze, V., Flaum, M., Yates, W., Arndt, S., & McChesney, C. (1990). Ventricular enlargement in schizophrenia evaluated with computed tomograph scanning: Effects of gender, age, and stage of illness. *Archives of General Psychiatry, 47,* 1008–1015.

Baron, M., Risch, N., Hamberger, R., Mandel, B., Kushner, S., Newman, M., Drumer, D., & Belmaker, R. (1987). Genetic linkage between X-chromosome marker and bipolar affective illness. *Nature, 236,* 289–292.

Berger, D., Nezu, S, Iga, T., Hosaka, T., & Nakamura, S. (1990). Information processing effect on saccadic reaction time in schizophrenia. *Neuropsychiatry, Neuropsychology, and Behavioral Neurology, 3,* 80–97.

Berrelet, L., Ferrero, F., Szigethy, L., Giddy, C., & Pellizer, G. (1990). Expressed emotion and first admission schizophrenia: Nine month follow-up in a French cultural environment. *British Journal of Psychiatry, 156,* 357–362.

Bertelsen, A., Harvald, B., & Hauge, M. (1977). A Danish twin study of manic-depressive disorders. *British Journal of Psychiatry, 130,* 330–351.

Bertrando, P., Beltz, J., Bressi, C., Clerici, M., Farina, T., Invernizzi, G., & Cazzullo, C. (1992). Expressed emotion and schizophrenia in Italy: A study of an urban population. *British Journal of Psychiatry, 161,* 223–229.

Breslin, N., & Weinberger, D. (1990). Schizophrenia and the normal functional development of the prefrontal cortex. *Development and Psychopathology, 2,* 409–424.

Brown, G., & Birley, J. (1968). Crisis and life change and the onset of schizophrenia. *Journal of Health and Social Behavior, 9,* 203–214.

Brown, G., Carstairs, G., & Topping, G. (1958). The post hospitalization adjustment of chronic mental patients. *Lancet, ii,* 685–689.

Brown, G., Monck, E., Carstairs, G., & Wing, J. (1962). Influence of family life on the course of schizophrenic illness. *British Journal of Preventative and Social Medicine, 16,* 55–68.

Buchsbaum, M. (1990). The frontal lobes, basal ganglia, and temporal lobes as sites for schizophrenia. *Schizophrenia Bulletin, 16,* 379–389.

Buchsbaum, M., Nuechterlein, K., Haier, R., Wu, J., Sicotte, N., Hazlette, E., Asarnow, R., Potkin, S., & Guich, S. (1990). Glucose metabolic rate in normals and schizophrenics during the Continuous Performance Test assessed by positron emission tomography. *British Journal of Psychiatry, 156,* 216–227.

Cannon, T., Mednick, S., Parnas, J., Schulsinger, F., Praesthom, J., & Vestergaard, A. (1993). Developmental brain abnormalities in the offspring of schizophrenic mothers: I. Contributions of genetic and perinatal factors. *Archives of General Psychiatry, 50,* 551–564.

Cegalis, J., & Sweeney, J. (1979). Eye movements in schizophrenia: A quantitative analysis. *Biological Psychiatry, 14,* 13–26.

Clark, C., Klonoff, H., Tyhurst, J., Li, D., Martin, W., & Pate, B. (1989). Regional cerebral glucose metabolism in three sets of identical twins with psychotic symptoms. *Canadian Journal of Psychiatry, 34,* 263–270.

Clementz, B., Grove, W., Iacono, W., & Sweeney, J. (1992). Smooth-pursuit eye movement dysfunction and liability for schizophrenia: Implications for genetic modeling. *Journal of Abnormal Psychology, 101,* 117–129.

Clementz, B., McDowell, J., & Zisook, S. (1994). Saccadic system functioning among schizophrenic patients and their first-degree biological relatives. *Journal of Abnormal Psychology, 103,* 277–287.

Clementz, B., & Sweeney, J. (1990). Is eye movement dysfunction a biological marker for schizophrenia: A methodological review. *Psychological Bulletin, 108,* 77–92.

Clementz, B., Sweeney, J., Hirt, M., & Haas, G. (1990). Pursuit gain and saccadic intrusions in first-degree relatives of probands with schizophrenia. *Journal of Abnormal Psychology, 99,* 327–335.

Crow, T., Ball, J., Bloom, S., Brown, R., Bruton, C., Colter, N., Frith, C., Johnstone, E., Owens, D., & Roberts, G. (1989). Schizophrenia as an anomaly of development of cerebral asymmetry. *Archives of General Psychiatry, 46,* 1145–1150.

Davis, J. (1978). Dopamine theory of schizophrenia: A two-factor theory. In L. Wynne, R. Cromwell, & S. Matthysse (Eds.), *The nature of schizophrenia,* pp. 105–115. New York: Wiley.

Davis, K., Kahn, R., Ko, G., & Davidson, M. (1991). Dopamine in schizophrenia: A review and reconceptualization. *American Journal of Psychiatry, 159,* 319–324.

Degreef, G., Ashtori, M., Bogerts, B., Bilder, R., Jody, D., Alvir, J., & Lieberman, J. (1992). Volumes of ventricular system subdivisions measured from magnetic resonance images in first-episode schizophrenic patients. *Archives of General Psychiatry, 49,* 531–537.

Diefendorf, A., & Dodge, R. (1908). An experimental study of the ocular reactions of the insane from photographic records. *Brain, 31,* 451–489.

Egeland, J., Gerhard, D., Pauls, D., Sussex, J., & Kidd, K. (1987). Bipolar affective disorders linked to DNA markers on chromosome 11. *Nature, 325,* 783–787.

Farde, L., Wiesel, F., Halldin, C., & Sedvall, G. (1988). Central D$_2$-dopamine receptor occupancy in schizophrenic patients treated with antipsychotic drugs. *Archives of General Psychiatry, 45,* 71–76.

Fowles, D. (1992). Schizophrenia: Diathesis-stress revisited. *Annual Review of Psychology, 43,* 303–336.

Freedman, M., & Oscar-Berman, M. (1986). Bilateral frontal lobe disorder and selective delayed response deficits in human beings. *Behavioral Neuroscience, 100,* 337–342.

Garmezy, N. (1985). Stress-resistant children: The search for protective factors. In J. Stevenson (Ed.), *Recent research in developmental psychopathology, Journal of Child Psychology and Psychiatry Book Supplement No. 4* (pp. 213–223). Oxford: Pergamon Press.

Giordano, P., Fasullo, S., Rubino, M., & Cordovana, V. (1989). Use of CT and MRI in the neurobiological study of schizophrenia. *Psychiatry Research, 29,* 265–266.

Gold, J., Goldberg, T., & Weinberger, D. (1992). Prefrontal function and schizophrenic symptoms. *Neuropsychiatry, Neuropsychology, and Behavioral Neurology, 5,* 253–261.

Goldman-Rakic, P., & Brown, R. (1982). Postnatal development of monoamine content and synthesis in the cerebral cortex of rhesus monkeys. *Developmental Brain Research, 4,* 339–349.

Gottesman, I. (1991). *Schizophrenia genesis.* New York: W. H. Freeman.

Gottesman, I., & Shields, S. (1982). *Schizophrenia: The epigenetic puzzle.* Cambridge: Cambridge University Press.

Gur, R., & Pearlson, R. (1992). Neuroimaging in schizophrenia research. *Schizophrenia Bulletin, 19,* 337–353.

Healy, D. (1991). D_1 and D_2 and D_3. *British Journal of Psychiatry, 159,* 319–324.

Heritch, A. (1990). Evidence for reduced and dysregulated turnover of dopamine in schizophrenia. *Schizophrenia Bulletin, 16,* 605–615.

Holzman, P. (1987). Recent studies of psychophysiology in schizophrenia. *Schizophrenia Bulletin, 13,* 49–75.

Holzman, P., Kringlen, E., Matthysse, S., Flanagan, S., Lipton, R., Cramer, G., Levin, S., Lange, K., & Levy, D. (1988). A single dominant gene can account for eye tracking dysfuntions and schizophrenia in offspring of discordant twins. *Archives of General Psychiatry, 45,* 641–647.

Holzman, P., & Matthysse, S. (1990). The genetics of schizophrenia: A review. *Psychological Science, 1,* 279–290.

Holzman, P., Proctor, L., & Hughes, D. (1973). Eye tracking patterns in schizophrenia. *Science, 181,* 179–181.

Holzman, P., Proctor, L., Levy, D., Yasillo, N., Meltzer, H., & Hurt, S. (1974). Eye-tracking dysfunctions in schizophrenic patients and their relatives. *Archives of General Psychiatry, 31,* 143–151.

Holzman, P., Solomon, C., Levin, S., & Waternaux, D. (1984). Pursuit eye movement dysfunctions in schizophrenia. *Archives of General Psychiatry, 41,* 136–139.

Iacono, W., & Lykken, D. (1979). Eye tracking and psycho-pathology: New procedures applied to a sample of normal monozygotic twins. *Archives of General Psychiatry, 36,* 1361–1369.

Iacono, W., Moreau, M., Beiser, M., Fleming, J., & Lin, T. (1992). Smooth-pursuit eye tracking in first-episode psychotic patients and their relatives. *Journal of Abnormal Psychology, 101,* 104–116.

Jenkins, J. (1988). Conceptions of schizophrenia as a problem of nerves: A cross-cultural comparison of Mexican-Americans and Anglo-Americans. *Social Science Medicine, 26,* 1233–1244.

Jenkins, J., & Karno, M. (1992). The meaning of expressed emotion: Theoretical issues raised by cross-cultural research. *American Journal of Psychiatry, 149,* 9–21.

Katsanis, J., & Iacono, W. (1991). Clinical, neuropsychological, and brain structural correlates of smoother-pursuit eye tracking performance in chronic schizophrenia. *Journal of Abnormal Psychology, 100,* 526–534.

Kavanagh, D. (1992). Recent developments in expressed emotion and schizophrenia. *British Journal of Psychiatry, 160,* 601–920.

Klausner, J., Sweeney, J., Deck, M., Haas, G., & Kelly, A. (1992). Clinical correlates of cerebral ventricular enlargement in schizophrenia: Further evidence for frontal lobe disease. *Journal of Nervous and Mental Disease, 180,* 407–412.

Krantz, D., & Manuck, S. (1984). Acute psychophysiologic reactivity and risk of cardiovascular and methlodigic critique. *Psychological Bulletin, 96,* 435–464.

Kuipers, L., Korten, A., Ernberg, G., Day, R., Sartorius, N., & Jablensky, A. (1987). Expressed emotion and schizophrenia in north India. III: Influence of relatives' expressed emotionality on the course of schizophrenia in Chandigarh. *British Journal of Psychiatry, 151,* 166–173.

Leff, J., Berkowitz, R., Shavit N., Strachan, A., Glass, I., & Gaughn, C. (1989). A trial of family therapy versus a relatives group for schizophrenia. *British Journal of Psychiatry, 154,* 58–66.

Leff, J., Kuipers, L., & Berkowitz, R. (1983). Intervention in families of schizophrenics and its effects on relapse rate. In W. McFarlane (Ed.), *Family therapy in schizophrenia,* (pp. 173–187). New York: Guilford Press.

Leff, J., Wig, N., Bedi, H., Menon, D., Kuipers, L., Korten, A., Ernberg, G., Day, R., Sartorius, N., & Jablensky, A. (1990). Relatives' expressed emotion and the course of schizophrenia in Chandigarh: A two-year follow-up of a first-contact sample. *British Journal of Psychiatry, 156,* 351–356.

Levin, S. (1984). Frontal lobe dysfunctions in schizophrenia. II. Impairment of psychological and brain functions. *Journal of Psychiatric Research, 18,* 57–72.

Levy, D., Holzman, P., Matthysse, S., & Mendell, N. (1993). Eye tracking dysfunction and schizophrenia: A critical perspective. *Schizophrenia Bulletin, 19,* 461–536.

Luria, A. (1980). *Higher cortical functions in man (2nd ed.).* New York: Basic Books.

Mackert, A., & Flechtner, M. (1989). Saccadic reaction times in acute and remitted schizophrenics. *European Archives of Psychiatry and Neurological Sciences, 239,* 33–38.

Matthysse, S., & Holzman, P. (1987). Genetic latent structure models: Implication for research on schizophrenia. *Psychological Medicine, 17,* 271–274.

McGue, M. (1992). When assessing twin concordance, use the probandwise not the pairwise rate. *Schizophrenia Bulletin, 18,* 171–176.

McGue, M., & Gottesman, I. (1989). Genetic linkage in schizophrenia: Perspectives from genetic epidemiology. *Schizophrenia Bulletin, 15,* 453–464.

McGuffin, P., & Sargeant, M. (1991). Genetic markers and affective disorder. In P. McGuffin & R. Murray (Eds.), *The new genetics of mental illness* (pp. 165–181). Oxford: Butterworth-Heinemann.

McGuffin, P., Sargeant, M., Hetti, G., Tidmarsh, S., Whatley, S., & Marchbanks, R. (1990). Exclusion of a susceptibility gene from the chromosome 5q11-q13 region: New data and a reanalysis of previous reports. *American Journal of Human Genetics, 47,* 524–535.

Miklowitz, D. (1994). Family risk indicators in schizophrenia. *Schizophrenia Bulletin, 20,* 137–149.

Miklowitz, D., Goldstein, M., Nuechterlein, K., Snyder, K., & Doane, J. (1987). The family and the course of recent-onset mania. In C. Hahlweg & M. Goldstein (Eds.). *Understanding major mental disorder: The contribution of family interaction research* (pp. 195–211). New York: Family Process Press.

Miklowitz, D., Goldstein, M., Nuechterlein, K., Snyder, K., & Mentz, J. (1988). Family factors and the course of bipolar affective disorder. *Archives of General Psychiatry, 45,* 225–231.

Moline, R., Singh, S., Morris, A., & Meltzer, H. (1985). Family expressed emotion and relapse in schizophrenia in 24 urban American patients. *American Journal of Psychiatry, 142,* 1078–1081.

Montero, I., Gomez-Beneyto, M., Ruis, I., Puche, E., & Adam, A. (1992). The influence of family expressed emotion on the course of schizophrenia in a sample of Spanish patients: A two-year follow-up study. *British Journal of Psychiatry, 161,* 217–222.

Morice, R. (1986). Beyond language: Speculations on the prefrontal cortex and schizophrenia. *Australian and New Zealand Journal of Psychiatry, 20,* 7–10.

Morton, N. (1955). Sequential tests for the detection of linkage. *American Journal of Human Genetics,* 277–318.

Mozny, P., & Votypkova, P. (1992). Expressed emotion, relapse rate and utilization of psychiatric inpatient care in schizophrenia: A study from Czechoslovakia. *Social Psychiatry and Psychiatric Epidemiology, 27,* 174–179.

Nigg, J., & Goldsmith, H. (1994). Genetics of personality disorders: perspectives from personality and psychopathology research. *Psychological Bulletin, 115,* 346–380.

Parker, G., Johnston, P., & Hayward, L. (1988). Parental "expressed emotion" as a predictor of schizophrenic relapse. *Archives of General Psychiatry, 45,* 806–813.

Pearlson, G. (1991). PET scans in schizophrenia: What have we learned? *Annals of Clinical Psychiatry, 3,* 97–101.

Pierrot-Deseilligny, C., Rivaud, S., Gaymard, B., & Agid, Y. (1991). Cortical control of reflexive visually-guided saccades. *Brain, 114,* 1473–1485.

Reiss, S., Peterson, R., Gursky, D., & McNally, R. (1986). Anxiety sensitivity, anxiety frequency and the predictions of fearfulness. *Behavioural Research and Therapy, 24,* 1–8.

Risch, N. (1992). Genetic linkage: Interpreting LOD scores, *Science, 255,* 803–804.

Rosenthal, D. (1970). *Genetic theory and abnormal behavior.* New York: McGraw Hill.

Rushton, J., Russell, R., & Wells, P. (1985). Personality and genetic similarity theory. *Journal of Social and Biological Structures, 8,* 63–86.

Rutter, M. (1979). Protective factors in children's responses to stress and disadvantage. In M. Kent & J. Rolf (Eds.), *Aggression and antisocial behaviour in childhood and adolescence* (pp. 95–113). Oxford: Pergamon Press.

Schulsinger, F., Parnas, J., Petersen, E., Schulsinger, H., Teasdale, T., Mednick, S., Moller, L., & Silverton, L. (1984). Cerebral ventricular size in the offspring of schizophrenic mothers: A preliminary study. *Archives of General Psychiatry, 41,* 602–606.

Sedvall, G. (1990). PET imaging of dopamine receptors in human basal ganglia: Relevance to mental illness. *Trends in Neuroscience, 13,* 302–308.

Seeman, P., & Niznik, H. (1990). Dopamine receptors and transporters in Parkinson's disease and schizophrenia. *Federation of Associated Society of Experimental Biology, 4,* 2737–2744.

Sherrington, R., Brynjolfsson, J., Petursson, H., Potter, M., Dudleston, K., Barraclough, B., Wasmuth, J., Dobbs, M., & Gurling, H. (1988). Localization of a susceptibility locus for schizophrenia on chromosome 5. *Nature, 336,* 164–167.

Silverton, L., Mednick, S., Schulsinger, F., Parnas, J., & Harrington, M. (1988). Genetic risk for schizophrenia, birthweight, and cerebral ventricular enlargement. *Journal of Abnormal Psychology, 97,* 496–498.

Stirling, J., Tantum, D., Thomas, P., Newby, D., Montague, L., Ring, N., & Rowe, S. (1991). Expressed emotion and early onset schizophrenia: A one year follow-up. *Psychological Medicine, 21,* 675–685.

Straube, E., & Oades, R. (1992). *Schizophrenia: Empirical research and findings.* San Diego: Academic Press.

Sweeney, J., Clementz, B., Haas, G., Escobar, M., Drake, K., & Frances, A. (1994). Eye tracking dysfunction in schizophrenia: Characterization of component eye movement abnormalities, diagnostic specificity, and the role of attention. *Journal of Abnormal Psychology, 103,* 222–230.

Sweeney, J., Haas, G., & Li, S. (1992). Neuropsychological and eye movement abnormalities in first-episode and chronic schizophrenia. *Schizophrenia Bulletin, 18,* 283–293.

Tarrier, N., Barrowclough, C., Porceddu, K., Watts, S., Vaughn, C., Lader, M., & Leff, J. (1979). Bodily reactions to people and events in schizophrenia. *Archives of General Psychiatry, 36,* 311–315.

Thaker, G., Nguyen, J., & Tamminga, C. (1989). Saccadic distractibility in schizophrenic patients with tardive dyskinesia. *Archives of General Psychiatry, 46,* 755–756.

Torrey, E. (1992). Are we overestimating the genetic contribution to schizophrenia? *Schizophrenia Bulletin, 18,* 159–170.

Vaughan, K., Doyle, M., McConaghy, N., Blaszczynski, A., Fox, A., & Tarrier, N. (1992). The relationship between relative's expressed emotion and schizophrenic relapse: An Australian replication. *Social Psychiatry and Psychiatric Epidemiology, 27,* 10–15.

Vaughn, C., & Leff, J. (1976). The influence of family and social factors on the course of psychiatric illness: A comparison of schizophrenic and depressed neuropsychiatric patients. *British Journal of Psychiatry, 129,* 125–137.

Ventura, J., Nuechterlein, K., Lukoff, D., & Hardesty, J. (1989). A prospective study of stressful life events and schizophrenic relapse. *Journal of Abnormal Psychology, 98,* 407–411.

Volkow, N., Wolf, A., Van-Gelder, P., Brodie, J., Overall, J., Cancro, R., & Gomez-Mont, F. (1987). Phenomenological correlates of metabolic activity in 18 patients with chronic schizophrenia. *American Journal of Psychiatry, 144,* 151–158.

Waddington, J. (1993). Neurodynamics of abnormalities in cerebral metabolism and structure in schizophrenia. *Schizophrenia Bulletin, 19,* 55–69.

Walker, E., Downey, G., & Caspi, A. (1991). Twin studies of psychopathology: Why do the concordance rates vary? *Schizophrenia Research, 5,* 211–221.

Wei, J., Ramchand, C., & Hemmings, G. (1992). Studies on concentrations of NA and HVA and activity of DBH in serum from schizophrenic patients, first degree relatives and normal subjects. *Schizophrenia Research, 8,* 103–110.

Weinberger, D., Berman, K., & Illowsy, B. (1988). Physiological dysfunction of dorsolateral prefrontal cortex in schizophrenia: III. A new cohort and evidence for a monoaminergic mechanism. *Archives of General Psychiatry, 45,* 609–615.

Wesner, R., & Winokur, G. (1990). Genetics of affective disorders. In B. Wolman & G. Stricker (Eds.). *Depressive disorders* (pp. 125–146). New York: Wiley.

Wig, N., Menon, D., Bedi, H., Leff, J., Kuipers, L., Ghosh, A., Day, R., Korten, A., & Ernberg, G. (1987). II. Distribution of expressed emotion components among relatives of schizophrenic patients in Aarhus and Changigarh. *British Journal of Psychiatry, 151,* 160–165.

 Article Review Form at end of book.

How does the experience of major depression and schizophrenia
provide evidence for seasonal influences on platelet 5-HT levels?

Seasonal Influence on Platelet 5-HT Levels in Patients with Recurrent Major Depression and Schizophrenia

**Miro Jakovljević, Dorotea
Mück-Šeler, Nela Pivac,
Dulijano Ljubičić, Maja Bujas,
and Goran Dodig**

The influence of seasons on platelet serotonin (5-HT) concentration was determined in 88 unipolar depressed and 117 schizophrenic male inpatients, and 90 normal male controls. Platelet 5-HT concentrations showed moderate, but insignificant intragroup seasonal variations in healthy controls and in the groups of depressed (psychotic and nonpsychotic) and schizophrenic (positive and negative) patients. In spring, platelet 5-HT concentrations were higher in schizophrenic patients than in normal controls or in depressed patients, while in other seasons platelet 5-HT concentrations were not significantly different between the groups. Higher platelet 5-HT concentrations were detected in psychotic when compared to nonpsychotic depressed patients in summer, fall, and winter. Increased platelet 5-HT concentrations observed in schizophrenic patients with positive symptomes clearly separated these patients from patients with negative schizophrenia, especially in spring, summer, and fall. Our results indicate the necessity to match patients with regard to the season of the sampling, and to divide depressed and schizophrenic patients into subtypes. © 1997 Society of Biological Psychiatry

Biol Psychiatry 1997;41:1028–1034

Introduction

Over the past decade there has been expanding research on the possible involvement of serotonin (5-hydroxytryptamine, 5-HT) in the pathophysiology of major depression (Eriksson and Humble 1990; Siever et al 1991) and schizophrenia (Siever et al 1991; Breier 1995).

Blood platelets are used extensively as a model for central serotoninergic synaptosomes (Stahl 1985). Uptake, storage, and release of 5-HT into platelets and the kinetic and pharmacologic characteristics of platelet receptors resemble the corresponding processes and receptors in the central serotoninergic neurons (Stahl 1985; Andres et al 1993). There are contradictory results about platelet 5-HT levels in major depression (Le Quan-Bui et al 1984; Sarrias et al 1989; Mück-Šeler et al 1991; Mann et al 1992), as well as in schizophrenia (Stahl et al 1982; Mück-Šeler et al 1988; Bleich et al 1991; Mück-Šeler et al 1991; Jakovljević et al 1991, 1993). Explanation for these conflicting results may be sought in the influence of seasonal variations on the serotoninergic system. Namely, seasonal variations were already reported for some parameters related to 5-HT metabolism and function in humans (Carlsson et al 1980), including both platelet 5-HT uptake (Arora et al 1984; Egrise et al 1986; Codd et al 1988; Marazziti et al 1990), content (Wirz-Justice et al 1977; Wirz-Justice and Pühringer 1978; Mann et al 1992), plasma L-tryptophan (Maes et al 1995), and ^{3}H-imipramine binding (Egrise et al 1986; DeMet et al 1989, 1991).

There are only a few studies (Wirz-Justice et al 1977; Wirz-Justice and Pühringer 1978; Mann et al 1992) with controversial results about the presence of circannual changes in platelet 5-HT concentration in normal controls as well as in patients with psychiatric disorders. On the other hand, to our knowledge, there are no data of the seasonal effect on the platelet 5-HT in the subtypes of depression and schizophrenia. Therefore, the purpose of this study is to examine: a) platelet 5-HT concentrations in large groups of healthy controls, in psychotic and nonpsychotic subtypes of depression, and in positive and negative subtypes of schizophrenia, and b) seasonal effect on platelet 5-HT concentrations in healthy controls, depressed patients, schizophrenic patients, and their subtypes.

Method

Subjects

Subjects were recruited in the study during a two-year period. The population studied comprised of 117 male schizophrenic patients and 88 male inpatients with recurrent major depression. The control group consisted of 90 healthy male volunteers (mean age 31.3 ± 9.7, range 19–59 yrs) with no personal or family history of psychopathology and no medical treatment.

Clinical diagnosis of recurrent major depression and schizophrenia was made according to DSM-III-R criteria. The mean age $\pm$ SD in patients with recurrent major depression was 47.6 ± 9.0 (range 28–65 yrs). They were subdivided according to the psychotic features of disease into psychotic and nonpsychotic subtypes. There were 39 psychotic patients (mean age 49.7 ± 8.4, range 29–63 yrs) and 49 nonpsychotic depressed patients (mean age 45.9 ± 9.3, range 28–65 yrs).

The schizophrenic group consisted of patients with mean age 29.1 ± 7.8 (range 18–59 yrs). Schizophrenic patients were subdivided according to positive and negative symptoms into two subtypes: 72 patients with predominantly positive symptoms (mean age 30.2 ± 8.3, range 19–59 yrs) and 45 patients with predominantly negative symptoms (mean age 27.0 ± 6.1, range 18–42 yrs).

To test the influence of seasons on platelet 5-HT concentration, subjects were distributed according to the date of biological testing into four seasons: 1) spring (March 21–June 20), 2) summer (June 21–September 22), 3) fall (September 23–December 20), and 4) winter (December 21–March 20).

Ten patients had no previous therapy and the remaining patients had been taking different neuroleptics or antidepressant drugs (excluding chlorimipramine, fluoxetine, and amitriptyline). After admission the patients were not treated with any neuroleptic or antidepressant drugs for at least 7 days.

Biochemical Analysis

Blood sample (8 mL) was drawn from cubital vein at 8:00 AM in a plastic syringe with 2 mL of acid citrate dextrose (ACD) anticoagulant after washout period. Platelet-rich-plasma (PRP) was obtained by centrifugation ($935 \times g$) for 70 s at room temperature. Platelets were sedimented by further centrifugation of PRP at $10,000 \times g$ for 5 min. The platelet pellet was washed with saline and centrifugated again.

Platelet 5-HT concentrations were determined by the spectrofluorimetric method (Mück-Šeler et al 1988). Briefly, platelets were destroyed by sonication (20 KHz, amplitude 8×10^{-3} mm for 30 sec). Specimens of standard, blank (water) and platelet sonicates were analyzed in duplicate. All samples were deproteinized with 1 mL of 10% $ZnSO_4$ and 0.5 mL of 1 N NaOH. For the preparation of fluorophore, 0.2 mL of L-cysteine (0.1%) and 1.2 mL of orthophthalaldehyde (0.004%) were added to deproteinized samples. The measurement of the 5-HT fluorescence was performed on an Aminco-Bowman spectrofluorimeter. Platelet protein was determined by the method of Lowry et al (1951).

All biochemical determinations were performed by laboratory personnel who had no knowledge of clinical diagnosis. The biochemical data remained coded in the laboratory until an independent clinical diagnosis was made by clinicians who were unaware of the biochemical findings.

Statistical Analysis

The results are expressed as mean $\pm$ SD, except in Figures 1 and 2 where individual values are shown. One-way analysis of variance (ANOVA) followed by Tukey's honestly significant difference test was used (Daniel 1995).

Results

One-way ANOVA (F = 12.1; df = 2,292; $p < 0.001$) revealed that schizophrenic patients (1.51 ± 0.47 nmol/mg protein, $n = 117$) had significantly ($p < 0.01$, Tukey's test) higher platelet 5-HT concentrations than normal controls (1.26 ± 0.26 nmol/mg protein, $n = 90$) and depressed patients (1.26 ± 0.49 nmol/mg protein, $n = 88$). The mean platelet 5-HT concentration in depressed patients was similar to that in normal controls.

When platelet 5-HT levels were compared in normal controls, with depressed and schizophrenic patients during the seasons (Figure 1), there were significant differences among groups (ANOVA; F = 3.0; df = 11,283 $p < 0.001$). Detailed statistical analysis (Tukey's test) indicated significant differences between schizophrenic patients and normal controls ($p < 0.01$) or depressed patients ($p < 0.05$) in spring. In other seasons the variations in platelet 5-HT concentrations did not reach the level of significance.

One-way ANOVA (F = 27.6; df = 4,290 $p < 0.001$) showed significant differences in platelet 5-HT levels among the subtypes of depressed and schizophrenic patients, regardless of the season (Table 1). The highest 5-HT levels were observed in positive schizophrenic patients when compared with 5-HT concentrations in normal controls and negative schizophrenic patients (Table 1). Depressed patients with nonpsychotic features had significantly lower platelet 5-HT values than psychotic depressed patients.

Individual values of platelet 5-HT in psychotic and nonpsychotic depressed, and positive and negative schizophrenic patients in different seasons are presented in Figure 2. One-way ANOVA (F = 6.5; df = 15,189 $p < 0.001$) revealed significant differences among tested groups; however, no significant (Tukey's test) seasonal effect on platelet 5-HT levels within the subtypes of depressed or schizophrenic patients was observed. The significant (Tukey's test) differences were only found between various subtypes of the illnesses in a particular season. Positive schizophrenic patients had significantly higher platelet 5-HT levels than negative schizophrenic patients in spring, summer, and fall ($p < 0.05$). In summer, psychotic depressed patients had significantly ($p < 0.05$), while in

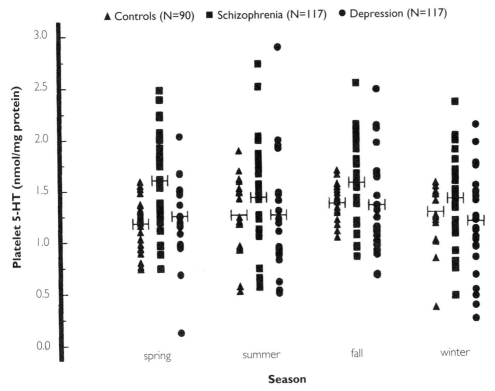

Figure 1. Individual platelet 5-HT concentrations in normal controls and schizophrenic and depressive patients in different seasons. The mean value in each group is indicated by horizontal line drawn through the corresponding data points.

fall and winter marginally higher 5-HT levels, than nonpsychotic depressed patients.

Discussion

In the present work we have confirmed our previously published results of platelet 5-HT concentrations in depressed and schizophrenic patients and in normal controls (Mück-Šeler et al 1988, 1991; Jakovljević et al 1991) and extended them with the research about seasonal influence on the platelet 5-HT concentrations.

Our results indicate nonsignificant intragroup seasonal variations of platelet 5-HT concentrations in healthy controls as well as in both groups of depressed and schizophrenic patients. On the other hand, significant intergroup differences were found between schizophrenic patients and both healthy controls and depressed patients in spring, but not in other seasons. These differences suggest an importance of seasonal influence on platelet 5-HT concentrations not only in healthy

controls and depressed patients (Mann et al 1992), but also in schizophrenic patients. This finding indicates that seasonality may be a far more general phenomenon in psychiatric disorders than originally thought.

The mean platelet 5-HT concentration in healthy controls was similar throughout the year; however, our finding of small, but insignificant peak of platelet 5-HT concentrations in the fall is partly in line with the higher platelet 5-HT levels (Wirz-Justice et al 1977), decreased plasma 5-HT level (Sarrias et al 1989), increased platelet 5-HT uptake (Egrise et al 1986), and maximal 5-HT concentration in postmortem human brain during October/November (Carlsson et al 1980). We failed to support the findings of significant intragroup seasonal variations of platelet or whole blood, 5-HT concentrations in healthy controls observed by Mann et al (1992). Our data could not support the hypothesis postulated by Sarrias et al (1989) that the decrease of plasma 5-HT ob-

served during spring and fall in the normal population may be related to the higher predisposition to depression in these periods of the year.

The reports regarding the seasonality of platelet 5-HT concentrations in depressed patients (Wirz-Justice and Pühringer 1978; Mann et al 1992) are scarce and inconsistent. We have been unable to replicate the finding of seasonal variations in whole blood and platelet 5-HT content in depressed subjects reported by Mann et al (1992). This disagreement could be explained by the different method used for platelet 5-HT determination or by the fact that our results were obtained on a larger number of patients. Wirz-Justice and Pühringer (1978) found semi-annual variations that were only related to the diurnal rhythm of platelet 5-HT in depressed patients. Their results were discussed in the light of the circadian desynchronization concept of depression. Since we observed the parallel seasonal oscillations of platelet 5-HT in depressed patients and healthy controls, seasonal desynchronization effect on platelet 5-HT was not found in our patients.

Depressed patients with psychotic and nonpsychotic features differ in symptomatology, clinical course, neurobiology, treatment responsivity, and etiology (for references see Leyton et al 1995). The present study is the first one that compares putative seasonality of platelet 5-HT levels within and between these subtypes of depressed patients. We have found nonsignificant seasonal oscillations in platelet 5-HT concentrations within particular subtypes of depressed patients; however, we have detected significantly different intergroup platelet 5-HT concentrations in various seasons. Psychotic depressed patients had significantly higher platelet 5-HT concentration than nonpsychotic depressed patients in summer, and marginally higher values in fall and winter. Seasonal variations of platelet 5-HT concentrations in psychotic and nonpsychotic depressed patients confirm the presumption that these sub-

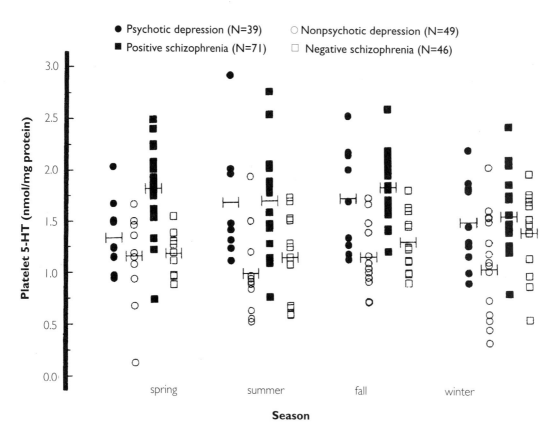

Figure 2. Individual platelet 5-HT concentrations in psychotic and nonpsychotic depressive, and positive and negative schizophrenic patients in different seasons. The mean value in each group is indicated by horizontal line drawn through the corresponding data points.

Table I	Platelet 5-HT Concentrations in Normal Controls, Psychotic and Nonpsychotic Depressive, and Positive and Negative Schizophrenic Patients		
		n^a	Platelet 5-HT (nmol/mg protein)
Normal controls		90	1.26 ± 0.26
Depressive patients			
Psychotic		39	1.51 ± 0.46
Nonpsychotic		49	1.05 ± 0.41[b]
Schizophrenic patients			
Positive		71	1.70 ± 0.43[c,d]
Negative		46	1.22 ± 0.35

[a]Number of subjects

[b]$p < 0.01$ vs psychotic depressive patients

[c]$p < 0.01$ vs normal controls

[d]$p < 0.01$ vs negative schizophrenic patients (ANOVA and Tukey's test)

types are two biologically distinct entities (Mück-Šeler et al 1991).

Schizophrenia is a disorder characterized by both positive symptoms (delusions, hallucinations, thought disorder, motoric symptoms) as well as negative symptoms (affective flattening, avolition/apathy, asociality) (Kendler 1986). Positive and negative types of schizophrenia differ in neurobiology, including the role of 5-HT and the treatment response (Hirsch and Weinberger 1995). We have found higher platelet 5-HT concentration in schizophrenic patients with dominantly positive symptoms compared to schizophrenic patients with dominantly negative symptoms. When analyzing results according to the particular season, we have observed significantly higher 5-HT concentrations in positive than in negative schizophrenic patients in all seasons except winter. This finding suggests that conflicting results of higher (Stahl et al 1983; Meltzer et al 1984; Mück-Šeler et al 1988, 1991) or unaltered (for references see Bleich et al 1991) platelet 5-HT concentrations in patients with schizophrenia, may be a consequence of different seasonal distributions of patients with positive and negative schizophrenic symptoms between particular studies.

The central 5-HT plays an important role in different physiological processes (mood, sleep, appetite, sexual functions, temperature regulation, pain, and circadian rhythms) (for references see Meltzer 1989; Wessemann and Weiner 1990), that show their own seasonality. In addition, different factors, that are also under the seasonal influence, like stress, nutritional habits, tryptophan availability, climatic variables, life events, and comorbidity, may affect 5-HT. A variety of similar factors, including seasonality, may also influence platelet 5-HT concentrations in psychiatric patients. In a recently published study (Jakovljević et al 1993), we have shown slightly higher platelet 5-HT levels in depressed patients with ulcer disease than in depressed patients without ulcer disease. Occurrence of mental disorders in spring and fall (Eastwood 1993) coincides with the occurrence of ulcer disease in the fall. The possible role of gastrointestinal 5-HT in ethiopathogenesis of ulcer disease, and the occurrence of ulcer in the fall, may be related to the higher platelet 5-HT values in depressed patients and healthy controls in the fall, observed in the present study.

In summary, our results show that various seasons did not affect significantly intragroup platelet 5-HT concentrations in healthy controls as well as in depressed and schizophrenic patients; however, significant differences in platelet 5-HT concentrations were observed between schizophrenic patients and both healthy controls and depressed patients in the spring. Significant variations in platelet 5-HT concentrations were also found between psychotic and nonpsychotic depressed, and positive and negative schizophrenic patients during particular seasons. Our results indicate the importance of matching patients with their controls in particular seasons, and the necessity of dividing depressed and schizophrenic patients into subtypes.

References

Andres AH, Rao MA, Ostrowitzki, S, Enzian W (1993): Human brain cortex and platelet serotonin² receptor binding properties and their regulation by endogenous serotonin. *Life Sci* 52:313–321.

Arora RC, Kregel L, Meltzer HY (1984): Seasonal variations of serotonin uptake in normal controls and depressed patients. *Biol Psychiatry* 19:795–804.

Bleich A, Brown SL, van Praag HM (1991): A serotonergic theory of schizophrenia. In Brown SL, van Praag HM (eds), *The Role of Serotonin in Psychiatric Disorders*. New York: Brunner/Mazel, Publishers, pp 183–214.

Breier A (1995): Serotonin, schizophrenia and antipsychotic drug action. *Schizophrenia Res* 14:187–202.

Carlsson A, Svennerholm L, Winblau B (1980): Seasonal and circadian monoamine variations in human brains examined postmortem. *Acta Psychiatr Scand* 61 (suppl. 280):75–85.

Codd EE, McAlister TW, Walker RF (1988): Factors affecting serotonin uptake into human platelets. *Psychopharmacology* 95:180–184.

Daniel WW (1995): *Biostatistics: A Foundation for Analysis in the Health Sciences*. Sixth edition. Chapter 8. New York: John Wiley & Sons, Inc. pp 295–298.

DeMet EM, Chicz-DeMet A, Fleiscmann J (1989): Seasonal rhythm of platelet ³H-imipramine binding in normal controls. *Biol Psychiatry* 26:489–495.

DeMet E, Reist C, Bell KM, Gerner RH, Chicz-DeMet A, Warren S, Wu J (1991): Decreased seasonal mesor of platelet ³H-imipramine binding in depression. *Biol Psychiatry* 29:427–440.

Eastwood MR (1993): Serotonin uptake blockers and biological rhythms in depression. In Mendlewicz J, Brunello N, Langer SZ, Racagni G (eds), *New Pharmacological Approaches to the Therapy of Depressive Disorders*, vol 5. Int Acad Biomed Drug Res, Basel: Karger, pp 37–47.

Egrise D, Rubinstein M, Schoutens A, Cantraine F, Mendlewicz J (1986): Seasonal variations of platelet serotonin uptake and ³H-imipramine binding in normal and depressed subjects. *Biol Psychiatry* 21:283–292.

Eriksson E, Humble M (1990): Serotonin in psychiatric pathophysiology. In: Lomax P, Vesell ES, (eds), *Progress in Basic and Clinical Pharmacology*, vol. 3, Basel: S. Karger, pp 66–119.

Hirsch SR, Weinberger DR (eds) (1995): *Schizophrenia* Blackwell Sci. Publ: Oxford.

Jakovljević M, Mück-Šeler D, Kenfelj H, Plavšić V, Biočina S, Kastratović D, Ljubičić (1991): Basal cortisol, dexamethasone suppression test and platelet 5-HT in recurrent (unipolar) major depression, schizophrenia and schizoaffective disorder. *Psychiatria Danubina* 3:389–414.

Jakovljević M, Mück-Šeler D, Jelovac N, Ercegović N, Plavšić V, Čulig J, Koršić M, Montani M (1993): Gastroduodenal ulcer disease in schizophrenia and major depression: Platelet 5-HT and plasma cortisol investigation. *Psychiatria Danubina* 5:277–294.

Kendler KS (1986): Phenomenology of schizophrenia. *Drug Dev Res* 9:3–8.

Le Quan-Bui KH, Plaisant O, Leboyer M, Gay C, Kamal L, Devynck MA, Meyer P (1984): Reduced platelet serotonin in depression. *Psychiatry Res* 13:129–139.

Leyton M, Corin E, Martial J, Meany M (1995): Psychotic symptoms and vulnerability to recurrent major depression. *J Affect Disord* 33:107–115.

Lowry OH, Rosenbrough NS, Farr AC, Randall RJ (1951): Protein measurement with the Folin phenol reagent. *J Biol Chem* 193:265–275.

Maes M, Scharpe S, Verkerk R, D'Hondt P, Peeters D, Cosyns P, Thompson P, De Meyer F, Wauters A, Neels H (1995): Seasonal variation in plasma L-tryptophan availability in healthy volunteers. *Arch Gen Psychiatry* 52:937–946.

Mann JJ, McBride PA, Anderson GM, Mieczkowski TA (1992): Platelet and whole blood serotonin content in depressed inpatients: Correlations with acute and life-time psychopathology. *Biol Psychiatry* 32:243–257.

Marazziti D, Falcone MF, Castrogiovaninni P, Cassano GB (1990): Seasonal serotonin uptake changes in healthy subjects. *Mol Chem Neuropathol* 13:145–153.

Meltzer HY, Arora MC, Metz J (1984): Biological studies of schizoaffective disorders. *Schizophr Bull* 10:49–70.

Meltzer HY (1989): Serotonergic dysfunction in depression. *Br J Psychiatry* 155 (suppl 8):25–31.

Mück-Šeler D, Jakovljević M, Deanović Ž (1988): Time course of schizophrenia and platelet 5-HT. *Biol Psychiatry* 23:243–251.

Mück-Šeler D, Jakovljević M, Deanović Ž (1991): Platelet serotonin in subtypes of schizophrenia and unipolar depression. *Psychiatry Res* 38:105–113.

Sarrias MJ, Artigas F, Martinez E, Gelpi E (1989): Seasonal changes of plasma serotonin and related parameters: Correlation with environmental measures. *Biol Psychiatry* 26:695–706.

Siever LJ, Kahn RS, Lawlor BA, Trestman RL, Lawrence TL, Coccaro EF (1991): Critical issues in defining the role of serotonin in psychiatric disorders. *Pharmacol Rev* 43:509–525.

Stahl SM, Ciarnello RD, Berger PA (1982): Platelet serotonin in schizophrenia and depression. In Ho BT, Scholar JC, Usdin E (eds), *Serotonin in Biological Psychiatry*. New York: Raven Press, pp 183–198.

Stahl SM, Woo DJ, Mefford IN, Berger PA, Ciaranello RD (1983): Hyperserotonemia and platelet serotonin uptake and release in schizophrenia and affective disorders. *Am J Psychiatry* 140:26–30.

Stahl SM (1985): Platelets as pharmacological models for the receptors and biochemistry of monoaminergic neurons. In Longenecker GL (ed), *Platelets: Physiology and Pharmacology*, New York: Academic Press, pp 307–340.

Wessemann W, Weiner N (1990): Circadian rhythm of serotonin binding in rat brain. *Prog Neurobiol* 35:405–428.

Wirz-Justice A, Lichtsteiner M, Feer H (1977): Diurnal and seasonal variations in human platelet serotonin in man. *J Neural Transm* 41:7–15.

Wirz-Justice A, Pühringer W (1978): Seasonal incidence of an altered diurnal rhythm of platelet serotonin in unipolar depression. *J Neural Transm* 42:45–53.

Article Review Form at end of book.

Summarize the psychophysiological findings (particularly, saccadic reaction time) associated with schizophrenia.

Manual and Saccadic Reaction Time with Constant and Variable Preparatory Intervals in Schizophrenia

Theodore P. Zahn, Bruce R. Roberts, and Carmi Schooler

National Institute of Mental Health

Rudolf Cohen

University of Konstanz

Saccadic reaction time (RT) has been shown to be unimpaired in schizophrenia. Could this be due to its not requiring controlled information processing? The authors gave 49 schizophrenia patients and 34 controls manual and saccadic RT tasks with preparatory intervals of 1, 3, and 5 s given in regular and irregular sequences. If saccades require mainly automatic processes, they should not be affected by variations in the preparatory interval that are mediated by controlled processing. The manual task showed typical slower RT and larger preparatory interval effects in patients than in controls. Although the saccadic task showed significant effects of both the preparatory interval and the preparatory interval on the preceding trial similar in kind to those in manual RT, there were no group differences in these or in RT. The results are attributed to greater

stimulus–response compatibility in the saccadic task, which puts fewer demands on working memory.

One of the earliest and most robust findings in schizophrenia research is slow reaction time (RT), measured by a manual response, in a variety of paradigms. The observation of slow RT per se, however, is considered to have limited value for understanding the pathogenesis of schizophrenia in part because persons with schizophrenia exhibit so many other deficits on experimental tasks. Slow RT has been considered part of a generalized deficit that is attributed to such factors as low motivation and lack of interest in the tasks presented. Therefore, the more recent and fairly consistently replicated findings of normal latencies of saccadic eye movements toward a visual target in schizophrenia are of considerable interest (Clementz, McDowell, & Zisook, 1994; Fukushima, Fukushima, Morita, & Yamashita, 1990; Hommer, Clem, Litman, & Pickar, 1991; Iacono, Tuason, & Johnson, 1981; Levin, Holzman, Rothenberg, & Lipton, 1981; Mather & Putchat, 1983). It seems reasonable

that understanding why saccadic RT is normal in schizophrenia might lead to a better understanding of why manual RT is so retarded in this disorder.

Another conception of the generalized deficit in schizophrenia is that it represents a disorder of controlled information processing—processes that make demands on attention and utilize limited-capacity resources (Callaway & Naghdi, 1981; Nuechterlein & Dawson, 1984). Such processes are necessary for the performance of the many tasks on which deficits are commonly observed in schizophrenia. Disorders of attention or preparatory sets (Shakow, 1962), working memory (Goldman-Rakic, 1994), and internal representation of context (J. D. Cohen & Servan-Schreiber, 1992) are among the specific mechanisms that have been proposed to account for the breadth of the nature of the schizophrenia deficits. Such processes are critical in most experimental tasks, and there is general agreement that they are impaired in schizophrenia. If saccadic RT is unimpaired in schizophrenia, then that task must have properties that

"Manual and Saccadic Reaction Time with Constant and Variable Preparatory Intervals in Schizophrenia," by Theodore P. Zahn, Bruce R. Roberts, Carmi Schooler, and Rudolf Cohen, *Journal of Abnormal Psychology,* Vol. 107, No. 2, 1998, pp. 328–337.

make the general motivational and cognitive deficits in schizophrenia less critical.

One hypothesis to account for normal saccadic RT in schizophrenia might be that because eye and hand movements are controlled by different cortical mechanisms, the differential impairments in schizophrenia suggest that only the brain areas involved in hand movements are seriously impaired in that disorder. However, that attentional factors are involved here is suggested by findings of schizophrenia impairment in the RT of antisaccades—movements away from a target stimulus—and in saccades to a location held in memory (Fukushima et al., 1990; Sereno & Holzman, 1995). Thus, the saccadic response can be disturbed in schizophrenia by introducing requirements for controlled information processing. This suggests that it is not the nature of the movement per se that eliminates the impairment of this response in schizophrenia. A similar argument could be made against the hypothesis that slow manual RT in schizophrenia is due to slow nerve-conduction velocity.

A seemingly more plausible hypothesis is that the saccadic RT task requires minimal controlled processing, being carried out mainly by automatic processes, which are thought to be unimpaired in schizophrenia (Callaway & Naghdi, 1981; Oltmanns, 1978). The shift of gaze to the location of a sudden event seems to be a very natural act that may be built into humans' evolutionarily determined adaptive capacities. This action is referred to as a *reflex* in the vision literature (Fischer, 1987). Neurophysiological support for this idea is evidence that although the saccadic system is mediated by both the frontal eye fields and the superior colliculus, lesions in the frontal eye fields do not seriously affect saccadic RT (Schiller, Sandell, & Maunsell, 1987). Similarly, despite the well-confirmed lack of impairment in saccadic RT, patients with schizophrenia had deficient activation of frontal eye fields during saccadic tasks as measured by regional cerebral blood flow (Nakashima et al., 1994). This suggests that saccadic RT may be controlled mainly by subcortical (i.e., brainstem) mechanisms,

which is consistent with interpreting this as an automatic response. The present study was designed to test this hypothesis by adding systematic variations in the preparatory interval (PI) to the saccadic RT paradigm. The reasoning behind this procedure is described below.

Variations in the PI have been long used to study attentional effects on simple warned manual RT in schizophrenia. The PI—the interval between a warning signal and the imperative stimulus—can be constant for a series of trials (regular series) or vary in an unpredictable fashion from trial to trial (irregular series). For PIs from about 1 s to 25 s duration, RT is an increasing function of the PI under the regular series but a decreasing function of the PI in the irregular series. In addition, irregular series RT is generally longer than that for the regular series, particularly at shorter PIs. In patients with schizophrenia, these relationships tend to be exaggerated compared to control participants. Moreover, although regular and irregular RT tends to approach equality at the longest PI in the series in controls, the curves for individuals with schizophrenia frequently tend to equalize or cross at an earlier point, a phenomenon referred to as *crossover*. Furthermore, in the irregular series, RT is influenced by the relationship of the PI on the current trial to the PI on the preceding trial (preceding PI, or PPI) such that RT is retarded when the PPI is longer than the PI. This effect is also more pronounced in schizophrenia (see reviews by Nuechterlein, 1977, and Rist & Cohen, 1991).

The PI effects in this paradigm have generally been attributed to their effects on preparation to respond (Niemi & Näätänen, 1981). The results of the schizophrenia studies have been taken to indicate that such patients have difficulty in maintaining preparation to respond for more than a short time, that they fail to take advantage of the information given by the regularity of the PI in the regular series (Shakow, 1962), that they are inordinately influenced by recent events in the irregular series, and that they are inordinately slowed in shifting attention to an unexpected stimulus (Zahn, Rosenthal, & Shakow, 1963). The premise of the

present study is that if saccadic RT does not require controlled processing, then it should not be affected by variations in parameters like the length and regularity of the PI, which influence preparation and expectancies. Additionally, to the extent that saccadic RT is influenced by PI and sequence effects, there should be a corresponding exaggeration in schizophrenia in those effects. The present study tested the effects of regular and irregular variations in the PI on both saccadic and manual RT in patients with schizophrenia and in normal controls.

Method

Participants

The patients with schizophrenia had hospital diagnoses of schizophrenia that were reconfirmed using the Structured Clinical Interview for *DSM-III-R* (SCID; Spitzer, Williams, Gibbon, & First, 1990) by Carmi Schooler and by an extensive reexamination of their records. The normal controls were screened by a clinical psychologist using the Non-Patient SCID (Spitzer et al., 1990) to eliminate those with histories of psychoses, mood disorders, alcohol dependence, psychoactive substance use disorder, anxiety disorders, or excessive use of drugs or alcohol.

One or both of the two RT tasks were given to 53 patients with schizophrenia and to 40 controls. There were no significant differences between the groups on age, race, sex, father's education, or mother's education (see Table 1). Of the schizophrenia group, 26 were inpatients at the National Institute of Mental Health (NIMH) research facility at St. Elizabeth's hospital in Washington, DC; 11 were inpatients in other parts of the same hospital; and 16 were outpatients being treated at that hospital's outpatient facility. The non-NIMH patients and the normal controls were paid for their participation. All participants gave written informed consent to participate in the study after the procedures were carefully explained to them. Of the total group, 49 patients and 34 controls did the saccadic RT task, 51 patients and 35 controls did the manual RT task, and 47 patients and 29 controls

Table 1 Characteristics of the Samples

Variable	Schizophrenia	Control
Number of participants	53	40
Mean age (years)	40.9 ± 8.2	37.6 ± 8.6
Percentage male	61	53
Percentage non-White	63	56
Father's education level[a] (M ± SD)	4.9 ± 2.0	4.6 ± 1.9
Mother's education level[a] (M ± SD)	5.0 ± 1.4	5.0 ± 1.3
BPRS total score	40.2 ± 13.6	

Note. Controls were not administered the Brief Psychiatric Rating Scale (BPRS).

[a]Education was coded on a 9-point scale (1 = *professional degree*, 9 = *no schooling*).

were given both procedures. The data for a few patients were not used because they had difficulties with the procedures as indicated below, so the final patient *n* s were 44 for saccadic RT, 49 for manual RT, and 41 for both procedures.

The patients with schizophrenia were all stabilized on therapeutic doses of conventional neuroleptic medications at time of testing. Ratings on the Brief Psychiatric Rating Scale (Overall & Gorham, 1962), made while patients were under this medication regimen, indicated a mean severity of illness between mild and moderate (see Table 1).

Apparatus

Eye movements were recorded using an infrared photoelectric limbus detection eye tracking device (Eye Trac, Model 210, Applied Sciences Laboratories, Waltham, MA). This device has a response time constant of 4 ms, an accuracy of better than 0.25° of visual angle and a range of 15° on each side of center. The participants were seated 43 cm in front of a video monitor on which the visual target was displayed. The targets were small bright white and blue squares that subtended a visual angle of about 0.5°, displayed against a dark background. The participant's head was secured by use of a bite bar. The infrared source and photodiode detectors were positioned in front of each eye just beyond the eyelashes at the level of the lower lid. Only horizontal eye movements were recorded. The analogue output of the infrared tracking device was sampled at 1000 Hz

and was stored in a computer for subsequent display and analysis. Before each run of data collection, the system was calibrated by asking the participant to look at targets in the center of the screen, 15° to the left and 15° to the right. When consistent values were obtained in each direction of gaze, these values were stored in the computer as reference points to calculate eye position and velocity. To minimize the participant's fatigue, data were collected only from the one eye for which the most rapid and accurate calibration could be obtained. The same eye was used for all studies of each participant.

The manual RT task was implemented by a MetraByte timing board in an IBM compatible personal computer.

Procedure

Manual RT

On each trial, a white dot appeared centrally on the screen for about 1 s to alert the participant that a new trial was to begin (see Figure 1). The white dot disappeared for about 0.5 s and was replaced by a blue dot. The blue dot persisted for the length of the PI and then disappeared. The imperative stimulus was the disappearance of the blue dot. Participants were instructed to push a black pushbutton as quickly as possible when the blue dot disappeared. There was a 2-s period allowed for a response to occur, and this was followed by the white prewarning light. RT was the time between the offset of the blue light and the button press measured in milliseconds.

In the regular series, the PI was constant for each block of 10 trials, and participants were informed of this before each block. Series with 1-, 3-, and 5-s PIs were given in that order. This was followed by an irregular series of three 10-trial blocks. Here, the three PIs were presented in a quasirandom order in which each PI followed each other PI, including itself, approximately an equal number of times. Participants were told that the blue light would come on for a random or unpredictable length of time in this case.

Saccadic RT

Participants were positioned in the headrest, and the equipment was calibrated as indicated above. White and blue dots were presented alternately 10° to each side of center (see Figure 1). As in the manual task, the blue dot remained on for the length of the PI, but the imperative stimulus included the simultaneous appearance of a white dot in the other position when the fixated blue dot disappeared. Participants were instructed that after a fixed (regular series) or random (irregular series) length of time, the light would go to the other side of the screen and that they were to just follow the dot and move their eyes to its new position as quickly as possible. The target (white) dot, now the prewarning signal, stayed on for about 1 s, then went off, and after a 0.5-s delay the blue PI light came on.

RT was measured offline from a visual display of the eye position, in which each data point represented the calculated mean eye position over an interval of 5 ms. RT was the time, to the nearest 5 ms, between the onset of the target and the point at which eye velocity toward the target attained 50° per second.

Trials on which participants failed to maintain fixation on the warning light for the duration of the PI were aborted and started again on the same side with presentation of the white light. For this task, blocks of 16–20 trials were given for the 1 and 3 s regular PIs and for the three irregular series trial blocks, but 7–9 trials were given for the 5 s regular PI because of difficulties in holding fixation for that long. At least 5 valid tri-

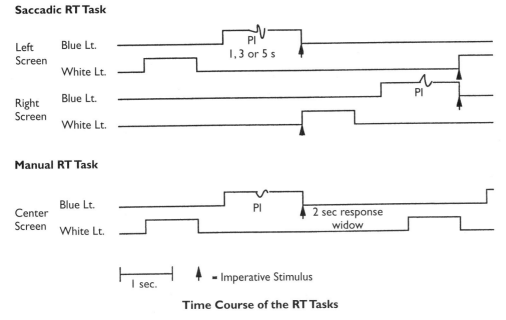

Saccadic RT Task

Left Screen — Blue Lt., White Lt.
Right Screen — Blue Lt., White Lt.

PI 1, 3 or 5 s

PI

Manual RT Task

Center Screen — Blue Lt., White Lt.

PI

2 sec response widow

⊢ 1 sec. ⊣   ↑ = Imperative Stimulus

Time Course of the RT Tasks

Figure I. Diagrammatic representation of the time course of the stimuli in the saccadic and manual reaction time (RT) tasks. Lt. = light; PI = preparatory interval; sec = seconds.

als were obtained at each PI for each participant. In the saccade task, the sequence in which the PPI was the same as the PI was about twice as frequent as the other sequences.

Data Analyses

The first trial for each series of trials was omitted from the analyses. RTs of less than 100 ms were omitted under the assumption that they were anticipatory responses. Trials on which a response did not occur within the 2 s response window were also omitted. The data for 2 patients who had more than 20 of these on the manual RT task were eliminated. Otherwise, these aberrant responses were not frequent and did not differ between groups. In the saccadic task, the data for 5 patients were discarded: 4 had difficulties with the procedure, leading to less than 65% of valid trials, and one was an outlier with saccadic RTs two to six times the next highest value.

RT distributions are typically skewed, so for each participant the median RT for each regular PI and for each irregular PI–PPI combination were computed. The data presented are the regular PI medians and the means of the three medians for each irregular PI and for each irregular PPI. However, we do note

when corresponding analyses of the mean RT led to a different conclusion. The major hypotheses of the study were tested by analyses of variance (ANOVAs). For more than two repeated measures (PI and PPI effects), the Huynh–Feldt epsilon correction to the degrees of freedom (Dixon, 1992) was used.

Results

Manual RT

Figure 2 shows manual RT (upper four curves) as a function of PI length and regularity of the series for the two groups. It can be seen that, as expected, the schizophrenia group had much longer RT and larger PI effects, especially for the irregular series, than did the control group. A Groups × PI × Sequence ANOVA showed that there was a main effect for groups on overall RT, $F(1, 82) = 25.14$, $p < .0001$; an interaction of groups with sequence, $F(1, 82) = 7.08$, $p < .01$; and an interaction of groups, sequence, and PI, $F(2, 164) = 4.34$, $p < .02$, $\varepsilon = .88$. ANOVAs on the regular and irregular series separately showed that PI did not differentiate the groups on the regular series ($F < 1$) but that the PI effect was greater in the patients in the irregular series (Group × PI), $F(2, 81) = 5.12$, $p < .02$, $\varepsilon = .76$. Note that

only the controls showed a crossover of the regular and irregular curves.

Analyses of the relationship between the PI and PPI (see Figure 3) showed an overall PI × PPI interaction, $F(4, 328) = 10.98$, $p < .0001$, $\varepsilon = .83$. This interaction appears greater in the patients, but the Groups × PPI × PI interaction did not reach significance for median RT, $F(4, 328) = 1.79$, $p < .15$. However, it was significant for mean RT, $F(4, 328) = 3.01$, $p < .02$, $\varepsilon = .96$. There were significant overall PPI effects at both 1-s ($p < .0001$) and 3-s ($p < .04$) PIs. For the 1-s PI only, the Group × PPI interaction for median RT approached significance, $F(2, 164) = 2.56$, $p = .08$, but for mean RT it was significant, $F(2, 164) = 3.81$, $p < .03$.

An analysis of the overall PPI effect, comparing PPI < PI, PPI = PI, and PPI > PI did show a significant Group × Condition relationship for RT medians, $F(2, 164) = 3.76$, $p < .04$, $\varepsilon = .78$.

The question has been raised as to whether these greater PI and PPI effects in schizophrenia are simply a function of their overall slowness. Indeed, Miller, Chapman, Chapman, and Kwapil (1993) found substantial correlations (.46–.69) between the PPI effect and mean RT in the irregular series in their patients and controls and that greater PPI effects for patients with schizophrenia than for controls in two studies were reduced to nonsignificance when adjusted for group differences in irregular series RT. However, as these investigators pointed out, a superior control would have been an independent measure of slowness rather than the mean of the same data from which the differences were obtained. In the present study, such an independent estimate is available: the RT in the regular series. Accordingly, we examined the relationships between the mean of the median RTs across PIs in the regular series and the PI effect (the difference between median RT at the 1-s and 5-s PI), the PPI effect (the difference between PPI < PI and PPI > PI), and the PPI effect just at the 1-s PI (difference between the 1-s and 5-s

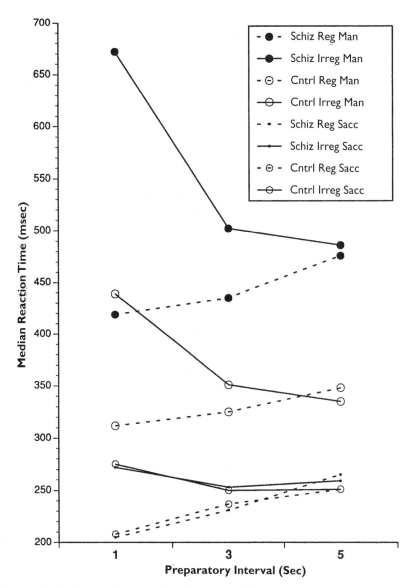

Figure 2. Median reaction time for the manual (Man; top four curves) and saccadic (Sacc; lower four curves) tasks for schizophrenia (Schiz) and control (Cntrl) groups. Results for the regular (Reg) and irregular (Irreg) series for each of the 3 preparatory intervals are plotted separately. Sec = seconds; msec = milliseconds.

regular RT was shorter than irregular RT, $F(1, 76) = 64.10$, $p < .0001$, and there was a PI × Sequence interaction, $F(2, 152) = 87.00$, $p < .0001$, $\varepsilon = .90$. For the simple effects for each group separately, both of these effects were significant at $p < .0001$. Neither of these effects showed a group difference ($F < 1$). Similarly, for the participants as a whole there were significant PI effects for both the regular series, $F(2, 152) = 65.80$, $p < .0001$, $\varepsilon = 1.0$, and the irregular series, $F(2, 152) = 15.90$, $p < .0001$, $\varepsilon = .93$. However, there was a trend for the patients to have a greater effect of the PI in the regular series (Group × PI), $F(2, 152) = 3.04$, $p < .06$. There was no group difference for the irregular series ($F < 1$).

The analyses of the PPI effects for each PI (see Figure 4) showed a PI × PPI interaction for both groups, $F(4, 304) = 27.89$, $p < .0001$, but no interaction with group ($F < 1$). The PI × PPI effect was significant at $p < .0001$ for each group separately. Simple effects of the PPI for each PI showed significant effects for each PI: at 1 s, $F(2, 152) = 41.80$, $p < .0001$, $\varepsilon = 1.0$; at 3 s, $F(2, 152) = 7.06$, $p < .002$, $\varepsilon = .93$; at 5 s, $F(2, 152) = 9.87$, $p < .0002$, $\varepsilon = .90$. Despite some apparent group differences in the shapes of the curves, none of these approached significance ($F < 1$). The analyses of the overall PPI effect, comparing RT when the PPI was shorter, equal, or longer than the PI, showed a significant PPI effect for the combined groups, $F(2, 152) = 43.88$, $p = .0001$, and for each group separately ($p < .0001$), but there was no group difference in this ($F < 1$).

Manual RT Versus Saccadic RT

It appears from Figure 2 that the two RT tasks were more different for the schizophrenia group than for the controls, both in RT level and in PI effects. This was tested by a Groups × Task × Sequence × PI ANOVA on the data for participants who did both procedures. A Groups × Task × Sequence × PI interaction, $F(2, 136) = 3.27$, $p < .05$, $\varepsilon = .89$, was based on a significant Task × Sequence × PI interaction for the patients, $F(2, 136) = 20.86$, $p < .0001$, $\varepsilon = .89$, but not for the controls. Thus differences between the two tasks in differential PI effects for the two sequences can be

PPI). Leverage analyses of the distributions of these four variables were done to check for extreme outliers that would distort the correlations, as recommended by Miller et al. (1993). The highest leverage score was .37 (for the schizophrenia group on the PPI effect), which is below the .5 cutoff that is cited as desirable to eliminate the outlier (Miller et al., 1993). The correlations of the three difference scores with regular RT were .10, .06, and .03, respectively, in the patients and −.21, .02, and .08 in the controls. None of these were significant nor were there any group differ-

ences in corresponding correlations. Thus, the group differences in the PI and PPI effects are independent of overall slowness as independently estimated by RT in the regular series.

Saccadic RT

It is clear from Figure 2 that saccadic RT for both groups is much faster than manual RT and that the group differences in overall RT and in PI and PPI effects are smaller. ANOVAs on saccadic RT found no significant group difference in RT level, $F(1, 76) < 1$. For the participants as a whole,

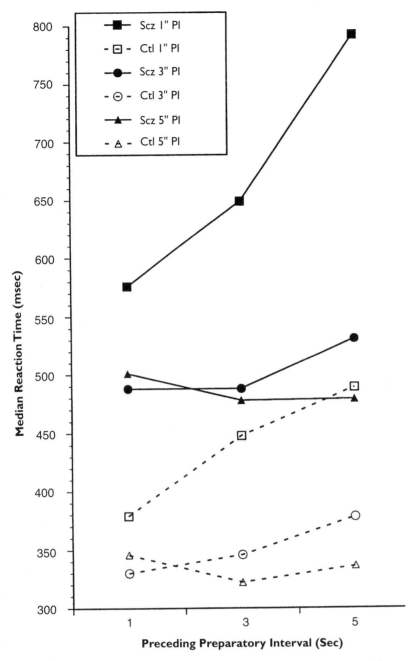

Figure 3. Median reaction time for the irregular series of the manual task for schizophrenia (Scz) and control (Ctl) groups. Results are plotted separately for each preparatory interval (PI) across the three preceding preparatory intervals. Sec = seconds; msec = milliseconds; " = seconds.

duction was significant for both patients, $F(1, 68) = 112.60$, $p < .0001$, and controls, $F(1, 68) = 14.96$, $p < .0002$.

Analyses of the PI–PPI combinations in the irregular series showed that the interaction between PI and PPI was reduced in the saccadic task for the participants as a whole, as shown by a Task × PI × PPI interaction, $F(4, 272) = 4.29$, $p < .004$, $\varepsilon = .85$, but there was only a marginal group difference in this, $F(4, 272) = 2.09$, $p < .10$. However, the triple interaction was significant for the schizophrenia group, $F(4, 272) = 6.94$, $p < .0001$, but not for the controls ($F < 1$). Thus, a reduction in the effects of the PPI on the PI in saccadic RT occurred only in the patients. Analyses of the PPI effect for each PI showed a Task × PPI effect for the 1-s PI, $F(2, 136) = 9.68$, $p < .0001$, $\varepsilon = 1.0$, but only a marginal group difference in this, $F(2, 136) = 2.66$, $p < .08$. This interaction was significant for both the schizophrenia, $F(2, 80) = 8.56$, $p < .0004$, $\varepsilon = 1.0$, and control, $F(2, 56) = 5.31$, $p < .009$, $\varepsilon = .97$, groups. For the 3-s and 5-s PIs, neither the Task × PPI nor Group × Task × PPI interactions were significant.

The overall PPI effect (comparing PPI less than, equal to, and greater than PI) was reduced in the saccadic task, $F(2, 136) = 30.30$, $p < .0001$, $\varepsilon = .77$. An interaction with group, $F(2, 136) = 5.55$, $p < .01$, reflected a larger effect in the patients, $F(2, 136) = 36.49$, $p < .0001$, than in the controls, $F(2, 136) = 4.79$, $p < .02$.

Discussion

Although not the novel focus of the present study, the results for the manual RT procedure are noteworthy in several respects. First, the two groups did not differ in the increment in RT as a function of the duration of the regular PI, in contrast to the results of many prior studies (e.g., Nuechterlein, 1977). Second, and possibly related to this, there were no differences in crossover, the data showing even a small reversal of the usual pattern of greater crossover in schizophrenia. This may be due partially to the maximum PI of 5 s used here. Most prior studies used a longer maximum PI. However, some previous manual RT studies using a similar range of PIs have found greater regular PI effects in schizophrenia than in controls (Borst &

shown only for the patients. However, this difference in PI effects occurred only for the irregular series. For the regular series, there was no task difference in the PI effect for either group or both groups combined. For the irregular series, a Groups × Task × PI interaction, $F(2, 136) = 6.09$, $p < .008$, $\varepsilon = .74$, indicated that the reduction in the PI effect in the saccadic task was more pronounced and sig-

nificant in the patients, $F(2, 136) = 39.86$, $p < .0001$, than in the controls, $F(2, 136) = 4.38$, $p < .03$. A Groups × Task × Sequence interaction, $F(1, 68) = 4.66$, $p < .04$, reflected a Task × Sequence effect, $F(1, 72) = 18.24$, $p < .0001$, in the patients but none in the controls. The patients had a greater reduction in overall RT than controls in the saccadic task (Group × Task), $F(1, 68) = 14.97$, $p < .0002$, but the re-

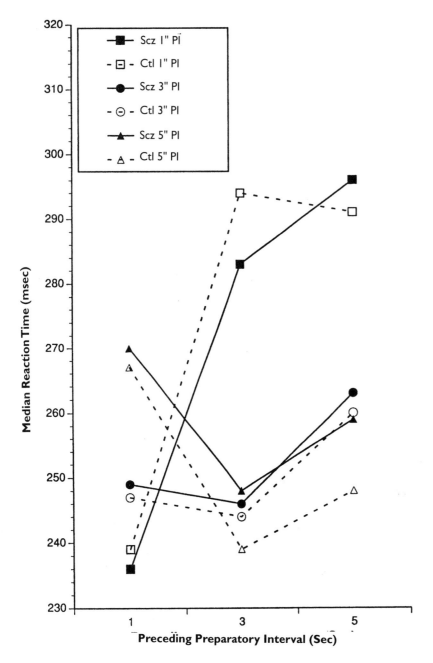

Figure 4. Median reaction time for the irregular series of the saccadic task for schizophrenia (Scz) and control (Ctl) groups. Results are plotted separately for each preparatory interval (PI) across the three preceding preparatory intervals. Sec = seconds; msec = milliseconds; " = seconds.

Cohen, 1989; R. Cohen, Hermanutz, & Rist, 1984), but not all (Borst & Cohen, 1987). All of those studies reported crossover in the patients. It seems more likely that the use of a keypress response instead of the usual key-release response contributed to both of these effects. Schneider & Cauthen (1982), using the embedded set paradigm (Bellissimo & Steffy, 1972), obtained

marked crossover with a key-release response but a difference in the opposite direction with a keypress response in the same patients with schizophrenia. The disproportionately long RT at longer regular PIs has been attributed to a build-up of inhibition due to PI redundancy (Bellissimo & Steffy, 1972). Eliminating the continuous reciprocal muscle tension during the PI should

thus eliminate the inhibitory effect on the RT response.

A third noteworthy feature is that the breakdown of the PPI effects by PI, which is infrequently done, shows how critical specific PI–PPI combinations may be in determining RT and differential RT in patients and controls. The present result of greater PPI effects at the 1-s PI than at longer PIs replicates an early study (Zahn et al., 1963). This has the methodological implication that unless the PI series is balanced, with an equal number of shorter, equal, and longer PPIs, the irregular PI RTs should be computed from the means or medians of each PI–PPI combination, as was done here. Moreover, studies without an equal PPI condition cannot be compared with studies that do include that condition on the irregular PI effect but only on PI–PPI combinations. Finally, the statistical independence of PI and PPI effects from an independent measure of slowness of response replicates a recent result with childhood-onset schizophrenia (Zahn et al., 1998) and contrasts with results obtained when the difference score (e.g., $A - B$) and slowness ($A + B$) measure shared a common component (Miller et al., 1993).

The marked slowness and greater irregular PI and PPI effects in schizophrenia for manual RT contrasts markedly with the lack of group differences in any of these effects in the saccadic RT task. The manual RT task was similar to the saccadic task in that the imperative RT stimulus was the offset of a light, although the simultaneous onset of a target light in a different location occurred in just the saccadic task. The lack of differences in overall RT is consistent with previous research using saccadic RT paradigms in schizophrenia.

This study was designed to test the hypothesis that saccadic RT is not impaired in schizophrenia because making a saccade to a target does not require controlled information processing and therefore does not tax the attention or limited capacity systems that are assumed to be defective in schizophrenia. This test is based on the assumption that if saccadic RT uses primarily automatic processing, akin to a reflex, then it should not be influenced by variations in the length, sequence, and context of the delay between a warning signal and the imperative stimulus (i.e., the PI).[1] However, for both groups, PI effects were very significantly present in both regular and irregular series of the saccadic task, and there were also significant PPI effects in the irregular series. In addition, in both groups, RT was longer in the irregular series, in which there was stimulus-onset uncertainty, compared to the regular series in which stimulus timing was predictable. All of these effects were qualitatively similar to those obtained with manual RT.

The positive slope of the regular series curve has been attributed to more accurate timing of peak preparation at shorter PIs (Niemi & Näätänen, 1981), and the longer irregular than regular RT at the shorter PIs is similarly due to the uncertainty of stimulus onset interfering with preparation. The PI and PPI effects similarly can be attributed to preparation being affected by distortions of time estimation, expectancies by long PPIs or both (Niemi & Näätänen, 1981). These effects suggest that performance of the saccadic RT task did require controlled information processing. The lack of impairment on this task in the schizophrenia group is evidence that the involvement of controlled processing is not a sufficient condition for a performance deficit in schizophrenia.

Note that this conclusion depends partly on the negative result of no group differences. Therefore, it may be asked if our sample size was adequate to detect a meaningful difference. An analysis of power (J. Cohen, 1969) shows that the power (probability) of detecting a moderate effect size (means separated by .5 SD) with the Ns used for the saccadic RT paradigm was .70.[2] At 80% power the critical effect size would be .59. With the obtained pooled standard deviation for the grand mean of the medians across regular and irregular PIs (37.4) there was a 70% chance of detecting a difference in RT as small as 19 ms and an 80% chance of detecting a difference of 22 ms. This difference is less than 10% of the obtained mean and would be considered a small difference in RT compared to most studies of schizo-

phrenia. The obtained difference was 2 ms. The other negative results for saccadic RT cited earlier strengthen the conclusion that if a difference exists it is very small.

What other feature could explain the lack of differential RT and PI effects in the saccadic task in schizophrenia? One possibly relevant feature is its high stimulus–response (S-R) compatibility. Although the requirement to move one's finger to the offset of a light is quite arbitrary, and requires keeping in mind the instruction to do so, moving one's eyes to a spot in peripheral vision is a natural act that requires minimal mnemonic strain. In manual RT, the response must be guided by a representation in memory, whereas in saccadic RT, the response is guided by the stimulus. High S-R compatibility does not necessarily imply automatic processing of the entire S-R sequence, but it does put fewer demands on remembering what to do at the onset of the stimulus. Working memory has been hypothesized to be a general source of schizophrenia impairment (Goldman-Rakic, 1994). It is conceptualized as a process that is mediated by "cortical processing networks by which the prefrontal cortex 'accesses' and holds 'on-line' representational knowledge of the outside world [such as instructional sets] through its connections with parietal and limbic centers" (Goldman-Rakic, 1994, p. 355). It differs from other types of memory in that its duration is brief, on the order of seconds.

A deficiency in working memory may be able to account for many of the specific RT deficits in schizophrenia. Impairments in working memory might take the form of a failure or delay in accessing longer term memory after the warning signal prompt, a faster decay during the PI, and/or a weaker or less accurate representation (J. D. Cohen & Servan-Schreiber, 1992), which is more subject to interference by PI effects. If working memory is impaired, then when S-R compatibility is low, as in manual RT (and in antisaccadic RT), RT is delayed because the responder must refresh it by accessing other parts of the cortical network at the onset of the RT stimulus before beginning to organize a response, a process that is not required or is begun sooner in persons with adequate working

memory function. With saccadic RT the instructional set is in large part congruent with the responder's natural response tendency, so it can be greatly simplified, and the step of refreshing working memory may be essentially bypassed. Thus, in both controls and patients RT is faster for the saccadic condition, but more so in the patients.

That there were PI effects in both groups in the regular series of the saccadic RT task suggests the operation of a preparatory process that could involve either programming the motor system or a shift of attention to the expected new location. The saccadic data suggest that the accuracy of the timing of peak preparation is better at shorter PIs, as in manual RT. The reduction in RT in the saccadic task together with the constancy of the PI effect suggests that these preparatory processes are more-or-less independent of the purely mnemonic function of working memory.

There was a marginally greater effect of the duration of the regular PI for the schizophrenia group than for the controls in the saccadic task. If this were to be confirmed in later studies, it would be difficult to attribute it to an impairment in timing accuracy because of the lack of differential regular PI effects in the manual RT. If this effect is real, it might be due to the saccadic task requiring fixation to one side during the PI, and a shift in gaze to the opposite side as the imperative response. This is somewhat analogous to the press–release sequence in the conventional manual version of this task and could theoretically lead to a greater buildup of inhibition in the patients (Bellissimo & Steffy, 1972).

In contrast, the irregular PI and PPI effects were about equal in the two groups for saccadic RT, but the patients showed a greater reduction in them compared to manual RT. In the manual task, the elevated RTs at the shorter PIs in all participants have usually been attributed to the high stimulus-onset uncertainty and its reduction with the passage of time or to a distortion of time estimation at those PIs, especially when the PPI is longer (Niemi & Näätänen, 1981). If it is less critical to have the knowledge of what to do on-line as a representation in working memory, as in the highly S-R compatible saccadic RT task, then inadequate preparation is less critical. Therefore, PI effects and the schizophrenia disadvantage in these are reduced. Because the short PI effects are potentiated by longer PPIs, no additional explanatory processes are required to account for the PPI effects.

Individuals with schizophrenia may be particularly susceptible to the effects of S-R compatibility. In studies of choice RT, task complexity has consistently been found to have a greater effect in schizophrenia than in controls only under conditions of low S-R compatibility (Hemsley, 1976). Greater effects of S-R compatibility in choice RT in childhood-onset schizophrenia than in controls was recently reported by Zahn et al. (1998). Hemsley attributed the greater effects of S-R compatibility in schizophrenia to a deficit at the stage of response selection, which bears some resemblance to the position taken here.

Many of the performance deficits in schizophrenia on tasks that require controlled information processing have been attributed to diminished processing capacity (Callaway & Naghdi, 1981; Nuechterlein & Dawson, 1984; Oltmanns, 1978). If saccadic RT puts fewer demands on working memory because of its high S-R compatibility, as proposed here, this should free processing capacity to deal with other aspects of the situation. Thus, specific deficits in preparation and their influence by variations in the PI in manual, simple, warned RT tasks may be apparent in schizophrenia mainly because of the relatively greater demands on working memory (and thus on processing capacity) required to perform the task. This type of explanation is compatible with the fact that the PI effects are quantitatively, but not qualitatively, different in schizophrenia as compared to controls (Rist & Cohen, 1991). The same holds for manual versus saccadic RT. The extent to which these group differences can be attributed to a specific deficit in working memory in schizophrenia (Goldman-Rakic, 1994), deficiencies in the internal representation of context (J. D. Cohen & Servan-Schreiber, 1992), or more generally to diminished capacity or to impaired atten-

tion cannot be decided from the present data alone. The working memory hypothesis has the advantage of not only fitting the present data, but it seemed more adequate than alternative hypotheses in explaining recent data on interference and facilitation in a Stroop procedure (Schooler, Neumann, Caplan, & Roberts, 1997), and it is compatible with the increasing evidence of frontal dysfunction in schizophrenia. A resolution of this question is still for future studies to determine.

Nevertheless, the present findings seem to cast strong doubt on the generality of previous delineations of impairments in schizophrenia that were based on the evidence from RT studies with constant and variable PIs. They suggest that the validity of attributions to schizophrenia of essentially cognitive deficits in attention or preparatory processes that have been inferred from RT studies, depends critically on the type of response, the relationship between the stimulus and response, or both. Thus, future studies would do well to pay more attention to the response facets of their paradigms rather than focusing exclusively on their information processing aspects.

Notes

1. Of course, one should keep in mind that the saccades in this task are not true reflexes in that they are voluntary (i.e., nonobligatory) responses.
2. This is based on a one-tailed test at $p < .05$. The one-tailed test seems justified because the null hypothesis of interest was that there would be no deficit in saccadic RT in the schizophrenia group.

References

Bellissimo, A., & Steffy, R. A. (1972). Redundancy-associated deficit in schizophrenic reaction time performance. *Journal of Abnormal Psychology, 80,* 299–307.

Borst, U., & Cohen, R. (1987). Impact of time estimation on the crossover effect in schizophrenics. *Psychiatry Research, 22,* 331–339.

Borst, U., & Cohen, R. (1989). Filling the preparatory interval with temporal information or visual noise: Crossover effect in schizophrenics and controls. *Psychological Medicine, 19,* 865–876.

Callaway, E., & Naghdi, S. (1981). An information processing model of

schizophrenia. *Archives of General Psychiatry, 39,* 339–347.

Clementz, B. A., McDowell, J. E., & Zisook, S. (1994). Saccadic system functioning among schizophrenia patients and their first-degree relatives. *Journal of Abnormal Psychology, 103,* 277–287.

Cohen, J. (1969). *Statistical power analysis for the behavioral sciences.* New York: Academic Press.

Cohen, J. D., & Servan-Schreiber, D. (1992). Context, cortex, and dopamine: A connectionist approach to behavior and biology in schizophrenia. *Psychological Review, 99,* 45–77.

Cohen, R., Hermanutz, M., & Rist, F. (1984). Zur Spezifität sequentieller Effekte in den Reaktionszeiten und ereignisbezogenen Potentialen chronisch Schizophrener [Specific sequential effects on the reaction times and event-related potentials of chronic schizophrenics]. In F. Hopf & H. Beckmann (Eds.), *Forschungen zur biologischen psychiatrie* (pp. 24–34). Berlin: Springer.

Dixon, W. J. (1992). *BMDP statistical software manual.* Berkeley: University of California Press.

Fischer, B. (1987). The preparation of visually guided saccades. *Review of Physiological and Biochemical Pharmacology, 106,* 1–34.

Fukushima, J., Fukushima, K., Morita, N., & Yamashita, I. (1990). Further analysis of the control of voluntary saccadic eye movements in schizophrenic patients. *Biological Psychiatry, 30,* 779–794.

Goldman-Rakic, P. S. (1994). Working memory dysfunction in schizophrenia. *Journal of Neuropsychiatry, 6,* 348–357.

Hemsley, D. R. (1976). Stimulus uncertainty, response uncertainty, and stimulus–response compatibility as determinants of schizophrenic reaction time performance. *Bulletin of the Psychonomic Society, 8,* 425–427.

Hommer, D. W., Clem, T., Litman, R., & Pickar, D. (1991). Maladaptive anticipatory saccades in schizophrenia. *Biological Psychiatry, 30,* 779–794.

Iacono, W. G., Tuason, V. B., & Johnson, R. A. (1981). Dissociation of smooth-pursuit and saccadic eye tracking in remitted schizophrenics. *Archives of General Psychiatry, 38,* 991–996.

Levin, S., Holzman, P. S., Rothenberg, S. J., & Lipton, R. B. (1981). Saccadic eye movements in psychotic patients. *Psychiatry Research, 5,* 47–58.

Mather, J. A., & Putchat, C. (1983). Motor control of schizophrenics—I. Oculomotor control of schizophrenics: A deficit in sensory processing, not strictly in motor control. *Journal of Psychiatric Research, 17,* 343–360.

Miller, M. B., Chapman, L. J., Chapman, J. P., & Kwapil, T. R. (1993). Slowness and the preceding preparatory interval effect in schizophrenia. *Journal of Abnormal Psychology, 102,* 145–151.

Nakashima, Y., Momose, T., Sano, I., Katayama, S., Nakajima, T., Niwa, S., & Matsushita, M. (1994). Cortical control of saccade in normal and schizophrenic subjects: A PET study using a task-evoked rCBF paradigm. *Schizophrenia Research, 12,* 258–264.

Niemi, P., & Näätänen, R. (1981). Foreperiod and simple reaction time. *Psychological Bulletin, 89,* 133–162.

Nuechterlein, K. H. (1977). Reaction time and attention in schizophrenia: A critical evaluation of the data and theories. *Schizophrenia Bulletin, 3,* 373–428.

Nuechterlein, K. H., & Dawson, M. E. (1984). Information processing and attentional functioning in the developmental course of schizophrenic disorders. *Schizophrenia Bulletin, 10,* 160–203.

Oltmanns, T. F. (1978). Selective attention in schizophrenic and manic psychoses: The effect of distraction on information processing. *Journal of Abnormal Psychology, 87,* 212–225.

Overall, J. E., & Gorham, D. R. (1962). The brief psychiatric rating scale. *Psychological Reports, 10,* 799–812.

Rist, F., & Cohen, R. (1991). Sequential effects in the reaction times of schizophrenics: Crossover and modality shift effects. In

S. R. Steinhauer, J. H. Gruzelier, & J. Zubin (Eds.), *Handbook of schizophrenia: Vol 5. Neuropsychology, psychophysiology and information processing* (pp. 241–271). Amsterdam: Elsevier Science.

Schiller, P. H., Sandell, J. H., & Maunsell, J. H. R. (1987). The effect of frontal eye field and superior colliculus lesions on saccadic latencies in the rhesus monkey. *Journal of Neurophysiology, 57,* 1033–1049.

Schneider, R. D., & Cauthen, N. R. (1982). Locus of reaction time change in schizophrenics and normal subjects. *Journal of Nervous and Mental Disease, 170,* 231–240.

Schooler, C., Neumann, E., Caplan, L. J., & Roberts, B. R. (1997). A time course analysis of Stroop interference and facilitation: Comparing normal and schizophrenic individuals. *Journal of Experimental Psychology: General, 126,* 19–36.

Sereno, A. B., & Holzman, P. S. (1995). Antisaccades and smooth pursuit eye movements in schizophrenia. *Biological Psychiatry, 37,* 394–401.

Shakow, D. (1962). Segmental set: A theory of the formal psychological deficit in schizophrenia. *Archives of General Psychiatry, 6,* 1–17.

Spitzer, R. L., Williams, J. B. W., Gibbon, M., & First, M. B. (1990). *SCID: User's guide for the Structured Clinical Interview for DSM–III–R.* Washington, DC: American Psychiatric Press.

Zahn, T. P., Jacobsen, L. K., Gordon, C. T., McKenna, K., Frazier, J. A., & Rapoport, J. L. (1998). Attention deficits in childhood-onset schizophrenia: Reaction time studies. *Journal of Abnormal Psychology, 107,* 97–108.

Zahn, T. P., Rosenthal, D., & Shakow, D. (1963). Effects of irregular preparatory intervals on reaction time in schizophrenia. *Journal of Abnormal and Social Psychology, 67,* 44–52.

 Article Review Form at end of book.

WiseGuide Wrap-Up

All of the disorders you are learning about from your textbook and this book can reach a state of florid symptomology if left untreated. Despite this, nothing is as severe as a schizophrenia disorder. Check out the resources in your career services office/department to set up a field visit to learn about the current care of this disabling condition.

R.E.A.L. Sites

This list provides a print preview of typical **Coursewise** R.E.A.L. sites. (There are over 100 such sites at the **Courselinks**™ site.) The danger in printing URLs is that web sites can change overnight. As we went to press, these sites were functional using the URLs provided. If you come across one that isn't, please let us know via email to: webmaster@coursewise.com. Use your Passport to access the most current list of R.E.A.L. sites at the **Courselinks** site.

Site name: Department of Health and Human Services

URL: http://www.os.dhhs.gov/

Why is it R.E.A.L.? This is a resource for health-related material; some resources about independent living may be in this site as well.

Key topics: expressed emotion, schizophrenia

Site name: Behavioral & Brain Sciences

URL: http://www.princeton.edu/~harnad/bbs.html

Why is it R.E.A.L.? This site provides articles and peer commentaries in areas of psychology.

Key topics: neuroscience findings, psychophysiological factors

section

5

Learning Objectives

- The student will become familiar with advanced concepts, such as "markers."

- The student will be able to identify the factors that predict and track depression symptomology.

Questions

Reading 14. What are heritability symptoms of depression and how are they investigated?

Reading 15. How does cognitive theory of pessimism inform us about the experience of depression?

Reading 16. Identify the path by which negative affect influences mood disorders. Comment on the theme of "autonomic arousal" in your response.

Depression

 **WiseGuide Intro**

The three articles in this section provide a resource of some of the key concepts related to the topic of depression. The practioner is in a position in which he or she needs to determine each patient's experience of depression.

The first reading in this section presents the results of a large-scale twin study. The registry of twins in Denmark is quite specific and affords research scientists with exact information. While this particular scientific technique is not without some limitations, the results yield valuable information about behavior. Given the rise in the number of cases reporting depression in our country among the elderly, causes need to be identified.

One of the newer conceptual frameworks of treatment effectiveness is the theory of pessimism and optimism. The researchers in the second reading provide a clear account of the presence of pessimism in depressed persons. The implications of this article are quite striking—they suggest that providing another opportunity after a failure can mediate depression.

The Brown and associates reading underscores the need to think about the disorders in a multidimensional fashion. The presence of autonomic arousal and negative affect are linked to the "emotion" conditions (i.e., anxiety disorders). The researchers used an advanced correlational technique called linear structural equations to identify this relationship.

This section is less specific to general information about the disorder of depression and more specific to salient concepts that will enrich your thinking as a student and future practitioner.

What are heritability symptoms of depression and how are they investigated?

Genetic and Environmental Contributions to Depression Symptomatology:

Evidence from Danish Twins 75 Years of Age and Older

Matt McGue

*University of Minnesota,
Twin Cities Campus*

Kaare Christensen

*Odense University Medical School and
Danish Epidemiology Science Centre*

The heritability symptoms of depression were investigated in a sample of 406 same-sex Danish twin pairs 75 years of age and older. Twins completed an interview assessment that included symptoms of depression, which were scored on the following 3 scales: Somatic, Affect, and Total. Heritability estimates (h^2) for the Total ($h^2 = .34$), Somatic ($h^2 = .31$), and Affect ($h^2 = .27$) scales were all moderate and statistically significant. For not one of the scales did h^2 vary significantly over the age range sampled, and although the observed twin correlations were substantially smaller among men as compared with women, none of the sex differences in heritability were statistically significant. Multivariate analyses indicated that all of the heritable effects on the Affect and Somatic subscales could be attributed to a single genetic factor. Depression symptoms in older adults may thus be more heritable than indicated in previous studies, although nonshared environmental factors clearly account for a majority of the variance. The implications of these findings for understanding the nature of late-life depression symptomatology are discussed.

Depression is one of the most prevalent psychiatric problems among older adults. Although rates vary from study to study (Snowdon, 1990), approximately 10% to 20% of older adults suffer clinically significant levels of depression or symptoms of depression (e.g., Blazer & Williams, 1980; Gurland et al., 1983; Lindsay, Briggs, & Murphy, 1989). The significance of late-life depression and depression symptomatology derives not only from its frequency and relatively direct effect on individuals' perceived quality of life but also from its possible prognostic associations with functional impairment (Berkman et al., 1986), health services utilization (Livingston, Hawkins, Graham, Blizzard, & Mann, 1990), and even mortality (Rabins, Harvis, & Doven, 1985). Despite considerable clinical interest, however, much remains to be determined about the nature and causes of late-life depression.

Remarkably, one issue that has not been fully resolved concerns simply whether the rate of depression among older adults differs from the rates observed in other age groups. Newman (1989), in her careful review of cross-sectional studies of community-dwelling U.S. adult samples, concluded that although the rate of clinically diagnosed depression appeared to decline substantially after age 60 years, the rate of depression symptom endorsement appeared to increase. Similarly, Blazer (1989) concluded that although epidemiological studies indicate that clinical depression is less common among older adults than among other age groups, "the majority of older adults suffering depressive symptoms are not captured by *DSM-III*, or *DSM-III-R* [*Diagnostic and Statistical Manual of Mental Disorders*, 3rd edition, or 3rd edition, revised] diagnostic categories" (p. 198). Studies published subsequent to the Newman and Balzer reviews have tended to confirm the pattern of relatively low rates of diagnosed depression (e.g., Girling et al., 1995) but relatively high rates of depression symptomatology (e.g., Kessler, Foster, Webster, & House, 1992) in late life, although it should be noted that most of these studies have not adequately sampled very old persons (i.e., individuals older than 80 years) and frequency of clinical depression may be very high in this age group (Kay et al., 1985).

Several researchers have speculated that the apparent dissociation of rate of clinical depression with mean level of depression symptom endorsement in older adults may reflect a measurement artifact. Specifically, the relatively high rate of depression symptom reporting may reflect age-related increases in cognitive and somatic complaints that are not related to affective state and therefore do not produce an increased rate of clinical depression (e.g., Zemore & Eames, 1979). Although the specific endorsement of cognitive and somatic symptoms certainly contributes to the relatively high rate of depression symptoms in older adults, the observation that purely affective symptoms also increase in frequency with age (Gatz & Hurwicz, 1990; Kessler et al., 1992) indicates that the increased rate of symptom reporting is not entirely conflicting age-normative changes in physical health with symptoms of depression.

Alternatively, some gerontologists have speculated that the distinctive association between age and depression may reflect the unique nature of late-life depression. Specifically, the cognitive and somatic symptoms of depression may become more salient with age either because depressed affect in the elderly may be a reaction to physical maladies (Berkman et al., 1986; Kennedy, Kelman, & Thomas, 1990) or because the elderly are relatively more likely to experience a qualitatively distinct form of depression when physical symptoms are primary rather than secondary (some-

times called the *depletion syndrome*; Fogel & Fetwell, 1985; Newman, Engel, & Jensen, 1991). In the present investigation, we explored the relationship between affective and somatic symptoms of depression in an elderly sample of twins. The twin study design not only allowed us to investigate the contribution of genetic and environmental factors to the variance in the number of affective and somatic symptoms, but it also allowed us to determine whether the association between the two types of symptoms was mediated primarily because of common genetic or common environmental effects.

Although there is substantial evidence indicating that genetic factors affect both the rate of clinical depression (Moldin, Reich, & Rice, 1991) and the expression of depression symptomatology (Jardine, Martin, & Henderson, 1984; Kendler, Heath, Martin, & Eaves, 1987) in young and middle-aged adult samples, relatively little is known about the genetic determinants of depression and depression symptomatology among older adults. The observation from family studies that the rate of depression among the relatives of depressed probands is significantly lower when the proband has an age of onset after, as compared with before, 60 years (Maier et al., 1991) has led some to suggest that genetic factors may exert less of an influence on depression among older adults than at other stages of the life span (e.g., Krishnan, 1991). The finding of low familial transmission of late-onset clinical depression is consistent with the finding by Gatz, Pedersen, Plomin, Nesselroade, and McClearn (1992) of a heritability (i.e., proportion of variance associated with genetic factors) of only 16% for the Center for Epidemiologic Studies–Depression scale (CES-D) in a sample of adult reared-apart and reared-together older Swedish twins (average age of 61 years). It is interesting to note that these latter investigators also reported that the heritability of some of the CES-D subscales, especially the Psycho-motor Retardation subscale, was greater for twins older, as compared with younger, than age 60 years.

The present investigation involved the assessment of symptoms of depression in a sample of 406 same-sex Danish twin pairs 75 years

of age and older. The study was undertaken to address the following questions:

1. What is the heritability of symptoms of depression in the elderly?

2. Does the heritability of depression symptoms vary by gender?

3. Is the relationship between somatic and affective symptoms of depression mediated primarily by common genetic factors or primarily by common environmental factors?

Method

Sample

The study sample was drawn from the participants of the Longitudinal Study of Aging Danish Twins (Christensen, Holm, McGue, Corder, & Vaupel, 1997). The sample for the larger longitudinal study was drawn from the population of all twins (regardless of co-twin status) living in Denmark who were 75 years of age or older by February 1, 1995. The residences of 3,099 individual twins meeting these criteria were identified by using the Danish Central Person Registry. Of this 3,099-participant target sample, 21 (1%) died before an interview could be completed. Of the remainder, 2,188 (71%) completed an in-person interview, 213 (7%) were assessed by proxy, 279 (9%) provided general health information only, and 398 (13%) were not interviewed. Details of the ascertainment procedures are summarized in Christensen et al. (1997), who also compare study participants with nonparticipants on information obtained from the Danish registry system. Briefly, when compared with nonparticipants, study participants had a slightly (although not significantly) greater number of hospitalizations during the 1977–1994 period and were more likely to be male (6% of participants versus 29% of nonparticipants). Nonparticipants and participants differed minimally in age and in whether they were monozygotic (MZ) or dizygotic (DZ).

The sample used in the present study was drawn from the 2,188 twins who completed the interview (i.e., depression symptomatology was not assessed by proxy). For purposes of twin analysis, we excluded the following participants from the interview sample: single twins whose cotwin was either deceased, assessed through proxy, or did not participate ($n = 1,330$); a twin pair whose zygosity could not be unambiguously determined; 16 different-sex twin pairs; and 6 same-sex twin pairs where one or both members did not complete the depression section but were otherwise interviewed. This left a sample of 406 same-sex twin pairs (115 female MZ, 173 female DZ, 52 male MZ, and 66 male DZ) where both members of the pair had complete data on the depression section of the assessment. The zygosity of these twins had been established by earlier questionnaire methods, when the sample was in middle age. The questionnaire methods used to determine zygosity in the Danish Twin Registry have been validated against serological methods and found to result in misclassification rates of less than 5% (Hauge, 1981). Table 1 gives descriptive characteristics of the sample.

The four groups of twins all had an average age of approximately 80 years, and the vast majority of twins had had 8 or fewer years of education. The majority of male twins were married and living with others, and the majority of female twins were widowed and living alone. Few of the twins were living in institutional settings. The twins reported having an average of 2.5 to 3.3 chronic illnesses or conditions (from a list of 34), with female twins reporting significantly more illnesses on average than male twins, $F(1, 811) = 11.60$, $p = .001$, but with no significant difference in the self-reported illness rate of MZ and DZ twins, $F(1, 811) = 0.01$, $p = .97$.

Procedure

The in-person interview lasted approximately 1 hr; generally took place in participants' residences; and included assessment of health, diseases, medication use, activities of daily living, cognitive functioning, depression symptomatology, and life circumstances and events. The interviews were administered by 100 interviewers who were employed by the Danish National Institute of Social Research and who lived throughout Denmark. Whereas the interviewers did not have any formal training in

medicine or psychology, the Institute of Social Research was established to undertake research on health and social circumstances and has had extensive experience in assessing the elderly (e.g., Kjoller, 1996; Platz, 1989, 1990). All 100 interviewers were trained by Kaare Christensen during January and February 1995 and were closely monitored during the 3-month period during which interviews were completed (February through April 1995). The members of intact twin pairs were each interviewed by different interviewers. A small number of participating twins ($n = 79$) completed the interview assessment during a pilot phase in November 1994; a few of these twins had not yet turned 75 (i.e., their birthday was in November, December, or January). Because the pilot assessment and protocol was nearly identical to the assessment and protocol used in the main survey, these twins were included in the present sample.

Measures

Because the depression section from the Cambridge Mental Disorders of the Elderly Examination (CAMDEX; Roth et al., 1986) had been used in a previous epidemiological survey of Danish elderly, we assessed depression symptomatology with an adaptation of this measure. Specifically, the 21 depression-related items from the CAMDEX were supplemented with an additional 11 items so as to provide a more comprehensive assessment of history of clinically relevant depression (e.g., whether the respondent had ever been treated for depression) as well as current affective state. For identification of meaningful subscales, the 21 items from the interview that directly assessed current depression symptomatology (including 16 of the original CAMDEX items and 5 of the supplementary items; see Table 2) were factor analyzed by using a principal-axes procedure with an oblique, oblimin rotation (as implemented in the Statistical Package for the Social Sciences [SPSS] for Windows, Norussis, 1993). All items except two were rated on a scale 3-point with the response options 1 = *no*, 2 = *sometimes*, and 3 = *most of the time*. The remaining two items (numbered 6 and 8 in Table 2) were rated dichotomously (1 = *no*, 2 = *yes*). To assess

factor replicability, we first derived a provisional factor solution on the sample of first-born twins ($n = 1,005$) and then replicated on the sample of second-born twins ($n = 1,069$); scaling of items was based on the entire sample of 2,074 individual twins, however.

On the basis of interpretability, replicability across the two samples, and agreement with previous factor analyses of depression symptom scales in the elderly (e.g., Kessler et al., 1992), a two-factor solution was adopted. The factor pattern matrix from the full-sample solution is given in Table 2; the correlation between the two factors in this solution was .591. Nine of the 21 symptoms loaded primarily on the first factor; these symptoms are distinguished by their affective content and lack of well-being. The first factor score derived from the solution in the sample of first-born twins correlated .997 with the first factor score derived from the solution in the sample of second-born twins, indicating an extremely high degree of factor replicability. Eight of the 21 symptoms loaded primarily on the second factor; these symptoms dealt primarily with cognitive difficulties, slowing, and loss of energy. The replicability correlation for this second factor was .994, also extremely high. Finally, four symptoms, dealing mostly with sleep and appetite disturbance, did not load at least .30 on either of the factors.

Scales for the two factors were constructed by summing the ratings for all symptoms that loaded at least .30 in absolute value on that factor; ratings for symptoms that loaded negatively were reflected prior to forming scale composites. If a respondent answered all but one of the symptoms on a scale, the mean symptom response for same-sex twins was substituted for the missing item in computing that individual's scale score. Failing to answer more than one symptom on a scale, however, resulted in a missing scale score. Three scales were formed. The first scale, labeled Affect, consisted of the sum of the 9 symptoms that loaded primarily on Factor 1 in Table 2. Internal consistency reliability estimates for the Affect scale were .76 and .81 in the male and female samples, respectively. The second scale, labeled Somatic, consisted of the sum of the 8

Table 1 Characteristics of the Danish Twin Sample

	Men		Women	
Measure	MZ	DZ	MZ	DZ
No. of pairs	52	66	115	173
Age (years)				
M	80.0	79.0	80.0	79.8
SD	4.3	3.8	4.1	3.9
Range	75–96	74–89	74–93	75–92
Education (%)				
8 years or less	74.0	79.5	82.1	85.0
Living situation (%)				
Living alone	29.8	28.0	67.4	66.2
Living with others	67.3	69.7	30.0	29.8
Institutionalized	2.9	2.3	2.6	4.0
Marital status (%)				
Married	62.5	62.9	26.5	25.4
Widowed	25.0	19.7	62.6	59.5
Nonwidowed single	12.5	17.4	10.9	15.0
Number of illnesses				
M	2.7	2.5	3.1	3.3
SD	2.2	2.0	2.5	2.4
Depression scale scores				
Affect				
M	11.7	10.7	11.5	12.2
SD	3.1	2.1	3.0	3.5
Somatic				
M	11.2	10.5	10.7	10.8
SD	3.4	3.1	3.0	3.2
Total				
M	22.9	21.2	22.2	23.0
SD	5.9	4.7	5.4	6.0

Note. MZ = monozygotic; DZ = dizygotic.

symptoms that loaded primarily on the second factor in Table 2. Internal consistency reliability estimates for the Somatic scale were .82 and .80 in the male and female samples, respectively. Finally, a Total scale was computed by summing the 17 total symptoms on the Affect and Somatic subscales. The internal consistency reliability estimate for the Total scale was .86 in both the male and female samples.

Depression scale means and standard deviations for the twin samples at given in Table 1. Because the depression scores were substantially positively skewed, scores were log-transformed prior to statistical analysis. None of the scale means differed significantly by zygosity. Women scored significantly higher than men on the Affect subscale, $t(810) = 3.24$, $p < .001$, standardized effect size = .24, but the gender effect was nonsignificant for both the Somatic subscale, $t(810) = 0.08$, $p = .94$, standardized effect size = .00, and the Total scale score $t(810) = 1.83$, $p = .07$, standardized effect size = .14. All three scales were significantly, but modestly, correlated with age (correlations of .09, .12, and .13 for the Affect, Somatic, and Total scales, respectively) and significantly and

moderately correlated with number of self-reported illnesses (.25, .27, and .29, respectively). Because, age–sex effects can bias analysis of twin resemblance (McGue & Bouchard, 1984), scores were adjusted for the effects of age and sex by subtracting an age–sex group-specific mean from each log-transformed score prior to undertaking the twin analyses. Eight age–sex groups were used in the adjustment (both sexes by the following four age groups: 79 years and younger, 80–84, 85–89, and 90 years and older). All analyses of twin similarity reported here are based on the log-transformed, age–sex adjusted scores.

Results
Univariate Analysis of Twin Depression Scores

Twin intraclass correlations for the three log-transformed and Age–Sex-Adjusted Depression scale scores are given in Table 3. Whereas all of the MZ correlations were significantly greater than zero, none of the DZ correlations were significant. In six of the nine comparisons summarized in Table 3, the MZ correlation significantly exceeded the corresponding DZ correlation, but in the remaining three comparisons, all involving the male subsample, the two correlations were not significantly different even though the MZ correlation exceeded the DZ correlation. The consistent observation of greater MZ than DZ twin resemblance implicates heritable effects on the depression scales. Moreover, the relative magnitude of the MZ twin correlations suggests that the heritability may be greater for the Somatic scale as compared with the Affect scale and greater in women as compared with men.

To estimate the heritability of the individual depression scales, we analyzed the twin data with biometric models. Following standard biometric practice (Neale & Cardon, 1992), we assumed that the total variance (V) in a scale could be decomposed as follows:

$$V = A + D + C + E, \quad (1)$$

where A refers to the variance contribution of additive genetic effects, D refers to the variance contribution of

		Loading	
Depression symptom		**Factor 1**	**Factor 2**
1. How often do you feel happy?[a]		−.81	.09
2. Do you feel sad, depressed, or miserable?		.71	−0.5
3. Are you happy and satisfied with your life at present?[a]		−.71	−0.3
4. Do you feel lonely lately?[a]		.62	−.13
5. How do you feel about your future?		−.57	−.06
6. Do you sometimes feel that life is not worth living?		.56	−.03
7. Do you feel tense and do you worry more than usual. . . .?		.41	.12
8. Do you consider yourself a nervous person?		.35	.08
9. Do you feel worthless. . . ?		.34	.03
10. Do you find it difficult to concentrate. . . ?		−.01	**.69**
11. Do you sometimes feel that you think more slowly. . . ?		−.11	**.68**
12. Do you find it more difficult to make decisions. . . ?		.08	**.62**
13. Do you find you have lost energy recently. . . ?		.15	**.59**
14. Do you find it more difficult to cope with things. . . ?		.12	**.57**
15. Have you lost pleasure or interest in doing things. . . ?		.19	**.50**
16. Do you speak more slowly than usual?		−.03	**.45**
17. Do you have extraordinarily long sleep?[a]		−.01	**.32**
18. Have you preferred to be more on your own recently?		.23	.14
19. Do you have less appetite or are you often more hungry. . . ?		.18	.17
20. Within the last 6 months, have you lost or gained substantial weight?		.18	.08
21. Do you wake up early in the morning unable to fall asleep again?[a]		.17	.03

Table 2 Depression Symptoms and Factor Pattern Matrix as Measured by an Adapted Form of the Depression Section of the CAMDEX

Note. Wording is a paraphrase of the actual interview item; numbering does not correspond to numbering in the interview. Loadings are based on the two-factor oblique solution in the total sample of interviewed twins ($N = 2,074$); the two factors correlated .591 in that solution. Scales for each factor were formed by summing items that loaded .30 or more in absolute value on that factor (loadings are in boldface in the table). The first nine symptoms form the Affect scale, the next eight symptoms form the Somatic scale, and the final four symptoms were not used in this report. The Total scale score was computed as the sum of the Affect and Somatic scale scores. CAMDEX = Cambridge Mental Disorders of the Elderly Examination.

[a] Item was one of those added to the CAMDEX depression interview for this study.

genetic dominance, C refers to the variance contribution of shared environmental effects (i.e., environmental factors that are shared by reared-together twins and are thus a source of their behavioral similarity), and E refers to the variance contribution of nonshared environmental effects (i.e., environmental factors that are not shared by reared-together twins and are thus a source of their behavioral dissimilarity). Assuming that

shared environmental effects contribute equally to the resemblance of MZ and DZ twins, the expected twin covariances are given by

$$covariance = \begin{cases} A + D + C \text{ for MZ twins} \\ (1/2)A + (1/4)D + C \text{ for DZ twins.} \end{cases} \quad (2)$$

Variance components were estimated from the observed twin variances and covariances by the method of maximum likelihood with the Mx

software package (Neale, 1994). With observations on reared-together MZ and DZ twins only, D and C cannot be simultaneously estimated. Consequently, the following five models, identified by the components estimated, were fit to the twin data: ACE, ADE, AE, CE, and E. We first fit models that allowed for sex differences in the variance component estimates and then determined whether the sex differences were significant by constraining the parameter estimates to be equal in the two samples. For each scale, a model was evaluated in terms of whether it both fit the data well (i.e., had a nonsignificant chi-square goodness-of-fit test statistic) and was parsimonious (i.e., none of the parameters in the model could be deleted without a significant increase in chi-square). The Akaike information criterion (AIC = $\chi^2 - 2 \ dfs$; Akaike, 1983) provides a summary index of both fit and parsimony, with models that have large negative AIC values preferred over models having smaller negative or positive AIC values. Table 4 summarizes the results from the univariate analyses.

For all three subscales, the estimates of the C parameter in the ACE model and the A parameter in the ADE model converged to zero, a pattern of results that is to be expected when the MZ correlation exceeds the DZ correlation by more than a factor of four, as it does in every comparison here. Failure to include a genetic component in the model (i.e., by fitting either a CE or an E model) always resulted in a significant increase in the chi-square test statistic relative to models that included a genetic component. Consequently, Table 4 provides test statistics and the variance component and heritability (i.e., proportion of variance associated with genetic factors) estimates for the two models, AE and DE, that fit the data well.[1] In every case, the DE model fit the data better (by AIC) than the AE model.

Although heritability estimates were consistently lower among men as compared with women, in no case was this difference statistically significant, as a common model (i.e., where variance component estimates were constrained to be equal for men and women) did not fit significantly more poorly than a sex-differences model

Table 3 — Twin Intraclass Correlations for Age–Sex Adjusted Depression Scores in the Male, Female, and Total Samples

Scale	Male Sample MZ (n = 52)	Male Sample DZ (n = 66)	p	Female Sample MZ (n = 115)	Female Sample DZ (n = 173)	p	Total Sample MZ (n = 167)	Total Sample DZ (n = 239)	p
Affect	.22*	.01	.13	.32*	.07	.01	.31*	.06	.01
Somatic	.22*	.02	.14	.46*	.03	<.001	.38*	.02	<.001
Total	.25*	.00	.09	.47*	.05	<.001	.41*	.04	<.001

Note. p gives the one-tailed p value for testing the difference in the MZ and DZ twin correlations. MZ = monozygotic; DZ = dizygotic.

* Correlation significantly different from 0 at $p < .05$, one-tailed.

Table 4 — Parameter Estimates and Test Statistics for Sex-Differences and No-Sex-Differences (Common) Univariate Models for the Three Depression Scales

Model	Women Gen.	Women Env.	Women h^2	Men Gen.	Men Env.	Men h^2	χ^2 (N = 406)	df	p	AIC
Affect										
Sex differences										
AE	.181	.445	.289	.107	.417	.208	3.08	8	.93	−12.92
DE	.208	.419	.331	.122	.402	.233	1.55	8	.99	−14.45
Common										
AE	.158	.439	.265				5.64	10	.85	−14.36
DE	.180	.416	.302				4.19	10	.94	−15.81
Somatic										
Sex differences										
AE	.245	.401	.379	.119	.550	.178	7.53	8	.48	−8.47
DE	.288	.357	.447	.134	.535	.200	2.52	8	.96	−13.48
Common										
AE	.201	.451	.308				10.25	10	.42	−9.75
DE	.233	.417	.358				6.44	10	.78	−13.56
Total										
Sex differences										
AE	.325	.475	.406	.164	.622	.208	7.54	8	.48	−8.46
DE	.375	.423	.537	.193	.592	.245	2.50	8	.96	−13.50
Common										
AE	.271	.524	.341				9.70	10	.47	−10.30
DE	.316	.478	.398				5.30	10	.87	−14.70

Note. The AE model included an additive genetic and a nonshared environmental component; the DE model included a genetic dominance and nonshared environmental component. h^2 is the heritability, or proportion of variance associated with genetic factors (A or D as appropriate). Parameter estimates were allowed to differ in the male and female samples in the sex-differences model, but constrained to be equal under the common model. In the latter case, the common variance component estimates are given in columns labeled for Women. AIC = Akaike information criterion; A = variance contribution of additive genetic effects, D = variance contribution of genetic dominance; E = variance contribution of nonshared environmental effects; Gen. = genetic; Env. = environmental.

(i.e., where the estimates were allowed to vary). The common heritability estimates were generally moderate, ranging from a low of approximately 30% for the Affect subscale to a high of approximately 40% for the Total scale.

To determine whether the heritability of the depression scales varied with age, for each of the three depression scales we correlated the absolute MZ twin pair difference with twin pair age. As any difference between the two members of an MZ twin pair must be environmental in origin, a pattern of, for example, increasing heritability with age would be reflected in a significant negative correlation between pair age and pair difference. For none of the three scales was this correlation significant (all three correlations were positive and less than .11), suggesting that the heritability of depression symptomatology is relatively constant over the age ranges sampled.

Given some evidence that degree of social contact might influence twin resemblance for some personality factors (e.g., Rose & Kaprio, 1988), we also explored whether the amount of social contact between the members of an MZ twin pair significantly moderated their similarity in depression symptomatology. Social contact was assessed by using twins' responses to a single item ("How often do you meet your twin?"), rated on an 8-point scale (from *never* to *live together*). The correlation between the two members of a twin pair for this item was extremely high in both the MZ (r = .927) and DZ (r = .907) samples, indicating a high degree of respondent reliability. A pair's social contact score was defined as the average of the two twins' ratings. In general, social contact scores were low (only 8% of MZ and 6% of DZ twins reported seeing each other at least once a day), and the mean contact score for MZ twins (M = 2.90, SD = 1.49, n = 167) did not differ significantly from the mean for DZ twins (M = 2.75, SD = 1.36, n = 239). We divided the MZ sample roughly in half by defining a low-contact group (the 80 pairs who reported seeing each other never or seldom) and a high-contact group (the 87 pairs who reported seeing each other at least once a month). MZ

twins correlations for the three depression symptomatology scales did not differ significantly as a function of this classification. For example, the MZ twin correlation for the Total depression score was .422 in the high contact group and .392 in the low contact group.

Multivariate Analysis of Twin Depression Scores

Table 5 gives the within-person and cross-twin (i.e., one twin's Affect score with co-twin's Somatic score) correlations between the Affect and Somatic scales. Consistent with previous studies that report correlations between the two scales in the .5 to .6 range (e.g., Berkman et al., 1986; Kessler et al., 1992), we observed a substantial within-person correlation between the Somatic and Affect scales in both the male and female samples. Analysis of the cross-twin correlations can help to characterize the basis for the within-person association (Plomin, DeFries, & McClearn, 1990). If the relationship between the Affect and Somatic scales primarily reflects nonshared environmental effects, then both the MZ and DZ cross-twin correlations should be near zero. Alternatively, if the relationship between the two scales is largely genetically mediated, the MZ cross-twin correlation should exceed the DZ cross-twin correlation and approximate the within-person correlation. The observation in Table 5 that the MZ cross-twin correlation substantially and consistently exceeded the DZ cross-twin correlation suggests that genetic factors do contribute to the association between the two scales.

To formalize the impressions gained from the informal analysis of the cross-twin correlations, we fit a two-factor Cholesky model (Figure 1) to the observed twin data (Neale & Cardon, 1992). As explained by Loehlin (1996), although the ordering of the variables in a two-factor Cholesky model is arbitrary with respect to how well the model fits the observed data (i.e., both orderings fit equally well), it is not arbitrary with respect to the parameter estimates that are produced. We were interested in determining the extent to which genetic effects on the Somatic

scale could account for genetic effects on the Affect scale. Consequently, priority was accorded the Somatic scale, and it is represented on the left-hand side of Figure 1. In this case, the genetic and environmental variance in the Affect scale was decomposed into components attributable to the genetic and environmental effects on the Somatic scale (represented as a_{21} and e_{21}, respectively, in Figure 1), whereas there is no decomposition of genetic environmental effects on the Somatic scale (which are represented as a_{11} and e_{11} in Figure 1). From the estimated parameters, statistics were derived as follows: the heritability of the Somatic scale (h_1^2), the heritability of the Affect scale, both overall (h_2^2) as well as decomposed into a portion attributable to genetic effects on the Somatic scale (h_s^2) and a residual component (h_r^2), the correlation between the genetic components for the two scales (r_e), the correlation between the two environmental components (r_g), and the bivariate heritability (i.e., the proportion of the phenotype correlation accounted for by genetic factors).

On the basis of the univariate results, we fit two-factor AE and DE Cholesky models, first allowing the male and female parameter estimates to differ and then constraining them to be equal. The derived parameter estimates and model-fit statistics for the multivariate models are summarized in Table 6. As was the case with the univariate models, constraining parameter estimates to be equal in the male and female samples in the multivariate models did not result in a significant increase in the chi-square test statistics and produced models that fit the data better (by AIC) than models where parameter estimates were allowed to differ in the two samples. Consequently, our discussion is focused on models where parameter estimates have been constrained to be equal in the two samples. Although the DE models fit the data better than the AE models, the pattern of results for the two models was very similar, with the single exception that heritability estimates were modestly larger in the DE as compared with the AE models.

Not unexpectedly, estimates of the total heritability of the Somatic and Affect scales in the multivariate

Table 5	Within-Person and Cross-Twin Correlations between Affect and Somatic Scales					

		Cross-Twin			
Sample	Within-Person	MZ	DZ	z	p
Women	.544*	.348*	.015	2.88	.002
Men	.541*	.218*	−.022	1.30	.09
Total	.543*	.313*	.007	3.13	<.001

Note. The cross-twin correlation is the correlation between the Affect score of the first member of a twin pair and the Somatic score of the second member, z is the (standard normal) test statistic used to test the significance of the difference between the MZ and DZ cross-twin correlations, and p is the corresponding one-tailed p-value. MZ = monozygotic; DZ = dizygotic.

*Correlation significantly different from zero at p < .05, one tailed.

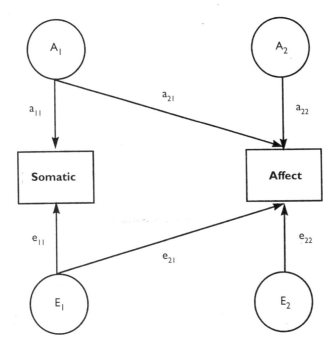

Figure 1. The two-factor AE (additive genetic and nonshared environmental) Cholesky model. The genetic and environmental effects on the Affect scale are decomposed into components in common with (a_{21} and e_{21}) and independent of (a_{22} and e_{22}) the genetic and environmental components underlying variance on the Somatic scale. The two-factor DE (genetic dominance and nonshared environmental) Cholesky model has the same form as the model depicted in the figure.

models were very similar to the heritability estimates from the univariate models. The unique contribution of the multivariate models is not in providing more precise estimates of heritability, however, but rather in helping to characterize the nature of the relationship between the two measures. The total heritability of the Affect scale can be attributed almost entirely to genetic effects on the Somatic scale; the residual component of heritability is consistently small (h_s^2 was less than .10) and the genetic correlation is uniformly high (r_g exceeds .80). Indeed, constraining the residual genetic component of variance to be equal to zero (by constraining either a_{22} or d_{22} to zero, in which case $r_g = 1.0$) did not result in a significant increase in the goodness-of-fit statistic in either the

AE, χ^2 (1, $N = 406$) = 2.2, $p > .05$, or the DE model, χ^2 (1, $N = 406$) = 1.6, $p > .05$. That is, we could not reject the hypothesis that all of the genetic effects for the Affect scale overlap the genetic effects for the Somatic scale.

Although genetic factors contributed substantially to the association, the correlation between the two depression subscales is not due entirely to common genetic effects, as setting e_{21} to zero (in which case the environmental correlation, r_e, equals zero), resulted in significant increases in the model test statistic for both the AE model, χ^2 (1, $N = 406$) = 46.3, $p < .001$, and the DE model, χ^2 (1, $N = 406$) = 41.4, $p < .001$. Plomin et al. (1990) proposed a useful statistic for gauging the extent to which the correlation between two variables is mediated genetically. The bivariate heritability is the proportion of the phenotypic correlation that can be attributed to common genetic effects. For the Affect and Somatic scales, the derived bivariate heritability estimates were all moderate (Table 6) and indicate that environmental and genetic effects shared by the two scales contribute roughly equally to the phenotypic correlation.

Discussion

The present study involved the analysis of twin resemblance for depression symptomatology in a sample of Danish twins 75 years of age and older. These analyses revealed that (a) depression symptomatology is moderately heritable in late life; (b) even though twin correlations suggested differences in heritability, we could not reject the possibility that the heritability of depression symptoms was the same in the male and female samples on the basis of standard statistical criteria; and (c) heritable effects on the Affect scale could be attributed entirely to genetic effects in common with the Somatic scale. Each of these findings has implications for understanding the nature of late-life depression symptomatology.

Estimates of the heritability of the Total depression scale score in the combined female and male sample were moderate, equaling .341 in the AE model and .398 in the DE model. These estimates are similar in magni-

Table 6

Parameter Estimates and Model-Fit Indices for
Two-Factor Cholesky Models

Measure	Sex-Differences Model		Common Model	
	AE	DE	AE	DE
Heritability Estimate				
Women				
Somatic				
Total (h_1^2)	.389	.454	.315	.365
Affect				
Total (h_2^2)	.306	.344	.271	.309
Attributable (h_s^2)	.229	.270	.197	.237
Residual (h_t^2)	.077	.074	.076	.072
Bivariate	.547	.644	.458	.541
Men				
Somatic				
Total (h_1^2)	.180	.201		
Affect				
Total (h_1^2)	.206	.235		
Attributable (h_s^2)	.134	.168		
Residual (h_r^2)	.072	.067		
Bivariate	.285	.337		
Correlation Estimate				
Women				
Genetic (r_g)	.865	.887	.850	.875
Environmental (r_e)	.380	.324	.417	.377
Men				
Genetic (r_g)	.807	.844		
Environmental (r_e)	.334	.461		
Test Statistic				
χ^2 ($N = 406$)	27.7	21.6	33.7	29.0
df	28	28	34	34
p	.48	.80	.48	.71
AIC	−28.3	−34.4	−34.3	−39.0

Note. AE refers to models that include additive genetic and nonshared environmental components; DE refers to models that include genetic dominance and nonshared environmental components; AIC = Akaike information criterion. Parameter estimates in the female and male samples were allowed to differ in the no-sex-differences models but constrained to be equal in the common models; estimates for the common model are given in rows labeled Women. In the Cholesky model (Figure 1), the total heritability in the Affect scale is decomposed into a component that is attributable to genetic effects on the Somatic scale (h_s^2), and a residual genetic component (h_r^2). The bivariate heritability is the proportion of the phenotypic correlation that can be accounted for by genetic effects common to the two scales.

tude to heritability estimates for depression symptomatology in young adult and middle-aged samples (Jardine et al., 1984) but substantially larger than the heritability estimate reported in the only other twin study of depression symptoms in older adults. Gatz et al. (1992) adminis- tered the CES-D to a Swedish sample of 68 MZ and 161 DZ reared-together twin pairs. The estimated heritability for the total CES-D score from this study was only .16. Of interest is that although the average age in the Swedish sample was 61 years, the sample ranged in age from 29 to 87 years. When the sample was divided into those older versus younger than age 60, the heritability of the CES-D was significantly higher in the older ($h^2 = .18$) than in the younger ($h^2 = .03$) cohort. Our sample is decidedly older than the older cohort (average age of 70 years) in the Gatz et al. study, perhaps explaining our larger estimate of heritability. Nonetheless, the correlation between MZ twin pair difference and twin age was not significant, suggesting that the heritability of depression symptomatology was relatively constant over the age range of our sample. Despite our larger heritability estimate, the present study and the Swedish study are consistent in implicating environmental factors as the major source of variance in depression symptoms among the elderly.

Twin correlations and heritability estimates for all three of the depression scales suggested that depression symptomatology may be more heritable in women than men; MZ correlations and heritability estimates in the male sample were about half as large as the corresponding correlations and estimates in the female sample. Nonetheless, when compared with models where parameter estimates were allowed to vary, constraining parameter estimates to be equal in the male and female samples produced both a nonsignificant increment in chi-square and a smaller AIC, indicating that the sex differences we observed were not statistically significant. Our power to detect significant sex differences in heritability was necessarily constrained by the size of our twin sample (especially the size of the male sample, which is quite a bit smaller than the female sample because of differential mortality patterns). We are currently planning a second-wave assessment of the current sample to take place during the winter of 1997, at which time we will also assess a new cohort of older twins. These additional data should provide us with greater power than we had in the present study to investigate sex differences in heritability.

In multivariate analyses of the Affect and Somatic scales, estimates of the correlation between the genetic effects on the two scales were consistently high (>.80) and not significantly less than unity. That is, all of the heritable variance on the scales could be attributed to a single common factor. We believe that the finding of a strong common genetic core between the Affect and the Somatic scales suggests that their association, rather than being artifactual, is fundamental. One or more mechanisms may underlie this association. First, the association may reflect a direct effect of poor physical health on both somatic and affective symptoms, a proposition that has a long tradition in psychological gerontology (e.g., Murrell, Himmelfarb, & Wright, 1983). Alternatively, depressed affect might influence the risk of somatic symptoms, perhaps indirectly through lifestyle choices (e.g., Aneshensel, Frerichs, & Huba, 1984). Finally, the association may reflect a core depressive syndrome that primarily afflicts older adults and in which somatic symptoms are primary (e.g., Newman et al., 1991). Although the present investigation was not designed to unambiguously determine from among these alternatives mechanisms for the observed association between somatic and affective symptoms, we favor the latter possibility, for several reasons. First, self-reported physical illness was only moderately correlated with all of the depression scales (all correlations were less than .30) and thus does not appear to constitute a major determiner of late-life depression symptomatology, at least in our sample. Second, many of the standard somatic symptoms of depression, and moreover the symptoms most likely to be confounded with physical illness (e.g., sleep and appetite disturbance), did not load on the factor that we labeled Somatic. Rather, the Somatic factor primarily reflected symptoms of lack of energy and cognitive disturbance. Newman et al. (1991) have argued that the increases in depression symptomatology that occur in late life are primarily increased expressions of feelings of en-

ervation and loss of interest, a profile that they term the "depletion syndrome" to convey the hypothesized unique origins of late-life depression symptomatology (cf. Fogel & Fretwell, 1985). Our finding that a single common genetic factor could account for all the heritable effects on both the Affect and Somatic scales is consistent with the existence of a core genetic component that underlies this unique pattern of late-life depression symptomatology. Nonetheless, a better understanding of the relationship among age, symptom type, and genetic factors should be facilitated by the planned longitudinal assessment of our twin sample.

Several limitations of the present investigation warrant mention. First, this study of reared-together twins carries with it all the well-known limitations of that research design (Plomin et al., 1990). Of special note is the critical assumption that any greater MZ than DZ phenotypic similarity must be attributed to their greater genetic, and not environmental, similarity (often called the equal environmental similarity assumption). The major concern with the equal environmental similarity assumption has been whether parents and teachers treat MZ twins more similarly than DZ twins, a possibility that seems to hold little significance in the present sample of older adult twins who, presumably, long ago went their separate ways. Moreover, we found no evidence that recent social contact moderated MZ twin resemblance in depression symptomatology, although, admittedly, recent contact is a very poor indicator of similarity in experience over a lifetime. In any case in their study of reared-together and reared-apart older Swedish twins, Gatz et al. (1992) did find evidence of a common rearing effect on the CES-D total scale score. Whereas the Gatz et al. finding runs counter to a substantial body of research documenting the limited effect of common rearing, especially on measures of affect and disposition (McGue, Sharma, & Benson, 1996; Plomin & Daniels, 1987), the present finding of moderate heritable effects on depression symptoms in the elderly certainly needs to be replicated in different samples with alternative designs.

Second, this investigation is limited in its assessment of depression. Out of respect for the private nature of the Danish, rather than use one of the standard depression interviews used in the United States, we elected to use the CAMDEX because it had been previously translated and used successfully in Danish populations. Although the CAMDEX has been widely used in western Europe, we have no evidence for how our version of this interview relates to clinician-diagnosed depression, and thus the clinical significance of the depression scores we observed is undetermined.

In summary, depression symptomatology was assessed in a sample of 406 same-sex Danish twin pairs 75 years of age and older. Analyses revealed that the heritability of the total depression score was moderate (approximately 35%) and did not appear to vary over the age range of the sample. Analyses of subscale scores revealed that somatic symptoms were somewhat more heritable than affective symptoms and that all of the heritable variance on the affective symptoms and somatic symptoms could be attributed to a single genetic factor.

Note

1. The generation of significant genetic dominance variance in the complete absence of additive genetic variance, although theoretically possible, is practically unlikely. Consequently, behavioral geneticists do not usually fit a DE model. In the present application, however, the parameter A in the three-parameter ADE model always converged to the boundary value of 0, leaving, in effect, the two-parameter DE model, from which we report results in Table 4. The superiority of the DE relative to the AE model for our data may reflect the existence of higher order genetic interactions that result in correlations that can be substantial for MZ twins but near zero for DZ twins (e.g., Lykken, Bouchard, McGue, & Tellegen, 1993). In any case, because the DE model is not a standard model fit by behavioral geneticists, we report findings for both the DE and AE models, the latter of which is a standard model. As is apparent from the results we present, findings from the two models are quite similar even though the DE models consistently fit the data somewhat better than the AE models.

References

Akaike, H. (1983). Information measures and model selection. *Bulletin of the International Statistical Institute, 50,* 277–290.

Aneshensel, C. S., Frerichs, R. R., & Huba, G. J. (1984). Depression and physical illness: A multiwave, non recursive causal model. *Journal of Health and Social Behavior 25,* 350–371.

Berkman, L. F., Berkman, C. S., Kasl, S., Freeman, D. H., Leo, L., Ostfeld, A. M., Cornoni-Huntley, J., & Brody, J. A. (1986). Depressive symptoms in relation to physical health and functioning in the elderly. *American Journal of Epidemiology, 124,* 372–384.

Blazer, D. (1989). Depression in late life: An update. In M. Powell Lawton (Ed.), *Annual review of gerontology and geriatrics* (pp. 197–215). New York: Springer.

Blazer, D., & Williams, C. D. (1980). Epidemiology of dysphoria and depression in an elderly population. *American Journal of Psychiatry, 137,* 439–444.

Christensen, K., Holm, N., McGue, M., Corder, L., & Vaupel, J. W. (1997). *A Danish population-based twin study on self-rated health in elderly.* Manuscript submitted for publication.

Fogel, B. S., & Fretwell, M. (1985). Reclassification of depression in the medically ill elderly. *Journal of the American Geriatrics Society. 42,* 446–448.

Gatz, M., & Hurwicz, M.-L. (1990). Are old people more depressed? Cross-sectional data on the Center for Epidemiological Studies Depression Scale factors. *Psychology and Aging, 5,* 284–290.

Gatz, M., Pedersen, N. L., Plomin, R., Nesselroade, J. R., & McClearn, G. E. (1992). Importance of shared genes and shared environments for symptoms of depression in older adults. *Journal of Abnormal Psychology, 101,* 701–708.

Girling, D. M., Barkley, C., Paykel, E. S., Gehlhaar, E., Brayne, C., Gill, C., Mathewson, D., & Huppert, F. A. (1995). The prevalence of depression in a cohort of the very elderly. *Journal of Affective Disorders, 34,* 319–329.

Gurland, B. J., Copeland, J., Kuriansky, J., Kelleher, M., Sharpe, L., & Dean, L. L. (1983). *The mind and mood of aging.* London: Croon Helm.

Hauge, M. (1981). The Danish Twin Register. In S. A. Mednick, A. E. Baert, & B. P. Bachmann (Eds.), *Prospective longitudinal research* (pp. 217–222). Oxford, England: Oxford Medical.

Jardine, R., Martin, N. G., & Henderson, A. S. (1984). Genetic covariation between neuroticism and the symptoms of anxiety and depression. *Genetic Epidemiology, 1,* 89–107.

Kay, D. W. K., Henderson, A. S., Scott, R., Wilson, J., Rickwood, D., & Grayson, D. A. (1985). The prevalence of dementia and depression among the elderly living in the Hobart community: The effect of diagnostic criteria on the prevalence rates. *Psychological Medicine, 155,* 317–329.

Kendler, K. S., Heath, A. C., Martin, N. G., & Eaves, L. J. (1987). Symptoms of anxiety and symptoms of depression: Same genes, different environments? *Archives of General Psychiatry, 44,* 451–457.

Kennedy, G. J., Kelman, H. R., & Thomas, C. (1990). The emergence of depressive symptoms in late life: The importance of declining health and increasing disability. *Journal of Community Health, 15,* 93–104.

Kessler, R. C., Foster, C., Webster, P. S., & House, J. S. (1992). The relationship between age and depressive symptoms in two national surveys. *Psychology and Aging, 7,* 119–126.

Kjoller, M. (1996). *Health and morbidity in Denmark, 1994.* Copenhagen, Denmark: Danish Institute for Clinical Epidemiology.

Krishnan, K. R. R. (1991). Organic bases of depression in the elderly. *Annual Review of Medicine, 42,* 261–266.

Lindsay, J., Briggs, K., & Murphy, E. (1989). The Guy's Age Concern Survey: Prevalence rates of cognitive impairment, depression and anxiety in an urban elderly community. *British Journal of Psychiatry, 155,* 317–329.

Livingston, G., Hawkins, A., Graham, N., Blizzard, B., & Mann, A. (1990). The Gospel Oak Study: Prevalence rates of dementia, depression and activity limitation among elderly residents in inner London. *Psychological Medicine, 20,* 137–146.

Loehlin, J. C. (1996). The Cholesky approach: A cautionary note. *Behavior Genetics, 26,* 65–69.

Lykken, D. T., Bouchard, T. J., Jr., McGue, M., & Tellegen, A. (1993). Emergenesis: Genetic traits that may not run in families. *American Psychologist, 47,* 1565–1577.

Maier, W., Lichtermann, D., Minges, J., Henn, R., Hallmayer, J., & Klingler, T. (1991). Unipolar depression in the aged: Determinants of familial aggregation. *Journal of Affective Disorders, 23,* 53–61.

McGue, M., & Bouchard, T. J. (1984). Adjustment of twin data for the effects of age and sex. *Behavior Genetics, 14,* 325–343.

McGue, M., Sharma, A., & Benson, P. (1996). The effect of common rearing on adolescent development: Evidence from a U.S. adoption cohort. *Developmental Psychology, 32,* 604–613.

Moldin, S. O., Reich, T., & Rice, J. P. (1991). Current perspective on the genetics of unipolar depression. *Behavior Genetics, 21,* 211–242.

Murrell, S. A., Himmelfarb, S., & Wright, K. (1983). Prevalence of depression and its correlates in older adults. *American Journal of Epidemiology, 117,* 173–185.

Neale, M. C. (1994). *MX: Statistical modeling* (2nd ed.). Richmond, VA: Medical College of Virginia, Department of Psychiatry.

Neale, M. C., & Cardon, L. R. (1992). *Methodology for genetic studies of twins and families.* Dordrecht, The Netherlands: Kluwer Academic.

Newman, J. P. (1989). Aging and depression. *Psychology and Aging, 4,* 150–165.

Newman, J. P., Engel, R. J., & Jensen, J. E. (1991). Changes in depressive-symptom experiences among older women. *Psychology and Aging, 6,* 212–222.

Norussis, M. (1993). *SPSS for Windows: Base system user's guide: Release 6.0.* Chicago, IL: SPSS.

Platz, M. (1989). *The elderly in their homes: Vol. 1. Living conditions.* Copenhagen, Denmark: Danish National Institute of Social Research.

Platz, M. (1990). *The elderly in their homes: Vol. 2. How do they cope?* Copenhagen, Denmark: Danish National Institute of Social Research.

Plomin, R., & Daniels, D. (1987). Why are two children in the same family so different from each other? *Behavioral and Brain Sciences, 10,* 1–16.

Plomin, R., DeFries, J. C., & McClearn, G. E. (1990). *Behavioral genetics: A primer* (2nd ed.). New York: Freeman.

Rabins, P. V., Harvis, K., & Doven, S. (1985). High fatality rates of late-life depression associated with cardiovascular disease. *Journal of Affective Disorders, 9,* 165–167.

Rose, R. J., & Kaprio, J. (1988). Frequency of social contact and intrapair resemblance of adult monozygotic cotwins. *Behavior Genetics, 18,* 309–328.

Roth, M., Tym, E., Mountjoy, C. Q., Huppert, F. A., Hendrie, H., Verma, S., & Goodard, R. (1986). CAMDEX: A standardised instrument for the diagnosis of mental disorder in the elderly with special reference to the early detection of dementia. *British Journal of Psychiatry, 149,* 698–709.

Snowdon, J. (1990). The prevalence of depression in old age. *International Journal of Geriatric Psychiatry, 5,* 141–144.

Zemore, R., & Eames, N. (1979). Psychic and somatic symptoms of depression among young adult, institutionalized aged and noninstitutionalized aged. *Journal of Gerontology, 34,* 716–722.

Article Review Form at end of book.

How does cognitive theory of pessimism inform us about the experience of depression?

Cognitive Theory and the Generality of Pessimism among Depressed Persons

Sanford Golin, Steven Jarrett, Mark Stewart, and Wanda Drayton

University of Pittsburgh

Depressed and nondepressed college students were given a series of anagrams to solve. A one-chance subgroup was informed that they would win a free movie ticket if they were successful in the anagram task. A second-chance subgroup received the same instructions as the one-chance subgroup but were also informed that if they failed the anagram task, they would have another opportunity in a different, undefined task to win the ticket. The subjects were subdivided into success and failure subgroups that either succeeded or failed the anagram task. Immediately after the anagram task, subjects reported their emotional state on the Multiple Affect Adjective Check List. Depressed subjects reported greater depression, anxiety, and hostility than nondepressed subjects in the one-chance condition but not in the second-chance condition; this interaction occurred independent of the subjects' success or failure in the anagram task. The results are viewed as indicating that current cognitive theories about the generality of pessimism in depression are incomplete. An explanation of the results in terms of the saliency of future reward opportunity is suggested as a basis for further study.

Contemporary cognitive theories view depressed persons as generally pessimistic (Abramson, Seligman, & Teasdale, 1978; Beck, 1976). In order to test this view, the present experiment posed the following question: Suppose that prior to engaging in a goal-attainment task subjects are informed that should they fail, they will have a second chance with a different task to attain the goal; what effect can such an instruction be expected to have on depressed persons? To the extent that a "second chance" instruction cognitively redefines the task so as to increase the individual's expectancy for success, it would be expected to reduce stress resulting from involvement in the task (e.g., Goldfreid, Linehan, & Smith, 1978). Contemporary cognitive theories of depression, however, suggest that because the global pessimism of depressed persons would presumably generalize to future undertakings, the opportunity for a second chance would be unlikely to attenuate signs of stress among such persons. Beck (1976) has described the process thus:

The depressed patient judges that, since he cannot achieve a major goal now, he never will. He cannot see the possibility of substituting other rewarding goals. Moreover, if a problem appears insoluble now, he assumes that he will never be able to find a way of working it out or somehow bypassing it. (p. 117)

One would intuitively expect an individual to be more sanguine about the prospects for success with two opportunities to attain a goal than with merely one opportunity. For this reason, despite the apparent contrary prediction implied by contemporary cognitive theories, it was hypothesized that a second-chance redefinition of a goal-attainment task would in fact attenuate signs of stress among depressed subjects. To test this prediction, the stress reactions of depressed and nondepressed persons were compared under two conditions, a *one-chance* and a *second-chance* condition, as described below.

Method

Subjects

Consistent with previous usage (e.g., Golin, Hartman, Klatt, Munz, & Wolfgang, 1977), depression was measured by a trait form of the Beck Depression Inventory (BDI; Beck, 1967), which has been shown to be a valid measure of depression among college students (Bumberry, Oliver, & McClure, 1978). From 287 undergraduates enrolled in introductory psychology classes at the University of Pittsburgh, 38 who scored 10 or more on the BDI were designated as depressed (D; *M* BDI = 15.10) and 52 who scored 6 or less were designated as nondepressed (ND; *M* BDI = 2.97).

These subjects were then randomly assigned to either a one-chance (OC) or a second-chance (SC) condition and were further randomly subdivided into success (S) and failure (F) conditions, as described below. The ns of each of the subgroups were: D–OC–S, 11 (5 male, 6 female); D–OC–F, 8 (4 male, 4 female); D–SC–S, 9 (4 male, 5 female); D–SC–F, 10 (5 male, 5 female); ND–OC–S, 14 (7 male, 7 female); ND–OC–F, 14 (7 male, 7 female); ND–SC–S, 12 (6 male, 6 female); ND–SC–F, 12 (6 male, 6 female).

Procedure

Subjects were informed by tape-recorded instructions that they would be given a series of 10 anagrams to solve. Each anagram was presented for 10 sec by a tachistoscope, and subjects were required to solve the anagram during these 10 sec. Subjects were informed that if they did well on this task they would win a free ticket to a movie shown on campus. One-chance subjects were given these instructions only; second-chance subjects were given the same instructions and also informed that if they did not win the movie ticket on the anagram task they would have another opportunity to win the ticket with a second task that would be described to them later. Easy and difficult anagrams, based on normative data presented by Tresselt and Mayzner (1966), were selected for use. All subjects received the same anagrams for the first six trials; these were, BEAHC (beach), NTGIA (giant), HOCAR (roach), GSRUA (sugar), AEWTR, (water), OARLB (labor). Subjects in the success condition were then told that they would have to get one of the four remaining anagrams correct in order to win the movie ticket. Four trials of the following easy anagrams were then presented: EGUJD (judge), ODELM (model), NTRAI (train), IFNLG (fling). Failure-condition subjects were told that they would have to get the remaining four anagrams correct in order to win the ticket; four trials of the following four difficult anagrams were then presented: BAROC (cobra), AITOP (patio), DTUAI (audit), SPEUA (pause). In all cases success subjects succeeded, and in no case did a failure subject win the movie ticket.

The self-reported depression, anxiety, and hostility occurring in reaction to the task were employed as a measure of stress (see Geen, 1976). Immediately following the last anagram, subjects were administered the Today form of the Multiple Affect Adjective Check list (MAACL; Zuckerman, Lubin, & Robins, 1965). In order to obtain a measure of the effectiveness of the success–failure manipulation, subjects were next instructed to rate the extent to which they were satisfied with their performance on the anagram task on a 10-point scale that ranged from not at all satisfied (1) to extremely satisfied (10).

Following completion of the ratings, subjects were debriefed and informed about the nature of the experiment including the actual nature of the success–failure condition. All subjects were given a free movie ticket.

Results

In order to check the effectiveness of the success–failure manipulation, an unweighted-means analysis of variance of the performance satisfaction ratings as a function of the depression, success–failure, sex, and one-chance–second-chance factors was carried out. A significant main effect of success–failure, $F(1, 74) = 77.55$, $p < .001$ (success $M = 6.41$; failure $M = 3.01$), was found. There were no other significant effects of the analysis. It was thus shown that the success–failure manipulation was successful in producing its intended effects.

The MAACL depression, anxiety, and hostility scores were subjected to unweighted-means analyses of variance. The analysis of variance of the depression scores yielded a significant main effect of success–failure, $F (1, 74) = 9.91$, $p < .01$ (success $M = 14.84$; failure $M = 17.68$). A significant Depression × One-Chance–Second Chance interaction, $F (1, 74) = 4.04$, $p < .05$, which is illus-

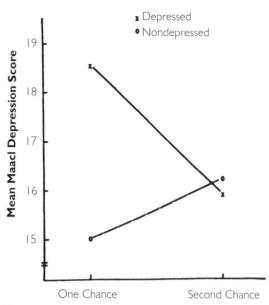

Figure I. Mean Multiple Affect Adjective Check List depression scores of depressed and nondepressed subjects in the one-chance and second-chance conditions.

trated in Figure 1, was also obtained. No other significant effects were found. Planned comparisons by one-tailed t tests among the means of the Depression × One-Chance–Second-Chance interaction showed the mean depression score of the depressed–one-chance subgroup ($M = 18.53$) to be significantly greater than both that ($M = 15.02$) of the nondepressed–one-chance subgroup, $t(45) = 2.69$, $p < .005$, and that ($M = 15.90$) of the depressed–second-chance subgroup, $t(36) = 1.85$, $p < .05$. No other significant differences among the means were found. As can be seen in Figure 1, the hypothesis that the second-chance condition would reduce the stress-related emotional reactions of depressed subjects was supported.

The analyses of variance of the anxiety and hostility scores yielded results quite similar to those obtained for the depression scores, that is, significant main effects of success–failure, $F(1, 74) = 9.82$, $p < .01$ (success $M = 7.87$; failure $M = 9.98$) for anxiety; $F(1, 74) = 17.46$; $p < .001$ (success $M = 8.00$; failure $M = 10.66$) for hostility; and Depression × One-Chance–Second-Chance interactions, $F(1, 74) = 4.06$, $p < .05$ for anxiety; $F(1, 74) = 3.57$, $p < .07$, for hostility. The hostility score analysis also yielded a main effect of depression, $F(1, 74) = 3.95$, $p < .05$ (depressed $M = 10.08$; nondepressed $M = 8.73$). No other effects approaching significance were found for these measures. The Depression × One-Chance–Second-Chance interactions for the anxiety and hostility scores were similar to the interaction obtained for the depression measure. That is, planned one-tailed t tests showed that the means of the depressed–one-chance subgroup (anxiety $M = 10.05$; hostility $M = 10.89$) were greater than those of both the nondepressed–one-chance subgroup (anxiety $M = 8.36$, hostility $M = 8.43$), $t(45)$ 1.71, $p < .06$, for the anxiety measure, $t(45)$ 2.59, $p < .01$, for the hostility measure, and those of the depressed – second-chance subgroup (anxiety $M = 8.21$; hostility $M = 9.26$), $t(36) = 1.71$, $p < .06$, for the anxiety measure; $t(36) = 1.57$, $p < .07$, for the hostility measure. No other differences among the means for the anxiety and hostility measures approached significance.

A composite emotionality score was also computed for each subject as the sum of the subject's depression, anxiety, and hostility scores. An unweighted-means analysis of variance of the composite emotionality scores again showed a significant effect of success–failure, $F(1, 74) = 14.78$, $p < .001$ (success $M = 30.71$; failure $M = 38.32$), and a significant Depression × One Chance–Second Chance interaction, $F(1, 74) = 6.55$, $p < .02$, but no other significant effects. Planned one-tailed t tests showed that the mean composite emotionality score of the depressed–one-chance subgroup ($M = 39.25$) was significantly greater than that of both the nondepressed–one-chance subgroup ($M = 31.56$), $t(45) = 2.69$, $p < .005$, and the depressed–second-chance subgroup ($M = 32.70$), $t(36) = 2.15$, $p < .01$. No other significant differences among the means were found.

Discussion

The results of this research demonstrated that depressed subjects were less depressed, anxious, hostile after completing a goal attainment task when that task was preceded by second-chance instructions than when the task ostensibly represented a single opportunity to attain the goal in question. In addition, depressed subjects were more emotional than nondepressed subjects following the one-chance task but not following the second-chance task. Apparently, the second-chance redefinition of the task served to prevent the emotionality engendered in depressed subjects by the anagram task under one-chance conditions. This prophylactic effect of a second-chance redefinition of the task indicates that depressed subjects were not particularly pessimistic about their prospects for success in the undefined second-chance task. Hence, the present results are not in accord with contemporary cognitive theories that view depressed persons as generally pessimistic (Abramson et al., 1978; Beck, 1976).

Why were depressed subjects more emotional than nondepressed subjects following the one-chance task? It is possible that this result may have partly reflected a general tendency of depressed subjects to obtain higher scores on the MAACL. However, because second-chance instructions resulted in relatively reduced emotionality among depressed subjects, the greater emotionality of one-chance depressives appears to have been due at least partly to a reaction to the anagram task. It will be recalled that the anagram task required subjects to solve each anagram in a brief time period; further, subjects were given three difficult anagrams during the first six trials so that all subjects experienced at least some failure on individual anagrams. It is likely that the greater emotionality of one-chance depressives resulted from the cumulative effects of the time pressure and occasional failure on individual anagrams. The results, therefore, suggest that the anagram task was more stressful for depressed subjects than nondepressed subjects under one-chance conditions but not under second-chance conditions.

To the extent that this interpretation is correct, it raises the question of the nature of the cognitions by which the emotionality of depressed subjects might have been reduced in the second-chance condition, in addition to contraindicating the generality of depressive pessimism.

Although the present study was not designed to answer this question, one ad hoc hypothesis about the nature of this process can be formulated from an observation made by Beck (1976), who has noted that the depressed patient is preoccupied with ideas such as "The game is over . . . . I don't have a second chance. Life has passed me by . . . . It's too late to do anything about it" (p. 118). This observation, considered in the light of the present results, suggests that depressed persons may experience stress because they are prone to believe that important goals they pursue must be attained by means of a single effort and that the absence of reward associated with potential failure may be permanent and irreversible. The prevention of stress in the second-chance condition can be viewed from this perspective as having occurred simply because the second-chance instructions made the possibility of future reward salient for depressed subjects.

In the present study the failure condition, as expected, resulted in greater emotionality than success; success–failure, however, did not interact significantly with depression. The finding that depressed subjects did not show a greater reaction than nondepressed subjects to failure to attain the goal is in accord with other results based on self-report data but is not consistent with results based on psychophysiological measures of emotionality (cf. Golin et al., 1977).

It should be noted that the design of the present study did not include a nonnormal, nondepressed group. Hence, the finding that second-chance instructions reduced the emotionality of depressives cannot be viewed as necessarily uniquely characteristic of depressed persons relative to other nonnormal groups. Further, since the subjects in this research were mildly to moderately depressed college students, the extent to which the current findings are applicable to a clinical population with its various possible subgroups (see Huesmann, 1978) also remains an open question.

In summary, the present research demonstrated that informing depressed subjects about a second chance to obtain a goal resulted in less emotionality consequent to their first try at attaining the goal. This finding was not in agreement with the view that depressed persons are generally pessimistic. The results suggest, as a basis for further study, the hypothesis that depressed persons may perceive the possibility of failure as particularly stressful, because they believe that goals they pursue must be attained on their first attempt.

References

Abramson, L. Y., Seligman, M. E. P., & Teasdale, J. D. Learned helplessness in humans: Critique and reformulation. *Journal of Abnormal Psychology*, 1978, *87*, 49–74.

Beck, A. T. *Depression:* New York: Hoeber, 1967.

Beck, A. T. *Cognitive therapy and the emotional disorders.* New York: International Universities Press, 1976.

Bumberry, W., Oliver, J. M., & McClure, J. N. Validation of the Beck Depression Inventory using psychiatric estimate as the criterion. *Journal of Consulting and Clinical Psychology*, 1978, *46*, 150–155.

Geen, R. G. *Personality—The skein of behavior.* St. Louis, Mo.: Mosby, 1976.

Goldfried, M. R., Linehan, M. M., & Smith, J. L. Reduction of test anxiety through cognitive restructuring. *Journal of Consulting and Clinical Psychology*, 1978, *46*, 32–39.

Golin, S., Hartman, S. A., Klatt, E. N., Munz, K., & Wolfgang, G. L. Effects of self-esteem manipulation on arousal and reactions to sad models in depressed and nondepressed college students. *Journal of Abnormal Psychology*, 1977, *86*, 435–439.

Huesmann, L. R. Cognitive processes and models of depression. *Journal of Abnormal Psychology*, 1978, *87*, 194–198.

Tresselt, M. E., & Mayzner, M. S. Normative solution times for a sample of 134 solution words and 378 associated anagrams. *Psychonomic Monograph Supplements*, 1966, *1*, 293–298.

Zuckerman, M., Lubin, B., & Robins, S. Validation of the Multiple Affect Adjective Check List in clinical situations. *Journal of Consulting Psychology*, 1965, *29*, 594.

Article Review Form at end of book.

Identify the path by which negative affect influences mood disorders.
Comment on the theme of "autonomic arousal" in your response.

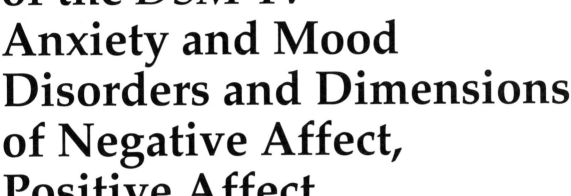

Structural Relationships among Dimensions of the *DSM-IV* Anxiety and Mood Disorders and Dimensions of Negative Affect, Positive Affect, and Autonomic Arousal

Timothy A. Brown

Center for Anxiety and Related Disorders

Bruce F. Chorpita

University of Hawaii

David H. Barlow

Center for Anxiety and Related Disorders

Using outpatients with anxiety and mood disorders (N = 350), the authors tested several models of the structural relationships of dimensions of key features of selected emotional disorders and dimensions of the tripartite model of anxiety and depression. Results supported the discriminant validity of the 5 symptom domains examined (mood disorders; generalized anxiety disorder, GAD; panic disorder; obsessive–compulsive disorder; social phobia). Of various structural models evaluated, the best fitting involved a structure consistent with the tripartite model (e.g., the higher order factors, negative affect and positive affect, influenced emotional disorder factors in the expected manner). The latent factor, GAD, influenced the latent factor, autonomic arousal, in a direction consistent with recent laboratory findings (autonomic suppression). Findings are discussed in the context of the growing literature on higher order trait dimensions (e.g., negative affect) that may be of considerable importance to the understanding of the pathogenesis, course, and co-occurrence of emotional disorders.

Over the past few decades, the number of diagnostic categories has increased markedly with each edition of the major classification systems for mental disorders (e.g., the *Diagnostic and Statistical Manual of Mental Disorders, DSM,* and the *International Classification of Diseases,* World Health Organization, 1993). For instance, with regard to the anxiety disorders alone, only 3 relevant categories existed in the second edition of the *DSM* (*DSM–II,* American Psychiatric Association, 1968), compared with the 12 categories that currently exist in the fourth edition of this system (*DSM–IV,* American Psychiatric Association, 1994). This increase could be viewed as signifying greater precision in the classification of disorders. However, many researchers (e.g., Andrews, 1996) have expressed concern that the expansion of our nosologies has come at the expense of less empirical

"Structural Relationships among Dimensions of the *DSM-IV* Anxiety and Mood Disorders and Dimensions of Negative Affect, Positive Affect, and Autonomic Arousal," by Timothy A. Brown, Bruce F. Chorpita, and David H. Barlow, *Journal of Abnormal Psychology,* 107 (2), 1998, pp. 179–192. Copyright © 1998 by the American Psychological Association. Reprinted with permission.

consideration of shared or overlapping features of emotional disorders that, relative to unique features of specific disorders, may have far greater significance in the understanding of the prevention, etiology, and course of disorders, and in predicting their response to treatment.

Of further concern is the possibility that our classification systems have become overly precise to the point that they are now erroneously distinguishing symptoms and disorders that actually reflect inconsequential variations of broader, underlying syndromes. Findings indicating that a variety of *DSM* disorders respond similarly to the same drug or psychosocial treatment have been offered in support of this position (e.g., Hudson & Pope, 1990; Tyrer et al., 1988). Moreover, consistent findings of high comorbidity among anxiety and mood disorders (T. A. Brown & Barlow, 1992), as well as emerging data that comorbid diagnoses often remit after psychosocial treatment of another anxiety disorder (Borkovec, Abel, & Newman, 1995; T. A. Brown, Antony, & Barlow, 1995), may also be reflective of poor discriminant validity of current classifications. However, conclusions about the validity of current classification systems cannot be drawn from the descriptive evidence of high rates of co-occurrence and covariation among disorders, given the multiple conceptual explanations for diagnostic comorbidity (cf. Blashfield, 1990; Frances, Widiger, & Fyer, 1990). Indeed, these explanations are sufficiently wide-ranging to either support or invalidate present nosologies (e.g., supportive explanation: two disorders co-occur because they share the same diathesis or because the features of one disorder act as risk factors for another disorder; nonsupportive explanation: high comorbidity is due to artificial separation of a broader syndrome or unnecessary overlap in definitional criteria).

Of studies that bear on the validation of the classification of anxiety and mood disorders, the majority have been conducted at the diagnostic level (e.g., family and twin studies; Andrews, Stewart, Morris-Yates, Holt, & Henderson, 1990; Kendler, Neale, Kessler, Heath, & Eaves, 1992) or have examined dimensional fea-

tures within a diagnostic category (e.g., psychometric evaluations of constituent features within a *DSM* disorder; Marten et al., 1993). As we have discussed at length elsewhere (T. A. Brown, 1996; T. A. Brown & Chorpita, 1996), the categorical approach to analysis has many limitations (cf. Livesley, Schroeder, Jackson, & Jang, 1994). For instance, studies conducted at the diagnostic level (e.g., comorbidity, genetic or familial aggregation, across-diagnosis comparisons) are restricted by their adherence to the disorders defined by the classification system; that is, by using diagnoses as the units of analysis, researchers are implicitly accepting or are bound to the nosology they are evaluating. Moreover, in view of evidence that anxiety and depression symptoms operate on a continuum, analyses at the diagnostic level rely largely on data that do not reflect the dimensional nature of these features.[1] Categorization of dimensional variables usually forfeits meaningful information by artificially (and often erroneously) collapsing variability above and below an arbitrary threshold (e.g., presence vs. absence of a *DSM–IV* disorder). Conversely, if assessment were performed at the dimensional level, the interrelationships among symptoms and syndromes could be examined, as could the extent to which the latent structure of these features corresponds to the structure forwarded by major classification systems such as *DSM–IV*.

Although this form of analysis has occurred in some areas of psychopathology (e.g., personality disorders; Moldin, Rice, Erlenmeyer-Kimling, & Squires-Wheeler, 1994), research of this nature for the anxiety and mood disorders has been sparse. However, a recent example in the area of anxiety and mood disorders is a study by Zinbarg and Barlow (1996). In this study, an exploratory factor analysis of various questionnaires of features of anxiety disorders produced a factor structure that was largely consistent with the *DSM–III–R* (*DSM*, 3rd ed., rev.; American Psychiatric Association, 1987) nosology (i.e., Social Anxiety, Generalized Dysphoria, Agoraphobia, Fear of Fear, Obsessions and Compulsions, Simple Fears). Support

for *DSM–III–R* was also provided by discriminant function analyses indicating that selected diagnostic groups (defined by principal diagnoses established by structured interviews) evidenced characteristic profiles in factor scores generated from a higher order factor analysis. Although encouraging, as noted by Zinbarg and Barlow, these findings were limited by the preponderant use of self-report measures (e.g., method variance could account, in part, for the structure observed) and the poor representation of mood disorders (e.g., depressive symptoms were assessed by a single measure with a scale under psychometric development). The latter limitation is noteworthy given evidence that mood disorders (i.e., major depression, dysthymia) may pose greater boundary problems for certain anxiety disorders than do other anxiety disorders (cf. T. A. Brown, Marten, & Barlow, 1995; T. A. Brown, Anson, & DiBartolo, 1996).

Unfortunately, specific disorders are often evaluated in isolation (Watson, Clark, & Harkness, 1994). For instance, the associated symptom criterion for *DSM–IV* generalized anxiety disorder was revised (i.e., autonomic arousal symptoms were eliminated) without empirical consideration of how this might further obfuscate its boundary with the mood disorders (T. A. Brown, Barlow, & Liebowitz, 1994). Comprehensive evaluations of the structure and construct validity of anxiety disorders should entail features of both anxiety and depression given the strong relationship and potential overlap of these domains (cf. Kendall & Watson, 1989).

Indeed, although anxiety and depression have historically been regarded as distinct at the conceptual level, dimensional measures of these constructs have evidenced considerable overlap (L. A. Clark & Watson, 1991; Kendall & Watson, 1989). Such findings, as well as data on the high co-occurrence at the syndromal level, have led investigators to question whether clinical anxiety and depression are in fact empirically distinct phenomena. On the basis of a review of the literature, L. A. Clark and Watson (1991) concluded that although anxiety and depression share a significant nonspecific component encompassing general affective distress and other common symptoms, the two constructs can be distinguished by certain unique features. L. A. Clark and Watson proposed a tripartite structure of anxiety and depression consisting of general distress or negative affect (shared by anxiety and depression), physiological hyperarousal (specific to anxiety), and an absence of positive affect (specific to depression). Sophisticated studies have begun to emerge in support of the tripartite structure (e.g., Joiner, Catanzaro, & Laurent, 1996; Watson, Clark, et al., 1995), though most of this work has been in analogue samples or clinical samples in which anxiety and mood disorders were not highly represented (Joiner, 1996; Watson, Weber, et al., 1995).

Nevertheless, in addition to explicating the shared and distinctive features of anxiety and depression, the tripartite model may have considerable importance in the understanding of the pathogenesis of anxiety and mood disorders. For instance, the dimension of negative affect may represent a key vulnerability factor for the development of both anxiety and depression (L. A. Clark, Watson, & Mineka, 1994; Watson & Clark, 1984; Watson et al., 1994). The collective evidence indicates that negative emotionality and related constructs (e.g., neuroticism) are heritable and temporally stable (e.g., Costa & McCrae, 1988; Tellegen et al., 1988; Watson & Clark, 1984). Ultimately, the construct of negative affect may prove empirically consistent with conceptual models (e.g., Barlow, Chorpita, & Turovsky, 1996) and genetic evidence (e.g., Kendler et al., 1992) suggesting that although differentiation among anxiety and mood disorders is warranted (e.g., the disorders differ on important dimensions that have implications for treatment), these syndromes are closely related because they share common diatheses (i.e., biological or trait vulnerabilities). Moreover, these positions provide a compelling account for the high rates of comorbidity observed among anxiety and mood disorders (i.e., the disorders co-occur because of the influence of the same underlying, causal factors). Similarly, low positive affect may op-

erate as a vulnerability dimension specific to depression, although existing data are less compelling relative to the accumulated knowledge on negative affect. Current data suggest that the third component of the tripartite model, autonomic arousal, may not be reflective of a trait vulnerability dimension of emotional disorders, although further research is needed (L. A. Clark, Watson, & Mineka, 1994).

With these issues in mind, the present study had several aims. Using a large sample of patients with anxiety and mood disorders ($N = 350$) who were assessed with a variety of self-report and clinician rating measures, it was predicted that confirmatory factor analysis would support a factor structure that corresponded to the *DSM–IV* typology of selected disorders (panic disorder, generalized anxiety disorder, social phobia, obsessive–compulsive disorder, and mood disorder) over models in which disorders were collapsed. After conducting analyses that were expected to confirm a factor structure consistent with the tripartite model, we comparatively evaluated structural models of the relationships among the *DSM–IV* disorders and tripartite factors. Of these models, it was predicted that the best fitting would entail the following: (a) significant paths from a higher order factor, Negative Affect, to each of the *DSM–IV* disorder factors, in accord with theory and evidence that negative affect represents a vulnerability dimension common to the anxiety and mood disorders (cf. Watson et al., 1994); (b) a significant path from the higher order factor, Positive Affect, to *DSM–IV* Depression, on the basis of evidence that low positive affect is a feature specific to depression and may act as a diathesis to mood disorders; and (c) paths from the *DSM–IV* anxiety disorder factors, but not from *DSM–IV* Depression, to the lower order factor of Autonomic Arousal that are significant and associated with good model fit (consistent with the prediction of the tripartite model that although autonomic arousal is not likely to be a trait vulnerability dimension, it distinguishes the anxiety disorders from the mood disorders; cf. L. A. Clark, Watson, & Mineka, 1994).

Method

Participants

Participants were 350 patients presenting for assessment and treatment at the Center for Stress and Anxiety Disorders, University at Albany, State University of New York. Women constituted the larger portion of the sample (61.7%); the average age of the sample was 35.56 years ($SD = 10.96$, range = 18–64).[2] Diagnoses were established with the Anxiety Disorders Interview Schedule for *DSM–IV*. Lifetime Version (ADIS-IV-L; Di Nardo, Brown, & Barlow, 1994), a structured interview designed to comprehensively evaluate current and lifetime *DSM–IV* anxiety, mood, and substance use disorders, as well as selected somatoform disorders (e.g., hypochondriasis); it was also designed to be a screen for the presence of other major disorders (e.g., psychosis). Findings of an initial study ($N = 72$) of the diagnostic reliability of the ADIS-IV-L for principal *DSM–IV* anxiety and mood disorders (i.e., calculated on the basis of two independent interviews) indicated good to excellent levels of interrater agreement (Di Nardo, Brown, Lawton, & Barlow, 1995; κ = .93 for panic disorder and panic disorder with agoraphobia, 1.00 for specific phobia, .83 for generalized anxiety disorder, .90 for obsessive–compulsive disorder, .64 for social phobia, .85 for mood disorder, either major depression or dysthymia). When the patient was deemed to have met criteria for two or more diagnoses, the principal diagnosis was the one that received the highest ADIS-IV-L clinical severity rating (CSR; a 9-point scale ranging from 0, *none*, to 8, *very severely disturbing/disabling*) that indicated the diagnostician's judgment of the degree of distress and interference in functioning associated with the diagnosis. Patients' *DSM–IV* principal diagnoses were as follows: panic disorder with or without agoraphobia ($n = 120$), generalized anxiety disorder ($n = 30$), social phobia ($n = 52$), specific phobia ($n = 30$), obsessive–compulsive disorder ($n = 22$), mood disorder (collapsed across major depressive disorder and dysthymia, n = 26), other (e.g., post-traumatic stress disorder, anxiety disorder not otherwise specified, co-principal diagnoses; n = 70).

Per guidelines of ADIS-IV-L administration and scoring, disorders that met or surpassed the threshold for a formal *DSM–IV* diagnosis were assigned CSRs of 4 (*definitely disturbing /disabling*) or higher (i.e., clinical diagnoses). When the key features of a disorder were present but were not extensive or severe enough to warrant a formal *DSM–IV* diagnosis (or for *DSM–IV* disorders in partial remission), CSRs of 1 to 3 were assigned (subclinical diagnoses). When no features of a given disorder were present, CSRs of 0 were assigned. For the five disorders examined in the present study, the total frequency of their occurrence at the clinical level was as follows: mood disorder (n = 137), generalized anxiety disorder (n = 93), panic disorder/agoraphobia (n = 166), obsessive–compulsive disorder (n = 36), and social phobia (n = 115).

Model Indicators

ADIS-IV-L ratings and questionnaires were collected and analyzed as indicators for the latent variables examined in the structural and measurement models. Latent factors were the *DSM–IV* disorders of Depression (DEP), Generalized Anxiety Disorder (GAD), Panic Disorder/Agoraphobia (PD/A), Obsessive–Compulsive Disorder (OCD), and Social Phobia (SOC); tripartite model latent factors were Negative Affect (NA), Positive Affect (PA), and Autonomic Arousal (AA).

ADIS-IV-L. ADIS-IV-L CSRs were used as indicators for each of the five disorders evaluated: DEP (collapsed across major depression, dysthymia, and depression not otherwise specified), GAD, PD/A, OCD, and SOC. In many sections of the ADIS-IV-L, diagnosticians made dimensional ratings (0–8 scales) of the key features of the disorder in question, irrespective of whether the disorder was ultimately assigned. These ratings were available for all patients as indicators for the latent variables GAD, OCD, and SOC. In the GAD section of the ADIS-IV-L, clinicians made excessiveness ratings for seven common worry spheres (e.g., minor

matters, family, finances), using a 0 (*no worry*) to 8 (*constantly worried*) scale. In the OCD section, nine obsessions (e.g., doubting, contamination, nonsensical impulses) were rated on a 0 (*never/no distress*) to 8 (*constantly/extreme distress*) persistence and distress scale. In this section, the frequency of six common compulsions (e.g., counting, checking, washing) was also rated on a 0 (*never*) to 8 (*constantly*) scale. In the SOC section, patients' fear of 13 social situations was rated using a 0 (*no fear*) to 8 (*very severe fear*) scale. For each set of ratings, average scores were used as indicators in the various models.

Depression Anxiety Stress Scales (DASS: S. H. Lovibond & P. F. Lovibond, 1995). The DASS is a 42-item instrument measuring current (over the past week) symptoms of depression, anxiety, and stress. The three psychometrically distinct scales consist of 14 items each, which are rated on a scale from 0 (*did not apply to me at all*) to 3 (*applied to me very much, or most of the time*); the range of scores for each scale is 0–42. The DASS–Depression and DASS–Anxiety scales were used as indicators for the latent variables *DSM–IV* DEP and AA, respectively. The DASS–Depression scale consists of items emphasizing dysphoria, hopelessness, self-deprecation, lack of interest and involvement, and so forth. The DASS–Anxiety scale consists of items assessing autonomic arousal and fearfulness. Large-sample studies of clinical and non-clinical participants have provided strong support for the psychometric properties of the DASS (e.g., T. A. Brown, Chorpita, Korotitsch, & Barlow, 1997; P. F. Lovibond & S. H. Lovibond, 1995).

Beck Anxiety and Depression Inventories (BAI, BDI; Beck & Steer, 1987, 1990). The BAI and BDI are widely used measures of current (over the past week) anxiety and depression. Both scales consist of 21 items, which are responded to on a 0–3 scale. Total scores range from 0 to 63. The BDI and BAI were used as indicators for the latent variables of *DSM–IV* DEP and AA, respectively. Guided by results of a factor analysis (T. A. Brown et al., 1996) indicating a two-factor solution (Cognitive–Affective,

Nonspecific–Somatic), the BDI was scored using only the 10 items that loaded on the factor deemed to be specific to the key features of mood disorders (i.e., the Cognitive–Affective factor: Items 1–9 and 13; e.g., depressed mood, sense of hopelessness, feelings of failure). Thus, this rescoring eliminated nonspecific items of general distress and negative affect (e.g., irritability, sleeplessness, fatigability) in line with our objective to use indicators of key features of the selected *DSM–IV* constructs under study.

Albany Panic and Phobia Questionnaire (APPQ; Rapee, Craske, & Barlow, 1995). The APPQ is a 27-item measure of situational interoceptive fear. Patients responded to items using a 0 (*no fear*) to 8 (*extreme fear*) scale, on the basis of how much fear they would expect to experience if they encountered the situation or activity during the next week. These items form three subscales: Agoraphobia (APPQ-A), composed of 9 items reflecting common agoraphobic situations (e.g., "going long distances from home alone"); Social Phobia (APPQ-S), composed of 10 items representing situations that can cause social phobia (e.g., "meeting strangers"); and Interoceptive (APPQ-I), composed of 8 items measuring fear of activities that cause physical sensations (e.g., "playing a vigorous sport"). Evidence from clinical samples supports the reliability, factor structure, and convergent and discriminant validity of the APPQ (Rapee et al., 1995). The APPQ-A and APPQ-I scales were used as indicators of the latent variable *DSM–IV* PD/A. The APPQ-S scale was used as an indicator of the latent variable *DSM–IV* SOC.

Anxiety Sensitivity Index (ASI; Peterson & Reiss, 1992). The ASI is a widely used measure of the construct of anxiety sensitivity—fear of the symptoms of anxiety. It consists of 16 items, which are responded to on a 0–4 scale, yielding a possible range of scores between 0 and 64. The ASI was used as an indicator for the latent variable *DSM–IV* PD/A.

Penn State Worry Questionnaire (PSWQ; Meyer, Miller, Metzger, & Borkovec, 1990). The PSWQ is a widely used measure of the trait on worry. It consists of 16 items, which are rated on a 1–5 scale; total scores range from 16 to 90. Evidence from clinical and nonclinical samples supports the reliability, unidimensional structure, and convergent and discriminant validity of the PSWQ (T. A. Brown, Antony, & Barlow, 1992; Meyer et al., 1990). The PSWQ was used as an indicator of the latent variable *DSM–IV* GAD.

Worry Domains Questionnaire (WDQ; Tallis, Eysenck, & Mathews, 1992). The WDQ is a 25-item measure assessing the extent to which a person worries about various content areas (e.g., relationship, finances). Items are rated on a 0 *(not at all)* to 4 *(extremely)* scale. In addition to a total score, the items of the WDQ can be scored into five subscales: Relationships, Lack of Confidence, Aimless Future, Work, and Financial (5 items each). Although initial evidence, primarily from nonclinical samples, indicates that the WDQ has favorable psychometric properties (Tallis, Davey, & Bond, 1994), recent data from our laboratory (T. A. Brown et al., 1996) have indicated that some WDQ items have low convergent and discriminant validity (e.g., items from the Aimless Future scale are more strongly associated with hopelessness and DEP than with GAD worry). On the basis of these findings, only one subscale (Work) was selected from the WDQ as an indicator of the latent variable *DSM–IV* GAD.

Maudsley Obsessive–Compulsive Inventory (MOCI: Hodgson & Rachman, (1977). The MOCI is a widely used measure of obsessive–compulsive symptoms. It consists of 30 items that are responded to using a true–false scale. The MOCI provides five scores: Total Obsessional Score, Checking, Washing, Slowness–Repetition, and Doubting–Conscientiousness. However, some items contribute to more than one subscale (e.g., some items from the Slowness–Repetition scale are also used in the Checking and Washing scales). In the present study, the Checking scale (MOCI-C, 9 items) and the Doubting–Conscientiousness scale (MOCI-D, 7 items) were used as indicators of the latent variable *DSM–IV* OCD, because these scales do not possess overlapping items (item overlap would artificially enhance loading on the same factor) and because these

subscales evidence favorable psychometric properties (Emmelkamp, 1988).

Social Interaction Anxiety Scales (SIAS; Mattick, Peters, & Clarke, 1989). The SIAS is a 20-item measure of social interaction anxiety (i.e., distress when initiating and maintaining conversations with friends, strangers, potential mates, etc.). Items are rated using a 0 *(not at all characteristic or true of me)* to 4 *(extremely characteristic or true of me)* scale. Total scores range from 0 to 80. Several studies have provided evidence attesting to the sound psychometric properties of the SIAS (e.g., E. J. Brown et al., 1997; Mattick et al., 1989). The SIAS was used as an indicator of the latent variable *DSM–IV* SOC.

Self-Consciousness Scale (SCS; Fenigstein, Scheier, & Buss, 1975). The SCS is a 23-item measure that yields three subscale scores: (a) Private Self-Consciousness, (b) Public Self-Consciousness, and (c) Social Anxiety. Items are rated on a 0 *(extremely uncharacteristic)* to 4 *(extremely characteristic)* scale. Although all three scales are widely used and possess favorable psychometric qualities (e.g., Fenigstein et al., 1975; Hope & Heimberg, 1988), only the 6-item Social Anxiety scale was selected for use in the present study, given its appropriateness as an indicator for the latent variable *DSM–IV* SOC.

Positive and Negative Affect Scales (PANAS; Watson, Clark, & Tellegen, 1988). The PANAS is a 20-item measure of two primary dimensions of mood: Positive Affect (PANAS-P, 10 items) and Negative Affect (PANAS-N, 10 items). Items are rated on a 1 *(very slightly or not at all)* to 5 *(extremely)* scale (total scores range from 10 to 50). The PANAS can be administered with various instructional sets reflecting different time frames (e.g., state vs. trait versions); in the present study, patients responded to PANAS items on the basis of how they felt in general. The PANAS-P and PANAS-N were used as indicators for the latent variables PA and NA, respectively.

Approach to Structural Modeling

The sample variance–covariance matrix of the aforementioned indicators was analyzed using a linear struc-

tural relations program and a maximum-likelihood solution (LISREL 8.12a; Jöreskog & Sörbom, 1993). In models involving more than one latent X variable (e.g., the five-factor model of *DSM–IV* disorders), the X factors were permitted to be intercorrelated. Goodness-of-fit was evaluated using the following: the comparative-fit index (CFI; Bentler, 1990), the incremental-fit index (IFI; Bollen, 1989), the root mean square error of approximation (RMSEA; Steiger, 1990), and the goodness-of-fit index (GFI; Bentler & Bonett, 1980). Multiple indices were selected because they provide different information for evaluating model fit (i.e., absolute fit, fit adjusting for model parsimony, fit relative to a null model); used together, these indices provide a more conservative and reliable evaluation of the various models (cf. Jaccard & Wan, 1996).

When competing models were nested (e.g., various measurement models of the *DSM–IV* anxiety and mood disorders), comparative fit was evaluated using nested chi-square tests. When competing models were not nested, comparative fit could not be evaluated using significance testing.[3] Therefore, the following criteria were used in the identification of best model fit: (a) overall fit (e.g., CFI, IFI); (b) the lowest chi-square with the most model parsimony (i.e., fewest number of paths), as quantified by Akaike's information criterion (AIC; Akaike, 1987); and (c) interpretability and strength of the various parameter estimates.

Results
Measurement Models for the DSM–IV Disorder Factors

Confirmatory factor analysis was performed to test the hypothesis that a five-factor model (corresponding to the *DSM–IV* disorders DEP, GAD, PD/A, OCD, and SOC) would provide an acceptable fit for the data, in comparison to a unifactorial model representing a general anxious–depressive syndrome and a two-factor model corresponding to depression and anxiety disorders (i.e., GAD, PD/A, OCD, and SOC collapsed under a single factor). Each *DSM–IV* latent variable was associated with three or more indicators, with at least one clinician rating and one questionnaire indicator (see Table 1). In all models, the theta-delta matrix was programmed to estimate correlated error among the ADIS-IV-L ratings within a given DSM–IV disorder (e.g., correlated error between ADIS-IV-L CSR-GAD and ADIS-IV-L Worry) on the basis of the expectation that individual symptom ratings for a disorder would influence the CSR that was ultimately assigned to it.

First, the five-factor model was fitted to the data. Fit indices indicated that this model provided an acceptable fit to the data $\chi^2(174)$, $N = 350) = 475.18$, CFI = .92, IFI = .92, RMSEA = .070, GFI = .89 ($N = 350$ for all chi-square analyses reported). However, inspection of modification indices and standardized residuals suggested that model fit could be improved if correlated error was estimated between the MOCI-C and MOCI-D scales, and among the three APPQ scales (highest modification index = 24.88). Thus, the five-factor model was refitted to the data with these adjustments (specifying correlated method variance among subscales). Fit indices for the revised model indicated improved fit, $\chi^2(170) = 401.20$, CFI = .94, IFI = .94, RMSEA = .062, GFI = .90. This was confirmed by a statistically significant decrease in the chi-square value, $\chi^2_{\text{diff}}(4) = 73.98$, $p < .001$. Factor loadings (completely standardized estimates from the lambda-X matrix) are presented in Table 1. All of these loadings, as well as the specified correlated errors (which ranged from .11 to .51), were statistically significant.

Next, the one-factor model was fitted to the data; this model included the same error theory (correlated error among certain indicators) used in the revised five-factor model. This model fit the data poorly, $\chi^2(180) = 1,623.65$; a nested chi-square test indicated that this model degraded fit significantly, $\chi^2_{\text{diff}}(10) = 1,222.45$, $p < .001$. Whereas the two-factor model improved fit relative to the one-factor model, $\chi^2_{\text{diff}}(1) = 478.87$, $p < .001$, it too fit poorly and was inferior to the revised five-factor model, $\chi^2_{\text{diff}}(9) = 743.58$, $p < .001$.

Table 2 presents the intercorrelations among the DSM–IV disorder factors from the revised five-factor

Table 1 Factor Loadings (Completely Standardized Estimates) for the DSM–IV Disorder Measurement Model

Latent Factor and Measure	Factor Loading
DSM–IV Depression	
DASS-Depression	.86
Beck Depression Inventory (Items 1–9, 13)	.92
ADIS-IV-L CRS–Mood	.71
DSM–IV Generalized Anxiety Disorder	
Penn State Worry Questionnaire	.88
Worry Domains Questionnaire–Work	.61
ADIS-IV-L Worry	.59
ADIS-IV-L CSR-GAD	.41
DSM–IV Panic Disorder/Agoraphobia	
Anxiety Sensitivity Index	.86
APPQ–Interoceptive	.62
APPQ–Agoraphobia	.57
ADIS-IV-L CSR-PD/A	.61
DSM–IV Obsessive–Compulsive Disorder	
MOCI–Doubting	.87
MOCI–Checking	.94
ADIS-IV-L CSR-OC	.41
ADIS-IV-L Obsessions	.45
ADIS-IV-L Compulsions	.46
DSM–IV Social Phobia	
Social Interaction Anxiety Scale	.91
APPQ–Social	.85
Self-Consciousness Scale–Social Anxiety	.83
ADIS-IV-L CSR-SOC	.64
ADIS-IV-L Social Fear	.79

Note. DSM–IV = Diagnostic and Statistical Manual of Mental Disorders (4th ed.); DASS = Depression Anxiety Stress Scales; ADIS-IV-L = Anxiety Disorders Interview Schedule for DSM–IV: Lifetime version; CSR = clinical severity rating; CSR–Mood = ADIS-IV-L CSR of mood disorders (major depression, dysthymia, and depression not otherwise specified); ADIS-IV-L Worry = average ADIS-IV-L rating of seven worry spheres; CSR-GAD = ADIS-IV-L CSR of generalized anxiety disorder; APPQ–Albany Panic and Phobia Questionnaire; CSR-PD/A = ADIS-IV-L CSR of panic disorder/agoraphobia; MOCI = Maudsley Obsessive–Compulsive Inventory; CSR-OCD–ADIS-IV-L CSR of obsessive–compulsive disorder; ADIS-IV-L Obsessions = average ADIS-IV-L rating of nine obsessions; ADIS-IV-L Compulsions = average AIDS-IV-L rating of six compulsions; CSR-SOC = ADIS-IV-L CSR of social phobia; ADS-IV-L Social Fear = average ADIS-IV-L rating of fear of 13 social situations.

model (i.e., completely standardized coefficients from the phi matrix). As can be seen in Table 2, the highest correlation between DSM–IV factors was for DEP and GAD (.63), consistent with previous evidence that generalized anxiety disorder may overlap more with the mood disorders than with its fellow anxiety disorders (cf. T. A. Brown et al., 1996;

T. A. Brown, Marten, & Barlow, 1995). This finding raised the possibility that model fit would not be degraded (or would perhaps be improved) if DEP and GAD were collapsed into a single factor. Accordingly, a four-factor model (DEP–GAD, PD/A, OCD, and SOC) was fitted to the data. A nested chi-square test indicated that this

Table 2

Zero-Order Intercorrelations Among the Five *DSM–IV* Disorder Latent Factors

Latent Factor	DEP	GAD	PD/A	OCD	SOC
DEP	—				
GAD	.63	—			
PD/A	.44	.50	—		
OCD	.43	.52	.29	—	
SOC	.39	.37	.22	.30	—

Note. Correlations are based on the results of the revised five-factor measurement model. *DSM–IV* = *Diagnostic and Statistical Manual of Mental Disorders* (4th ed.); DEP = depression (*DSM–IV* mood disorders); GAD = generalized anxiety disorder; PD/A = panic disorder with or without agoraphobia; OCD = obsessive–compulsive disorder; SOC = social phobia.

four-factor model produced a significant degradation in model fit, relative to the five-factor model, χ^2_{diff} (4) = 152.83, $p < .001$.[4]

Measurement Models for the Tripartite Model Factors

Prior to examining the various structural models involving the *DSM–IV* disorder and tripartite model factors, the structure of the tripartite factors was first evaluated with confirmatory factor analysis. Because the latent variables NA and PA were assessed with single indicators, the PANAS-N and PANAS-P were randomly split-halved for inclusion in these analyses (because of the need for at least two indicators per latent variable to prevent model underidentification). As noted earlier, the BAI and DASS-A were used as indicators for the latent variable AA. Three models were evaluated: (a) the predicted three-factor model (NA, PA, and AA), (b) a two-factor model (NA–PA and AA, given the possibility that the PANAS-N and PANAS-P would cluster together because they were derived from the same instrument), and (c) a one-factor model. The one- and two-factor solutions were poor fitting, $\chi^2(9) = 434.48$ and $\chi^2(8) = 317.69$, respectively. Conversely, the hypothesized three-factor model provided an excellent fit for the data, $\chi^2(6) = 3.83$, CFI = 1.00, IFI = 1.00, RMSEA = 0, GFI = 1.00. Each of the six indicators had strong and statistically significant loadings ($ps < .001$) on their respective latent factors: NA = .90, .86; PA = .98, .81; AA = .91 (BAI), .86 (DASS-A). The in-

tercorrelations among these factors (completely standardized estimates from the phi matrix) were –.35 (NA–PA), –.30 (PA–AA), and .77 (NA–AA; all $ps < .001$). To rule out the possibility that the strong correlation between the NA and AA factors indicated that these latent variables could be collapsed, a fourth model was fit to the data. This two-factor model (i.e., NA–AA and PA) resulted in a degradation in fit, thereby providing further support for the tripartite measurement model, $\chi^2_{\text{diff}}(3) = 117.51$, $p < .001$.

Structural Models Using the DSM–IV Disorder and Tripartite Factors

As noted earlier, of the various models involving structural relationships among the tripartite and *DSM–IV* disorder factors, it was predicted that the best fitting model would entail (a) significant paths from a higher order factor, NA, to each of the five *DSM–IV* disorder factors (and paths from NA to AA); (b) a significant path from a higher order factor, PA, to DEP; and (c) significant paths from GAD, PD/A, OCD, and SOC to AA ("hypothesized model"; see Figure 1). This model was viewed to be consistent with the following: (a) The general distress symptoms shared by the various anxiety and mood disorders are best conceptualized as trait NA, a chronic feature that represents a vulnerability dimension for the development of emotional disorders; (b) the influence of trait PA is specific to DEP; and (c) the anxiety disorders, but not

DEP, influence AA (i.e., the absence of a path from DEP to AA would not strain model fit because AA is specific to anxiety disorders). Although the hypothesized model contained a path from GAD to AA, it was uncertain whether this path would be significant given evidence that GAD and worry may be associated with autonomic suppression (e.g., Borkovec, Lyonfields, Wiser, & Diehl, 1993; Hoehn-Saric, McLeod, & Zimmerli, 1989); however, other data indicate that patients with GAD endorse autonomic symptoms frequently; e.g., T. A. Brown, Marten, & Barlow, 1995.

The hypothesized model was compared with two competing models (see Figure 1): (a) In Competing Model 1, the five *DSM–IV* disorder factors were specified as higher order factors, and the tripartite factors were specified as first-order factors (i.e., NA and PA, as well as AA, were influenced by the *DSM–IV* disorders), suggesting that although the tripartite model constructs characterize the shared (NA) and unique (PA and AA) symptoms of anxiety and depression, none represent trait dimensions that influence these disorders; and (b) in Competing Model 2, NA, PA, and AA were each specified as higher order factors, and the *DSM–IV* disorders were specified as first-order factors, signifying that in addition to NA and PA, AA was a traitlike variable that could predict variability in the *DSM–IV* disorder factors (this model was included because of empirical and conceptual uncertainty about whether, along with NA and PA, AA represents a trait vulnerability dimension of emotional disorders; L. A. Clark, Watson, & Mineka, 1994).

In both competing models, the patterns of paths between the tripartite and *DSM–IV* factors were the same (e.g., the *DSM–IV* anxiety disorder factors each had paths to AA, or vice versa). In all three models, the latent factors NA and PA were specified with single indicators (the full-scale PANAS-N and PANAS-P, respectively); however, measurement error was modeled in these factors by constraining the theta-delta and theta-epsilon matrices to predetermined values (i.e., estimates of error variance were calculated using internal consistency estimates of the PANAS-N and PANAS-P in the pre-

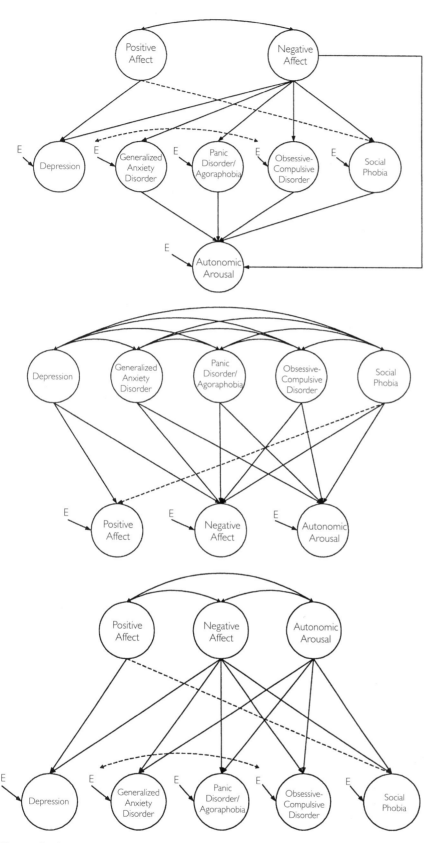

Figure 1. Structural models of *DSM–IV* disorder and tripartite model factors: hypothesized model (top), Competing Model 1 (middle), Competing Model 2 (bottom). Dotted lines indicate paths that were added after fit diagnostics of the initial model. *DSM–IV = Diagnostic and Statistical Manual of Mental Disorders* (4th ed.); E= residual.

sent sample).[5] Moreover, each of the structural models was evaluated with the error theory used in the *DSM–IV* measurement models (e.g., correlated error among the APPQ scales and between the MOCI-C and MOCI-D), and the theta-delta-epsilon matrix was programmed to estimate correlated error between the DASS–Anxiety and DASS–Depression scales (i.e., nonrandom measurement error attributable to subscales from the same measure).

Hypothesized Model

Indices of overall fit indicated that the hypothesized model provided a good fit for the data, $\chi^2(255) = 579.36$, CFI = .94, IFI = .94, RMSEA = .060, GFI = .89. Modification indices pertaining to the measurement aspect of the model indicated no points of ill fit due to the addition of the tripartite indicators to the five *DSM–IV* disorder factor model (e.g., despite a zero-order factor correlation between PD/A and AA of .89, see Table 3; lambda-*Y* modification indices for both AA indicators and the PD/A factor were 0.14). However, inspection of modification indices for various aspects of the structural model revealed two points of strain. First, these indices suggested that fit could be improved if a path were freed between GAD and OCD (modification index = 19.31 in both the beta and psi matrices). Second, a high modification index (21.53) was observed in the gamma matrix for the PA and SOC factors. Results suggesting an association between GAD and OCD were interpreted as consistent with earlier findings indicating that these syndromes may be neighboring disorders in the context of other anxiety disorders (e.g., because of the potential similarities or overlap in chronic worry and certain types of obsessions; cf. T. A. Brown, Moras, Zinbarg, & Barlow, 1993; Turner, Beidel, & Stanley, 1992). Although counter to our initial predictions, further review of the literature indicated that the second strain in model fit was in fact consistent with prior evidence that social phobia is associated with low PA (Amies, Gelder, & Shaw, 1983; Watson, Clark, & Carey, 1988). Thus, the hypothesized model was refitted to the data with the additions of a path estimating corre-

Table 3 Zero-Order Intercorrelations Among *DSM–IV* Disorder and Tripartite Model Latent Factors

Tripartite Model Factor	DSM–IV Disorder Factor				
	DEP	**GAD**	**PD/A**	**OCD**	**SOC**
NA	.77$_a$	.74$_a$	.65$_b$	.43$_c$	.41$_c$
PA	−.53$_a$	−.27$_c$	−.23$_{c,d}$	−.16$_d$	−.39$_b$
AA	.60$_b$	.48$_c$	.89$_a$	.31$_d$	.31$_d$

Note. Correlations were derived from the revised hypothesized structural model. Correlations sharing the same subscript letter do not differ in their relative magnitude as determined by the z test procedure (α = .05) presented by Meng, Rosenthal, and Rubin (1992); for example, although significantly (p < .05) different from PD/A, OCD, and SOC, the DEP and GAD factors do not differ in their strength of associations with NA. *DSM–IV* = *Diagnostic and Statistical Manual of Mental Disorders* (4th ed.); DEP = depression (*DSM–IV* mood disorders); GAD = generalized anxiety disorder; PD/A = panic disorder with or without agoraphobia; OCD = obsessive–compulsive disorder; SOC = social phobia; NA = negative affect; PA = positive affect; AA = autonomic arousal.

lated residuals between the GAD and OCD factors and a path from PA to SOC.

The revised hypothesized model is presented in Figure 2. The zero-order factor correlation matrix for the tripartite and *DSM*–IV disorder factors is presented in Table 3, along with the results of tests of the differential magnitude of the associations between the *DSM*–IV disorder factors and the tripartite factors. This model provided a significantly improved fit for the data, $\chi^2_{\text{diff}}(2) = 43.76$, $p < .001$. Overall fit indices were $\chi^2(253) = 535.60$, CFI = .95, IFI = .95, RMSEA = .057, GFI = .89. Inspection of modification indices and standardized residuals indicated no strains in the structural model. As shown in Figure 2, completely standardized paths from NA to the various *DSM*–IV disorder factors were of the expected relative magnitude (e.g., the highest paths from NA were to GAD and DEP), and all were statistically significant ($ps < .001$). As expected, a statistically significant ($ps < .001$) path was observed from PA to DEP (completely standardized estimate = −.29). A statistically significant path ($p < .001$) was also observed from PA to SOC (−.28). Consistent with the tripartite model, modification indices from the gamma matrix involving potential paths from PA to GAD, PD/A, and OCD were uniformly low (range = 0 to 0.47), which is indicative of a lack of relationship between PA and these disorders.

As suggested by the initial model, the residuals between the GAD and OCD factors were correlated significantly (.18, $p < .001$). Strong and statistically significant paths from PD/A and NA to AA were obtained (path coefficients = .67 and .50, respectively; $ps < .001$). It is interesting that a statistically significant ($p < .001$) path from GAD to AA was also observed; however, this path was negative (−.22), indicating that an increase in GAD was associated with a decrease in AA, despite the fact that the zero-order factor correlation between GAD and AA was positive (.48, see Table 3). Thus, a suppressor effect was operative in this aspect of the model: Specifically, the strong association between the predictors NA and GAD (zero-order factor correlation = .74) masked the true association between GAD and AA (cf. Cohen & Cohen, 1983). In other words, when variance from NA was removed, the true relationship between GAD and AA was elucidated (in this instance, the direction of the association was reversed).[6]

As shown in Figure 2, nonsignificant paths to AA were obtained for both OCD and SOC, a finding that was counter to expectation. However, consistent with our prediction and the tripartite model, results indicated that fit would not be improved if a path was added from DEP to AA (beta modification index = 2.46; standardized expected change = 0).

Competing Models

The two competing models were fitted to the data (incorporating the structural modifications suggested by the initial hypothesized model; e.g., the path linking PA and SOC) to determine whether the revised hypothesized model indeed best accounted for the interrelationships among the tripartite and *DSM*–IV disorder factors. Competing Model 1 (in which the *DSM*–IV disorder factors were predictors) generally fit the data well, $\chi^2(246) = 561.10$, CFI = .94, IFI = .94, RMSEA = .061, GFI = .89. However, although significance testing could not be used (i.e., the various models were not nested; see the Method section), it is interesting to note that relative to the hypothesized model, this model produced a higher chi-square value (561.10 vs. 535.60), despite having fewer degrees of freedom (246 vs. 253); AIC = 719.10 and 679.60 for Competing Model 1 and the hypothesized model, respectively. The reduction in degrees of freedom in Competing Model 1 was due to the specification of the *DSM*–IV disorder factors as predictors; thus, all correlations among these disorders (see Table 2) were estimated in the phi matrix. Therefore, it is surprising that Competing Model 1 produced an increase in chi square given that the intercorrelations among the *DSM*–IV disorder factors were fully modeled, especially in context of the more stringent hypothesized model, in which the intercorrelation among *DSM*–IV disorder factors could be accounted for only by their associations with NA and PA (and the correlated residuals of GAD and OCD). On the basis of these considerations, in tandem with the observation of nonsignificant paths between some *DSM*–IV disorder factors and NA (e.g., −.02 for OCD, .09 for SOC), Competing Model 1 was rejected because it was not equivalent or superior to the hypothesized model.

A similar result was obtained for Competing Model 2 (which specified all three tripartite dimensions as higher order factors to the *DSM*–IV disorder factors). Whereas this model generally fit the data well, $\chi^2(252) = 542.84$, CFI = .94, IFI = .94, RMSEA = .058, GFI = .89, compared with the hypothesized model it too produced a higher chi-square value (542.84 vs.

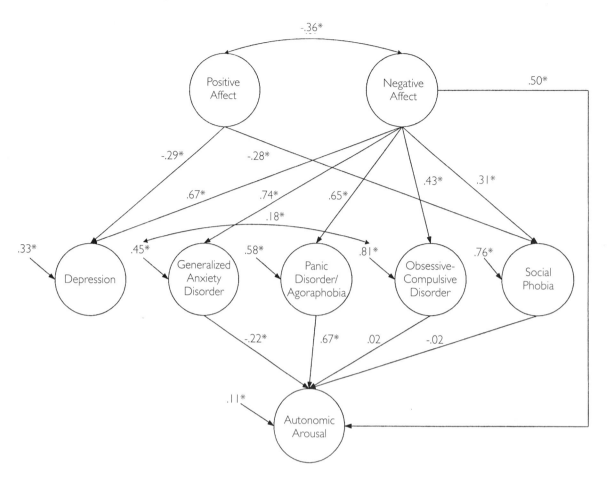

Figure 2. Completely standardized solution of hypothesized structural model—revised. *$p < .01$.

535.60) with fewer degrees of freedom (252 vs. 253); AIC = 688.84 and 679.60 for Competing Model 2 and the hypothesized model, respectively. Although associated with fewer counterintuitive path estimates than Competing Model 1 (though several poor estimates did exist; e.g., NA to PD/A = −.09), this model was also rejected because of its inferior interpretability and parsimony (i.e., higher chi-square and AIC values), relative to the hypothesized model.

Discussion

For the five *DSM–IV* anxiety and mood disorder constructs examined, confirmatory factor analysis of a variety of dimensional symptom measures provided empirical support for the discriminant validity of these disorders. While upholding the exploratory factor structure reported by Zinbarg and Barlow (1996), the present findings extend these prior results with the inclusion of model

indicators assessed by multiple methods (questionnaires, clinician ratings) and the inclusion of a *DSM–IV* mood-disorder latent factor. As expected from these analyses, the highest factor correlation observed was between GAD and DEP (.63), supporting previous contentions that relative to the other anxiety disorders, the features of generalized anxiety disorder have the most overlap with the mood disorders (in fact, the correlation between GAD and DEP was higher than the correlations between GAD and PD/A, between GAD and OCD, and between GAD and SOC). It is also interesting to note that the relative magnitudes of other zero-order factor correlations generated from the five-factor solution (see Table 2) were in accord with previously observed or hypothesized points of overlap among these disorders (e.g., the OCD factor had its strongest correlation with GAD; cf. T. A. Brown et al., 1993). Nevertheless, in addition to its superiority to

the one- and two-factor models, the five-factor model was significantly better fitting than a four-factor model (in which GAD and the mood disorders were collapsed as a single latent factor), thereby providing support for the distinction of these domains.

Although the five-factor *DSM–IV* disorder model fit the data well and was superior to competing models, these analyses could be viewed as a somewhat liberal test of the *DSM* structure given that most indicators assessed key features of the disorders (e.g., chronic worry, depressive affect) rather than potentially less distinguishable associated symptoms (e.g., the somatic symptoms of GAD and the mood disorders were not modeled). This issue seems less germane to three of the five disorders analyzed (PD/A, OCD, and SOC) because their *DSM–IV* definitions are based on key features and do not include associated symptom criteria. Yet it is likely that inclusion of associated symptoms for GAD and DEP would have increased the correlation between these latent factors (and would have degraded model fit unless double-loading indicators were specified), given the definitional overlap in many of these features (e.g., sleep disturbance, fatigue, restlessness). This potential problem in differential diagnosis is handled in two ways by *DSM–IV*: (a) a hierarchical rule specifying that GAD should not be assigned if its features occur exclusively during a mood disorder, and (b) to count toward GAD or a mood disorder, the associated symptoms must accompany the key features of the disorder (e.g., in GAD, worry is associated with sleep disturbance, restlessness, etc.).

Whereas the distinguishability of generalized anxiety disorder from other anxiety and mood disorders was supported by the superiority of the five-factor measurement model, these data also indicated that of the *DSM–IV* constructs examined, GAD evidenced the highest degree of overlap with the other *DSM–IV* disorder factors (i.e., the latent factor *DSM–IV* GAD consistently had the strongest zero-order correlations with other *DSM–IV* disorder factors; see Table 2). Moreover, at the zero-order level and in the best fitting structural model (see Figure 2); *DSM–IV* GAD evidenced a strong association with the nonspecific dimension of NA (.74). Although suggesting that the construct of *DSM–IV* GAD had poorer discriminant validity relative to other disorders, these collective findings could be viewed as consistent with conceptualizations of generalized anxiety disorder as the basic emotional disorder because it is composed of features (chronic worry, negative affect) that are present to varying degrees in all emotional disorders and that reflect key vulnerability dimensions of these syndromes (which also may account for the high comorbidity rates associated with this disorder; cf. T. A. Brown et al., 1994). In light of these findings and conceptual arguments, an important direction for future inquiry is the examination of the structural longitudinal relationships among dimensions of generalized anxiety disorder and dimensions of trait vulnerability (e.g., negative affect, neuroticism). This research would evaluate whether the features of generalized anxiety disorder are best subsumed under these personality dimensions (consistent with the view that *DSM–IV* generalized anxiety disorder reflects a trait of nonspecific vulnerability rather than an Axis I disorder) or whether generalized anxiety disorder represents a distinct *DSM–IV* Axis I type construct that along with (but to a greater extent than) other anxiety and mood disorders, is influenced by these higher order dimensions (T. A. Brown, in press).

Similarly, whereas the present findings support the distinguishability of the five *DSM–IV* constructs examined, these results should not be interpreted as bearing directly on the validity of the *DSM–IV* organizational scheme (i.e., the grouping of PD/A, GAD, OCD, etc. under the broad category of *anxiety disorders;* the grouping of major depression, dysthymia, etc. under the broad heading of *mood disorders).* In future research, a more comprehensive evaluation of the *DSM–IV* nosology would use confirmatory factor analyses of data in which all constituent criteria of the anxiety and mood disorders were dimensionalized, perhaps by specifying multiple-factor loadings for indicators of shared associated symptoms and single-factor loadings for key features. Moreover, the current results could be extended with the inclusion of indicators for additional disorders (e.g., posttraumatic stress disorder, specific phobia) and the use of hierarchical factor analysis to examine if the *DSM–IV* anxiety and mood disorder constructs load onto higher order factors in a manner consistent with the *DSM–IV* organizational scheme.

Despite being the most stringent of the three structural models involving the relationships of the *DSM–IV* disorder and tripartite dimensions, the hypothesized model produced the lowest chi-square and AIC values with the greatest degree of parsimony (i.e., the smallest number of paths). It could be argued that because chi-square and AIC values did not vary substantially in the models tested (e.g., χ^2 range = 535.60 to 561.10), fit was generally equivalent across models. However, substantial fluctuations in overall fit indices are not expected in instances in which small alterations are evaluated in the context of a large model with a good fit to the data. Such was the case in the present study in which minor, yet theoretically important, structural variations (in general, the *direction* but not the *existence* of paths varied across models) were evaluated within a good-fitting measurement model. As noted earlier, this underscores the importance of considering other parameters of fit besides indices of overall fit (e.g., model parsimony, interpretability of path coefficients). Even when these parameters were considered, the hypothesized model was regarded as superior to the competing models (e.g., it produced the lowest chi-square and AIC values even though the correlations among *DSM–IV* disorder factors could be accounted for in the model only by the paths from NA and PA). Nevertheless, the lack of marked differences in fit across models may have also been due, in part, to reciprocal relationships among some factors (e.g., NA may influence the *DSM–IV* disorders, which in turn influence NA; cf. L. A. Clark, Watson, & Mineka, 1994). This possibility could not be addressed in the present cross-sectional study because specification of reciprocal paths would have led to model underidentification. Evaluation of this speculation, as well as a more definitive analysis of negative and positive affect as dispositional vulnerability dimensions of the emotional disorders, awaits longitudinal investigation.

Nevertheless, the current analyses produced several interesting findings regarding the relationships among the tripartite model dimensions and the *DSM–IV* anxiety and mood disorders. It is noteworthy that the factor correlation between NA and PA (–.36) was quite consistent with prior findings (e.g., D. A. Clark, Steer, & Beck, 1994; Watson et al., 1988), indicating that the relationship between these dimensions is relatively stable across samples, instruments, and data analytic strategies. Consistent with the tripartite model in which negative affect is viewed as a factor common to anxiety and depression, all paths from NA to the *DSM–IV* disorder factors were statistically significant. The relative magnitudes of these paths were also concordant with prediction. For instance, the largest paths from NA (and zero-order factor correlations) were to GAD and DEP, factors that correspond to *DSM–IV* disorders that are often considered to have the strongest associations with negative affect. In addition, the smaller factor correlations and path coefficients observed between NA and certain *DSM–IV* factors (e.g., SOC) align with earlier evidence that the nature and strength of the relationship of negative affect may vary across the different anxiety disorders (L. A. Clark, Watson, & Mineka, 1994).

The notion that the tripartite factors may have differential relevance or relationships to the anxiety disorders was also observed in paths and correlations involving the latent variable of AA. Findings indicating degradations in model fit and interpretability when AA was specified as a higher order factor could be taken in support of prior conclusions that of the three tripartite factors, autonomic arousal is the least related to dimensions of personality (L. A. Clark, Watson, & Mineka, 1994). Consistent with current conceptualizations that AA is of central importance to panic disorder (Barlow et al., 1996; L. A. Clark, Watson, & Mineka, 1994), the strongest paths to and factor correlations with AA were found for the latent factor PD/A. On the other hand, paths from the *DSM* disorder factors of OCD and SOC to AA were nonsignificant. In addition, these factors were weakly correlated with AA at the zero-order level (all $rs = .31$). These results suggest that, though generally unrelated to mood disorders (i.e., results indicated no improvement in model fit with the addition of a path from DEP to AA), autonomic arousal symptoms may be weakly related or of less discriminant value for certain anxiety disorders (e.g., discrete social phobias). Although not addressed in the present study, this would also seem to be the case for specific phobia given evidence that persons with this disorder often score within the normal range on measures of autonomic arousal or fear and general distress (T. A. Brown, Chorpita, et al., 1997).

Accordingly, the current findings highlight a possible refinement of the tripartite model with regard to autonomic arousal. Although autonomic arousal had been initially posited to be a discriminating feature for the entire range of anxiety disorders, these data suggest that the relevance of autonomic arousal may be limited primarily to panic disorder/agoraphobia. Although this interpretation is generally in accord with recent reconsiderations of the tripartite model (L. A. Clark, Watson, & Mineka, 1994), additional research is needed to examine the replicability of these results in other samples and with other indicators of AA (e.g., to rule out the possibility that the high representation of panic disorder in the sample and use of the BAI as an indicator of AA—cf. Cox, Cohen, Direnfeld, & Swinson, 1996; Steer & Beck, 1996—may have augmented the differential association between PD/A and AA in the present study).

Nowhere was the potential differential relationship of the anxiety disorders with autonomic arousal more evident than in the path from the GAD factor to AA. Indeed, the suppressor effect observed in the hypothesized structural model (path = –.22, despite a zero-order correlation of .48) may help to account for the conflicting findings regarding the association between generalized anxiety disorder and symptoms of autonomic arousal. As discussed earlier, although patients with generalized anxiety disorder endorse these symptoms frequently (T. A. Brown, Marten, & Barlow, 1995), recent data indicate that these patients may respond to psychological stress with autonomic inflexibility (Borkovec et al., 1993; Hoehn-Saric et al., 1989). Our findings suggest that autonomic symptoms in this disorder may be due to high levels of negative affect (i.e., in addition to GAD being associated with the highest levels of NA—cf. T. A. Brown et al., 1996, T. A. Brown, Chorpita, et al., 1997—both GAD and AA are strongly correlated with NA). However, after accounting for variance in AA due to NA, the true direct influence of GAD on AA may have been illuminated in these analyses; namely, the disorder-specific features of GAD (i.e., worry; most of the GAD indicators were measures of worry) act to decrease (suppress) autonomic arousal.[7] If interpreted in this manner, this attests to the robustness of the association between worry and autonomic suppression given the disparate method-ologies that have produced this result (i.e., structural equation modeling vs. laboratory challenges).

As was true for the higher order latent factor NA, results involving PA were generally consistent with our predictions. Comparisons of the various models indicated that model fit and interpretability of the resulting path estimates were optimal when PA was specified as a higher order factor to the *DSM–IV* disorder factors. Moreover, support for the tripartite model was obtained by findings of a significant negative path from PA to DEP and low modification indices, indicating that model fit would not improve (i.e., the paths would be nonsignificant) if paths were added from PA to GAD, PD/A, or OCD. Such findings support the contention that low positive affect is more specifically linked to depression. However, counter to our expectations, inspection of fit diagnostics of the initial hypothesized model revealed that fit would improve with the specification of a path from PA to SOC. In addition, SOC had a significantly stronger zero-order association with PA than did the other anxiety disorder factors (see Table 3). In fact, unbeknownst to us when the initial hypothesized model was constructed, previous research has found an association between social phobia and lower levels of PA (Amies et al., 1983; Watson, Clark, & Carey, 1988). The unique relationship of social phobia and PA relative to the other anxiety disorders has been interpreted as being based on the interpersonal character of low PA (e.g., low confidence, unassertiveness; L. A. Clark, Watson, & Mineka, 1994). The addition of this path in the revised model was statistically significant and in the direction (i.e., negative) consistent with prior findings. However, somewhat counter to the tripartite model, which asserts that PA is more strongly linked to depression than to the anxiety disorders, this path (–.28) was virtually identical to the path from PA to DEP (–.29), suggesting no differential influence of PA on DEP and SOC after controlling for variance in NA (although DEP was more strongly correlated with PA than SOC at the zero-order level; see Table 3). These results underscore the importance of examining the influence of these dimensions at the multivariate level given the complexity of their posited interrelationships (e.g., hierarchical structure, differential strength of influence) and potential overlap in their underlying domains (e.g., zero-order relationships of the tripartite dimensions to emotional disorder symptoms and syndromes are affected to varying degrees by shared variance in NA, PA, and AA).

Results of multiple regression analyses reported in Watson, Clark, and Carey (1988), in which PA and NA were entered as predictors of major depression, dysthymia, and social phobia, did reveal greater differential magnitudes of the paths (standardized regression coefficients) of PA and depression (–.26) and PA and social phobia (–.19). However, inconsistent with predictions of the tripartite model and the results of the present study, Watson et al. found that NA did not add to the prediction of social phobia after controlling for variance in PA. It is also interesting to note that, although of similar relative magnitude, the zero-order factor correlations and path coefficients among the tripartite and DSM–IV disorder factors in the present study were generally stronger than the zero-order correlations and regression coefficients obtained by Watson et al. Possible reasons for these differences include (a) the use of a categorical versus a dimensional approach to the assessment of DSM–IV disorders (diagnoses were scored dichotomously as absent or present in Watson et al.), and (b) control versus no control of measurement error (because standard correlational and regression analyses were used in Watson et al., the resulting correlations and path coefficients were not adjusted for measurement error). Thus, it could be contended that the structural-modeling approach of the present study provided a better analysis for the multivariate relationships of the tripartite and DSM–IV dimensions for such reasons as (a) the dimensional nature of psychopathology (i.e., key features of DSM–IV disorders) was retained, and (b) the interrelationships among the DSM–IV and tripartite dimensions were examined after accounting for the influence of measurement error in the quantification of these domains (cf.

Bagozzi, 1993; Green, Goldman, & Salovey, 1993). Also, it is possible that other methodological differences, such as sample composition and the measurement of PA and NA (these traits were assessed using the Multidimensional Personality Questionnaire in Watson et al.), were partly responsible for these differential results.

Although the present investigation evaluated one of the most appropriate samples to be studied to date (e.g., prior studies have often used samples in which anxiety and mood disorders were not well represented), certain disorders occurred infrequently in our data set (e.g., obsessive–compulsive disorder; although mood disorders occurred frequently, most patients with a depressive disorder had an anxiety disorder principal diagnosis). In this light, it would be of interest to examine the structural and parameter equivalence of our revised model (Figure 2) in other samples (e.g., inpatient populations). Moreover, as noted earlier, structural research of longitudinal data would be of considerable value in the verification of NA and PA (or related constructs; cf. Carver & White, 1994) as higher order dimensions exerting strong influence on the pathogenesis, course, and treatment response of the emotional disorders.

Notes

1. Nevertheless, the issue of the qualitative versus quantitative nature of emotion disorders continues to be debated in the literature (cf. Flett, Vredenburg, & Krames, 1997). Moreover, although considerable consensus exists for the conclusion that measures of psychopathological symptoms operate dimensionally, expression of symptoms along a continuum alone cannot be taken to confirm or refute the absence of an underlying taxon (e.g., quantitative indicators can have dichotomous latent influences such as the presence or absence of a gene; cf. Meehl, 1995).

2. The samples used in the current study and in Zinbarg and Barlow's (1996) study did not overlap.

3. The chi-square difference test is inapplicable in situations where the structures of competing models vary substantially (e.g., in models where latent factors vary between being X and Y variables) and models are not nested (i.e., a nested model is one that has a

subset of the free parameters of a parent model).

4. Given the possibility that inclusion of ADIS-IV-L diagnosis severity ratings biased the results in favor of the five-factor model (because ADIS-IV-L CSRs reflect dimensional severity ratings based on the DSM–IV classification scheme), confirmatory factor analyses of the DSM–IV measurement models were reconducted excluding ADIS-IV-L CSRs. Once again, the five-factor model provided the best fit for the data, $\chi^2(89) = 183.83$, CFI = .97, IFI = .97, RMSEA = .055, GFI = .94, relative to the one-factor model, $\chi^2(99) = 1,085.90$, the two-factor model, $\chi^2(98) = 811.03$, and the four-factor model, $\chi^2(93) = 328.27$; for example, a five- versus a four-factor model: $\chi^2_{diff}(4) = 144.44$, $p < .001$.

5. Internal consistencies (Cronbach's alphas) for the PANAS-N and PANAS-P in the present sample were .88 and .90, respectively. The single indicator approach was selected over a split-half approach because measurement error could be modeled more accurately (i.e., Cronbach's alpha represents an average of all possible split-halves).

6. To examine the possibility that we concluded erroneously that NA was chiefly responsible for the suppressor effect observed in the relationship between GAD and AA, a simplified model was evaluated with LISREL: NA was specified as a predictor with paths to the GAD and AA factors, and a path was specified from GAD to AA. This model provided an excellent fit to the data, $\chi^2(11) = 31.25$, CFI = .98, IFI = .98, RMSEA = .073, GFI = .98, and the same suppressor effect was obtained (the completely standardized path from GAD to AA was –.15).

7. Similarly, the high zero-order factor correlation between DEP and AA (.60) could have been due to the strong relationships between DEP and NA (.77) and AA and NA (.77). This conclusion was supported by small modification indices from the structural model indicating that adding a path from DEP to AA would not improve model fit (i.e., the path would be nonsignificant) because DEP could not account for additional variance in AA.

References

Akaike, H. (1987). Factor analysis and AIC. *Psychometrika*, 52, 317–332.

American Psychiatric Association. (1968). *Diagnostic and statistical manual of mental disorders* (2nd ed.). Washington, DC: Author.

American Psychiatric Association. (1987). *Diagnostic and statistical manual of mental disorders* (3rd ed., rev.). Washington, DC: Author.

American Psychiatric Association. (1994). *Diagnostic statistical manual of mental* disorders (4th ed.). Washington, DC: Author.

Amies, P. L., Gelder, M. G., & Shaw, P. M. (1983). Social phobia: A comparative clinical study. *British Journal of Psychiatry, 142,* 174–179.

Andrews, G. (1996). Comorbidity in neurotic disorders: The similarities are more important than the differences. In R. M. Rapee (Ed.), *Current controversies in the anxiety disorders* (pp. 3–20). New York: Guilford Press.

Andrews, G., Stewart, G., Morris-Yates, A., Holt, P., & Henderson, S. (1990). Evidence for a general neurotic syndrome. *British Journal of Psychiatry, 157,* 6–12.

Bagozzi, R. P. (1993). An examination of the psychometric properties of measures of negative affect in the PANAS-X scales. *Journal of Personality and Social Psychology, 65,* 836–851.

Barlow, D. H., Chorpita, B. F. & Turovsky, J. (1996). Fear, panic, anxiety, and disorders of emotion. In D. A. Hope (Ed.), *Perspectives on anxiety, panic, and fear* (Vol. 43, pp. 251–328). Lincoln, NE: University of Nebraska Press.

Beck, A. T. & Steer, R. A. (1987). *Manual for the revised Beck Depression Inventory.* San Antonio, TX: Psychological Corporation.

Beck, A. T. & Steer, R. A. (1990). *Manual for the Beck Anxiety Inventory.* San Antonio, TX: Psychological Corporation.

Bentler, P. M. (1990). Comparative fit indices in structural models. *Psychological Bulletin, 107,* 238–246.

Bender, P. M., & Bonett, D. G. (1980). Significance tests and goodness of fit in the analysis of covariance structures. *Psychological Bulletin, 88,* 588–606.

Blashfield, R. K. (1990). Comorbidity and classification. In J. D. Maser & C. R. Cloninger (Eds.), *Comorbidity of mood and anxiety disorders* (pp. 61–82). Washington, DC: American Psychiatric Press.

Bollen, K. A. (1989). *Structural equations with latent variables.* New York: Wiley.

Borkovec, T. D., Abel, J. L., & Newman, H. (1995). Effects of psychotherapy on comorbid conditions in generalized anxiety disorder. *Journal of Consulting and Clinical Psychology, 63,* 479–483.

Borkovec, T. D., Lyonfields, J. D., Wiser, S. L., & Diehl, L. (1993). The role of worrisome thinking in the suppression of cardiovascular response to phobic imagery. *Behaviour Research and Therapy, 31,* 321–324.

Brown, E. J., Turovsky, J., Heimberg, R. G., Juster, H. R., Brown, T. A., & Barlow, D. H. (1997). Validation of the Social Interaction Anxiety Scale and the Social Phobia Scale across the anxiety disorders. *Psychological Assessment, 9,* 21–27.

Brown, T. A. (1996). Validity of the *DSM–III–R* and *DSM–IV* classification systems for anxiety disorders. In R. M. Rapee (Ed.), *Current controversies in the anxiety disorders* (pp. 21–45). New York: Guilford Press.

Brown, T. A. (in press). Generalized anxiety disorder and obsessive–compulsive disorder. In T Millon, P. H. Blaney, & R. Davis (Eds.), *Oxford textbook of psychopathology.* New York: Oxford University Press.

Brown, T. A., Anson, A. M., & DiBartolo, P. M. (1996). *The distinctiveness of DSM–IV generalized anxiety disorder from major depression and dysthymia.* Manuscript in preparation.

Brown, T. A., Antony, M. M., & Barlow, D. H. (1992). Psychometric properties of the Penn State Worry Questionnaire in a clinical anxiety disorders sample. *Behaviour Research and Therapy, 30,* 33–37.

Brown, T. A., Antony, M. M., & Barlow, D. H. (1995). Diagnostic comorbidity in panic disorder: Effect on treatment outcome and course of comorbid diagnoses following treatment. *Journal of Consulting and Clinical Psychology, 63,* 408–418.

Brown, T. A., & Barlow, D. H. (1992). Comorbidity among anxiety disorders: Implications for treatment and *DSM–IV. Journal of Consulting and Clinical Psychology, 60,* 835–844.

Brown, T. A., Barlow, D. H., & Liebowitz, M. R. (1994). The empirical basis of generalized anxiety disorder. *American Journal of Psychiatry, 151,* 1272–1280.

Brown, T. A., & Chorpita, B. F. (1996). On the validity and comorbidity of the *DSM–III–R* and *DSM–IV* anxiety disorders. In R. M. Rapee (Ed.), *Current controversies in the anxiety disorders* (pp. 48–52). New York: Guilford Press.

Brown, T. A., Chorpita, B. F. Korotitsch, W., & Barlow, D. H. (1997). Psychometric properties of the Depression Anxiety Stress Scales (DASS) in clinical samples. *Behaviour Research and Therapy, 35,* 79–89.

Brown, T. A., Marten, P. A., & Barlow, D. H. (1995). Discriminant validity of the symptoms constituting the *DSM–III–R* and *DSM–IV* associated symptom criterion of generalized anxiety disorder. *Journal of Anxiety Disorders, 9,* 317–328.

Brown, T. A., Moras, K., Zinbarg, R. E., & Barlow, D. H. (1993). Diagnostic and symptom distinguishability of generalized anxiety disorder and obsessive–compulsive disorder. *Behavior Therapy, 24,* 227–240.

Carver, C. S., & White, T. L. (1994). Behavioral inhibition, behavioral activation, and affective responses to impending reward and punishment: The BIS/BAS scales. *Journal of Personality and Social Psychology, 67,* 319–333.

Clark, D. A., Steer, R. A., & Beck, A. T (1994). Common and specific dimensions of self-reported anxiety and depression: Implications for the cognitive and tripartite models. *Journal of Abnormal Psychology,103,* 645–654.

Clark, L. A., & Watson, D. (1991). Tripartite model of anxiety and depression: Psychometric evidence and taxonomic implications. *Journal of Abnormal Psychology, 100,* 316–336.

Clark, L. A., Watson, D., & Mineka, S. (1994). Temperament, personality, and the mood and anxiety disorders. *Journal of Abnormal Psychology, 103,* 103–116.

Cohen, J., & Cohen, P. (1983). *Applied multiple regression/correlation analysis for the behavioral sciences* (2nd ed.). Hillsdale, NJ: Erlbaum.

Costa, P. T. & McCrae, R. R. (1988). Personality in adulthood: A six-year longitudinal study of self-reports and spouse ratings on the NEO Personality Inventory. *Journal of Personality and Social Psychology, 54,* 853–863.

Cox, B. J., Cohen, E., Direnfeld, D. M., & Swinson, R. P. (1996). Does the Beck Anxiety Inventory measure anything beyond panic attack symptoms? *Behaviour Research and Therapy, 34,* 949–954.

Di Nardo, P. A., Brown, T. A., & Barlow, D. H. (1994). *Anxiety Disorders Interview Schedule for DSM–IV: Lifetime Version (ADIS-IV-L).* San Antonio, TX: Psychological Corporation.

Di Nardo, P. A., Brown, T. A., Lawton, J. K., & Barlow, D. H. (1995, November). *The Anxiety Disorders Interview Schedule for DSM–IV Lifetime Version: Description and initial evidence for diagnostic reliability.* Paper presented at the 29th annual meeting of the Association for Advancement of Behavior Therapy, Washington, DC.

Emmelkamp, P. M. G. (1988). Maudsley Obsessional–Compulsive Inventory. In M. Hersen & A. S. Bellack (Eds.), *Dictionary of behavioral assessment techniques* (pp. 294–295). New York: Pergamon Press.

Fenigstein, A., Scheier, M. F., & Buss, A. H. (1975). Public and private self-consciousness: Assessment and theory. *Journal of Consulting and Clinical Psychology, 43,* 522–527.

Flett, G. L., Vredenburg, K., & Krames, L. (1997). The continuity of depression in clinical and nonclinical samples. *Psychological Bulletin, 121,* 395–416.

Frances, A., Widiger, T. & Fyer, M. R. (1990). The influence of classification methods on comorbidity. In J. D. Maser & C. R. Cloninger (Eds.), *Comorbidity of mood and anxiety disorders* (pp. 41–59). Washington, DC: American Psychiatric Press.

Green, D. P., Goldman, S. L., & Salovey, P. (1993). Measurement error masks bipolarity in affect ratings. *Journal of Personality and Social Psychology, 64,* 1029–1041.

Hodgson, R. J., & Rachman, S. J. (1977). Obsessional–compulsive complaints. *Behaviour Research and Therapy, 15,* 389–395.

Hoehn-Saric, R., McLeod, D. R., & Zimmerli, W. D. (1989). Somatic manifestations in women with generalized anxiety disorder: Psychophysiological responses to psychological stress. *Archives of General Psychiatry, 46,* 1113–1119.

Hope, D. A., & Heimberg, R. G. (1988). Public and private self-consciousness and social phobia. *Journal of Personality Assessment, 52,* 626–639.

Hudson, J. I., & Pope, H. G. (1990). Affective spectrum disorder: Does antidepressant response identify a family of disorders with a common pathophysiology? *American Journal of Psychiatry, 147,* 552–564.

Jaccard, J. C., & Wan, C. K. (1996). *LISREL approaches to interaction effects in multiple regression.* Thousand Oaks, CA: Sage.

Joiner, T. E. (1996). A confirmatory factor-analytic investigation of the tripartite model of depression and anxiety in college students. *Cognitive Therapy and Research, 20,* 521–539.

Joiner, T. E., Catanzaro, S. J., & Laurent, J. (1996). Tripartite structure of positive and negative affect, depression, and anxiety in child and adolescent psychiatric inpatients. *Journal of Abnormal Psychology, 105,* 401–409.

Jöreskog, K., & Sörbom, D. (1993). LISREL 8.12a [Computer software]. Chicago: Scientific Software.

Kendall, P. C., & Watson, D. (Eds.). (1989). *Anxiety and depression: Distinctive and overlapping features.* San Diego, CA: Academic Press.

Kendler, K. S., Neale, M. C., Kessler, R. C., Heath, A. C., & Eaves, L. J. (1992). Major depression and generalized anxiety disorder: Same genes, (partly) different environments? *Archives of General Psychiatry, 49,* 716–722.

Livesley, W. J., Schroeder, M. L., Jackson, D. N., & Jang, K. L. (1994). Categorical distinctions in the study of personality disorder: Implications for classification. *Journal of Abnormal Psychology, 103,* 6–17.

Lovibond, P. F., & Lovibond, S. H. (1995). The structure of negative emotional states: Comparison of the Depression Anxiety Stress Scales (DASS) with the Beck Depression and Anxiety Inventories. *Behaviour Research and Therapy, 33,* 335–342.

Lovibond, S. H., & Lovibond, P. F (1995). *Manual for the Depression Anxiety Stress Scales* (2nd ed.). Sydney, Australia: Psychological Foundation of Australia.

Marten, P. A., Brown, T. A., Barlow, D. H., Borkovec, T. D., Shear, M. K., & Lydiard, R. B. (1993). Evaluation of the ratings comprising the associated symptom criterion of *DSM–III–R* generalized anxiety disorder. *Journal of Nervous and Mental Disease, 181,* 676–682.

Mattick, R. P., Peters, L., & Clarke, J. C. (1989). Exposure and cognitive restructuring for social phobia: A controlled study. *Behavior Therapy, 20,* 3–23.

Meehl, P. E. (1995). Bootstraps taxometrics: Solving the classification problem in psychopathology. *American Psychologist, 50,* 266–275.

Meng, X.-L., Rosenthal, R., & Rubin, D. B. (1992). Comparing correlated correlation coefficients. *Psychological Bulletin, 111,* 172–175.

Meyer, T. J., Miller, M. L., Metzger, R. L., & Borkovec, T. D. (1990). Development and validation of the Penn State Worry Questionnaire. *Behaviour Research and Therapy, 28,* 487–495.

Moldin, S. O., Rice, J. P., Erlenmeyer-Kimling, L., & Squires-Wheeler, E. (1994). Latent structure of *DSM–III–R* Axis II psychopathology in a normal sample. *Journal of Abnormal Psychology, 103,* 259–266.

Peterson, R. A., & Reiss, S. (1992). *Anxiety Sensitivity Index manual* (2nd ed.). Worthington, OH: IDS Publishing.

Rapee, R. M., Craske, M. G., & Barlow, D. H. (1995). Assessment instrument for panic disorder that includes fear of sensation-producing activities: The Albany Panic and Phobia Questionnaire. *Anxiety, 1,* 114–122.

Steer, R. A., & Beck, A. T. (1996). Generalized anxiety and panic disorders: Response to Cox, Cohen, Direnfeld, and Swinson (1996). *Behaviour Research and Therapy, 34,* 955–957.

Steiger, J. H. (1990). Structural model evaluation and modification: An interval estimation approach. *Multivariate Behavioral Research, 25,* 173–180.

Tallis, F., Davey, G. C. L., & Bond, A. (1994). The Worry Domains Questionnaire. In G. Davey & F. Tallis (Eds.), *Worrying: Perspectives on theory, assessment, and treatment* (pp. 285–297). New York: Wiley.

Tallis, F., Eysenck, M. W., & Mathews, A. (1992). A questionnaire for the measurement of nonpathological worry. *Personality and Individual Differences, 13,* 161–168.

Tellegen, A., Lykken, D. T., Bouchard, T. J., Wilcox, K. J., Segal, N. L., & Rich, S. (1988). Personality similarity in twins formed apart and together. *Journal of Personality and Social Psychology, 54,* 1031–1039.

Turner, S. M., Beidel, D. C., & Stanley, M. A. (1992). Are obsessional thoughts and worry different cognitive phenomena? *Clinical Psychology Review, 12,* 257–270.

Tyrer, P., Seivewright, N., Murphy, S., Ferguson, B., Kingdon, D., Barczak, B., Brothwell, J., Darling, C., Gregory, S., & Johnson, A. L. (1988). The Nottingham study of neurotic disorder: Comparison of drug and psychological treatments. *Lancet, 2,* 235–240.

Watson, D., & Clark, L. A. (1984). Negative affectivity: The disposition to experience aversive emotional states. *Psychological Bulletin, 96,* 465–490.

Watson, D., Clark, L. A., & Carey, G. (1988). Positive and negative affectivity and their relation to the anxiety and depressive disorders. *Journal of Abnormal Psychology, 97,* 346–353.

Watson, D., Clark, L. A., & Harkness, A. R. (1994). Structures of personality and their relevance to psychopathology. *Journal of Abnormal Psychology, 103,* 18–31.

Watson, D., Clark, L. A., & Tellegen, A. (1988). Development and validation of brief measures of positive and negative affect: The PANAS scales. *Journal of Personality and Social Psychology, 54,* 1063–1070.

Watson, D., Clark, L. A., Weber, K., Assenheimer, J. S., Strauss, M. E., & McCormick, R. A. (1995). Testing a tripartite model: II. Exploring the symptom structure of anxiety and depression in student, adult, and patient samples. *Journal of Abnormal Psychology, 104,* 15–25.

Watson, D., Weber, K., Assenheimer, J. S., Clark, L. A., Strauss, M. E., & McCormick, R. A. (1995). Testing a tripartite model: I. Evaluating the convergent and discriminant validity of anxiety and depression symptom scales. *Journal of Abnormal Psychology, 104,* 3–14.

World Health Organization. (1993). *The ICD-10 classification of mental and behavioural disorders: Diagnostic criteria for research.* Geneva, Switzerland: Author.

Zinbarg, R. E., & Barlow, D. H. (1996). Structure of anxiety and anxiety disorders: A hierarchical model. *Journal of Abnormal Psychology, 105,* 181–193.

Article Review Form at end of book.

WiseGuide Wrap-Up

Review the treatment for depression in your textbook and from the readings in this section. If you plan to apply your knowledge of abnormal psychology to your worksite, you will encounter depression and can then make a referral for treatment. Given the responsiveness of SSRDs to alleviating symptomology, investigate the role of medication in treatment.

R.E.A.L. Sites

This list provides a print preview of typical **Coursewise** R.E.A.L. sites. (There are over 100 such sites at the **Courselinks**™ site.) The danger in printing URLs is that web sites can change overnight. As we went to press, these sites were functional using the URLs provided. If you come across one that isn't, please let us know via email to: webmaster@coursewise.com. Use your Passport to access the most current list of R.E.A.L. sites at the **Courselinks** site.

Site name: Mental Health Net
URL: http://www.cmhc.com/
Why is it R.E.A.L.? This is a voluminous resource of sites and links for depressive disorders and others.
Key topics: pessimism, depression

Site name: Helplessness-L
URL: Send email to: Listserv@netcom.com
Why is it R.E.A.L.? Dr. Martin Seligman owns and operates this site. Applications of helplessness to areas such as depression are discussed.
Key topics: depression

section 6

Child and Adolescent Pathology

This section is slightly longer to accommodate articles in the child and adolescent areas. In practice with children, the issues of attention and hyperactivity surface. Unfortunately, there has been an increase in instances of adolescent aggressive acts.

Samuel and colleagues present remarkable findings about cultural differences in the presentation of attention deficit hyperactivity disorder in children. The authors report comorbidity with other behavior disorders, such as oppositional defiant disorder, as well.

The topic of adolescent sexual aggression is treated by van Eys in the second article of this section. She correctly points out that little data/research exists to understand this disturbing condition. One of the many values of this article is the comprehensive treatment outcome review that is presented. Social skills treatment is highlighted; this is likely to be an approach used at agencies, practices, and hospital settings that you are exposed to in your field studies.

Adolescent suicide is second in prevalence to that of elders and represents a serious and compelling clinical challenge. Culp and colleagues present the results of a respected measure of depression. The results, as you will read, are alarming. The table in the article provides specific information about the problems that adolescents experience that trigger depression.

The last article in this section, by Heatherton and associates, provides the results of a carefully conducted survey study. The strength of this study is further enhanced with a remeasurement of the variables ten years later. This longitudinal approach revealed that body dissatisfaction remains a problem and disordered eating declines as adolescents transition to young adults.

The readings in this section highlight issues that a practitioner planning to work with children will need to consider.

Learning Objectives

- The student will begin to develop a view of cultural factors influencing the expression of symptoms in children.

- The student's interest in practitioner issues will increase with the study of the various treatment approaches to child/adolescent pathology explained in the readings.

- The student will become familiar with the adolescent manifestation of major pathologies such as sexual expression and affective disorders.

? Questions ?

Reading 17. What are the public health implications to working with African American children with attention deficit hyperactivity disorder?

Reading 18. Do treatment models of empathy building work?

Reading 19. How does a depressed adolescent ask for help?

Reading 20. Explain the body dissatisfaction that eating-disordered individuals express and comment on how a longitudinal study is able to identify this phenomenon.

What are the public health implications to working with African American children with attention deficit hyperactivity disorder?

Clinical Characteristics of Attention Deficit Hyperactivity Disorder in African American Children

Valerie J. Samuel, Ph.D.,
Joseph Biederman, M.D.,
Stephen V. Faraone, Ph.D.,
Patricia George, B.A.,
Eric Mick, B.A.,
Ayanna Thornell, B.A.,
Shannon Curtis, B.A.,
Andrea Taylor, B.A.,
and Deborah Brome, Ph.D.

Objective

*The authors' goal was to explore the nature of attention deficit hyperactivity disorder (ADHD) in African American children, which has received scant attention by psychiatric researchers. **Method:** Subjects were 19 African American children with DSM-III-R ADHD and 24 African American children without ADHD. Ethnically sensitive methods were used to evaluate the children comprehensively. The findings were compared with those from an earlier study of Caucasian children with ADHD. **Results:** African American children with ADHD had higher levels of psychiatric disorders other than ADHD than did African American children who did not have ADHD. **Conclusions:** Among African American children, ADHD may be characterized by a narrower pattern of psychiatric comorbidity and dysfunction than has been observed in Caucasians. Given the small number of subjects studied, these findings are preliminary and must be replicated to confirm their validity.*

(Am J Psychiatry 1998; 155:696–698)

In contrast to thousands of scientific articles on attention deficit hyperactivity disorder (ADHD) in Caucasians, there is limited information about ADHD among African Americans. In an earlier review,[1] we identified only 17 articles about ADHD in African Americans and only a handful having a focus on ethnicity. Since ADHD is a substantial disorder of childhood,[2] the absence of meaningful information relevant to African Americans has clinical and public health implications.

To help fill this lacuna in the literature, we studied ADHD in African American children using an ethnically sensitive design. We hypothesized that African American children with ADHD would have higher levels of psychiatric dysfunction than African American children who did not have ADHD.

Method

The study design and methodology closely followed our earlier studies of Caucasian children.[3,4] In addition, ethnically sensitive accommodations were made for this study based on recommendations from an advisory committee of 14 African American researchers and mental health professionals. This committee reviewed our methodology for cultural appropriateness.

We recruited African American children between the ages of 6 and 17 who did (N=19) or did not (N=24) have DSM-III-R ADHD. The children with ADHD came from pediatric and psychiatric referral sources. The pediatric source was a large health maintenance organization; the psychiatric source was our pediatric psychopharmacology unit. Subjects were excluded from the study if they had been adopted, their nuclear family was not available, or they had paralysis, deafness, blindness, psychosis, autism, or a full-scale IQ less than 80.

Table 1	Comorbid Psychiatric Diagnoses of African American Children with and without Attention Deficit Hyperactivity Disorder (ADHD)		
Comorbid Diagnosis	**Children with ADHD (N=19)**	**Children without ADHD (N=24)**	**p (Fisher's exact test)**
Disruptive disorders			
Oppositional defiant disorder	4	0	0.03
Conduct disorder	3	1	0.31
Mood disorders			
Major depression (severe)	11	0	<0.001
Bipolar disorder	4	0	0.03
Dysthymia	2	0	0.19
Anxiety disorders			
Multiple anxieties (≥2)	2	1	0.40
Panic disorder	1	1	1.00
Agoraphobia	2	1	0.58
Overanxious disorder	1	0	0.44
Simple phobia	4	3	0.68
Social phobia	1	1	1.00
Separation anxiety	4	0	0.03
Substance disorders			
Alcohol abuse	1	0	0.44
Drug abuse	1	1	1.00
Smoking	1	2	1.00
Other disorders			
Tic disorder	2	0	0.19
Enuresis	7	5	0.31
Encopresis	1	0	0.44
Language disorder	2	3	1.00
Stuttering	2	1	0.58

The African American children who did not have ADHD were selected from the pediatric medical clinics at the two ascertainment sites and from advertisements. All parents completed consent forms for themselves and their children. Assent forms were obtained from the children. The research project was reviewed and approved by our institutional review board.

Diagnostic assessments used structured interviews based on DSM-III-R. Psychiatric assessments of children used the Schedule for Affective Disorders and Schizophrenia for School-Age Children—Epidemiologic Version.[5] Diagnoses were based on independent interviews with all of the mothers and di-rect interviews with the children older than 12.

All assessments were made by six African American raters who were blind to the subject's diagnosis and ascertainment site. These raters were trained and supervised by project investigators (V.J.S., J.B., and D.B.). The ethnic validity model of Tyler et al.[6] was used to train the raters in cultural sensitivity. We com-puted kappa coefficients of agree-ment by having a board-certified child psychiatrist or a licensed clini-cal child psychologist diagnose chil-dren from audiotaped interviews made by the assessment staff. Based on 173 interviews from a larger data set, the median kappa for all diag-noses was 0.86, and the kappa for

ADHD was 0.98. In addition, we computed kappa separately for cases in which two African American raters rated an African American child. That kappa was 0.87.

Diagnoses were considered positive if DSM-III-R criteria were unequivocally met. All diagnostic un-certainties were resolved by a com-mittee of three board-certified or licensed clinicians (V.J.S., J.B., D.B.) who were blind to ascertainment group. For children older than 12, data from direct and indirect inter-views were combined by considering a diagnostic criterion positive if en-dorsed in either interview.

Data were analyzed by using t tests and Fisher's exact tests. All tests of significance were two-tailed, and significance was set at the 5% level.

Our findings for this group of African American children with ADHD were compared with those in our earlier study of Caucasian chil-dren,[7] which used an identical assess-ment battery.

Results

The children with and without ADHD did not differ in age (mean=13 years, SD=3, versus mean=12.6 years, SD=3, respectively) (p=0.70, Fisher's exact test), social class (mean=2.1, SD=0.9, versus mean=2.1, SD=0.9) (p=1.00, Fisher's exact test), or number with separated or divorced parents (12 versus 12) (p=0.50, Fisher's exact test).

Compared with children who did not have ADHD, the children with ADHD had higher lifetime rates of almost all of the evaluated psychi-atric disorders, but there were statis-tically significant differences only in oppositional defiant disorder, major depression, bipolar disorder, and separation anxiety disorder (table 1).

The mood disorder findings were consistent with those in our previously reported study of Caucasian children with ADHD,[7] who were assessed with an identi-cal assessment battery. In contrast, the rates of other disruptive behav-ior and anxiety disorders were com-paratively modest in the African American children. The comorbidity of ADHD with disruptive behavior disorders has been associated with poor prognosis, delinquency, and substance abuse in Caucasian children with ADHD.[8,9] Moreover, co-morbidity of ADHD with anxiety disorders has been associated with poor response to stimulant treatment.[10]

Discussion

These African American children with ADHD had the prototypical psychiatric correlates of the disorder: high rates of oppositional defiant, mood, and anxiety disorders. These preliminary findings suggest that the currently accepted definition of ADHD identifies a disorder in African American children with similar—but not identical—psychiatric correlates to those previously identified in Caucasians.

Although a preliminary finding, the modest levels of comorbidity in this study group may indicate that African American children have a potentially more manageable and treatment-responsive form of ADHD.

Our results must be interpreted in the context of methodological limitations. Because the number of subjects was relatively small, we had low statistical power to detect group differences. Moreover, because we made multiple comparisons, some of our results may be type II errors. Because the subjects with ADHD had been referred, our results may not generalize to all children with ADHD. They should, however, generalize to children seen in treatment settings. In addition, because the subjects were primarily from middle-class families, the findings may not generalize to children from other social strata.

Despite these limitations, to our knowledge this work is the first to use ethnically sensitive methods to study ADHD in African American children. Before drawing definitive conclusions, further work is needed to replicate this study with a larger group of African American children. If our findings are replicated, new avenues may be opened for clinicians in the assessment of and treatment planning for African American children with ADHD.

References

1. Samuel V, Curtis S, Thornell A, George P, Taylor A, Brome D, Biederman J, Faraone S: The unexplored void of ADHD and African-American research: a review of the literature. *J. Attention Disorders* 1997; 1(4):197–208
2. Cantwell D, Hanna G: Attention-deficit hyperactivity disorder, in *American Psychiatric Press Review of Psychiatry*, vol 8. Edited by Tasman A, Hales RE, Francis AJ. Washington, DC, American Psychiatric Press, 1989, pp. 134–161
3. Biederman J, Faraone SV, Keenan K, Benjamin J, Krifcher B, Moore C, Sprich S, Ugaglia K, Jellinek MS, Steingard R, Spencer T, Norman D, Kolodny R, Kraus I, Perrin J, Keller MB, Tsuang MT: Further evidence for family-genetic risk factors in attention deficit hyperactivity disorder (ADHD): patterns of comorbidity in probands and relatives in psychiatrically and pediatrically referred samples. *Arch Gen. Psychiatry* 1992; 49:728–738
4. Biederman J, Faraone S, Milberger S, Guite J, Mick E, Chen L, Mennin D, Marrs A, Ouellette C, Moore P, Spencer T, Norman D, Wilens T, Kraus I, Perrin J: A prospective four-year follow-up study of attention deficit hyperactivity and related disorders. *Arch Gen Psychiatry* 1996; 53:437–446
5. Orvaschel H: Psychiatric interviews suitable for use in research with children and adolescents. *Psychopharmacol Bull* 1985; 21:737–745
6. Tyler FB, Brome DR, Williams JE: *Validity, Ecology, and Psychotherapy: A Psychological Perspective.* New York, Plenum, 1991
7. Biederman J, Faraone SV, Mick E, Wozniak J, Chen L, Ouellette C, Marrs A, Moore P, Garcia J, Mennin D, Lelon E: Attention deficit hyperactivity disorder and juvenile mania: an overlooked comorbidity? *J Am Acad Child Adolesc Psychiatry* 1996; 35:997–1008
8. Gittelman R, Mannuzza S, Shenker R, Bonagura N: Hyperactive boys almost grown up, I: psychiatric status. *Arch Gen Psychiatry* 1985; 42:937–947
9. Mannuzza S, Gittelman-Klein R, Horowitz-Konig P, Giampino TL: Hyperactive boys almost grown up, IV: criminality and its relationship to psychiatric status. *Arch Gen Psychiatry* 1989; 46: 1073–1079
10. Spencer TJ, Biederman J, Wilens T, Harding M, O'Donnell D, Griffin S: Pharmacotherapy of ADHD across the lifecycle: a literature review. *J. Am Acad Child Adolesc Psychiatry* 1996; 35: 409–432

 Article Review Form at end of book.

Do treatment models of emphathy building work?

Group Treatment for Prepubescent Boys with Sexually Aggressive Behavior:

Clinical Considerations and Proposed Treatment Techniques

Patti P. van Eys

Peabody College of Vanderbilt University

Descriptive and treatment outcome studies regarding sexually aggressive prepubescent boys are lacking. Preliminary data, however, are available from five studies on this difficult-to-treat population. This article has multiple goals: 1) to summarize descriptive and treatment outcome data of problematic sexual behavior in children; 2) to describe general considerations regarding treatment for sexually aggressive prepubescent male children; 3) to address two traditional clinical goals (e.g., eliminating perpetration behavior and enhancing victim empathy) for treating sexual aggression; and 4) to broaden the concept of empathy as a treatment goal. In addition, useful activities are described and available resources are referenced for practitioner use.

Clinicians who treat sexually aggressive children are challenged with un-derstanding this difficult-to-treat clinical population without a strong theoretical or empirical basis for specific interventions. Although the emerging literature on treating aggressive children in groups with cognitive behavioral techniques is promising (Braswell, 1993; Kazdin, 1996; Kendall & Panichelli-Mindel, 1995; Lochman & Lenhart, 1993), it does not include empirical reviews of treating sexually aggressive children. According to William Friedrich, "The fact is, we don't know what works with these children" (1993a, p. xi). Whereas a practitioner task force has developed assumptions for the treatment of adolescent sexual offenders (National Adolescent Perpetrator Network, 1993), a similar task force has not been formed for treating prepubescent children with serious sexual behavior problems. Experts in the field emphasize the need to identify and treat young sexual offenders when the behavior first appears and before the perpetration patterns be-come ingrained and more resistant to treatment (e.g., Bonner, 1995).

In an attempt to spur discussion regarding mental health intervention for this population, this article presents some treatment issues inherent in clinical work with sexually aggressive children. Drawing from the nascent theoretical and empirical work in this area, analog literature on treatment for adult and adolescent sexual offenders, analog literature on treatment for adult and adolescent sexual offenders, analog literature on aggressive children, and the author's own experience with sexually aggressive boys aged 8 to 10, it appears that a comprehensive treatment package may be needed to reduce or eliminate sexually aggressive behavior. Therapeutic work in the following areas is proposed: caregiver treatment, perpetration behavior and distorted cognitions, perspective-taking and empathy development, socialization skills, and sexual education.

Theoretical and Treatment Outcome Review

Theoretical Review

A continuum of sexual behaviors derived from clinical observations (Johnson & Feldmuth, 1993) aids in grouping children with sexual behavior problems into typologies for treatment. Group I children are described as those who are developing sexual attitudes, considered normal, and exploring their emerging sexuality in a generally curious and spontaneous manner. Group II children, called "sexually reactive," are children who display more sexual behavior and intense sexual reactivity, compared with Group I children. This behavior may be triggered by the child's own history of sexual victimization or overstimulation (e.g., exposure to pornography). The sexual behavior is rarely aggressive and mostly self-directed (e.g., intense and frequent masturbation; preoccupation with sexual topics). When it is other-directed, this group engages in nonforceful and non-coercive sexual activity with same-age peers. Affect related to the offending behavior generally involves anxiety, guilt, shame, and confusion. Group II children are usually amenable to intervention that focuses on victim issues, with sexual reactivity being one symptom targeted for treatment.

Group III children fall in the "mutually sexually reactive behavior" category, and Group IV children are referred to as "children who molest" (Gil & Johnson, 1993). Group III children seek other children with whom to behave sexually. They have a more pervasive (e.g., across settings and times) and focused (e.g., more time spent planning sexual situations) sexual behavior pattern than Group II children, and may be less responsive to intervention. They usually do not coerce or use force, but use persuasion and can engage in a full range of sexual behaviors with other children. They usually exhibit an apathetic affect related to their sexualized behavior with other children.

Group IV children are those with a pervasive and consistent pattern of sexual offending. These children use force and coercion and engage in the full range of sexual behaviors. Affect related to perpetration is angry, agitated, and aggressive; accompanying behaviors are compulsive, impulsive, and rageful. These children have behavior problems across settings, and tend to have few, if any, friends. Some children vacillate between Groups III and IV.

In a Canadian pilot study of 60 sexually abused male children (ages 6 1/2 to 14) who were divided into these four typological categories, children in Groups III and IV shared certain features of their abuse histories (Hall, Mathews, & Pearce, 1997). Compared with Group I and II children, the children in Groups III and IV had histories of sexual abuse of higher frequency and duration; had experienced more sexual arousal during abuse; had the highest pain and fear during abuse; had the highest percentage of having watched the perpetrator in additional sexual activity; had been groomed by the perpetrator; and had multiple additional family problems, including the highest percentage of separations from or losses of primary caretakers.

Another study of children who would be classified in Groups III and IV (i.e., who were referred for sexual behavior problems that were repetitive, unresponsive to adult intervention, equivalent to adult sexual criminal offense categories, pervasive, and consisted of a diversity of sexual acts) showed that the children had similar histories to those in the Canadian study. This 5-year study of 72 sexually aggressive children (ages 6 to 12) in Vermont (Gray, Busconi, Houchens, & Pithers, in press) found that 93% of the males and 100% of the females were themselves reported victims of child sexual abuse. Final reports of this study are expected to produce empirically based typologies for sexually aggressive children, as well as treatment outcome information (A. Gray, personal communication, February 28, 1997). Preliminary data suggest that psychiatric diagnoses were found in 93% of the sample, with Conduct Disorder (73%), Attention-Deficit/Hyperactivity Disorder (ADHD; 41%), Oppositional Defiant Disorder (27%), and Posttraumatic Stress Disorder (PTSD; 17%) being the most common diagnoses. Sixty-two percent of the total sample exceeded clinical ranges on the Sex Problems scale of the Child Behavior Checklist-Revised (CBCL-R; Achenbach, 1991a).

Descriptive data from three small-scale studies of children with molesting behavior also show convergent findings (Friedrich & Luecke, 1988; Johnson, 1988, 1989a). In these studies, the majority of children evidenced striking sexual victimization histories and high incidence rates of psychopathology, particularly ADHD, Oppositional Defiant Disorder, and Conduct Disorder. It is important to note that careful empirical diagnostic studies of this population are not available. The clinical features in this population show both complex etiology (e.g., biological, environmental, contextual) as well as high comorbidity (e.g., ADHD with Conduct Disorder or PTSD with hyperkinetic features). Much needed research in this area would greatly aid our diagnostic understanding of these children.

Morenz and Becker (1995), in their review on characteristics of adolescent sexual offenders, add credence to these preliminary findings. They state, "the sex offense itself usually occurs as the culmination of a multifaceted process that may include family dysfunction, social isolation and deficits, physical and/or sexual abuse, poor school performance, and other factors unique to each individual offender" (p. 254).

Treatment Outcome

Treatment outcome data regarding children with sexual behavior problems is lacking. Although some empirical literature exists regarding adolescent sexual offenders and the promising outcomes of cognitive behavioral techniques in group therapy (e.g., Becker, 1990; Butler & Fontenelle, 1995; Camp & Thyer, 1993), there is a paucity of therapy outcome studies for adolescent perpetrators (Becker et al., 1995) and virtually no published studies of treatment outcomes for prepubescent children with sexual behavior problems. In a careful review of cognitive behavioral group treatment programs for adult sexual offenders, Marshall and Barbaree (1990) found that, although there are limitations to the research, particularly in terms of specific treatment component efficacy with various types of offenders, cognitive behavior treatment (CBT) appears to be effective in reducing recidivism of sexual offending.

Unpublished, preliminary data on 70 children (ages 5 to 12) referred for sexual behavior problems suggest that both cognitive behavioral group therapy and unstructured dynamic play therapy groups are successful in reducing inappropriate sexual behavior (Walker, Jean, Bonner, & Berliner, 1997). The participants included children with a wide range of sexual behavior problems (e.g., no contact to full contact) reported as problematic by parents through the CBCL-R (Achenbach, 1991a) and the Child Sexual Behavior Inventory-Revised (CSBI-R, Friedrich, 1993b). It is difficult to discern from this preliminary report how successful the treatment groups were for the sexually aggressive (Groups III and IV) children. It is possible that group means are skewed by Group II children whose prognosis in treatment is better, according to general clinical observation.

Two recent empirical studies involving sexually abused preschoolers in CBT treatment found significant reductions in sexual behavior problems as endorsed by parents on the CSBI both at posttreatment and follow-up measures (Cohen & Mannarino, 1997; Stauffer & Deblinger, 1996). One study compared nonstructured supportive individual therapy to CBT individual therapy and found significant differences between the two approaches on the CSBI, with CBT achieving significantly higher reductions of problematic sexualized behavior at posttreatment (Cohen & Mannarino).

These studies, although limited in generalization by several factors (e.g., age, severity of sexual behavioral problems, identified victims rather than offenders), lend support to the idea that CBT may effectively target inappropriate sexual behaviors.

Empathy, Social Isolation, and Social Skills
Literature Regarding Children with Abuse Histories: Impact on Empathy

Adult offender literature acknowledges particular difficulties in empathy and intimacy, as is so clearly stated in the following quote: "Exposures to the experience typical of a sex offender's childhood . . . can be expected to make them relatively unable to develop intimacy and to feel empathy, and it leaves them socially inept, lacking in confidence, self-centered, hostile, aggressive . . ." (Marshall & Barbaree, 1990, p. 263). In general, a striking characteristic of Group III and IV children, like these adults, is their lack of empathy or perspective-taking (Gil & Johnson, 1993). Compared with nonabused children, however, abused children of any type tend to lack empathy. Straker and Jacobson (1981), for example, reported that physically abused boys and girls between ages 5 and 10 show less empathy than a carefully matched sample of nonabused children. In a sample of moderately aggressive preadolescent and adolescent boys, proactive aggression was predicted by parental physical aggression directed toward their offspring (Lochman & Lenhart, 1993). In another study, adolescent males who were sexually abused and did not abuse others tended to exhibit more empathy than sexually abused male adolescents who did abuse others (Arundell, 1992). Jordan's unpublished work (as cited by Goldstein & Michaels, 1985) hypothesizes that, in general, males may tend to have greater difficulty with empathic responding because it may imply, for them, passivity, loss of objectivity, and loss of control.

This notion is corroborated by the finding that aggressive boys place more value than nonaggressive boys on gaining control of a victim, and indicate feeling less concern about the suffering of the victim (Boldizar, Perry, & Perry, 1989). Aggressive boys endorse dominance and revenge as motivational factors for their behavior to a significantly greater extent than non-aggressive boys (Lochman & Lenhart, 1993). Given that most Group III and IV boys have been overpowered by an abuser, and are most likely experiencing a sense of powerlessness (e.g., Finkelhor & Browne, 1986), empathic responding and its concomitant implications could further threaten them. If, as is hypothesized by some researchers, these former victims may be attempting to recover lost control, power, and mastery by abusing others (e.g., Burgess, Hartman, & McCormack, 1987; Tharinger, 1990), the emergence of empathy may be antithetical to their goals of regaining power. This creates a clinical challenge, in that victim empathy has been theorized as a central factor in preventing future sexually aggressive behavior (e.g., Gilgun & Conner, 1990; Gray & Pithers, 1993; Ingersoll & Patton, 1990; Marshall & Barbaree, 1990, Murphy, 1990; Salter, 1995). Gray and Pithers caution that without the development of victim empathy, adolescent offenders may intellectually encode relapse prevention skills, but may lack the motivation to use this knowledge to avoid reoffending.

Social Isolation

Retrospective accounts of adult offenders underscore the profound sense of isolation these men felt as children and continue to experience as adults, and isolation is noted as a key factor to address in treatment (Ballard et al. 1900; Gilgun & Conner, 1990; Justice & Justice, 1979). Likewise, the adolescent sexual offender literature lists social isolation as especially problematic (Awad & Saunders, 1989; Barbaree & Cortoni, 1993; Fehrenbach, Smith, Monastersky, & Deisher, 1993). Marshall, Laws, and Barbaree (1990) elaborated on this sense of isolation from a developmental perspective, stating that if children do not develop strong and positive attachment bonds, they may never develop the capacity for intimacy. This, in turn, may create loneliness, which has been shown to be highly related to hostility and aggression.

Given this thinking, it follows that children who are already isolated and sexually aggressive must experience some reduction of isolation to begin taking the perspective of their victim(s). Children's self-statements of "I belong" are fundamental to later identification of others' feelings and an understanding of the consequences of one's actions on another. Although it is hoped that the group milieu will inherently foster community building and reduce isolation, the typically serious issues of abuse histories, damaged trust, and often disrupted attachment histories in this population necessitate a more creative and intentional treatment component to inculcate group connection and identity. Friedrich (1993a) wrote, "The more corrective the attachment experience, the more children can develop the 'internal working model' of relatedness that enables them to view other children accurately, and not as victims" (p. xii).

Social Skills Treatment

Given the above review, it is not surprising that social skills training is one of the more commonly prescribed treatments for sexual offenders (Bonner, 1995; McFall, 1990; Morenz & Becker, 1995; Murphy, 1990). However, social skills training has not been specifically tested as a treatment component for sexual offending (McFall). Practitioner consensus regarding treating adult and adolescent sexual offenders has maintained that targeting areas such as problem-solving, assertiveness, and conflict resolution enhances treatment outcome.

Treatment Models of Empathy Building

This paper introduces some general principles in treating boys with sexually aggressive behavior, undergirded with the belief that general empathy experienced as a part of the group context must be an explicit, foundational goal in treatment to foster the desired goal of victim empathy.

A three-component model of empathy (Feshbach & Feshbach, 1982) includes (1) the capacity to discriminate another's emotional state (affect identification); (2) the ability to assume the perspective and role of another (cognitive perspective-taking); and (3) the ability to respond emotionally (affective responsivity). This model includes several cognitive and affective skills that must be rehearsed in an interpersonal interaction. A developmental analysis of empathy (Hoffman, 1987) proposes that early in life (age 2), a child may experience empathic affect without a cognitive understanding that the other is separate from self. Later (ages 6 to 9), children see others as distinct entities with unique histories. This awareness progresses into more

complex levels of cognitive processes (including perspective-taking) that mediate and shape empathic responses. It follows, then, that it is precisely in this period of development (older childhood) that cognitive training may most greatly influence the development and refinement of empathic responding. Support for the Feshbach and Feshbach model exists in the adult sexual offender literature. Salter's (1995) team's unpublished empirical work regarding empathy in adult sexual offenders found that even individuals with a capacity for empathy were unaffected by the pain of others if they did not take the others' point of view and correctly identify the feelings. These researchers concluded that both perspective-taking and empathic concern are necessary to alter the behavior of offenders toward would-be victims.

The Feshbach and Feshbach (1982) model may be put into practice by training children to sequentially identify and label feelings in general, in themselves, and in others. Structured behavioral rehearsal in group discussions and activities (presented below) facilitates the safety needed to label and explore feelings in the self and then identify a similar feeling in other group members. Group members receive positive reinforcement for empathic perspective-taking and responding, such as identifying frustration in a group member and responding by helping that member with his task, or facilitating a conflict resolution within the group. Within a parent group component of treatment, caregivers are taught specific strategies for fostering and reinforcing empathic responses in their children.

An advantage of group treatment for empathy training is that the group may provide the objectivity and perspective needed for victim empathy. For example, by hearing group members discuss their perpetration of anonymous children, psychological distance is created. Group members have the opportunity to discuss how someone else's victim might have felt, or how another group member might have felt when abused. It is difficult to attain this level of objectivity in an individual treatment mode.

Treatment
Screening and Orientation

Careful screening is imperative for a successful group experience. Separate clinical interviews with parents and children elicit information regarding not only sexual offending behavior, but also the child's general behavioral and cognitive, emotional, and social development. Because interviewer anxiety can greatly limit information gathering and future group participation, clinicians working with this population must be knowledgeable about and comfortable with normative childhood sexual development, and must exhibit a calm concern for the perpetrating child. To establish permission to discuss sexuality, it is helpful to be direct with the children about the purpose of the interview and group. An example follows.

I am talking with you and other boys your age about being in a group. In this group, all of the boys have had a problem with sexual touching. Together, we will work on solving this problem. Today, I want to get to know many things about you. The sexual touching problem will be one of the things we will talk about, but we will also talk about other things, like what you like to do and what music you like best.

In keeping with this direct approach, if the interviewer has information from the child abuse investigative system, parents, or teachers, it is recommended to disclose this to the child. This approach models openness and facilitates trust.

I have talked with Investigator John. I understand that you have had some of your touching trouble with Susie. This is the place to talk about that problem so we can begin to make it better.

This statement gives the child permission to talk about the presenting problem by addressing relevant information in a matter-of-fact way.

Group Configuration

Gil and Johnson (1993) outlined important details for starting a group that closely match this author's approach in group treatment for Group III and IV children. Important factors to match in child clients are size, age (no more than 2-year spans are recommended), gender, status (e.g., disabled/non-disabled, high intelligence/lower intelligence, etc.) and sexual behavior group typology. Although it seems best to match children into their group types, this author's experience is that some Group III and IV children can be matched into a single group. If a Group IV child is much larger, or has a much higher status, and is also more aggressive, Group III children should not be included, to avoid setting up a power differential that can be countertherapeutic and potentially retraumatizing.

Group treatment may not be appropriate for some children. It is important to keep in mind that dyad or individual treatment may be more appropriate for children who may not match easily into a forming group. Factors such as power (aggressive) differentials, cognitive limitations, psychotic behaviors, or various disabilities (e.g., hearing impaired) may indicate the need for alternative treatment. The following vignette provides an example.

Danny, age 11, entered the group as a Group IV child. He was immature, emotionally and socially, but quite large and aggressive. He had forced intercourse on his younger sister repeatedly. He displayed aggressive conduct at home and at school, threatening both children and adults. Another group member, Stevie, age 10, was also a Group IV child. He had been hospitalized following his victim's disclosure of rape. He was hostile and aggressive, but also very slight and short in stature. A third group member, James, age 10, was a Group III child who was cognitively underdeveloped compared to the rest of the group. The fourth member, Tim, age 11, was a larger child (but not as large as Danny) who vacillated between Group III and IV behaviors. The last group member, Andy, age 9, was a Group III child who was cognitively bright, but physically small. In the first group session, Danny began victimizing the group members, mostly with verbal threats and aggressive physical gestures. Although the therapists kept the group physically safe, the boys were not emotionally safe. After the first session, Danny was asked to leave the group and was subsequently placed in individual treatment. At the following group session, the boys processed the initial session. Each member was able to admit how frightened he had felt and each expressed relief that Danny had been asked to leave the group.

Although this incident established the trust in the group leaders that was necessary for the boys to progress in treatment, the event could have been avoided with a more careful screening evaluation.

Issues of Group Safety: Group Size and Therapist Issues

Aside from matching group members, the author recommends groups be small (4 to 6 members) and led by 2 therapists (mixed gender) for role-modeling purposes. Other clinicians who work with behaviorally disordered children concur with this proposed small group size (e..g, Braswell, 1993), and those in the field of sexual offender treatment concur with the idea of a male and female co-leader team (e.g., McFall, 1990). The first group this author conducted had 4 group members and 1 therapist. The high level of anxiety in the group members, coupled with general hyperactivity, created behaviors difficult to control. The need to strip the room of "projectiles" was quickly recognized. Group materials (e.g., pencils) were introduced into the room only as projects required. This initial group treatment experience highlighted the importance of heightened structure and the value of a co-therapist. In the second group, the presence of Joe, a male co-therapist, facilitated group containment and group process. In terms of containment, the physical and vocal presence of the male (perceived by the children as more powerful) provided a natural inhibiting stimulus for group members' disruptive behavior. Additionally, the male co-therapist provided a natural and positive role model for appropriate social and empathy skills, as well as acceptable treatment of children and the modeling of an egalitarian relationship with the female co-therapist.

Although the male presence provides gender role modeling, it may also raise anxiety by serving as a stimulus for memories of past abuse by a male. In the first session of the group, for example, the boys explored the context by asking Joe if he had been abused as a child. The therapists interpreted this question as a safety check. Their response addressed the possible concern regarding safety.

Joe and I are both safe leaders. We will not hurt you or touch you in uncomfortable or sexual ways. We will not allow you to hurt each other or touch in sexual ways. We know many of you have been sexually misused by men [in our groups this had been 100%], and it makes sense that you would have worries about being here with a man and other boys who have been sexual with others.

In addition to having provided a corrective experience with a male, this experience also served as an entree to establish and post group rules about touching boundaries and other boundaries (e.g., appropriate language) that would keep the group safe.

In keeping with safety issues, 2 male therapists could be overwhelming, as the stimulus for fear would not be counterbalanced by an adult female presence. For most children, sexual abuse does not occur in the presence of a female (in the groups discussed in this paper, this was 100% the case). The children may have perceived that abuse would not occur in the presence of a female. For some children, of course, this may not be the case; some children are sexually abused by a female or with a female present. These considerations highlight the importance of knowing as much as possible about the particular abuse histories of the children in a group so that the various abuse stimuli can be minimized, discussed, and so that real and perceived safety can be achieved in the group milieu.

Caregiver Interview

During the caregiver interview, the therapist/interviewer gathers information, calms anxieties, and begins to educate the child's legal guardian. Two helpful and inexpensive resources for caregivers are the booklets *Children Who Molest: A Guide for Parents of Young Sex Offenders* (Gil, 1987) and *From Trauma to Understanding: A Guide for Parents of Children With Sexual Behavior Problems* (Pithers, Gray, Cunningham, & Lane,

1993). In this author's clinical experience, these materials appear to present realistic perceptions of the treatment process and emphasize the importance of parental supervision in the life of the offending child. The caregiver interview offers a good opportunity to reinforce the very important role of the parent or parent figure in meeting treatment goals (e.g., the offending child should not be left alone with other children until treatment goals are reliably met).

The first meeting with supportive caregivers clarifies expectations about the children's and parents' groups, including details about the sexuality portion of the education. Informing parents that they will be exposed to the same sexuality curriculum as the children may encourage further parent-child communication about sexuality outside the group. Caretakers often have questions such as, "Is my child going to continue to abuse children when he grows up?" or "Is my child going to be gay?" It is advisable to offer realistic answers to these and other anxiety-laden questions during the initial interview with caretakers. Some effective responses may include, "Research tells us that although there is a greater proportion of sexual offenders who were abused as children, the majority of sexually abused children do not develop into sexual offenders" and "The majority of gay and lesbian persons in the general population were not sexually abused as children. We know that sexual abuse does not directly cause homosexuality."

During the screening interview(s), it is important to document a thorough psychosocial history, as well as specific information regarding the child offender's sexual behavior and sexual knowledge. General measures of child functioning (e.g., CBCL-R; Achenbach, 1983) are always useful. The Child Sexual Behavior Checklist Second Revision (CSBCL; Johnson, 1995), a specific structured interview, is a useful tool for initial interviewing. The CSBCL is a non-normed, theoretically driven structured interview that facilitates gaining in-depth information regarding the parental perspective on the child's sexual knowledge and behavior. This measure can be used in conjunction with Johnson's parent

surveys, which are useful tools for gathering information on parental beliefs about childhood sexuality; for understanding parental responses to sexual behavior in children and family practices in areas of privacy, nudity, hygiene; and for gaining a history of parental sexuality from parents' own childhood experiences. In addition, information from child protective service records, law enforcement reports, school reports, past mental health records, and medical evaluations is invaluable in planning the young client's therapeutic course.

A specific sexual behavior assessment instrument is the CSBI (Friedrich, 1993a; Friedrich, in press; Friedrich, Grambsch, Broughton, Kuiper, & Beilke, 1991). The CSBI has high inter-item and test-retest reliability, as well as discriminative validity between abused and non-abused children (Friedrich et al., 1992). The CSBI discriminates normative and non-normative sexual behavior (e.g., general psychiatric, non-abused, abuse) specific to ages and gender.

Caregiver Treatment Component

The most striking deficiency in CBT programs and research up to this point has been the neglect of children's caregivers, although it is generally believed that intervening with these caregivers is a critical factor in both strengthening and maintaining generalization of treatment effects over time (e.g., Kendall, 1991). Additionally, CBT with non-offending parents of sexual abuse victims has promising empirical support in terms of symptom reduction in both the child victims and their parents (Deblinger, Lippmann, & Steer, 1996; Stauffer & Deblinger, 1996).

Although there is no treatment outcome literature of parent management therapy for parents of sexually aggressive children, behavioral parent training has been documented as the most effective treatment for childhood aggression (Kazdin, 1987; Lochman, 1990; McMahon & Wells, 1989). Recent data suggest parent management training combined with problem-solving skills training for children with conduct disorder produces more symptom reduction as measured by the CBCL-R and Teacher Report Form (TRF; Achenbach, 1991b;

Edelbrock & Achenbach, 1984) than either method alone (Kazdin, 1996). These proven models for parent management of aggression require parental knowledge of the child's misconduct, parents' availability to act cross-situationally as agents of change, and, perhaps most importantly, parents' investment in the treatment of their children. In working with sexually aggressive children, parents often are not aware of their children's offending behaviors, which typically occur in private settings designed by the child. Thus, "catching" a child in order to mete out immediate consequences may be difficult, creating a challenge to parental management. Furthermore, Group III and Group IV boys may have a complex history with state child protection services and juvenile justice systems. Accessible caregivers for these child clients may be temporary foster or group care "parents" whose investment is inherently limited. Finally, some families may be non-supportive of treatment because they continue to remain loyal to an adult perpetrator when legal evidence has been too scanty to obtain conviction of guilt in criminal or family court.

Even when caregivers are supportive of treatment efforts, they are often psychosocially limited. Families of sexually aggressive children are frequently characterized as multi-problem families in which the family has a high tolerance for aggression, sexually explicit material is available to the child, and the maternal-child relationship is described as "problematic" in several areas, including boundary-setting and child management skills (Hall et al., 1997). Although one could argue that this research provides rationale for parent treatment, the fact is that basic parenting must be taught before the more intense sexual offending and abuse dynamics portions of the treatment can be addressed. Thus, parent training and mental health treatment for these kinds of caregivers is more complex and may warrant longer treatment duration (Kendall, 1991).

Finally, even when parents are available, invested, and motivated to help their child by participating in treatment, caregivers may be strapped financially, have transportation obstacles, need child care, or be psychologically depleted or impaired. Despite these hindrances, it is essential that an attempt be made to include the available caregivers in an adjunct treatment module while the boys are in treatment. Some agencies provide child care and transportation. Other agencies work with child protection services or the juvenile justice system to meet these needs for clients.

Parent training components for children with sexual behavior problems have been formally designed but not yet published (A. Gray, personal communication, February 28, 1997; C. E. Walker, personal communication, January 28, 1997). This article is not intended to address the scope of a parent training module; however, the areas to cover with parents are introduced.

Parents may need education and treatment in the following areas: (1) explanation of the group (outline of the sessions and topics that will be covered with the boys); (2) context and impact of abusive behaviors (sexual, physical, and emotional); (3) sexual offending behaviors and cognitions (e.g., examples of sexual abuse cycle models); (4) sexual education (e.g., the curriculum to which their children are exposed, how to verbally follow up with their children regarding the sexual education curriculum, exploration of parental attitudes and beliefs regarding sexuality); (5) behavior management techniques for aggressive and sexualized behavior (e.g., parents are given specific strategies for supervising their child and for dealing with reoffending behavior if it occurs); and (6) recognition of their own histories of violence and problem-solving strategies, and alterations of their own schema and behavioral repertoire in these areas, where indicated. The message inherent in the parent training module is that parents are social role models for their children. As such, they can help children generalize and maintain their newfound skills only if they have also changed their beliefs and actions in the various treatment areas described above.

Child Treatment Component
Treatment Structure

Once a group is carefully configured, issues of group structure arise.

Again, guidelines provided by Gil and Johnson (1993) are helpful. The authors suggest that children be part of a weekly 1.5 hour group for 1 to 1.5 years in order to maximize learning and change behaviors to eliminate perpetration behavior. This time frame is longer than that typical of even the longer duration CBT programs for aggressive children, which loosely range from 18 (e.g., Braswell, 1993; Lochman, 1985) to 20 sessions (e.g., Blonk, Prins, Sergeant, Ringrose & Brinkman, 1996). Time frames for adult offender treatment range from 4 to 30 months (Marshall & Barbaree, 1990). The Oklahoma Health Sciences Center model for adolescent offenders requires a minimum of 1 year of weekly 1.5 hour sessions for the boys, and required monthly sessions for the parents, with an option of attending weekly 1.5 hour parent groups (Bonner, 1995). Group session duration may be limited by agency or financial resources. Treatment providers may need to implement creative solutions, such as grant funding or offering the group in 12-week treatment units with "rest time" built in, that might be more financially manageable.

Within each session, a set structure has been useful in the current author's experience, and reported as useful by others who work with youngsters with disruptive behavior problems (e.g., Braswell, 1993; Morenz & Becker, 1995). Such a structure provides an anticipated schema, which may reduce anxiety and facilitate maintenance of control. Structure includes a beginning format (e.g., a group game or sharing time), snack, lesson with discussion or an experiential component, large group social skills practice (e.g., non-competitive game) with discussion, and a ritualized good-bye, such as clean-up or circle time to review goals for the week.

Group Treatment Techniques
Cognitive Behavioral Therapy Modifications to Existing Resources

In this author's work with 8- to 10-year-old male children with sexual behavior problems, she has relied

heavily on cognitive behavioral techniques; however, she has found that CBT has been most workable with this energetic child population when offered in active, hands-on modalities. These children have a high incidence of learning problems and school failure. This author recommends that written work or other "school-like" activities be minimized or modified. Three activity resource books for this population, often used with modification, have been quite useful (see Cunningham & MacFarlane, 1991; Johnson, 1995; MacFarlane & Cunningham, 1988). In *Steps to Healthy Touching* (MacFarlane & Cunningham), children work through 12 written steps in areas such as victim empathy; perpetration thoughts, feelings, and actions; social support system; and changing critical thinking. All work is in the form of written assignments. Practicing new behaviors is built in as homework. Because follow-through on written assignments is poor, it is recommended that these 12 steps be adapted to minimize the written component. An example of such a modification is in the area of identification and labeling of feelings. Empirical research indicates that aggressive boys, as compared to nonaggressive boys, overendorse happiness as an affect in hypothetically negative situations (Lochman & Dodge, 1994). These researchers hypothesize that the boys minimize their emotions (e.g., fear) so they do not feel vulnerable. The authors conclude that, regardless of the sources, the implication is that the boys may be ill-prepared to cope with their affective reactions, possibly being flooded by affect, which preempts their information processing systems. The danger, of course, with sexually aggressive boys, is automatic offending behaviors might override affect (e.g., fear), thus reinforcing sexual offending behavior.

To work with the concept of identifying and labeling feelings, drawing a picture of "taking off your mask," from *Steps to Healthy Touching* (MacFarlane & Cunningham, 1988, p. 30), can be substituted by having the group members create masks that they can actually put on and take off in the context of group. Role plays around the artful "feeling masks" (e.g., papier-mâché or paper bags) can be directed by the leaders or by the group itself. For example, one boy said he shows a happy mask to the world, while actually feeling very sad inside. The children are encouraged to discuss what they think and do when they present a "happy" mask and what they think and do when they present the more authentic "sad" feelings. They are challenged to change their thoughts and behaviors to be consistent with their feelings. This exercise leads into discussions about how their angry thoughts and behaviors that are precipitants to their sexual offending may be thoughts and behaviors that cover up their hurt, sad, or scared feelings and thoughts. Later, the children will be encouraged to generate alternative behaviors for dealing with sad, angry, hurt, and scared feelings. Exercises like this one lay the groundwork for the later, more applied, behavioral change work and is consistent with CBT groundwork with children who have been sexually abused who tend to distance themselves from authentic emotions (Deblinger & Heflin, 1996).

The following examples are samples of other modifications that can extend written exercises in *Steps to Healthy Touching* (MacFarlane & Cunningham, 1988). The idea is to create therapeutic tasks that actively engage children's minds and bodies around their thoughts, feelings, and behaviors related to the sexual acting out. One example is to substitute for the written exercise for thoughts and feelings connected to before, during, and after the offending behavior (pp. 66, 71–72) by creating several large wall murals upon which children write "graffiti" about feelings and thoughts regarding their perpetration behavior. Different walls are designated for thoughts and feelings before, during, and after the offending behavior. An additional wall might be designated for graffiti showing external consequences to their offending behavior. This activity gives opportunities for movement, colorful expression, and a group activity (peer modeling) as the children record their thoughts and feelings. Further, the ABCs of their offending behavior are now in the form of visual cues within the group room, to be used for later discussions. Another simple modification of a written exercise is for children to

make a large STOP sign from poster board and a dowel stick to put in their rooms as a visual cue each day to STOP and THINK or to STOP their perpetration behavior (p. 54).

Other resource books offer a variety of valuable treatment activities. In *When Children Molest Children* (Cunningham & MacFarlane, 1991), activities fall in the following areas of therapeutic focus: self-esteem, anger, problem-solving skills, victimization, perpetration, empathy, and healthy sexuality. This manual has been recently updated and revised, bearing a new title, *Children Who Abuse* (Cunningham & MacFarlane, 1996). Finally, Johnson's (1995) *Treatment Exercises for Child Abuse Victims and Children With Sexual Behavior Problems* has several family-focused exercises and parent exercises that offer an additional angle for treating this population. These resources have several stories that can be successfully modified as role plays or puppet plays, as well as a wealth of games, role plays, and group exercises.

Specific Treatment Techniques for Sexually Aggressive Children

For adolescent and adult sexual offenders, primary treatment goals have been to (a) reduce perpetration behavior and (b) increase victim empathy. Secondary goals have included anger modulation, social skills enhancement, healthier sexual attitudes, and increasing social support networks (e.g., Marshall, Laws, & Barbaree, 1990). This author's experience suggests that a mediating third goal, general empathy and a feeling of group identity, operationalized as vicarious conditioning, facilitates reaching all other goals. The next sections describes specific treatment techniques to (a) increase prosocial, empathic responses within the group setting and to foster group identity; (b) to reduce perpetration behaviors; and (c) to increase victim empathy.

Techniques for Increasing Perspective-Taking and General Empathy through Group Work

General empathy and group identification has not been emphasized as a

specific treatment goal for children who molest, thus, less resources exist for the therapist. To reach the primary goals of eliminating perpetration behaviors and gaining victim empathy, this therapist has been guided by the principle that the boys must feel a sense of general connection to and identity with others. As previously stated, models of empathy in children focus on perspective-taking or taking the role of another as a key for empathy and prosocial behavior (e.g., Bengtsson & Johnson, 1992; Feshbach, 1975; Hoffman, 1975; Macorov, 1978). Within group sessions, focus is on teaching prosocial skills through such techniques as role playing, skill teaching and rehearsal, thought stopping, anger management, and problem-solving. A specific model, such as interpersonal cognitive problem-solving skills (Spivack, Platt, & Shure, 1976), can be used as a base (e.g., Utay & Lampe, 1995). This model details five specific skills, including (1) to view the self in relation to others, along with recognizing that how one relates can lead directly to positive or negative results; (2) to generate alternative solutions to problems; (3) to verbalize a step-by-step plan for solving an interpersonal problem; (4) to take into consideration consequences of social behavior on the self and others; and (5) to understand that how one feels and behaves may influence the feelings and actions of others. These five specific skills can be taught and reinforced throughout the group experience through role plays and in vivo activities. A specific technique that has been clinically useful, but has not been empirically tested, is non-competitive, or cooperative, group games and therapeutic activities. Within these activities, the five above steps can be implemented.

Non-Competitive Group Games and Activities

Cooperative problem-solving games such as Circle the Circle (Rohnke, 1984), Warp Speed (Rohnke, 1989), Group Juggling (Rohnke, 1984), and others (e.g., Fluegelman, 1976) are useful group starters. Such starters set a non-competitive climate in which prosocial skills and empathy are taught, modeled, and rehearsed. The idea is to give these typically aggressive boys an opportunity to create new schemas within a meaningful peer relationship context; one in which the children need each other to reach the goals of the activity. Theoretically, as the group works together to attain mutual goals, feelings of isolation will be reduced, and competency, trust, and skills in communication and cooperation will increase. The five steps of interpersonal problem-solving can be reinforced, as the group must communicate about solving problems and become aware of how their actions may impact the group goal.

As a simple example of a "win-win" game, the therapist starts a group session by offering a beach ball and asking, "How long can the group keep the ball in the air today? How many group hits before it touches the floor?" The next week the group tries to break the record; they problem-solve as a group (hopefully using some of their new skills) to work together keeping the ball in the air. The boys quickly see that their impulsive, aggressive style will not facilitate "winning" for the group. Following the games, structured discussion can reinforce the prosocial skills with questions such as, "Who did you notice using assertive communication today?"; "How did it go with John taking the leader role today?"; "What thoughts did you have when you were the one who allowed it to hit the floor?" Positive comments such as, "I liked the way there were no put-downs even when the ball hit the floor"; "Wow! You guys figured out that gently hitting the ball rather than slamming it helps you break your group record!" reinforce specific skills in development of group cooperation.

An example of a cooperative therapeutic activity that implements CBT principles, and can serve as the basis for the group "lesson," is the traditional Blindfold Trust Walk. This activity allows the children to experience arousal (e.g., anxiety or fear) while they are being led blindfolded through an obstacle course by the group leader. The adult can model effective communication while leading the boys to a prize (e.g., candy) that awaits as a positive reinforcer. Through taking turns, group members can practice communication and leadership skills and then receive feedback from the group. Using the five steps of interpersonal cognitive problem-solving, the boys can generate strategies for more effective communication and discuss how their behavior and communication to the group either helped or hindered the process. This activity is also a natural gateway to perspective-taking by creating an arousing emotional circumstance within which to practice labeling and identifying feelings such as fear and powerlessness as well as competency and control in self and others.

Eliminating Perpetration Behavior

In general, perpetration behaviors are eliminated through (a) recognizing internal and external cues and conditions that signal the reoffending cycle and (b) generating new behavioral and cognitive strategies that can counteract the antecedent feelings, behaviors, or thoughts that precede or accompany the offending behavior (e.g., Pithers, 1990).

Reducing or preventing perpetration behavior is interwoven throughout the group treatment during all modules. In addition, teaching about appropriate sexuality (e.g., Johnson, 1989b) is another avenue to influence the perpetration cycles. Some ideas for direct work on perpetration behaviors follow.

Physical Boundaries

Direct education regarding physical boundaries is imperative. Sexually aggressive children have distorted perceptions and beliefs about appropriate and inappropriate physical touch. Likely, their own boundaries have been invaded by older persons in their histories. One in vivo exercise that demonstrates, behaviorally, the significance of boundaries is Face Space (T. Boatmun, 1994). This exercise serves to raise arousal, as the children are asked to move in and out of their physical comfort zones. The boys can become aware of thoughts and behaviors as they become aroused by physical closeness. The details of this exercise (below) serve to illustrate how Face Space can be used in the context of CBT with sexually aggressive boys.

Group members form dyads and are given 3 feet of yarn. Participants wrap one end of the yarn around their index fingers and place it on their stomachs. They stand far enough apart so that their string is taut. Group members must discover their "face space," or the distance between two persons talking. Silently, the pairs move towards each other, wrapping the yarn around their index fingers in order to keep it tight. Once they find their "face space," they are directed to stop. When they are comfortable with this distance, their arousal is raised by having them take one step closer. The participants then think about how this makes them feel and where they feel it in their bodies. They notice their thoughts. Then, the leader has them step back out, and think about how it feels to be back in their comfortable space. Again, participants are asked to notice their thoughts. These steps are repeated and followed by discussion focused on identifying and respecting personal physical boundaries. The children can learn to identify where their physical boundaries are for social interactions and what it feels like when those boundaries are being invaded. They can learn to understand that all people have different boundaries. They may begin to discuss times when their physical boundaries have been violated. They may be able to discus feeling sexual arousal when they were close and what thoughts or environmental constraints inhibited sexual behavior. Such an experience is helpful in pointing out that they can be close to a peer and not be sexual; that they do have some internal control.

Sexual Abuse Cycles

Adult and adolescent sexual offender treatment experts recommend working with perpetrators directly on sexual abuse cycles (e.g., Gilgun & Connor, 1990; Ryan, Lane, Davis, & Isaac, 1987) in order for offenders to have a framework for understanding the behavioral, psychological, situational, and social factors that led to their offense. For children, there are several useful models that explain a sequence of behaviors that characterize sexual perpetration. Cunningham and MacFarlane (1991) offer two possible models of perpetration cycles: "Sexual Abuse for Kids" (p. 172) and

"Sexual Abuse Cycle/Steps to Getting in Trouble" (p. 173). Johnson (1995) provides an alternative model (e.g., pp. 154–161; see Appendix A for one model).

The sexual abuse cycle model creates a visual and verbal representation of the steps in each child's sexual offending pattern. The sexual abuse cycle concept helps children become more aware of the many factors in their sexual offending behavior. This awareness will then be used to develop strategies to stop the behaviors at certain points in their unique cycles. The boys will ultimately sequence the emotions, thoughts, and behaviors that occur in their individual perpetration cycles. They also identify the contextual cues or triggers to their abusive behaviors that may influence the onset, maintenance, and cessation of the sexual offending behaviors.

Although none of the general models listed above will reflect a child's exact sexual abuse sequence, these models can be used to demonstrate how thoughts and feelings lead to choices for abusive behaviors. The boys are introduced to the generic cycles, followed by stories to illustrate the cycles. Examples of abuse cycle stories are in Appendix B. The first, "The Angry Baseball Player" (Cunningham & MacFarlane, 1991, p. 174), is best used initially. It depicts an anger cycle with consequences that closely follow the sexual abuse cycle. The second story, "The Babysitting Disaster" (Cunningham & MacFarlane, pp. 175–176), includes angry and sexual feelings and actions.

These stories can be readily adapted into role plays by the group with variations suggested by the director (usually the therapist; sometimes a group member). The director will "rerun" the story with directives of "Stop the action!" at different decision-making points. The character then generates a new solution. Videotaping these role plays is quite useful for later group discussion of various solutions and choices the boys generate. The boys "rehearse" their solutions by watching themselves and peers in the role plays and then discussing the action at various therapist-driven choice points.

When the group members have mastered the cycle, steps, or road map concept, each child is given the task of detailing his own sexual abuse cycle. A useful way to depict the sequences of behaviors and thoughts is through cartooning. Cartoons naturally provide the schema for behaviors through pictures, and thoughts through thought bubbles. Additionally, group members can put each behavioral frame on a separate index card so that the cards can be laid out in order to chronicle their unique perpetration behaviors and thoughts. As the boys learn new strategies for dealing with feelings (e.g., talking to someone; relaxation), thoughts (e.g., thought-stopping or channel-switching), and situational factors (e.g., avoid certain situations, don't be alone with younger children), they can create a new cartoon frame to reflect their new skill, which is aimed at interrupting the perpetration cycle. The boys are encouraged to present their completed cycles at various therapeutic stages to the whole group. Group members can then ask questions, offer suggestions, and positively reinforce the work effort. Strong social learning through peer modeling can occur for the group as certain group members model positive changes in their behavioral repertoires.

Victim Empathy

In working with this population, it is important to be ever mindful that our child clients are themselves victims (emotional, physical, and/or sexual). Work with adult and adolescent sexual offenders highlights the offender's own victimization as a topic for clinical intervention (e.g., Ryan et al., 1987). Group leaders can begin by introducing activities such as "I'm OK, You're OK" (Aiken, 1993) that address difference, perspective-taking, and empathy, and later can directly educate the group members about the impact of abuse, helping the children remember their own abuse experiences cognitively and affectively. This sets the stage for facilitating the reinterpretation of group members' own victimization experiences into new schemas (e.g., "even though I became sexually aroused, that does not mean I asked for the experience or even that I liked what was happening"; "I blamed myself because I really needed that relationship and even enjoyed the contact, but I see now that I was confused and really didn't have any other person that understood me . . . maybe I'm not so bad for having those feelings"). The leaders then can model compassion for the boys' victimization, demonstrating the very behaviors expected from the children toward their victims. Furthermore, by offering the opportunity to safely express feelings related to prior victimization, the children have a substitute behavior for dealing with their intense affect and cognitions around their own abuse, theoretically reducing their impulse to repeat their victimization experience with other children. Deblinger and Heflin (1996) offer a chapter on CBT with sexually abused children that can be used as a guide for the children's own victimization work.

Caution is advised, however, for it is important to continue to focus on the main goal of reducing perpetration behavior. Thus, therapists are advised to achieve a balance between victim and offender issues in which accountability for offending behaviors is balanced with empathy and compassion for the child offender's own victimization. The videotapes *A Time to Tell* (Boy Scouts of America, 1989) and *Scared Silent: Exposing and Ending Child Abuse* (Shapiro Productions, 1992) are tools used to bridge offending/victimization issues. The boys can clearly discuss and identify with both the offending patterns of those depicted, as well as the victimization issues. Seeing both sides may be important for two reasons. First, the boys can understand themselves as victims in order to develop self and victim empathy and they can understand perpetration behavior more fully, noticing the motivations of the offender. Second, empirical research with nonperpetrating children (ages 10 to 11) indicates that children who can reflect on the inner experiences of both the victim and the victimizer are more prosocial in their actions (Bengtsson & Johnson, 1992). (Note: In using *Scared Silent,* only the segment of a juvenile offender telling her offending and victimization history is appropriate for this purpose. It is a highly affectively charged scenario, and likely should be introduced into the group only after trust has been established and when the boys have a groundwork in expressing some of their feelings regarding their perpetrating behavior.)

Again, the activity manuals previously listed include exercises for developing victim empathy. Activities focus on perspective-taking and empathy through role plays within the group setting. Exercises such as identification of victims, identification of victims' feelings, and writing amends letters are included. Stories can also be included to underscore the victim-to-victimizer process (Davis, 1990; see Appendix C, "The Scorpion Bunny"). An example of an activity that has provided a foundation for victim perspective-taking through role playing and discussion in these groups is an interactive story called "Bruno the Bobcat" (Cunningham & MacFarlane, 1991, pp. 177–178; see Appendix D). This story allows for group reflection concerning the role of the victim turned victimizer. Following the story, the children take turns role-playing the part of the baby monkey whom Bruno victimizes. The story is processed by asking the children how they felt when they were the monkey and asking them for ideas about what the bobcat could do to make it up to the monkey. The group is then led to consider what the other animals in the forest could do to let the monkey know that they understand how he feels. Finally, the children can discus the concept of making amends after someone has hurt someone else. This exercise encourages empathy when the children project themselves into another's shoes. Many stories or short scenarios can be used therapeutically in this way or expanded through artwork.

Experiential Victim Empathy Exercise: Paper People

A victim empathy exercise called "Paper People" has been developed by the current author (van Eys & Hoffman, 1992). This exercise is used when the group members have achieved a substantial level of maturity in their understanding of their victims' experiences and their own perpetration cycle. "Paper People" takes advantage of a documented developmental change in older children wherein they are more likely to explain their empathic feelings by referring to the internal psychological perspective of the target person

(Hughes, Tingle, & Sawin, 1981). A concrete target person enhances the children's ability to conceptualize thoughts and feelings of the victim.

Before engaging in this activity, the child should demonstrate the following: (a) child is able to admit he has sexually perpetrated; (b) there is no overt victim-blaming (e.g., "it was her idea") but there may continue to be subtle victim-blaming (e.g., "it was my choice and my fault, but Susie really liked it"); (c) child has at least rudimentarily detailed his own sexual abuse cycle, with at least an emerging awareness of the antecedent thoughts, feelings, and behaviors that evoke his cycle; (d) child has demonstrated prosocial skills and contributed in the group meetings consistently for several weeks; and (e) there have been no reports of sexual offending for several weeks. The experiential exercise is analogous to an adult offender group exercise in which the clients write and then read a diary account or letter "as if" from their victim's perspective (e.g., Ingersoll & Patton, 1990). The adult offender "victim diary" was modified to be more developmentally appropriate for children, because they need to be more concrete, visual, and interactive in their approach to problem solving. The "Paper People" activity offers group members and leaders a gauge to the therapeutic progress of the offending behaviors and attitudes. Has the child stopped the more subtle victim-blaming? Does the child understand all the damage that has occurred as a result of his perpetration? Is there any evidence of denial, minimization, rationalization, or continued cognitive distortion? The "Paper People" exercise, like the adult offender victim diary exercise, is thought by this author to be a promising tool for assessing the status of cognitive, affective, and behavioral components of the offending behavior in child perpetrators.

In the "Paper People" exercise, the group member(s) is asked to construct on butcher paper a life-size drawing of his victim(s) and encouraged to think carefully about just how this person looks and dresses. The child is asked to spend quite a bit of time making the victim(s) as life-like and size-appropriate as possible. It is useful to provide drawing materials as well as fabric and but-

tons for clothing and yarn or drapery cord for hair. Poster board may be used to bolster the backside of the "people."

Although the children may be simultaneously asked to create their paper people, only one or two group members will present their victim's experience during any given weekly session. This activity occurs late in the group process (e.g., when there is evidence of a growing level of victim empathy) and may occur sooner for some group members than others. When a group member is ready to present his story, he sits in a chair with his life-size person in front of him so that the rest of the group sees only the paper figure. The child then speaks from behind the paper person as if he were the victim, telling the whole story, focusing in on the feelings. Group members ask questions of the "victim." The questions not only reveal the spotlighted child's progress and current understanding, but also the group members' distortions, understandings, motivations, and areas of misunderstanding. For example, a common question from the group is, "Why did he do it?" This interest in motivation for offending often prompts therapeutic group discussion, and may enlighten group leaders to greater awareness of group members' continued areas of cognitive distortion. An example of a child's "Paper People" exercise follows.

Stevie, age 10, told Mary's story. "I (Mary) wanted to do the sex thing too." This concerned the therapists initially, who thought Stevie was blaming the victim or minimizing his responsibility. However, therapist concern dissipated when a group member asked "Mary, did you like it?" and the offender child (as "Mary") answered, "No, it hurt and I cried." It became apparent that, with this offense, the dynamics were like Group III dynamics—the set-up had been mutual, but the victim did not fully understand the "sex thing." By this point in treatment, Stevie had been able to understand that even though his victim had agreed to "sex things" without overt coercion, she had not enjoyed the experience, and, indeed, it had hurt her. Stevie appeared to have some genuine understanding of his victim. Following this scenario, Stevie then said that there was another victim that he had previously not disclosed. The experience of being empathic and receiving group support had permitted him to name another victim.

This level of victim empathy follows much preparatory work on the part of the presenting group member. The ability to engage fully in this exercise would indicate readiness for "graduation" from the program.

Conclusion and Discussion

In the absence of empirical literature, this paper has presented a tentative, untested model for treating prepubescent boys with aggressive sexual behavior. The nascent theoretical and descriptive literature served as a base for the current model, and depicts these boys as coming from multi-troubled backgrounds. Group treatment for sexually aggressive boys creates unique challenges for mental health practitioners. Careful screening with a thorough intake assessment specific to this population is imperative to ensure an effective group configuration. Understanding the group typologies of children with sexual behavior problems is important. Small groups (4 to 6 children) matched for age and gender with two leaders of different genders are advised. A concurrent parent group appears to be an important adjunct to treatment. Effective group leaders are those with a comfortable tolerance for and understanding of children, sexuality, and challenging behavior, as well as the confidence to directly approach these issues in a nonjudgmental manner. A background in implementing CBT techniques and an experiential, playful spirit also seem to be crucial leadership qualities.

Three primary goals of this logically derived proposed multi-component treatment model are reducing perpetration behaviors, increasing general empathy and perspective-taking, and increasing victim empathy. Secondary goals include anger management, building social skills, strengthening social support, and developing healthy sexuality. Specific resources for group curriculum are detailed (e.g., Cunningham & MacFarlane, 1991, 1996; Johnson, 1995; MacFarlane & Cunningham, 1988). Cooperative

group games, structured role plays, stories, and exercises such as "Paper People" (van Eys & Hoffman, 1992) give the children active modalities in which to practice perspective-taking, social skills, and empathy skills.

Through this multi-component treatment model, the boys in this author's experience eliminated perpetration behavior (as measured by self-report, parental report, and no further victim allegations at 1-year follow-up). Furthermore, in this author's experience, the boys in group achieved heightened general empathy responses observable within the group setting, as well as victim empathy observable through certain therapeutic activities (e.g., "Paper People"). Treatment outcome studies that will follow the boys into the adolescent and adult years are needed for this population.

Methodological Issues

This population is both difficult to treat and study due to factors such as low parental motivation, the transient nature of living situations (e.g., multiple foster placements or transient families), inconsistent attendance, and questionable reliability of self and parental report regarding recidivism. Another constraint is that most communities do not have specific treatment programs for prepubescent children who are sexually aggressive. Thus, finding participants for such research is limited. Given that early intervention with this population could prove to decrease later sexual offenses, it would be wise community policy to (a) screen all alleged maltreated children for the possibility of sexual and aggressive reactivity and (b) create specific community programs for sexually aggressive children that will be court-mandated and monitored by the court or child protective system. Once a child is entered into a community program, various supports such as transportation, child care or therapeutic groups for siblings, and financial assistance are a few ways to reduce barriers to treatment.

Research issues for sexually aggressive children are similar to those outlined in a review of CBT interventions for children (Ager & Cole, 1991). Key issues in their review included discerning the critical components of cognitive behavioral inter-

ventions, determining what variables increase generalization and maintenance effects, and developing socially valid outcome measures. Other important issues are comorbidity and clinical significance (Kendall & Panichelli-Mindel, 1995).

Concerning the proposed treatment model, the above recommendations are important. Research is needed to determine which specific components (e.g., sexual education, perspective-taking, group problem-solving, sexual abuse cycle, parental component) of this comprehensive treatment package are most effective singly and in combination, and for what subtypes of children (e.g., Group III and Group IV; boys and girls; children with various comorbid conditions; children with various abuse histories; children with either invested or non-invested caregivers; early elementary or older elementary; etc.).

In terms of measuring treatment effectiveness, issues of clinically and socially meaningful outcomes, as well as comprehensive and meaningful outcome measures, are at issue. It is recommended that child self-reports and reports and records of sexual behavior and allegations of offending (sexual and nonsexual) behavior be obtained from parents, teachers, mental health counselors, child protective service, law enforcement, probation officers, and the courts. Formal measures, such as assessing the amount of information a child has learned in group, or measures, such as the CBCL-R and the CSBI, that provide clinically useful norms, are potential pre- and post-test measures. Finally, pre- and post-test peer acceptance ratings within the group and school settings add additional, potentially useful information. In the social skills training literature, peer acceptance has been the most resistant measure to change (Zaragoza, Vaughn, & McIntosh, 1991). Because isolation and peer rejection have been identified as major issues for this population, it is important to try to effect changes in this area; however, guarded optimism is cautioned in terms of large treatment effect sizes. In this light, it would be interesting to test this proposed model that emphasizes group problem-solving, non-competitive activities, in-depth perspective-taking and victim empathy against a more skills-oriented social skills training model to see if peer acceptance ratings, perpetration recidivism, and other clinically and socially meaningful measures differ between these types of interventions.

Appendix A
Sexual Abuse Cycle/Steps to Getting in Trouble

This chart [see below] is adapted with permission from *The Sexual Abuse Cycle in the Treatment of Adolescent Sexual Abusers* (Videotape reference materials), by Connie Isaac and Sandy Lane (© 1990 by The Safer Society Press, PO Box 340, Brandon, VT 05733). The case example was furnished by a 9-year-old offender. As printed in "Group Treatment for Prepubescent Boys with Sexually Aggressive Behavior: Clinical Considerations and Proposed Treatment Techniques," by Patti P. van Eys, *Cognitive and Behavioral Practice, 4,* 1997, pp. 349–382.

Appendix B
The Angry Baseball Player

There was a boy named Andy who didn't feel very good about himself. The only thing Andy thought he was good at was baseball. Andy *was* an excellent hitter. One day, Andy had a bad game. He struck out every time he was at bat. He said to himself, "I can't do anything right. I can't even hit anymore." He figured that everyone watching thought he was a lousy hitter (even though he didn't ask them what they thought). He felt so bad about himself that he kept away from the other team members and didn't talk to anyone when he got home.

After a while, Andy began to blame Sam, the pitcher for the other team, for his strike-outs. He thought about it all the time. He started to think about how much bigger and stronger he was than Sam. Then Andy started to think about hurting Sam for making him look bad. In fact, that's *all* he thought about.

One day Andy made a plan to get even. He decided to beat Sam up before the next baseball game. He knew where the team was playing, so he rode his bike over there early and started a fight with Sam. Andy gave Sam a black eye. As Andy was riding away, he began to worry that his coach would find out about what he did and kick him off the team.

The coach *did* find out and suspended Andy for one game. Andy felt bad about it—but only for a little while. Then he started to think to himself, "Sam really deserved it; what I did was okay." As time went on, he forgot all about it.

Discussion: As you can see, the story follows the sexual abuse cycle. Some questions for discussion include:

1. What could Andy have done or said to himself to keep from feeling so bad?

2. What could Andy's parents or team members have done to help Andy when he started to keep away from other people?

3. Why did Andy start to blame Sam?

4. How could Andy stop himself from thinking about hurting Sam and getting even? (thought stopping)

5. How did Andy end up victimizing someone else?

6. How do you think Sam felt?

After discussing Andy's story, have the children give examples of times that they have been on the sexual abuse cycle. Gradually bring in the issue of sexual acting out. Help the children chart their sexual acting out. The issues of fantasies and thought-stopping should also be addressed

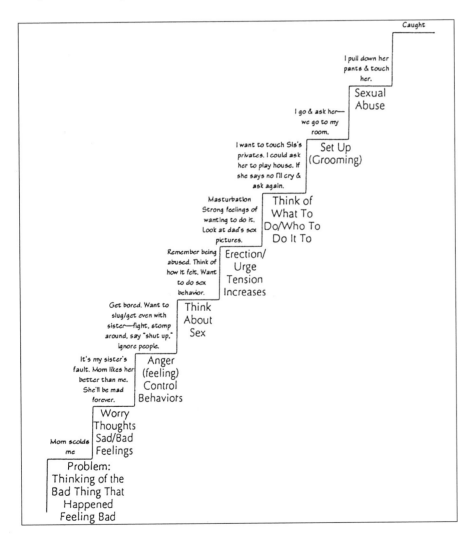

Caught

I pull down her pants & touch her.

Sexual Abuse

I go & ask her—we go to my room.

Set Up (Grooming)

I want to touch Sis's privates. I could ask her to play house. If she says no I'll cry & ask again.

Think of What To Do/Who To Do It To

Masturbation Strong feelings of wanting to do it. Look at dad's sex pictures.

Erection/ Urge Tension Increases

Remember being abused. Think of how it felt. Want to do sex behavior.

Think About Sex

Get bored. Want to slug/get even with sister—fight, stomp around, say "shut up." ignore people.

Anger (feeling) Control Behaviors

It's my sister's fault. Mom likes her better than me. She'll be mad forever.

Worry Thoughts Sad/Bad Feelings

Mom scolds me

Problem: Thinking of the Bad Thing That Happened Feeling Bad

(e.g., "When you start thinking about victimizing or molesting someone, what can you do?").

Note: It is a good idea to present The Sexual Abuse Cycle to parents at the same time that you present it to the children. Parents can learn to identify when their children are on the steps or in the cycle and help them interrupt it.

The Babysitting Disaster

Mark, who is 12 years old, was really looking forward to the senior high football game tonight. All of his friends were going, and his girlfriend was going to be there, too. After the game Mark and his friends were going to a party. Mark had been looking forward to it for a long time.

He also was hoping that he'd get home before his report card did. "Please, please, please," he prayed, "let the mail be slow so my report card comes tomorrow. Let the Post Office lose my report card . . ." He knew that his grades were going to be pretty bad. On his way home, Mark was thinking about all the different ways he could talk his mom into letting him go to the game even after she saw how bad his grades were.

As soon as Mark opened the front door, he saw his mom waiting for him in the front hall with his report card in her hand. "This is the worst report card you've ever gotten," she yelled.

Mark tried to calm his mother down. "I'll do better next time, I promise, Mom."

But his mother kept yelling at him. "You're right, you're going to do better—you're grounded! Starting tonight, you stay home every night and study. Wait until your father finds out about this!"

Mark felt his stomach go into a knot. "But Mom," he pleaded, "what about the game tonight—*please?*"

"No way!" she declared. Mark was really upset and really angry. He had planned to go to the game for a long time. What would his friends think? What would his girlfriend think?

When Mark's father came home, the angry shouting started all over again. Mark felt pretty bad after listening to his father yell, "You'll *never* amount to *anything*!" Then his parents decided to go out and made him stay home to babysit his 5-year-

old brother Jimmy. He hated to babysit.

After his parents left, Mark thought about the game he was missing, and what a good time his friends and his girlfriend were probably having, and how they were probably thinking he was a baby who couldn't go out by himself at night. He got angrier and angrier inside. He *really* wanted to get even with his parents. "I *hate* them," he thought to himself.

Everything Jimmy said or did irritated Mark. The *last* person he wanted to be with was his brother. *Finally* it was 8 o'clock—time for Jimmy to take a bath and get ready for bed.

Mark got Jimmy's bath water ready. He thought about making it too hot, just to get even with his parents, but he decided that would get him into too much trouble. While Mark was helping his brother get undressed for the bath, he started to get a different kind of feeling inside—a warm feeling. He was still mad, but there was something else, too. Mark thought about how he usually felt better when he touched his penis, how it made him feel grown up and not like the baby his parents seemed to think he was.

After Jimmy got in the bathtub, Mark still had that funny feeling. He felt his penis getting hard. Then Mark decided he was going to touch Jimmy's penis. He pretended to help Jimmy wash himself, but after helping him wash, Mark started to touch Jimmy's penis. Jimmy yelled, "I don't like this! I'll tell Mommy!"

"Oh yeah?" Mark said. "I'll say that you *asked* me to touch you, and if you tell Mom, you're going to get into a lot of trouble. Mom will believe me because I'm older." Jimmy looked scared and promised that he wouldn't tell.

After Jimmy went to bed, Mark felt strange and confused inside. He was terrified that his parents would find out. What if Jimmy told? He would be in *big* trouble.

What do you think will happen next?

Appendix C
The Scorpion Bunny

Once upon a time a soft, furry and gentle bunny was born. It lay in the soft grass beside its mother, helpless

as little bunnies are, wanting very, very much to be loved and cared for. But something happened to the mother rabbit. She was confused, and she gave the bunny away. She made sure that the little one had enough food to keep him alive, but no one gave the bunny the love and care he needed: no one told him he was special, no one hugged him or nurtured him, no one comforted him when he cried in pain or was scared.

And so, after a long period of feeling that no one loved him, the little bunny decided to be a scorpion. A scorpion is a very hard and dangerous creature, stinging and hurting its victims. It lives alone and has a hard shell to keep others away. This scorpion-bunny was confused, and began to hurt those around him. He felt that perhaps, if he caused others enough pain, someone would recognize that he was miserable, and somehow this would make him feel better. He gave others pain to ease his pain, but *it never worked.* Sometimes after he stung someone he felt better for awhile, but that feeling didn't last, and then all he could think of was seeking someone else to hurt. Sometimes his pain was even greater because he hated himself for his thoughts and behaviors. He felt lonely and sometimes wondered if he was "crazy."

Now it happened that some adults discovered that he was hurting little bunnies, and they became very angry with him. This caused the scorpion-bunny even more pain, and he tried to make his shell harder and his stinger more pointed. The scorpion-bunny thought that the whole world was mad at him, until one day an older bunny named Molly came to talk to him.

Molly Bunny understood what was happening in the heart of the scorpion-bunny. So she let him know that being a scorpion who hurts people would never help him to find love because scorpions don't have love or give love, so they can never feel it. She told him that if he could find the power to change back into a bunny, she would help him to learn to stop using his stinger to attack. When he learned that lesson she would help him to love himself and others.

The little scorpion-bunny was very afraid to trust, and he thought and thought about whether he would allow Molly Bunny to help him. Finally his longing to be loved and cared for and free of pain was greater than his fear, and he found the courage to ask for her help. Gently but firmly, she let him see that the shell was not really a part of him, and she took it away, showing him that he was really a little bunny underneath, not a scorpion at all. Then she put the shell away where the little bunny would never have to use it again. At first this caused him to feel very afraid, because without his shell he felt weak and unprotected.

But Molly Bunny gave him much love and talked to him about many things to help him understand his power as an individual and his own ability to love himself. She taught him the difference between a power that hurts and a power that loves. She helped him to understand how to be a bunny, who became wise, caring and filled with joy.

And as he learned more and more he came to understand that he truly *was* a bunny! With Molly Bunny's help, he realized that he no longer wanted to be a scorpion, covered with that shell and isolated from everyone—he wanted to be soft and caring and connected with other bunnies.

Every day after that, the bunny learned more about his own power and about loving himself and being kind and caring. And wherever he went he took with him a picture of a scorpion, to remind him of just how much he had changed.

"The Scorpion Bunny," by Dr. Nancy Davis, from *Once upon a time therapeutic stories (Rev. ed.)*. Reprinted by permission of the author.

Appendix D
Bruno the Bobcat

Deep in the forest lived Bruno the bobcat. Bruno spent weeks and weeks building himself a home where he could be safe and warm. He took special pride in his sleeping place where he put straw and leaves to make his very own private spot. No one else could enter without his permission.

One day while Bruno was peacefully sleeping, a huge gorilla—twice Bruno's size—barged into Bruno's safe space without even knocking. With a loud grunt, the gorilla kicked Bruno out of bed and plopped himself down right in the middle of Bruno's special spot.

Bruno wandered around the forest, feeling like he wanted to cry. But everybody in the forest knew bobcats were strong, so Bruno was afraid to cry. He felt sad and confused and didn't know what to do. Rather than feeling sad and crying, Bruno got mad instead. Every time he thought about that gorilla taking over his special place, he got angrier and angrier and began to growl louder and louder.

One day as he was sitting alone in the forest, he spotted his friend Mickey the monkey sitting in a tree. Mickey had built his own special place, just like the one that Bruno used to have. Bruno thought to himself, "Mickey looks just like that gorilla, only he's much smaller." In a flash, Bruno growled and kicked Mickey out of his home. Bruno curled up in Mickey's nest. For a while he felt better and more powerful. He thought to himself, "At least I don't feel like a helpless wimp anymore."

But somehow, it just didn't feel right. Bruno knew exactly what it was like to have someone take advantage of him. Bruno was sure that Mickey was feeling just as sad and angry as he had felt when it happened to him.

Bruno left Mickey's tree and started walking in the forest. Once again, Bruno felt as if he wanted to cry, but he didn't want to show his feelings. A little further away, Bruno spotted Mother Monkey with her new baby. Mother Monkey asked, "Bruno, could you watch my baby monkey for a minute while I hunt for some bananas?"

It felt good for Bruno to feel important. He said, "Sure."

After just a few minutes of playing with the baby monkey, Bruno suddenly felt angry again. He began to think about hurting the baby. Suddenly, he kicked the baby monkey out of the nest. The baby fell and broke his leg. When Mother Monkey came back, she gasped and asked Bruno to tell her what happened to the baby. Bruno lied and said, "Baby monkey fell down."

Bruno felt guilty because he lied. He also felt bad because he had hurt the baby. And most of all, he felt confused and upset. He ran away, lay down in the forest, and cried and cried.

A little while later, Bruno heard a "Whoooooooo" sound. It was Ozzie Owl. He asked Bruno, "Why you are so sad?" Bruno answered, "Someone took my home and now I don't know what to do."

Ozzie asked, "Do you think that kicking others out of their homes will get you your home back?" Bruno was startled. "How did you know . . . ?" Then Bruno hung his head and mumbled his answer. "No. . . . But I just get so angry that I can't stop."

Ozzie said, "It's okay to feel sad, and it's okay to cry. It's okay to feel angry too. But hurting others isn't okay. It isn't fair to them and it makes you feel guilty."

"What should I do?" Bruno asked.

Ozzie thought a moment and then said, "Use your words, not your muscles. Talk to the other animals who are older and wiser than you about what happened to you and what you did. They will help you."

So Ozzie Owl helped Bruno tell Lennie the Lion and Terry the Tiger what happened. They went back to Bruno's home, where they were big enough, strong enough, and wise enough to get the gorilla to go with them to a place where he could get help for his problem.

Then Ozzie Owl went with Bruno to visit Mickey Monkey. "Bruno has something to say to you, Mickey," Ozzie began. "I'm sorry for taking your nest," Bruno apologized. "It was really mean. You must have felt really bad. I'd like to help you make your nest nice gain, that is, if it's okay with you." Mickey said he would think about it.

Bruno and Ozzie went to see Mother Monkey, too, so Bruno could apologize for hurting Baby Monkey and then lying about it. Bruno offered to find bananas two days a week for Mother Monkey since she didn't feel that it was safe for Bruno to babysit anymore. He could understand that. It took a while for Bruno to feel safe again, too.

Apologizing was really hard, but eventually, it helped Bruno feel better about himself. He learned that it's okay to feel sad and that it's okay to cry. He learned that you can get help if you ask for it. He also learned that it's better to talk about the hurt than to hurt others, and that when you hurt others, you're also hurting yourself.

References

Achenbach, T. M. (1983). *Manual for the Child Behavior Checklist*. Burlington: University of Vermont.

Achenbach, T. M. (1991a). *Manual for the Child Behavior Checklist/4-18 and 1991 Profile*. Burlington: University of Vermont.

Achenbach, T. M. (1991b). *Manual for the teacher's report form & 1991 profile*. Burlington: University of Vermont.

Ager, C. L., & Cole, C. L. (1991). A review of cognitive-behavioral interventions for children and adolescents with behavioral disorders. *Behavioral Disorders, 16*, 276–287.

Aiken, J. (1993). *Harvest of hope*. USA: The Refuge. (Available from The Refuge/Nature's Classroom, P.O. Box 400, Mentone, AL 35984)

Arundell, R. M. (1992). The relationships of empathy, social support, trauma symptoms and family violence in the victim to victimizer process in adolescent males. *Dissertation Abstracts International, 52*, 4965.

Awad, G. A., & Saunders, E. (1989). Adolescent child molesters: Clinical observations. *Child Psychiatry and Human Development, 19*, 195–206.

Ballard, D. T., Blair, G. D., Devereaux, S., Valentine, L. K., Horton, A. L., & Johnson, B. L. (1990). A comparative profile of the incest perpetrator: Background characteristics, abuse history, and use of social skills. In A. L. Horton, B. L. Johnson, L. M. Roundy, & D. Williams (Eds.), *The incest perpetrator* (pp. 43–64). Newbury Park, CA: Sage.

Barbaree, H. E., & Cortoni, F. A. (1993). Treatment of the juvenile sex offender within the criminal justice and mental health system. In H. E. Barbaree, W. Marshall, & S. M. Hudson (Eds.), *The juvenile sex offender* (pp. 243–263). New York: Guilford Press.

Becker, J. V. (1990). Treating adolescent sexual offenders. *Professional Psychology, 21*, 362–365.

Becker, J. V., Alpert, J. L., Subia Bigfoot, D., Bonner, B. L., Geddie, L. F., Henggeler, S. W., Kaufman, K. L., & Walker, C. E. (1995). Empirical research on child abuse treatment: Report by the Child Abuse and Neglect Treatment Working Group, American Psychological Association. *Journal of Clinical Child Psychology, 24* (Suppl.), 23–46.

Bengtsson, H., & Johnson, L. (1992). Perspective taking, empathy, and prosocial behavior in late childhood. *Child Study Journal, 22*, 11–22.

Blonk, R. W. B., Prins, J. M., Sergeant, J. A., Ringrose, J., & Brinkman, A. G. (1996). Cognitive-behavioral group therapy for socially incompetent children: Short-term and maintenance effects within a clinical sample. *Journal of Clinical Child Psychology, 25*(2), 215–224.

Boatmun, T. (1994, March). Using games and activities with sexually abused adolescents. Workshop at the Tenth National Symposium on Child Sexual Abuse, Huntsville, AL.

Boldizar, J. P., Perry, D. G., & Perry, L. C. (1989). Outcome values and aggression. *Child Development, 60*, 571–579.

Bonner, B. L. (1995). Adolescent sex offenders: Current treatment approaches. *The Quarterly, 18*(4), 5–8.

Boy Scouts of America (Producer). (1989). *A time to tell* [Video]. Irving, TX: Author (Available from [241] 580-2598).

Braswell, L. (1993). Cognitive-behavioral groups for children manifesting ADHD and other disruptive behavior disorders. *Special Services in the Schools 8*, 91–117.

Burgess, A., Hartman, C., & McCormack, A. (1987). Abused to abuser: Antecedents of socially deviant behavior. *American Journal of Psychiatry, 144*, 1431–1436.

Butler, S. F., & Fontenelle, S. F., III. (1995). Cognitive-behavioral group therapy: Application with adolescents who are cognitively impaired and sexually act out. *The Journal for Specialists in Group Work, 20*, 121–127.

Camp, B. H., & Thyer, B. A. (1993). Treatment of adolescent sex offenders: A review of empirical research. *The Journal of Applied Social Sciences, 17*, 191–206.

Cohen, J. A., & Mannarino, A. P. (1997, January). *A treatment study for sexually abused preschool children: Outcome during a one year follow-up*. Paper presentation at the Conference on Responding to Child Maltreatment, San Diego.

Cunningham, C., & MacFarlane, K. (1991). *When children molest children: Group treatment strategies for young sexual abusers*. Orwell, VT: Safer Society Press.

Cunningham, C., & MacFarlane, K. (1996). *Children who abuse*. Charlotte, NC: KIDSRIGHTS.

Davis, N. (1990). *Once upon a time therapeutic stories* (Rev. ed.). Oxon Hill, MD: Psychological Associates of Oxon Hill. (Available from Psychological Associates of Oxon Hill, 6178 Oxon Hill Road, Suite 306, Oxon Hill, MD 20745)

Deblinger, E., & Heflin, A. F. (1996). Child intervention: Therapeutic components. In *Treating sexually abused children and their nonoffending parents: A cognitive-behavioral approach* (pp. 49–111). Thousand Oaks, CA: Sage.

Deblinger, E., Lippmann, J., & Steer, R. (1996). Sexually abused children suffering posttraumatic stress symptoms: Initial treatment outcome findings. *Child Maltreatment, 1*, 310–321.

Edelbrock, C., & Achenbach, T. A. (1984). The teacher version of the child behavior profile: I. Boys aged 6–11. *Journal of Clinical and Consulting Psychology, 52*, 207–217.

Fehrenbach, P. A., Smith, W., Monastersky, C., & Deisher, R. W. (1993). Adolescent sexual offenders: Offender and offense characteristics. *American Journal of Orthopsychiatry, 56*, 225–233.

Feshbach, N. D. (1975). Empathy in children: Some theoretical and empirical considerations. *Counseling Psychologist, 5*, 25–30.

Feshbach, N. D., & Feshbach, S. (1982). Empathy training and the relation of aggression: Potentialities and limitations. *Academic Psychology Bulletin, 4*, 399–413.

Finkelhor, D., & Browne, A. (1986). Initial and long-term effects: A conceptual framework. In D. Finkelhor, S. Aruji, L. Baron, A. Browne, S. D. Peters, & G. E. Wyatt (Eds.), *A sourcebook on child sexual abuse* (pp. 180–198). Newbury, CA: Sage Publications.

Fluegelman, A. (Ed.). (1976). *The new games book*. Garden City, NY: Headlands Press Books.

Friedrich, W. N. (1993a). Forward. In E. Gil & T. C. Johnson (Eds.), *Sexualized children: Assessment and treatment of sexualized children and children who molest* (pp. x–xii). Rockville, MD: Launch Press.

Friedrich, W. N. (1993b). Sexual behavior in sexually abused children. *Violence Update, 3*, 160–165.

Friedrich, W. N. (in press). *Child Sexual Behavior Inventory*. Odessa, FL: Psychological Assessment Resources.

Friedrich, W. N., Grambsch, P., Broughton, D., Kuiper, K., & Beilke, R. L. (1991). Normative sexual behavior in children. *Pediatrics, 88*, 456–464.

Friedrich, W. N., Grambsch, P., Damon, L., Hewitt, S., Koverola, C., Lang, R., Wolfe, V., & Broughton, D. (1992). The child sexual behavior inventory: Normative and clinical findings. *Psychological Assessment, 4*, 303–311.

Friedrich, W. N., & Luecke, W. (1988). Young school-age sexually aggressive children. *Professional Psychology Research and Practice, 19*, 155–164.

Gil, E. (1987). *Children who molest: A guide for parents of young sex offenders*. Walnut Creek, CA: Launch Press.

Gil, E., & Johnson, T. C. (1993). *Sexualized children: Assessment and treatment of sexualized children and children who molest*. Rockville, MD: Launch Press.

Gilgun, J. F., & Conner, T. M. (1990). Isolation and the adult male perpetrator of child sexual abuse: Clinical concerns. In A. L. Horton, B. L. Johnson, L. M. Roundy, & D. Williams (Eds.), *The incest perpetrator* (pp. 74–87). Newbury Park: Sage.

Goldstein, A. P., & Michaels, G. Y. (1985). *Empathy: Development, training, and consequences*. Hillside, NJ: Lawrence Erlbaum.

Gray, A., Busconi, A., Houchens, P., & Pithers, W. D. (in press). Children with sexual behavior problems and their caregivers: Demographics, functioning, and clinical patterns. *Sexual Abuse: A Journal of Research and Treatment.*

Gray, A., & Pithers, W. D. (1993). Relapse prevention with sexually aggressive adolescents and children: Expanding treatment and supervision. In H. E. Barbaree, W. L. Marshall, & S. M. Hudson (Eds.) *The juvenile sex offender* (pp. 289–319). New York: Guilford Press.

Hall, D., Mathews, F., & Pearce, J. (1997, January). *The development of intrusive sexuality in children and youth: The DISC project.* Paper presentation at the Conference on Responding to Child Maltreatment, San Diego.

Hoffman, M. L. (1975). Developmental synthesis of affect and cognition and its implications for altruistic motivation. *Developmental Psychology, 11,* 607–622.

Hoffman, M. L. (1987). The contribution of empathy to justice and moral judgement. In N. Eisenberg & J. Strayer (Eds.), *Empathy and its development* (pp. 47–80). Cambridge: Cambridge University Press.

Hughes, J. R., Tingle, B. A., & Sawin, D. B. (1981). Development of empathic understanding in children. *Child Development, 52,* 122–128.

Ingersoll, S. L., & Patton, S. O. (1990). *Treating perpetrators of sexual abuse.* Lexington, MA: Lexington Books.

Johnson, T. C. (1988). Child perpetrators— children who molest other children: Preliminary findings. *Child Abuse and Neglect, 12,* 219–229.

Johnson, T. C. (1989a). Female child perpetrators: Children who molest other children. *Child Abuse and Neglect, 13,* 571–585.

Johnson, T. C. (1989b). *Human sexuality curriculum for parents and children in troubled families.* (Available from Children's Institute International, Marshall Resource Library, 711 South New Hampshire Avenue, Los Angeles, CA 90005)

Johnson, T. C. (1995). *Treatment exercises for child abuse victims and children with sexual behavior problems.* (Available from Toni Cavanaugh Johnson, Ph.D., 1101 Fremont Avenue, Suit 101, South Pasadena, CA 91030)

Johnson, T. C., & Feldmuth, J. R. (1993). Sexual behaviors: A continuum. In E. Gil & T. C. Johnson (Eds.), *Sexualized children: Assessment and treatment of sexualized children and children who molest* (pp. 41–52). Rockville, MD: Launch Press.

Justice, B., & Justice, R. (1979). *The broken taboo: Sex in the family.* New York: Human Sciences Press.

Kazdin, A. E. (1987). Treatment of antisocial behavior in children: Current status and future directions. *Psychological Bulletin, 102,* 187–203.

Kazdin, A. E. (1996). Problem solving and parent management in treating aggressive and antisocial behavior. In E. D. Hibbs & P. S. Jensen (Eds.), *Psychosocial treatments for child and adolescent disorders: Empirically based strategies for clinical practice* (pp. 377–408). Washington, DC: American Psychological Association.

Kendall, P. C. (Ed.) (1991). *Child and adolescent therapy: Cognitive-behavioral procedures.* New York: Guildford Press.

Kendall, P. C., & Panichelli-Mindel, S. M. (1995). Cognitive-behavioral treatments. *Journal of Abnormal Child Psychology, 23,* 107–124.

Lochman, J. E. (1985). Effects of different treatment lengths in cognitive behavioral interventions with aggressive boys. *Child Psychiatry and Human Development, 16,* 45–56.

Lochman, J. E. (1990). Modification of childhood aggression. In M. Hersen, R. Eisler, & P. M. Miller (Eds.), *Progress in behavior modification: Vol. 25* (pp. 47–85). Newbury Park, CA: Sage.

Lochman, J. E., & Dodge, K. A. (1994). Social-cognitive processes of severely violent, moderately aggressive, and nonaggressive boys. *Journal of Consulting and Clinical Psychology, 62,* 366–374.

Lochman, J. E., & Lenhart, L. A. (1993). Anger coping intervention for aggressive children: Conceptual models and outcome effects. *Clinical Psychology Review, 13,* 785–805.

MacFarlane, K., & Cunningham, C. (1988). *Steps to healthy touching: A treatment workbook for kids who have problems with sexually inappropriate behavior.* Mount Dora, FL: KIDSRIGHTS.

Macarov, D. (1978). Empathy: The charismatic chimera. *Journal of Education for Social Work, 14,* 86–92.

Marshall, W. L., & Barbaree, H. E. (1990). An integrated theory of the etiology of sexual offending. In W. L. Marshall, D. R. Laws, & H. E. Barbaree (Eds.), *Handbook of sexual assault: Issues, theories and treatment of the sex offender* (pp. 252–275). New York: Plenum Press.

Marshall, W. L., Laws, D. R., & Barbaree, H. E. (1990). *Handbook of sexual assault: Issues, themes and treatment of the sex offender.* New York: Plenum Press.

McFall, R. M. (1990). The enhancement of social skills: An information-processing analysis. In W. L. Marshall, D. R. Laws, & H. E. Barbaree (Eds.), *Handbook of sexual assault: Issues, theories and treatment of the sex offender* (pp. 311–330). New York: Plenum Press.

McMahon, R. J., & Wells, K. C. (1989). Conduct disorders. In E. J. Mash & R. A. Barkley (Eds.), *Treatment of childhood disorders* (pp. 73–134). New York: Guilford Press.

Morenz, B., & Becker, J. V. (1995). The treatment of youthful sexual offenders. *Applied & Preventive Psychology, 4,* 247–256.

Murphy, W. D. (1990). Assessment and modification of cognitive distortions in sex offenders. In W. L. Marshall, D. R. Laws, & H. E. Barbaree (Eds.), *Handbook of sexual assault: Issues, theories, and treatment of the sex offender* (pp. 331–342). New York: Plenum Press.

National Adolescent Perpetrator Network. (1993). The revised report from the National Task Force on juvenile sexual offending. *Juvenile and Family Court Journal, 44,* 1–120.

Pithers, W. D. (1990). Relapse prevention with sexual aggressors. In W. L. Marshall, D. R. Laws, & H. E. Barbaree (Eds.), *Handbook of sexual assault: Issues, theories, and treatment of the sex offender* (pp. 343–361). New York: Plenum Press.

Pithers, W. D., Gray, A. S., Cunningham, C., & Lane, S. (1993). *From trauma to understanding: A guide for parents of children with sexual behavior problems.* Brandon, VT: The Safer Society Press.

Rohnke, K. (1984). *Silver bullets: A guide to initiative problems, adventure games and trust activities.* Dubuque, IA: Project Adventure, Inc.

Rohnke, K. (1989). *Cowstails and cobras II: A guide to games, initiatives, ropes courses, and adventure curriculum.* Dubuque, IA: Project Adventure, Inc.

Ryan, G., Lane, S., Davis, J., & Isaac, C. (1987). Juvenile sex offenders: Development and correction. *Child Abuse and Neglect, 11,* 385–395.

Salter, A. C. (1995). *Transforming trauma.* Thousand Oaks, CA: Sage.

Shapiro Productions (with USAA; Producers). (1992). *Scared silent: Exposing and ending child abuse* [Video]. Hollywood, CA: National Committee to Prevent Child Abuse.

Spivack, G., Platt, J. J., & Shure, M. B. (1976). *The problem-solving approach to adjustment.* San Francisco: Jossey-Bass.

Stauffer, L. B., & Deblinger, E. (1996). Cognitive behavioral groups for nonoffending mothers and their young sexually abused children: A preliminary treatment outcome study. *Child Maltreatment, 1,* 65–76.

Straker, G., & Jacobson, R. S. (1981). Aggression, emotional maladjustment, and empathy in the abused child. *Developmental Psychology, 17,* 762–765.

Tharinger, D. (1990). Impact of child sexual abuse on developing sexuality. *Professional Psychology: Research and Practice, 21,* 331–337.

Utay, J. M., & Lampe, R. E. (1995). Use of a group counseling game to enhance social skills of children with learning disabilities. *The Journal for Specialists in Group Work, 20,* 114–120.

van Eys, P. P., & Hoffman, C. F. (1992). *Paper people* (unpublished therapeutic technique). Huntsville, AL: National Children's Advocacy Center. (Available from P. P. van Eys, GPC 512, Vanderbilt University, Nashville, TN 37203.)

Walker, C. E., Jean, V. M., Bonner, B. L., & Berliner, L. (1997, January). *Treatment of children with sexual behavior problems: An empirically based design.* Paper presentation at the Conference on Responding to Child Maltreatment, San Diego.

Zaragoza, N., Vaughn, S., & McIntosh, R. (1991). Social skills interventions with children with behavior problems: A review. *Behavioral Disorders, 16,* 260–275.

Article Review Form at end of book.

How does a depressed adolescent ask for help?

Adolescent Depressed Mood, Reports of Suicide Attempts, and Asking for Help

**Anne McDonald Culp,
Mary M. Clyman,
and Rex E. Culp**

Abstract

Subjects of this study were 220 students in the 6th through 12th grades. Results indicate that 57% of the students reported symptoms of depressed mood (CES-D); 33% had thought of suicide; and 6% had attempted suicide. Depressed mood scores were significantly different between those students who had attempted suicide and those who had not. Loneliness was identified as a problem among 66% of the students, along with school-related problems and not feeling good about oneself. Fifty percent of the middle school students and 40% of the high school students were unaware of services in their school. Among the students with symptoms of depressed mood, 49% did not ask for help. Of those who did not seek help, 68% believed they had to take care of their problems themselves. Adolescents who have symptoms of depressed mood and who believe they must take care of their own problems are overrepresented among teenagers who think of attempting suicide.

Studies of normal adolescent populations indicate that many experience biological, physiological, and social changes (Conger & Peterson, 1984; Simmons, Burgenson, Carlton-Ford, & Blyth, 1987) without any major psychological or emotional problems (Petersen, Compas, Brooks-Gunn, Stemmier, Ey, & Grant, 1993). However, responses to these changes vary; many adolescents experience only mild forms of anxiety (Larson & Ham, 1993; Rutter, Graham, Chadwick, & Yule, 1976) and demonstrate adequate coping skills which enable them to address these developmental changes with minimal turmoil (Offer, 1967; Weiner, 1990). Petersen and her colleagues (1993) have defined adolescent depression at three levels: (1) depressed mood, (2) depressive syndrome, and (3) clinical depression. Depressed mood is sadness at various times in response to an unhappy situation; it is measured by self-report checklists, and is "the single most powerful symptom in differentiating clinically referred and nonreferred youth" (Achenbach, 1991). Adolescents who report both anxiety and depression along with other symptoms such as feeling sad, lonely, unloved, and worthless are considered to have depressive syndrome. Adolescents who manifest five or more depressive symptoms which impair their current functioning and last for at least two weeks are considered clinically depressed. (See Petersen et al., 1993 for a review.)

Recent literature on adolescent development has emphasized the need for parents, teachers, counselors, and clinicians to pay close attention to adolescent symptomatology so that help can be offered early on, thus minimizing the chances of more serious problems, such as suicide attempts (Davis, Sandoval, & Wilson, 1988; Jones, 1990; Taylor, Miller, & Moltz, 1991).

Although studies on adolescent depression involve varying populations and measurement (Roberts, Andrews, Lewinsohn, & Hops, 1990), significant percentages of depressive symptomatology have been reported: 50% (Schoenbach, Kaplan, Grimson, & Wagner, 1982); 48% (Kashani, Beck, Hoeper, Fallahi, Corcoran, McAllister, Rosenberg, & Reid, 1987); 46% for males and 56% for females (Roberts et al., 1990); and a median of 35% across 14 studies (Petersen et al., 1993). Gender differences appear to be genuine: females have a greater tendency toward depressive and mood disorders during adolescence (Petersen, Kennedy, & Sullivan, 1991). Findings on race differences have been inconclusive (Petersen et al., 1993).

Over the past three decades the rate of suicide has increased dramatically among 15- to 24-year-olds and is the third leading cause of death in this age group (Henry, Stephenson,

"Adolescent Depressed Mood, Reports of Suicide Attempts, and Asking for Help," by Anne McDonald Culp, Mary M. Clyman, and Rex E. Culp, *Adolescence, 30* (120), Winter 1995, pp. 827–837. Reprinted by permission of Libra Publishers.

Hanson, & Hargett, 1993). In 1988, 2,296 adolescents committed suicide in the United States (National Center for Health Statistics, 1991). From 1960 to 1970 to 1986 the rate has continued to increase from 3.6 to 7.2 to 10.2 deaths per 100,000 (National Commission on Children, 1991). By 1988, the rate among the 15- to 24-year-olds was 13.2 per 100,000 (U.S. Department of Commerce, 1991). Considering the literature indicating adolescents' limited utilization of resources in the school (Leviton, 1977; Wells & Ritter, 1979; Hutchinson & Buttorff, 1986), the question of how adolescents are coping with their problems is raised.

This study was undertaken to investigate (1) the prevalence of depressive symptomatology among a specific adolescent population, (2) the incidence of personal problems the adolescents, their families, and closes friends had experienced in the past year, (3) how the adolescents deal with their problems, (4) their level of awareness and use of school resources for addressing personal problems, and (5) reports of attempted suicide and depressive symptomatology.

Method

Subjects

Two hundred and twenty students (over 50% of the total student population) in two midwestern parochial schools participated in the study. Of these, 186 (84.5%) were in grades 9–12 (high school) and 34 (15.5%) were in grades 6–8 (middle school). The students ranged in age from 11 to 18 with a mean age of 15 years. The sample consisted of 71% Anglo-American, 11% Mexican-American, 6% African-American, 3% Asian-American, and 9% from multiple-ethnic backgrounds. There were more females (64%) than males (36%); 83% were Catholic.

Family demographics indicated that approximately 80% of the students' parents were married, including those who had remarried; 20% were separated or divorced. Household size ranged from 2 to 14 individuals, with a mean of 5 members; 81% fathers and 72% mothers had at least some college education; 93% considered their family to be financially well off or comfortable.

Procedures

Data were collected utilizing a questionnaire and the Center for Epidemiological Studies Depression Scale (CES-D; Radloff, 1977, 1991). The questionnaire solicited information on the following: (a) demographic data; (b) student's awareness of counseling services available at school; (c) specific problems the student, the student's family, and the student's closest friend had experienced in the past year; (d) how the student dealt with personal problems, and (e) whether the student had or had not attempted or had thoughts of suicide during the past year. The CES-D, a self-administered 20-item inventory designed to measure levels of depressive symptomatology, primarily depressed mood and affect, was used. Respondents indicate how often they experienced each of the 20 items during the past week. Higher scores indicate both the presence and persistence of the symptoms. Based upon a 0–3 response rate with 0 indicating "rarely or none of the time" and 3 indicating "most of the time," a total symptom score (range 0–60) is obtained. A score of 16 or higher indicates depressive symptomatology (Radloff, 1977, 1991; Roberts, 1987; Roberts et al., 1990). According to Weissman, Sholomskas, Pottenger, Prusoff, and Locke (1977), validation studies indicate that the CES-D scale helps to identify persons "at-risk" for clinical depression, and is a valuable tool for studying the relationships between depressive symptoms and other variables (Radloff, 1977, 1991).

Validation studies of the CES-D with adolescents indicate high internal consistency with coefficient alphas above .80 (Schoenbach et al., 1982); and above .87 (Roberts et al., 1990). In addition, Tolor and Murphy (1985) and Roberts et al. (1990) found an acceptable test-retest reliability coefficient alpha above .50 in adolescent populations. Studies of clinical and community populations, including adolescents and three major social/ethnic groups (whites, blacks, and Hispanics), indicate that the scale has a high level of internal consistency, acceptable test-retest reliability, good concurrent validity as assessed by clinical and self-report criteria, and considerable construct

validity (Radloff, 1977; Roberts, 1980; Schoenbach et al., 1982; Weisman et al., 1977).

Efforts were made to prevent students from sharing information with one another about the questionnaires which could bias the findings. High school faculty administered the two questionnaires to all subjects at the high school during the same class period. In the middle school, due to schedule differences, the two questionnaires were distributed by the second author to each class during three consecutive classroom periods. Following completion of the study, information on various mental health resources in the metropolitan area was distributed to the students.

Results

The primary variables measured include: (1) the rate of depressive symptomatology among the sample population of middle and high school students, (2) personal problems experienced by the student, the student's family or closest friend in the past year, (3) how they dealt with these problems, (4) the student's awareness and utilization of various school resources for addressing personal problems, including depression, and (5) rates of attempted suicides and thoughts of suicide, depressive symptomatology, and asking for help.

Depressive symptomatology. Overall, the mean CES-D score for the total population was 18.4, with a standard deviation of 9.9 and a range of 0 to 49. Scores of 16 and above have been identified as indicating depressive symptomatology or depressed mood in previous studies using the CES-D with adolescents and adults (Radloff & Teri, 1986; Radloff, 1991; Roberts, 1987; Roberts et al., 1990). Of the total student sample, 57% had CES-D scores of 16 and above; 42% had scores of 20 and above; 26% had scores of 25 and above.

T tests of significance comparing the CES-D scores of the following groups were performed: (a) females vs. males, (b) middle school vs. high school students, (c) students who reported attempting suicide vs. those who reported not attempting suicide, and (d) those who had asked for help for personal problems they had experienced in the past year vs. those who had not.

1. When the sample was divided by gender, the CES-D scores did not significantly differ between females (M = 19.1) and males (M =17.2), $t(215)$ = 1.34, $p < .17$.

2. CES-D scores did not significantly differ between the middle school students (M = 17.3) and the high school students (M = 18.6) $t(217)$ = .8, $p < .40$. Sixty-two percent of the middle school students and 57% of the high school students had scores of 16 and above ($\chi^2(1, N = 219)$ = .33, $p < .55$).

3. When the sample was divided by whether or not the student reported having attempted suicide in the past year, 94% reported not attempting suicide, while 6% reported that they had attempted suicide. The CES-D scores of students who reported not having attempted suicide (M = 17.8) were significantly lower than the scores of those who reported having attempted suicide (M = 28.5), $t(217)$ = 3.7, $p < .0001$.

4. When the sample was divided by whether the students indicated they had asked for help regarding personal problems experienced in the past year and those who had not, the scores of those who had asked for help (M = 18.9) were not significantly different from the CES-D scores of those who had not asked for help (M = 18), $t(217)$ = .71, $p < .48$. Fifty-six percent of those seeking help had CES-D scores of 16 or above, while 58% of those not seeking help had CES-D scores of 16 or above. The CES-D scores among the students with depressive mood who has asked for help (M = 25.7) did not differ significantly from students with depressive mood who had not asked for help (M = 24.7), $F(1, 121)$ = 6.2, $p < .43$.

Problems experienced in the past year. Students were asked to identify from a list which problems they, their families, and their closest friend had experienced in the past year. Among the 219 students completing this task,

the five problems they themselves experienced most often were loneliness (66%), school-related problems (64%), not feeling good about yourself (55%), depression (54%), and problems with friends (50%).

As shown in Table 1, the five most common problems students identified in relation to their family were: family problems (44%), loss of someone close to you (39%), medical problems/serious illness (27%), depression (27%), and loneliness (25%).

The five most common problems experienced by their closest friend were: school-related problems (50%), loneliness (45%), depression (43%), breakup of a relationship (43%), and problems with friends (38%). In addition, 11% of the students reported having used drugs twice a month as compared to 20% who reported that their closest friend used drugs twice a month. Additionally, 39% of the students reported having used alcohol twice a month as compared to 33% who reported that their closest friend used alcohol twice a month.

How students dealt with personal problems. Among the 216 students who responded to the question of whether they had sought help for personal problems during the past year, only 113 (52%) reported seeking help. Of the 113 students who had asked for help, 102 students gave reasons; the three most common were: (a) they needed and wanted the help (n = 41, 40%); (b) they wanted advice and assistance in figuring out their problems (n = 16, 16%); and (c) they wanted to feel better and were concerned about their well-being (n = 14, 14%). Of the 103 students who reported not asking for help, the three most common reasons were: (a) they felt it was their responsibility to deal with their own problems (n = 32, 31%); (b) their problems were not that important (n = 19, 19%); and (c) they did not think they needed help (n = 18, 18%).

Of the 180 students who responded to the question of whether or not they had ever seen a professional for any personal reasons, 87 (48%) indicated they had. Of the 87 students who had seen a professional, 24 students (28%) had seen church-affiliated professionals (nun, priest, or other church person), and

23 students (26%) had seen school counselors; 40 students (46%) reported seeing at least one of the following professionals: social worker, psychologist, psychiatrist or a family therapist.

Of the 123 students with CES-D scores of 16 or above, 63 students (51%) reported asking for help and 60 students (49%) had not asked for help. Of the 63 students asking for help and with CES-D scores 16 or above, 29 (46%) reported that they had sought help because they needed and wanted help; 35 (56%) reported that they wanted advice on figuring out their problems; and 50 (79%) reported that they wanted to feel better and were concerned about their well-being. Of the 60 students not seeking help and with CES-D scores of 16 or above, 41 (68%) reported that they had not sought help because they felt it was their responsibility to figure out their own problems; 35 (58%) reported that their problems were not important; and 20 (33%) reported that they did not think they needed help.

Students awareness and utilization of resources. Among the 32 middle school students who responded to the question of what counseling services were available at their school, 10 students (31%) indicated they were aware the school offered guidance and counseling services, and 16 (50%) indicated they did not know what services were available. Among the 185 high school students who responded to the same question, 111 (60%) indicated they were aware that the school offered guidance and counseling services; 74 (40%) indicated they did not know what counseling services were available.

Students' reports of suicide attempts or thoughts. Sixty-five students (30%) indicated that they had thoughts of suicide, and 12 (6%) had attempted suicide. The number of students who indicated that their closest friend had attempted suicide (11%) was approximately twice as large as the number who indicated that they had attempted suicide (6%).

The CES-D scores were significantly different between the twelve students who attempted suicide (M = 28.5) and the remainder of the sample (M = 17.8) $t(217)$ = 3.7 $p < .001$. Of the 12 students who reported

Table I Problems Experienced in the Past Year as Cited by Students

Loneliness	66	25	45
School-related problems	64	15	50
Not feeling good about yourself	55	14	32
Depression	54	27	43
Problems with friends	50	8	38
Breakup of a relationship	44	7	43
Alcohol use (2× a month or more)	39	18	33
Concerns about sex	36	8	33
Loss of someone close to you	33	39	25
Family problems	33	44	31
Financial problems	23	31	16
Alcohol use (1× a week or more)	21	14	23
Medical problems/serious illness	14	27	12
Drug use (2× a month)	11	5	20
Other	11	15	12
Divorce of parents	7	8	11
Drug use (1× a week or more)	6	4	11
Legal problems	6	12	10

$N = 129$ for each group.

suicide attempts, all had CES-D scores above 19. There were no significant gender differences: four males (5.2%) and eight females (5.8%) reported having attempted suicide, $\chi^2(1, N = 216) = .03, p < .86$. Six students (50%) indicated they had not asked for help, and five students (42%) had never seen a professional regarding personal concerns. In addition, there were no significant differences in rates of attempted suicide between those who asked for help and those who did not ($F = (1, 121) = .01, p < .91$).

Discussion

The findings from this study contribute to the body of knowledge regarding the rate of depressed mood, awareness and use of counseling services, and reported suicide attempts and thoughts in adolescent populations. Over half of the 220 subjects who completed the CES-D had scores of 16 and above, which confirmed results obtained in previous studies using the CES-D with adolescent populations (Radloff, 1991; Roberts et al., 1990; Schoenbach et al., 1982; Tolar & Murphy, 1985) that a high percentage of adolescent populations report symptoms of depressed mood. Based on these results, the usefulness of separating students based on depressed mood (scores of 16 or above) was investigated. This study found neither gender differences among the adolescents experiencing depressive mood nor school level differences. Contrary to previous studies, the males were just as likely to report depressed mood as were the females.

As indicated by CES-D scores, a large number of adolescents are experiencing depressive symptomatology. For some adolescents those feelings may be temporary and in response to the developmental changes occurring during this age period. For others those symptoms may indicate more serious symptomatology. Although questions regarding whether these feelings are temporary or chronic or whether they reflect normal or psychopathological development are important areas of investigation, these data indicate that students are indeed experiencing them. Further investigation into how adolescents cope with these feelings and their utilization of existing resources may be a more efficient method for identifying youth who are unable to cope with these feelings

and who may resort to more risk-taking behavior or suicide.

The percentage of students who identified problems experienced by their own family was often lower than the percentage reporting problems they themselves or their closest friend had experienced. The percentage of students who reported that they personally had experienced loneliness, depression, problems with friends, and school-related problems was between 10 and 20% higher than the percentage of students who reported that their closest friend had experienced these same problems.

Despite the fact that counseling services were provided to the students at both the middle and high school, many students did not know that the services were available. In the middle school, teachers were assigned a specific number of students and served in an advisory capacity on both school and personal issues. In the high school, one full-time and one part-time counselor were assigned specific grade levels to assist students with school and personal issues. A third counselor was available once a week to assist students with personal issues. It is clear from these data that approximately half the adolescents in this sample were not aware of the services available to them. The need for services in this sample is apparent; however, not knowing about the availability and location of existing services reflects poorly on the schools and community. The results of this study should encourage schools and communities to evaluate whether adolescents know about the services and whether the mental health needs of students populations are being adequately addressed.

Students who reported that they did not ask for help indicated that they were responsible for dealing with their own problems and that their problems lacked importance.

In this cohort of adolescents, 6% had attempted suicide, and within that 6%, males were as well represented as females; half of the attempters did not ask for help; less than half had seen a professional; and all reported high depression scores. This draws a picture of isolation for a significant number of youth who are at high risk of killing themselves.

More work is needed on the prevalence of depression in

adolescence (Petersen et al., 1993), and these data bring to light issues for further investigation. One issue involves the type of messages young people are receiving about the problems they are experiencing and how they should deal with them. If young people feel they need to handle their own problems, the question remains whether they are capable of doing so. Educating youth about expected developmental changes and the problems that may result, is an obvious need.

Another issue involves adolescents' feelings about seeking help for their problems and the factors that influence their decisions. Knowing from whom adolescents feel comfortable seeking help and what contributes to that comfort would assist professionals in developing appropriate support services for this population.

References

Achenbach, T. B. (1991). *Manual for the Child Behavior Checklist and 1991 Profile.* Burlington: University of Vermont, Department of Psychiatry.

Conger, J., & Peterson, A. (1984). *Adolescence and youth.* New York: Harper & Row.

Davis, J. M., Sandoval, J., & Wilson, M. P. (1988). Strategies for the primary prevention of adolescent suicide. *School Psychology Review, 17,* 559–569.

Henry, C. S., Stephenson, A. L., Hanson, M. F., & Hargett, W. (1993). Adolescent suicide and families: An ecological approach. *Adolescence, 28,* 291–308.

Hutchinson, R. L., & Bottorff, R. L. (1986). Selected high school counseling services: Student assessment. *The School Counselor, 33,* 350–354.

Jones, R. M. (1990). Merging basic with practical research to enhance the adolescent experience. *Journal of Adolescent Research, 5,* 254–262.

Kashani, J. H., Beck, N. C., Hoeper, E. W., Fallahi, C., Corcoran, C. M., McAllister, J. A., Rosenberg, T. K., & Reid, J. C. (1987). Psychiatric disorders in a community sample of adolescents. *American Journal of Psychiatry, 144,* 584–589.

Larson, R., & Ham, M. (1993). Stress and "storm and stress" in early adolescence: The relationship of negative events with dysphoric affect. *Developmental Psychology, 29,* 130–140.

Leviton, H. S. (1977). Consumer feedback on a secondary school guidance program. *Personnel and Guidance Journal, 55,* 242–244.

National Center for Health Statistics. (1991). *Vital statistics of the United States: 1988,* Vol. II, morality, part A (DHHS Publication No. PHS 91-1101). Washington, DC: U.S. Government Printing Office.

National Commission on Children. (1991). *Beyond rhetoric: A new American agenda for children and families.* Washington DC: National Commission on Children.

Offer, D. (1967). Normal adolescents. *Archives of General Psychiatry, 17,* 285–290.

Petersen, A. C., Kennedy, R. E., & Sullivan, P. (1991). Coping with adolescence. In M. E. Colton, & S. Gore (Eds.), *Adolescent stress: Causes and consequences* (pp. 93–110). New York: Aldine deGruyter.

Petersen, A. C., Compas, B. E., Brooks-Gunn, J., Stemmler, M., Ey, S., & Grant, K. E. (1993). Depression in adolescence. *American Psychologist, 48,* 155–168.

Radloff, L. (1977). The CES-D Scale: A self-report depression scale for research in the general population. *Applied Psychological Measurement, 1,* 385–401.

Radloff, L. S., & Teri, L. (1986). The use of The Center for Epidemiologic Studies Depression Scale with older adults. In T. L. Brink (Ed.), *Clinical gerotology: A guide to assessment and intervention.* New York: Haworth Press.

Radloff, L. (1991). The use of the Center for Epidemiologic Studies Depression Scale in adolescents and young adults. *Journal of Youth and Adolescence, 20,* 149–166.

Roberts, R. (1980). Reliability of the CES-D scale in different ethnic contexts. *Psychiatry Research, 2,* 125–134.

Roberts, R. E. (1987). Epidemiological issues in measuring preventive effects. In R. F. Munoz (Ed.),*The prevention of depression: Research and directions* (pp. 45–75). Washington DC: Hemisphere.

Roberts, R. E., Andrews, J. A., Lewinsohn, P. M., & Hops, H. (1990). Assessment of depression in adolescents using the Center of Epidemiologic Studies Depression Scale. *Journal of Consulting and Clinical Psychology, 2,* 122–128.

Rutter, M., Graham, P., Chadwick, O. F. D., & Yule, W. (1976). Adolescent turmoil: Fact or fiction? *Journal of Child Psychology and Psychiatry and Allied Disciplines, 17,* 35–56.

Schoenbach, V. J., Kaplan, B. H., Grimson, R. C., & Wagner, E. H. (1982). Use of a symptom scale to study the prevalence of a depressive syndrome in young adolescents. *American Journal of Epidemiology, 116,* 791–800.

Simmons, R. G., Burgeson, R., Carlton-Ford, S., & Blyth, D. A. (1987). The impact of cumulative change in early adolescence. *Child Development, 58,* 1220–1234.

Taylor, D. K., Miller, S. S., & Moltz, K. A. (1991). Adolescent health care: An assessment of referral activities. *Adolescence, 26,* 717–725.

Tolor, A., & Murphy, V. M. (1985). Stress and depression in high school students. *Psychological Reports, 57,* 535–541.

U.S. Department of Commerce (1991). *Statistical abstract of the United States 1991: The national data book.* Economics and Statistics Administration, Bureau of the Census, Washington, DC.

Weiner, I. B. (1990). Distinguishing healthy from disturbed adolescent development. *Journal of Developmental and Behavioral Pediatrics, 11,* 151–154.

Weismann, M. M., Sholomskas, D., Pottenger, M., Prusoff, B. A., & Locke, B. Z. (1977). Assessing depressive symptoms in five psychiatric populations: A validation study. *American Journal of Epidemiology, 106,* 203–214.

Wells, C. E., & Ritter, K. Y. (1979). Paperwork, pressure, and discouragement: Student attitudes toward guidance services and implications for the profession. *Personnel and Guidance Journal, 58,* 242–244.

 Article Review Form at end of book.

Explain the body dissatisfaction that eating-disordered individuals express and comment on how a longitudinal study is able to identify this phenomenon.

A 10-Year Longitudinal Study of Body Weight, Dieting, and Eating Disorder Symptoms

Todd F. Heatherton

Dartmouth College

Fary Mahamedi

Harvard University

Meg Striepe

Hahnemann University

Alison E. Field

*Harvard Medical School
and Brigham and Women's Hospital*

Pamela Keel

*University of Minnesota,
Twin Cities Campus*

This article describes a 10-year longitudinal study of eating attitudes and behaviors. A sample of 509 women and 206 men completed a detailed survey in 1982 while they were in college. The authors contacted participants 10 years later and administered a 2nd questionnaire to assess stability and change in eating behaviors that occurred during the transition to early adulthood. Women in the study had substantial declines in disordered eating behavior as well as increased body satisfaction. However, body dissatisfaction and desires to lose weight remained at relatively high levels. Men, who rarely dieted or had eating problems in college, were prone to weight gain following college, and many of them reported increased dieting or disordered eating. The authors conclude that disordered eating generally tends to decline during the transition to early adulthood. However, body dissatisfaction remains a problem for a substantial segment of the adult population.

Although disordered and chaotic eating behaviors are common among young women, relatively little is known about the natural course or progression of these eating problems over time. A substantial number of young girls begin dieting before adolescence, and by the time they are in high school many of them have become chronic dieters (Heatherton & Polivy, 1992; Rosen & Gross, 1987). Moreover, many young women engage in a variety of disordered eating behaviors, such as binge eating or purging (Leon, Fulkerson, Perry & Cudeck, 1993). Likewise, eating disorders are especially prevalent during adolescence and early adulthood, with the most common onset reported to occur around age 18 (Thelen, Mann, Pruitt, & Smith, 1987). Thus, by late adolescence many young women experience a variety of eating disturbances. However, few studies have examined whether these eating problems remain stable over long periods of time or whether they abate as individuals mature into adulthood. Although a number of risk factors for eating disorders have been identified, the factors that promote or sustain abnormal eating are poorly understood. This article describes a 10-year longitudinal study of eating behavior and eating disorder symptoms. The goal of this research was to examine the stability of these behaviors during the transition to adulthood.

A few recent studies have begun to examine the long-term outcome of having a clinical eating disorder. In general it appears that eating disorders fluctuate over time, with individuals sometimes meeting clinical criteria and other times falling short of a clinical diagnosis (Fairburn & Beglin, 1990). Relapse is quite common in individuals treated for eating disorders, although some evidence indicates that the prognosis is better for bulimia nervosa than for anorexia nervosa (Herzog et al.,

1993). Studies that have followed patients for the longest periods have tended to find that eating disorder symptoms often abate over time. For instance, Collings and King (1994) followed 50 people with bulimia for 10 years following pharmacological treatment. They found that 52% recovered completely, whereas 39% continued to experience some symptoms and 9% remained bulimic. Similarly, Norring and Sohlberg (1993) found that although relapse was common, 77% of their bulimic sample did not meet criteria for an eating disorder 6 years after treatment. Johnson-Sabine, Reiss, and Dayson (1992) found that nearly half of their bulimic sample was judged to have a good behavioral outcome after 5 years (with nearly one third showing a complete recovery). Thus, these long-term results suggest that a substantial number of patients seem to get better within 5 years. Note that all of the participants in these studies received treatment for their eating disorders. To date there have been no long-term studies examining the natural history of eating disorders.

Although much of the research has focused on clinical eating disorders, which affect 1–5% of young women and less than 1% of men (American Psychiatric Association, 1994; Fairburn & Beglin, 1990), there exists a wide spectrum of disordered eating that falls short of clinical diagnosis. For instance, one recent study found that close to 30% of college women and just about 10% of college men reported current or past problem binge eating (Heatherton, Nichols, Mahamedi, & Keel, 1995). Moreover, body dissatisfaction and chronic dieting are extremely common among young women, and many of them experience at least some degree of disordered eating (Heatherton & Baumeister, 1991; Polivy & Herman, 1987; Striegel-Moore, Silberstein, & Rodin, 1986). Many researchers have called for longitudinal studies on the natural course of eating problems among those who do not have full-blown eating disorders (see Leon, Fulkerson, Perry, & Early-Zald, 1995). In their review of the epidemiological literature, Fairburn and Beglin (1990) concluded "it is time for a shift in

emphasis away from prevalence per se toward studies of the nature, course, and etiology of the full spectrum of disturbance that exists in the community" (p. 407).

In spite of theoretical interest in the topic, there has been little empirical examination of the natural course or history of the full range of eating disturbances. Leon et al. (1995) categorized adolescents into one of four disordered eating risk categories and found an impressive degree of stability over 2 years, with most respondents staying in the same risk category (47% for girls and 45% for boys) or moving up or down the risk hierarchy by only one group (27% for girls and 40% for boys). Drewnowski, Yee, Kurth, and Krahn (1994) reported on a 6-month longitudinal study of 557 college women. They classified respondents into one of five categories (nondieters, casual dieters, intensive dieters, dieters at risk, and bulimic) and found that there was a great deal of shifting from one category to another over 6 months, although usually the shifts were to an adjacent category. However, this study followed participants for only a very short period, and it is possible that classifications would be more stable over longer periods. Accordingly, the primary goal of the current study was to examine stability and change in a wide spectrum of eating behaviors over a reasonably long period.

Dieting and Long-Term Weight Change

Dieting is a notoriously ineffective means of achieving weight loss. Some 95% of those who lose weight will regain the weight within a few years, and many will gain more weight than they originally lost (National Institutes of Health Technology Assessment Conference Panel, 1993). Moreover, many of those who diet are not overweight, and therefore it seems unlikely that they will achieve substantial weight loss.[1] Indeed, one study found that average-weight chronic dieters did not lose any weight over a 6-month period (Heatherton, Polivy, & Herman, 1991), and a recent study

found that even overweight chronic dieters did not lose weight over a 30-month period (Klesges, Klem, Epkins, & Klesges, 1991). Note that in the Klesges et al. study there was a tendency for all participants to gain weight over time, and in this respect there were no differences between dieters and nondieters. Thus, the data indicate that most diets are doomed to fail (Garner & Wooley, 1991). One goal of the current study was to assess the long-term effects of dieting behavior on body weight.

The Transition to Adulthood

This study examines eating behaviors during the transition from college to young adulthood. Anecdotal, clinical, biographical, and empirical evidence suggests that this is a period of major life change (Caspi, 1993; Costa & McCrae, 1994; Heatherton & Weinberger, 1994; Helson & Stewart, 1994; Levinson, Darrow, Klein, Levinson, & McKee, 1978; McCrae & Costa, 1990; Vaillant, 1977). During this period individuals begin to settle down, get married, have children, and establish careers, and they usually develop a strong and coherent sense of identity. To the extent that changes in role status (e.g., from student to professional) reflect simultaneous change in life goals, it might be expected that the importance of physical appearance diminishes as people approach their thirties (when other goals become more important). Moreover, this transitional period is marked by growing autonomy from parents and peers, and therefore any influence that they have over physical appearance standards should also tend to diminish. It is also common for individuals to enter long-term, committed relationships during their mid to late twenties (Erikson, 1968). To the extent that relationship partners are supportive and nurturing, they may encourage increased self-acceptance. Hence, the various tasks and challenges associated with making the transition to adulthood might assuage the widespread preoccupation with physical appearance and thereby lessen the motivation for constant dieting. From this perspective one might expect eating disturbances and eating disorders to be less common among adults than among adolescents or college students, and indeed a variety of evidence indicates that this is true (Bushnell, Wells, Hornblow, Oakley-Browne, & Joyce, 1990; Fairburn & Beglin, 1990).

A relatively low rate of eating disorders among adults (older than college students) may reflect developmental processes (as suggested above), but it may also reflect cohort changes in abnormal eating patterns. That is, individuals who passed through adolescence during the 1960s and early 1970s (when eating disorders were relatively uncommon) may hold very different attitudes about body weight and physical appearance than those who were adolescents during the late 1970s and 1980s (when eating disorders were much more prevalent, see Heatherton et al., 1995). Thus, the extant literature does not allow an assessment of cohort effects, which have been shown to be extremely important in understanding behavioral and personality change over the life course (Caspi, 1993; Elder & Caspi, 1992). To the extent that the sociocultural milieu affects individual attitudes about physical appearance and the desirability of being thin, growing up during an apex of pressures to be thin may instill values and beliefs about body weight that last a lifetime.

Current Study

This research follows a cohort who were teenagers in the late 1970s and early 1980s, a period when dieting, eating disturbances, and eating disorders were highly prevalent (Halmi, Falk, & Schwartz, 1981). The current sample had participated in a study of eating behavior while they were college students, and findings from that study indicated that the prevalence of eating problems and eating disorder symptoms was similar to that reported for other college campuses at that period of time (Zuckerman, Colby, Ware, & Lazerson, 1986). We contacted participants 10 years after their original participation and examined their current eating habits and eating-related attitudes in some depth. We expected eating problems (such as chronic dieting) to diminish during the transition to adulthood.

Method

Participants

Participants in this study ($N = 715$) had been college students (freshmen or seniors) at a selective northeastern college in 1982. This sample comprised 509 women and 206 men, ranging in age from 27 to 55, ($M = 30.0$, $SD = 2.0$). This group was 80% White, 6% Black, 8% Asian, and 4% Hispanic (1% other).

Procedure

In the spring of 1982, researchers affiliated with the Henry Murray Center of Radcliffe College sent out a survey to a randomly selected sample of 800 women and 400 men from a selective northeastern college, half of whom were freshmen and half of whom were seniors. The response rate was 78% for women ($N = 625$) and 69% for men ($N = 276$). The questionnaire included demographic background information, items assessing height and weight, and items assessing general eating patterns (such as meal frequency). Respondents were also asked about dieting history, body weight and shape concerns, and abnormal eating behaviors (binging, vomiting, laxative and diuretic use, and fasting). Respondents also indicated whether they had engaged in these behaviors in the past (but not now) or whether the behaviors were ongoing. Those who reported current regular binge eating were asked to specify the frequency of their binges, as well as how much control they had over the binges and how troubled or worried they were by the binges. Respondents were also asked about the type of food that they consumed during a typical binge. Finally, participants completed 26 items from the Eating Disorder Inventory (EDI; Garner, Olmsted, & Polivy, 1983). These items are the principal items for five of the EDI subscales (Drive for Thinness, Bulimia, Maturity Fears, Perfectionism, and Interpersonal Distrust). Results from this study indicated that the prevalence of eating disorders in this sample was very similar to those reported in other studies of college students (Zuckerman et al., 1986).

During the spring of 1992 we attempted to identify and follow up all the participants from the first study ($N = 901$). We received responses from 515 (82%) women and 209 (76%) men. Of those who did not respond, 4 had died (2 men and 2 women) and the remainder were either untraceable or did not respond to the survey (we mailed two follow-up surveys in order to maximize participation). Three of those who responded returned blank forms and therefore were excluded. Moreover, 6 participants were excluded because the information in their 1992 questionnaire did not correspond with the information in the 1982 questionnaire, leading us to believe that the follow-up data were not from the initial respondent. The final sample consisted of 509 women and 206 men.

The 1992 survey was based closely on the 1982 survey (in order to make direct comparisons we asked the questions in the same manner). In addition to the questions that were asked in the 1982 survey, we also asked about marital status, education, career, income, exercise history, and children. Moreover, we asked participants to recall their weights and dieting histories while they had been in college.[2]

Classifications

Body mass index (BMI; calculated as weight in kilograms divided by height in meters squared) was calculated for each participant. They were also classified as underweight, average weight, overweight, or obese on the basis of standards adapted from the National Health and Nutrition Examination Survey (NHANES; Kuczmarski, 1992; Kuczmarski, Flegal, Campbell, & Johnson, 1994). Men scoring under 20.7 and women scoring under 20.0 were considered underweight. BMI cutoffs for overweight were 27.8 for men and 27.3 for women, and BMI cutoffs for obesity were 31.1 for men and 32.3 for women.

All participants were classified into one of five groups for both 1982 and 1992; nondieters, dieters, problem dieters, subclinical eating disordered, and eating disordered. Classifications were made by raters unaware of year of participation. We used *Diagnostic and Statistical Manual of Mental Disorders* (3rd ed., revised; *DSM–III–R*; American Psychiatric

Association, 1987) criteria for bulimia nervosa to classify participants into the *eating disordered* category, and these participants had to report (a) regularly binge eating twice or more per week as well as regular purging (typically vomiting or fasting); (b) feeling out of control during a binge (4 or 5 on a 5-point scale); (c) being extremely worried about their binge eating (4 or 5 on a 5-point scale); (d) being in the top 25th percentile of the EDI measures of drive for thinness and bulimia; (e) regular dieting; and (f) dissatisfaction with their current appearance and desire to lose weight. The latter measures helped identify a preoccupation with dieting and physical appearance. Participants classified as having *subclinical eating disorders* were those who reported regularly binge eating (at least once a week) but who did not meet one or more of the criteria for an eating disorder. Most often these individuals reported binge eating only once per week or did not report regular use of purgatives. These participants had to report at least moderate worry about their binge eating and report being somewhat out of control during a binge. *Problem dieters* were those who reported sometimes or often dieting, who scored above the median on EDI measures of drive for thinness and bulimia, and who reported some symptoms of an eating disorder (most commonly bingeing). However, these participants reported feeling moderately in control during a binge and did not report being overly concerned about their binge eating. *Dieters* were those who reported sometimes or often dieting, who also reported body dissatisfaction, but who reported minor or no eating disorder symptoms. *Nondieters* were those who reported rarely or never dieting and who reported no symptoms of eating disorders. We followed the conservative strategy of moving participants to a less disordered category if there were any questions about classification.

Results

Preliminary analyses were conducted to examine potential differences between those who responded to the survey and those who did not. Although the participation rate was greater for women (82%) than for men (76%), χ^2 (1, $N = 901$) = 6.1, $p < .02$, there were no other demographic differences that predicted participation. In terms of dieting and eating disorder symptoms, the responders were generally more concerned about body weight and more likely to have some sort of eating problem while they were in college. Specifically, the participation rates for frequent dieters (85%) were higher than for those who reported never dieting (75%), χ^2(1, $N = 901$) = 12.6, $p < .01$. This pattern was significant only for women. Similarly, the participation rates for dieters, problem dieters, subclinical eating disordered, and eating disordered (range from 82 to 88%) were higher than for those with no symptoms of eating problems (74), χ^2(1, $N = 901$) = 17.9, $p < .01$. Thus, nondieting participants without any eating difficulties were somewhat less inclined to participate in the follow-up survey.[3]

Physical Changes

Height

As might be expected, height did not change for either men or women between 1982 and 1992 (*ns*). Average height was 70.8 in. (179.8 cm, $SD = 6.68$) for men and 65.3 in. (165.8 cm, $SD = 7.1$) for women in both 1982 and 1992. Moreover, there was a great deal of relative stability in self-reports of height, $r(713) = .98$, $p < .0001$.

Weight

A two-way analysis of variance (ANOVA) using repeated measures on body weight revealed an interaction between sex and weight change over the 10 years of the study, $F(1, 706) = 36.8$, $p < .0001$. Overall, there was a main effect such that both men and women gained weight over the 10 years, $F(1, 706) = 142.9$, $p < .0001$. On average, women were 4 lbs (8.81 kg) heavier in 1992 ($M = 132.4$, $SD = 22.8$) than in 1982 ($M = 128.1$, $SD = 17.5$), $t(502) = 6.88$, $p < .0001$. Men, however, gained a lot more weight than did women—nearly 12 lbs (5.44 kg) between 1982 ($M = 161.8$, $SD = 22.7$) and 1992 ($M = 173.3$, $SD = 24.2$), $t(204) = 11.3$, $p < .0001$. However, rank orderings for body weight were quite reliable, $r(501) = .79$, for women and, $r(203) = .81$, for men.

Participants were divided into one of three groups: those who lost 10 or more pounds, those who gained 10 or more pounds, and those who stayed the same. A much larger proportion of men gained weight (55%) than did women (28%), χ^2(2, $N = 708$) = 48.6, $p < .0001$, whereas relatively few men (5%) or women (11%) lost weight. The majority of men gained at least 10 lbs, and indeed this group had a mean weight gain of 21.1 lbs ($SD = 14.4$, range = 10–88 lbs).

An exploratory stepwise regression analysis was conducted to examine the best predictors of weight gain. All eating habit, dieting, body satisfaction, eating disorder symptom, and eating attitude variables from 1982 were used to predict change in BMI over the 10 years. For women, the best predictors of weight gain were the discrepancy between 1982 weight and highest past reported weight (i.e., the most that participants in 1982 reported that they had ever previously weighed), $\beta = .07$, $t(492) = 4.8$, $p < .0001$, and 1982 Drive for Thinness scores from the EDI, $\beta = -.06$, $t(492) = 3.8$, $p < .0001$. Together these variables accounted for 6% of the variance in BMI change, $F(2, 492) = 16.0$, $p < .0001$. Thus, weight gain for women was associated with a past history of weighing more and being less concerned about being thin in 1982. For men, the best predictors of weight gain were 1982 body weight, $\beta = -.03$, $t(200) = 4.0$, $p < .0001$, and 1982 Drive for Thinness scores, $\beta = .09$, $t(200) = 2.7$, $p < .001$. Together these variables accounted for 9% of the variance in BMI change, $F(2, 200) = 9.9$, $p < .0001$. Thus, for men weight gain was associated with lower body weight and greater concern about being thin.

Although our participants gained weight, they are, on average, quite thin as a group. Recent studies have found that 20–35% of American adults are overweight or obese (Kuczmarski et al., 1994). Our participants were students at a prestigious university where even moderate overweight is quite rare. Indeed, as may be seen in Table 1, less than 2% of students were overweight in 1982, and nearly one third of the women were underweight by population standards. In 1992, even after weight gain, fewer than 10% of the participants were overweight or obese.

Nonetheless, this group shows a similar trend in weight gain as has been observed in more representative samples of American adults (Williamson, Kahn, Remington, & Anda, 1990).

Body Satisfaction and Dieting

Although very few of our participants were actually overweight while in college (compared to representative samples), many of them, and especially women, believed themselves overweight and wished to lose at least 10 lbs. In 1982, more women viewed themselves as overweight or very overweight than average weight or underweight , and only 1 woman in over 500 viewed herself as very underweight (see Table 1). Indeed, the vast majority of women reported wanting to lose weight, and very few reported wanting to gain weight. Ten years later, these women were much less likely to report themselves as overweight, χ^2 (16, $N = 504$) = 189.3, $p < .0001$, and also less likely to report wanting to lose weight, $\chi^2(4, N = 508)$ = 97.1, $p < .0001$. As may be seen in Table 1, the number of women who reported themselves as overweight dropped in half between 1982 and 1992 and the modal woman in 1992 described herself as average weight. Of those women who viewed themselves as overweight in 1982, more than half (55%) viewed themselves as average weight in 1992, suggesting that either they had lost weight or that their standards for judging overweight had changed (and given the weight findings, the latter appears to be the better explanation).

A different picture emerges for men. As may be seen in Table 1, the vast majority of men in 1982 viewed themselves as average weight or slightly underweight, and the men were roughly equally divided in their desires to gain weight, lose weight, or stay the same. Given the weight gain noted above, it is not surprising that significantly more men saw themselves as overweight in 1992 than did in 1982, $\chi^2(12, N = 204)$ = 249.5, $p < .0001$, and significantly more men wanted to lose weight than gain weight in 1992, $\chi^2(4, N = 202)$ = 67.8, $p < .0001$. Men who wanted to lose weight in 1982 continued to want to lose weight in 1992 (81%). Interestingly, 47% of the men who were happy with their weight in 1982, and 28% of the men who wanted to

| Table 1 | Changes in Overall Weight and Dieting Behavior for Men and Women: 1982 to 1992 |

	Women				Men			
	1982		**1992**		**1982**		**1992**	
Measure	**n**	**%**	**n**	**%**	**n**	**%**	**n**	**%**
Weight group[a]								
Underweight	158	31.2	145	28.7	43	21.0	11	5.3
Average	342	67.5	328	65.0	157	76.6	174	84.5
Overweight	5	1.0	21	4.2	5	2.4	17	8.3
Obese	2	0.4	11	2.2	0	0.0	4	1.9
Self-categorization[a]								
Very underweight	1	0.2	2	0.4	1	0.5	0	0.0
Underweight	11	2.2	39	7.7	27	13.2	12	5.8
Average	230	45.5	317	62.5	148	72.2	142	69.3
Overweight	248	49.0	129	25.4	28	13.7	50	24.4
Very overweight	16	3.2	20	3.9	1	0.5	1	0.5
Desire to[a]								
Lose weight	417	82.1	346	67.9	75	37.1	114	55.4
Stay same	75	14.8	151	29.7	81	40.1	66	32.0
Gain weight	16	3.2	12	2.4	46	22.8	26	12.6

[a]Significant difference for women and for men (using chi-square analysis).

gain weight in 1982, subsequently wanted to lose weight in 1992.

In terms of dieting behavior, the majority of women in 1982 reported dieting at least sometimes or often (see the marginals reported in brackets in Table 2). Ten years later, there was a strong trend for less frequent dieting, $\chi^2(9, N = 502)$ = 84.3, $p < .0001$, and constant dieting dropped in half. As may also be seen in Table 2, of those who were sometimes dieting in 1982, more than half reported never or rarely dieting in 1992, and of those who were always dieting in 1982, almost half reported never or rarely dieting in 1992. Thus, whereas 18% of women became more intense dieters between 1982 and 1992, 37% remained at the same level and 45% decreased their dieting intensity. In contrast, men were much more likely to stay at the same level of dieting intensity (61%) or increase dieting (31%), χ^2 (2, $N = 202$) = 86.3, $p < .0001$. Of course, given that the baseline prevalence of dieting among men was low in 1982, it is not completely surprising that dieting frequency increased or remained the same. As may be seen in Table 2, fewer than 1 in 4 men reported any dieting in 1982, but by 1992 nearly half reported dieting, $\chi^2(9,$

$N = 205$) = 67.0, $p < .0001$. Thus, compared to 1982, men in 1992 reported weighing more, wanting more to lose weight, and were also more likely to be on a diet. Unfortunately, the nature of these data do not allow us to assess whether the weight gain preceded or followed efforts at dieting, although common sense might suggest that the weight gain occurred first.

Eating Disorder Attitudes and Symptoms

A major goal of the study was to examine changes in eating disorder attitudes and symptoms in the 10 years following college. Eating disorder attitudes were obtained through scores on a modified version of the EDI (Garner et al., 1983), and eating disorder symptoms were obtained through a symptom checklist (that asked for occurrence and frequency of a variety of disordered behaviors). Subsidiary items were used to assess the intensity and problematic nature of these symptoms.

Attitudes

Two-factor (sex and time of survey) repeated measures ANOVAs were used to assess changes for each of the

Table 2 Changes in Dieting Status for Men and Women: 1982 to 1992

1982 Dieting Status	Percentage Reported Dieting Status in 1992			
	Never	**Rarely**	**Sometimes**	**Often**
Women	(32.5)	(29.9)	(27.0)	(10.6)
Never (25.1)	56.3	26.2	13.5	3.9
Rarely (15.1)	43.4	31.6	19.7	5.3
Sometimes (37.1)	20.4	35.5	34.4	9.7
Often (22.7)	18.4	23.7	35.1	22.8
Men	(52.2)	(23.4)	(18.5)	(5.9)
Never (75.6)	63.9	20.6	10.9	4.5
Rarely (9.8)	30.0	40.0	25.0	5.0
Sometimes (13.2)	7.4	29.6	55.6	7.4
Often (1.4)	0.0	0.0	33.3	66.6

Note. Numbers in parentheses refer to overall percentage selecting specific category in that year (i.e., 25.1% of women reported never dieting in 1982, whereas 3.25% reported never dieting in 1992).

Table 3 Changes in Modified Eating Disorder Inventory Subscale Scores for Women and Men: 1982 to 1992

Subscale	Women		Men	
	1982	**1992**	**1982**	**1992**
Bulimia				
M	14.3	11.0****	10.4	9.6****
SD	5.1	4.3	3.4	3.2
Drive for thinness				
M	16.1	12.6****	8.9	9.6**
SD	6.4	5.6	4.3	4.6
Perfectionism				
M	23.0	24.1***	22.9	23.6*
SD	5.4	5.2	5.0	5.0
Maturity fears				
M	10.3	9.7**	10.4	10.1
SD	3.1	3.4	2.9	3.4
Interpersonal distrust				
M	12.3	11.8	13.2	13.3
SD	4.0	3.6	4.0	3.9

Note. Significance tests refer to within-sex contrasts.
*$p < .05$. **$p < .01$. ***$p < .001$. ****$p < .0001$.

EDI subfactors (bulimia, drive for thinness, perfectionism, interpersonal distrust, and maturity fears). As may be seen in Table 3, attitudes related to eating behavior changed substantially for men and women. For instance, there was an overall decrease in bulimic attitudes, $F(1, 696) = 260.3$, $p < .0001$, although the effect was stronger for women, $t(496) = 15.9$, $p < .0001$, than for men, $t(200) = 3.92$, $p < .0001$, interaction $F(1, 696) = 46.35$, $p < .0001$.

As might be expected from the dieting data, a repeated measures ANOVA on drive for thinness scores resulted in an interaction between sex and year of survey,

$F(1, 697) = 79.25$, $p < .0001$. Although women showed a strong decline in drive for thinness, $t(495) = 12.80$, $p < .0001$, men showed a moderate increase in drive for thinness, $t(202) = 2.25$, $p < .01$.

In terms of the EDI scales that did not directly assess eating attitudes, there was an overall increase in perfectionism, $F(1, 697) = 26.04$, $p < .0001$, and an overall decrease in maturity fears, $F(1, 690) = 12.17$, $p < .0005$, although sex did not interact with year of survey on either measure. Finally, there were no significant changes in self-reports of interpersonal distrust. Thus, the major changes on the EDI scales were in those items related to eating attitudes.

Symptoms and Classification

Respondents were asked to indicate whether they currently engaged in a list of disordered eating behaviors. As may be seen in Table 4, women engaged in fewer disordered eating behaviors in 1992 than they did in 1982. Specifically, women reported declines in binge eating, $t(490 = 6.8$, $p < .0001$; fasting, $t(459) = 5.2$, $p < .0001$; and laxative use, $t(476) = 1.95$, $p < .05$. Women also reported nonsignificant declines in diet pill use, $t(465) = 1.8$, $p < .10$; diuretics, $t(473) = 1.4$, $p > .10$; and vomiting, $t < 1$. Note that very few men reported eating disorder symptoms in either 1982 or 1992, and although the percentage reporting binge eating dropped, this decline was not significant, $t(190) = 1.4$, $p > .10$.

As may be seen in Table 5, the percentage of women classified as having any sort of eating problem (problem dieter, subclinical, or clinical) dropped from more than 40% to just over 15%, $\chi^2(16, N = 509) = 115.80$, $p < .0001$. Thus, the modal woman (46%) moved to a lower eating category, whereas 41% stayed in the same category and 14% moved to a more disordered category. Very few men reported any form of eating problem, and 72% stayed in the same eating category for both 1982 and 1992, with the remainder evenly split between moving to a less severe eating category (13%) or to a more severe eating category (16%). Note that most men who increased in eating category went from being nondieters to being dieters (see Table 5).

Relation between Changes in Eating Behaviors and Attitudes

One goal of the current study was to examine how changes in eating disorder risk factors (e.g., dieting, body image, and body weight) were related to changes in disordered eating attitudes and behaviors. Change scores (1982–1992) were calculated for dieting behavior, body dissatisfaction, body weight, EDI Drive for Thinness, EDI Bulimia, and eating disorder classification, and the correlations between these variables are shown in Table 6 (separately for men and women). Note that all of the variables were significantly correlated for women ($p < .0001$), whereas all but the relation between changes in EDI Bulimia and changes in body weight were significant for men ($ps < .05–.0001$).

Discussion

The results of our longitudinal study demonstrate that for our sample of women, body dissatisfaction, chronic dieting, and eating disorder symptoms generally diminished in the 10 years following college. Rates of apparent eating disorders dropped by more than half, and the prevalence of binge eating and purging declined substantially. These findings are similar to studies of long-term outcome for those who have clinical eating disorders (Collings & King, 1994; Norring & Sohlberg, 1993). This pattern suggests that maturing into adulthood and getting away from the enormous social influences that emphasize thinness (such as being on a college campus) help most of the women escape from chronic dieting and abnormal eating. These results also imply that, for some women, disordered eating behaviors may be part of a temporary phase. Indeed, some of our participants included personal letters that commented on how dieting became much less important to them when they gained some distance—both geographically and emotionally—from the college experience.

A substantial number of women, however, continued to have eating problems 10 years after college. Thus, the results of the current study have elements that are both encouraging and discouraging. Although very few of the women who were satisfied with their body weight or shape in college went on to develop serious eating problems, many of those who were dissatisfied with their bodies continued dieting

Table 4 Eating Disorder Symptoms for Men and Women: 1982 and 1992

Disordered Behavior	Women 1982 n	Women 1982 %	Women 1992 n	Women 1992 %	Men 1982 n	Men 1982 %	Men 1992 n	Men 1992 %
Binge eating[a]	132	26.9	59	12.0	27	14.1	19	9.9
Diuretics	6	1.3	2	0.4	1	0.5	0	0.0
Diet pills	13	2.8	6	1.3	2	1.0	0	0.0
Laxatives[a]	10	2.1	3	0.6	0	0.0	0	0.0
Fasting[a]	79	17.2	30	6.5	12	6.3	13	6.8
Vomiting	9	1.9	6	1.3	0	0.0	1	0.5

[a]Significant difference for women.

Table 5 Changes in Eating Disorder Classification for Men and Women: 1982 to 1992

1982 Category	Percentage Reported in 1992 Nondieter	Dieter	Problem Dieter	Subclinical	Clinical
Women	(55.8)	(28.3)	(7.1)	(5.9)	(2.9)
Nondieter (33.4)	77.6	17.6	1.8	1.8	1.2
Dieter (26.3)	50.8	37.3	7.5	4.5	0.0
Problem dieter (22.0)	44.6	33.0	9.8	9.8	2.7
Subclinical (11.0)	44.6	32.1	8.9	10.7	3.6
Clinical (7.3)	24.3	24.3	18.9	10.8	21.6
Men	(72.8)	(18.4)	(4.4)	(2.4)	(1.9)
Nondieter (77.2)	82.4	12.0	3.1	1.3	1.3
Dieter (10.7)	31.8	63.6	4.5	0.0	0.0
Problem dieter (7.2)	46.7	26.7	6.7	6.7	13.3
Subclinical (3.4)	42.9	14.3	14.3	28.6	0.0
Clinical (1.5)	66.7	0.0	33.3	0.0	0.0

Note. Number in parentheses refer to overall percentage classified into a specific category in that year (i.e., 7% of women were classified as having an eating disorder in 1982, compared with 3% in 1992).

Table 6 Relation between Changes in Eating Attitudes and Behaviors: 1982 to 1992

Change	1	2	3	4	5	6
1. ΔDieting	—	.36	.26	.57	.40	.57
2. ΔBody dis.	.23	—	.57	.39	.40	.33
3. ΔWeight	.25	.38	—	.25	.31	.24
4. ΔEDI-DT	.48	.29	.14*	—	.62	.54
5. ΔEDI-B	.19	.25	.11†	.49	—	.63
6. ΔEating dis.	.51	.16*	.16*	.47	.37	—

Note. Numbers above the diagonal are for women, and numbers below diagonal are for men. All correlations for women are $p < .0001$. All correlations for men are $p < .001$, except where noted.

ΔDieting = change in frequency of dieting; ΔBody dis. = change in body dissatisfaction; ΔWeight = change in body weight; ΔEDI-DT = change in eating Disorder Inventory Drive for Thinness; ΔEDI-B = change in EDI Bulimia; ΔEating dis. = change in eating disorder classification.

*$p < .05$. †Nonsignificant.

and engaging in disordered eating during the 10 years after college. Indeed, more than one in five of the women who met clinical criteria for an eating disorder in college also met criteria for an eating disorder 10 years later.

Although there was a general reduction in eating problems for women, a very different picture emerged for the men in our sample. In the 10 years following college, more than half of the men gained at least 10 lbs, and body weight concerns, desires to lose weight, and dieting behavior increased accordingly. These increases in desire to lose weight and dieting were associated with increased eating-disordered attitudes and behaviors (although, overall, binge eating showed a modest decline for men). Although these data do not allow for a complete determination of the sequence of these events, common sense suggests that weight gain preceded dieting and that dieting preceded eating problems. Although it is possible that eating problems preceded dieting for the men in our sample, that scenario strikes us as unlikely. Undoubtedly many of the men who gained weight were overeaters, but their overeating episodes probably did not include the psychological mindset of the binge eater (i.e., feeling out of control during the binge and being extremely worried about the binge eating behavior). It is important to distinguish between simple overeating and binge eating; although they both might be

unhealthy and contribute to weight gain, simple overeating lacks the psychological distress that accompanies binge eating.

There are a number of possible explanations for the weight gain among men (e.g., increased alcohol intake, decreased exercise, increased consumption of fattening foods, change in metabolic rate), although we do not have the data in the current study to identify the relative importance of these various explanations. The different weight change patterns for men and women provide at least one plausible explanation for why men gained more weight than women. Women are socialized from a young age to watch their weight; men are not given the same message. Perhaps the women put more effort into maintaining their weight, whereas the men did not realize that as they moved to more sedentary lifestyles (associated with having a full-time job) they would gain weight if they did not decrease their caloric intake or stay active. Unfortunately, the data do not appear to support such a scenario. The only significant predictors of increased weight gain, for men, were lower body weight and heightened desires to be thin. This suggests that the men who gained weight were actually more concerned about being thin than the men who did not gain weight. However, it is important to note that the predictors of weight gain in our study explained only a modest amount of variance (less than

10%), and therefore it is premature to draw any specific conclusions about why men in our study gained weight.

It is also interesting to note that the overall trend for weight gain is similar to that found for members of this age group in the general population (Kuczmarski et al., 1994; Williamson et al., 1990). Thus, even though research has demonstrated that the growth in obesity is related to socioeconomic status (Kuczmarski, 1992), there does appear to be a general trend that crosses social strata.

Why Did Eating Difficulties Decrease for Women?

We have argued that eating problems diminish in the 10 years following college—at least for women—primarily because of maturational processes and changes in role status. It is also possible, however, that our findings reflect a more general societal trend. Heatherton et al. (1995) compared eating behavior on college campuses for students in 1982 and 1992 and found that eating disorder symptoms, dieting, and body dissatisfaction declined during that decade. For instance, in 1982, approximately 7% met clinical criteria for an eating disorder and 26% reported some form of binge eating. In contrast, rates of clinical eating disorders for students at the same college in 1992 were just over 5% and binge eating was reported by 19%. Thus, although eating disorders remain a serious and widespread problem on college campuses, it is possible that the findings in the current study reflect a general decline in the prevalence of disordered eating behaviors. However, the decline in disordered eating was greater in the current sample than in our cross-sectional study, suggesting that there is an age-related decline in disordered eating.

Heatherton et al. (1995) proposed a number of possible reasons for this decline in disordered eating behavior. For instance, information about eating disorders has been widely disseminated in the media. There have been public health advertisements, international "no diet" days, television "movies of the week," numerous talk shows on anorexia nervosa and bulimia, as well as noted celebrity sufferers (e.g., Princess Diana) and even celebrity deaths (e.g., Karen Carpenter). This increased media focus on eating disorders may have increased awareness of the potential consequences of fasting, bingeing, and purging. There has also been an increasing emphasis on healthful eating and regular exercise, and nutritionists have tended to emphasize low-fat rather than low-calorie diets. Thus, sociocultural messages about the importance of thinness, long blamed for cultivating eating disorders, may have changed between the early 1980s and the 1990s.

Another possible explanation for the decline in self-reports of eating problems is that participants may be more reluctant to report eating problems in 1992 than they were in 1982. Women who are approaching their thirties may be embarrassed to admit that they are experiencing problems typically associated with adolescence. Moreover, *dieting* has become a dirty word, mainly because of the failures typically associated with conventional dieting, and therefore our participants may have reframed their *dieting* to refer to *lifestyle modifications*, in which one diets to be healthy rather than to be thin (although all of the behaviors and consequences are the same). Finally, it is also possible that women in the 1990s may have a better understanding of the behaviors and terminology of eating disorders. For instance, there may be better agreement on what is meant by binge eating, and fewer women may feel that their occasional bouts of overeating are pathological. Thus, there may be a growing sophistication in how people refer to eating difficulties. However, given that participants reported consistent declines in all behaviors and attitudes related to body weight issues, including those that are more objective and easy to define (i.e., diet pill use, vomiting, answers to EDI items), we believe that our findings represent a genuine decrease in disordered eating in the 10 years following college.

This study is also limited by its reliance on self-reports, which have been criticized because they are prone to self-presentational bias (Fairburn & Beglin, 1990). We were limited by the methods and items used in the 1982 study, and we needed to follow those methods as closely as possible to en-

sure that any differences were not due to changes in item definition or method used to assess symptoms. Although clinical interview methods may have been preferable to self-reports, they were not possible in the current study. To our knowledge this is the first study that follows a large sample of participants during the transition from late adolescence to early adulthood. Therefore, we believe that our results may provide valuable information about eating problems during the transition to adulthood that might be confirmed by future interview studies.

Conclusions

Our study demonstrates that eating difficulties appear to lessen, especially for women, in the decade following graduation from college. These results suggest that at least some degree of disordered eating may be normative for college women, and that it is also normative for these problems to diminish after graduation. However, body dissatisfaction and chronic dieting remain a problem for a substantial number of women. For men, the decade after college is typically a period of weight gain, accompanied by increased dieting and, for some, the development of disordered eating. Understanding the mechanisms by which maturational processes influence the maintenance or change in eating attitudes and behaviors is an important goal for future research.

Notes

1. Although it is possible that some individuals diet to avoid weight gain (rather than to lose weight), the majority of women who diet report wanting to lose at least 10 lbs (Heatherton et al., 1995). Thus, although average-weight women may want to lose less weight than overweight women, weight loss is still the primary motive for their dieting efforts.

2. Reliabilities for recall of college weight were $r(692) = .95$; $r(489) = .92$ for women and $r(201) = .89$ for men. This issue is considered in greater detail (for women) in Field, Colditz, Herzog, and Heatherton (1996).

3. Note that other studies have found that severity of eating problems predicts decreased likelihood of research participation (e.g., Fairburn, Jones, Peveler, Hope, & O'Connor, 1993).

References

American Psychiatric Association. (1987). *Diagnostic and statistical manual of mental disorders* (3rd ed., rev.). Washington, DC: Author.

American Psychiatric Association. (1994). *Diagnostic and statistical manual of mental disorders* (4th ed.). Washington, DC: Author.

Bushnell, J. A., Wells, J. E., Hornblow, A. R., Oakley-Browne, M. A., & Joyce, P. (1990). Prevalence of three bulimic syndromes in the general population. *Psychological Medicine, 20,* 671–680.

Caspi, A. (1993). Why maladaptive behaviors persist: Sources of continuity and change across the life span. In D. C. Funder, R. D. Parke, C. Tomlinson-Keasey, & K. Widam (Eds.), *Studying lives through time* (pp. 343–376). Washington, DC: American Psychological Association.

Collings, S., & King, M. (1994). Ten-year follow-up of 50 patients with bulimia nervosa. *British Journal of Psychiatry, 164,* 80–87.

Costa, P. T., Jr., & McCrae, R. R. (1994). Set like plaster? Evidence for the stability of adult personality. In T. F. Heatherton & J. L. Weinberger (Eds.), *Can personality change?* (pp. 21–40). Washington, DC: American Psychological Association.

Drewnowski, A., Yee, D. K., Kurth, C. L., & Krahn, D. D. (1994). Eating pathology and *DSM–III–R* bulimia nervosa: A continuum of behavior. *American Journal of Psychiatry, 151,* 1217–1219.

Elder, G. H., Jr., & Caspi, A. (1992). Studying lives in a changing society: Sociological and personological explorations. In R. A. Zucker, A. I. Rabin, J. Aronoff, & S. Frank (Eds.), *Personality structure in the life course* (pp. 276–322). New York: Springer.

Erikson, E. H. (1968). *Identity: Youth and crisis.* New York: Norton.

Fairburn, C. G., & Beglin, S. J. (1990). Studies of the epidemiology of bulimia nervosa. *American Journal of Psychiatry, 147,* 401–408.

Fairburn, C. G., Jones, R., Peveler, R. C., Hope, R. A., & O'Connor, M. (1993). Psychotherapy and bulimia nervosa; Longer-term effects of interpersonal psychotherapy, behavior therapy, and cognitive behavior therapy. *Archives of General Psychiatry, 50,* 419–428.

Field, A. E., Colditz, G. A., Herzog, D. B., & Heatherton, T. F. (1996). Disordered eating: Can women accurately recall their bingeing and purging behaviors ten years later? *Obesity Research 4,* 153–159.

Garner, D. M., Olmsted, M. P., & Polivy, J. (1983). Development and validation of a multidimensional eating disorder inventory for anorexia nervosa and bulimia. *International Journal of Eating Disorders, 2,* 15–34.

Garner, D. M., & Wooley, S. C. (1991). Confronting the failure of behavioral and dietary treatments for obesity. *Clinical Psychology Review, 11*, 729–780.

Halmi, K. A., Falk, J. R., & Schwartz, E. (1981). Binge-eating and vomiting: A survey of a college population. *Psychological Medicine, 11*, 697–706.

Heatherton, T. F., & Baumeister, R. F. (1991). Binge eating as an escape from self-awareness. *Psychological Bulletin, 110*, 86–108.

Heatherton, T. F., Nichols, P., Mahamedi, F., & Keel, P. K. (1995). Body weight, dieting, and eating disorder symptoms among college students 1982 to 1992. *American Journal of Psychiatry, 152*, 1623–1629.

Heatherton, T. F., & Polivy, J. (1992). Chronic dieting and eating disorders: A spiral model. In J. H. Crowther, S. E. Hobfall, M. A. P. Stephens, & D. L. Tennenbaum (Eds.), *The etiology of bulimia nervosa: The individual and familial context* (pp. 133–155). Washington, DC: Hemisphere Publishers.

Heatherton, T. F., Polivy, J., & Herman, C. P. (1991). Restraint, weight loss, and variability of body weight. *Journal of Abnormal Psychology, 100*, 78–83.

Heatherton, T. F., & Weinberger, J. L. (Eds.). (1994). *Can personality change?* Washington, DC: American Psychological Association.

Helson, R., & Stewart, A. (1994). Personality change in adulthood. In T. F. Heatherton & J. L. Weinberger (Eds.), *Can personality change?* (pp. 201–226). Washington, DC: American Psychological Association.

Herzog, D. B., Sacks, N. R., Keller, M. B., Lavori, P. W., von Ranson, K. B., & Gray, H. M. (1993). Patterns and predictors of recovery in anorexia nervosa and bulimia nervosa. *Journal of the American Academy of Child and Adolescent Psychiatry, 32*, 835–842.

Johnson-Sabine, E., Reiss, D., & Dayson, D. (1992). Bulimia nervosa: A follow-up study. *Psychological Medicine, 22*, 951–959.

Klesges, R. C., Klem, M. L., Epkins, C. C., & Klesges, L. M. (1991). A longitudinal evaluation of dietary restraint and its relationship to changes in body weight. *Addictive Behaviors, 16*, 363–368.

Kuczmarski, R. J. (1992). Prevalence of overweight and weight gain in the United States. *American Journal of Clinical Nutrition, 55*, 495S–502S.

Kuczmarski, R. J., Flegal, K. M., Campbell, S. M., & Johnson, C. L. (1994). Increasing prevalence of overweight among U.S. adults: The national health and nutrition examination surveys, 1960 to 1991. *Journal of the American Medical Association, 272*, 205–211.

Leon, G. R., Fulkerson, J. A., Perry, C. L., & Cudeck, R. (1993). Personality and behavioral vulnerabilities associated with risk status for eating disorders in adolescent girls. *Journal of Abnormal Psychology, 102*, 438–444.

Leon, G. R., Fulkerson, J. A., Perry, C. L., & Early-Zald, M. B. (1995). Prospective analysis of personality and behavioral vulnerabilities and gender influences in the later development of disordered eating. *Journal of Abnormal Psychology, 104*, 140–149.

Levinson, D. J., Darrow, C. N., Klein, E. B., Levinson, M. H., & McKee, B. (1978). *The seasons of a man's life.* New York: Ballantine.

McCrae, R. R., & Costa, P. T., Jr. (1990). *Personality in adulthood.* New York: Guilford Press.

National Institutes of Health Technology Assessment Conference Panel. (1993). Methods for voluntary weight loss and control. *Annals of Internal Medicine, 199*, 764–770.

Norring, C. E., & Sohlberg, S. S. (1993). Outcome, recovery, relapse and mortality across six years in patients with clinical eating disorders. *Acta Psychiatrica Scandinavica, 87*, 437–444.

Polivy, J., & Herman, C. P. (1987). Diagnosis and treatment of normal eating. *Journal of Consulting and Clinical Psychology, 55*, 635–644.

Rosen, J. C., & Gross, J. (1987). Prevalence of weight reducing and weight gaining in adolescent girls and boys. *Health Psychology, 6*, 131–147.

Striegel-Moore, R. H., Silberstein, L. R., & Rodin, J. (1986). Toward an understanding of risk factors for bulimia. *American Psychologist, 41*, 246–263.

Thelen, M. H., Mann, L. M., Pruitt, J., & Smith, M. (1987). Bulimia: Prevalence and component factors in college women. *Journal of Psychosomatic Research, 31*, 73–78.

Vaillant, G. E. (1977). *Adaptation to life.* Boston: Little, Brown.

Williamson, D. F., Kahn, H. S., Remington, P. L., & Anda, R. F. (1990). The 10-year incidence of overweight and major weight gain in U.S. adults. *Archives of Internal Medicine, 150*, 665–672.

Zuckerman, D. M., Colby, A., Ware, N. C., & Lazerson, J. S. (1986). The prevalence of bulimia among college students. *American Journal of Public Health, 76*, 1135–1137.

 Article Review Form at end of book.

WiseGuide Wrap-Up

The area for greatest advancement in child/adolescent psychopathology is likely to be cultural diversity. The experience and expression of symptomology within the context of development are complicated.

Advances in understanding childhood and adolescence in general will occur from longitudinal cross-cultural studies of pathology.

R.E.A.L. Sites

This list provides a print preview of typical **Coursewise** R.E.A.L. sites. (There are over 100 such sites at the **Courselinks**™ site). The danger in printing URLs is that web sites can change overnight. As we went to press, these sites were functional using the URLs provided. If you come across one that isn't, please let us know via email to: webmasters@coursewise.com. Use your Passport to access the most current list of R.E.A.L. sites at the **Courselinks** site.

Site name: Psychology Self-Help Resources

URL: http://www.psychwww.com/resource/selfhelp.htm

Why is it R.E.A.L.? This site contains information about child and adolescent behavior disorders and other disorders.

Key topics: cultural factors and ADD, eating disorders, mood, sexual aggression

Site name: American Academy of Child & Adolescent Psychiatry

URL: http://www.aacap.org/

Why is it R.E.A.L.? Facts for families and other information on topics related to adolescence are covered at this site.

Key topics: cultural factors and ADD, eating disorders, mood, sexual aggression

section

7

Learning Objectives

- The student's knowledge on what therapy is, who seeks help, and who are service providers will be enhanced.

- The student will learn various types of treatment.

? Questions ?

Reading 21. Summarize the contributions from software/computers to psychotherapy.

Reading 22. Does therapy help? Whom does it help?

Treatment

In teaching abnormal psychology over the years, I have been frequently made aware of the student's interest in treatment. The curiosity extends to questions of what goes on in therapy, how does it transpire, and does it really work. Your textbook provides an overview of the results of treatment outcome studies specific to each disorder. The articles in this section represent some extensions of the general idea of what goes on in treatment.

The Bloom article gives a good general account of how practitioners use computers. The second table in the article is a segment of a script used in a cognitive behavioral intervention. The step-by-step presentation in this table will give you an idea of that treatment approach and how clients may respond. Besides computer-assisted psychotherapy, Bloom describes assessment and training using computers. Centers with a large volume of clients will probably be more acclimated to using computer approaches, although the rapid, accurate means of data collection makes it worthwhile in every setting.

The next article in this section received a lot of attention in popular and professional circles. Seligman conducted a study on therapy for *Consumer Reports*. Many responses were generated to his approach to interpreting the data. The result that therapy work and the types of therapists that were reported as effective are quite interesting.

The prospective practitioner will find this section to be very interesting. The enacted techniques and the way they are put into operation are discussed in the articles.

Summarize the contributions from software/computers to psychotherapy.

Computer-Assisted Psychological Intervention:

A Review and Commentary

Bernard L. Bloom

University of Colorado

Abstract

This paper reviews the 25-year history of computer-assisted psychological intervention, with particular emphasis on the current status of the computer in psychotherapy. The computer is playing an increasingly important role in personality and behavioral assessment, diagnostic interviewing and history taking, health education, mental health consultation, and clinical training. In these areas, the reliability, validity, and utility of the computer compares very favorably with that of the clinician. Evaluations of the use of the computer with psychiatric patients conclude that even those who are quite disturbed interact very successfully with computers, including many patients who are unable to interact with mental health personnel. Computer-assisted psychotherapy programs have been most successfully implemented in the areas of cognitive and behavioral psychotherapy. In the case of psychodynamic psychotherapy, computer programs appear to be limited by our failure to make fully explicit the rules governing therapist behavior and by the continuing inability of computers to comprehend natural language.

Twenty-five years ago, Weizenbaum (1966) and Colby, Watt, and Gilbert (1966) startled the therapeutic world with their descriptions of software programs that enabled people to discuss their personal problems with a computer. The participant could use natural language: that is, ordinary words, punctuation, and sentence structure. The conversations were typed at a teletype keyboard connected to a mainframe computer (these programs were written long before the development of microcomputers and video display terminals), and responses were printed at teletype speed one character at a time in hard copy on the same keyboard. According to Colby et al., these computer programs were designed to "communicate an intent to help, as a psychotherapist does, and to respond as he does by questioning, clarifying, focusing, rephrasing and occasionally interpreting" (1966, p. 149).

Both Weizenbaum and Colby acknowledged that their reports were preliminary, and both expressed concern about a number of aspects of their work. Colby et al. were concerned primarily with the effectiveness of such computer programs. They wrote, "If the method proves beneficial, then it would provide a therapeutic tool which can be made widely available to mental hospitals and psychiatric centers" (1966, p. 152).

In contrast, Weizenbaum was primarily concerned with ethical issues associated with the use of the computer as a psychotherapist. He expressed considerable doubt about what he called the illusion of understanding created by the computer program. Indeed, Weizenbaum himself (1967) provided an illustration of this illusion in the form of an anecdote that has become part of the oft-quoted early history of computer psychotherapy—

My secretary watched me work on this program over a long period of time. One day she asked to be permitted to talk with the system. Of course, she knew she was talking to a machine. Yet, after I watched her type a few sentences she turned to me and said "Would you mind leaving the room please?" (pp. 477–478)

Ultimately, Weizenbaum (1976) concluded that it would be immoral to substitute a computer for a human function that "involves interpersonal respect, understanding, and love" (1976, p. 269). Needless to say, Weizenbaum rejected Colby's proposal that computers be used for psychotherapeutic purposes, presumably even if it could be shown that such uses were genuinely helpful

(Colby, 1980; DeMuth, 1984; McGuire, Lorch, & Quarton, 1967; O'Dell & Dickson, 1984; Wagman, 1988, pp. 27–30).

The idea of using the computer as psychotherapist still precipitates a good deal of derision if not alarm on the part of mental health professionals, although, as we will see, the issues are more equivocal than one might initially think (see Cogswell, 1983; Colby, 1980; Colby, Gould, & Aronson, 1989; Erdman, Klein, & Greist, 1985; Greist, 1980; Lester, 1977; Plutchik & Karasu, 1991; Sampson & Pyle, 1983; Spero, 1978; Stodolsky, 1970; Trappl, 1981; Wagman, 1988).

In a way, it was unfortunate that the computer entered the psychological intervention domain as a potential psychotherapist, since of all the tasks that the computer can be asked to perform, the role of psychotherapist is surely the most difficult and most controversial. Far less complex and controversial roles, such as in personality and behavioral assessment, diagnostic interviewing, history taking, consumer health education, mental health consultation, clinical training, and specific forms of behavior modification are currently gaining considerable popularity and are making their way into the standard armamentarium of the mental health professional both in the United States and abroad (Elwork & Gutkin, 1985; Erdman, Greist, Klein, Jefferson, & Getto, 1981; Greist, Klein, & Erdman, 1978; Hedlund, 1978; Johnson, 1978; Johnson, Giannetti, & Williams, 1976; Klein, Greist, & Van Cura, 1975; Kratochwill, 1982; Kratochwill, Doll, & Dickson, 1985; McCullough, Farrell, & Longabaugh, 1986; McGuire, 1971; Monnickendam, 1990; Rokeach, 1975; Schwartz, 1984).

Four substantive domains have been identified as appropriate for the computer in supplementing the traditional psychotherapeutic relationship: (1) consumer health education, including orienting the patient to the psychotherapeutic relationship and to the process of psychotherapy; (2) psychological assessment: that is, providing a rationale for the process followed by the administration, scoring, and interpretation of appropriately selected test instruments; (3) development of a psychosocial history and expansion of psychological mindedness on the part of the patient through the creation of an increasingly precise statement of the presenting problem and by exploring alternative explanations of why the problem has arisen; and (4) providing specific interventions that are supplementary to the work of the therapist, by identifying and correcting cognitive distortions, or expanding the availability and variety of behavioral choices when there is evidence that patients are unduly limited in their approaches to dealing with complex interpersonal issues (Sampson, 1986).

Research studies and reviews report with remarkable regularity that resistance to computers in the mental health field comes primarily from clinicians, not from patients (Ben-Porath & Butcher, 1986; Erdman et al., 1981, 1985; Greist, 1980; Hedlund, 1978; Space, 1981; Wagman, 1983). Computer interviews with psychiatric patients appear to yield reliable and accurate results, and most patients find interacting with the computer highly acceptable: sometimes more acceptable than interacting with mental health professionals (Erdman et al., 1981; Lawrence, 1986; Plutchik & Karasu, 1991; Zarr, 1984). Even markedly disturbed psychiatric inpatients can interact successfully with computers (Burda, Starkey, & Dominguez, 1991; Matthews, De Santi, Callahan, Koblenz-Sulcov, & Werden, 1987), and it has been found that 85% or more of psychiatric patients can complete a computer interview at the time they are admitted into an inpatient facility.

Uses of Computers in Patient Assessment and Management

Before examining the field of computer psychotherapy in greater detail, it would be useful to provide a brief overview of other better-established uses of the computer in the general field of psychological intervention (Butcher, 1987; Farrell, 1989; Greist, Carroll, Erdman, & Klein, 1987; Hedlund & Vieweg, 1984; Hedlund et al., 1981; Sampson, 1983; Space, 1981).

Psychological Assessment

Psychological testing or assessment can be subdivided into two component parts—(1) test administration and scoring; and (2) test interpretation. The terms "testing" and "assessment" are used interchangeably in this paper, but Matarazzo (1990) makes the important distinction that testing involves "little or no continuing relationship or legally defined responsibility between the examinee and examiner," while assessment is "geared specifically to the benefit and needs of the particular patient" (p. 1000). Defining the nature of the ongoing responsibility between the examinee and the examiner is indeed an important professional consideration regardless of how psychological test instruments are administered or scored.

Virtually every major psychological assessment procedure, including those that measure academic aptitude, vocational and professional interest patterns, cognitive and psychophysiological functioning, and personality functioning (using both objective and some projective approaches) can be administered and scored by computer.

Under most circumstances, computer-based test administration and interpretation have a number of obvious advantages. Computer-based assessment is ordinarily faster and far less expensive than traditional methods. Since such procedures can be staffed by clerical personnel, the psychologist is freed up for more complex duties. Computer-based procedures allow patients to go at their own pace in taking tests. Errors in recording test responses are minimized, and the reliability of test administrations and test interpretations is increased. Some psychological tests are not only time consuming to score manually but may also be very difficult to score. Computer-based scoring minimizes such problems. Test responses can be stored and accumulated and can become an invaluable clinical resource. Optimal decision-making rules can be consistently employed in test interpretations (Jackson, 1985; Space, 1981).

Computer-administered test instruments must be comparable with traditionally administered tests, not only in terms of actual scores in individual cases, but also in terms of distribution of scores within groups of people. On the basis of the research that has been reported thus far (French & Beaumont, 1989; Honaker, 1988; Honaker, Hector, & Harrell, 1986; Jackson, 1985; Lukin, Dowd, Plake, & Kraft, 1985; Moreland, 1985b; Waller & Reise, 1989; Wilson, Genco, & Yager, 1985), meaningful differences in test scores do not relate on how the test is administered or scored.

Computer-based psychological assessment programs are very well developed, but while employing the computer for test administration and scoring seems well accepted (according to Schoenfeldt, 1989, most psychological tests administered in the United States are scored by computer), some doubt has been expressed about the validity of computerized test interpretation programs (see, for example, Burke & Normand, 1987; Groth-Marnat & Schumaker, 1989; Matarazzo, 1985, 1986; Moreland, 1985a, 1985b; Space, 1981; Zachary & Pope, 1984).

In spite of these doubts, however, computer software and commercial services for providing psychological test administration, scoring, and interpretations are rapidly increasing in availability and quality (Schoenfeldt, 1989). Even the most vocal critics of computer-generated test interpretations seem to agree that it is only a matter of time before computerized test interpretations will be demonstrably more valid than those generated by clinicians (Ben-Porath & Butcher, 1986; Butcher, Keller, & Bacon, 1985; Matarazzo, 1985; Moreland, 1985a).

Questions have been raised about the potential for overly aggressive marketing of test interpretation software programs in the absence of clearly established validity (Blois, 1980; Hofer & Green, 1985; Kiesler & Sproull, 1986; Lanyon, 1984; Matarazzo, 1986). Most evidence suggests, however, that there is relatively little basis for these concerns, and that computer-generated test report developers are providing empirical information about the relative validity of their computer-generated test reports as contrasted with those produced by clinicians (Fowler, 1985; Fowler & Butcher, 1986; Klepsch, 1990; Moreland & Onstad, 1987; Roid,

1985). The very high level of professional vigilance over test administration and interpretation software undoubtedly accounts for the fact that computerized assessment programs have received such high marks.

Computer programs that provide test interpretations are more complex than simple scoring programs, since they must accurately reflect the reasoning of clinicians who examine test results and make interpretations based upon test scores viewed singly and in combination with each other. Essentially, test interpretation programs are organized as a series of if-then statements. If the score on scale A is within a certain range, then print a specified statement. If the score on scale A is within a certain range, while the score on scale B is within another range, and the score on scale C is within another range, and so forth, then print another statement. If the scores on scales A and B are within certain ranges, print a specified statement, unless the score on scale C is within a certain range, in which case print a different specified statement.

The computer's ability to juggle if-then statements is unlimited. The task of the computer programmer is to emulate the clinician as accurately as possible. If the clinician can articulate the rules that are used in preparing a test interpretation, however complicated or subtle those rules are, the computer can be programmed to follow the same rules in the preparation of test reports. It should be cautioned, however, that any test interpretation, computerized or otherwise, that does not include appropriate consideration of clinical and case history material is entirely inadequate.

History Taking and Diagnostic Interviewing

Reports of computer use in history taking and diagnostic interviewing have appeared since the late 1960s, and while the clinical acceptance of computer interviewing has been slower than anticipated, it is growing, triggered mainly by the accumulating evidence that such interviews (even if they are quite long) have a very high level of patient acceptance and validity and often uncover important aspects of a patient's life that

are missed by the clinical interview (Angle, Ellinwood, & Carroll, 1987; Barron, Daniels, & O'Toole, 1987; Carr, Ghosh, & Ancill, 1983; Greist, Klein, & Van Cura, 1973; Jackson, 1985; Maultsby & Slack, 1971; McLean, Foote, & Wagner, 1975; Slack & Slack, 1972).

Several programs have been designed to take a psychiatric or medical history or provide a psychiatric diagnosis (Colby & Parkinson, 1985; Greist, Klein, Erdman, & Jefferson, 1983; Kleinmuntz & McLean, 1968; Lucas, Card, Knill-Jones, Watkinson, & Crean, 1976; Maultsby & Slack, 1971; Slack, Leviton, Bennett, Fleischman, & Lawrence, 1988; Slack & Van Cura, 1968; Spitzer & Endicott, 1969; Yokley & Reuter, 1989), generally with results quite comparable to the efforts of clinicians.

The computer has also been effectively used to collect routine intake interview data (Barron et al., 1987; Haug et al., 1987), to predict the risk of suicide (Greist, Gustafson, Stauss, Rowse, Laughren, & Chiles, 1973), and to assess social adjustment, symptom change, drug and alcohol abuse, sexual dysfunction, and lifestyle health risk factors (Greist & Klein, 1980; Stroebel & Glueck, 1970). In all of these efforts, patients have reported that the computer is a very acceptable modality for data collection, and analyses of results have shown that actuarial predictions and assessments are at least as valid as predictions and assessments made by clinicians. Put in a different way, computer diagnoses and predictions agree with clinical diagnoses and predictions at about the same level as clinicians agree with each other (Hedlund, Evenson, Sletten, & Cho, 1980).

What has made computer-based history taking feasible, and what distinguishes it from more traditional test administration, scoring, and interpretation, has been the potential of the computer program to branch, that is, to follow different pathways depending on answers to particular questions (Baccara, 1985; Greist & Klein, 1980; Weiss, 1985). While computer-based testing involves administration of a standard test or test battery, history taking is far more flexible, with the result that no patients may have the identical set of questions asked of them. For example, if the program asks patients if they are currently employed, subsequent questions are posed depending on how they answer that question. If the patient answers the employment question positively, follow-up questions may deal with the nature of that employment. If the patient answers the employment question negatively, follow-up questions may deal with the reasons for the unemployment. If patients are asked if they have any trouble sleeping and they answer negatively, the computer program can skip directly to the next major question. If a patient answers in the affirmative, the computer program can continue by exploring the nature of the sleep difficulties.

There is evidence that branching procedures have to be used prudently since specific problems may be missed if patients answer more general questions in the negative (Angle et al., 1978; Farrell, Camplair, & McCullough, 1987). But because computer-based interviews have such high acceptability, and because the computer can obtain and retain so much information, most researchers are quite optimistic about the potential of the computer for routine initial interviewing and clinical assessment of both medical and psychiatric patients.

Consumer Health Education
The computer is being used in two different aspects of health education that parallel the two branches of the field—education of the consumer (usually called consumer health education) and education of the health professional (usually referred to as continuing education, staff development, or in-service training). Most computer programs designed to help patients are sensitive to the fact that consumer health education is more than the provision of information. Rather, a useful consumer health education program must also aspire to affect health-related attitudes and to change health-related behavior (Bloom, 1988, chapter 4).

Computer-assisted educational programs have been used in relatively successful efforts to prevent alcohol and drug abuse (Moncher et al., 1989; Raines & Ellis, 1982), to increase responsible sexual behavior (Deardorff, 1986; Kann, 1987), to pre-

vent delinquent behavior (Cassel & Blum, 1969), to enhance self-esteem (Robertson, Ladewig, Strickland, & Boschung, 1987), to modify self-destructive lifestyles (Hawkins, Bosworth, Chewning, Day, & Gustafson, 1985), and to reduce disruptive classroom behavior (Tombari, Fitzpatrick, & Childress, 1985), as well as to supplement treatment programs for medical patients (Chambers, Balaban, Carlson, Ungemack, & Grasberger, 1989; Ellis, Raines, & Hakanson, 1982; Lilford & Chard, 1982; McDowell, Newell, & Rosser, 1989; Russell, 1983; Sheppard, Kirklin, & Kouchoukos, 1974; Siegel & Strom, 1974; Sittig, Pace, Gardner, Beck, & Morris, 1989). Gustafson, Bosworth, Chewning, and Hawkins (1987) believe that the full potential of computer-based health promotion has yet to be realized, primarily because the unique advantages of computers in assisting the learning process and in facilitating behavioral change have not been fully explored.

Training Clinical Practitioners
Two approaches to computer-based clinical training have been reported in the literature: (1) computer-based clinical consultation; and (2) simulation of the encounter between the health care provider and the patient, in which the computer is programmed to take the role of the patient. The computer as teacher/consultant plays a major role in primary medical care—perhaps an even more important role than in the education of mental health professionals (Lappe et al., 1990; Piemme, 1988).

Computer-Based Clinical Consultation
In situations in which there is a large knowledge base and precise rules for using that base in the formulation of a diagnosis, a classification, or a recommended course of action, the computer can be used to implement an expert system for aiding in decision making. Such expert, or knowledge-based, systems have been developed, for example, to assist in medical diagnosis and therapeutic planning, in determining the structure of complex organic molecules, in evaluating mineral sites, and in identifying children with reading problems and prescribing a remedial program for them (Barnett, 1984; Bleich, 1974; Golferini

& Facchin, 1987; Langlotz, Fagan, Tu, Sikic, & Sortliffe, 1987; Miller, Pople, & Myers, 1982; Potter & Ronan, 1990; Sicoly, 1989; Uplekar, Antia, & Dhumale, 1988; Wagman, 1988, pp. 71 ff.; Werner, 1987). When experts agree on the rules for converting facts into decisions or courses of action, such expert systems have been shown to have very acceptable validity.

When the recipients of such computer-assisted consultations are themselves not experts and when expert help is not otherwise available, there appears to be an unusually high readiness to use this consultation in decision making. A compelling example of such a consultation program in dealing with emotional crises has recently been presented by Hedlund, Vieweg, and Cho (1987). The setting for such computer-based consultation is a U.S. nuclear submarine, and the consultees are enlisted medical corpsman who ordinarily have first-line responsibility for any medical emergencies while at sea.

The computer-supported assessment and treatment consultation for emotional crises (CATCEC) is designed to help the medical corpsman evaluate and treat emotional and behavioral emergencies by helping to collect information and by making treatment suggestions. Final decisions regarding diagnosis and treatment remain in the hands of the medical corpsman.

In implementing the CATCEC system, the corpsman administers a structured paper and pencil interview schedule, enters the patient's responses into the computer along with the results of physical examinations, and any other collateral information, and receives in return a printed patient summary that includes a probable diagnosis and treatment suggestions. Additional information may be entered into the computer at any time. Supplementing the diagnosis and treatment program suggestions is a computer-assisted instructional program covering general emergency treatment principles and specific information about eight common emergency situations: the belligerent patient, the violent patient, the psychotic or delirious patient, the hyperactive or grandiose patient, the severely anxious patient, the severely depressed patient, the suicide attempt, and the unresponsive mute patient.

Hedlund and his colleagues validated the CATCEC against the opinions of seven experienced psychiatrists and clinical psychologists and found that 56% of the recommendations were judged to be "fully consistent with typical emergency practice" (p. 117), 28% were "reasonable and appropriate for the special submarine setting" (p. 117), and 14% required minor revisions such as different suggested doses of certain medications or wording changes to improve the clarity of instructions to the medical corpsman.

An example of a computer-based medical diagnostic system can be found in the work of Shortliffe (1976) and his colleagues, who have developed a computer program called MYCIN that provides diagnostic and treatment recommendations for patients with infectious diseases. The program requests clinical and laboratory data, attempts to determine whether a treatable infection is present, identifies the likely organism, and then recommends an appropriate antimicrobial regimen. In addition, alternate therapeutic recommendations can be requested, and the program can provide a teaching function by describing the reasoning processes it invoked in coming to its diagnostic and treatment conclusions.

In an examination of the MYCIN computer program, Yu, Buchanan, Shortliffe, Wraith, Davis, Scott, and Cohen (1979) selected 15 patients at the Stanford University Medical Center on the basis of evidence of some microbial agent present in blood samples, and evaluated them with the computer program and by ten physicians who were infectious disease experts. Three measures were developed: (1) the significance of the organism (whether treatment of any kind was necessary); (2) the identity of the infectious organism; and (3) selection of the most efficacious treatment.

The ten physicians agreed with the MYCIN conclusion regarding the necessity of treatment in 97% of the cases. The computer program and the physicians agreed that no treatment was indicated in 4 of the 15 patients. Identification of the organism provided by MYCIN was essentially identical to that provided by the physicians in 77% of the instances and the majority of physicians agreed with the MYCIN results in 91% of the cases. Finally, as to treatment selection, the physicians accepted the MYCIN recommendation in 8 out of the 11 cases requiring treatment. In one case the infectious disease experts were divided as to whether the treatment recommendation was appropriate, and in two cases the experts disagreed with the computer recommendation. Changes in the rules governing the MYCIN program were subsequently made in response to these two cases.

The MYCIN program's accuracy approaches that of infectious disease experts and probably surpasses the accuracy of nonexpert practicing physicians. Yu et al. (1979) suggested, however, that in spite of these findings, the program needs further improvement. For the program to gain more acceptability, its accuracy needs to be improved, its domain of competence needs to be expanded, the time required to use the program needs to be reduced, and it needs to be more easily understood by physicians (also see Alperovitch, Le Minor, & Lellouch, 1976; Rennels & Shortliffe, 1987; Shortliffe, 1987).

Simulating the Clinical Encounter

Friedman (1973) reported an informative example from the field of general medicine of a computer simulation that had an instructional objective. In this simulation, the objective was to enhance physicians' diagnostic accuracy and efficiency. After a brief initial training session, participants were provided with a medical background statement about a particular patient who represented a diagnostic problem, and were then invited to request any test that they felt might assist in formulating a diagnosis. Participants were to formulate the diagnosis as efficiently as possible and were told that their patients were extremely sick and could expire if the correct diagnosis were not made quickly enough. Penalties were assigned for incorrect diagnoses as a function of the judged severity of the misdiagnosis. Physicians were kept continually oriented to date and hour and to the cost of each diagnostic test procedure that was requested. Tests that were requested outside of normal laboratory working hours were more expensive if requested immediately than if the results could wait until the next day.

To evaluate this computer simulation, three medical cases of graded difficulty were prepared, and 25 physicians of varying degrees of experience, ranging from medical student to house staff to senior staff, in a number of different specialties were invited to evaluate the program by agreeing to complete at least one case. The high level of acceptance of the simulation can be judged by the fact that all but three of the physicians subsequently requested permission to complete all three cases.

As expected, the more difficult diagnostic problems took longer, were more expensive to resolve, and resulted in more fatalities prior to formulation of the correct diagnosis than were the easier diagnostic problems. Also, as expected, in comparison with house staff and senior staff, medical students required the longest amount of time to arrive at a diagnosis, and spent the most money on their work-ups. Surprisingly, however, house staff were the most efficient in formulating correct diagnoses, and, according to Friedman, may have been less hampered than senior staff because of their limited medical specialty training.

From the point of view of the usefulness of such computer simulation in the study of the cognitive processes that take place when physicians are faced with a diagnostic problem was the finding that after presentation of the medical history and request for a physical examination, no two work-ups followed the same pattern or included the same set of diagnostic tests. Thus, with such enormous variability in the behavior of physicians, it would be possible to examine how the establishment of a correct diagnosis related to characteristics of medical training or of the participating physicians (also see Bellman, Friend, & Kurland, 1966; Miller et al., 1982).

In a more recent development of computer simulation for use in the training of counselors, Lichtenberg, Hummel, and Shaffer (1984) have developed the first of what they hope will be a number of computer clients. CLIENT 1 is a reasonably verbal, motivated, and trusting 30-year old man who has a number of problems in the areas of work, family, emotions, and social relationships. The problems are not equally important to him, and one problem in particular is his primary concern. The student counselor's task is to engage the computer client with sufficient skill so that the problem of greatest importance will be revealed. Thus, CLIENT 1 is a computer model of an initial interview.

The program generates client statements and then allows the student counselor to respond to these statements on the basis of choices that can be made by selecting specific emotions, content, and persons from a large array of possibilities. Subsequent computer client statements depend on the statements of the student counselor. The grammar of the program is somewhat primitive, but quite intelligible. The following example of a CLIENT 1 interview (see Table 1) shows how the client's problem can be revealed by a skillful counselor.

Lichtenberg et al. (1984) believe that CLIENT 1 can be used both for counselor education and for research. The program lends itself to many forms of modification that can result in a variety of cases and challenges to the student. Because the rules governing the behavior of CLIENT 1 are completely explicit, it is possible to develop and test different counseling theories. The program allows the student to disaggregate the counseling process into a series of components. The program will tolerate counselor errors that most clients will not. Feedback in the form of client response is immediate. The process can be stopped at any time to allow for discussion. As for research, CLIENT 1 provides a standardized problem stimulus for counselors, and, as such, can yield important data about counselor behavior.

Computer Psychotherapy and Counseling

We have seen that the computer is being used as a tester, report writer, interviewer, diagnostician, educator,

Table 1 Example of Interview with CLIENT 1

Client: Work seems to be going OK for me most of the time, but sometimes I have trouble coping with it.

Counselor: You feel a sense of uncertainty about work situation.

Client: The trouble is that I am caught in the work situation and I do not know what to do.

Counselor: I am not sure, but I think you feel anxiety about work situation.

Client: I especially feel this way when I work around the secretaries.

Counselor: You feel tense with secretaries.

Client: When I am around the secretaries, I am uncertain of just how to act . . . what to do.

Counselor: You are telling me about a sense of uncertainty about behavior with secretaries.

Client: I guess it is not all the secretaries though . . . I feel most tense around my own secretary.

Counselor: I think it would be a good idea if you could tell me about anxiety about secretary.

Client: I really feel wound up when I have to work around my secretary. It is not that she is a bad secretary . . . in fact, in some ways she makes me feel kind of secure at work.

Counselor: I am not sure, but I think you feel affection for secretary.

Client: You know, it is strange but I want to be around her more and more of the time. It is when I get to feeling those things about my secretary that I get all wound up inside.

Reprinted from "CLIENT 1: A Computer Simulation for Use in Counselor Education and Research," by J. M. Lichtenberg, T. J. Hummel, and W. F. Shaffer. *Counselor Education and Supervision, 24,* 1984, page 61. © ACA. Reprinted with permission. No further reproduction authorized without written permission of the American Counseling Association.

trainer, and consultant. Furthermore, we have seen that evaluations of these various uses generally conclude that the procedures have satisfactory validity and reliability, and high acceptance among patients. With this brief review behind us, we can now return to the use of the computer in psychotherapy.

The potential pros and cons of computer psychotherapy have been well articulated in the existing literature:

The disadvantages involve lack of nonverbal communication, and the lack of direct contact with another human being, who can serve as a model or mentor. What seems to characterize all successful therapies is an intentional helping relationship. Can this relationship develop between patient and therapist through the communicative medium of a computer system? The advantages of a computer psychotherapist would be several. It does not get tired, angry, or bored. It is always willing to listen and to give evidence of having heard. It can work at any time of day or night, every day and every month. It does not have family problems. It does not try to perform when sick or hungover. It has no facial expressions of contempt,

shock, surprise, etc. It is polite, friendly, and always has good manners. It is comprehensible and has a perfect memory. It does not seek money. It will cost only a few dollars a session. It does not engage in sex with its patients. It does what it is supposed to do and no more. (Colby, 1979, pp. 155–156; also see Colby, Gould, & Aronson, 1989; Slack & Slack, 1977)

Cognitive and Behavioral Psychotherapy Computer Programs

While computerized therapy research spans the full spectrum of psychotherapeutic theory, it is "more attuned to brief, focused therapies of cognitive or behavioral inclination, those that claim to be independent of nonspecific aspects of therapy and that expect new relationships or behaviors to be experienced mainly outside the therapeutic setting" (Servan-Schreiber, 1986, p. 200). Wagman suggests that "in contrast to the psychoanalytic psychotherapist, the psychoeducational technologist has the role of an instructor in the procedures of systematic desensitization, an advisor in reconstruing and modifying maladaptive cognitive behavior and a guide in the acquisition and the application of effective methods of problem-solving" (1988, p. 18). Such approaches generally have a somewhat formalized and didactic quality, and include the use of computer games (Allen, 1984; Aradi, 1985; Clarke & Schoech, 1984; Colby, 1968, 1973), biofeedback, and computer-assisted instruction (Lawrence, 1986; Zarr, 1984).

To the extent that a patient's personal problems are related to skill or knowledge deficiencies, or to dysfunctional attitudes, the computer can be used to deal with the cognitive components of those deficiencies, allowing the therapist to confront the affective and motivational issues that prevent the patient from functioning optimally. Computer-based instructional programs can provide pertinent information and can improve the patient's abilities to plan, solve problems, and make decisions.

The Dilemma Counseling System

A good example of a computerized cognitive approach to psychotherapy can be found in the Dilemma Counseling System developed by Wagman (1984; see also Wagman, 1980, 1988; Wagman & Kerber, 1980). The dilemma is a central concept in most approaches to psychotherapy (Wagman, 1984, pp. 36–64), and, as the term is used by Wagman, describes a situation in which a person must choose between what are thought of as two undesirable alternatives. In Wagman's words, "If I make a decision for action p, then unhappy consequence r will occur; and if I make a decision for action q, then unhappy consequence s will occur. But, I must do either p or q, and so one of these unhappy consequences, r or s, must occur" (1980, p. 18).

Five steps are involved in resolving a dilemma: (1) formulating the problem as a psychological dilemma; (2) developing an extrication route for each component of the dilemma; (3) identifying a line of inquiry that will help negotiate the extrication route; (4) generating solutions for each line of inquiry; and

(5) ranking and evaluating the various proposed solutions. The Dilemma Counseling System presents an overview of the dilemma counseling method and procedure, gives practice in phrasing dilemmas and in generating solutions, and then provides an opportunity for patients to apply the method to problems of their own. The procedure requires about 2 hours to learn the dilemma counseling method and about 1 hour to apply the method to a self-selected psychological dilemma.

Wagman (1980) and Wagman and Kerber (1980) evaluated the procedure with a sample of college undergraduates who were randomly assigned to either the Dilemma Counseling System or to a control group after having identified several troublesome dilemmas they were facing. Members of the group who had been assigned to the dilemma counseling method reported significantly greater improvement than did members of the control group in coping with these dilemmas both 1 week and 1 month after the computerized procedure, and generally viewed the procedure very favorably. Students found interacting with the computer to be highly stimulating and interesting, and, contrary to some predictions, most students did not find that the procedure was too impersonal (also see Wagman, 1984, pp. 192–200; Wagman, 1988, pp. 110 ff.).

Therapeutic Learning Program

Colby et al. (1989) have recently described a method of short-term computer-assisted psychotherapy for stress-producing problems in interpersonal living that combines use of the computer with direct contact with a psychotherapist in a group setting. The method, called the Therapeutic Learning Program, requires 5 2-hour or 10 1-hour sessions that can be conducted weekly, or even daily. The patients meet in groups of 6 to 10 people and each patient has access to a personal computer during the sessions. After each step in the process is introduced and explained, each patient works with the computer and receives a printout that is discussed with the therapist while the other patients in the group listen. The method, according to Colby et al., represents a "type of in-

dividualized therapy in a group setting" (p. 105). The patients tend to think of themselves as a class taking part in a learning experience.

The steps in the therapeutic learning program are as follows: 1. Identify the demand inherent in the patient's interpersonal problem situation that is not being addressed effectively. . . . 2. Identify new proactive behavior (action steps) that might effectively address the dissatisfied state. . . . . . 3. Clarify the suitability of the new proactive behavior and identify the inhibited function that results from the patient's prediction of feared adverse consequences. 4. Identify the incorrect beliefs (thinking errors) that link catastrophic predictions to an action intention. 5. Help the patient to understand the historical origin of thinking errors in childhood adaptations and to sort out present realities from past realities. . . . . 6. Help the patient understand that childhood thinking is no longer appropriate for adult decision making in interpersonal problem situations. 7. When the predicted adverse consequences are accepted as incorrect, the patient's fears of transgressing rigid command rules diminish and the patient is more likely to carry out the required proactive behavior. 8. The recovery of an inhibited function becomes a part of the patient's positive self-concept as a functioning adult. (Colby et al., 1989, p. 105)

After initial encouraging results with a small group of six patients using the Therapeutic Learning Program, a more extensive evaluation was undertaken with a sample of 278 patients who were part of a health management organization. The results were very positive. A drop in distress was reported by 78% of the participants. Over 95% reported improvement in their ability to handle the problem situation that brought them to the therapy, and 78% reported a high level of satisfaction with the procedure.

Behavior Modification Programs

A number of recent publications have described computer psychotherapy programs that focus on behavior changes. Among such programs are those that treat depression (Selmi, Klein, Greist, Johnson, & Harris, 1982; Selmi, Klein, Greist, Sorrell, & Erdman, 1990) test anxiety (Biglan, Villwock, & Wick, 1979), obesity (Burnett, Taylor, & Agras, 1985; Porter, 1978; Slack, 1978; Slack et al.,

1976; Witschi et al., 1976), excessive smoking (Schneider, 1986; Schneider, Walker, & O'Donnell, 1990), failure to adhere to medication regimens (Sorrell, Greist, Klein, Johnson, & Harris, 1982), sexual dysfunction (Binik, Servan-Schreiber, Freiwald, & Hall, 1988; Binik, Westbury, & Servan-Schreiber, 1989; Servan-Schreiber & Binik, 1989), and phobias (Chandler, Burck, & Sampson, 1986; Chandler, Burck, Sampson, & Wray, 1988; Ghosh, Marks, & Carr, 1984). The studies that have been reported in the literature generally provide good descriptions of the computer programs and should be examined not only because of their specific properties but also because they illustrate a very wide variety of computer-based psychotherapy programs that can be developed to meet specific objectives.

Schneider (1986) has described a 5-week long computer-assisted smoking-cessation program that is designed to help clients who do not choose to attend face-to-face meetings. This program was initially accessed through a small electronic bulletin board system available to any computer owner in a section of New Jersey. Bulletin boards of this kind are becoming increasingly popular across the country and are easily contacted by computer owners with the use of a telephone modem. Participants can communicate with each other in writing through the bulletin board as if it were a large party line, and they also can take advantage of any computer programs that are made available.

Smokers were recruited by a notice posted on the bulletin board and a total of 28 volunteered. When a participant typed the single word "smoker," a menu of six choices was made available: (1) stop-smoking conference; (2) enter diary reports; (3) stop-smoking instructions; (4) overcome strong urge now; (5) get earlier instruction; and (6) overall progress report. The first choice provided an opportunity for smoking cessation program participants to describe their reactions to the program and to make comments to each other and share their observations and experiences. Daily cigarette consumption was entered using the second menu choice.

The third choice provided daily messages through the 5-week program. The first message each week posed a number of questions, and the rest of the messages for that week were tailored to the program participant's response to the questions. Smokers were taught to recognize when feelings and activities associated with smoking took place and how to prepare for these moments by preparing substitute behaviors and thoughts that were antagonistic to smoking. The fourth menu choice provided a number of suggestions for overcoming a strong urge to smoke. The fifth menu choice allowed participants to re-read earlier instructions, and the final choice provided a group progress report. The program was available 24 hours a day.

Three months after the program had been concluded an effort was made to contact all participants. Subjects who could not be reached were assumed to be smoking. Of the 28 participants, 10 had quit smoking at the end of the program and, of these 10, 7 had not relapsed at the 3-month follow-up contact. This success rate compares very favorably with a number of face-to-face smoking cessation programs that are far more expensive and labor intensive. Schneider subsequently inaugurated a far larger trial of this computer-assisted program based in a nationwide electronic bulletin board service with more than 300,000 members. A subsequent controlled evaluation (Schneider, Walker, & O'Donnell, 1990) provided additional confirmation or the effectiveness of the smoking cessation program, particularly when the full program was made available.

Selmi et al. (1982) developed a short-term computer-based cognitive therapy program for depression based on the work of Beck (1976; see also Beck, Rush, Shaw, & Emery, 1979). Three principles govern the cognitive therapy approach: (1) moods are created by thoughts; (2) depressive thoughts are negative; and (3) negative thoughts are distorted. The basic goal of cognitive therapy for depressives is to modify dysfunctional thoughts by using behavioral and cognitive therapeutic techniques. The computer-assisted

treatment program that Selmi et al. developed requires six to eight 40- to 50-minute sessions over a 6-week period.

The computer program uses case vignettes, multiple-choice items, and generalized approaches to identifying and dealing with dysfunctional thoughts. The Beck Depression Inventory (Beck, Ward, Mendelson, Mock, & Erbaugh, 1961) is administered as part of each session. Session 1 is used to build rapport and to introduce the cognitive theory of emotion. Multiple-choice questions are provided to assess the patient's understanding of the material, and feedback is given for each answer. Homework is assigned depending on the individual needs of each patient. Session 2 reviews and clarifies the material presented at the first session and initiates agenda setting with the patient. In Session 3 homework assignments are reviewed, dysfunctional automatic thoughts that can produce depression are discussed with the use of case examples, and the patient is asked, as a homework assignment, to identify specific situations that precipitate feelings of depression. The remaining sessions emphasize identifying automatic thoughts, defining cognitive distortions, and teaching the patient how to respond more appropriately to automatic thoughts. At the final session the patient is prepared for termination and given suggestions for dealing with future depressions. An example taken from Selmi et al. (1982) of a small section of the second session is shown in Table 2.

To evaluate this computer-assisted cognitive-behavioral treatment program, Selmi et al. (1990) contrasted the outcome of this six-session treatment program in three groups of volunteer patients (36 cases in all) who met criteria for current major or minor depression. Patients were randomly assigned to either (1) the computer-assisted cognitive-behavioral treatment program; (2) the same program conducted by a therapist; or (3) a waiting list control condition. At the end of treatment, and 2 months later, both treatment groups improved significantly more than controls on a number of standard measures of depression and dysfunctional cognitions. The two treatment

Table 2 Excerpt of Selmi et al. (1982) Cognitive Therapy Program for Depression

Computer: Last week, we talked about the principles of Cognitive Therapy. If you recall, Principle 1 stated that feelings are caused by cognitions or thoughts. Today, I want us to examine this principle in greater detail. How does this sound to you?

1. Sounds fine. Let's continue.

2. I would like a brief review of the major points you made last week, before continuing.

Patient: 1

Computer: Good. Let's try a few examples. If a person were to think to him or herself "I am inferior," what is likely to occur?

1. The person would compare himself to others and find faults in himself and feel bad.

2. Probably would feel real low about himself.

3. He would get angry.

[Choose the best answer(s)]

Patient: 1, 2

Computer: You're right, John. By saying to himself, "I'm inferior," he would compare himself to others, be very critical of himself, and probably get depressed. Let's try another. Suppose a boss gets upset and starts yelling at an employee. The employee thinks: "I know it. I can't do anything right!" How will the employee feel?

1. Anxious

2. Depressed/low

3. Angry

Patient: 2

Computer: Good Work! Now, suppose a boss starts yelling at the employee and the employee thinks: "That guy has got the nerve! I won't stand for this!" How will the employee feel?

1. Anxious

2. Depressed/low

3. Angry

Patient: 2

Computer: No, he wouldn't feel depressed, John. He would be angry, because the employer has put him down and the employee won't stand for that. Perhaps the employee has thought that the "put down" was unjustified. Can you see from this example that different thoughts about the same situation can produce different feelings?

From "An Investigation of Computer-Assisted Cognitive-Behavior Therapy in the Treatment of Depression," by P. M. Selmi, M. H. Klein, J. H. Greist, J. H. Johnson, and W. G. Harris, *Behavior Research Methods & Instrumentation, 14,* p. 184. Copyright © 1982. Reprinted by permission of Psychonomic Society, Inc.

groups did not differ from each other either at the end of treatment or at the follow-up 2 months later. Thus, the two treatment programs appeared to be equally effective and long-lasting. The authors believe that their results support the position that computer-assisted psychotherapy can provide effective, efficient, and economical treatment.

Biglan et al. (1979) described a short-term relaxation training and systematic desensitization program for the treatment of test anxiety with a sample of nine college students who obtained scores in the 75th percentile or higher on a standard measure of test anxiety. The program comprised audiotaped relaxation training plus computer-controlled desensitization. In the computer-controlled program, a standard hierarchy of 20 items related to test anxiety was presented one at a time on a video display terminal, and the students were instructed to imagine the item while relaxing for a predetermined time period. If during that time period students felt any discomfort, they pressed a key marked "Discomfort." The computer then presented the instruction "RELAX" and waited 30 seconds before presenting the next item in the hierarchy. If no discomfort was reported, the period of imagination lasted 30 seconds, after which the student pressed a key to indicate whether they were comfortable or uncomfortable at the end of the 30-second exposure period. If they indicated that they felt comfortable, the instruction "GOOD, RELAX" was presented, and an additional 30 seconds of relaxation time was made available. If they indicated that they felt uncomfortable at the end of the original exposure period, the instruction "RELAX" was presented followed by an additional 30-second relaxation period. On average, there were four desensitization sessions lasting about 30 minutes each.

Scores on the test anxiety scale demonstrated a highly significant drop from pre-treatment to post-treatment. In addition, students reported increased comfort in a number of different aspects of the academic examination process. Completion of the entire relaxation and desensitization program required less than 2 hours and was directed by specially trained undergraduate assistants. Thus, very little therapist time was required once the program was written and the assistants trained.

Chandler, Burck, Sampson, and Wray (1988; Chandler, Burck, & Sampson, 1986) have recently described a computer-based program that is designed to help in the systematic desensitization of any phobia that is not based solely on misinformation. The program can be personalized by participants who can create their own individualized phobic hierarchy that is then presented to them upon demand. The therapeutic package consists of a computer program, an audio tape for relaxation training, and printed information summaries.

After determining that the computer-assisted treatment approach is suitable for the patient, the program first provides a learning theory perspective for understanding and solving the phobic condition and instruction in the use of the relaxation procedure. The patient is instructed to use the relaxation procedure for a minimum of five training sessions. Then the patient is instructed in how to create his or her unique phobic hierarchy—a list of situations that are arranged in gradually increasing order of severity in terms of their ability to create a phobic response in the patient. The situations in this list are subsequently presented to the patient with instructions to think about them without becoming anxious.

The situations are interspersed with neutral situations that do not produce phobic reactions, and gradually the patient learns to imagine the anxiety-provoking situations without becoming anxious. After mastering the entire hierarchy, the patient is instructed to deal with these same hierarchical situations in real life.

All five participants in an early test of the computer-assisted therapy program improved dramatically. These results are particularly remarkable because only one patient had any prior experience using a computer. One patient, for example, who could not go to a grocery store by herself and was unable to drive comfortably in heavy traffic, was able to go shopping by herself and drive comfortably at the conclusion of the treatment program. Another patient, who was phobic for medical or dental care and who fainted at the sight of blood, was able to get a complete physical examination, including immunizations, was able to go to the dentist, and gave blood after completing the treatment program. In addition, several patients reported that they liked the sense of control that they felt over the therapeutic process and that they noted improvement in other areas of their lives.

A controlled study of the effectiveness of another computer program in the treatment of phobics was reported by Ghosh et al. (1984). These researchers contrasted book instruction, computer instruction, and clinician instruction in a sample of 71 phobic patients who were randomly assigned to the three treatment conditions. Patients who were treated by book instruction were given a self-help book that explained how patients can help themselves by devising a program of graded exposure to their feared situations, setting up their own homework tasks, and enlisting relatives and friends as cotherapists. Computer-instructed and clinician-instructed patients received the same general instructions as the book-instructed patients, except that the instruction was provided either by a computer or by a clinician. Patients in these two groups were treated individually and received between 3 and 10 treatment sessions that averaged 40–60 minutes in duration. The patients were evaluated at the conclusion of the treatment and at 1, 3, and 6-months post-treatment using a variety of objective questionnaires. In all three groups, improvement was dramatic during the course of the treatment and was maintained throughout the 6 months of follow-up. No differences in treatment effectiveness were found among the three treatment groups. Thus, as in the case of the Chandler et al. study, the desensitization program did not appear to require interpersonal interaction with a therapist in order to be successful.

Another domain in which successful computer-based behavior modification has been employed is in the field of dietary counseling. One example is in the work of Slack and his colleagues (Porter, 1978; Slack, 1978; Slack et al., 1976; Witschi et al., 1976), who have developed a dietary counseling program designed to increase people's awareness of their own eating habits and to change those habits, specifically in an effort to reduce caloric intake.

The counseling system is totally computerized and is divided into three sections: (1) a dietary history; (2) analysis of typical daily food intake; and (3) a diet and menu planner. The dietary history includes questions about eating behavior, weight patterns, and problems related to the control of weight. A written summary of the information obtained in this section is made available to the patient, physician, and nutritionist. The second section provides the opportunity for the patient to list the type and amount of all foods eaten at meals and snacks during a typical day. The computer program calculates the caloric content of the reported food intake and the printed report provides caloric information for each meal and snack of the day as well as for the total day. The final section of the computer program allows the patient to plan meal by meal menus for one or more days within a range of 1200 to 1700 calories.

After an initial evaluation of the program by 25 volunteers who were not themselves overweight, the program was revised and then made available to 64 randomly selected overweight patients who also met with one of two nutritionists. Order of the procedures was balanced, so that in half of the cases the meeting with the nutritionist preceded participation in the computer-based program while in the other half the meeting with the nutritionist took place after completion of the computer-based dietary counseling program.

From the nutritionists' point of view, prior completion of the computer program provided useful summary information, saved time, and increased the impact of the nutritional consultation that was provided to the patients. From the patients' point of view, the computer program was particularly valued because it helped them gain increased understanding about the nature of their own caloric intake. Concern that had been expressed about the depersonalizing influence of the computer was unfounded; most participants found the experience with the computer to be pleasant as well as informative. Initial follow-up interviews conducted 3 months after completion of the nutritional consultations indicated that most patients had lost weight and that the patients continued to express favorable opinions about their participation in the experiment.

Another example of a dietary counseling program can be found in the work of Burnett, Taylor, and Agras (1985), who developed a particularly innovative computer-based procedure designed to help reduce obesity that made use of a light-weight portable computer. The computer was used to provide immediate feedback on goal attainment, response-contingent positive reinforcement, and instructions to increase the effects of monitoring weight-related behavior.

Six pairs of women between the ages of 30 and 50, weighing at least 35% over their optimal weight, were randomly assigned to the computer-assisted therapy program and to a control treatment condition. Women in the computer-assisted condition prepared self-reports about food consumption during and between meals and about their exercise patterns. In reporting food consumption into the computer, study participants were trained to enter food and portion codes. For physical activity reports, study subjects entered exertion levels and duration. Upon entering this information, the computer provided feedback regarding total and cumulative daily meal or snack calories, percentage of daily caloric intake limit already consumed, remaining caloric intake limit for the day, as well as similar information about physical activity self-reports. In addition, the computer provided contingent praise and additional instructions as needed. Women in the control group participated in the same treatment program without computer assistance.

Dramatic differences in weight loss were found when the experimental and control groups were contrasted. At the end of the 8-week treatment program, average weight loss in the experimental group was 8.1 pounds and in the control group 3.3 pounds. Eight months later, average weight loss in the experimental group was 17.7 pounds and only 2.3 pounds in the control group. While members of the control group were unable to lose any additional weight after the end of the treatment program, the experimental group members whose treatment was computer-assisted continued to lose weight in almost linear fashion, with rate of continued weight reduction slowing down only after more than 20 weeks of observation.

Binik, Servan-Schreiber, and their colleagues (Binik et al., 1988; Binik et al., 1989; Servan-Schreiber & Binik, 1989) have developed a computer-based tutoring system for the assessment and treatment of sexual dysfunction. Sexual dysfunction lends itself to a cognitive treatment program because: (1) it is frequently viewed as a cognitive-behavioral program; (2) there is an already well-developed set of therapeutic interventions; and (3) there is a tradition of self-help in the area of sex therapy.

The tutoring program is designed to deal with couples, although it can deal with an individual. During the 1-hour initial session, the program attempts to identify sexual dysfunctions and place them in their interpersonal and historical context. Possible causes and perpetuating factors are investigated, and the effects of the sexual dysfunction on the dyadic relationship are investigated and discussed with the couple. At the end of the initial session, the program may recommend an individualized treatment program (based on well-established cognitive-behavioral interventions) that the couple may elect to accept or reject.

The individualized treatment program takes into account the information that has been provided at the initial session, including information about the couple's overall relationship and patterns of sexual behavior. If the couple proceeds with the treatment program, the computer will monitor treatment progress and will try to discover why the couple is unable to complete or succeed in some specific exercise, if such failures are reported.

Empirical evaluation of the tutoring program has thus far been very favorable. In the initial study, individuals interacted with the program for about 20 minutes. Two comparison groups were created: in one group individuals interacted with a computer program unrelated to sexual dysfunction; in the other, individuals completed a paper and pencil sex-related questionnaire that was patterned after the computer program. Significantly positive attitude shifts toward computerized sex therapy were found in the experimental group, but not in either control group. Members of the experimental group also commented on how human the computer program seemed to them.

Most interesting to the investigators were the results of their examination of two couples who permitted their interactions with the computer program to be videotaped.

Many aspects of the computer session seemed similar to the interactions normally seen between a couple and a sex therapist. The couples were clearly engaged in the process, seriously discussed their sex life and their relationship with each other as well as their reactions to the comments and suggestions made by the computer. In addition, the couples reported that they discussed sexual issues with each other after the computer session that they had not previously talked about, and that as a consequence they experienced increased intimacy, openness, and comfort with their sexual feelings.

Dynamic Psychotherapy Computer Programs

In examining the limited progress that has been made in the past quarter century in the development of psychodynamic psychotherapy computer programs, two facts compel our immediate attention. First, no computer can yet understand natural language. Indeed, a major aspect of the newly emerging field of artificial intelligence is in the development of computer programs that have language-comprehension capabilities (Wagman, 1988, pp. 39 ff.). The failure to understand natural language is not for want of trying (see, for example, Barnett, Knight, Mani, & Rich, 1990; Barr & Feigenbaum, 1981, Chapter 4; Colby & Enea, 1967; Helm, 1968; Lawrence, 1986; Parkison, Colby, & Faught, 1977; Rich, 1983, Chapter 9; Schank & Abelson, 1977; Servan-Schreiber, 1986; Stone, Dunphy, Smith, & Ogilvie, 1966; Winston, 1984, Chapter 9; Zarr, 1984). While understanding natural language may seem simple enough to a normal adult, and even to a 6-year-old child, the contextual rules governing that understanding have proven far too complex to put into a computer program, at least for computers that currently exist.

Consider, for example, these four short sentences: (1) I am taking out Sally; (2) I am taking out the trash; (3) I am taking out that defenseman; and (4) I am taking out a loan. The phrase "taking out" has four very different meanings, yet the average adult has no difficulty making the necessary distinctions that are required to understand the sentences. Within each sentence are other words to provide a sufficient context for understanding the complex verb "take out." But teaching a computer to make these same distinctions is a task of extraordinary complexity (Nelson, 1982).

Or consider the many possible meanings of the simple sentence "Mary had a little lamb." It could conceivably mean any of the following: (1) Mary once owned a little lamb; (2) Mary gave birth to a little lamb; (3) Mary ate a small amount of lamb; or even (4) Mary engaged in sexual intercourse with a little lamb. Which of these interpretations is correct depends on the larger context within which the sentence is embedded. Most natural language is context-bound, a fact that makes computer programming of natural language far more difficult than one would initially think. It is this difficulty that leads to such hilarity in the back-translation literature, as in the sentence "The spirit is willing, but the flesh is weak" that is back-translated as "The wine is good, but the meat is spoiled."

Even when words themselves have unequivocal meaning, true understanding may elude the computer programmer. " 'The coffee is hot' may be an observation, a hint, a request, an explanation, an excuse, a warning—or hallucinated" (Cavell, 1988, p. 131). There is no question that human beings have the capacity not only to understand but to be moved by words and phrases that they have never previously heard in the way just presented. Indeed, when the wonderfully subtle complexities of natural language are contemplated—literary writing, poetry, idioms, dialect, humor, double entendres—it is easy to conclude that computers may never be able to understand natural language.

Weizenbaum (1967) dealt with this issue of understanding in the following way:

When a person enters a conversation he brings his belief structures with him as a kind of agenda. . . . Since, in the last analysis, each of our lives is unique, there is a limit to what we can bring another person to understand. There is an ultimate privacy about each of us that absolutely precludes full communication of any of our ideas to the universe outside

ourselves and which thus isolates each one of us from each other . . . object in the world. There can be no total understanding and no absolutely reliable test of understanding. . . . This issue must be confronted if there is to be any agreement as to what machine "understanding" might mean. What the above argument is intended to make clear is that it is too much to insist that a machine understands a sentence (or a symphony or a poem) only if that sentence invokes the same imagery in the machine as was present in the speaker of the sentence at the time he uttered it. For by that criterion no human understands any other human. Yet we agree that humans do understand one another to *within acceptable tolerances.* . . . When, therefore, we speak of a machine understanding, we must mean understanding as limited by some objective. (p. 476)

The second fact, that serves as a potential antidote for the first, is that writing *any* computer program requires no more than understanding the rules governing the process to be programmed. With regard to creating computer psychotherapy, Colby (1979) puts this principle as follows:

These decision-making rules will be complex and will reflect the human therapist's view of what should take place in therapy. Of the many schools of therapy which currently exist, cognitive therapy seems the best candidate for programming because it tries to be explicit about what is said and done. But any therapeutic system that can be formulated in terms of rules could be implemented on a computer system. (p. 154)

Earlier, Bellman et al. (1966) described the process of psychotherapy in similar language:

There are various types of interviewing policies. One policy would be for the psychiatrist to say and do almost nothing in the course of the interview. Other policies that he might follow are: to ask set questions independent of the responses of the patient; to repeat the last sentence or phrase to the patient; to limit his verbalizations to encouraging but nonspecific phrases such as "uh-huh" or "I see." More complex policies involving the actual information pattern are: repetition of key words of the patient, repetition of words descriptive of the patient's affective state, or a varying mixture of these policies. . . . Indeed, one of the purposes of developing simulation processes is to provide a tool for the identification and testing of different types of policies. (p. 390)

Another example of the same general point of view is provided by Cogswell (1983):

What I foresaw was the possibility of developing understanding through the process of simulating the counselor with the computer. I reasoned that the process of observing and analyzing the counselor in the detail required for computer simulation would demand a precision in detail heretofore not tried. Consequently, we would be forced to explicate the counseling operations in a way that allow precise formulation of the rules as well as an excellent means for replication. The successive iterations in computer programs required to approximate the human counselor would provide us with increasing statements of accuracy as to what the counseling process is. (pp. 61–62)

If useful computer psychotherapy is to be developed, at least for the present, the task of programming the computer must proceed in a different way. The importance of these views of the psychotherapeutic process is that many of the rules of therapy, once articulated, are programmable, and do not require the computer to understand natural language. If the rules governing a therapist's behavior can be made explicit (see, for example, Carkhuff, Pierce, & Cannon, 1980; Danish, D'Augelli, & Hauer, 1980; Evans, Hearn, Uhlemann, & Ivey, 1989; Hilf, 1972; Martin, 1983; Okun, 1982), it should be possible to program a computer to follow those rules (see also Karasu, 1977; Servan-Schreiber, 1986).

General Programming Strategies

The original procedure for writing a computer psychotherapy program was described by Weizenbaum as follows:

The text [written by the patient] is read and inspected for the presence of a key word. If such a word is found, the sentence is transformed according to a rule associated with the key word; if not, a content-free remark or, under certain conditions, an earlier transformation is retrieved. A rule-cycling mechanism delays repetition of responses to identical keys as long as possible. The text so computed or retrieved is then printed out. (1967, p. 475)

This approach, in increasingly sophisticated form (Colby, 1975, Chapter 4; DeMuth, 1984), has been used for the development of computer programs for the past two decades. An alternative strategy employed by Balis Computing (1984) in their program called PSYCHE groups key words into specific subject areas and prints responses depending on the key word and subject area. This program is unusually flexible and allows the operator to add or delete subject areas, to add or delete key words for each subject area, to assign differential weights to key words (so that if more than one key word appears in the same statement, the one with the higher weight will be selected), and, finally, to modify responses for any key word or subject area. In addition to the ability to add, delete, or modify responses, the program permits use of responses that include the key word itself or the entire previous text entered by the patient. For example, if the patient writes, "I have been feeling very sad lately," the computer can respond, "How do you mean 'sad'?" Or, alternatively, the computer can respond, "What are your feelings in saying that you have been feeling very sad lately?"

In addition to specific responses that are triggered by key words, responses are created for text that does not include any key words, as well as for text that ends with a question mark or an exclamation point. A program like PSYCHE has the special advantage of being written to meet a therapeutic theory or strategy or set of conceptualized therapeutic rules.

For example, the PSYCHE program has been modified by the author so that the computer therapist consistently explores the meaning and significance of what the patient has just written—using such questions as "How do you mean?", "How would you describe your feelings?", "Could you express that a little differently?", "Could you give me an example?", or "How is the situation you mention a problem?" Alternatively, responses can be prepared to emulate a supportive and empathic therapist, or a therapist who attends only to feelings.

Below is an example of a portion of a PSYCHE interview in which the computer program is designed to

Table 3   Excerpt of PSYCHE Computer Program

Patient: I am feeling very sad.

Computer: How do you mean, "sad"?

Patient: I cry almost every day, and I am having trouble sleeping.

Computer: Perhaps it would help if you told me more about the trouble.

Patient: It has been going on for months, and I cry mostly at night when I am getting ready for bed.

Computer: How are these feelings related to your problems?

Patient: I have been sad ever since I retired from the university.

Computer: What do you mean when you say that you have been sad ever since you retired from the university?

Patient: I mean that I thought I wouldn't miss teaching, but now I feel that I think all the time about my students and my years of teaching.

Computer: Could you tell me more about what you mean by "you mean that you thought you would not miss teaching but now you find that you think all the time about your students and your years of teaching"?

Patient: Well, I have been teaching for nearly 25 years and I was enjoying it less and less. I also was not enjoying most other aspects of university life.

Computer: How do you mean?

Patient: I didn't enjoy the conflict among my colleagues, the competition for limited funds, and the fact that I never could get all things I need to do done.

Computer: "Never"? Do you really mean, "never"?

Patient: I mean that I was always behind in my work, and I felt that if I retired, I could limit myself to just doing a few things and I would be able to do them well.

Computer: How would you describe your feelings?

Patient: At the time I retired, I felt hopeful, but lately, as I said, I have begun to feel that I made a mistake by retiring.

Computer: What sort of mood are you experiencing at the moment?

Patient: At the moment I am very sad, and I am beginning to feel worried about that.

Computer: Could you say a little more about that?

Patient: I am worried because I may have made a mistake that I cannot reverse.

Computer: What are you feeling when you say "worried?"

Patient: I am frightened and uneasy about my own judgment.

Computer: Could you give me an example?

Patient: Well, I wonder if I made a mistake because I am getting older and my judgment is not as good as it used to be.

recreate the therapist who functions solely as an explorer. In this example, the patient makes a connection between his depression and his aging (see Table 3).

Computer-assisted psychotherapy programs that encourage the patient toward continuing exploration of particular behaviors or attitudes may be effective on the basis of the manifest characteristics of their comments, even in the absence of underlying hypotheses. Indeed,

computer-assisted psychotherapy programs cannot yet develop a model of the patient. But if the computer therapist asks patients to think more deeply about themselves, such requests may have significant therapeutic potential particularly because they provide an opportunity for patients that is rarely present in normal social interactions. Consistent exploration can lead to discoveries about oneself that can clarify and demystify. Freud's early theories of psychotherapy make this point very clearly. Describing his view of the difference between the conscious and the unconscious, Freud noted that everything conscious is subject to a process of wearing away, while what is unconscious is relatively unchangeable. Pointing out to a patient the antiques standing about in his office, Freud (1909/1953) reconstructed his comments as follows: "They were, in fact, I said, only objects found in a tomb, and their burial had been their preservation: the destruction of Pompeii was only beginning now that it had been dug up" (p. 313; also see Malcolm, 1987).

Another alternative that can be used in writing a computer-assisted psychotherapy program is to use a language such as CONVERSE (Bloom, White, Beckley, & Slack, 1978) or PC/PILOT (Washington Computer Services, 1989) that allows the programmer to create branchable pages of text that can be used in situations where the psychotherapy lends itself to a cognitive or instructional approach. A number of examples of such programs have already been provided in this review.

Concluding Comments

The computer is making an impact in virtually every aspect of psychological intervention, and that impact will continue to expand as additional progress is made in conceptualizing the work of the clinician and in converting those conceptualizations into rigorous rules. This review has provided a sense of the current vigor of clinical and research activity in the field of computer-assisted psychological intervention.

It seems only a matter of time before virtually all psychological assessment procedures will be administered, scored, and interpreted by computer. Rational test interpretation, even including interpretations that attend to the external life history or life circumstances of the patient, can and should be converted to computerized format. It is already clearly feasible to take a psychiatric or medical history, to identify and assess the severity of physical or psychiatric symptoms, and to conduct diagnostic interviews by computer. These successes are particularly remarkable in

view of the tolerance of a very wide variety of psychiatric and medical patients for computer-based assessment. The computer has been underused in the role of teacher (either of patients or of mental health professionals), and we can expect considerably more activity in that domain in the near future.

In the case of computer-assisted psychotherapy, the future is somewhat more clouded. The field of computer-assisted psychotherapy still needs more research, more program evaluation (see O'Dell & Dickson, 1984), more innovative experimentation, more theory building, and more conceptualization.

Some programs that have been described in this review can function without the direct participation of a clinician. Such programs have economy on their side. Other programs require the presence of the clinician for all or for part of the time, and thus have fewer time-saving advantages (Colby et al., 1989). In the case of such computer-assisted psychotherapy programs, the fundamental issue is one of efficacy. If the general psychotherapy evaluation literature has a parallel in the future computer-assisted psychotherapy evaluation literature, cognitive approaches to computer psychotherapy that have already proven feasible and successful may turn out to be just as effective as dynamic approaches when they have also become feasible and successful.

In this context, Wagman (1988) distinguishes between what he calls a level one and a level two computer counselor. A level one computer counselor "possesses a theory of its own reasoning that includes a representation of the client's personality structure and dynamics and applies techniques as tactics within the overall structure of its model of its therapeutic domain" (p. 199). The level one computer counselor is a hypothesis-generating, model-building therapist—clearly more difficult to emulate with a computer. In the case of a level two computer counselor, "techniques are applied in the absence of the computer counselor's possession of models of its therapeutic domain and the effects of the techniques are processed largely by the client's models of therapy and per-

sonality problem domains" (p. 199). Thus, the level two computer counselor can be programmed for counseling technique—for identifying faulty assumptions, exploring, pointing out feelings, clarifying, comparing and contrasting, supporting, and so forth.

Another promising area for further research in computer-assisted psychotherapy is in following up the early work of Slack (1971) who demonstrated that the computer could be programmed to attend to nonverbal behavior as well as to keyboard responses. This initial work has not had the continued attention it justifies. Slack showed that the computer could attend to heart rate and to keyboard response latency, and could be programmed to respond to increases in both. In his branching program designed to conduct a medical history and mental status interview, the respondent's heart rate is monitored by two chest electrodes. Response latency is continually monitored by the computer.

Heart rate and response latency values can be used to determine branching moves in the questionnaire. If the heart rate exceeds a predetermined value, the computer can be programmed to skip certain questions, to offer suggestions for relaxation, or to inquire whether the particular question is a disturbing one to the respondent. If the question is acknowledge to be disturbing, further branching moves can be invoked to conduct additional inquiry into the particular subject. High response latency can signal fluctuating attention or depressed mood. Consistently high response latency across a number of subjects would suggest that the particular question may be too difficult or poorly worded. George and Skinner (1990) have recently reported that there is some evidence that response latency may be longer when subjects provide honest self-reports than when they fake good feelings.

In 1979, Colby noted that the early hopes of computer researchers about the possibility of creating a world class chess-playing computer program did not come true because too few people were working on the problem. In the late 1970s, however, a burst of energy in the development of chess-playing programs took place that led to the development of programs that were so sophisticated that many chess grandmasters refused to compete against them. Colby concluded, "The moral is simple: for problems-within-reach to be solved, people must work on them. If no one works on computer psychotherapy, then there will be none. This is admittedly a tautology but some tautologies are more instructive than others" (p. 155). As this review indicates, we may now be witnessing an equivalent burst of energy in the field of computer-assisted psychological intervention.

References

Allen, D. H. (1984). The use of computer fantasy games in child therapy. In M. D. Schwartz (Ed.), *Using computers in clinical practice: Psychotherapy and mental health applications* (pp. 329–334). New York: Haworth.

Alperovitch, A., Le Minor, M., & Lellouch, J. (1976). Three examples of computer-aided medical decision. In F. T. de Dombal & F. Grémy (Eds.), *Decision making and medical care: Can information science help?* (pp. 143–151). Amsterdam: North-Holland.

Angle, H. V., Ellinwood, E. H., & Carroll, J. (1978). Computer interview problem assessment of psychiatric patients. In F. H. Orthner (Ed.), *Proceedings: The Second Annual Symposium on Computer Applications in Medical Care* (pp. 137–148). Long Beach, CA: IEEE Computer Society.

Aradi, N. S. (1985). The application of computer technology to behavioral marital therapy. *Journal of Psychotherapy and the Family, 1,* 167–177.

Baccara, J.-P. (1985). "Psychosom", questionnaire informatise et épidémiologie psychiatrique. In P. F. Channoit & J. de Verbizier (Eds.), *Informatique et épidémiologie psychiatrique.* Toulouse, France: Érès.

Balis Computing. (1984). *PSYCHE talks back.* Boca Raton, FL: Author.

Barnett, G. O. (1974). The use of a computer-based system to teach clinical problem solving. In R. W. Stacy & B. D. Waxman (Eds.), *Computers in biomedical research* (pp. 301–319). New York: Academic Press.

Barnett, J., Knight, K., Mani, I., & Rich, E. (1990). Knowledge and natural language processing. *Communications of the ACM, 33,* 50–71.

Barr, A., & Feigenbaum, E. A. (Eds.). (1981). *The handbook of artificial intelligence* (Vol. 1). Stanford, CA: HeurisTech Press.

Barron, M. R., Daniels, J. L., & O'Toole, W. M. (1987). The effect of computer-conducted versus counselor-conducted initial intake interviews on client expectancy. *Computers in Human Behavior, 3,* 21–28.

Beck, A. T. (1976). *Cognitive therapy and the emotional disorders.* New York: International Universities Press.

Beck, A. T., Rush, A. J., Shaw, B. F., & Emery, G. (1979). *Cognitive therapy of depression.* New York: Guilford.

Beck, A. T., Ward, C. H., Mendelson, M., Mock, J., & Erbaugh, J. (1961). An inventory for measuring depression. *Archives of General Psychiatry, 4,* 561–571.

Bellman, R., Friend, M. B., & Kurland, L. (1966). Simulation of the initial psychiatric interview. *Behavioral Science, 11,* 389–399.

Ben-Portah, Y. S., & Butcher, J. N. (1986). Computers in personality assessment: A brief past, an ebullient present, and an expanding future. *Computers in Human Behavior, 2,* 167–182.

Biglan, A., Villwock, C., & Wick, S. (1979). The feasibility of a computer controlled program for the treatment of test anxiety. *Journal of Behavior Therapy and Experimental Psychiatry, 10,* 47–49.

Binik, Y. M., Servan-Schreiber, D., Freiwald, S., & Hall, K. S. (1988). Intelligent computer-based assessment and psychotherapy: An expert system for sexual dysfunction. *Journal of Nervous and Mental Disease, 176,* 387–400.

Binik, Y. M., Westbury, C. F., & Servan-Schreiber, D. (1989). Interaction with a "sex-expert" system enhances attitudes toward computerized sex therapy. *Behavior Research and Therapy, 27,* 303–306.

Bleich, H. L. (1974). Automated instructional programs for advanced medical education. In R. W. Stacy & B. D. Waxman (Eds.), *Computers in biomedical research* (pp. 289–300). New York: Academic Press.

Blois, M. S. (1980). Clinical judgment and computers. *New England Journal of Medicine, 303,* 192–197.

Bloom, B. L. (1988). *Health psychology: A psychosocial perspective.* Englewood Cliffs, NJ: Prentice-Hall.

Bloom, S. M., White R. J., Beckley, R. F., & Slack, W. V. (1978). Converse: A means to write, edit, administer, and summarize computer-based dialogue. *Computers and Biomedical Research, 11,* 167–175.

Burda, P. C., Starkey, T. W., & Dominguez, F. (1991). Computer administered treatment of psychiatric inpatients. *Computers in Human Behavior, 7,* 1–5.

Burke, M. J., & Normand, J. (1987). Computerized psychological testing: Overview and critique. *Professional Psychology: Research and Practice, 18,* 42–51.

Burnett, K. F., Taylor, C. B., & Agras, W. S. (1985). Ambulatory computer-assisted therapy for obesity: A new frontier for behavior therapy. *Journal of Consulting and Clinical Psychology, 53,* 698–703.

Butcher, J. N. (Ed.). (1987). *Computerized psychological assessment.* New York: Basic Books.

Butcher, J. N., Keller, L. S., & Bacon, S. F. (1985). Current developments and future directions in computerized personality assessment. *Journal of Consulting and Clinical Psychology, 53,* 803–815.

Carkhuff, R. R., Pierce, R. M., & Cannon, J. R. (1980). *The art of helping: IV.* Amherst, MA: Human Resources Development Press.

Carr, A. C., Ghosh, A., & Ancill, R. J. (1983). Can a computer take a psychiatric history? *Psychological Medicine, 13,* 151–158.

Casel, R. N., & Blum, L. P. (1969). Computer assist counseling (COASCON) for the prevention of delinquent behavior among teenagers and youth. *Sociology & Social Research, 54,* 72–79.

Cavell, S. (1988). *In quest of the ordinary: Lines of skepticism and romanticism.* Chicago: University of Chicago Press.

Chambers, C. V., Balaban, D. J., Carlson, B. L., Ungemack, J. A., & Grasberger, D. M. (1989). Microcomputer-generated reminders: Improving the compliance of primary care physicians with mammography screening guidelines. *Journal of Family Practice, 29,* 273–280.

Chandler, G. B., Burck, H., & Sampson, J. P. (1986). A generic computer program for systematic desensitization: Description, construction, and case study. *Journal of Behavior Therapy and Experimental Psychiatry, 17,* 171–174.

Chandler, G. M., Burck, H., Sampson, J. P., & Wray, R. (1988). The effectiveness of a generic computer program for systematic desensitization. *Computers in Human Behavior, 4,* 339–346.

Clarke, B., & Schoech, D. (1984). A computer-assisted therapeutic game for adolescents: Initial development and comments. In M. D. Schwartz (Ed.), *Using computers in clinical practice: Psychotherapy and mental health applications* (pp. 335–353). New York: Haworth.

Cogswell, J. F. (1983). Reflections of a grandfather. *Counseling Psychologist, 11*(4), 61–63.

Colby, K. M. (1968). Computer-aided language development in nonspeaking children. *Archives of General Psychiatry, 19,* 641–651.

Colby, K. M. (1973). The rationale for computer-based treatment of language difficulties in nonspeaking autistic children. *Journal of Autism and Childhood Schizophrenia, 3,* 254–260.

Colby, K. M. (1975). *Artificial paranoia: A computer simulation of paranoid processes.* New York: Pergamon.

Colby, K. M. (1979). Computer simulation and artificial intelligence in psychiatry. In E. A. Serafetinides (Ed.), *Methods of biobehavioral research* (pp. 145–156). New York: Grune & Stratton.

Colby, K. M. (1980). Computer psychotherapists. In J. B. Sidowski, J. H. Johnson, & T. A. Williams (Eds.), *Technology in mental health care delivery systems* (pp. 109–117). Norwood, NJ: Ablex.

Colby, K. M., & Enea, H. (1967). Heuristic methods for computer understanding of natural language in context-restricted on-line dialogues. *Mathematical Biosciences, 1*, 1–25.

Colby, K. M., Gould, R. L., & Aronson, G. (1989). Some pros and cons of computer-assisted psychotherapy. *Journal of Nervous and Mental Disease, 177*, 105–108.

Colby, K. M., & Parkison, R. (1985). Linguistic conceptual-patterns and key-idea profiles as a new kind of property for a taxonomy of neurotic patients. *Computers in Human Behavior, 1*, 181–194.

Colby, K. M., Watt, J. B., & Gilbert, J. P. (1966). A computer method of psychotherapy: Preliminary communication. *Journal of Nervous and Mental Disease, 142*, 148–152.

Danish, S. J., & D'Augelli, A. R., & Hauer, A. L. (1980). *Helping skills: A basic training program.* New York: Human Sciences Press.

Deardorff, W. W. (1986). Computerized health education: A comparison with traditional formats. *Health Education Quarterly, 13*, 61–72.

DeMuth, P. (1984). Eliza and her offspring. In M. D. Schwartz (Ed.), *Using computers in clinical practice: Psychotherapy and mental health applications* (pp. 321–327). New York: Haworth.

Ellis, L. B. M., Raines, J. R., & Hakanson, N. (1982). Health education using microcomputers: II. One year in the clinic. *Preventive Medicine, 11*, 212–224.

Elwork, A., & Gutkin, T. B. (1985). The behavioral sciences in the computer age. *Computers in Human Behavior, 1*, 3–18.

Erdman, H. P., Greist, J. H., Klein, M. H., Jefferson, J. W., & Getto, C. (1981). The computer psychiatrist: How far have we come? Where are we heading? How far dare we go? *Behavior Research Methods & Instrumentation, 13*, 393–398.

Erdman, H. P., Klein, M. H., & Greist, J. H. (1985). Direct patient computer interviewing. *Journal of Consulting and Clinical Psychology, 53*, 760–773.

Evans, D. R., Hearn, M. T., Uhlemann, M. R., & Ivey, A. E. (1989). *Essential interviewing: A programmed approach to effective communication* (3rd ed.). Pacific Grove, CA: Brooks/Cole.

Farrell, A. D. (1989). Impact of computers on professional practice: A survey of current practices and attitudes. *Professional Psychology: Research and Practice, 20*, 172–178.

Farrell, A. D., Camplair, P. S., & McCullough, L. (1987). Identification of target complaints by computer interview: Evaluation of the computerized assessment system for psychotherapy evaluation and research. *Journal of Consulting and Clinical Psychology, 55*, 691–700.

Fowler, R. D. (1985). Landmarks in computer-assisted psychological assessment. *Journal of Consulting and Clinical Psychology, 53*, 748–759.

Fowler, R. D., & Butcher, J. N. (1986). Critique of Matarazzo's views on computerized testing: All sigma and no meaning. *American Psychologist, 41*, 94–96.

French, C. C., & Beaumont, J. G. (1989). A computerized form of the Eysenck Personality Questionnaire: A clinical study. *Personality and Individual Differences, 10*, 1027–1032.

Freud, S. (1953). Notes upon a case of obsessional neurosis. In A. Strachey & J. Strachey (Eds.), *Sigmund Freud, M.D., LL.D. Collected papers* (Vol. 3, pp. 296–383). London: Hogarth Press. (Original work published 1909).

Friedman, R. B. (1973). A computer program for simulating the patient-physician encounter. *Journal of Medical Education, 48*, 92–97.

George, M. S., & Skinner, H. A. (1990). Using response latency to detect inaccurate responses in a computerized lifestyle assessment. *Computers in Human Behavior, 6*, 167–175.

Ghosh, A., Marks, I. M., & Carr, A. C. (1984). Controlled study of self-exposure treatment for phobics: Preliminary communication. *Journal of the Royal Society of Medicine, 77*, 483–487.

Golferini, F., & Facchin, P. (1987). Computer diagnosis of primary headaches in children. *Computers and Biomedical Research, 20*, 55–63.

Greist, J. H. (1980). Computer therapy. In R. Herink (Ed.), *The psychotherapy handbook* (pp. 111–114). New York: New American Library.

Greist, J. H., Carroll, J. A., Erdman, H. P., & Klein, M. H. (1987). *Research in mental health computer applications: Directions for the future* (DDHS Publication No. ADM 87-1468). Washington, DC: U.S. Government Printing Office.

Greist, J. H., Gustafson, D. H., Stauss, F. F., Rowse, G. L., Laughren, T. P., & Chiles, J. A. (1973). A computer interview for suicide-risk prediction. *American Journal of Psychiatry, 130*, 1327–1332.

Greist, J. H., & Klein, M. H. (1980). Computer programs for patients, clinicians, and researchers in psychiatry. In J. B. Sidowski, J. H. Johnson, & T. A. Williams (Eds.), *Technology in mental health care delivery systems* (pp. 161–181). Norwood, NJ: Ablex.

Greist, J. H., Klein, M. H., & Erdman, H. P. (1978). Computer interviewing: Beyond data collection. In. F. H. Orthner (Ed.), *Proceedings: The Second Annual Symposium on Computer Applications in Medical Care* (pp. 227–230). Long Beach, CA: IEEE Computer Society.

Greist, J. H., Klein, M. H., Erdman, H. P., & Jefferson, J. W. (1983). Computers and psychiatric diagnosis. *Psychiatric Annals, 13*, 785, 789–792.

Greist, J. H., Klein, M. H., & Van Cura, L. J. (1973). A computer interview for psychiatric patient target symptoms. *Archives of General Psychiatry, 29*, 247–253.

Groth-Marnat, G., & Schumaker, J. (1989). Computer-based psychological testing: Issues and guidelines. *American Journal of Orthopsychiatry, 59*, 257–263.

Gustafson, D. H., Bosworth, K., Chewning, B., & Hawkins, R. P. (1987). Computer-based health promotion: Combining technological advances with problem-solving techniques to effect successful health behavior changes. *Annual Review of Public Health, 8*, 387–415.

Haug, P. J., Warner, H. R., Clayton, P. D., Schmidt, C. D., Pearl, J. E., Farney, R. J., Crapo, R. O., Tocino, I., Morrison, W. J., & Frederick, P. R. (1987). A decision-driven system to collect patient history. *Computers and Biomedical Research, 20*, 193–207.

Hawkins, R. P., Bosworth, K., Chewning, B., Day, P. M., & Gustafson, D. H. (1985). Adolescents' use of computer-based health information: The BARN project. In M. Chen & W. Paisley (Eds.), *Children and microcomputers: Research on the newest medium* (pp. 228–245). Beverly Hills, CA: Sage.

Hedlund, J. L. (1978). Computers in mental health: An historical overview and summary of current status. In F. H. Orthner (Ed.), *Proceedings: The Second Annual Symposium on Computer Applications in Medical Care* (pp. 168–183). Long Beach, CA: IEEE Computer Society.

Hedlund, J. L., Evenson, R. C., Sletten, I. W., & Cho, D. W. (1980). The computer and clinical prediction. In J. B. Sidowski, J. H. Johnson, & T. A. Williams (Eds.), *Technology in mental health care delivery systems* (pp. 201–235). Norwood, NJ: Ablex.

Hedlund, J. L., & Vieweg, B. W. (1984). Computers in mental health: A selected bibliography. In M. D. Schwartz (Ed.), *Using computers in clinical practice: Psychotherapy and mental health applications* (pp.481–495). New York: Haworth.

Hedlund, J. L., Vieweg, B. W., & Cho, D. W. (1987). Computer consultation for emotional crises: An expert system for "non-experts." *Computers in Human Behavior, 3*, 109–127.

Hedlund, J. L., Vieweg, B. W., Wood, J. B., Cho, D. W., Evenson, R. C., Hickman, C. V., & Holland, R. A. (1981). *Computers in mental health: A review and annotated bibliography* (DHHS Publication No. ADM 81–1090). Washington, DC: U.S. Government Printing Office.

Helm, C. E. (1968). Natural language processing in behavioral research. In N. S. Kline & E. Laska (Eds.), *Computers and electronic devices in psychiatry* (pp. 20–33). New York: Grune & Stratton.

Hilf, F. D. (1972). Partially automated psychiatric interviewing—A research tool. *Journal of Nervous and Mental Disease, 155*, 410–418.

Hofer, P. J., & Green, B. F. (1985). The challenge of competence and creativity in computerized psychological testing. *Journal of Consulting and Clinical Psychology, 53*, 826–838.

Honaker, L. M. (1988). The equivalency of computerized and conventional MMPI administration: A critical review. *Clinical Psychology Review, 8*, 561–577.

Honaker, L. M., Hector, V. S., & Harrell, T. H. (1986). Perceived validity of computer- versus clinician-generated MMPI reports. *Computers in Human Services, 2,* 77–83.

Jackson, D. N. (1985). Computer-based personality testing. *Computers in Human Behavior, 1,* 255–264.

Johnson, J. H. (1978). Computers in mental health: Where are we now? In F. H. Orthner (Ed.), *Proceedings: The Second Annual Symposium on Computer Applications in Medical Care* (pp. 104–108). Long Beach, CA: IEEE Computer Society.

Johnson, J. H., Giannetti, R. A., & Williams, T. A. (1976). Computers in mental health care delivery: A review of the evolution toward interventionally relevant on-line processing. *Behavior Research Methods & Instrumentation, 8,* 83–91.

Kann, L. K. (1987). Effects of computer-assisted instruction on selected interaction skills related to responsible sexuality. *Journal of School Health, 57,* 282–287.

Karasu, T. (1977). Psychotherapies: An overview. *American Journal of Psychiatry, 134,* 851–863.

Kiesler, S., & Sproull, L. S. (1986). Response effects in the electronic survey. *Public Opinion Quarterly, 50,* 402–413.

Klein, M. H., Greist, J. H., & Van Cura, L. J. (1975). Computers and psychiatry: Promises to keep. *Archives of General Psychiatry, 32,* 837–843.

Kleinmuntz, B., & McLean, R. S. (1968). Computers in behavioral science: Diagnostic interviewing by digital computer. *Behavioral Science, 13,* 75–80.

Klepsch, R. (1990). Is computer assessment of obsession and compulsion applicable in obsessive-compulsive disorder?: Preliminary results using the Hamburg Obsession Compulsion Inventory—Computer short form (HOCI-CS). *Computers in Human Behavior, 6,* 133–139.

Kratochwill, T. R. (1982). Advances in behavioral assessment. In C. R. Reynolds & T. B. Gutkin (Eds.), *Handbook of school psychology* (pp. 314–350). New York: Wiley.

Kratochwill, T. R., Doll, E. J., & Dickson, W. P. (1985). Microcomputers in behavioral assessment: Recent advances and remaining issues. *Computers in Human Behavior, 1,* 277–291.

Langlotz, C. P., Fagan, L. M., Tu, S. W., Sikic, B. I., & Shortliffe, E. H. (1987). A therapy planning architecture that combines decision theory and artificial intelligence techniques. *Computers and Biomedical Research, 20,* 279–303.

Lanyon, R. I. (1984). Personality assessment. *Annual Review of Psychology, 35,* 667–701.

Lappe, J. M., Dixon, B., Lazure, L., Nilsson, P., Thielen, J., & Norris, J. (1990). Nursing education application of a computerized nursing expert system. *Journal of Nursing Education, 29,* 244–248.

Lawrence, G. H. (1986). Using computers for the treatment of psychological problems. *Computers in Human Behavior, 2,* 43–62.

Lester, D. (1977). *The use of alternative modes for communication in psychotherapy: The computer, the book, the telephone, the television, the tape recorder.* Springfield, IL: C. C. Thomas.

Lichtenberg, J. M., Hummel, T. J., & Shaffer, W. F. (1984). CLIENT 1: A computer simulation for use in counselor education and research. *Counselor Education and Supervision, 24,* 155–167.

Lilford, R. J., & Chard, T. (1982). Computers in antenatal care. *British Journal of Hospital Medicine, 28,* 420–426.

Lucas, R. W., Card, W. I., Knill-Jones, R. P., Watkinson, G., & Crean, G. P. (1976). Computer interrogation of patients. *British Medical Journal, 2,* 623–625.

Lukin, M. E., Dowd, E. T., Plake, B. S., & Kraft, R. G. (1985). Comparing computerized versus traditional psychological assessment. *Computers in Human Services, 1,* 49–58.

Malcolm, J. (1987, April 20). J'appelle un chat un chat. *The New Yorker* pp. 84–92, 95–102.

Martin, D. G. (1983). *Counseling and therapy skills.* Monterey, CA: Brooks/Cole.

Matarazzo, J. D. (1985). Clinical psychological test interpretations by computer: Hardware outpaces software. *Computers in Human Behavior, 1,* 235–253.

Matarazzo, J. D. (1986). Computerized clinical psychological test interpretations: Unvalidated plus all mean and no sigma. *American Psychologist, 41,* 14–24.

Matarazzo, J. D. (1990). Psychological assessment versus psychological testing: Validation from Binet to the school, clinic, and courtroom. *American Psychologist, 45,* 999–1017.

Matthews, T. J., De Santi, S. M., Callahan, D., Koblenz-Sulcov, C. J., & Werden, J. I. (1987). The microcomputer as an agent of intervention with psychiatric patients: Preliminary studies. *Computers in Human Services, 3,* 37–47.

Maultsby, M. C., & Slack, W. V. (1971). A computer-based psychiatry history system. *Archives of General Psychiatry, 25,* 570–572.

McCullough, L., Farrell, A. D., & Longabaugh, R. (1986). The development of a microcomputer-based health information system: A potential tool for bridging the scientist-practitioner gap. *American Psychologist, 41,* 207–214.

McDowell, I., Newell, C., & Rosser, W. (1989). Computerized reminders to encourage cervical screening in family practice. *Journal of Family Practice, 28,* 420–424.

McGuire, M. T. (1971). The ultimate role of the computer in psychiatry. *Psychiatric Opinion, 8,* 28–33.

McGuire, M. T., Lorch, S., & Quarton, G. C. (1967). Man–machine natural language exchanges based on selected features of unrestricted input—II. The use of the time-shared computer as a research tool in studying dyadic communication. *Journal of Psychiatric Research, 5,* 179–191.

McLean, E. R., Foote, S. V., & Wagner, G. (1975). The collection and processing of medical history data. *Methods of Information in Medicine, 14,* 150–163.

Miller, R. A., Pople, H. E., & Myers, J. D. (1982). Internist-I, an experimental computer-based diagnostic consultant for general internal medicine. *New England Journal of Medicine, 307,* 468–476.

Moncher, M. S., Parms, C. A., Orlandi, M. A., Schinke, S. P., Miller, S. O., Palleja, J., & Schinke, M. D. (1989). Microcomputer-based approaches for preventing drug and alcohol abuse among adolescents from ethnic-racial minority backgrounds. *Computers in Human Behavior, 5,* 79–93.

Monnickendam, M. (1990). Computers in social work: Values, concepts, processes and techniques. In B. Marin (Ed.), *The use of computers in social work* (Eurosocial Report 35: pp. 4–22). Vienna, Austria: European Centre for Social Welfare and Research.

Moreland, K. L. (1985a). Computer-assisted psychological assessment in 1986: A practical guide. *Computers in Human Behavior, 1,* 221–233.

Moreland, K. L. (1985b). Validation of computer-based test interpretations: Problems and prospects. *Journal of Consulting and Clinical Psychology, 53,* 816–825.

Moreland, K. L., & Onstad, J. A. (1987). Validation of Millon's computerized interpretation system for the MCMI: A controlled study. *Journal of Consulting and Clinical Psychology, 55,* 113–114.

Nelson, H. (1982, April). Artificial intelligence after 25 years. *Microcomputing,* pp. 32–34, 36.

O'Dell, J. W., & Dickson, J. (1984). Eliza as a "therapeutic" tool. *Journal of Clinical Psychology, 40,* 942–945.

Okun, B. F. (1982). *Effective helping: Interviewing and counseling techniques* (2nd ed.). Monterey, CA: Brooks/Cole.

Parkison, R. C., Colby, K. M., & Faught, W. S. (1977). Conversational language comprehension using integrated pattern-matching and parsing. *Artificial Intelligence, 9,* 111–134.

Piemme, T. E. (1988). Computer-assisted learning and evaluation in medicine. *Journal of the American Medical Association, 260,* 367–372.

Plutchik, R., & Karasu, T. B. (1991). Computers in psychotherapy: An overview. *Computers in Human Behavior, 7,* 33–44.

Porter, D. (1978). Patient responses to computer counseling. In F. H. Orthner (Ed.), *Proceedings: The Second Annual Symposium on Computer Applications in Medical Care* (pp. 233–237). Long Beach, CA: IEEE Computer Society.

Potter, B., & Ronan, S. G. (1990). Computer diagnosis of skin disease. *Journal of Family Practice, 30,* 201–210.

Raines, J. R., & Ellis, L. B. (1982). Conversational microcomputer based health risk appraisal. *Computer Programs in Biomedicine, 14,* 175–183.

Rennels, G. D., & Shortliffe, E. H. (1987). Advanced computing for medicine. *Scientific American*, **257**, 154–161.

Rich, E. (1983). *Artificial intelligence*. New York: McGraw-Hill.

Robertson, E. B., Ladewig, B. H., Strickland, M. P., & Boschung, M. D. (1987). Enhancement of self-esteem through the use of computer-assisted instruction. *Journal of Educational Research, 80,* 314–316.

Roid, G. H. (1985). Computer-based test interpretation: The potential of quantitative methods of test interpretation. *Computers in Human Behavior, 1,* 207–219.

Rokeach, M. (1975). Long-term value change initiated by computer feedback. *Journal of Personality and Social Psychology, 32,* 467–476.

Russell, G. K. G. (1983). Computers in medicine. *New Zealand Medical Journal,* **96,** 813.

Sampson, J. P. (1983). An integrated approach to computer applications in counseling psychology. *Counseling Psychologist, 11,* 65–74.

Sampson, J. P. (1986). The use of computer-assisted instruction in support of psychotherapeutic processes. *Computers in Human Behavior, 2,* 1–19.

Sampson, J. P., & Pyle, K. R. (1983). Ethical issues involved with the use of computer-assisted counseling, testing, and guidance systems. *Personnel and Guidance Journal, 61,* 283–287.

Schank, R. C., & Abelson, R. P. (1977). *Scripts, plans, goals and understanding*. Hillsdale, NJ: Lawrence Erlbaum.

Schneider, S. J. (1986). Trial of an on-line behavioral smoking cessation program. *Computers in Human Behavior, 2,* 227–286.

Schneider, S. J., Walker, R., & O'Donnell, R. (1990). Computerized communication as a medium for behavioral smoking cessation treatment: Controlled evaluation. *Computers in Human Behavior, 6,* 141–151.

Schoenfeldt, L. F. (1989). Guidelines for computer-based psychological tests and interpretations. *Computers in Human Behavior, 5,* 13–21.

Schwartz, M. D. (Ed.). (1984). *Using computers in clinical practice: Psychotherapy and mental health applications*. New York: Haworth.

Selmi, P. M., Klein, M. H., Greist, J. H., Johnson, J. H., & Harris, W. G. (1982). An investigation of computer-assisted cognitive-behavior therapy in the treatment of depression. *Behavior Research Methods & Instrumentation, 14,* 181–185.

Selmi, P. M., Klein, M. H., Greist, J. H., Sorrell, S. P., & Erdman, H. P. (1990). Computer-administered cognitive-behavioral therapy for depression. *American Journal of Psychiatry, 147,* 51–56.

Servan-Schreiber, D. (1986). Artificial intelligence and psychiatry. *Journal of Nervous and Mental Disease, 174,* 191–202.

Servan-Schreiber, D., & Binik, Y. M. (1989). Extending the intelligent tutoring system paradigm: Sex therapy as intelligent tutoring. *Computers in Human Behavior, 5,* 241–259.

Sheppard, L. C., Kirklin, J. W., & Kouchoukos, N. T. (1974). Computer-controlled interventions for the acutely-ill patient. In R. W. Stacy & B. D. Waxman (Eds.), *Computers in biomedical research* (pp. 135–148). New York: Academic Press.

Shortliffe, E. (1976). *Computer-based medical consultations: MYCIN*. New York: American Elsevier.

Shortliffe, E. H. (1987). Computer programs to support clinical decision making. *Journal of the American Medical Association,* **258,** 61–66.

Sicoly, F. (1989). Computer-aided decisions in human services: Expert systems and multivariate models. *Computers in Human Behavior, 5,* 47–60.

Siegel, J. H., & Strom, B. L. (1974). An automated consultation system to aid the physician in the care of the desperately sick patient. In R. W. Stacy & B. D. Waxman (Eds.), *Computers in biomedical research* (pp. 115–134). New York: Academic Press.

Sittig, D. F., Pace, N. L., Gardner, R. M., Beck, E., & Morris, A. H. (1989). Implementation of a computerized patient advice system using the HELP clinical information system. *Computers and Biomedical Research, 22,* 474–487.

Slack, W. (1971). Computer-based interviewing system dealing with nonverbal behavior as well as keyboard responses. *Science,* **171,** 84–87.

Slack, W. V. (1978). Patient counseling by computer. In F. H. Orthner (Ed.), *Proceedings: The Second Annual Symposium on Computer Applications in Medical Care* (pp. 222–226). Long Beach, CA: IEEE Computer Society.

Slack, W. V., Leviton, A., Bennett, S. E., Fleischmann, K. H., & Lawrence, R. S. (1988). Relation between age, education, and time to respond to questions in a computer-based medical interview. *Computers and Biomedical Research,* **21,** 78–84.

Slack, W. V., Porter, D., Witschi, J., Sullivan, M., Buxbaum, R., & Stare, F. J. (1976). Dietary interviewing by computer. *Journal of the American Dietetic Association,* **69,** 514–517.

Slack, W. V., & Slack, C. W. (1972). Patient-computer dialogue. *New England Journal of Medicine, 286,* 1304–1309.

Slack, W. V., & Slack, C. W. (1977). Talking to a computer about emotional problems: A comparative study. *Psychotherapy: Theory, Research and Practice, 14,* 156–164.

Slack, W. V., & Van Cura, L. J. (1968). Patient reaction to computer-based medical interviewing. *Computers and Biomedical Research, 1,* 527–531.

Sorrell, S. P., Greist, J. H., Klein, M. H., Johnson, J. H., & Harris, W. G. (1982). Enhancement of adherence to tricyclic antidepressants by computerized supervision. *Behavior Research Methods & Instrumentation, 14,* 176–180.

Space, L. G. (1981). The computer as psychometrician. *Behavior Research Methods & Instrumentation, 13,* 595–606.

Spero, M. H. (1978). Thoughts on computerized psychotherapy. *Psychiatry, 41,* 279–288.

Spitzer, R. L., & Endicott, J. (1969). DIAGNO II: Further developments in a computer program for psychiatric diagnosis. *American Journal of Psychiatry, 125,* (Suppl.), 12–21.

Stodolsky, D. (1970). The computer as psychotherapist. *International Journal of Man-Machine Studies, 2,* 327–350.

Stone, P. J., Dunphy, D. C., Smith, M. S., & Ogilvie, D. M. (Eds.). (1966). *The general inquirer: A computer approach to control analysis*. Cambridge, MA: M.I.T. Press.

Stroebel, C. F., & Glueck, B. C. (1970). Computer derived global judgments in psychiatry. *American Journal of Psychiatry, 126,* 1057–1066.

Tombari, M. L., Fitzpatrick, S. J., & Childress, W. (1985). Using computers as contingency managers in self-monitoring interventions: A case study. *Computers in Human Behavior, 1,* 75–82.

Trappl, R. (1981). Computer psychotherapy: Is it acceptable, feasible, advisable? *Cybernetics and Systems: An International Journal, 12,* 385–394.

Uplekar, M. W., Antia, N. H., & Dhumale, P. S. (1988). Sympmed I: Computer program for primary health care: *British Medical Journal, 297,* 841–843.

Wagman, M. (1980). PLATO DCS: An interactive computer system for personal counseling. *Journal of Counseling Psychology, 27,* 16–30.

Wagman, M. (1983). A factor analytic study of the psychological implications of the computer for the individual and society. *Behavior Research Methods & Instrumentation, 15,* 413–419.

Wagman, M. (1984). *The dilemma and the computer: Theory, research, and applications to counseling psychology*. New York: Praeger.

Wagman, M. (1988). *Computer psychotherapy systems: Theory and research foundations*. New York: Gordon and Breach.

Wagman, M., & Kerber, K. W. (1980). PLATO DCS, an interactive computer system for personal counseling: Further development and evaluation. *Journal of Counseling Psychology, 27,* 31–39.

Waller, N. G., & Reise, S. P. (1989). Computer adaptive personality assessment: An illustration with the absorption scale. *Journal of Personality and Social Psychology, 57,* 1051–1085.

Washington Computer Services. (1989). *PC/PILOT general information*. Bellingham, WA: Washington Computer Services.

Weiss, D. J. (1985). Adaptive testing by computer. *Journal of Consulting and Clinical Psychology, 53,* 774–789.

Weizenbaum, J. (1966). ELIZA—A computer program for the study of natural language communication between man and machine. *Communications of the Association for Computer Machinery, 9,* 36–45.

Weizenbaum, J. (1967). Contextual understanding by computers. *Communications of the Association for Computing Machinery, 10,* 474–480.

Weizenbaum, J. (1976). *Computer power and human reason: From judgment to calculation.* San Francisco: W. H. Freeman.

Werner, G. (1987). Methuselah—An expert system for diagnosis in geriatric psychiatry. *Computers and Biomedical Research, 20,* 477–488.

Wilson, F. R., Genco, K. T., & Yager, G. G. (1985). Assessing the equivalence of paper-and-pencil vs. computerized tests: Demonstration of a promising methodology. *Computers in Human Behavior, 1,* 265–275.

Winston, P. H. (1984). *Artificial intelligence* (2nd ed.). Reading, MA: Addison-Wesley.

Witschi, J., Porter, D., Vogel, S., Buxbaum, R., Stare, F. J., & Slack, W. (1976). A computer-based dietary counseling system. *Journal of the American Dietetic Association, 69,* 385–390.

Yokley, J. M., & Reuter, J. M., (1989). The computer-assisted child diagnostic system: A research and development project. *Computers in Human Behavior, 5,* 277–295.

Yu, V. L., Buchanan, B. G., Shortliffe, E. H., Wraith, S. M., Davis, R., Scott, A. C., & Cohen, S. N. (1979). Evaluating the performance of a computer-based consultant. *Computer Programs in Biomedicine, 9,* 95–102.

Zachary, R. A., & Pope, K. S. (1984). Legal and ethical issues in the clinical use of computerized testing. In M. D. Schwartz (Ed.), *Using computers in clinical practice: Psychotherapy and mental health applications* (pp. 151–164). New York: Haworth.

Zarr, M. L. (1984). Computer-mediated psychotherapy: Toward patient-selection guidelines. *American Journal of Psychotherapy, 38,* 47–62.

Article Review Form at end of book.

Does therapy help? Whom does it help?

Mental Health:

Does Therapy Help?

Our groundbreaking survey shows psychotherapy usually works. This report can help you find the best care.

Coping with a serious physical illness is hard enough. But if you're suffering from emotional or mental distress, it's particularly difficult to know where to get help. You may have some basic doubts about whether therapy will help at all. And even if you do decide to enter therapy, your health insurance may not cover it—or cover it well.

As a result, millions of Americans who might benefit from psychotherapy never even give it a try. More than 50 million American adults suffer from a mental or addictive disorder at any given time. But a recent Government survey showed that fewer than one-third of them get professional help.

That's a shame. The results of a candid, in-depth survey of Consumer Reports subscribers—the largest survey ever to query people on mental-health care—provide convincing evidence that therapy can make an important difference. Four thousand of our readers who responded had sought help from a mental-health provider or a family doctor for psychological problems, or had joined a self-help group. The majority were highly satisfied with the care they received. Most had made strides toward resolving the problems that led to treatment, and almost all said life had become more manageable. This was true for all the conditions we asked about, even among the people who had felt the worst at the beginning.

Among Our Findings

- People were just as satisfied and reported similar progress whether they saw a social worker, psychologist, or psychiatrist. Those who consulted a marriage counselor, however, were somewhat less likely to feel they'd been helped.

- Readers who sought help from their family doctor tended to do well. But people who saw a mental-health specialist for more than six months did much better.

- Psychotherapy alone worked as well as psychotherapy combined with medication, like *Prozac* or *Xanax*. Most people who took drugs like those did feel they were helpful, but many people reported side effects.

- The longer people stayed in therapy, the more they improved. This suggests that limited mental-health insurance coverage, and the new trend in health plans—emphasizing short-term therapy—may be misguided.

- Most people who went to a self-help group were very satisfied with the experience and said they got better. People were especially grateful to Alcoholics Anonymous, and very loyal to that organization.

Our survey adds an important dimension to existing research in mental health. Most studies have started with people who have very specific, well-defined problems, who have been randomly assigned to a treatment or control group, and who have received carefully scripted therapy. Such studies have shown which techniques can help which problems (see "What Works Best?," page 236), but they aren't a realistic reflection of most patients' experiences.

Our survey, in contrast, is a unique look at what happens in real life, where problems are diverse and less well-defined, and where some therapists try one technique after another until something works. The success of therapy under these real-life conditions has never before been well studied, says Martin Seligman, former director of clinical training in psychology at the University of Pennsylvania and past president of the American Psychological Association's division of clinical psychology.

Seligman, a consultant to our project, believes our readers' experiences send "a message of hope" for other people dealing with emotional problems.

Like other surveys, ours has several built-in limitations. Few of the people responding had a chronic, disabling condition such as schizophrenia or manic depression. We asked readers about their past experiences, which can be less reliable than asking about the present. We may have sampled an unusually large number of people in long-term treatment. Finally, our data comes from the readers' own perceptions, rather than from a clinician's assessment. However, other studies have shown that such self-reports frequently agree with professionals' clinical judgments.

Who Went for Help

In our 1994 Annual Questionnaire, we asked readers about their experiences with emotional problems and their encounters with health-care providers and groups during the years 1991 to 1994. Like the average American outpatient client, the 4000 readers who said they had sought professional help were mostly well educated. Their median age was 46, and about half were women. However, they may be more amenable to therapy than most.

Many who went to a mental-health specialist were in considerable pain at the time they entered treatment. Forty-three percent said their emotional state was either very poor ("I barely managed to deal with things") or fairly poor ("Life was usually pretty tough").

Their reasons for seeking therapy included several classic emotional illnesses: depression, anxiety, panic, and phobias. Among the other reasons our readers sought therapy: marital or sexual problems, frequent low moods, problems with children, problems with jobs, grief, stress-related ailments, and alcohol or drug problems.

The Results: Therapy Works

Our survey showed that therapy for mental-health problems can have a substantial effect. Forty-four percent of people whose emotional state was "very poor" at the start of treatment said they now feel good. Another 43 percent who started out "fairly poor" also improved significantly, though somewhat less. Of course, some people probably would have gotten better without treatment, but the vast majority specifically said that therapy helped.

Most people reported they were helped with the specific problems that brought them to therapy, even when those problems were quite se-

vere. Of those who started out "very poor," 54 percent said treatment "made things a lot better," while another one-third said it helped their problems to some extent. The same pattern of improvement held for just about every condition.

Overall, almost everyone who sought help experienced some relief—improvements that made them less troubled and their lives more pleasant. People who started out feeling the worst reported the most progress. Among people no longer in treatment, two-thirds said they'd left because their problems had been resolved or were easier to deal with.

Whom Should You See?

In the vast field of mental health, psychiatrist, psychologists, and clinical social workers have long fought for turf. Only psychiatrists, who are medical doctors, can prescribe drugs and have the training to detect medical problems that can affect a person's mental state. Otherwise, each of these professionals is trained to understand human behavior, to recognize problems, and to provide therapy.

Historically, social workers have been the underdogs and have had to fight for state laws requiring insurance companies to cover their services. But many of today's budget-minded insurers *favor* social workers—and psychiatric nurses—because they offer relatively low-cost services.

In our survey, almost three-quarters of those seeking professional help went to a mental-health specialist. Their experiences suggest that any of these therapists can be very helpful. Psychiatrists, psychologists, and social workers received equally high marks and were praised for being supportive, insightful, and easy to confide in. That remained true even when we statistically controlled for the seriousness and type of the problem and the length of treatment.

Those who went to marriage counselors didn't do quite as well, and gave their counselors lower grades for competence. One reason

may be that working with a fractured couple is difficult. Also, almost anyone can hang out a shingle as a marriage counselor. In some states the title "marriage and family therapist" is restricted to those with appropriate training. But anyone can use other words to say they *do* marriage therapy, and in most places the title "marriage counselor" is up for grabs.

What about Doctors?

Many people are more comfortable taking their problems to their family doctor than to a psychologist or psychiatrist. That may work well for some people, but our data suggest that many would be better off with a psychotherapist.

Readers who exclusively saw their family doctor for emotional problems—about 14 percent of those in our survey—had a very different experience from those who consulted a mental-health specialist. Treatment tended to be shorter, more than half of those whose care was complete had been treated for less than two months. People who went to family doctors were much more likely to get psychiatric drugs—83 percent of them did, compared with 20 percent of those who went to mental-health specialists. And almost half the people whose doctors gave them drugs received medication without the benefit of much counseling.

The people who relied on their family doctors for help were less distraught at the outset than those who saw mental-health providers; people with severe emotional problems apparently get themselves to a specialist. Even so, only half were highly satisfied with their family doctor's treatment (compared with 62 percent who were highly satisfied with their mental-health provider). A significant minority felt their doctor had neither the time nor temperament to address emotional issues. In general, family doctors did help people get back on their feet—but longer treatment with a specialist was more effective.

However, if you begin treatment with your family doctor, that's where you're likely to stay. Family doctors referred their patients to a

The worse people felt at the start of therapy, the greater their gains.

Private insurers have always covered mental disorders and substance abuse more grudgingly than medical illness, either by building in limits or by interposing a case manager between you and your benefit. And very few plans deal well with the lifelong needs of people with chronic, severe mental illness. On the whole, says Kathleen Kelso, executive director of the Mental Health Association of Minnesota, "insurers would just as soon cover us from the neck down."

Almost all traditional fee-for-service plans pay 80 percent or more of the fee when you visit the doctor with a medical problem. But for outpatient therapy, the majority pay just 50 percent, and frequently that's after "capping" bills at well below the therapists' actual fees—which range on average from $80 to $120 according to Psychotherapy Finances, an industry newsletter. Most insurance plans also impose one or more other limits on mental-health coverage, such as the number of outpatient visits and hospital days they will pay for. In addition, many plans have annual or lifetime dollar maximums; for outpatient care, it can be as low as $1000 and $10,000, respectively. In recent years consumer advocates have lobbied for state laws that would equalize coverage for psychiatric and other illnesses. So far, just six states—Maine, Maryland, Minnesota, New Hampshire, Rhode Island, and Texas—have passed so-called "parity" laws. Consumers Union supports such laws, and has actively worked for their passage.

Health maintenance organizations (HMOs) also limit access to psychiatric services, typically providing a maximum of 20 outpatient visits and 30 hospital days a year. Patients usually have to go through their family physician or another gatekeeper to gain access to those benefits, and may get less than the maximum.

In our survey of mental-health care, respondents whose coverage limited the length and frequency of therapy, and the type of therapist, reported poorer outcomes. (However, we found no clear difference in outcome between people with fee-for-service coverage and those in HMOs and preferred provider plans.) Paying for therapy on their own was clearly a hardship for many: Twenty-one percent cited the cost of therapy as a reason for quitting.

To hold down spending, increasing numbers of employers, HMOs, and fee-for-service plans are turning to specialized managed-care companies to run their mental-health benefit. These specialty firms refer patients to a network of clinicians who must adhere to strict treatment guidelines. And they *have* reined in spending, saving some employers as much as 30 percent in the cost of mental-health care.

But many patients—and their therapists—feel they're being shortchanged. Psychiatrists complain about the difficulty of extending a hospital stay for patients considered too sick to leave and the challenge of getting approval for more than brief outpatient care.

Although many plans run by managed-care firms nominally have generous benefits, reality may fall somewhat short. All services must be authorized by a case manager. To get approval for additional sessions, therapists must provide details about a patient's problems and the course of treatment.

With scores of managed-care companies nationwide, there's great variability in how they tend to the needs of their subscribers. Even critics acknowledge that some plans are quite accommodating, and that some overly stringent practices have been curbed. But concern about heavy-handed practices has prompted several states to enact laws regulating managed-care services.

How to Choose a Plan

If you're picking a health-care plan and are concerned about mental-health coverage, you should ask some pointed questions:

- **What are the stated benefits?** Pay close attention to the benefit limits, including co-payments, limits on the number of hospital days and outpatient sessions, and annual or lifetime dollar maximums. A typical plan with limits covers 30 days of inpatient care and 50 or fewer outpatient visits. But the cap it sets on covered charges may be low, and the copayments high.

- **If the benefits cover only "medically necessary" treatment, who makes that determination?** It's best if that decision is left to you and your therapist. But in many managed-care plans it's a case manager who decides whether you need therapy or hospitalization, and how long it should last.

- **What are your rights of appeal if coverage is denied or cut short?** In many plans the grievance process consists of a single appeal.

- **In a managed-care plan, how large is the provider panel?** The more therapists in your area, the more likely you'll find one whose personality and expertise are a good match for you.

- **Will the plan add new providers to its panel?** This can be important if you're already seeing a therapist who's not part of the plan but is willing to join.

- **Which facilities are approved by the plan?** Be sure there's a hospital that's convenient and that offers a broad spectrum of mental-health and substance-abuse services. Also look for transitional and intermediate-care programs, such as mental-health day centers.

---

mental-health specialist in only one out of four cases, even when psychotherapy might have made a big difference. Only half of those who were severely distressed were sent on, and 60 percent of patients with panic disorder or phobias were never referred, even though specific therapies are known to work for those problems.

Other research has shown that many family doctors have a poor track record when it comes to mental health. They fail to diagnose some 50 to 80 percent of psychological problems, and sometimes prescribe psychiatric drugs for too short a time or at doses too low to work.

The Power of Groups

It was 60 years ago that a businessman and a physician, both struggling with alcoholism, realized they could

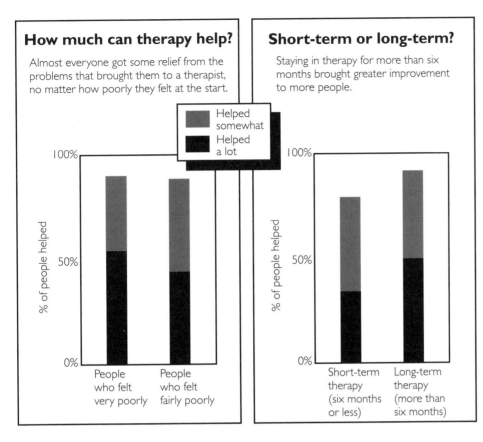

How much can therapy help?

Almost everyone got some relief from the problems that brought them to a therapist, no matter how poorly they felt at the start.

Legend:
- Helped somewhat
- Helped a lot

% of people helped (y-axis: 0% to 100%)

- People who felt very poorly
- People who felt fairly poorly

Short-term or long-term?

Staying in therapy for more than six months brought greater improvement to more people.

% of people helped (y-axis: 0% to 100%)

- Short-term therapy (six months or less)
- Long-term therapy (more than six months)

Drugs, Pro and Con

For decades, drug therapy to treat problems such as depression carried a raft of unpleasant, sometimes dangerous side effects. Then came *Prozac* (fluoxetine), launched in 1988. Safer and easier to take than previous antidepressants, *Prozac* and other drugs in its class—including sertraline (*Zoloft*) and paroxetine (*Paxil*)—have radically changed the treatment of depression. Along the way, people have claimed that *Prozac* seems to relieve a growing list of other complaints—from eating disorders to shyness to, most recently, premenstrual syndrome.

In our survey, 40 percent of readers who sought professional help received psychiatric drugs. And overall, about 60 percent of readers who took drugs said the medication helped a lot.

However, many of our readers did well with psychotherapy alone; in fact, people who received only psychotherapy improved as much as those who got therapy plus drugs.

For many people, having the option of talk therapy is important because every psychiatric drug has potential side effects that some individuals find hard to tolerate. Almost half of all our respondents on medication reported problems with the drug. Drowsiness and a feeling of disorientation were the most common complaints, especially among people taking the older antidepressants such as amitriptyline (*Elavil*).

stay sober by talking to one another. They talked to other alcoholics, too, and eventually worked out the system of long-term recovery known as Alcoholics Anonymous, or AA. Today there are over a million active AA members in the U.S., and attending an AA group is often recommended as part of professional treatment. The AA format has also been adopted by dozens of other self-help groups representing a wide spectrum of dysfunctional behavior, from Gamblers Anonymous to Sex and Love Addicts Anon. Support groups also bring together people who are dealing with medical illness or other trials.

One-third of our survey respondents went to a group, often in addition to individual psychotherapy. Overall, they told us, the groups seemed to help.

Readers who went to AA voiced overwhelming approval. Virtually all endorsed AA's approach to treatment, and most said their struggle with addiction had been largely successful. In keeping with AA's principle that recovery is a lifelong process, three-quarters of our readers had been in the group for more than two years, and most were still attending. Most of those who had dropped out said they'd moved on because their problems had improved.

Certainly not everyone who goes to AA does as well; our sampling method probably over-represented long-term, and thus successful, AA members. AA's own surveys suggest that about half of those who come to the program are gone within three months. Studies that follow people who have undergone treatment for alcoholism find that AA is no more or less effective than other programs: A year after entering treatment, about half the participants are still in trouble.

Nevertheless, AA has several components that may maximize the chance of success. In general, most alcoholics do well while they are being actively treated. In AA, members are supposed to attend 90 meetings in the first 90 days, followed by three meetings a week for life.

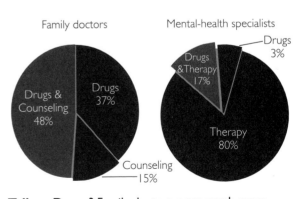

Family doctors

- Drugs & Counseling 48%
- Drugs 37%
- Counseling 15%

Mental-health specialists

- Drugs 3%
- Drugs & Therapy 17%
- Therapy 80%

Talk or Drugs? Family doctors were much more likely to dispense mostly medication or a mix of drugs and talk. Very few mental-health therapists relied mainly on drugs; the vast majority provided psychotherapy.

Until a decade or so ago, any evidence that psychotherapy worked came from the testimonials of therapists and their patients. But today, controlled studies have shown that psychotherapy does make a difference: People with a broad range of problems can usually benefit from psychological treatment. More important, for certain conditions researchers have homed in on specific therapies and drugs that can bring swift improvement for the majority of sufferers.

Here is a summary of the top treatment options for four common problems. It was compiled from the scientific literature by psychologist Martin Seligman and reviewed by psychiatrists Stewart Agras of Stanford University and Jesse Schomer of Cornell University, and by social worker Eleanor Bromberg of The Hunter School of Social Work in New York. (For a comprehensive look at treatments that work, see Seligman's book, *What You Can Change & What You Can't*, Ballantine Books, New York, 1995.)

Depression

More than the passing blues, depression can sap you of pleasure, hope, and vitality, upend your eating and sleeping habits, and draw a veil of despair that lasts for months or years. In bipolar depression, also called manic-depression, the laws alternate with excessive, frenetic highs. Most of the time, depression can be cut short and considerably relieved.

With **cognitive therapy,** you learn to recognize and change the negative assumptions and beliefs that color your emotions and shape your world view. If, for example, you react to small setbacks by thinking you can't do anything right, you'll learn to focus on evidence to the contrary—your recent promotion at work, for instance. Cognitive therapy brings considerable relief to about 70

percent of depressed people. It takes about a month to start working, and typically involves a few months of weekly sessions.

Interpersonal therapy is just as effective and runs about as long, but focuses instead on the difficulties of personal relationships. You'll examine current conflicts and disappointments, learn how they sow depression, and work on successful ways of relating to other people.

Drug therapy is about as effective as these psychotherapies. Each of the three major classes of antidepressant drugs works equally well. People who don't respond to one type of drug may respond to another; overall, 60 percent to 80 percent of depressed people get marked relief within three to six weeks. However, the classes differ significantly in their adverse effects: Fluoxetine (*Prozac*) and related drugs tend to be better tolerated, though they frequently produce insomnia, restlessness, and sexual problems. The older, "tricyclic" antidepressants such as amitriptyline (*Elavil*) can cause drowsiness, tremor, weight gain, and heart-rhythm changes. For people with manic-depression, treatment with the drug lithium carbonate (*Escalith, Lithane*) is clearly the best route.

Electroconvulsive therapy is used for severely depressed people who can't take, or don't respond to, antidepressant drugs. Electrodes placed on the head transmit bursts of electricity believed to affect many of the same brain chemicals as antidepressant drugs. The "dosage" has been greatly reduced from the jolts used in the past. Repeated several times over the course of a week, ECT quickly relieves severe depression about 75 percent of the time. The downside is the risk of anesthesia and the side effects—temporary, but disturbing—of memory loss and confusion.

Although the problems associated with psychiatric drugs are well-known, 20 percent of readers said their provider never discussed them—a disturbing lapse in communication. Equally disturbing was the finding that 40 percent of the people taking antianxiety drugs had done so for more than a year—25 percent for more than two years—even though long-term use results in habituation, requiring larger and larger doses.

Antianxiety medications such as *Xanax* and *Valium* can provide relief if used for a short time during a particularly stressful period, such as the death of a parent. But they haven't been well tested for generalized anxiety—a kind of chronic, excessive worrying combined with physical and emotional symptoms—and therapists have found them only erratically effective.

Xanax is approved by the U.S. Food and Drug Administration for panic disorder, which causes repeated bouts of unbearable anxiety; studies show that it acts quickly to reduce panic attacks. But after two months, *Xanax* apparently performs little better than a placebo. (See CONSUMER REPORTS, January 1993.) The reason many people take antianxiety drugs for so long is that they're extremely hard to kick; if the drug is stopped, symptoms return in full force.

People in therapy more than six months reported the most progress.

How Long Will It Take?

When a person needs psychotherapy, how much do they need? That has become a critical question—both for

clinicians and for the insurers that pay for therapy. And it's a hard one to answer.

Nationally, most people who get therapy go for a relatively short time—an average of four to eight sessions. It's not clear, however, whether people stop going because they have been helped enough, because they don't think the therapy is working, or because they've run out of money. Controlled studies of specific kinds of therapy usually cover only 12 to 20 visits. While brief therapy often helps, there's no way to tell from such studies whether 30 or 40 sessions, or even more, would be even more effective.

For the people in our survey, longer psychotherapy was associated with better outcomes. Among people

Anxiety

Unlike ordinary worrying, clinical anxiety is irrational, freezes you into inaction, or dominates your life.

Tranquilizers such as diazepam (*Valium*) and alprazolam (*Xanax*) can provide quick relief, but the benefit ends when the drug is stopped. Extended use may result in tolerance, which diminishes the benefit, and also produces dependency, making it hard to quit.

Everyday anxiety often yields to self-help techniques. Simple forms of **meditation** can be useful. So can various forms of **relaxation,** such as progressive relaxation. Some therapists teach these techniques, or you can check a local YMCA, community hospital, or yoga institute for courses.

If your anxiety is intense and unyielding, it may need professional attention. Cognitive-behavioral therapy is often helpful; you'll learn to counter the irrational thoughts that provoke anxiety and to overcome fears.

Panic

A panic attack isn't easily forgotten. It produces chest pain, sweating, nausea, dizziness, and a feeling of overwhelming dread. Millions of people suffer such episodes repeatedly and unexpectedly.

Antidepressant drugs and the anti-anxiety drug *Xanax* can dampen or even prevent panic attacks in the majority of people. But side effects include drowsiness and lethargy, and panic rebounds about half the time when therapy is stopped.

An alternative approach is cognitive therapy, which provides relief to almost all panic sufferers. Treatment is based on the idea that panic occurs when a person mistakes normal symptoms of anxiety for symptoms of a heart attack, going crazy, or dying. The fear that something is wrong can escalate into a full-fledged panic attack. In cognitive therapy you'll learn to short-circuit that reaction by interpreting anxiety symptoms for what they are.

Phobias

Strong, irrational fears affect more than 10 percent of American adults. Some fear specific objects, such as animals, snakes, or insects; even more can't bear crowded places or open spaces, a condition called agoraphobia. Still others with social phobia recoil from situations involving other people.

Two behavior therapies are now used, with considerable success, to treat phobias. In both, you'll have to confront what you most fear. The more gradual technique is systematic desensitization. After learning progressive relaxation, you'll construct a fear hierarchy with the most terror-inducing situation at the top. In the first of a series of steps, you'll go into a relaxed state, then vividly imagine the least fearsome situation—or face it in real life. Gradually you'll move up the hierarchy and face more frightening situations.

During flooding, the other therapy, you're thrown in immediately with the thing that scares you; a cat phobic, for instance, will sit in a room full of cats. The goal is to stay for an agreed-upon length of time while the anxiety ebbs.

Behavior therapy is most successful with object and social phobias, producing lasting results in the majority of cases in a matter of weeks or months. In agoraphobia, behavior therapy is best combined with an antidepressant drug to control panic.

---

who entered therapy with similar levels of emotional distress, those who stayed in treatment for more than six months reported greater gains than those who left earlier. Our data suggest that for many people, even a year's worth of therapy with a mental-health specialist may be very worthwhile. People who stayed in treatment for more than two years reported the best outcomes of all. However, these people tended to have started out with more serious problems.

We also found that people got better in three distinct ways, and that all three kinds of improvement increased with additional treatment. First, therapy eased the problems that brought people to treatment. Second, it helped them to function better, improving their ability to relate well to others, to be productive at work, and to cope with everyday stress. And it enhanced what can be called "personal growth." People in therapy had more confidence and self-esteem, understood themselves better, and enjoyed life more.

Despite the potential benefit of long-term therapy, many insurance plans limit mental-health coverage to "medically necessary" services—which typically means short-term treatment aimed at symptom relief. If you want to stay in therapy longer, you may have to pay for it yourself.

Our findings complement recent work by psychologist Kenneth Howard of Northwestern University. By following the progress of 854 psychotherapy patients, Howard and his associates found that recovery followed a "dose-response" curve, with the greatest response occurring early on. On average, 50 percent of people recovered after 11 weekly therapy sessions, and 75 percent got better after about a year.

Recommendations

Emotional distress may not always require professional help. But when problems threaten to become overwhelming or interfere with everyday life, there's no need to feel defeated.

Our survey shows there's real help available from every quarter—family doctors, psychotherapists, and self-help groups. Both talk therapy and medication, when warranted, can bring relief to people with a wide range of problems and deep despair.

With such clear benefits to be had, the strict limits on insurance coverage for mental-health care are cause for concern. As the debate over health care continues, we believe that improving mental-health coverage is important.

If you want to see a therapist, you should approach therapy as an active consumer. In our survey, the more diligently a person "shopped" for a therapist—consulting with several candidates, checking their experience and qualifications, and speaking to previous clients—the more they ultimately improved. Once in treatment, those who formed a real partnership with their therapist—by being open, even with painful subjects, and by working on issues between sessions—were more likely to progress.

When you look for a therapist, competence and personal chemistry should be your priorities. You'll be sharing your most intimate thoughts and feelings, so it's important to choose someone who puts you at ease.

Many people first consult their family doctor, who has already won their confidence and trust. If you decide to stay with your physician for treatment, bear in mind that the approach will probably be medically based and relatively short.

If you would prefer to work with a therapist, ask your doctor for a referral. Other good referral sources are national professional associations or their local or state chapters. For information or referrals you can call the American Psychiatric Association, at 202 682-6220; the American Psychological Association, 202 336-5800; the National Association of Social Workers, 800 638-8799, ext. 291; the American Association for Marriage and Family Therapy, 800 374-2638; and the American Psychiatric Nurses Association, 202 857-1133. Also contact local universities, hospitals, and psychotherapy and psychoanalytic training institutes. For general information on mental illness, call the National Alliance for the Mentally ill, 800 950-6264.

The Types of Therapies and Therapists

If you're considering mental-health treatment, you're facing a wide choice of therapies and practitioners. Many therapists favor a particular theoretical approach, though often they use a combination.

In psychoanalysis, Freud's classical technique employing a couch and free association, patients explore and confront troubling childhood experiences. In psychodynamic therapy, the emphasis is on discovering unconscious conflicts and defense mechanisms that hinder adult behavior. The goal of interpersonal therapy is to enhance relationships and communication skills. Cognitive therapy is aimed at helping people recognize and change distorted ways of thinking. Behavioral therapy seeks to replace harmful behaviors with useful ones.

As for choosing a therapist, be careful. Anyone can legally be called a psychotherapist, whether or not he or she has received the training and supervision needed to competently practice. Look for someone licensed or certified in one of the following fields:

- **Psychiatrists** are physicians who have completed three years of residency training in psychiatry following four years of medical school and a one-year internship. All are trained in psychiatric diagnosis and pharmacotherapy, but only some residency programs provide extensive experience in outpatient psychotherapy.

- **Psychoanalysts** have a professional degree in psychiatry, psychology, or social work, plus at least two years of extensive supervised training at a psychoanalytic institute.

- **Psychologists** with the credential Ph.D., Psy.D., or Ed.D. are licensed professionals with doctoral-level training, typically including a year of clinical internship in a mental-health facility and a year of supervised post-doctoral experience.

- **Social workers** typically train in a two-year master's degree program that involves fieldwork in a wide range of human services, including mental health settings. Those who seek state certification or licensing as a clinical social worker need two years of supervised post-grad experience and must pass a statewide exam.

- **Marriage and family therapists** may have a master's or doctoral degree from an accredited graduate training program in the field, or may have another professional degree with supervised experience in the specialty.

- **Psychiatric nurses** are registered nurses who work in mental-health settings, often as part of a therapeutic team. Advanced practice nurses have a master's degree and can provide psychotherapy.

Family and friends may also know of reputable therapists; try to get several names to consider. Our readers who located therapists through personal or professional references felt better served than those who relied on ads, their managed care company's roster, or local clinics.

 Article Review Form at end of book.

WiseGuide Wrap-Up

Construct a grid of the following topics: type of treatment, effectiveness, and relevant disorders. As you read further in this area, think about treatment in this format. Also, several journals are specifically designed to review treatment; consider a review of recent issues of *Journal of Consulting and Clinical Psychology* and *Clinical Psychology: Research and Practice.*

R.E.A.L. Sites

This list provides a print preview of typical **Coursewise** R.E.A.L. sites. (There are over 100 such sites at the **Courselinks**™ site.) The danger in printing URLs is that web sites can change overnight. As we went to press, these sites were functional using the URLs provided. If you come across one that isn't, please let us know via email to: webmaster@coursewise.com. Use your Passport to access the most current list of R.E.A.L. sites at the **Courselinks** site.

Site name: PharmInfoNet

URL: http://pharminfo.com

Why is it R.E.A.L.? This site is a large database on drugs and their effects; it is sponsored by the Pharmaceutical Information Network.

Key topic: Does therapy work?

Site name: Eliza

URL: http://www-ai.ijs.si/eliza/eliza.html

Why is it R.E.A.L.? This is a computerized Rogerian counselor; you type in your problems and "she" replies.

Key topic: computers in therapy

Index

Note: Names and page numbers in **bold** type indicate authors and their articles; page numbers in *italics* indicate illustrations; page numbers followed by *t* indicate tables.

harm avoidance, 15, *16*
health education, computerized, 212
health maintenance organizations, 230
health-related concerns about alcohol, 61–62
heart rate, computerized assessment of, 222
Heatherton, Todd F., **197**
helping relationships, 61
Helplessness-L, 170
help-seeking, 194
heredity. *See* genetics
hierarchical agglomerative cluster analysis, 102, 103
Hispanics
    prevalence of disorders among, 35*t*, 36*t*, 37
    psychotherapy for, 2–12
history taking, computerized, 211–12
homophony, 10
horizontal credibility, 7
Hughes, Michael, **29**
hypochondriasis, 46*t*, 47*t*

I

if-then statements, 211
immaturity, and temperament, 17
impulse disorders, 53
income level, and prevalence of psychiatric disorders, 35*t*, 36*t*, 37
individual differences, and recovery from alcohol problems, 63–64
information processing deficits, 128–29
insight, 9
insurance coverage, 228, 230, 233
intermediacy, 24, 26*t*
interpersonal cognitive problem-solving skills, 182
interpersonal therapy, 232, 234
intersubjective school of psychoanalysis, 8
interviewing, computerized, 211–12
intimacy, among sexually abused children, 177
introversion, 88–89. *See also* extraversion
intuition, 4–5
isolation, 177–78

J

Jakovljević, Miro, **123**
Jarrett, Steven, **151**
Jenike, Michael A., **69**

K

Keel, Pamela, **197**
Kendler, Kenneth S., **29**
Kessler, Ronald C., **29**
Keuthen, Nancy J., **69**
knowledge
    unconscious, 9
    views of, 3–5
Korten, Ailsa, **42**

L

Lacanian theory, 3–12
lalangue, 9
late-life depression, 140–49
late-life recoveries, 58
learning, and personality, 14
level 1 and 2 computer counselors, 222
Life History Questionnaire, 83
lifetime disorders, demographic correlates of, 35*t*
Ljubičić, Dulijano, **123**
Llamas, Michael, **81**
loneliness, among sexually aggressive children, 177–78

M

Mahamedi, Fary, **197**
major depressive episode. *See* depression
managed care, 230
manual reaction time, and schizophrenia, 128, 130, 131–36
marriage and family therapists, 229, 234
"master's discourse," 3
Maudsley Obsessive-Compulsive Inventory, 159
McGonagle, Katherine A., **29**
McGue, Matt, **140**
medical corpsmen, computerized training for, 212–13
medical diagnoses, computerized, 213
medications
    with CBT for anxiety disorders, 81–87
    frequency of prescribing, 229
    predicting effectiveness from personality, 21
    pros and cons of, 231–32
    Web sites about, 235
meditation, 23–24, 233
memory impairments, 135
mental health insurance, 230
Mental Health Net Web site, 170
mental health services
    patient satisfaction with, 229
    shopping for, 234
    utilization rates for, 34, 38–39
mental illness. *See* psychiatric disorders
Mick, Eric, **172**
minorities. *See* ethnic minorities
modeling, 159–67
modernity, 3
Moncayo, Raul, **2**
mood disorders
    and ADHD, 173
    classifying, 155–57, 164–76
    See also anxiety disorders; psychiatric disorders
moods, and personality, 17
Mück-Šeler, Dorotea, **123**
MYCIN, 213
mythical thought, 4, 5

N

National Comorbidity Survey (NCS)
    methodology of, 30–32, 37–38
    results of, 29, 32–37, 38–39
natural language, computerized understanding of, 219–20
natural recovery, 55–65
negative affect, influence on DSM-IV emotional disorders, 157, 161–67
Nelson, Christopher B., **29**
neurasthenia, 45, 46*t*, 47*t*
neuroticism, anxiety and, 88–90, 93–96
nonaffective psychosis, 32*t*, 33
non-competitive group games, 182–83
nondefensive ego functioning, 8–9
nondieters, 200
nondirective dynamic-humanistic-interpersonal therapy, 22–23
nonverbal behavior, computerized assessment of, 222
novelty seeking, 15, *16*
number symbolism, 10–11
nurses, stress and coping behavior among, 100–112

O

Oei, Tian P.S., **81**
Oldehinkel, Tineke, **42**
older adults, depression among, 140–41, 149
oncology nurses, stress and coping behavior among, 100–112
Ormel, Johan, **42**
O'Sullivan, Richard L., **69**
the Other, 8

P

panic disorder
    prevalence of, 32*t*, 46*t*, 47*t*
    treatments for, 81–87, 233
"Paper People," 185
parents
    of compulsive gamblers, 77–78
    of sexually aggressive children, 179–81
pathological gambling, 72–78
Penn State Worry Questionnaire, 159
persistence, 15–17
personality
    and alcohol problems, 64
    anxiety and, 88–97
    basing therapy on, 21–28
    and depression, 92, 93*t*
    psychobiological model of, 13–21
personality assessments, 13–14
personal space, 183
pessimism, 151–54
PharmInfoNet Web site, 235
phobias, 218, 233
physical abuse, 19–20
physical boundaries, 183

physical illness, and disability, 50–51
physicians, mental health services from, 229–31
Pini, Stefano, 42
Pivac, Nela, 123
platelet serotonin concentration, 123–27
positive affect, influence on DSM-IV emotional disorders, 157, 161–67
Positive and Negative Affect Scales, 159
postmodernism, 3, 4–5, 11
pregnancy, and alcohol consumption, 58
preparatory interval, 129, 130–36
prevalence of disorders
    across cultures, 42–51
    in U.S., 29–39
problem dieters, 200
problem-solving games, 182–83
procedural learning, 14
Prochaska's change model, 60–61, 138
professional services, utilization rates for, 34, 38–39
programming, for computerized psychotherapy, 220–22
propositional learning, 14
Prozac, 231
PSYCHE, 221
psychiatric disorders
    demographic correlates of, 35t, 36t
    diagnosing, 50
    prevalence across cultures, 42–51
    prevalence in U.S., 29–39
    See also anxiety disorders; mood disorders; panic disorder; schizophrenia; treatments
psychiatric nurses, 234
psychiatrists, 229, 234
psychoanalysis, 2–12, 234
psychobiology, 13–21
psychodynamic therapy, 234
psychologists, 229
Psychology Self-Help Resources Web site, 53, 113, 207
psychotherapy. *See* treatments
psychotic disorder, 31, 94–95

R

race, and prevalence of psychiatric disorders, 35t, 36t
race discrimination, and alcohol problems, 57
racing, 76t
rarity, 24, 26t
rationalism, 3–4
reaction time, 128–36
R.E.A.L. sites
    Addict-L, 79
    American Academy of Child and Adolescent Psychiatry Homepage, 207
    APA's Psychnet, 53, 79
    The Atlantic Monthly, 53
    Behavioral and Brain Sciences, 138
    Behavior Online, 79
    Cyber-Psych, 138

Department of Health and Human Services, 138
Eliza, 235
Helplessness-L, 170
Mental Health Net, 170
PharmInfoNet, 235
Psychology Self-Help Resources, 53, 113, 207
Support LISTSERV for Depression, 170
Yanx-Dep, 113
region, disorder prevalence by, 35t, 36t, 37
reinforcement management, 61
relational school of psychoanalysis, 8
relaxation training, 217–18, 233
religion, 23
repression, 8–9
response latency, 222–23
reward dependence, 15, *16*
Roberts, Bruce R., 128
Rodriguez, Dayami, 69
role incompatibility, 62
role selection, 62
role socialization, 62
role transitions, 62–63, 198–99
rural areas, comorbidity in, 39

S

saccadic movements, 117–18, 128–36
Samuel, Valeria J., 172
schizophrenia
    biological factors in, 115–18, 123–27, 128–36
    effect of seasons on, 123–27
    prevalence in U.S., 33
    psychological factors in, 118
    symptoms of, 126
Schooler, Carmi, 128
scientific tradition, 3–4
"The Scorpion Bunny," 188–89
seasons, 123–27
second chances, 151–54
self-confidence, 21
Self-Consciousness Scale, 159
self-control, 54
self-directedness, 15t, *16*, 17, 60–61
self-help groups, 231
self-liberation, 61
self-recognition, 61, 64
self-reevaluation, 61
self-transcendence, 15t, *16*, 17
serotonin levels, 123–27
services, utilization rates for, 34, 38–39
sex differences
    in depression, 144, 145t, 148
    in gambling behavior, 75
    in post-college weight gain, 200–201
    in prevalence of disorders, 33, 34, 35t, 36t
    in recovery from alcohol problems, 58
sexual abuse
    and personality development, 19–20
    and sexually aggressive children, 176, 177, 179

sexual abuse cycles, 183–84, 187–90
sexual dysfunctions, computerized treatment of, 219
sexually aggressive boys
    attributes of, 175, 176
    focus of treatments for, 177–87
    sample activities for, 187–90
    treatment outcomes for, 176–77
sexual reactivity, 176
Shanyang Zhao, 29
Sher, Kenneth J., 55, 88
smoking, 64, 216
smooth pursuit eye movement, 117–18
social deviance, 24, 26t
Social Disability Schedule (SDS), 44
Social Interaction Anxiety Scales, 159
social isolation, 177–78
social liberation, 61
social phobia, 32t
social skills training, 178
social workers, 229, 234
socioeconomic status, 6–8, 35t, 36t
software. *See* computers
somatization disorder, 46t, 47t
South Oaks Gambling Screen (SOGS), 72, 73–74, 76, 78
spirituality, 23–24
sports betting, 76t
"Steps to Getting in Trouble," 187
Steps to Healthy Touching, 181, 182
Stewart, Mark, **151**
stimulus control, 61
stimulus-response model of stress, 100–101
Stinchfield, Randy, 72
stories of abuse, 184, 187–90
stress
    cognitive appraisals of, 109–10
    coping behaviors for, 106–7, 110–11
Striepe, Meg, 197
structural modeling, 159–67
subclinical eating disorders, 200
substance use disorders
    and alcohol problems, 64
    and compulsive gambling, 72–73, 77t
    prevalence in U.S., 32t, 33
suicide attempts, 192–96
Suinn, Richard M., 115
superego, 9
supportive-realistic therapy, 21–22
Support LISTSERV for Depression, 170
Survey Research Center, 31
Svrakic, Dragan M., 13
systematic desensitization, 217–18, 233

T

Taylor, Andrea, 172
temperament
    in canonical sequence, 18–21
    dimensions of, 14–17
Temperament and Character Inventory (TCI), 13
    canonical sequence in, 18–21
    in case example, 24–27

Putting it in *Perspectives*
-Review Form-

Your name:_____   Date: _____

Reading title: _____

Summarize: Provide a one-sentence summary of this reading: _____

_____

_____

_____

Follow the Thinking: How does the author back the main premise of the reading? Are the facts/opinions appropriately supported by research or available data? Is the author's thinking logical?

_____

_____

_____

_____

_____

Develop a Context (answer one or both questions): How does this reading contrast or compliment your professor's lecture treatment of the subject matter? How does this reading compare to your textbook's coverage?

_____

_____

_____

_____

_____

Question Authority: Explain why you agree/disagree with the author's main premise.

_____

_____

_____

_____

_____

_____

COPY ME! Copy this form as needed. This form is also available at http://www.coursewise.com
Click on: *Perspectives*.